Y0-BZT-584

...ceepoked... her

...Hamburg

918) as their

...7 brought hi...

...ept. the boy

...rest sweetes...

ever met. We

...d of him

...died of

...losis on Jun...

...weeks' illne...

Dr Freud

Dr Freud

A Life

Paul Ferris

A Cornelia and Michael Bessie Book

COUNTERPOINT

WASHINGTON, D. C.

The endpapers show an extract from a letter from Freud to his nephew Sam, reproduced in full in the illustrations, courtesy of The John Rylands University Library, Manchester.

Copyright © 1997 by Paul Ferris

First American edition 1998 by Counterpoint. First published in the United Kingdom in 1997 by Sinclair-Stevenson, Random House, London.

All rights reserved under International and Pan-American Copyright Conventions. No part of this book may be used or reproduced in any manner whatsoever without written permission from the Publisher, except in the case of brief quotations embodied in critical articles and reviews.

Library of Congress Cataloging-in-Publications Data

Ferris, Paul, 1929–
    Dr. Freud, a life / Paul Ferris. — 1st American ed.
    (   )
    "A Cornelia and Michael Bessie Book"
    Includes bibliographical references and index.
    1. Freud, Sigmund, 1856–1939.   2. Psychoanalysts—Austria—
Biography. I. Title.
    BF109.F74F465 1998
    150.19'52'092—dc21
    [B]   97-51677

ISBN 1-887178-72-4 (hardcover: alk. paper)

Jacket design by Wesley B. Tanner / Passim Editions

Printed in the United States of America on acid-free paper that meets the American National Standards Institute Z39-48 Standard.

A Cornelia and Michael Bessie Book
COUNTERPOINT
P.O. Box 65793
Washington, D.C. 20035-5793
Counterpoint is a member of the Perseus Books Group.

10 9 8 7 6 5 4 3 2 1

FIRST PRINTING

For Bryn and Griff Ferris

Contents

List of Illustrations

The Freuds, *c.*1898 *(Freud Museum, London / Sigmund Freud Copyrights)*

postcard from Philipp Freud *(Freud Museum, London / Sigmund Freud Copyrights)*

Second eight-page section:

Carl Jung

Emma Jung

Karl Kraus *(Bildarchiv der Österreichische National Bibliothek)*

Fritz Wittels *(Sigmund Freud Museum Archives, Vienna)*

Wilhelm Stekel

Ernest Jones *(Institute of Psycho-Analysis, London)*

Anna Freud's alien's certificate *(Freud Museum, London / Sigmund Freud Copyrights)*

Sándor Ferenczi *(Institute of Psycho-Analysis, London)*

Serge Pankejeff, the 'Wolf man'

Lou Andréas-Salomé *(Freud Museum, London / Sigmund Freud Copyrights)*

Freud and Sophie *(Freud Museum, London / Sigmund Freud Copyrights)*

letter from Freud to his nephew Sam *(The John Rylands University Library, Manchester)*

Freud with Anna *(Freud Museum, London / Sigmund Freud Copyrights)*

The 'secret committee' *(Freud Museum, London / Sigmund Freud Copyrights)*

Horace Frink and Freud *(The Alan Mason Chesney Medical Archives of the Johns Hopkins Medical Institutions / Sigmund Freud Copyrights)*

Marie Bonaparte *(Freud Museum, London / Sigmund Freud Copyrights)*

Amalie Freud with her five daughters *(Freud Museum, London / Sigmund Freud Copyrights)*

Freud, *c.* 1935 *(Freud Museum, London / Sigmund Freud Copyrights)*

extract from Freud's diary, May–June 1938 *(Mary Evans / Sigmund Freud Copyrights)*

Marie Bonaparte, Prince George of Greece, Freud and Hanns Sachs *(Freud Museum, London / Sigmund Freud Copyrights)*

Introduction

A century ago the man from Vienna was about to emerge from the basements of psychological medicine and become a figure that an occasional German-speaking poet, journalist or well-read lay person had heard of. He was approaching middle age, 'an old, somewhat shabby Jew' in his sardonic estimation. *The Interpretation of Dreams* (1900) began the slow awakening of popular interest. Long before he died (in his bed, in London, in 1939), everyone knew who he was, or thought they did.

Those who insist that Freud 'diagnosed the problems of humankind' in exemplary fashion carry no more and no less conviction today than the revisionists of recent years who say he was a resourceful charlatan, manipulating the evidence. In between are those who recognise Freud's insights, often casually expressed, the truth of which they understand at once in the way that a line of poetry or a sentence in a novel illuminates a thought you almost had yourself, but were never able to frame.

My sympathies as an onlooker are with those who find the flawed Freud more interesting, because more believable, than the traditional figure. 'Charlatan' is too strong for my taste; 'ruthless' and 'devious' seem acceptable, as long as they are words intended not to diminish Freud's stature but on the contrary to suggest the scale of his endeavour to explain our nature: the end which he saw as justifying the means. Freud was an extraordinary figure even though his general theory of the mind is now widely regarded as deficient.

The claims of psychoanalysis are so decisive that to see them questioned is intolerable to many believers. The movement came under attack from the start – the vehemence of the opposition probably helped it cohere, and certainly helped Freud present himself as a messianic figure, persecuted for his convictions.

European psychiatrists had a vested interest in attacking these upstarts who, they feared, wanted to steal their patients (unlike American doctors later who were more inclined to become upstarts themselves). As 'Freudism' spread, it became a more obvious target. For years before the First World War, Karl Kraus, the Viennese iconoclast who ran the magazine the *Torch*, was peppering psychoanalysis with epigrams, some quite nasty: 'If mankind, with all its repulsive faults, is an organism, then the psychoanalyst is its excrement.'

Freud, and the movement in general, responded to hostility by deciding that only the converted were capable of understanding the system. Dissent from the rubric of analysis was called 'resistance', and dismissed as error which could be corrected only by a dose of the very thing under attack, psychoanalysis: a splendid gambit, still in use.

In terms of biography, powerful inhibitions have been at work, and until the 1970s no one had the stomach to re-investigate aspects of the life described in the three-volume official version by Ernest Jones twenty years earlier. Those with the scholarly opportunities to look for evidence of a different story usually lacked the boldness to imagine alternative Freuds. A censorship arose from misplaced piety and has not entirely vanished. There is something about all this in Chapter 32.

More insidious than the restraints imposed by the Sigmund Freud Archives has been an apparent indifference to the historical record. One of the areas now receiving belated attention is the overall integrity of Freud's methods. His approach to well-known episodes and cases is being re-examined, too, among them the 'Seduction Theory', Anna O. (who was not his patient) and the Wolf Man. Cases that are less well-known – the Austrian Emma Eckstein, the American Harold Frink – are under scrutiny. So is the sexuality of the early analysts, including Freud himself. As Professor Edward Timms said at a London conference in 1993, 'the history of the movement has been systematically desexualised', a history that has been 'written from the inside by those with a vested interest in propping up Freud's prestige'. Altogether there is a new curiosity about Freud. But most of it has arisen outside the movement.

Unanalysed as I am, my psychological qualifications for writing Freud's biography amount to a healthy (or unhealthy) interest in people's mental quirks, including my own. As a child it occurred to me that when I wrote the 'P' of my given name precisely under a capital 'D' in the line above, the 'D' stood for Death and was best avoided. This wasn't hard to fix – a gap of a quarter-inch, and Death was defeated. But the persistence in one's life of illogical compulsions and private rituals is a reminder of the peculiar other-world *out there*, or rather *in here*, that the man from Vienna made his province. For years the middle-aged Freud saw omens of his death around him, even in a telephone number and the number of his hotel room. From time to time he believed in telepathy. Behind the eventual eminence were the usual uncertainties.

Working on this book has taught me the inexhaustible nature of the subject. Freud is what you want him to be.

Boughrood and London, 1993–1997

Acknowledgements

I am grateful to the staff at the Archives of the British Psycho-Analytical Society, and in particular Jill Duncan; Thomas Roberts, archivist, Sigmund Freud Copyrights, in Wivenhoe, Essex; Erica Davies and Michael Molnar of the Freud Museum; Ingrid Scholz-Strasser and Doris Fritsche of the Sigmund Freud House at Berggasse 19, Vienna; David W. C. Stewart and Robert Greenwood at the Royal Society of Medicine Library, London. Two analysts and writers from very different disciplines, Anthony Stadlen and Anthony Storr, let me consult them at length. So did Hugh Freeman, Eric Rayner and Edward Timms. Hanns W. Lange, meticulous genealogist of the Freuds, supplemented his family trees with family tales. The book was suggested by Christopher Sinclair-Stevenson, and my greatest debt is to him.

Others I want to thank are: Stephen Barlay, Fred W. Bauman Jr (Library of Congress), John Beloff, Wolfgang Berner, Julia Cave, Christopher Cordess, Rhian Davies, Rosina Davies, T. G. Davies, Walford Davies, Esmond Devas, Alice Eisler, Georg Eisler, Allen Esterson, Alice Feldman, John Fforde, Armond Fields, Sophie Forrester, Joan Freeman, Sophie Freud, John E. Gedo, Marlene Hobsbawm, Han Israëls, Mervyn Jones, Andreas Kafka (Austrian Broadcasting Corporation), Heinz Katschnig, Crawford Keenan (Johns Hopkins Medical Institutions), Pearl King, Sue King (Police College Library, Bramshill, Hampshire), Harald Leupold-Löwenthal, Karen Llewellyn, John McGarry, Jeffrey Masson, Peter Nathan, Tom Philby, Dilys Rayner, J. Russell Rees, Paul Ries, Gloria Roberts (Planned Parenthood Federation of America), Charles Rycroft, Wilhelm Schlag, Tom Scott, Riccardo Steiner, Peter Swales, Edith Wolzl, John Riddington Young.

Mrs Helen Frink Kraft gave me permission to consult the Horace W. Frink and Doris Best Frink Papers, and the Horace W. Frink correspondence in the Adolf Meyer Papers, all at the Alan Mason

Chesney Medical Archives of the Johns Hopkins Medical Institutions at Baltimore, Maryland, to whose trustees I am also grateful.

Libraries and archives not already mentioned whose help is gratefully acknowledged are the British Medical Association Archives, Leo Baeck Institute, Wellcome Institute for the History of Medicine, Wiener Library, all in London; John Rylands University Library, Manchester; and Southport and Crosby public libraries.

I am grateful to the following for granting permission to quote from copyright material: Faber & Faber Ltd for permission to quote nine lines of 'In Memory of Sigmund Freud' by W. H. Auden, from *Collected Shorter Poems*, copyright © The Estate of W. H. Auden, 1966; Harvard University Press for permission to quote from *The Complete Letters of Sigmund Freud to Wilhelm Fliess 1887–1904*, translated and edited by Jeffrey Moussaieff Masson, copyright © The Belknap Press, Harvard University Press, 1985; from *The Correspondence of Sigmund Freud and Sándor Ferenczi*, Volume 1, edited by Eva Brabant, Ernst Falzeder and Patrizia Giampieri-Deutsch and translated by Peter T. Hoffer, and Volume 2, edited by Ernst Falzeder and Eva Brabant and translated by Peter T. Hoffer, both copyright © The Belknap Press, Harvard University Press, 1993; from *The Complete Correspondence of Sigmund Freud and Ernest Jones 1908–1939*, edited by R. Andrew Paskauskas, copyright © The Belknap Press, Harvard University Press, 1993 and 1996; and from *The Letters of Sigmund Freud to Eduard Silberstein 1871–1881*, edited by Walter Böhlich and translated by Arnold J. Pomerans, copyright © The Belknap Press, Harvard University Press, 1990; The Estate of Carl Jung, The Hogarth Press and Routledge & Kegan Paul, for permission to quote from *The Freud–Jung Letters: The Correspondence between Sigmund Freud and C. G. Jung*, edited by William McGuire, translated by Ralph Manheim and R. F. C. Hull, copyright © The Hogarth Press and Routledge & Kegan Paul, 1974; Mark Paterson & Associates for quotations from *The Standard Edition of the Complete Psychological Works of Sigmund Freud* (The Hogarth Press, London, & W. W. Norton & Co., New York, 1953–1974); unpublished Sigmund Freud material © A. W. Freud et al, by arrangement with Mark Paterson & Associates.

Every attempt has been made to trace holders of copyright material. I much regret if any inadvertent omissions have been made, but these can be rectified in future editions.

1: Tales from the Vienna Woods

B aedeker's *Austria*, ninth edition, 1900, has the authority assumed by guidebooks from self-assured times. When it describes a short excursion from the capital to the summit of a nearby hill called the Kahlenberg, the account crammed into one of its tiny pages has a definitive air, disposing of paths, inns, vineyards and views in a once-and-for-all fashion. From the summit at 1,580 feet, spurs of the Carpathians can be seen to the east in clear air, with some Alps away to the south-west.

> Lastly, in the centre of the extensive landscape (900 sq. M.), the imperial city of Vienna, with the new channel of the Danube and its five bridges.

Various ways up are offered. Walkers can take the steam-train to Nussdorf, in the 19th District, and approach along a valley 'by a shady path called the *Beethoven-Gang*, with a bronze bust of the great composer, who made this a frequent resort'. Shady path and great composer are still there, the head dark and weathered, rising above a bush of squashed purple berries that have stained his plinth. Boy cyclists sweep past. There is a distant smell of barbecue from someone's lawn.

Tens of thousands must have passed this way and paid their respects in the days when statues, like portrait photographs, were thought to have something important to say. Among them, more than once, was the young Sigmund Freud, who liked to walk in suburban Vienna because he couldn't afford to walk anywhere else. He left a record of one such occasion in 1882 when he was taking his German sweetheart, Martha (she came from Hamburg), to visit places he knew. It was a day in summer, and Martha's sister Minna was there to act as chaperone as they proceeded up Beethoven Walk, where no doubt they admired the head, unveiled two decades earlier, and talked of the composer's life in Vienna. Sigmund had other things on his mind. Aged twenty-six, a penniless doctor and in love, he couldn't help looking every time Martha turned aside to pull up her stockings. She seems to have done this rather often. He was still thinking about it a year later, and mentioned the stockings in a letter, apologising to her for being so bold, at the same time getting some mileage from the memory. It wasn't much of an event even for the prudish times they lived in, but Freud was a late developer in these matters.

Around the Kahlenberg and its surrounding hills are the beech-covered slopes of the Vienna Woods, once preserved for imperial hunting purposes, now picnic country, much of it deserted in the way of countryside on the edge of cities, too near to be taken seriously. Dr Freud used to go mushrooming there with his children. He had married the girl from Hamburg. To begin with they lived in an apartment on a boulevard, and he began to carve a decent career as a private physician; though not half decent enough for someone with such complicated dreams. When he came to make his private imagination (or some of it) public in his books, the dreams had traces of a childhood with a hard-up father presiding over the Freuds at various shaky addresses in the Jewish quarter; as well as traces of his own longing to succeed.

During the long summer breaks, which the Viennese take seriously, Sigmund and Martha were soon able to afford family holidays in the Semmering, a mountainous region fifty miles south-west of the capital. They usually stayed at Reichenau, once a village with iron-ore mines, 1,600 feet above sea level. Freud tramped up to the barren mountain plateaux, wearing tweedy clothes with a collar and tie as people used to, even on holiday; Schneeberg, Snow Mountain, the highest in Lower Austria, and one of his favourites, reaches 6,800 feet, an exhilarating wasteland in the sky. This is the section of Alps visible in clear weather from Vienna's Kahlenberg.

High country appealed to Freud. The Austrians, like the Swiss, feel about mountains as the British do about coasts. 'There is no sin in the mountains,' they say hopefully in Vienna. On one of these Semmering holidays, in 1893, Freud had an adventure on the Rax, the mountain next to Schneeberg. It was an adventure in the special sense of Freud's adventures in psychology: vivid, a trifle odd, without witnesses. He was approached by an innkeeper's daughter, a sulky adolescent who consulted him on the mountain about anxiety attacks. Freud soon winkled out the problem. She had an 'uncle' (it was really her father) who made sexual advances to her and her cousin. Her symptoms, he decided, were neurotic, reproducing the anxiety she felt when father/uncle struck. Freud used this early case history in a book, and 'Katharina — —' became famous in the literature.

The encounter may have been shaped by Freud to make it read like a short story (which it does), but Katharina of course existed; her name was Aurelia Kronich, and there is even a photograph of her, together with one of the wicked father, Julius, a man with a small moustache that makes him look like Hitler. Her identity, and the photographs, were dug out a century later by Peter Swales, a maverick Freudian scholar who pursues Freud from story to story, questioning his integrity with a ruthless inventiveness that in a strange fashion mirrors Freud's own way of working.*

Freudian scholarship broods at enormous length over those early years, when psychoanalysis was in the making. It becomes difficult to separate the man who met Katharina on the mountain top, who watched Martha Bernays adjust her clothes in Beethoven Walk, from the reconstructed Freud, endlessly dwelt upon. Places with associations – a landscape, a room, an as-it-was-once that survives – offer the biographer some comfort; perhaps illusory.

Freud wanted to change the world by giving it a universal theory of human behaviour, and he has to be looked for in terms of his certainty that this was possible, and that he was the man to do it. Anyone who has such ambitions and makes such claims invites scepticism. But Freud's attempt was on a mighty scale. If human personality was too much for him in the end, at least his running commentaries on the lives we lead were full of insights and ingenious explanations of mysteries that, even when they became mysteries of another kind in his hands, added to our knowledge of ourselves. If he used ruthless means – guile, deception, deviousness – to achieve the ends he believed in, it is no more than most innovators have to do. Only an unusual being of iron will could have kept it up: a sort of Oedipus (as he saw himself) who knew that he knew the answer to the riddle of the Sphinx. The figure in the landscape is never quite what he seems.

* Peter J. Swales, born 1948 in Haverfordwest, Wales, was educated at the local grammar school and later, after a 'spiritual crisis', turned himself into a one-man centre of excellence in Freudian studies, based in New York.

Tucked away among the meadows and vineyards lower down the slopes of the Kahlenberg and its adjoining hills were various choice properties, among them the Schloss Bellevue, a house on a connected ridge to the south-west at about 1,200 feet that the Freuds came to know. The 1900 Baedeker ignores it. Grinzing, a village a mile below, gets a mention ('Berger's Restaurant, shady garden and good wine'), and there is a passing reference to 'numerous villas' in the area. A City of Vienna tramline terminates there now, and the place is dotted with shady gardens where tourists are pressed to guzzle the *Heuriger*, the young local wine. Beethoven Walk is half a mile distant, to the east.

Just below Grinzing is a public park, on land where the Turkish Army that besieged Vienna for months in 1683 was camped. One autumn morning the imperial army and its Polish allies came charging over the Kahlenberg, and that was the end of the Turks, though fear of invasion from the east kept defence works in place, cramping the city inside them, for another two centuries. When Freud was a child, the military had just relinquished tracts of inner-city land, and Vienna was seized with building mania. Near the end of his life, in 1937, when the Nazis were figuratively at the gates, Freud drew a parallel with 1683, writing sadly that this time no one was going to come riding over the Kahlenberg.

Short of funds for a family holiday in 1895, Freud decided to forgo the Alps and settle for the Kahlenberg area. Bellevue, owned by a family called Schlag, was not an hotel and had no public restaurant, and the owners thought of it as a house that took guests; they obviously paid but the transaction was veiled in gentility. The building was unusual, squat and vaguely Italianate from the front, with a pair of thin towers enclosing the upper storey at each end. It was built earlier in the century as a place of entertainment – receptions, dances, gambling – and the rooms were unusually spacious. At the back of the main building were two wings that stretched back from the frontal extremities, trailing behind the preposterous façade. Three big upper windows dominated the front, looking out over Vienna, the rooms where the best guests stayed; the Freuds must have qualified, but their name meant little at the time, and only a dim memory of the family as paying guests survives among the Schlags. Above the three windows, large and not very genteel letters across the house proclaimed BELLE VUE.

The Freuds went there early, at the end of May, no doubt organising a horse and cart for the luggage and a servant, and a closed carriage for themselves and their five children. Martha had been pregnant with a sixth child since March, an unwelcome event. 'On Monday we move to Heaven,' Freud wrote to a friend; Himmel Strasse, or Heaven Street, being the road up from Grinzing that passes Bellevue on its way to Heaven, an estate further up the hill. Freud had no time for Heaven just then. Until Vienna's summer holidays began, he commuted between Heaven and their city apartment, by this time at Berggasse, or Hill Street, where the patients and the income were.

Freud was uneasy that spring. Less keen by this time to continue as a general physician, though no less dependent on the fees, he had ideas that cruel colleagues in Vienna would soon be smiling at. A few days before the family went to Bellevue he told his friend Dr Wilhelm Fliess in Berlin that 'a man like me' couldn't live without a consuming passion. He claimed to have found it in psychology. The study of 'mental functioning', he said, normal and abnormal, had become a tyrant that tormented him.

Nothing out of the ordinary except Freud himself seems to have nourished this passion and what it implied: the search for an explanation of how the mind worked down to the last detail, and for ways of treating its malfunctions. Dr Freud's clinical material was modest. It consisted of the mixed bag of neurotic middle-class Viennese he had been seeing for nine years who kept practices like his going. Their problems were real enough but their treatment was haphazard.

One didn't see the properly mad; they went into private clinics if they were well-off and unsavoury hospital wards if they weren't, where they were assumed to have inherited bad blood from their parents and were, with any luck, soon forgotten. The neurotics, the walking-wounded of psychiatry, were more amenable because they were less abnormal. These were the ones with anxiety attacks and phobias – who were afraid of horses or the dark, who felt inadequate, who suffered indigestion and bad legs and backaches – for which there was no particular diagnosis except the vague but popular 'neurasthenia' or, in severe cases, 'hysteria'. This itself was an ill-defined condition, a favourite nineteenth-century affliction that struck middle-class women in particular and may have owed its ubiquity to the lives the women led.

No tranquillisers or anti-depressants were available; for most doctors these patients with 'nerves' were on the margins of real medicine, though pleasingly lucrative. Freud took their money, but he paid attention to what they told him as well and his observations made him curious about the personality of patients who were disturbed, who were 'not themselves'. The nature of consciousness was a popular subject for philosophic debate in the nineteenth century. By Freud's time psychologists and psychiatrists had begun to take a technical interest, and many were convinced that a sub- or un-conscious part of the mind existed. Most people took the idea of a divided consciousness for granted. When Thomas Hardy wrote in *The Return of the Native* that 'men are drawn from their intentions even in the course of carrying them out', he expressed an elementary truth that his Victorian readers of 1878 would have recognised. What Freud did was seize on this growing perception of a mind within a mind and, using a mixture of intuition and observation, begin to elaborate an all-embracing scheme that used neurotics as its raw material but set out to explain human behaviour in general.

This was a tall order. He had his own state of mind to go on, but that was itself part of the wider mystery. 'Internal perception cannot claim to be "evidence",' he told his friend Fliess. He frequently felt uneasy. This didn't stop him plunging ahead.

His credibility wasn't helped, when people happened to hear of him, by a conviction that sex was the principal preoccupation of this other self. His first book, *Studies on Hysteria*, written with a senior colleague whose name preceded his on the title page, was published in the same month, May 1895, and contained the cryptic remark, in italics, that *'Hysterics suffer mainly from reminiscences'*. (One of the patients he wrote about was Katharina, the girl on the mountain.) Freud's speculations in the book about the nature of the reminiscences were muted, but he believed they were to do with sexual matters.

Sex also dominated his view of milder mental problems, such as neurasthenia, in which people had 'trouble with their nerves'. Either the evidence of patients or his own inclinations – Freud implied the former, the facts suggest the latter – led him to condemn masturbation and the use of condoms as dangerous practices that gave people bad nerves and debilitated them. Doctors and clergymen commonly denounced anything that made sex sound a pleasure instead of a duty. Freud didn't think (or if he did, he didn't say) that these practices were immoral. What they did was blight one's life by causing neurasthenia. Since Vienna had a prosperous middle class that suffered with its nerves and had done plenty of forbidden things in the past, there was no shortage of patients to whom he could apply the solution. But it would be wrong to see Freud as a doctor inventing treatments. He believed that he had a profound answer, a special key.

He also had a personal interest. His own marital situation as a father of five, nearly six, with a wife who shrank from continual pregnancies, gave him reason for a morbid concern with contraception or the lack of it. Bursts of optimism (he was 'wild and yearning' for the spring, he told his Berlin friend in April) alternated with gloom. A fluttering heart and burning pains in the chest made him into a hypochondriac; he was taking cocaine and smoking heavily; aged thirty-nine, he was convinced he would be dead at fifty-one, a date that had mysterious significance. He knew he was neurotic.

Bellevue in the summer was remote, its meadows and gardens floating above the city's dust, the air heavy-scented with the wild roses that grew around the house. A north-easterly wind blew faint music from the military band that played at the Hotel Kahlenberg on Thursdays and Sundays, but nothing much intruded on Bellevue. Trespassers from Heaven Street got shouted at by Herr Schlag through a megaphone.

In July Freud was there more often. In between walking and strawberrying, he dwelt on the stories of sexual experiences in childhood that he heard, or thought he was hearing, from patients. There were other things on his mind. His wife had had thrombosed veins in her legs during a previous pregnancy, and Freud was worried about a recurrence. She was still a young woman in today's terms, approaching her thirty-fourth birthday on 26 July, for which celebrations were planned at Bellevue. On 23 July a friend and younger colleague, Oscar Rie, called to see them, and made a remark about one of Freud's patients, 'Irma', that implied criticism of her treatment.

Martha's pregnancy, the forthcoming birthday, the colleague's visit, the size of the reception rooms at Bellevue and his professional uncertainties were about to be worked into a dream that Freud made famous. He claimed to unravel a meaning, and used the result as a first proof that dreams were serious scientific business, soon to be indispensable to his brand-new, as yet unheard-of psychology. Far from being indiscriminate, dreams, he thought, revealed aspects of the dreamer that could be understood by someone who could break their code. Freud was the someone.

The Bellevue dream came to acquire the touch of drama that proved so useful all his life. It occurred early in the morning of 24 July. Freud was in a large hall, Bellevue-like, receiving guests, among them the patient he disguised as 'Irma'. Alarmed at her condition, he looked down her throat and saw peculiar lesions. Colleagues were present and the case was discussed. They concluded that Irma's infection was due to an injection not long before, probably given by Dr Rie with a dirty syringe.

That was all. Four years passed before he published it in *The Interpretation of Dreams* at the turn of the century, where he set out to capture an audience beyond medicine. The summary there ran to a few hundred words. He called it a 'specimen dream', examining it carefully and in the process inviting readers to plunge into the 'minutest details' of his life.

The thoughts aroused by the dream revolved around Freud's competence as a doctor. Martha's putative thrombosis was connected to the hypodermic syringe that injected Irma. The associations go on for pages. Freudian scholarship has been at work ever since, thickening the broth. To Freud it was a dream about his professional standing, measuring himself against colleagues and concluding that he was not, after all, to blame for Irma's condition. 'The dream represented a particular state of affairs as I should have wished it to be. *Thus its content was the fulfilment of a wish and its motive was a wish.*' Freud made this into one of the universal truths he was after. His conviction that all dreams were purposeful, and that they were always an attempt at the fulfilment of a wish, however obscure, provided him with technical knowledge that he could use when evaluating the dreams he encouraged his patients to tell him.

Whether or not dreams are really about fulfilling wishes, a minority view today, those 'minutest details' have left the dreamer more exposed than he intended. Guarded as he was, Freud nevertheless kept leaving clues – in dreams, in letters, in his voluminous works – that encourage discovery. Friends tried to dissuade him, but he had an urge for autobiography, and some of the 'scientific' writings with which he set out to conquer the world still glitter with his hints and asides. Most lives are measured by outward events. Much of Freud's life was inward, and it may be that it was an unconscious need to reveal – lest there be too little to satisfy his biographers – that led him to leave clues that don't always show him to advantage. Freud revealed things about himself to which he was the only witness. This has had the odd consequence that his enemies draw much of their firepower from the weapons that he provides.

The 'Irma' dream and his commentary betray signs of guilt. Was it Martha's tendency to superficial vein thrombosis that worried him? Or was it the fact that after being sexually abstinent for much of the time since their fifth child was born in 1893 – thanks to a reluctance to use contraception – he had impregnated her yet again in March 1895? 'I am again a human being with human feelings,' he wrote triumphantly to Dr Fliess on 15 March, a day or two after the probable night when number six was conceived.

There were other things to feel guilty about. One of the women concealed behind 'Irma' was Emma Eckstein, a patient with menstrual problems. Freud was analysing her and may have thought that the root of her trouble was masturbation. Earlier in the year he sent her to Dr Fliess, whose mind seethed with as many ideas as Freud's and who thought that a sympathetic connection existed between nose and sexual organs (they were strange times in medicine). Fliess operated on Eckstein's nose but he botched the surgery. Returning to Vienna, she haemorrhaged several times and nearly died. In public Freud wouldn't hear a word against Fliess, whose friendship as a fellow pioneer he badly needed. But in the dream it could have been different.

'Irma's injection' was a turning-point for Freud – the vision, it has been said, of a middle-aged man, creatively inclined, lonely and frustrated in his attempts to explain human nature, who was taught by a dream what insights the unconscious has to offer. He may even have dreamt it to order. Patients are apt to have dreams that the analyst finds useful. For a few years after 1895, Freud's mind kindly sprouted the dreams he needed to help him understand his most important patient, himself.

In June 1900, writing (again from Bellevue) to Fliess, Freud wondered if 'someday' a marble tablet would say:

In this house, on July 24 1895
the secret of dreams was
revealed to Dr Sigm. Freud

It took a long time, but most of the wish, Freud-like in its intensity, was fulfilled in 1977 on the 121st anniversary of his birth. A plaque on a pedestal was set up in a corner of what had been the Bellevue meadow, below the house, where the ground is already sliding away towards Vienna. The monument, which reproduces the sentence from the letter to Fliess, stands in the middle of nowhere. Bellevue has gone.

The Schlags left it long ago. After their time it was a children's sanatorium. In 1945 Russian soldiers were in occupation. Refugees from the east took refuge there for a while. Later someone tried to bring the ruin back to life as a restaurant, without success. Finally it was knocked down. Bellevue is now the name of a location on a ridge between two valleys. Where the house stood there are irregularities in the ground among the trees that have taken root; nothing more.

2: Out of the East

Two shabby men with a horse and cart, taking dyed cloth into the coldest corner of Europe and bringing back wool and honey in exchange, will do as a caricature of the world Freud came from. The time is the 1840s. The nag is slow, the weather nasty. There are three or four hundred miles to cover. The Carpathians head off warm airs from the south. Possibly a wolf or two howl. Reliable reports of travellers devoured by wolves are rare, but in distant Galicia a hundred and fifty years ago, *Wanderjuden*, travelling Jews, might have been an at-risk category. Wolves or no, it sounds a bleak enterprise.

The lands the wagon crossed belonged to the Austrian Empire. The imperial writ ran east from Vienna, through Bohemia, Moravia, Silesia, Hungary and eventually Galicia, which the Empire acquired from Poland in the eighteenth century; only Hungary is left. Seen from Vienna, with its palaces and violins, Galicia was a dirty, far-off place. The humming bureaucracy sent garrisons to keep order and officials to raise taxes, especially taxes from the Jews, 200,000 of whom were acquired along with Galicia, more than doubling their numbers in the Empire. People from the east were regarded with suspicion in Vienna, and Jews were not popular wherever they came from; their apartness saw to that. The job lot who came with Galicia were greeted with severe laws and taxes to make them cost-efficient, and if possible to keep their numbers down. Marriage, candles and kosher meat were taxed. Their faith was subordinate to the State religion, Roman Catholicism. Even their surnames had a price, since Galician Jews were ordered to have Germanic names in 1787, and officials could be bribed to approve something agreeable. It was worth paying money to be a Blumenthal, a Valley of Flowers, or a Schonberg, a beautiful mountain.

The travellers in the wagon – an old man called Siskind Hofmann and a young man called Jacob Freit, or Freud – would have kept their eyes lowered at the sight of anyone in uniform, not because they were acting illegally but because humility was prudent. Their temporary passports had to be ready for inspection, tucked away inside oilskin to keep them dry. Jews had even fewer rights than Polish peasants. Traces of Siskind and Jacob's travels survive only because the Austrian bureaucracy had an appetite for permits and passports, and went on hoarding records long after the Empire ceased to exist.

The name Freud means 'joy' in German, perhaps another hopeful invention. Jacob Freud lived in difficult times that he would have seen as perfectly normal. For a thousand years eastern Europe had been filled with disparate peoples, arranged and rearranged within autocratic empires – Turkish, Russian, Austrian. These mixed populations fostered prejudice, and the Jews were always there, distinctive and visible, to be on the receiving end of it. Reviled from early times by Christian propagandists as the persecutors of Christ, barred from the learned professions and driven to be self-sufficient, they learned to handle goods and money, which was clever of them but provoked envy. So did sharp Semitic wits, bred into the culture by a respect for learning that encouraged bright boys to study religion and laid upon affluent Jews the duty of subsidising it.

The farther east a particular Jew originated, the greater the suspicions he aroused. This trend grew through the nineteenth century and into the twentieth, as population shifts from east to west took place, and the 'assimilated' – westernised – Jews found the *Ostjuden* a useful stereotype to distance themselves from. Among the Empire's Jews, those from Galicia were regarded with special distaste. Even in the 1840s, there would have been Jews in Vienna who viewed their Galician brethren as primitives with greasy hair, speaking a weird vernacular, Yiddish, instead of decent German. These perceptions influenced Sigmund Freud. His parents eventually came up in the world a bit, settling in Moravia, a long way to the west of Galicia, before he was born. As a socially-conscious teenager he made more than one cutting remark about those other Jews who were not his sort at all.

The 1900 Baedeker observed that most of Galicia's shop- and innkeepers were Jews: 'They differ in their dress and the mode of wearing their hair from the other inhabitants, who despise them but are financially dependent on them.' The same guidebook mentioned the Northern Railway's route across Galicia, from Tarnopol, now in the Ukraine, to Oświęcim, now in Poland. Forty years later the Nazis had occupied Poland and Germanised the place-names. Oświęcim became Auschwitz. Sigmund Freud's birthplace, near the Moravian border with Silesia, is an hour or two's drive today from Oświęcim and the ruined crematoria. Four of his sisters, by then in their eighties, were put to death by gassing in 1942, three years after he died in his bed in London. Some say that Rosa was murdered at Auschwitz; Paula, Mitzi and Dolfi at extermination camps farther to the north. The rattle of bones can be heard behind Freud's story.

Jacob, born 1815, was to be Sigmund's father. Otherwise the wagon would have proceeded across the frame of the landscape and into oblivion. The old man, Siskind Hofmann, was Jacob's maternal grandfather, forty or so years his senior. Jacob's father, Salomon, was another associate of Siskind. Salomon is only a shadow, but we know that his son had a peaceful nature, resigned and hopeful. It was probably the Hofmanns who drove the business, not the Freuds. In 1844, applying for tax relief, Siskind told the authorities he was seventy-six (adding a few years for effect), 'bent by age' and too infirm to carry on alone. Jacob had complementary reasons for relief. He was 'only a beginner', his trade 'insignificant'. The officials had heard it all before; the application failed.

The Freuds' roots were in Galicia, traceable into the eighteenth century. Tysmenitz, Galicia, today Tysmienica, Poland, was Jacob's birthplace, a small trading town within forty miles of the Russian border, on a north–south road in a country where the imperial highways ran east–west. Jacob (who had two brothers and a sister) acquired an education. Tysmenitz had some standing as a centre for Jewish studies, and his schooling was presumably religious in the special Jewish sense, involving close study of the Bible and the Talmud. At the end of it Jacob could read Hebrew, but for business he used German.

Before he was seventeen, in 1832, Jacob was married off to a woman called Sally Kanner; an arranged Jewish marriage at an early age was normal for the time. Before he was eighteen, Jacob had a son, Emmanuel, followed by a second, Philipp, within a year. Two other children seem to have died in infancy.

For twenty years, while his sons grew up, Jacob went on travelling and trading; or so it's assumed. His grandfather's western base was another small commercial town, Freiberg in Moravia, now Příbor in Czechoslovakia, but their official place of residence remained Tysmenitz. To be in Freiberg at all they needed temporary permits. Jews were thinner on the ground in Moravia and most of the population spoke German or Czech. Western culture was nearer – Vienna, down the imperial highway to the south-west, was less than 150 miles away. According to a document of April 1844, Siskind had been visiting Freiberg on and off for decades. He rented a room and two cellars for the business, and lodged at the town hostelry. No doubt Jacob did the same. By Galician standards they were men of the world.

Jacob's private life is a mystery. Was Sally alive and bringing up the boys in Tysmenitz? Did Jacob return home each autumn with gifts and traveller's tales? Whatever was happening, around the middle of the century his life changed decisively, along with the lives of many. Revolutions, predicted for years, swept through Europe in 1848, bringing reforms of a sort. Austria had already tasted trouble when the peasants rose in Galicia in 1846. Now the revolution reached Vienna, and the imperial court and government fled in October. They were back again three weeks later, executing rebels but ultimately more open to argument.

With Austria shifting towards an industrialised society, the Jewish condition improved, slowly, as a by-product of change. In 1848 Jacob was still having to reapply for permission to spend short periods in Freiberg, but four years later he had gone to live there permanently. So had his sons Emmanuel (married by now) and Philipp. So, confusingly, had his wife Rebekka. This is a further mystery. Had Sally died? Was there really a Rebekka as well, or only a confusion over names? Either way, by 1855 both Sally and Rebekka, if there was a Rebekka, were dead (or even divorced). Jacob, described as a widower since 1852, was getting married again that summer, this time in Vienna.

Jacob was forty years old, about to become the grandfather of Emmanuel's first child. His bride was nineteen, a pretty Galician Jewess called Amalie Nathansohn who had been living in Vienna with her parents. The Nathansohns must have seen Jacob as a man of means or they wouldn't have given their daughter to someone of his age. They may in the end have been disappointed, which suggests how personable Jacob must have been to convince them in the first place.

A rabbi with reformist tendencies married them. Amalie's husband, who took her to live in Freiberg, was on the way to becoming, or had become already, an emancipated Jew, anxious to live in the West and conform to its values. Slim and fair-haired, he comes into focus at last. The caftan, the long tunic with a girdle that was the conventional wear for Jewish men in Galicia, turns into a suit. Yiddish is replaced by German. The Nathansohns, sure to be useful allies in business, are established in Vienna, and the new man, revitalised by a woman who is younger than his sons, sets about having a second family.

Jacob and Amalie lived in a rented room above a blacksmith; the house is still there. Amalie was pregnant at once, and the child, a boy covered in dark hair and with a membranous 'caul' adhering to the head, supposedly a charm against drowning, was born on 6 May 1856. He was circumcised a week later and given two names: Salomon, in honour of Jacob's father, and Sigismund, for no known reason. Sigismund was an unfortunate choice, a comic name popular in German-language jokes about Jews. Freud's mother called him 'Sigi', but when he was sixteen he amended Sigismund to the more dignified Sigmund.

Amalie was a strong-willed, difficult woman, an unreconstructed Galician, a 'tornado' according to one of her grandchildren, Sigmund Freud's son Martin; she had 'little grace and no manners'.* In photographs her husband looks almost soft-hearted and she looks almost cruel, with narrow features and deep-set eyes. Her birthplace, Brody, was farther east than Tysmenitz, and she spent some of her girlhood at Odessa, on the Black Sea. She continued to speak Yiddish and broken German for the rest of her long life.

Amalie's first-born, her 'golden Sigi', had his first experiences above the flying sparks of Zajic the blacksmith, at the top of the narrow stairs. Eight months after Sigmund's birth, Amalie was pregnant again, and a second son, Julius, was born in October

---

* Martin Freud, who ended his life as an Englishman with a tobacconist's shop opposite the British Museum, had harsh words for Galician Jews, a 'peculiar race' who were 'absolutely different from Jews who had lived in the West for some generations'. This racial snobbery lives on. One of the few psychoanalysts still practising in Vienna told me (making prejudice sound like fact) that 'merchants' was too grand a word for Jacob Freud and Siskind Hofmann. They were *Ostjuden* riff-raff, dealers in old clothes.

1857. Sigmund was jealous of him, and the death of the new brother six months later left him with 'the germ of self-reproach'; it was all in his dreams later on. In this respect Freud's early infancy was unusual: he claimed to remember more of it than most people do.

'Infantile amnesia', still not satisfactorily explained, erases the memory of all but fragments of what happens before the age of five or six. Few adults can remember sufficient moments of early infancy to add up, in the real time of the original experience, to half an hour. Freud, intrigued by this 'strange riddle', tried to overcome his own amnesia, hoping that if he could uncover early memories he would learn more about his own nature, and thus about everyone else's. Dreams were the most promising source, as long as they were interpreted in the right way. Wherever they came from, memories didn't fall into one's hands ready made; if they seemed to, it was a delusion. They had to be reconstructed. He believed there was raw material to be recovered from the void, and that he was the man to do it. Freud's claims that he could uncover elements of his patients' early lives have been disputed. But his compulsive need to advance into this strange territory is not in doubt. What survives is the force of his curiosity.

Before the baby died, Amalie was into her third pregnancy. The Freuds had a maid or nursemaid – the details are obscure – who may have been called Resi. Freud recalled her as his 'nurse' and said she 'told me a great deal about God Almighty and hell', so presumably she was a Roman Catholic. When he grew up, Freud's mother told him that the woman was 'always carrying you off to some church'. The maid's non-Jewishness was apparently no obstacle. She may have worked exclusively for the Freuds, or have been shared with Emmanuel and his wife who lived nearby. The Emmanuel Freuds already had two children: John, a few months older than his uncle Sigmund, and Pauline, a few months younger. Resi may have been a maid-cum-wet nurse who breastfed Sigmund, and who looked after Emmanuel's children as well when the Freud women were helping in cellar or shop or wherever the men worked.

A series of dreams, forty years after the events he hoped to recall, was devoted to her. Freud concluded that the servant had been 'my teacher in sexual matters', though he failed to explain what he meant.

Because infantile sexuality was central to his theories, researchers have looked for evidence from his own early life, wondering whether he saw his parents sexually engaged in the one-room dwelling. He never referred to it. But as an analyst he took a keen interest in the 'primal scene', the fantasy that an infant creates (they say) around its dim perception of adults performing some incomprehensible act in bed. His famous analysis of Serge Pankejeff, the 'Wolf Man', uncovered or invented an episode in which the patient saw his parents copulate when he was eighteen months old. Pankejeff didn't remember; nor was it likely that the parents, wealthy Russians, would have had a child's cot in their bedroom. Freud told him it had happened, interpreting a dream about wolves to arrive at the explanation. Did a memory of his own infancy from the room above the blacksmith's insinuate itself into the analysis?

Current psychology offered Freud few rules for how to proceed in anything. Relying on intuition, he convinced himself that his results were universal. Sometimes they were.

Family life in Freiberg drifted back in memory. He dreamt that the maid had been dishonest, and his mother confirmed it was true. A day when he played in a field of dandelions with John and Pauline came back to him. The naughty boys stole the girl's flowers, but the memory appeared to conceal something less innocent. He attributed the episode to an unnamed man when he wrote a paper in 1899, 'Screen Memories', in which a forbidden fantasy of ravishment and wedding nights, buried in the unconscious, 'slips away into a childhood memory' – the memory of the game and the flowers – and so is made acceptable. The man was Freud himself; a shrewd follower, Siegfried Bernfeld, worked it out after his death.

Freud and his past are elusive. The story of the flowers has more detail than you expect but less clarity than you would like. Memory and its consequences were at the core of his thinking, and his own memories of childhood were dredged for significant detail over a period of four or five years when he was in his late thirties and early forties. Some of the results appeared in print, notably in *The Interpretation of Dreams* (published soon after 'Screen Memories'), but they were often worked-on memories, put together and made part of a narrative with ulterior motives. Some of the memories occur in letters he had no intention of publishing, or were attributed to someone else. Even where he appears to be frank and revelatory, Freud is concealing information or editing it. His reticence is easily overlooked, thanks to his seductive air of openness.

The dandelion memory contained information about himself that he had no intention of making public. Others have obliged, elaborating on the probable fantasies that excited him as an adolescent and a young man. His critics, in turn, write narratives of their own with ulterior motives, which include the demystifying of Freud to show what kind of private life inspired the creator of psychoanalysis. The truth is what you want it to be.

Life in Freiberg lasted three years, time for Sigmund's next sibling to be born – a girl, Anna, on New Year's Eve 1858 – and for another to be conceived. In 1859 the Freuds decided to leave. No one is sure why. In one possible scenario the cloth business was in decline, and the Czechs who made up most of the population were complaining about the Jews; in another, Emmanuel and Philipp put family money into South African ostrich farming and came unstuck; or perhaps the brothers feared conscription into the imperial army, since Austria was engaged in a short war with Italy.

When the Freuds left Freiberg they went to Leipzig in Germany. Whether or not they were avoiding the draft, Sigmund's half-brothers may have been the catalysts who moved the family on. The amiable Jacob never made much of his life, and there is no reason to suppose he was any different in Freiberg as he approached middle age and fathered a new brood. His grown-up sons were still in their twenties, and Emmanuel at least was to prosper in business. Freud liked and admired Emmanuel all his life. Philipp is a darker and less certain figure, ignored and perhaps actively disliked by Freud. It has been suggested, on slender evidence, that Philipp (who was unmarried when he lived in Freiberg) and Amalie, his young stepmother, had an illicit relation-ship; even, that this lay behind the departure from Freiberg.

At the start of 1859 Amalie was twenty-three, Philipp twenty-four (and Jacob forty-four). A relationship is not impossible, although given her non-stop pregnancies Amalie might have felt that one virile man was enough. The case against Philipp is feeble but persistent. Because Jacob had two (or three) wives, and two sets of children separated by more than twenty years, Freud the child was confused about relationships. He said once that he had believed that his half-brother had something to do with the baby sister who appeared in December 1858. That sounds innocent enough, but a nightmare he had as a child of about nine, which he described thirty years later, has been analysed by others to suggest an adult uneasiness about Philipp.

In the dream his mother was being carried by men with birds' beaks who laid her on a bed, at which he woke screaming. Freud said it was fear of his mother dying. His 'associations' to the dream, the thoughts it led to, included a boy he played with who taught him a slang word, 'vogeln', meaning 'to fuck', derived from 'Vogel', 'a bird'. The boy was called Philipp, but Freud failed to report any association that led to his half-brother. Since this was an obvious connection to make, Freud could have had something to hide, either from himself or from his readers.

This is plausible if far-fetched. Ernest Jones, Freud's friend and colleague, made an oblique comment in the official biography, hinting that he, too, found it odd. Jones often knew more than he said, and he kept his mouth shut about many things, at the same time letting people know he was the insider, last survivor of Freud's henchmen. Perhaps he suspected that a sexual scandal lay buried in Freiberg.

Whatever happened, if anything did, the two brothers broke away from the family. From Leipzig they went to live in Manchester, the centre of the textile trade in England, and sent back remittances that helped keep the Freuds afloat.

Freiberg became the place that Freud looked back to, the necessary Eden: 'Deeply buried within me there still lives the happy child of Freiberg,' he wrote in old age when the town honoured him, as any famous citizen might do. A horse and cart took them away, on the first stage of the journey to Leipzig. He recalled Breslau station, which the train passed through at night, and the gas flames that made him think of the spirits burning in hell that the maid had told him about.

Soon after Emmanuel and Philipp had gone their own way, Jacob and Amalie were back in Austria with their two small children, Sigmund and Anna, living now in Vienna. Amalie's family, the Nathansohns, may have offered a degree of security. Their first address, probably in 1860, was across the Danube Canal from Leopoldstadt, the Jewish quarter, north-east of central Vienna, apparently as sub-tenants of another Freud, a distiller. Presently they left the city side of the canal for Leopoldstadt proper, between the canal and the river, where odorous smoke and steam from basement workshops blew into the overcrowded tenements that overhung the streets. The district, only a stroll from the city centre, had some elegant houses, and at one end, beyond a railway station and the marshalling yards, it opened into the Prater, the pleasure park of Vienna; but Leopoldstadt grew more crowded with every train that brought in hopefuls from the east.

The poorest rented a portion of a room, each plot delineated by chalkmarks, or merely the right to sleep in a bed when the previous occupant vacated it. The Freuds were not as desperate as that. But they were nearer the bottom of the heap than the top.

They were in Vienna for good. Freud would live in the city for eighty years, until his life was nearly over. Often he cursed it, made fun of it, was disgusted by it. He once wrote to his fiancée about the 'grotesque and animal-like faces' one saw about the place, the 'deformed skulls and potato noses'. But he could never be parted from it for long. He came to define a particular Vienna where young bourgeois women who lived in men's shadows confessed their fears and dreams to the brooding Jewish doctor, and where, amid the thick-layered subterfuge and hypocrisy (but was it so different from New York's and London's?) he found what he needed to drive his fantasies and pursue his unsettling experiments with people.

3: The Field of Flowers

Jacob and Amalie would have wanted the best for their children but there is no evidence they were imaginative or far-sighted parents. A scholar is supposed to have figured in Amalie's genealogy; on Jacob's side were the dim forebears who bought and sold things. Jacob's ambitions were large but unfocused. Being an optimist he may have seen the rosy outline of a career in trade, even in a profession, for the boys – or the boy, since his wife, after producing Sigmund (and Julius, who died), gave birth to a succession of girls. He is unlikely to have seen a specifically Jewish future for any of his children. The future lay with emancipation, with embracing the Austrian tradition that looked towards Germany.

Financial security for Sigmund would benefit the parents, as well as the sisters if they were not lucky enough to find husbands. Jacob had no visible means of support, and how he managed to seem as tolerably well-off in Vienna as he did is a mystery. According to city records he had no taxable income. The sons in Manchester helped, and so probably did the Nathansohns, until its head, another Jacob, died in 1865. Sigmund – as merchant, banker or professional man with stiff collar and cylinder hat – would be a valuable addition to his father's system of muddling through.

The earliest family photographs reach out for respectability. The fact that they were taken at all is a sign of progress. A pair dating from 1864, when Sigmund was eight years old, has the usual studio furniture; portrait photography had caught on in all the European capitals. Sigmund appears in both pictures, self-assured, head possibly gripped by a hidden neck clamp, hair glossy from the brush, hands like flippers, placed at the photographer's instruction. Jacob, in one of the pair, is the minor businessman with the close-trimmed beard. Amalie, in the other, dark-dressed and with two daughters alongside as well as her son, has an autocratic air.

A few years later, someone made an oil painting of the entire brood: Sigmund, five sisters and a final brother, at last, Alexander, born in 1866. The heads don't match the bodies, so the portraitist must have been learning his trade. Even so, having children in oils was a step up.

Sigmund had to be the favoured one; his sisters, when they were old enough for it to register, would have expected nothing else. The evidence is still available to show him as a child of fortune, gliding through his education, serious beyond his years, subject of approving glances. By the time he was eleven or twelve, his parents liked to take him with them on evening visits to a café in the Prater, another of the things that Jacob shouldn't have been able to afford but could. When an itinerant poet appeared, writing instant verse for customers, he did a poem for the Freuds and said their son would be a government minister. A preliminary career as a lawyer seemed to be indicated, and for some years that was what Sigmund intended.

His sister Anna wrote, late in life, that when she was eight years old her brother complained he couldn't live in the apartment because of her piano lessons. He had his own study, she said, narrow and cut off from the other rooms, with a window looking out on the street. When she was eight, he was ten. The piano had to go.

Anna liked to gild the family circumstances, but no doubt she was right about the deference Sigmund received. She had other stories about the big brother. When she was fifteen he stopped her reading Balzac and Dumas because they were improper. At sixteen her mother's rich uncle, a widower, arrived from Russia wanting to marry her, promising a horse, new dresses and a warm welcome from his six married children. The rich uncle was aged fifty-nine. According to Anna, Amalie didn't reject the idea out of hand but consulted Sigi; one assumes that Jacob was being offered a financial contribution he couldn't refuse. Sigmund said the kind uncle or old lecher could go back to Russia. He would then have been in his first year at university.

Jacob liked to walk around Vienna with his son. He told him how once, as a young man in Freiberg, he wore a new fur cap on the Sabbath. A Christian knocked the cap into the mud and told him to get off the pavement. *Sigmund*: 'What did you do?' *Father*: 'I went into the roadway and picked up my cap.' The story shocked the boy, with its glimpse of arrogant Roman Catholicism lording it over the Jews in the shape of his beloved father.

Freud's account, written in 1900, described a boyhood fantasy of revenge in which he was Hannibal, warrior of the Carthaginians – a Semitic people – whose father Hamilcar made him swear to take revenge on the Romans. The fantasy extended into adult life. Freud remembered Hannibal, who crossed the Alps in triumph with his army and the elephants in 218 BC but hesitated before Rome, and never reached it. Freud too hesitated, and it was years after he first visited Italy that he managed to reach the city. By describing the projection into the future of a schoolboy's wish, stubbornly adhered to, Freud added significance to his childhood, something he did more than once. Destiny appealed to him. On another occasion, aged six, his mother told him that we are made of dust, and to dust we shall return. Sigmund was dubious. She rubbed her hands together as though making dumplings, and showed him the flakes of grey skin. At once he understood.

Perhaps the lives of great men start reminding them at an early age of the need to accumulate evidence. When Freud was still in his twenties, an unknown doctor without prospects, he announced to his fiancée, Martha the German girl who had trouble with her stockings, that he had destroyed all his papers of the past fourteen years. 'As for the biographers,' he added, 'we have no desire to make it too easy for them.' This was Freud being sardonic. Still, biography was serious. When he was old and disenchanted he said it was bunk: given to concealment, hypocrisy, flattery. A classical education had told him via Plutarch and his *Lives* that the object was to describe the admirable and give readers something to emulate. It was bunk, thought Freud, because it made the subject sound too good to be true. What he hardly envisaged was biography as a conspiracy against the subject to seek out imperfection in him and his family. Under those circumstances, Freud's childhood clouds over like everyone else's.

A wicked Uncle Josef has been hunted down in recent years. Freud's version was unexciting. Josef, ten years younger than Jacob, appeared in a not very important dream of Freud's, a man with a yellow beard who, 'in his eagerness to make money', transgressed and was punished. 'My father,' wrote Freud, 'whose hair turned grey from grief in a few days, used always to say that

Uncle Josef was not a bad man but only a simpleton.' The new evidence has improved the story. Josef, Jacob's brother, was the first Freud to get himself in the newspapers. In 1866 he was tried in Vienna for counterfeiting offences. A small fortune in forged Russian roubles was involved, and he was sent to prison for ten years. The trial implicated the brothers in Manchester. Sigmund, aged nine, is unlikely not to have known what was happening.

Originally a trader in English ironmongery, Josef was another Freud who came west, settling in Vienna in 1861, soon after Jacob. When he was arrested in June 1865 for trying to pass one hundred fifty-rouble notes, he was carrying 17,959 forged roubles, today worth £30,000. Josef and a collaborator called Weich had visited England, and police believed that the roubles were printed there from copperplate engravings. Compromising letters from the brothers in Manchester were referred to at the trial in February 1866 but not disclosed. Passing the money had been delegated to 'Israelites of Polish origin' (that is, Galician Jews, as the Freuds were). It was suggested that anti-Austrian revolutionaries in Poland were using the forgeries to finance their political aims.

Whether police ever came knocking on Jacob's door in Leopoldstadt, and whether it was more than fraternal grief that turned Jacob's hair grey, is unknown. But it was a major family scandal involving the kind of episode that the westernised Freuds, anxious to shake off racist canards about the swindling Jews from the east, must have found distressing. One possible consequence was Freud's venomous attitude as a young man towards eastern Jews (although dislike of them was common enough among those who had come west). Another was his uneasy attitude to money. He referred frequently to the family's poverty. 'From my youth,' he wrote in a letter (aged forty-three), 'I came to know the helplessness of poverty and continually fear it.' But the penury was relative; the evidence points to inconvenience, not desperation. Perhaps the hateful memories were fuelled by hateful knowledge or suspicion of something else: that ill-gotten gains had trickled into Leopoldstadt and helped keep the family afloat.

The case against the brothers in Manchester rested on an unproven allegation made in a court that had no jurisdiction in England. The rest is guesswork. If the Manchester connection did exist, Philipp might be the one to look for. Compared with Emmanuel, dealer in second-hand clothes to begin with, pillar of the Jewish community, who raised his children to be proudly English, Philipp is a shadowy figure, who was in the cheap-jewellery trade and married a toymaker's daughter from Birmingham.

Freud's education was the intensive exercise in self-betterment of the times. Formal lessons taught by Jacob began at home, followed by attendance at a private Jewish school until he entered the State-run high school in Leopoldstadt, which catered for both Jews and Gentiles, at the age of nine. Thereafter he won prizes and after a hesitant start was at or near the top of the class in the eight years before he left for university.

A patriot, like most boys, he relied on Germany for brave deeds. Austria was decaying, an empire long past its best, sharing its principal language with Germany and increasingly inclined to look to its neighbour for political and military will. When war broke out between Germany and France in August 1870, Sigmund, aged fourteen, kept up with the battles as the decadent French retreated. The following winter Paris was besieged. He had maps arrayed with flags on pins to mark the victorious German progress, and an admiring audience of sisters to be told what it all meant.

They were stirring times for victors and their friends. The spectacular defeat of France alerted Europe to Germany's rise. In London, Gladstone's government increased the armed forces budget. In Vienna, emancipated Jews saw even more clearly that their future lay with a Greater Germany.

Freud's first surviving letter dates from about this time, written to a school friend, Eduard Silberstein. Silberstein's father, a businessman in Romania, far to the east, had sent his son to Vienna to be educated. An undated letter, probably of 1870, is written in the mock-solemn style that the boys used:

> Herr and Frau Freud would be prepared to lodge him and his brother Karl and to provide them with a room in the new apartment to which they will be moving in two months' time, and also to sign their sick notes for school.

Sigmund and Eduard exchanged flowery letters about a fictitious Spanish Academy, lapsing into fanciful Spanish to guard against adult intruders. It was a game with private jokes and romantic secrets, in which girls were referred to as 'principles'. When Sigmund took a serious interest in a girl called Gisela Fluss – the sister of another boyhood friend, Emil – she was given a code-name in the correspondence. Fluss is German for 'river', so she became 'Ichthyosaura', a prehistoric fish.

Gisela is the only known romantic involvement of Freud's life apart from the woman he married, and the friendship didn't amount to much. She lived in Freiberg, the town the Freuds had left behind, where her father, Ignaz Fluss, was a textile manufacturer of the kind that Jacob had failed to be. Emil, like Eduard Silberstein, was sent to school in Vienna. The Freuds and the Flusses were on friendly terms, and Sigmund visited Freiberg to stay with the family at least twice, in the summers of 1871 and 1872. On the first visit Sigmund was sixteen and Gisela twelve. By the following year he was in love with her.

Before he visited Freiberg in 1871 he had stayed at the health resort of Roznau, in the hills fifteen miles to the south, where his mother and most of her children were installed at a guest house for the summer. Amalie had a weak chest and frequently went to Roznau after a hard winter, another of the expenses that Jacob could somehow afford and that Freud somehow overlooked when he spoke about hard times. The following year, in Freiberg again, he told Eduard that he had taken a fancy to Gisela, although 'knowing my character, Your Honour will rightly think that instead of approaching her I have held back'. His diffidence, 'the nonsensical Hamlet in me', stood in the way.

He waited till Gisela was no longer there before enthusing over aquiline nose, long black hair, firm lips and dark complexion. Even that sounded more polite than passionate. The only sensual reference came three years later, in 1875, when she was safely lost and he was teasing Eduard about some comparable experience. 'Only in summer does the delight of the principles come into bloom,' he wrote, recalling 'a so-called rose garden, a feast of dahlias', and the lure of 'walks, unconscious searching and undesired yet hotly desired discovery'.

Passion gave way to equanimity. The adolescent Sigmund, deep-eyed above plumpish cheeks, watch chain dangling from his waistcoat, had his future to think about. In March 1873, the year he would finish with high school, he wrote to Gisela's brother, Emil, that a matter of great importance to his 'miserable life' was in the process of being decided. In May he explained what it was: he had chosen to be a 'Natural Scientist', not a lawyer.

This didn't commit him to medicine. Darwin, then at the height of his fame, was a natural scientist. Sigmund could choose to become a zoologist or a chemist and spend his life in a laboratory. He told Fluss that what he feared was mediocrity; he also advised him to keep his letters – 'You never know!'

The Vienna World Fair, held in the Prater that year, enlivened the city and took schoolboys' minds off their exams. The Emperor Franz-Josef I opened it on a wet May Day, while artillery thundered in the distance and the crowned heads of Europe sheltered under umbrellas. Sigmund wrote a sardonic letter to Fluss about newspaper reports of cheering crowds, who were, he said, so busy keeping dry that they hardly raised their hats. His Majesty, he added, looked about as regal as a crossing-sweeper.

Beyond the plumed helmets was sterner stuff: industrial pavilions filled with machines and gadgets, one of them an oil lamp with chains to raise and lower it above the dining-room table, which appealed to the Freuds so much that they bought one. Austria was anxious to show that it was becoming a modern State. Some of the exhibiting nations obliged by not keeping up with their hosts. The British, complaining that their exhibits had been 'unreasonably delayed' on the continental roads, draped Union flags over the empty spaces and hoped no one would notice.

The 1873 Fair was an excuse for the Viennese to show off a redesigned city. Liberalising influences had prompted a programme to rebuild Vienna. On the eve of the opening, visiting reporters were taken up to the rooftops at night, and marvelled at the sinuous avenues, brilliantly lit by thousands of gas lamps. The central city had been a tangle of impacted streets, enclosed within a belt of green fields that was kept undeveloped so that the army could defend it against Turks or their modern equivalents. The suburbs were outside the defensive zone. This was hardly the way to run a modern city. Finally an imperial decree broke the deadlock. The army was made to give up its land, and a great boulevard around the old city, the Ringstrasse, studded with clusters of public buildings, was put in hand. 'The Ring' and its triumphalist style came to define the new Vienna.

Sigmund and his father would have seen it slowly taking shape when they went for their walks, a good omen for all progressives, its broad perspectives fading into sunlight, snow or rain with equal splendour. The army had made the best of a bad job by insisting the road width of the Ring be as great as possible, to inhibit barricades and make sure troops had a good view of troublemakers if they needed to be shelled with grapeshot.

Sigmund, taking his examinations in June, found time to keep visiting the Fair. 'It is a show for the world of the aesthete,' he wrote grandly to Emil Fluss, 'the sophisticated, unthinking world, which also for the most part makes up its visitors.' The letters of Abraham Lincoln, on display in facsimile, impressed him, and he could be heard reciting them to his audience of sisters.

By the middle of July he had his results, a matriculation certificate with distinction; the papers included Greek, Latin and mathematics, and an essay, 'On the Considerations in the Choice of a Profession'. His mother was in Roznau again, but he stayed in Vienna, walking in the hills by himself, unable to accompany her. 'My father does not wish it,' he told Silberstein, 'and though I long for [Roznau] for one hour each day, I cannot seriously plan to do what he for good reasons opposes.' Nor was he able to go to England which he had hoped to visit for the first time that year; no reason was given. There is nothing about Gisela except a line in a letter to Eduard to say he has given up 'the attachment' that bound him to her.

As relationships go, it left barely a biographical ripple on the surface, except that Freud, with his appetite for self-examination, wrote about it in 'Screen Memories', where his patient, 'a man of university education', was really himself. Its broad conclusion was that childhood memories are modified by unconscious forces. Freud suggested the term 'screen memory' to describe an early impression that – perhaps unknown to the individual – is a screen for earlier or subsequent events, which are linked, via personal associations, with the memory that is being recalled. The screen memory is illusion but behind it is reality.

In the 1899 paper, the screen memory – supposedly the Educated Man's, in fact Freud's – was about a meadow of dandelions where he and a second infant stole the flowers of the latter's sister. They threw away their own flowers and ran to a peasant woman, who gave them slices of unforgettably delicious bread. We know that Freud and his nephew John were the children, that the girl was John's sister, Pauline, and the place was Freiberg.

Connected with this memory was a later recollection of the man revisiting the town. This was Freud going back to Freiberg when he was a teenager. As the Educated Man tells it, the family had left the place because of a business 'catastrophe'; thereafter he longed for the countryside near his birthplace. Returning there aged seventeen to stay with friends who had risen in the world, he fell in love with the daughter of fifteen. This was Gisela Fluss, actually aged thirteen. When she returned to school, leaving the lovesick youth at her parents' house, he 'passed many hours in solitary walks through the lovely woods that I had found once more and spent my time building castles in the air'. These were fantasies of 'if only': if only he had remained in his birthplace, grown up in the country, followed his father's occupation and married her! Thereafter anything yellow reminded him of the yellow dress she was wearing when he first saw her.

A further set of memories was drawn in, concerning a visit three years later to his 'uncle' who had prospered in a 'far-distant city', in reality Freud's half-brother Emmanuel in Manchester. There he met the children whom he had played with in the meadow. Freud, alias the Educated Man, believed that father and half-brother had concocted a plan for him to 'exchange the abstruse subject of my studies for one of more practical value', that is, to settle down in Manchester and marry Pauline.

These memories swam together, the yellow of the flowers, the yellow of Gisela's dress, the hallucinatory bread that tasted so sweet because it represented the pleasures of living in the country with Gisela, the flowers-for-bread exchange that stood for Jacob's idea of giving up unpractical aims and finding a bread-and-butter occupation. Snatching the flowers from Pauline meant deflowering her – or, since the past and present were interchangeable, deflowering Gisela, which is what the Educated Man concedes that he wanted to do as a youth. What any man finds seductive when he contemplates marriage, says Freud, writing it down as dialogue between himself and his non-existent patient, is the wedding night. What does he care about the aftermath? The fantasy of 'gross sexual aggression' is so coarse, he suggests, that it must have found its way under a 'flowery disguise' into the scene of childhood innocence in the meadow – a scene that very likely took place, but came to be remembered only because it made a suitable resting place for the other memories.

Behind the technical content of the paper is the incidental biography, telling us something of Freud as a teenager, that he dreamt of women and had fantasies of what he would like to do to them. This is unremarkable information about an adolescent, as are the oblique references to masturbation. But the adolescent happened to be Freud. As a psychologist he was driven to look for the origins of human behaviour in sexual instincts. This was courageous and far-sighted; even if he overstated his case, his insight helped people admit the truth about themselves, a process that has preoccupied the twentieth century. But when Freud came to examine his own sexuality he implied a certain self-exemption from the ordinary run of people. His insistence, when developing the methods that became psychoanalysis, that sexual matters brought themselves to his reluctant notice, was meekly accepted and became part of the legend.

Freud liked to appear as austere and inviolate, someone who turned aside from common temptations. There was enough truth in this to make it plausible. The character he strove for rested on austerity, on an ideal of noble rationality, but there is always the shadow of someone more vulnerable at his elbow. This other Freud was, among other things, the young man who felt hesitant and uneasy with women. If his nature had let him be bolder with Gisela instead of making him a 'nonsensical Hamlet', dithering and doing nothing, sex might have turned out to be less of an inner torment. No doubt he would still have invented psychoanalysis had he managed to ravish a Gisela or two, since he saw his life as a mission to explain human nature, but the way he configured the system might have been different.

4: Dissection

The University of Vienna admitted Freud as a student in autumn 1873. He said afterwards that he decided on medicine because he was moved by 'a sort of curiosity'. To begin with he chose the natural sciences without being sure that medicine would be the outcome, telling his friend Emil Fluss that he hoped to 'gain insight into the age-old dossiers of Nature, perhaps even eavesdrop on her eternal processes'. His university education was financed with difficulty, but he took his time over it; later there were grants from charitable bodies, not talked about by Freud. Aged seventeen, he had a 'largish account' at the bookseller's that his father had to pay. If there was family money to be spared, it went in his direction.

Letters to Silberstein during his second year show him unsure and restless, attending lectures in January 1875 on anatomy, physiology, zoology, physics, mathematics and 'Darwinism'.

> A poor troubled medical student is done an injustice if . . . he is said to have a will of his own. Rather, he is a drop of liquid pumped by complicated pressure devices from one lecture theatre to the next . . . and forced, by the laws of mechanics, to traverse his path with minimum friction and in the shortest possible time.

He was 'semi-nocturnal', studying from ten in the evening until two a.m. or later. In February he said he had been overdoing things and missed lectures for a few days, 'roaming instead through the streets of Vienna studying the masses'. Was the superfluous 'of Vienna' added as a literary touch to create an image of the young scientist, alone and secretive in the city? By March he had attended philosophy lectures by Professor Franz Brentano, a former priest with literary connections, and decided that a PhD in philosophy and zoology was the answer, putting logic on the list and informing Silberstein in April that for the first time he was experiencing 'academic happiness . . . close to the source from which science springs at its purest'.

By the middle of June 1875, now aged nineteen, he was planning to spend the long vacation at home in Vienna with microscope and pile of books, working on zoology and histology. This picture of diligence was compromised a fortnight later by his admission that 'I am not insensitive to the reproach that I divide my modest forces among a host of heterogeneous subjects.'

Then, as the academic year ended, another life beckoned in the shape of a business career. The student was packed off to England and the Manchester Freuds, as 'Screen Memories' describes in code. The decision was either taken quickly or was kept from Sigmund till the last minute. At the end of June he was still planning his vacation studies; by the middle of July he was telling Silberstein of his imminent departure.

Freud only inferred that Emmanuel and his father were plotting a life in commerce, so presumably the matter was never pressed on him. The likelihood is that Jacob, his mysterious finances stretched to the limit by a son who needed microscopes and books as well as tuition fees and who was visibly not striding towards a future as a famous physician, put the thought into Emmanuel's head. Perhaps Emmanuel was already contributing to Sigmund's upkeep and was willing to consider that another bright boy about the place might help him expand the business. When he saw the mature Sigmund for himself, he realised that something better was called for. There is a hint of this in a letter he sent to Jacob during the visit, which sounds like a reproof:

> He is a splendid specimen of a fine human being, and if I had the pen of a Dickens, I could well make a hero of him . . . All your descriptions of him have been worthless; only now, since he is with us, do we see him as he really is.

This recognition by Emmanuel, and his likely support for a continuing education, may explain Freud's lifelong admiration. Emmanuel saw what Jacob missed.

The visit, which lasted nearly seven weeks, did little for zoology but gave Sigmund a new context in which to see himself. On a day trip to the coast he spent hours on a beach, collecting marine animals washed up from the Irish Sea. A small girl saw him with a starfish and asked, 'Is it alive?' 'Yes, he is alive,' he answered, a foreigner's grammatical error that vexed him so much, it came back to him in a dream after twenty-five years. At Emmanuel's house in Ardwick, a suburb of Manchester, he lived alongside John, Pauline and their English-born brother, Sam. Pauline (he told Silberstein) was 'beautiful', John 'an Englishman in every respect, with a knowledge of languages and technical matters well beyond the usual business education'. Both his half-brothers were respected shopkeepers, not rich, and Philipp had married 'an intelligent and lovable wife' three years earlier.

England to Sigmund was beyond criticism. Manchester was an immigrant city, popular throughout the nineteenth century with Germans and Jews, who flooded in at all levels – typesetters, tailors, labourers, pawnbrokers, doctors. This smoky paradise delighted Sigmund. One of the possible lives he might have lived made a brief appearance. When he returned to Vienna in September, he wrote to Silberstein, by the light of 'a miserable, eye-destroying paraffin lamp (in England, every beggar uses gas)', to say he would 'sooner live there than here, rain, fog, drunkenness and conservatism notwithstanding'. A favourable wind might even blow him over to England for 'practical work', once he had finished his studies:

> If I wished to influence a large number of people instead of a small number of readers or fellow scientists, England would be just the place ... A respected man, supported by the press and the rich, could do wonders in alleviating physical ills, if only he were enough of an explorer to strike out on new therapeutic paths.

At last there was a possible future: practising private medicine among the merchants and manufacturers of northern England. Did Emmanuel suggest it in the gas-lit parlour at Ardwick, pointing out how reputation and a secure income could go hand in hand, and how splendid it would be to have a new generation of Freuds growing up there? But no more was heard of it. Sigmund got on with his multiple subjects.

Gisela Fluss had not entirely gone away. She was in Vienna with her sister on New Year's Eve, 1874, apparently being entertained by the Freuds. The following month the two girls were at dancing classes and Sigmund refers to 'the pleasure ... of "touching" Gisela, something which I have less motive and occasion to do'. Not long after, he was advising Silberstein how to behave with a girl aged sixteen in whom his friend was showing an interest, warning him not to encourage the 'imprudent affection' of someone whose gender had 'no inherent ethical standard; [a woman] can act correctly only if she keeps within the bounds of convention, observing what society deems to be proper'. Sigmund had taken the then popular idea of inborn female immorality to heart, presenting sexual restraint as a kindness to women. 'You do harm to the poor things when you accustom them to flattery and gallantries,' he wrote, shining with virtue. But Gisela was still in his thoughts, and no doubt his dreams.

Early in October, not long after he returned from Manchester, Sigmund sent Silberstein a poem, in the form of an 'epithalamium' or nuptial song, on the occasion of Ichthyosaura's marriage to a man called Rosenzweig. This was strange, because she didn't marry anyone for another six years (and then his name was Popper). She was now sixteen. Presumably young Hamlet wanted to exorcise her – or young women in general who aroused lubricious thoughts – once and for all, and decided to do it in ironic verse. The imaginary Rosenzweig was mocked for caring about money, Gisela for being not very clever but good in the kitchen ('Nimbly she cuts through the herring'). A draft of the poem spoke ironically of his abominable fate and the pain searing his breast, not to mention cyanide, razor blades and revolvers. Sigmund wanted to be seen hardening his heart against eroticism. Behind the irony were thwarted feelings. But the poem seems to have worked. A postscript to the letter that accompanied it spelt out his new mood, using language that a Freudian might have smiled at, if sexual symbolism had been invented at the time:

> I now bury the magic wand that aided her education, and may a new age begin without forces working in secret, that has no need of poetry and fantasy!

No more was heard of Gisela. Whatever dreams she gave rise to were buried.

The following March, 1876, Freud travelled again, this time as part of his zoology studies, on a grant that let him do research for a month in a laboratory at Trieste, on the Adriatic. For the first time he visited the south. In those days Trieste belonged to Austria and was the Empire's principal seaport, but the history and spirit of the place were Italian.

The project was organised by Carl Claus, Professor of Comparative Anatomy in the university, who had set up a small institute for zoological experiments at Trieste the previous year. Claus, an authority on hermaphroditism in lower animals, set Freud to investigate the sexual life of the eel, in particular to discover if the male eel had testicles, something that had so far eluded science.

The institute occupied a small house with a garden on the shore, 'five seconds from the last Adriatic wave', and Freud spent long hours poring over bits of eel, the deep-blue bay shining outside the window. Every day when the fishing boats came in the zoologists hurried to the courtyard to collect fresh baskets of sea creatures. Freud cheerfully dissected sharks and rays as well, but it was male eels he was after. 'All the eels I cut open are of the gentler sex,' he wrote to Silberstein, pointing out that this had been the problem for Aristotle, who was forced to conclude that eels had no males and sprang from mud.

The description of his working quarters that he gave Silberstein savoured the details; he was a scientist at last. His work-table faced the window, a second table was for books, there were three chairs, shelves with twenty test tubes, microscope on the left-hand corner of the work-table, dissection dish on the right, four pencils and drawing paper in the centre, and at the front an array of glass vessels and pans containing small creatures or bits of larger ones in seawater, surrounded by instruments, needles and microscope slides. There wasn't room for him to put a hand on the table. Each day he sat there from eight till twelve and one till six, practising his

> beast-killing science . . . hands stained with the white and red blood of marine animals, cell detritus swimming before my eyes, which disturbs me even in my dreams, in my thoughts nothing but the great problems connected with the words ducts, testicles and ovaries, world-renowned words.

The street he lodged in was named after an Italian saint, as were most of the streets; the Roman Catholic presence struck him more forcibly than it did in Vienna. He noticed a plaque in a neighbouring town commemorating a sixteenth-century mayor who 'had the Jews expelled and all vileness removed'. He also noticed the southern women and for a day was entranced by slim, tall creatures whom he described for Silberstein, their slender faces, dark eyebrows and small protruding upper lips making them 'lovely specimens'. Trieste, he decided, was inhabited by 'Italian goddesses'. But they left him 'filled with apprehension', and after the first day they seemed to have disappeared. What he noticed now were women with fine heads of hair who let a lock of it dangle over one eye, a fashion that extended to 'the more dubious classes of society'. Evidently the goddesses had become prostitutes.

When he and a colleague took a steam-ship to the fishing port of Muggia one Sunday, he saw three signboards advertising the services of midwives, 'a striking number for so small a place'. Visiting an inn and then a café he noticed that in both cases the landlady was pregnant and made a joke about it to Silberstein, saying that he hadn't bothered to check 'whether the local women, perhaps influenced by the marine fauna, bear fruit the whole year round, or whether they only do so at certain times and all together'.

There was no shortage of pregnant women (or prostitutes) in Vienna. Here, in a southern city, they made a different impression. He was in Trieste for a month, returning in September with a further grant to carry on the good work in the house by the sea. Perhaps female flesh disturbed him again; this time there are no letters to Silberstein.

He was left with a memory of Trieste (I think) that found its way into an essay he wrote thirty-three years later. The essay was 'The "Uncanny"', published in autumn 1919. In it Freud described how, one hot summer's afternoon, he walked 'through the deserted streets of a provincial town in Italy which was unknown to me', and found himself in the brothel district, where 'painted women' sat at the windows of little houses. He hurried away but got lost and found himself back in the street, 'where my presence was now beginning to excite attention'. Again he wandered off, again he arrived at the brothels.

> Now, however, a feeling overcame me which I can only describe as uncanny, and I was glad enough to find myself back at the piazza I had left a short while before, without any further voyages of discovery.

Freud liked to play with the unknowable, then nail down the ghost with psychoanalytic explanation. This is what he was doing in 'The "Uncanny"', which concerned unfamiliar events and their capacity for causing unease. But he ignored the Freudian reading of the episode: that he kept returning to the street because he wanted to visit a brothel.

The setting could have been one of several Italian cities he visited over the years, but the story doesn't seem to be about a mature traveller. A brothel quarter with women on show fits Trieste, which, like all seaports, catered for the passing trade. Although it was Austrian in 1876, it would have felt like Italy to Freud. When he wrote 'The "Uncanny" ' in 1919 the city had just been taken away from Austria, which was on the losing side in the First World War, and given to Italy, one of the winners. This painful reminder of Austrian defeat was probably what brought back the memory of Trieste and led him to add the anecdote of the 'hot summer afternoon' to an existing manuscript – which is thought to have been drafted earlier, then rewritten in the spring of 1919 – where it sits awkwardly in the text, a scrap of personal history.

Freud, as disheartened as most of Vienna's middle class in 1919, would have read about Trieste in the newspapers and remembered the place as he once knew it. An article in the *Neue Freie Presse* that April lamented the government's apathy, complaining that without the port, Italy would have Austria at its mercy. In May, Freud came across the unpublished essay in a drawer and reworked it.

He believed that nothing in our thoughts is arbitrary, that mankind is subject to 'the demand of a determinism whose rule extends over mental life'. To forget a name or make a slip of the tongue was to betray an inner conflict. So to be drawn back to the street of painted women suggests a conflict between the good intentions that kept him walking and the base reality that kept bringing him back.

If it occurred to Freud in 1919 that psychoanalytic readers might spot this connection, he knew that all it would reveal was someone who couldn't be tempted, who was above such things. A visit to a prostitute was unexceptional for an educated young man who had a few florins in his pocket, so by resisting temptation Freud had proved himself a model of self-discipline. I think he was proud of his achievement that stifling afternoon, the sun above the roofs, a woman's shadow on the stairs. But he would have liked to do it, all the same.

5: Vocation

Knowledge poured out of Europe's laboratories in the second half of the nineteenth century like an invisible accompaniment to the smoke belching from industrial chimneys. Much of it was biological and medical. The human body as a machine had come into its own, burning its gases, circulating its energies, as unable to escape the rules of matter as a locomotive. Eventually there would be perfect knowledge and so perfect understanding. There was no occult and no mystery, merely an absence of correct information.

The human body was scrutinised alive or dead, but especially dead, since treating it for disease was more difficult than cutting it open and looking inside. In Vienna brigades of doctors and students hurried to the autopsy rooms before the corpses were cold to see if the diagnoses could be confirmed; Carl Rokitansky, Professor of Pathological Anatomy in the university, was said to have studied a hundred thousand cadavers. Ernst Brücke, Professor of Physiology in Vienna, encouraged his students to stare through microscopes at tissue and taught that 'no other forces than the common physico-chemical ones are active within the organism'. This was the doctrine of the 'positivist' school, where Sigmund served his apprenticeship and learned that the management of those never-ending flows of energy was what constituted life. At the same time Darwinism had explained how evolution produced these biological machines. Researchers young and old were inspecting birds' wings and rabbits' nerves (and if possible eels' testicles) to see how the grand design worked.

Ernst Wilhelm von Brücke (1819–92) became Sigmund's mentor, encouraging his scientific papers, paying him cold compliments, providing a dependable presence that would have him referred to by others as a 'father figure' for Freud, when Freud came to popularise the term. His presence was intimidating – a north-German Protestant with red hair and a dangerous smile who had no patience with lax Viennese ways. Students shrivelled under his gaze.

Brücke's department operated from dismal premises in an old arms factory. His classes were compulsory. Freud did research in other departments but it was in Brücke's that he settled in 1876, and it was there that he had his interest focused on the central nervous system, thus pointing him in the general direction of studies that would eventually connect with neurology and beyond that the problematic regions of psychology.

Favoured by Brücke, in so far as Brücke favoured anyone, Freud remained the struggling student. His poverty was against him; so was his race. More enlightened times favoured the middle classes, but would they favour middle-class Jews to the same extent? Although Jewish scientists and doctors were common in the new, enlightened Austria, they could meet subtle difficulties, and the higher they rose in the academic hierarchies the more obstacles they encountered. Like many of his generation, Freud was not a Jew in any religious sense. He became a lifelong atheist who concerned himself with the social and psychological aspects of religion, which he explained away as human desperation and neurosis.

How religious the Freuds were as a family in his early years is uncertain. Attempts have been made to claim Sigmund's parents as enthusiastic believers or, at the other extreme, as 'enlightened' Jews who had thrown off all traces of the past. Neither is likely to have been true. Jacob had a sentimental regard for his race. Amalie was an old-fashioned Galician, but her granddaughter, Mathilde (Freud's eldest daughter, born 1887), wrote, 'I don't think that any question about religion worried her very much.' She kept the important Jewish holidays 'in a casual way', and they meant little to her.

They evidently meant even less to the eighteen-year-old Sigmund. As his second year at university began, in September 1874, he wrote casually to Eduard Silberstein about Rosh Hashanah, the Jewish New Year. The Freuds had been celebrating the festival, and 'even the God-denier who is fortunate enough to belong to a tolerably pious family cannot deny the holiday when he puts a New Year's Day morsel to his lips'. Sigmund poked fun at Jewish festivals and their 'alliance between religion and the stomach'. The Passover had 'a constipating effect due to unleavened bread and hardboiled eggs.' As for the forthcoming Yom Kippur, the Day of Atonement, it was 'so lugubrious a day not so much through God's wrath as through the plum jam and the evacuation it stimulates'. In the kitchen, 'the death rattle of two fishes and a goose' told him that the Day was at hand.

Before he left high school, Freud had known what it was to be a Jew in a non-Jewish society. Vienna was the most anti-Semitic city in Europe, the place that poor Jews driven from the east by poverty or curiosity descended on, upsetting the natives. He was circumcised, he lived in Leopoldstadt, his parents came from far-off places. 'I began to understand for the first time what it meant to belong to an alien race, and anti-Semitic feelings among the other boys warned me that I must take up a definite position.' This was written in maturity. So was his account of arriving at Vienna University, his disappointment at finding he was 'expected to feel myself inferior and an alien because I was a Jew. I refused absolutely to do the first of these things.'

He took avoiding action where he could. He joined a radical students' society that was dedicated to political union with Germany (and kept quiet about it later) to help distance himself from the least popular Jews, those who came from the eastern provinces. A Viennese-born Jew was thought to be better prepared for life, socially and academically. Freud was only one generation away from Galicia.

These were Jewish concerns as often as they were Gentile. At the university it was wiser not to be seen as one of the *Ostjuden*. Meeting in June 1875 a student who spoke four languages and wrote literary essays, Sigmund pronounced him 'undoubtedly brilliant, but unfortunately a Polish Jew'. Had he replaced 'Polish' with the less damaging 'Moravian' he could have been describing himself.

Jews behaving badly on trains formed a category that Sigmund noticed more than once when he was young. Trains represented the new freedom. They were also a place where people were shut up together, with nothing to do but scrutinise one another. In September 1872, a year before he went to university – when he was returning to Vienna from the Freiberg visit on which he thought himself in love with Gisela – he encountered a family of Jews and thought them worth describing to Emil Fluss.

They were from Moravia and the father spoke 'in the same way as I had heard thousands of others talk before, even in Freiberg'. He didn't elaborate; it was enough that they were the wrong kind of Jew. The son was 'cut from the cloth from which fate makes swindlers when the time is ripe: cunning, mendacious'. From their conversation Sigmund learned that 'Madame Jewess and family hailed from Meseritsch [a town on the Freiberg–Vienna railway line]: the proper compost-heap for this sort of weed.'

Such views were not held casually; they had survival-value. Freud had not been long at university when one of its luminaries, Theodor Billroth, an innovative German surgeon and polymath (he wrote music and knew Brahms), declared himself unhappy with the number of Jews from the east – specifically from Hungary and Galicia – who were entering medical school in Vienna. He proposed a quota system to save the university from these culturally deprived immigrants who, 'even if they speak and think more beautifully and better in the German language than many Teutons of the purest water', could never be truly German. Billroth's conclusion would have gone down well in Berlin sixty years later: after giving the matter careful thought, he was unable to deny 'the cleavage between pure German and pure Jewish blood'.

There is no evidence that Freud's other professors said anything comparable, and Billroth himself apologised later, after he had ignited student riots in which Jews were dragged from lecture rooms and knocked about.* The Jewish members of the radical student body appear to have gone out of their way to say that Billroth was right. The episode is never mentioned by Freud.

'Bad blood', with each generation polluting the next, was seen as a scientific diagnosis. It had racial undertones; the Jews were accused of mental instability. One of Freud's motives for seeking the roots of neurosis in the individual's childhood, not in his ancestry, may have been to demonstrate that Jews and Gentiles had the same psychological machinery. As a young man he thought there was tainted blood on Jacob's side. The family he watched on

---

* What the Gentile students shouted was 'Jews get out.' They were still shouting it at the Vienna medical school before the Second World War, 'after which, of course,' as the Jewish writer Emmanuel Rice pointed out, 'there remained no Jews to shout at'.

the train to Vienna was 'mendacious' and inclined towards crime. His remark about swindlers conjures up Uncle Josef, passer of bad money, modest-sized skeleton in the cupboard. The family of another of Jacob's brothers, Abraham, who lived in Breslau and had feeble-minded children, was suspect in Freud's eyes. He knew about the sinister belief that the Jews as a race were diseased and immoral. His unhappy uncles were too near the bone.

As a poor Jew he could look to charities for help with books and tuition fees, although some poverty-relief was available only after police inquiries and the issue of a certificate of impecuniousness. Freud avoided this humiliation and with Brücke's help obtained grants from two private Jewish foundations in 1878 and 1879, worth between them rather more than £1,000 a year today, and not requiring a certificate. He never referred to them afterwards.

His student years dragged on. No decision about whether to be a doctor or a researcher was taken. The Vienna skyline was changing as public buildings and private apartments took shape along the Ring. Freud saw them daily as he emerged from the crowded apartment in the Jewish quarter and crossed the canal into modern Vienna. Dust from the building sites, from the granite road-surface, from the powdered excrement of horses, drifted through the streets. Coarseness, vulgarity, were all around him. On a boiling hot day he was overwhelmed by the sight of people – 'I wish,' he wrote to Silberstein on 15 August 1877, 'for all the rabble found on this earth to be struck down by heavenly thunder and the world to become so depopulated that one would encounter just one human being every three miles.'

In ill-lit laboratories smelling of gas he examined nerve cells in the spinal cords of fish and demonstrated their affinity with the nervous system of higher animals; an audience applauded when he read his paper. When Professor Rokitansky died in July 1878 he attended the funeral, then went to the Prater with a fellow student, Josef Bettelheim. They joined a Bettelheim family party, but Freud was dismayed to find that the father was another of the wrong sort of Jew, who poked fun at a hunchbacked woman. That summer, for a change, he studied nerves in salivary glands and contemplated experiments on dogs. In August he speculated in a jocular way whether his real work lay in flaying animals or torturing people; that is, in zoology or medicine.

His friends included one of Brücke's senior assistants, Ernst Fleischl von Marxow, an urbane young Jew with powerful connections whom Freud admired. Fleischl knew everyone; as the unprivileged Freud put it, 'he frequents the most exclusive society'. Through Fleischl he made contact with a network embracing science and the arts. He met Theodor von Gomperz, an academic who was editing the works of J. S. Mill, recently dead, and was given a volume to translate. That earned him a little money. He also borrowed from Fleischl, his senior in the department, and from Josef Paneth, his junior. Another influential friend who belonged to the Brücke and Fleischl connection was Josef Breuer. Breuer, a fashionable physician with a scientific reputation, was a family man who introduced Freud to the pleasures of a bourgeois household. Fourteen years older, he would be the most important of the early friends.

Some time in 1879, when he was twenty-three, Freud began a year's military service, although for a medical student this meant no more than being available at a hospital. The following year he sat Parts 1 and 2 of his final examinations for a medical degree, followed by Part 3 in March 1881, when, after seven years as a student, he became Sigmund Freud MD. Although licensed to practise, Freud knew virtually nothing about clinical medicine, and perhaps didn't want to. He continued to work in Brücke's laboratory, a calm, articulate man, apparently content to work for a pittance at a bench, who would eventually become an assistant and, if fortunate, a senior academic of some kind, far in the future.

Among those who attended his graduation in March 1881 were the parents of Gisela Fluss; she had married her Mr Popper the previous month. Following Freud's insipid relationship with her when he was sixteen, women are absent from the record. In 1881 he was twenty-five: healthy, well-built, good-looking and, as far as anyone knows, still a virgin. He may have remained so until he was thirty: not unheard of even today, but an interesting curiosity in Freud's case, since the psychology that he spent most of his life developing revolved around sex. The combination of inward absorption in the subject and outward inhibition may be what made his eventual concerns run so deep.

There are insubstantial stories that Freud had extra-marital sexual experiences. In one he is said to have told a patient, Marie Bonaparte, that he was not a virgin when he married; her journals, where the fact might be recorded, are largely unpublished and impossible to access. In another, the American author and analyst John E. Gedo cites a 'personal communication' from the late Bruno Bettelheim quoting a Viennese uncle who 'claimed to have gone to the brothels' with Freud. Bettelheim's anecdotes were not always reliable; he had uncles in Vienna, although Freud's fellow student Josef Bettelheim, mentioned above, is unlikely to have been one of them. The anecdote was communicated in conversation, at a party; Gedo didn't follow it up.*

Whatever Freud did or didn't do, references in his work to lust suggest he thought it was demeaning, or that it could have demeaning consequences. A career was a safer preoccupation. In his phrase, one 'sublimated' the sexual drive, redirecting it to other ends. Auto-eroticism was another matter. 'You have to know how to do it well,' he was once reported as saying of masturbation. As a doctor he took the unexceptional view of those days that 'self-abuse' was a problem, and wrote about it extensively in his early works.

Diffident and priggish in sexual matters, Freud had to wait until April 1882 before he found a suitable partner with whom he could enjoy a constrained relationship that had marriage at the end of it. Her name was Martha Bernays; she was born in July 1861 (and so was five years younger than Sigmund), an obedient, dark-haired young woman who lived a circumscribed life in Vienna with widowed mother, sister Minna and brother Eli. Her family was Orthodox Jewish. There was a friendship between the two families, perhaps among the daughters, another hint that the Freuds had not forgotten their Jewishness. The first time Sigmund saw Martha, when he arrived home one evening, she, and probably her sister, were sitting around the table with the family. Since the Bernays followed the strict dietary code, it suggests the Freuds must have done so too.

Martha was peeling an apple. Sigmund was smitten. That at any rate is the story. There were scholars in her family, and perhaps that was part of the attraction to someone without much of a

---

* Casual sex was in good supply in Vienna. A local author whom Freud later admired, and who admired him, Arthur Schnitzler, took a professional interest in neurotic lusts and sombre outcomes that was not unlike Freud's. But Schnitzler was a participant. Six years younger – a doctor's son, and himself training to be a doctor – he was already chasing shop assistants before he was twenty. His stories are the kind a more pleasure-seeking Freud might have written.

background at all. The Bernays were the dominant family, socially and intellectually. Martha's paternal grandfather, Isaac Bernays, had been chief rabbi of Hamburg. Two of his sons became distinguished university teachers, but the distinction ran out with a third son, Martha's father, Berman, who was described, optimistically, as a 'merchant'. He, his forthright wife and the three children had moved to Vienna in 1869, living there in straitened circumstances for ten years until he had a heart attack in the street and died, just before Christmas 1879. It was just over two years later that Martha and Sigmund met.

'Freshness' and 'sweetness' were the qualities he noted, the ones that men were supposed to look for. Soon he was sending a red rose every day. They 'walked out' together, visiting nearby beauty spots, among them Grinzing below the Kahlenberg. She baked him a cake; he sent her *David Copperfield*. There was some hand-pressing under the table, and Sigmund wrote his first love letter on 15 June. 'How you have changed my life,' he said, adding how wonderful it had been to visit her home. Eli left them alone for a moment, but Sigmund refrained from doing what he was tempted to do. That, whatever that was – a clasp, a kiss – would have been 'a violation of the hospitality so warmly accorded, and I would not do anything base when near you'. Two days later he secretly proposed and was secretly accepted.

The Bernays' religious leanings can't have appealed to Freud any more than an atheist can have appealed to them. Martha had to hide in the garden to write him letters on the Sabbath. Later he tried to persuade her not to fast on the Day of Atonement because she was too thin. It may be that he took pleasure in seizing this docile young woman, as he thought of her, and rescuing her from error, and there were bitter rows with the Bernays before their courtship was over.

Martha's family, like Sigmund's, harboured a scandal. Her late father was an Uncle Josef figure – though not on Josef's scale – who had been imprisoned for fraudulent bankruptcy. In Hamburg his interests had included selling securities and advertising health spas. Money had gone missing and he was gaoled for a year in 1868. When he came out, an advertising firm he had worked for offered him a job in Vienna, which was why the family had moved there. His wife, Emmeline, who like many north Germans suspected the Viennese of frivolity, never liked the place. If Sigmund knew about the erring Mr Bernays, it might have aroused protective feelings towards Martha.

It would be nine years, Freud calculated, before he could afford to marry, by which time he would be thirty-five and she would be thirty. They settled down to wait, as people did, but he had second thoughts about his career. When he met Martha in the spring his post in the laboratory was that of 'demonstrator', the lowliest of all, for which he had a State grant worth about £2,000 a year today. No promotion was in sight, or was likely to be as long as Fleischl and another assistant were still there. As soon as he got engaged, Freud did as juniors were expected to and told his professor. Brücke held realistic views on young men in badly-paid jobs. He had once recommended Freud for an assistant's post in the provinces, describing him as 'a very poor Jew, who would have to live on his salary, which, incidentally, he would manage easily, given his simple and regular way of life'. When he heard the word 'marriage' he advised his demonstrator to give up full-time research.

That may have been Freud's own intention, and falling in love with Martha part of a strategy for rearranging his life by escaping into a world that was more like the one that his friend Breuer lived in. In any event, research soon ceased to be the goal.

They began an intensive correspondence. Most of his letters exist, but only a few of them are available. He adopted a superior tone, dominant man addressing compliant girl. He felt obliged to tell her that she was not beautiful in an artist's sense, adding condolences about 'the magic of your being'. When she rebuked him for sending her a present, the finger wagged: 'Martha must give up saying so categorically "You mustn't do that".' At times another voice can be heard, saying 'I have such unruly dreams.' His ardour was never in doubt, and he made no attempt to conceal it. When Martha went to Wandsbek, near Hamburg, to spend the rest of summer 1882 at an uncle's home (perhaps packed off for safety), Freud borrowed money and went after her, jealous of men in her past, real or imagined.

This had to be done without her uncle getting to hear of it. With Eli supplying a ticket to the German border, he set off quoting Shakespeare ('What is love? 'tis not hereafter'), the railway timetables in his head, her photograph in his wallet. He had to meet her without being seen, but they seem to have managed it more than once. They sat in a park, she in a brown dress and a big hat, he bearded and proprietorial in his shabby jacket, black hair neatly parted, likening the spot to Eden: free of angels with flaming swords, he wrote to her later, having 'only one little delicate angel with emerald eyes and two sweet lips'. From now on, he said, warning her not to fight the inevitable, she was 'but a guest' in her family: a jewel he had pawned, to be redeemed when he was rich.

His career-plan took effect. Immediately after the trip to Hamburg he went to the Vienna General Hospital to become a physician and earn some money. Clinical medicine was to be the way out of poverty. He didn't give up research at once, but continued to experiment in Brücke's laboratory as well.

The hospital meant a different sort of drudgery. The wards were gloomy, the patients poorly nursed (many had to administer their own medicine), the physicians accustomed to giving their juniors the same hard time that they had endured. One of Freud's chiefs told him cheerfully that in the old days his lunch consisted of two boiled eggs. This came as little surprise to Freud, who took an ironic pride in telling Martha about the sixpence he had just spent on cigars or the twopence on chocolate. For months he had no salary at all, and after that it was only a nominal amount.

Loans from Fleischl and Paneth, who both had private means, helped keep him going; he called it 'the sponger's existence'. In addition there was the fatherly Breuer, ready with loans, hot meals and even hot baths. In sweaty weather he made available his plumbed-in bathtub, a luxury in a city where even the moderately well-off bathed in barrels of hot water brought to the premises or, at best, hired a cabin in the local bath-house. Freud described the Breuer bathroom to Martha and said they would have one too, 'no matter how many years it will take'.

Breuer was highly regarded, authoritative but genial, his balding head resting egg-like in a nest of beard. His father, a religious teacher, was an eastern Jew who came west to Vienna. At one time, while still practising as a physician, Breuer had worked as a scientist outside the university, with which he had a difficult relationship because he felt himself underrated. He discovered the reflex mechanism that controls breathing and made significant findings about the labyrinth of the ear and its function in maintaining balance. As a general physician he was in demand by university professors and their families as well as by the wealthy. There was a warmth about him that Freud responded to. And over a period of years Breuer let him run up debts of about £6,500 at today's values.

Sometimes Freud went with him on visits and they discussed the cases. One of Breuer's patients was a young woman called Bertha Pappenheim. Her case was closed by the time Freud heard about it, late in 1882, so he never met her, but they talked about her often and she became of major importance to Freud and the creation of psychoanalysis. An unhappy daughter of wealthy patients, struck with visions and nightmares, Breuer treated her mainly by letting her talk. It was a theatrical case, now somewhat discredited, but still important in the history of the movement, a legend that can't be dispensed with. In the literature she appears as 'Anna O.' More will be heard of her later.

Freud's relationship with Martha continued to meet difficulties. Following his visit to Hamburg in July 1882, she and her mother returned to Vienna in September. She had been there only a month when Mrs Bernays announced that in 1883 they would be going back to Hamburg for good. At Christmas Sigmund and Martha formally told her about their engagement. Mrs Bernays was not pleased. The news, if it was still news after six months of clandestine letters and meetings, didn't change her mind, and by June 1883 the Bernays had gone from Vienna. Sigmund was left to rage at long distance. He turned his anger against Martha, accusing her of cowardice, threatening to break off the correspondence. And if he did that, 'My stormy longing heart will then be dead.' They both drew back.

The love letters throughout are a matchless commentary on his private life, dwelling on Martha as much as on nature's secrets, hating poverty, resenting the grey ranks of humanity. Should they stay in Austria when they married? The thought of a grave in the Central Cemetery distressed him. He had sudden longings for England's 'sober industriousness'. Uncertain of Martha's affection, he consoled himself with Satan's injunction in *Paradise Lost* to

> Consult . . .
> What reinforcement we may gain from hope,
> If not what resolution from despair.

What will they need to be happy? he asks, and gives her the answer: Three rooms, a stove that never goes out, and a small larder in case of hunger or guests. What does he feel for her? Indescribable longing. Freud rages a little, knowing he has years to wait; but marriage at thirty or beyond was nothing unusual for middle-class men, who were first expected to establish themselves financially. If there were many Schnitzlers who did as they pleased in their twenties, there must have been many Freuds as well.

The need for propriety haunted him throughout the engagement. He forbade Martha to stay with a woman friend who had unforgivably 'married before her wedding'. He refused to let her go ice-skating if there was a chance of her linking arms and skating alongside a man. Having made her a gift of *Don Quixote*, he decided he had gone too far. 'You are quite right, little princess,' he wrote, 'it is no reading matter for girls.' He had forgotten, he said, the 'many coarse and in themselves nauseating passages when I sent it to you'. Freud the analyst would have said there was no such thing as innocent 'forgetting': if he gave it her, it was because he wanted her to read it.

With Mrs Bernays he was on edge, sometimes at war. She was a dogmatic, intelligent woman from a Scandinavian family, who liked to get the better of people and saw no reason to give up her daughter to this non-believer without a fight. On the other hand she knew that Freud, whatever his background, was not common-place. He had differences with Eli Bernays, a budding businessman whose schemes didn't appeal to him, compounded when Eli married his eldest sister, Anna, in October 1883. A full Jewish wedding was laid on in Hamburg. Sigmund didn't go.

His letters, sharply introspective, suggest a man simmering below the surface. 'I can hardly contain myself for silent savagery,' he told Martha in one letter; 'I am violent and passionate with all sorts of devils pent up that cannot emerge' in another, adding that if only he had some daring activity where he could 'venture and win', it might make him gentler; instead of which, and you can hear the pen digging into the paper, 'I am forced to exercise moderation and self-control.'

The world was disappointing. Mankind was not edifying. When Martha described a fair in Hamburg and its plebeian crowds he preached her a sermon on the unhappy spectacle of the mindless poor, with 'their thick skins and their easy-going ways', seizing the pleasures of the moment because they have nothing else to wait for. 'The poor are too helpless, too exposed, to behave like us.' Thus there is 'a psychology of the common man which differs considerably from ours'.

Freud portrayed the ascetic Us who couldn't bear to be like the feckless Them, in the process defining himself as a man apart. His pent-up devils were there, disguised as 'natural instincts'. The recognition of 'unpleasure' as the other side of 'pleasure' pointed to the conflict between desire and the need to repress it that would feature in his psychological system.

> The mob gives vent to its appetites, and we deprive ourselves. We deprive ourselves in order to maintain our integrity, we economise in our health, our capacity for enjoyment, our emotions; we save ourselves for something, not knowing for what. And this habit of constant suppression of natural instincts gives us the quality of refinement. We also feel more deeply and so dare not demand much of ourselves. Why don't we get drunk? Because the discomfort and disgrace of the after-effects give us more 'unpleasure' than the pleasure we derived from getting drunk. Why don't we fall in love with a different person every month? Because at each separation a part of our heart would be torn away. Why don't we make a friend of everyone? Because the loss of him or any misfortune befalling him would affect us deeply. Thus we strive more towards avoiding pain than towards seeking pleasure.

If he could speculate, he could also observe. In 1883 a hospital colleague called Nathan Weiss hanged himself at a public bath-house ten days after he and his wife returned from their honeymoon. Weiss, a neurologist, was a *privat dozent*, an unpaid university lecturer, the prerequisite for anyone who meant to build up a private practice. Freud returned from the funeral and mused on the dead man, restless and self-absorbed, son of a brutal father, tied to the hospital, who called himself a 'compromised central European' and reminded Breuer (said Freud) of the story of the old Jew who asks his son, 'What do you want to be?' and gets the answer, 'Vitriol, the stuff that eats its way through everything.'

Weiss had pressed on with marriage to a woman who didn't love him and returned unhappy from his honeymoon. 'I think he dropped his self-restraint too early, and physical aversion and moral disapproval quickly stifled all affection in the still cool and prudish girl.'

People were blaming the widow. Freud didn't agree:

> I believe that the realisation of an enormous failure, the rage caused by rejected passion, the fury at having sacrificed his whole scientific career, his entire fortune, for a domestic disaster, perhaps also the annoyance at having been done out of the promised dowry, as well as the inability to face the world and confess it all – I believe that all this,

following a number of scenes which opened his eyes to his situation, may have brought the madly vain man (who in any case was given to serious emotional upheavals) to the brink of despair. He died from the sum total of his qualities.

At the graveside a Weiss family spokesman, speaking with 'the ardour of the savage, merciless Jew', was heard to declare publicly that the widow's family were murderers. Weiss's death, wrote Freud, was like his life, 'cut to a pattern: he all but screams for the novelist to preserve him for human memory'. There was always a novelist in Freud, trying to get out.

6: Nerve Doctor

The general hospital in Vienna was outside the inner city, on a site of twenty-five acres in the 9th District, just beyond the north-west corner of the Ringstrasse. Occupying grandiose but dilapidated buildings, it was the largest public hospital in Europe. It was also the university's teaching hospital; celebrated doctors worked there, but medicine was a less effective science then, and for many of the patients in its 2,000 beds the real point of their being in hospital was to serve as teaching material. They lay in dimly-lit wards, giving the nurses gratuities if they wanted special attention, waiting uneasily for the next batch of students to come along and start prodding them.

Freud, hurrying about the place by the long courts between buildings and in through the narrow doorways, took the same detached, indifferent view of the patients as everyone else. When he progressed to 'nervous disorders' in January 1884, he quickly found the material for his first clinical publication, a tailor's apprentice who had a brain haemorrhage with 'interesting symptoms'. He told Martha how he sat at the bedside for hours, 'with the result that until his death at 8 p.m. nothing escaped my notice'. A short paper, duly published, was 'at least a beginning which should make the others take notice of me'. The room where he slept at the hospital had belonged to the Dr Weiss who hanged himself; his ghost, said Freud, posed no threat. Wood for the stove was provided free. He also received a salary, about the same as the lamplighter's.

Soon after the tailor's apprentice, Freud had his eye on an alcoholic innkeeper from Hamburg – 'He is moreover a nervous case and if he hangs on long enough I may write a paper on him, too.' He saw himself as a realist; being a 'good' or 'bad' doctor didn't come into it. Freud the psychoanalyst would go further and conclude that 'in the proper sense' he had never been a doctor at all, one who thought his job was to help 'suffering humanity'. That, he said, required an 'innate sadistic disposition' which he lacked. What he meant was that an apparent desire to help the sick was a device to conceal from oneself an unconscious desire to do the opposite. In its simplistic form, which Freud sometimes endorsed, it put good acts in a bad light: behind every kind doctor is a sadistic doctor; behind every hero is a coward. This dismaying piece of twentieth-century wisdom was still a long way off in 1884.

'Nervous diseases' became Freud's prime interest. By these, he and his colleagues meant problems of both mind and brain, but especially brain since this was the physical reality behind the mental process. Neurology was about brains and nerves, and so, confusingly, was psychiatry. (Things were different in Britain and America, where psychiatry as a separate specialty had been invented.) Professor Theodor Meynert, one of Freud's teachers and patrons at the hospital, published a textbook on psychiatry in 1884 subtitled *A Treatise on Diseases of the Forebrain*. Brain anatomy was crucial to the specialty. Freud, having worked at Brücke's laboratory on the central nervous system of fish, raised his sights when he reached the general hospital and applied himself to humans. In Meynert's laboratory for cerebral anatomy he dissected brain tissue and studied the medulla oblongata, where spinal cord becomes cerebrum. To mark off the nerve tracts he later devised a method of staining tissue with gold chloride that attracted attention. At the same time he was working in the wards, studying patients with brain lesions that affected their speech or movement. He was a neurologist in the making, a *Nervenarzt*, or 'nerve doctor'.

Brains, nerves and mental processes were an exotic subject, deeply confusing. Some of the figures in the field, not content with seeing the brain as an engine, tried to describe it in imaginative detail, producing a 'brain mythology' that only added to the uncertainties. Meynert was among them. A poet, a clever but difficult man, once a chloroform addict, he originally took up brain anatomy as a hobby, and claimed to see strange sights that eluded others. Freud admired him but kept his distance.

The nerve doctor's province extended to patients with minor disorders, odd habits and 'things on their mind', but they were matters that few serious doctors in the German-speaking countries bothered with. The English were pioneers in the field, having discovered the 'wear-and-tear' syndrome in the 1830s, proudly attributing it to the pressures of the industrial revolution in the country where it began. The Americans responded with 'neurasthenia', an improved version which quickly became the dominant complaint of its kind and a label for indeterminate ill-health, especially in those debilitated by 'modern life'.

It is unlikely that beds were found for sufferers at the general hospital. As for serious mental illness, patients usually went down the road to the more up-to-date Lower Austrian lunatic asylum at 14 Lazarethgasse, where 700 beds and extensive gardens for wandering about in awaited them. The inmates there were likely to be the chronically insane and the advanced syphilitics. Categories and definitions in mental illness have always been elusive. If the merely unstable and mysteriously disturbed were sent anywhere in Vienna in the 1880s, it was to a private clinic or a health spa. Without Breuer's patience and the family's money, the condition of Bertha Pappenheim, 'Anna O.', would have been invisible as far as medicine was concerned, unless it had landed her at 14 Lazarethgasse, thus making her a madwoman.

Meynert's laboratory, like Brücke's, may have appealed to Freud the research scientist, but a life treating patients was always the likely outcome. A plan emerged: improve his knowledge and status, become a nerve doctor, put up a brass plate in a fashionable Vienna street, and hope for the best. Working with microscopes and pickled brains or climbing slowly up the promotional ladder at the hospital were less attractive once there was a practical alternative.

He explained to Martha how important it was to be talked about. This was a constant need. No sooner had Meynert congratulated him on a lecture he gave than he was worrying he had to find something new to 'make the world sit up'. He was 'chasing after money, position and reputation'. His confidence fluctuated. One or two letters to Minna Bernays, Martha's younger sister, have touches of self-doubt. Minna's fiancé, Ignaz Schonberg, a friend of Freud's, was dying of tuberculosis, and she would never marry. She and Sigmund were relaxed and direct with one another. He sent her his photograph in August 1884 after he had been in temporary charge of a department – 'the picture of a dispossessed man of importance . . . as of today I am once more a poor little devil'.

Freud's life was a 'battle for a future' in Vienna. Years later, on his fiftieth birthday, he was disturbed when friends made him a surprise present of a medallion that showed Oedipus answering the

Sphinx, inscribed with a line from Sophocles: 'Who divined the famous riddle and was a mighty man'. In a 'strangled voice' he recalled day-dreaming in his youth, standing before busts of professors at the university and seeing his own alongside theirs inscribed with the words on the medallion. This coincidence left him 'pale and agitated'. His fantasies, then, had the power of prophecy. But the fact that he was consumed with ambition is not surprising; what is striking is that he denied it absolutely, as if it reduced his stature to be so commonplace. To be seen as a schemer in pursuit of fame was not to his taste.

The pace of discovery in medicine meant that many unknown doctors would be famous for something, so why not Freud? He was on the lookout for other people's success. He kept an eye on Professor Koch in Berlin who was claiming to have isolated the pathogen that caused tuberculosis. 'Is Master Koch of Berlin right?' he speculated to Martha. He was angry to see researchers making 'straight for the unexploited legacy of nervous diseases', the ones he had his eye on.

He was preoccupied with destiny and he wanted to get his hands on Martha; 'I will quench my thirst with your kisses,' he wrote, and for a while may have been driven by dreams of married bliss as much as by hopes of fame. Sigmund and Martha had been apart since June 1883 when she and her sister were taken off to live in Hamburg. Other people, he told Breuer, implicitly separating himself from ordinary mortals, would have been 'torn open by the traumatic events of my life'. What events did he have in mind, apart from the absence of his sweetheart? The dank apartments where they lived in Leopoldstadt, or little Gisela Fluss, or wicked Uncle Josef? But he had to energise his story and give it significance.

In April 1884, aged twenty-seven, he thought up a scheme that might change his life, sexually and professionally. He began to experiment with cocaine. This was not because he had any particular knowledge or original ideas. It was a drug that doctors and pharmacologists had been arguing about for a quarter of a century, and was widely available in Europe as the active ingredient of a popular 'health drink', Mariani Wine (and would soon be temporarily available in America in a smart new syrup, Coca-Cola). Freud had seen a report by a German army doctor who gave water and cocaine to tired soldiers on manoeuvres without telling them what it was, and claimed they were rejuvenated. He began reading up on cocaine, and ordered some from the manufacturer. One reason for his interest may have been that the leaves of the coca bush – from which cocaine was isolated earlier in the century – were traditionally believed by South American Indians to be aphrodisiac.

Something else he had read in the American literature was that cocaine could be used as a harmless agent to replace morphine and thus provide a cure for morphine addiction, a use first advocated by a Kentucky doctor four years earlier. Freud had an experimental subject to hand, his friend and benefactor Fleischl von Marxow, the impeccable scientist with the enviable social graces. Years earlier a wound on Fleischl's thumb became infected at a post-mortem. The thumb was amputated, but subsequent growths and surgery on his hand caused chronic pain, leading him to take morphine, to which he became addicted. He had told Freud in 1883 that when his parents were dead he would shoot himself.

Writing to Martha on 21 April 1884, Freud said he meant to use cocaine on Fleischl. It might not work, but who could tell? As he put it, 'We need no more than one stroke of luck of this kind to consider setting up house.' So Freud set off to seek his fortune with a gram of white powder from Merck & Co. of Darmstadt.

It was a muddled enterprise with lessons for Freud. He was a physician masquerading as a scientist, but this seemed to bother no one. Cocaine was a subject of broad interest on which he could exercise his skills as a writer and presenter, the first time this had happened. His method, once he had acquired the product, was to conduct 'experiments' that were intended to reinforce the view he began with, that cocaine was a drug with miraculous properties. The experiments consisted of handing out small doses among his friends and taking it himself. First reports were enthusiastic, although Breuer was not impressed. Among the conditions that Freud considered he might be able to treat were nervous exhaustion, neuralgia, heart disease, rabies and diabetes; he thought of simulating sea-sickness in a swing-boat on the Prater to see if that could be added to the list.

Martha was drawn into the circle of enchantment. Sigmund told her about a patient with stomach trouble who had been cured of pain. He himself, he wrote on 25 May 1884, soon after his twenty-eighth birthday, was taking 'very small doses' for depression and indigestion with 'brilliant success'. Martha was sent supplies 'to make her strong and give her cheeks a red colour'.

Its aphrodisiac qualities were hinted at. A visit by Freud to Wandsbek had been planned for the summer of 1884. Early in June he wrote:

> Woe to you, my Princess, when I come. I will kiss you quite red and feed you till you are plump. And if you are forward you shall see who is the stronger, a gentle little girl who doesn't eat enough or a big wild man who has cocaine in his body.

His fantasies of a woman taken by force surface as he dreams of what cocaine can do for him. For years to come Freud would find the drug a friend in need, though less for its sexual properties than for psychological support.

As well as his 'experiments' he was searching the literature and preparing a paper that was soon written, sent to a Vienna medical journal, and published in July as 'On Coca'. He dedicated it to his fiancée as 'a hymn in praise of that magical substance', a fair indication of what the reader was in for.

Its essence was a review of the literature, stylishly presented. From the history and use of the coca plant in Peru, its country of origin, Freud moved on to contemporary reports. Throughout, material was presented in a partisan way to make a case for cocaine's efficacy. According to Freud it changed the body's metabolism, enabling more work to be done for less food intake. While this is true in the short term (because cocaine stimulates production of adrenalin), Freud appeared to think it could act as a substitute for food, using unknown mechanisms that affected the central nervous system. He was believing in magic.

Some of the evidence evidently came from close to home. One-twentieth of a gram in water produced 'exhilaration and lasting euphoria, which in no way differs from the normal euphoria of the healthy person'; perhaps he was euphoric with cocaine when he wrote it. Self-control was enhanced. Not only was the capacity for work increased, but also 'vitality', that euphemism for 'sexual potency' as used in patent-medicine advertising. Freud reported knowing three people who were sexually excited by taking the drug; one of them is likely to have been him. Cocaine, he reassured his readers, was not addictive and left 'absolutely no craving'. This meant only that so far he knew of no evidence to the contrary.

None of this helped Freud be taken seriously, though it didn't harm him much either. Cocaine was a fashion. The author Conan Doyle, who probably took it himself, had made Sherlock Holmes a regular user by 1887, with Dr Watson watching disapprovingly as the great detective rolled up his sleeve thrice daily to reveal a sinewy forearm scarred with puncture-marks, and injected a seven-per-cent solution because he craved 'mental exaltation'. Freud merely joined the bandwagon.

His friend Fleischl was first treated early in May 1884, before 'On Coca' was written. At first Fleischl thought the cocaine had cured his morphine addiction as Freud said it would, but by 1885 he was addicted to the new drug and taking enormous doses. Fleischl's case was desperate all along, of the kind that makes any therapy worth trying. Otherwise men like Brücke and Breuer would not have agreed to the treatment; nor would Freud have attempted it on such a scale. But even when serious doubts were being raised about cocaine, Freud was adamant that he knew best.

For another year or two he continued to praise the virtues of cocaine, until in 1887 his last paper on the subject admitted that it could be dangerous if used with morphine addicts. By this time he had been accused (by Albrecht Erlenmeyer, a prominent psychiatrist) of helping unleash a 'scourge on humanity'.

The magical substance had let him down. Freud admitted it reluctantly. In an 1885 paper to the Vienna Psychiatric Society he recommended cocaine by subcutaneous injection 'without reservation'. By the 1887 paper he had changed his mind, and suggested that it was the method, injection (a way of delivering drugs that was not yet wholly accepted), that was at fault. After that it was necessary to suppress the 1885 paper which contained the earlier statement advocating injection, and he took steps to do so. As Ernest Jones pointed out, in *The Interpretation of Dreams* Freud wrote that he first recommended cocaine in 1885 instead of the correct year, 1884: betrayed (said Jones, making a Freudian diagnosis) by his unconscious, which knew he was guilty, and so prompted him to make a slip of the pen.

Freud met with a further set-back. In the summer of 1884, when he was in his first enthusiasm for cocaine, a younger colleague at the hospital, Karl Koller, whose specialty was ophthalmology, discovered something about it that Freud had missed. Anyone who took the drug orally found that it numbed lips and mouth. When Freud was considering its uses, he added eye complaints to the list, then did nothing more. But he spoke to Koller, who was already looking for a local anaesthetic, about its ability to numb tissue.

In September Freud visited Hamburg to see Martha as planned, although he went later than he intended because his department was short-staffed. He returned to find that Koller had used cocaine to anaesthetise eyes – a frog's, a rabbit's, a dog's and his own – and established his priority with a paper. Freud's part in drawing cocaine to his attention was acknowledged, but it was Koller who discovered local anaesthesia. In his 1925 *Autobiographical Study* Freud blamed Martha, saying that he stopped work on cocaine at short notice in order to visit her. This wasn't true.

Long after Freud's death his daughter Anna, the guardian of his memory, was encouraging friends to keep quiet about the cocaine story. Ernest Jones wrote about Freud's habit but played down its extent. In a private letter of 1952 to James Strachey, Freud's translator, he said that 'the way Freud thrust the cocaine on everybody must have made him quite a menace ... he was only interested in the magical effects of the drug, of which he took too much himself'. Cocaine came into Freud's dreams. Fleischl's ghost (he died in 1891) would be in them too. His photograph, black-bearded and handsome, hung on the wall of Freud's consulting room. It is still there in the Sigmund Freud House in Vienna.

The spring of 1885 marked a change in Freud's life. His application to become a *privat dozent*, which depended on the patronage of Brücke and Meynert as well as on his abilities, was sent in early that year. The plan to set up shop as a nerve doctor was taking shape. He applied for a travelling grant that would let him live in Paris and work under the illustrious neurologist, Charcot. On 10 March he gave the last of a course of lectures and told Martha that the day 'marks a clear dividing line in my life, all the old things have been finished, and I am in a completely new situation'.

Ten years earlier he said 'May a new age begin!' to his friend Silberstein when he told him (mistakenly) that Gisela Fluss was about to get married; another of his dramatic touches. In April 1885 he informed Martha that he had destroyed personal documents going back fourteen years, among them 'letters, scientific excerpts and the manuscripts of my papers'. Only letters from her and from his family were spared. Swales wondered if he was using cocaine when he did it, but his need for personal drama may have sufficed.

Martha was told that the story he saw his biographers writing, the one they would now have to produce without the help of his early papers, would be called 'The Development of the Hero'. So his theme had been defined. If it was meant to be a joke, it was also meant to be true.

With hindsight, auguries can be seen. When Breuer had been away in 1880 and Freud was looking after one of his patients, he told Martha that some cases had to be treated more with one's personality than with instruments. Again, when he was with a group of young hospital doctors, he heard them laughing over a midwife in training who had been asked why meconium – excreta – sometimes appeared in the water that came away with a birth. They thought her unsophisticated reply, 'It means the child's frightened,' was ridiculous. But Freud was on her side, believing that 'this poor woman from the humbler classes had laid an unerring finger on an important correlation'.

None of these idiosyncrasies amounted to much. Freud remained a conventional candidate for a conventional career, plodding on. When the faculty voted in summer 1885 to send his name forward as *privat dozent* for the State to approve, which it did after some bureaucratic hesitation, he was in his thirtieth year.

Conformity meant safety. Given the support of their peers, doctors were largely secure against criticism. Even the cocaine adventure came within the broad licence that medicine granted itself. The medical game of preserving the profession as a collegiate end in itself, as played with local variations in all the European capitals, was something that Freud, like his colleagues, saw the wisdom in continuing.

Among the conventions to be obeyed was dress. For the oral examination that was part of the *privat dozent* preliminaries, full evening dress was necessary, down to white gloves and silk hat. Freud liked the idea of dressing stylishly; rather than borrow a suit, he went to a tailor he couldn't afford. He had to wear much the same outfit when, that summer, he accepted the offer of a holiday job at a clinic run by Heinrich Obersteiner, a friend of Breuer and Fleischl.

The private-clinic way of life was another possibility for a poor young doctor like Freud who wanted to get ahead. Obersteiner's clinic was the oldest of the half-dozen private mental institutions in Vienna that catered for the middle classes. A variety of conditions flourished in these genteel settings: neurasthenia, drug and alcohol addiction, depression, sometimes raving madness in locked wards that were not talked about. Obersteiner's place was almost in the country. Five cows were kept so that there would always be fresh milk for patients who were having the fashionable fattening-up treatment imported from America. The clinic stood on a small hill in a park on the way to Grinzing and the Kahlenberg, near a route that the amorous Arthur Schnitzler often followed with his friends and their women, tearing off in a carriage and a cloud of dust to the nearby Casino Zögernitz. Such paths as Freud's and Schnitzler's didn't cross.

According to Freud, the 'mild' cases at the clinic, the neurasthenics, were all dilapidated nobility. He noted that none of them, 'mild' or 'serious', received more than cursory medical treatment for their condition. He was at the clinic for only two weeks in June, long enough for him to tell Martha what an idyllic life one might live there with 'wife and child', as undemanding as the civil service. If 'things outside' went badly, he might 'inquire of my little woman whether such an existence, in which she wouldn't have to worry even about the kitchen, would suit her. It has its pros and cons.'

But the care of decaying barons was unlikely to satisfy him whatever the circumstances. In the event, he got his university lectureship and heard that he had been awarded a small but sufficient travelling grant, and so could go to Paris. He was quite right; his life had changed. At the end of August he left the hospital for ever, spent six weeks in Hamburg with Martha and the Bernays, on better terms with Martha's mother at last, and arrived in Paris in the middle of October 1885. He had a letter of introduction to Charcot and his 600-gulden grant (£2,000 today); also a supply of cocaine to keep his spirits up.

7: French Lessons

Paris was a means to an end for Freud, a disturbing city where he felt alone among forbidden sights, and where the glamour of Charcot, the man he came to study, made him realise how far he had travelled from the sober world of his teachers in Vienna. Jean-Martin Charcot was sixty years old, the most famous (and most expensive) neurologist in Europe. His lectures and demonstrations at the Salpêtrière Hospital were public events, attended by journalists as well as doctors. To look at he was domineering, his features like a Roman emperor's on a coin – or like Napoleon's, a comparison he encouraged – and his style in handling people was a mixture of democratic affability and terror. He made Freud think of a worldly priest.

Since the 1860s Charcot had been classifying neurological disease, making his name with work on conditions like multiple sclerosis, aphasia and the complications of syphilis. More recently he had been studying hysterics. Because their symptoms were so varied – paralyses, convulsions, mood-changes – patients were often thought to be malingering. (Bertha Pappenheim might have been suspected of it by a doctor less sympathetic than Breuer.) Charcot disagreed; he believed the physical signs of hysteria were genuine, arising unbidden in the sufferer's mind or personality. They were mental phenomena that somehow infiltrated the body and did things to it. His investigative tool was hypnotism, which he took seriously and used at theatrical public lectures to make women hysterics go into convulsions or begin sleepwalking, demonstrating the connection between mind and matter.

Freud must have heard something of this; so must the faculty professors who gave him his grant and knew he was going to Paris. Charcot's reputation was probably proof against any rumours of eccentric goings-on that did reach Vienna. But Freud himself, whatever he knew beforehand, came to regard Charcot as a magician among nerve doctors.

At first Freud was on the edge of things. He presented Charcot with a letter of introduction and was politely accepted to do the work he had planned, on anatomical changes in children's brains, the kind of science that the Vienna school approved of. The laboratory was overcrowded and he soon tired of it. The only lectures he attended regularly, apart from Charcot's, were those at the Paris mortuary of P. C. H. Brouardel, a forensic psychiatrist whose cases included murder, child-rape and incest. An interest in sex and children could be seen as Freudian, but any connection with the Paris morgue is apparent only with hindsight, and his visits may have had no special significance. One of Brouardel's epigrams stuck in his mind: 'Dirty knees are the sign of a respectable girl.'

Freud was adrift again, missing Martha, self-conscious about speaking French, feeling himself so lonely in the street, he said, that without his beard and silk hat to comfort him on his first day there he would have wept. The French he found self-absorbed and hostile, their city 'a vast overdressed Sphinx who gobbles up every foreigner unable to solve her riddles'. They were a peculiar people, 'given to psychical epidemics, historical mass convulsions, and they haven't changed since Victor Hugo wrote *Notre Dame*'. Angry voices denounced opponents, while posters announced sensational novels. Shameless men *and women* crowded to see nudity; sex was being troublesome again, now that he was abroad. 'My heart is German provincial,' he sighed, 'and it hasn't accompanied me here.' It was Minna, the friend, who stirred up most of these observations in a letter of 3 December, not her sister Martha, the icon. He also gave Minna the good news that he managed to say 'croissants' to a waiter.

Relatives of Martha and even some colleagues from Vienna were in Paris at the same time as Freud, so there was company to be had. He was at museums and the theatre; he saw Sarah Bernhardt in a melodrama before going back to his hotel with a migraine. The loneliness was in his nature, or his nature then. The usual distance lay between him and his surroundings. The crowd was 'vulgar'; Vienna, Hamburg, Paris, it made no difference to Freud. There were hints of his impatience with himself for being so ill at ease, for being in an unexplored city he found 'magically attractive' as well as 'repulsive', yet a city he couldn't bring himself to embrace.

England hadn't aroused such feelings. The puritanical tone of the English character appealed to him; Cromwell was a hero. In Paris he breathed a more exotic air and was unsettled. Women were fleetingly referred to. A male relative of Martha asked him if he kept a mistress in Paris. He visited a restaurant with a former colleague from Vienna and his wife, and it turned out to be a brothel. 'I cannot deny myself a thing,' he told Martha defiantly, but he seems to have meant only eating and smoking, unless cocaine was an unspoken indulgence.

His fantasies, the non-sexual ones, were hinted at here and there. When he told Minna that Paris was 'simply one long confused dream', was it a figure of speech or did he mean something more definite? When, moving to a new hotel, he found that the bed-curtains were green, and applied chemical tests to see if the dye contained arsenic, was he taking a scientific precaution or indulging a neurotic fantasy?

Long after, Freud recalled how when he was in Paris he often heard his name called by 'an unmistakable and beloved voice'. Noting the time of the hallucinations (the word he used), he sent urgent inquiries to Vienna to see if anything had happened. Nothing had. Then there was the Paris day-dream in which he flung himself at a runaway horse and carriage, saved the life of the important occupant, and was told, 'You are my saviour. What can I do for you?' Freud remembered it fourteen years later in a roundabout way. While writing *The Interpretation of Dreams* he wanted to illustrate a point about day-dreams and recalled the story of the runaway horse. But he thought that it came from a novel by Daudet, *Le Nabab*, and concerned a poor book-keeper called Monsieur Jocelyn who habitually day-dreams as he walks around Paris. Returning to the novel, he couldn't find the episode. What he did find was that the book-keeper was called not Jocelyn but Joyeuse, the French equivalent of Freud. So (he reasoned, and was surely right) the fantasy of the runaway horse must have been his – invented in Paris when he walked the streets 'lonely and full of longings, greatly in need of a helper and protector, until the great Charcot took me into his circle'.

In a 1916 paper he said that day-dreams are where the child and the adolescent satisfy their need for power or love: '[The fantasies] persist until maturity is reached and are then either given up or maintained till the end of life.' If this is true, Freud's fantasies were lifelong. In Paris, in the first unhappy months, they just showed themselves more plainly than usual.

Freud had already despaired of the place when Charcot befriended him. Having arranged to spend Christmas 1885 with the Bernays in Hamburg, he had decided not to return to Paris in the New Year but to go to Berlin instead. In the second week of December, however, the 'stupid idea' occurred to him of offering to translate a volume of Charcot's lectures that had not appeared in German; he understood French better than he spoke it. Charcot was persuaded, so Freud changed his mind about Paris and early in January 1886 he was back. This time he drew closer to his patron.

What Freud admired was the theatrical Charcot who found an extra dimension in his hysterical patients that was not to be explained in physical terms. Hysteria rather than neurology may have been Freud's real interest in Paris. The letter of introduction that he had brought from Vienna in October was written by Moritz Benedikt, Professor of Neurology, who also used hypnotism, and thought that sex and hysteria were connected: an old-fashioned belief, out of favour in scientific circles. Meynert or Brücke would have been more appropriate names to sign a letter of introduction, so perhaps Freud asked Benedikt to sponsor him in order to impress a fellow hypnotist, Charcot. Or was Freud himself already drawn to hypnotism? The subject had been shunned in Vienna for years, but medical interest was stirring again in the 1880s. His friend Breuer had tried hypnosis with Bertha Pappenheim and had told Freud about his success in using it to lead her back through the history of her illness.

If Freud planned all along to study hypnotism and the 'mental' aspects of hysteria in Paris, was the investigation of children's brains meant to conceal his intentions from the Vienna medical faculty? The Pappenheim/Anna O. affair was on his agenda. He tried to interest Charcot in her, but the neurologist's thoughts 'seemed to be elsewhere'. Charcot saw hypnosis as a means of exploring hysterical behaviour, not the private histories of hysterics.

By the time Freud was in Paris, Charcot was engrossed in hysteria. It was a complaint that needed to be explained and fitted into a wider picture if nerve doctors were to have the clinical success and personal prestige being achieved in general medicine, where the discoveries about infectious disease were being made.

In the late nineteenth century hysteria was a condition with wonderfully dramatic symptoms, most of which would fade away after 1900 as if the illness was adapting itself to a more realistic century; although a new variety returned as 'shell-shock' in the First World War when soldiers faced with impossible situations responded with symptoms that might get them away from the trenches. In its heyday the paralysis was amazing to see, the blindness or dumbness baffling, the convulsions terrifying. All this gave a cheerful tyrant like Charcot a dramatic setting to help him crown his career. One line of inquiry convinced him that hypnotism could be used to produce hysterical paralysis in patients who were susceptible to the method, as he believed all hysterics were. Ultimately he claimed (as did Freud, at greater length) that it was the ideas implanted in the patient's mind that caused the paralysis, thus demonstrating that the hysteric could, and often did, develop paralysis and other symptoms for psychological reasons. This became a crucial insight for Freud in the 1890s, confirming the existence of powerful mental processes that were hidden from everyday consciousness.

Charcot is still admired as a clinical teacher. His work with the hypnotised hysterics that so entranced Freud and others hasn't worn so well. The displays that politicians and actors as well as doctors and students flocked to see were medical theatre. The women (as most of his hysterics were) gave such extravagant performances that some, at least, must have known what was expected of them. Not all were elderly residents of the Salpêtrière. There were special wards for hysterical patients, among them young women who enjoyed being celebrities in their own right.

Geneviève, who liked to show a silk-stockinged leg, had her portrait in magazines. Blanche, 'queen of the hysterics', found her way into more than one painting. The performances were orchestrated by Charcot and his assistants. A touch on the arm or leg was enough to send subjects into a trance. A gong sounded and the patient became cataleptic, unable to move (they did it once by mistake at a patients' ball and dancers were immobilised). Touching a muscle made limbs contract. A word would cause a woman to fall screaming to the floor. The author and doctor Axel Munthe who studied under Charcot in the 1880s thought the performances at the Salpêtrière farcical, 'a hopeless muddle of truth and cheating'. But Freud, who saw what he wanted to see, made Charcot one of his heroes.

Back in Paris after Christmas, Freud was accepted into the master's circle. He visited Charcot's 'magic castle', a mansion on the Boulevard St Germain, to discuss the translation, and soon progressed to an after-dinner visit – wearing a new shirt and new tail coat, his beard trimmed, his nerves calmed with cocaine. 'I drank beer,' he reported to Martha, 'smoked like a chimney, and felt very much at ease without the slightest mishap occurring.' He made a medical joke to Charcot, and left feeling satisfied with his achievements – or rather, as he said, the achievements of the drug.

More visits followed. Cocaine helped him cope with the rich and famous he met there, and perhaps with Martha as well. Scribbling his thoughts to her one evening in February before he left for Charcot's, he told her of his fear of the 'something alien' that people saw in him, regretting that he was not a genius, explaining his suspicion of strangers by the fact that 'common or bad people treat me badly'. Was this cocaine-induced reverie the truth or merely the expression of a mood? Something egged him on that evening; perhaps his Jewishness, which he kept in check with the anti-Semitic Charcot. Breuer, he wrote, once told him that

> hidden under the surface of timidity there lay in me an extremely daring and fearless human being. I had always thought so, but never dared tell anyone. I have often felt as though I had inherited all the defiance and all the passions with which our ancestors defended the Temple and could gladly sacrifice my life for one great moment in history. And at the same time I always felt so helpless and incapable of expressing these ardent passions even by a word or a poem. So I have always restrained myself, and it is this, I think, which people must see in me.

One subject that Freud and Charcot might have discussed, but never did, was sex. Charcot would have known the popular belief that behind hysteria was frustrated eroticism. (The origin of the word hysteria – from the Greek word for womb – hinted at the same idea.) Some thought that sexual intercourse was therapeutic. This folk-knowledge knocked about on the edge of medicine, but Charcot, although he recognised that hysterical patients might have sexual hallucinations, was not interested.

On one occasion Freud did hear him talk about sex, at a reception in the Boulevard St Germain. The host was telling Brouardel, the forensic psychiatrist, about a young married couple. The man was impotent and the woman distressed as a result. Charcot had told the husband, 'Go on trying! I promise you, you'll succeed.' Freud couldn't catch Brouardel's reply, but he seemed to be surprised that the wife was so upset. Then he heard Charcot cry, 'But in this sort of case it's always a question of the genitals – always, always, always!' Writing in 1914, Freud went on:

> He crossed his arms over his stomach, hugging himself and jumping up and down on his toes several times in his own characteristically lively way . . . for a moment I was almost paralysed with amazement and said to myself: 'Well, but if he knows that, why does he never say so?' But the impression was soon forgotten.

In February 1886 he said goodbye to Charcot, whom he never saw again. He spent a few weeks in Berlin studying children's diseases as part of his preparation for private practice, and was back in Vienna for the spring, being told by Breuer not to be hasty, making sour jokes about emigrating and becoming a waiter, counting his diminishing cash, and looking for a consulting room and the electrical apparatus that was essential for 'electrotherapy', the fashionable treatment for private patients with bad nerves.

Whatever Paris had taught him, Freud continued with his original plan – make a living, marry Martha – as if nothing had happened. It isn't clear when his new ideas about hysteria and psychology took shape. He encapsulated the most important in the observation that hysterical symptoms corresponded to the popular notion of what the nervous system was like, not to the reality. The patient dragged his leg in the way he expected – without knowing he was expecting it – that a bad leg would be dragged, not as the laws of physiology would make him drag it if there was anything organically wrong. It followed from this that hysteria was independent of the 'ordinary' self, suggesting that some different internal regime was involved. Beyond such ideas (which others as well as Freud were toying with) lay a new psychology, waiting to be invented.

Freud later claimed that he proposed a paper on these lines to Charcot before leaving Paris, to show that in hysteria 'paralyses and anaesthesias . . . are demarcated according to the popular idea of their limits and not according to anatomical facts'. We only have Freud's word for it; and by then he was anxious to date his own ideas earlier than anyone else's, in particular, earlier than an 1892 paper by another psychologist, the Frenchman Pierre Janet. It was 1893 before Freud's paper on the subject appeared. However, he did make a similar point about hysteria and anatomical reality, though less decisively, in an article of 1888, only three years after Paris.

This, significantly, was an unsigned contribution to an encyclopaedia. If we assume that Freud was actively developing the idea in private from 1885, it appears that in public he decided to put prudence first. He was a nerve doctor looking for patients in a competitive city. He didn't want to upset his prospects by promulgating strange theories. For the moment he kept his mouth shut.

By mid-April 1886 he had found two rooms to live in and practise from close to the Vienna Town Hall, a good professional address. Mrs Breuer fixed nameplates outside the apartment and in the street. A discreet item, announcing that Dr Freud, university lecturer in neuropathology, had returned from six months in Paris and was residing at No. 7 Rathausstrasse, appeared in the *Neue Freie Presse* on 25 April, Easter Sunday; perhaps an atheist's gesture. His thirtieth birthday was just over a week away.

From the start, patients came his way through colleagues. He saw the Portuguese ambassador. He used hypnotism on an Italian woman who went into convulsions if anyone said 'apples'; was he trying to see what she could remember about the start of her hysteria? Martha was told of a case with 'delicate aspects' that he was handling free of charge, an American physician whose 'nervous complaint' was complicated by his relationship with his attractive wife. Freud had seen her twice and on each occasion Martha's photograph fell off the table, something it had never done before. Twenty years on, his friend Carl Jung would be annoying him by claiming to produce paranormal phenomena in his study. In 1886 Freud enjoyed a little mystification. 'I don't like such hints,' he wrote, 'and if a warning were needed – but none is needed.'

Now that he was in practice and earning money, marriage later in the year became a possibility. A short, bitter quarrel with the Bernays family broke out in early summer. Martha had handed over part of her dowry to her canny brother, Eli, who found it came in handy for short-term investment. When he heard about it, Freud demanded she retrieve the capital – about £2,000 at today's values – and made himself unpleasant. He never liked Eli, who was clever and financially adept, and almost certainly he knew that Eli's father had gone to prison; it didn't help that Eli himself had been gaoled for two months the previous year for avoiding military service. The money was repaid; Martha was shocked at Sigmund's behaviour, but they patched up the quarrel, and got ready for a late-summer wedding.

A month of unexpected army service between August and September meant the date had to be postponed. Freud wrote to Breuer from a 'filthy hole' in Moravia, not far from his birthplace, where he spent his time being medical officer to a battalion, handing out notices telling men they had been wounded in blank-cartridge battles, laughing behind the back of the general who rode up on his horse and called, 'Men! Men! Where would you be if those things had been loaded?' But he added that military life had blown away his neurasthenia. It was the first time he mentioned it; he must have hoped that marriage would cure it for good.

The ceremony came in two parts: a civil marriage on 13 September 1886 at Wandsbek Town Hall and a Jewish religious ceremony the next day, forced on a reluctant Freud by the Bernays. Martha's Uncle Elias, who kept an eye on Martha – he once asked, 'Who is this Freud?' – coached him in the necessary prayers.

For their honeymoon they went first to Lübeck, an ancient river-port thirty miles away. Peter Swales has tracked him there through his dreams. Two years before he married Martha, Freud had told her of a dream induced by another coca-leaf derivative, ecgnonin; it was the year of the experiments. He dreamt that after taking the drug he walked for miles 'and finally came to a harbour with pretty gardens around and the Holstentor, whereupon I called out "Lübeck!"'

At the time of the dream they had already planned to begin the honeymoon there. The Holstentor is a Gothic structure of twin towers guarding the Holsten Gate, across the narrow harbour from the town itself. A man walking from Hamburg would see the two steep cones that crown the towers and pass through the rounded gateway between them before crossing the bridge into Lübeck. A Freudian imagination might see such artefacts – two cones above, rounded passageway below – as sexual symbols, and this is how Swales interprets the dream. The Holstentor is a woman reclining, ready for her lover. Freud was dreaming of deflowering his bride.

This interpretation makes generous use of a building with which Freud was already familiar. Since he happened to dream about Lübeck, might he not have reproduced the architecture he would have seen as he got there? Must a pair of rounded towers be Martha's breasts? Freudians will reply that buildings and landscapes are regularly used in sexual metaphor. Freud came to believe that doors and gates represented the female pudenda, as did gardens, like the 'pretty gardens' of the dream. Dream-towers would no doubt have qualified as breast-symbols, even if dream-apples and dream-peaches were more traditional.

These are unsolvable puzzles. Much of psychoanalysis involves an act of faith, not a scientific proof. Swales's approach to the dream is attractive, and it is tempting, even for a non-Freudian, to believe in the Freud who dreamt about his wedding night, using the symbols whose significance he had yet to recognise. The intricacies of dream symbolism have acquired the potency of myths. Symbolic breasts and symbolic everything abounded in the fables that Freud was to spend his life embroidering. The Freudian version of the dream makes a better story, even if it is one that he himself didn't tell; it offers a glimpse to add to all the other glimpses of this strange man beneath the skin.

Freud would have hated such retrospective prying. Even more, he would have hated his slow metamorphosis in recent times from scientist, man of unimpeachable theory, into monumental curiosity, storm-damaged and uneasy on his plinth. Neither of these futures would have seemed very likely as he relived his dream that night in Lübeck.

8: Secret Lives

Married life for the Freuds began in a four-room apartment on the Ringstrasse, the avenue that now encircled the old city. Its broad vistas and public buildings – museums, galleries, the opera, the administration – made it fashionable for those who wanted a good address. Some stretches were better than others. The apartment that Freud chose during the summer before getting married was in a new block on the north-eastern leg, near the Stock Exchange and the old cloth-makers quarter on the inner-city side and within easy walking distance of medical institutes and the general hospital outside the Ring; not quite the smartest district, but desirable. A police headquarters stands on the site today. When I spoke to the duty officer he said, 'Sigmund Freud? I don't know the name.'

The apartment building was entered from a parallel street, Maria-Theresienstrasse. Its official name was the *Kaiserliches Stiftungshaus*, the Imperial Memorial Building, and it occupied the site of a former theatre where fire had broken out during a performance five years earlier, and several hundred died.* It was known as the 'House of Atonement', and its history is said to have deterred would-be tenants. If the rents were low as a result, that would explain how Freud was able to afford it. At first he barely managed. He had to pawn a gold watch that had been a present from Emmanuel, as well as the gold watch he gave Martha when they married.

Survival was the priority, but before he lost himself in the daily grind he made a gesture towards the ideas he had brought back from Paris and hoped to develop in future. A report on his work

* People liked to say they had tickets for the fatal performance but failed for some reason to attend, thus being saved by a miracle. Martha, her brother Eli and Freud's sister Anna were allegedly among the small army who escaped death.

under Charcot was expected of him since the university had paid for his trip, and in October 1886 he read a paper to the Viennese Physicians' Society which was meeting for the first time after the summer break. The subject was male hysteria.

Freud was not very diplomatic. He presented Charcot's work with enthusiasm, informing his audience that hysteria was a specific disease, not an excuse used by malingerers, and that male hysterics were not as rare as doctors seemed to think. Whatever the merits of the work being done in Paris, Vienna resented having to listen to someone who sounded like Charcot's messenger.

Freud's reception was cool, though not as cool as he suggested in his autobiography, where he made it sound as if medical reactionaries had conspired against a young innovator whose ideas they refused to consider. In this retrospective account he spoke of an 'old surgeon' in Vienna who chided him at the time for ignoring the fact that 'hysteria' suggested 'womb', and could thus apply only to women. If this fossil existed outside Freud's imagination, he would have been untypical of Viennese medicine. But the more opposition Freud imagined, the easier it was to feel the hero, fighting the crowd.

He had another reason for looking back on the Vienna meeting with bitterness. Paris had provoked ideas, in particular the idea that symptoms of hysteria corresponded to the patients' perceptions of their anatomy, not to their anatomy as it really was. This was too tentative and sounded too eccentric to be aired at so distinguished a gathering, and in the event Freud didn't attach his name to it for years. What rankled in his memory was probably that he had not dared to address the real idea then, but told them a safer, clumsier story instead. Blaming the Viennese physicians for this was more acceptable than blaming himself.

The work Freud embarked on was not in the 'scientific' medicine he had learned under Brücke and Meynert. He might still have become a neurologist, dealing in physical diseases of the brain and nervous system. To do that, he would have needed an appointment to the university's Psychiatric-Neurological Clinic, where Gentiles were favoured over Jews. He was offered and accepted a part-time post at an institute for children's diseases. This was outside the university and the work lacked prestige and research opportunities, both necessary if he was to have a successful private practice in the specialty. Even so, for another ten years Freud was concerned with brain anatomy and neurological disease, and his publications made him a leading authority on the paralyses of childhood. Neurology was another career he might have had.* But self-employment in an imprecise discipline offered more scope for a man with unorthodox ideas than a salaried post in a central department of the university hospital.

Freud turned to the uncertainties of 'nervous complaints'. There was a good living to be made from unspecific ill-health, then as now. 'Nerves' were the coming thing, blamed for minor ailments that appeared to have no cause: tiredness, headache, tremors, backache, constipation, sleeplessness, loss of appetite. In his autobiography, Freud remembered the sufferers, 'the crowds of neurotics, whose number seemed further multiplied by the way in which they hurried, with their troubles unsolved, from one physician to another'. He ministered to them gravely, a figure of conventional dignity in dark clothes with a well-trimmed beard, attentive and occasionally humorous.

Neurotics were treated in general like children. Textbooks with a faint air of quackery described typical patients, such as the nervous woman who was 'thin and lacks blood . . . To read wearies her; to play the piano wearies her; to eat and even to speak weary her; and so the day passes, in dream-like monotony.'

Hardly anything is known about Freud's earliest patients. The 'rabble' that he did not care for was largely absent from the practice; apart from anything else they couldn't pay his bills. Later on he would insist that his patients be educated people, of 'reliable character' as he put it, but in the early days he had to take what he could get. Most are assumed to have been sent by medical friends, especially Breuer, whose well-connected circle was Freud's only contact with affluence. Women predominated. The unidentified 'Mrs A.' appears in a letter of November 1887 and subsequently in others, all of them written to Dr Wilhelm Fliess, a new friend in Berlin. Fliess, a German-Jewish nose and throat specialist two years younger than Freud, had visited Vienna in 1887 for postgraduate studies, when the two men met. The ubiquitous Breuer was the

---

* Freud's other life as a neurologist continued after he invented psychoanalysis. As a young man the conductor Bruno Walter consulted him because of cramp in his right arm. He expected to be questioned about sexual aberrations in infancy. Instead Freud examined his arm.

intermediary. Soon Freud was writing, 'I still do not know how I won you,' an admiring note that ran through their correspondence. Freud opened his heart in letters to his brilliant, touchy friend. Not published in full until the 1980s, they reveal more than Freud would have wished, and in his lifetime he tried unsuccessfully to buy them back.

Mrs A.'s problem was dizziness and weak legs. Freud decided she was suffering from neurasthenia, the fashionable aches-and-pains condition, and we hear that he was treating her with mild electric shocks, hydrotherapy and hypnosis.

The same letter spoke about Freud's practice, making it sound a burden. 'The carriage is expensive,' he said, meaning the light *fiacre* that a physician was expected to drive. And 'visiting and talking people into or out of things – which is what my occupation consists of – robs me of the best time for work'. By 'work' he meant his writing.

By February 1888, when the letter was written, Mrs A. was pregnant. Freud made a strange comment:

> It may be that I am in part responsible for this new citizen. I once spoke very strongly and not unintentionally in the patient's presence about the harmfulness of coitus reservatus.

This is the first sign of Freud's strong feelings about birth-control practices, now a forgotten part of his story. He thought they caused neurosis and menaced people; perhaps he thought they menaced him. 'Reservatus' is intercourse without male orgasm, usually seen as challenging rather than harmful. Freud, who wanted Mrs A. to know his views, was not going to be a Breuer or a Charcot when it came to advice about the marriage bed.

After its early appearance as the 'wear-and-tear' syndrome (England, 1831), neurasthenia was named and writ large by Dr George M. Beard (America, 1869). Beard said it was all to do with 'nerve force', which some people had too little of, like run-down batteries. He thought it affected more men than women, reversing the bias found in hysteria, though many doctors said otherwise. Disagreement over technicalities merely added substance to the literature that neurasthenia was soon generating.

Beard's triumph was to create a malady of modern life, the neurosis by which the age could know itself.* At first intellectuals

---

* A watered-down neurasthenia persisted into the twentieth century. It was neurasthenics who were sent on sea voyages to 'tone up the system' if they were

and busy professional men were thought to be most at risk from their nerves; after a while the labouring classes were reluctantly admitted to neurasthenic circles. Beard's followers had no trouble connecting disease and gross national product. A medical textbook of 1895 produced menacing comparisons. In 1840 the English posted 595 million letters. In 1891 it was one-and-a-quarter billion. More mail, more newspapers and more railway journeys meant more 'nerve work'. The inevitable outcome was more neurasthenia.

Freud the nerve doctor went with this tide. When a Viennese medical journal sent him a book about it to review in January 1887, his article described neurasthenia as 'the commonest of all the diseases in our society', which 'complicates and aggravates most other clinical pictures in patients of the better classes'. He also criticised 'scientifically educated physicians' who had never heard of it, and the 'so-called clinical education' that medical students received in hospitals as a result of such ignorance.

Treatment for nervous disorders was varied and expensive. An American doctor, S. Weir Mitchell of Philadelphia, made himself famous by treating bad nerves with months of disciplined bed-rest, isolation and big meals, interspersed with massage. This meant going to a sanatorium. As Freud once remarked, no general practitioner could make a living from seeing a patient once and sending him off to be cured by someone else. Another favourite method was hydrotherapy, treatment with water baths and water sprays. This usually meant sanatoriums too, and was highly thought of – Vienna had its own Professor of Hydrotherapy – although spas also had a reputation for casual sex.

Electrotherapy, which he had already used on hospital patients, was more to Freud's taste. Electricity was still a novelty. Arthur Schnitzler, staying at Berlin's Hotel Continental, enjoyed a room with electric lighting for the first time in 1888. Like most doctors Freud was excited by a new, apparently scientific, therapy which could be practised on the premises, and at first it was probably his favourite method. Patients felt they were being taken seriously when they saw the imposing apparatus – switchboard covered in dials and lamps, wires with electrodes and brushes on the end, wooden bathtub to soak in and receive tingling sensations. The new

---

wealthy enough to afford it, or given a bottle of 'tonic' if they weren't. The condition still appears in international disease-tables as 'chronic fatigue syndrome'.

specialty, electrotherapeutics, had an impressive technical vocabulary, and a prophet in the shape of Dr Wilhelm Erb, the distinguished neuropathologist of Leipzig, who claimed 'admirable results' in treating the 'thousand remarkable forms' of neurasthenia.

For a year or two Freud persevered with electricity, using Erb's complicated rituals. 'Unluckily,' Freud concluded, still sounding pained about the great Erb after decades had passed, 'what I had taken for an epitome of exact observations was merely the construction of fantasy.' Erb's *Handbook of Electrotherapeutics* was no better than 'some "Egyptian" dream-book, such as is sold in cheap book shops'.

The Freuds' first child, a girl, was born on 16 October 1887, around the time Freud met Fliess, and named Mathilde after Mrs Breuer. Martha was 'brave and sweet,' said Freud, 'and when she had to scream she apologised each time to the doctor and the midwife'.

Fresh expenses loomed up. He wrote to Fliess in May 1888 to say he had 'a lady in hypnosis lying in front of me and therefore can go on writing in peace', a nice economy of labour.* His family, he said, was

> living rather happily in steadily growing modesty ... In short, one manages; and life is generally known to be very difficult and very complicated and, as we say in Vienna, there are many roads to the Central Cemetery.

Income was needed and neurasthenia was a useful provider, but Freud was anxious to make more of it than a popular condition to be treated with palliatives. He not only thought it unwise of Mr A. to have intercourse without orgasm, but produced dogmatic theories about how harmful sex led to neurasthenia and an associated condition he called 'anxiety neurosis'.

These theories had nothing to do with those on which psychoanalysis would come to be based. Sex was crucial to psychoanalytic theory too, but there it was 'remembered' sex, part of the galaxy of

---

* The sentence was cut from the original English-language edition of the Freud–Fliess letters, approved by the family and published in 1954. Many passages failed to pass the censors and were silently omitted. A satisfactory edition had to wait until 1985, when the enterprising J. M. Masson, thanks to the position he held at the Sigmund Freud Archives before he fell out of favour, was able to publish the full correspondence. See Chapter 32.

past events that in adult life produced the conflicts that caused what Freud called 'psychoneurosis', principally hysteria and the obsessional neuroses: serious conditions, threatening well-being.

By harmful sex, which was supposed to be blighting the lives of Mr and Mrs A., Freud meant everyday behaviour such as imperfect coitus (whether interruptus or reservatus) and the use of condoms. Masturbation was also to be avoided; other doctors had often said the same, but Freud incorporated the view into his grand scheme for explaining neurasthenia and anxiety neurosis. He called them 'Actual Neuroses'.* By 1892–93 his letters to Fliess show him condemning an 'abnormal sex life' for causing them. This, not the pace of modern living, was to blame.

The story that Freud came to emphasise when he looked back on the early days concentrated on the business of 'remembered' sex, since this was essential to psychoanalysis; the Actual kind didn't affect the central theory and in the end was quietly forgotten, although Freud went on paying lip-service to it. But his later accounts failed to make clear how important the Actual Neuroses story had been at the beginning.

Freud's interest in psychoneurosis, typified by hysteria, proceeded in parallel. In 1888 he contributed an unsigned entry of several thousand words on 'Hysteria' to a medical textbook. There he described 'a method first practised by Josef Breuer in Vienna' in which '[we] lead the patient under hypnosis back to the psychical prehistory of the ailment and compel him to acknowledge the psychical occasion on which the disorder in question originated'. The 'prehistory' phrase was pure Freud. He was implying that when a traumatic memory was traced back to its source, the act of uncovering it somehow purged the patient of damaging emotions. The process later acquired the name 'catharsis', a special application of a common term. The model was Bertha Pappenheim, her case as yet unpublished and unknown. Breuer hadn't chosen to pursue the 'cathartic method' with other patients. Freud exploited it, moving cautiously at first, trying it with and sometimes without the use of hypnosis.

No one knew what to make of hypnosis, Freud included. Since the time of the Viennese Anton Mesmer, active in the late eighteenth century, who claimed that invisible fluids ('animal

---

* In German, *Aktualneurose*, literally 'present-day neurosis'.

magnetism') passed between the mesmerist and his subject, there had been sporadic interest in the 'magnetic sleep' that was reported, a state of altered consciousness for which a Scottish physician, James Braid, invented the term 'hypnotism' in 1842. Charlatans abounded. Mesmer himself was a wily showman with many idiosyncratic beliefs.

The medical community was suspicious of a technique that lent itself to stage performances and party games at home. Breuer, who found a serious use for hypnosis with Bertha Pappenheim, also thought that birds could be hypnotised. Animals were popular subjects. Before he become ill Fleischl performed at a private party, putting a chicken to sleep and persuading a crab to stand on its head. When Dr Arthur Schnitzler became an enthusiast, he suggested his own murder to a patient, who obediently came at him with a letter-opener the next day.

You never knew who was pulling whose leg. Charcot believed in hypnotism, but only for the weak-minded and for hysterics, such as the attention-seekers at the Salpêtrière who were no doubt sometimes busy pulling *his* leg. Freud, however, believed it was a route into 'psychical prehistory', and it was the more exotic hysterics who caught his imagination, especially women with strong characters whose florid symptoms had got the better of them.

For Freud, hysteria became the defining neurosis that he employed to peer back into early lives. He didn't worry that it might be connected with women's discontent; no serious feminist agenda existed, for nerve doctors or for anyone else. What interested him was unravelling the private thoughts.

This seems commonplace now that psychotherapy of one sort or another rules and we all believe in secret lives. At the time it was bold and imaginative. Curious to know what was going on inside his patients' heads, he listened to the things they told him, as Breuer had done with Anna O. Then he persuaded them to tell him more.

9: The Talking Cure

Of all the episodes in Freud's time as a young doctor, none made such an impression as the case that Breuer described to him in the days before he was married, the Bertha Pappenheim affair. It was Freud who persuaded Breuer to publish the case – years later, in 1895 – when they collaborated in *Studies on Hysteria*, the book that began Freud's career. Pappenheim was disguised there as 'Anna O.', and it is under this name that she became the famous patient, supposedly cured by Breuer, who gave Freud the inklings that led him to construct psychoanalysis.

Her real name didn't appear until Ernest Jones wrote Freud's biography in the 1950s, a disclosure that enraged her family since Bertha Pappenheim was eventually a famous social worker and feminist, which was how they wanted to remember her. Since Jones's time, unwelcome facts about the case that may or may not have been available to Freud have emerged. A sub-industry now exists, explicating Anna O. for the scholarly reader, and Freud can be seen exploiting the case for his own ends: which was the way he worked.

Breuer first mentioned her on 18 November 1882, the date fixed by a letter from Freud to Martha the next day. Strangely, Martha already knew Bertha. After Berman Bernays dropped dead in the street in 1879, Siegmund Pappenheim – Bertha's father – was made Martha's legal guardian.

The Pappenheims were a prominent Orthodox Jewish family. Bertha was born in Leopoldstadt in February 1859, about the time the Freuds arrived there with the three-year-old Sigmund. But the Freuds occupied a tenement, the Pappenheims a mansion. Later they moved across the canal into the 9th District. How much of the family background Freud knew or cared about is unknown.

Bertha had no interest in religion, but could do no more than offer silent opposition. She would have received the essential religious training, together with instruction to ready her for marriage including methods of food preparation and the complex rules governing menstrual hygiene. Her secular education, which probably ended when she was sixteen, included modern languages, and she spoke English, French and Italian as well as German. She rode, played the piano, attended concerts and the theatre, and in general lived a genteel life of the kind she later condemned as made up of 'insipid trivia', directed merely at 'passing the time'.

Neither her medical treatment nor the psychological assessments that Breuer made of the case seem ever to have considered her as a clever, wilful young woman of passionate feelings who contrived her condition as a way of escape from a life she hated. The nearest approach to this diagnosis, which appeals to the twentieth century but didn't to the nineteenth, was Breuer's comment that a 'monotonous family life' had left her with a surplus of energy to feed the imagination.

Her illness, as described by Breuer in *Studies on Hysteria*, was surreal and baffling. It began in July 1880, when she was twenty-one, with tiredness and hallucinations. The family was spending the summer at Ischl, a resort with mud and sulphur baths favoured by the Emperor and his family. Her father became seriously ill with a chest infection and Bertha, a devoted daughter, insisted on being at his bedside all night.

Her symptoms began at the same time as his illness. In one of her hallucinations a skull appeared in place of his head. In another, a surgeon had been summoned from Vienna to treat an abscess, and while Bertha was sitting with her father waiting for him to arrive after dark, she saw her fingers turn into snakes and her arm became paralysed. The whistle of the train bringing the surgeon broke the spell.

The hallucinations were described to Breuer retrospectively, and remembering them became part of the treatment. This complicates any account of what was happening, because most of the events were private phenomena that Bertha brought up later while experiencing further mood shifts and day-dreams that themselves became events in the illness. What Bertha developed in 1880 that came to the notice of the family was a nasty cough, and this is why Breuer was consulted and went to see her in November 1880.

From 11 December until 1 April 1881 she was ill in bed with

headaches, disturbances of vision, paralyses and peculiar states of consciousness in which she was unable to speak grammatically, and used a jargon made up of several languages. It occurred to Breuer that she might be organically ill, and he considered, but rejected, a diagnosis of tubercular meningitis, preferring to classify her under the catch-all heading of hysteria. Some commentators still argue for a physical illness, perhaps contracted from her father; although the general feeling is that whatever was wrong with Bertha Pappenheim, it would be an anticlimax if it turned out to be merely a germ.

Breuer, visiting her daily, found that in the late afternoon she became drowsy and fell into a trance-like state, which he called self-hypnosis, in which she told him her day-dreams – 'sad' stories, often about a girl who was unwell. She gave this process a name, 'chimney-sweeping', and described it as her 'talking cure'. Her condition improved.

We are not told what happened to Breuer's busy practice while he spent these hours at her bedside, listening; or why he felt the need to lavish so much attention on Bertha. One calculation is that he must have spent a thousand hours with her. Mental illness was not usually given this kind of encouragement by the science-minded 1880s. The long-winded 'psychological' approach was foreign to Western medicine: you were either mad or sane. Pappenheim was eventually in and out of private clinics, but the endless talking sessions were the root of the therapy. Had her parents not been able to afford them, and had Breuer not been interested in the experiment, the illness would have been different; her malady evolved in terms of the treatment she was being given.

She rose from her bed on All Fools Day 1881 (a coincidence or a clue), but her condition worsened almost immediately when, on 5 April, her father died. This produced a fresh crisis with more visions of skulls and skeletons, an inability to speak German (she used English instead) and long 'absences' in which she could recognise no one but Breuer. At one point he had to feed her. Anorexia, fits of anger and the hallucinations became so severe, accompanied by suicide attempts, that on two occasions he had her admitted to a sanatorium at Inzensdorf, outside Vienna. No one but Breuer could practise the talking method, and when he went on holiday she refused to co-operate with other doctors.

Amid this chaos, Breuer perceived something that was thera-
peutically more specific than the relief that Bertha apparently
found in random story-telling. One of her innumerable symptoms
was difficulty in swallowing water. Under self-hypnosis she
recalled seeing her 'companion', an Englishwoman, letting her dog
('horrid creature!') drink from a glass. Having told Breuer this, the
symptom disappeared. This got Breuer interested in her memories.

The illness moved into its crucial stage in the winter of 1881–82.
The deranged Bertha now seemed to have two exist-
ences: one in the present, the other in the past. When in 'past'
mode she was able to relive, in detail, events of exactly one year
before. Her mother was allegedly able to confirm these recollections
from her diary. Breuer spent months unpicking the memories,
one symptom at a time, in reverse chronological order. This
meant progressing from each manifestation of the symptom to its pre-
cursor until he reached the first time it occurred. Then it was cured.
Every symptom related to her father; his illness, or her relationship
with him, seemed to be at the root of her condition. This fact was
never explained. Perhaps her hysteria was a way of escaping the
nightmare of nursing him.

The 'symptoms' were undramatic. One was 'deafness brought on
by fright at a noise'. Thirty-seven instances of this were traced; the
origin was a choking fit of her father's. 'Not hearing when someone
came in, while her thoughts were abstracted' occurred 108 times,
back to its inception when her father came into the room and she
didn't hear. Whatever corroboration her mother's diary provided, it
can hardly have extended to 108 entries about this non-event.

The treatment lasted until June 1882 when Bertha reached the
origin of the illness, the vision of the skull. After this (as Breuer
said in his definitive account contributed to *Studies on Hysteria*
thirteen years later, written with Freud at his elbow), she was free
from the 'innumerable disturbances', although it was 'a considerable time before she regained her mental balance entirely. Since
then she has enjoyed complete health.'

By himself Breuer might have left the story untold. He wasn't in
the habit of publishing psychological case-histories. It was Freud
who encouraged him because he saw in Bertha Pappenheim a
theme to explore: the resonance of memory and the way it could be
exploited in the understanding and treatment of hysteria. He
would coin the phrase for *Studies on Hysteria* that became famous,

echoing through his work, even when it was superseded by more sophisticated formulas, that hysterics suffer mainly from reminiscences.

Pappenheim's was a bizarre case, typical of nothing but itself. No one, before or since, has produced comparable symptoms. Yet 'Anna O.' was held up as a classic case of hysteria, a neurotic in the grip of unconscious forces who manipulated all those around her. (It was she, rather than Breuer, who set the agenda for the talking cure.) The case was apparently unique in the literature of hysteria; few seem to have thought that its singularity diminished its authority.*

It goes without saying that both men, but especially Freud, saw in it what they wanted to see. Freud knew from Breuer in 1882 that Pappenheim was far from well when the treatment was supposed to have been finished. He told his fiancée in August 1883 that according to Breuer she was 'quite unhinged' and that he hoped she would die, 'so that the poor soul could be released from her suffering'.

By using the phrase about her recovery taking 'a considerable time', Breuer covered himself, up to a point, while leaving the impression of steady progress. In fact, Pappenheim had become addicted to drugs introduced into German psychiatry in the 1860s – chloral hydrate and morphine – which Breuer originally prescribed for her neuralgia. That didn't appear in the published version and nor did other facts about her true condition.

After she was freed from the 'innumerable disturbances' in June 1882, Breuer wrote in the *Studies* that she 'left Vienna and travelled for a while'. All she did, however, was travel to Switzerland, to the Bellevue Clinic at Kreuzlingen where Breuer had her admitted. She was there till October, ill for much of the time with neuralgia and many of the same psychological problems – mood changes, inability to speak German, her 'absences'. All this has been discovered since the 1970s when traces of a photographer's address were found on a picture of Bertha, and a town identified that pointed to the clinic at Kreuzlingen.

---

* Mikkel Borch-Jacobsen (1996) discredits the entire episode, regarding it as part of psychoanalysis's 'vast anthology of tall tales'. A sensational stage hypnotist who was at work in Vienna in 1880, Carl Hansen, is seen as the origin of ideas that the ingenious Pappenheim and the innocent Breuer conspired to make manifest in her illness and its treatment. Freud becomes a fantasist who turned the confusion to his own ends.

The director of the clinic, Robert Binswanger, suspected that Pappenheim had invented her illness. Breuer insisted this was not the case, 'even if individual elements are not genuine'. In a lengthy (though apparently unfinished) case-history that he prepared for Binswanger, no mention is made of the year-old memories that Pappenheim recalled. He told Binswanger about it in a separate document ('her actions were influenced day by day by the events of the same day in the previous year'), without giving it any particular significance. Perhaps it was Freud, obsessively interested in memory, who nudged Breuer into the emphasis he gave it in the *Studies* a dozen years later.

After Kreuzlingen, Pappenheim was admitted to the Inzensdorf sanatorium on at least three occasions over the next five years. Each time she left with the same diagnosis: 'hysteria'.

Breuer was obviously carried away by his treatment. The story, later circulated in private by Freud, was that Breuer was attracted to his patient. His wife became jealous and Breuer decided to end the treatment. Before he did, Pappenheim is supposed to have gone into imaginary labour with an 'hysterical childbirth', causing Breuer to panic and take his wife away to Venice on a second honeymoon, where their daughter Dora was conceived.

Pappenheim was certainly attracted to Breuer. A letter from Freud to Martha (October 1883), telling her that Breuer's marriage was threatened by it, caused Martha to panic and hope that the same would not happen to her and Sigmund. (He consoled her by replying, 'For that to happen one has to be a Breuer.') But the story of the honeymoon pregnancy can't be true, because the child was born in March 1882, three months before Pappenheim's Vienna treatment ended. This suggests to some critics that the entire 'hysterical childbirth' story is a lie, put about by Freud to show that Breuer was out of his depth when dealing with a sexually-repressed young woman.

Breuer wrote that Pappenheim's sexual side was 'astonishingly undeveloped', and that he believed sex played no part in her hallucinations. Freud had other ideas, complaining discreetly in the *Studies* that the case 'was not considered at all by its observer [Breuer] from the point of view of a sexual neurosis, and is now quite useless for this purpose'. The implication, convenient for Freud, is that Breuer failed with Anna O. because he wouldn't grasp the sexual nettle.

No doubt this is what Freud believed, later if not at the time. Nor is there anything unlikely about the idea that some of the frustrations in Pappenheim's life were sexual. In 1895, Freud could do little about it. When *Studies* was published, his beliefs about the inseparability of sex and the psyche were still half-formed, and in any case Breuer was his senior and stood in the way of his obsession. What Breuer did say, as the Kreuzlingen file shows, was that Pappenheim 'has never been in love to the extent that this has replaced her relationship to her father; it has itself, rather, been replaced by that relationship'.

This passionate attachment to a father looks more interesting now than it did at the time, and there has been speculation that she was sexually abused in childhood as a result of which she suffered from multiple personality disorder, a reputed sequel to child abuse. There is no evidence of this.

As far as Freud was concerned, the point of Bertha Pappenheim was that she generated quantities of data that lent themselves to imaginative interpretation. If, later on, he tailored the facts to make them fit, it was no more than he would do on other occasions when he convinced himself that ends justified means. Freud's summary of the case, written twenty years later, described how 'It was discovered one day [by Breuer] that the pathological symptoms of certain neurotic patients have a sense. On this discovery the psychoanalytic method of treatment was founded.' This implied that Anna O.'s treatment was a success. Freud, who knew it wasn't, might have argued that it was the insight into neurosis that mattered, not whether Bertha Pappenheim was cured.

Freud had strong, almost messianic views about the human condition, and his thinking was lit with flashes of intuition about why we have become what we are, and how we can best manage our imperfections and so become something else. Nothing was allowed to stand in the way of this vision, and it was as a visionary that he meant to be judged. To an extent he has succeeded. His way of seeing the world has crept into the way we think. But the evidence he used, especially in the early days, makes you wonder. Anna O. was a fishy business.

Josef Breuer, cautious and methodical, drew narrower conclusions from the case. For him the intimate relationship with a patient that the case demanded, together with his knowledge that the cure was not what it seemed, meant that he never repeated the experiment. Breuer (largely forgotten) lacked the adventurer's temperament. Freud (widely remembered) relied on it. For him and the movement he was to initiate, Anna O. became a powerful myth: an event that fell into the founder's lap, evidence from inside a mind of the games it could play. He could even say she was cured; a romantic lie, since it was her own efforts that turned her into the social worker whose interests (perhaps significantly) included orphan girls and international prostitution. But it is the myth of the tormented young woman and the magical talking cure, forerunner of a century of psychotherapy to come, that still touches a nerve.

10: Hysterical Women

Freud's ideas about the sexual background to neurosis of all kinds were taking shape by the 1890s. The early hysterics were being treated between about 1888 and 1893, and some striking cases were then written up in *Studies on Hysteria* which was published in 1895. In the *Studies* Freud said less than he had already learned; he was still the novice, and Breuer, his co-author, was uneasy about his nonconformity. But he must have recognised Freud's skill as a diagnostician.

One of the cases Breuer sent him was 'Emmy von N.', a woman of means whose troubles included phobias and terrors. Freud's carriage took him to spend long hours at her house, where he began by prescribing warm baths and body massage; then he used hypnosis. A widow in her early forties with two daughters, Emmy was terrified by fantasies almost on the Bertha Pappenheim scale: an oversized mouse ran over her hand; a monster with a vulture's beak tried to eat her; she saw bloodied heads floating in the sea.

When Freud wrote her up in the *Studies*, he described physical symptoms that included pains in leg and stomach, a facial tic and a compulsive clacking noise that she made with her mouth. Madness and asylums were much on her mind. She said herself that some of her terrors went back to childhood memories. Freud, exploring her past under hypnosis, claimed to have succeeded in wiping out many of her fears by tracing them back to some event and 'suggesting' to her that the fear was unjustified.

One strand of disagreeable memories concerned her late husband, an industrialist, much older than her, who had died of a stroke in 1874, after which his family accused her of poisoning him. Freud, who liked to be thought of as discreet when it came to patients' identities, included these true details in his account, and made it possible for anyone whose memory went back fifteen years to identify her. He was hungry for dramatic material, having seen what splendid psychological symptoms Bertha Pappenheim produced. Emmy von N. was not a Pappenheim, but her colourful story lent itself to the artistry of a writer who knew that extravagant hysterics rarely had their behaviour recorded with such attention to detail. Her outpourings were not treated as nonsense but examined for meaning. Freud was assuming that clinical material could be found in the unlikeliest of places, the things people said when they were emotionally disturbed.

Her real name, made public in recent times, was Fanny Moser, born 1848, the widow of a Russian-Swiss industrialist who married her when he was sixty-five and she was twenty-three. He made his fortune selling cheap watches in Russia and Central Asia, and the widow Moser was popularly known as 'the richest woman in Europe'. The 'poisoning' story that followed her husband's death was put about by her stepson after rat poison was found in the bedroom where his father died. An autopsy was performed, Moser's will was contested, and the widow was thereafter ostracised in the aristocratic circles she aspired to.

This is the life of outward events (few of them mentioned by Freud), not the inward chronicle that he was charting, but the one sits uneasily with the other. Freud mentions the 'poison' story but doesn't give it the significance that it may have assumed for Mrs Moser. What emerges in both versions is a strong character. She insisted on telling him her stories in her own way, without interruption. He was told to be quiet and hear her out, not keep 'asking her where this and that came from'. Her younger daughter, Mentona, a teenager at the time (later a writer and Communist who died at a great age in East Berlin in 1971), remembered him attending her mother, 'short and thin' with 'blue-black hair and big black eyes'. She said he looked shy and very young.

This uncharacteristic Freud, brought to order by a powerful patient, let Mrs Moser ramble on, sometimes without hypnosis. He listened and learned, with her and with others, finding, in their undirected thoughts, a stream of spontaneous memories and perceptions which revealed more about them than they intended, and suggested to him the future method of psychoanalysis, 'free association'.

Freud didn't claim to have cured her, although he thought her condition improved. He added a footnote in 1924, the year before she died, to say that no analyst could now read the case 'without a smile of pity', but it was 'the first case in which I employed the cathartic procedure to a large extent'. She was an experiment. So were they all.

Freud saw these early patients as source material for his writing. Moser/Emmy was one of four women he treated who were given a chapter apiece in *Studies on Hysteria*, alongside Breuer's chapter on Pappenheim, disguised as Anna O. Other Freud cases had shorter entries, among them a woman he called Cäcilie M. whose importance he emphasised, adding that 'personal considerations' made it impossible to report the case properly, despite the fact that he got to know her 'far more thoroughly' than any of the other early hysterics.

Cäcilie's identity has also been established.* She was Anna von Lieben, a banker's wife, and another woman of great wealth who could have been recognised if Freud gave too much detail: she was not only rich and well-known, but was connected with a medico-social network that nourished Freud's practice and took a personal interest in the von Liebens, a Jewish family that on both Anna and her husband's side displayed neurosis and mental instability. She was an aristocrat – a baroness in her own right, married to a baron – and a clever and accomplished woman. A surviving photograph shows a strong face with a large nose.

The von Liebens and their circle were too important to Freud's interests to risk upsetting. Among the interlocking names was that of the influential Gomperz family with which Freud had professional and personal connections and to which Anna was related. Freud's former university teacher Theodor Meynert had reputedly cured Anna's aunt, who presided over smart gatherings at the family palace in Vienna that Meynert and Breuer attended with other medical celebrities.

Beginning in 1888, Freud investigated her case jointly with Breuer, who left the labour-intensive work to his junior while he hovered in the background. After treating her for neuralgia, Freud found himself dealing with a ragbag of hysterical symptoms: 'hallucinations, pains, spasms and long declamatory speeches'. His journeys into her past in search of traumas involved seeing her

---

* By the dissident Peter Swales. The will to explore Freud's life and work and rescue it as history has come largely from outside the psychoanalytic community.

through many individual attacks, and Freud said that he was sent for on 'hundreds' of occasions. Perhaps Breuer left her to his friend because he was afraid she might be another Bertha Pappenheim. Swales thinks that Anna Lieben did more than any of Freud's patients to help him invent free association.

Freud's rapport with her was clearly of a different order to anything he achieved in Mrs Moser's case, but he is sparing with detail. The one hallucination he describes is not concerned with her past life. After he and Breuer had both refused to prescribe her a drug (perhaps morphine), she saw them 'hanging on two trees next to each other in the garden'.

Freud found a powerful allusion for Lieben and her hysteria. Her behaviour, he said, was 'an hysterical psychosis for the payment of old debts', that is, she was reliving and thus disposing of the traumas she had been accumulating throughout her life. She was forty-one years old in 1888, and her wealth, a distinguished marriage and children had failed to make her happy. Her sexual life was not mentioned in Freud's account, but he must have been aware of it.

Many have speculated about these hysterical Viennese and tried to explain them in terms of the city. Vienna was said to be a peculiarly sensual place behind the façade of a Habsburg bureaucracy that made an industry out of censorship and secretiveness. Were the consequent tensions somehow reflected in private lives?*

Similar tensions could be described in London, where there was no comparable political censorship, but rampant sexual hypocrisy instead. London prostitutes, kept busy by clients from the respectable classes, were regarded with sanctimonious horror; Vienna was less self-righteous, and Arthur Schnitzler could put loose women into his stories with a freedom that didn't exist in England.

As far as Freud was concerned, neurosis was the same wherever you lived. But Jews are sometimes said to be particularly susceptible to nervous illness. Since many of Freud's patients were Jews,

* The 'tragedy at Mayerling', the great Austrian scandal of the times, has been seen as an extreme case of something rotten in the imperial city. The heir to the throne, Crown Prince Rudolf, and his mistress, Baroness Maria Vetsera, aged seventeen, were found shot dead in a hunting lodge outside the city in January 1889. (The prince sometimes stayed at Bellevue, the house below the Kahlenberg, which thus might have become famous for the tragedy, instead of rather less famous for the dream of Irma's injection.) Probably it was a suicide pact; conceivably it was murder.

and he was one himself, perhaps that coloured the nature of his practice in Vienna and indeed of psychoanalysis.

Jews themselves have speculated about their psychopathology. Depression has been singled out and the troubled history of the race – the struggle to exist amid hatred which in Freud's time and in Vienna was also the struggle to achieve the same status as Gentiles – used to explain it. The Jewish religion has also been invoked. Freud eventually concluded that religion was best explained as a collective obsessional neurosis; so Jews, being a religious-minded people, could be seen as more likely to suffer from such a neurosis.

Altogether there is more speculation than fact, easily perverted. To describe psychoanalysis as 'the Jewish science' is not necessarily to denigrate it, but it is a two-edged phrase. Crude legends of the Jew as diseased and unwholesome still linger around the subject. They were widespread in Freud's Vienna, and later they came in useful for the Nazis.

Freud got on with treating his Jews and Gentiles as best he could. Apart from sitting and listening to what they said, all he could do at first was hypnotise them, if they were susceptible. While the phase lasted, he found it 'highly flattering to enjoy the reputation of being a miracle-worker'. Hypnotism was a kind of magic and Freud was ready to be seduced by it, as he had been with cocaine.

For a while Freud was convinced that as well as being used to look into the patients' pasts, hypnotism could plant ideas in their minds as well; although 'suggestibility' was an idea he embraced reluctantly, perhaps because it was someone else's. A school of hypnotists had emerged in the 1880s in the countryside near Nancy, where a village doctor, Ambroise Liébeault, had become famous locally for the type of hypnotism still found in stage and television shows: the gaze into the eyes, the trance, the suggestion that the subject will obey. In Liébeault's case he told patients that their symptoms had vanished. Headaches, arthritis, tuberculosis, all were treatable.

This simple therapist (he charged no fees) or dangerous quack (his family were peasants; his claims were preposterous) impressed the Professor of Medicine at Nancy, Hippolyte Bernheim, who took over Liébeault's principle of removing symptoms by suggestion and put it on a more professional footing. Eventually he began to dispense with hypnotism and concentrate on making suggestions to patients when they were wide awake. He called this method 'psychotherapeutics'. Liébeault and Bernheim were outsiders – mention of their names enraged Charcot, the man with a mansion and the most distinguished patients in Europe – but the Nancy method caught on. It was another of those false dawns in medicine.

In 1888 Freud translated a book by Bernheim, *On Suggestion*, telling Fliess that he was not much impressed; he was still a Charcot man. The following year he went to Nancy and changed his mind. Anna von Lieben was there as well. Freud travelled from Vienna via Switzerland, where he visited Fanny Moser who had an estate outside Zürich. She had recently returned there from a spell of treatment with Freud, so the visit may have been more social than professional. (How many patients became friends, and how deep the friendship was, no one knows. It may be that only Moser and Lieben qualified, and that even they were not friends in any real sense. He was a young doctor, useful to them; as they were to him.)

From Zürich he went straight to Nancy, where Lieben had agreed to join him, or perhaps had proposed it herself because she thought it might be amusing. Dozens of doctors went to Nancy, but none was as adept at acquiring what he needed as the nerve doctor from Vienna. He saw 'the moving spectacle of old Liébeault working among the poor women and children of the labouring classes'. He saw Bernheim hypnotise a patient into doing foolish things such as opening an umbrella when the doctor returned to the ward, another stage-hypnotist's trick. Freud wrote that he 'received the profoundest impression of the possibility that there could be powerful mental processes which nevertheless remained hidden from the consciousness of men'.

What he didn't see in Nancy was Bernheim hypnotising Anna von Lieben. The Frenchman failed to put her to sleep; there is evidence that Freud, too, found her a difficult subject for hypnosis. While they were in Nancy, a matter of a week or two, he seems to have visited her at her hotel every day for treatment.

Extracts from two letters that he wrote to his sister-in-law, Minna, have escaped the psychoanalytic censors and show him as the same lonely figure he was in Paris: although he would not be the first foreign traveller to paint a gloomy picture to conceal a more enjoyable reality from the people left behind. The thought of staying much longer made him sick, he wrote from Nancy at the end of July 1889. 'True, I spend my mornings very pleasantly, since, when I don't sleep through them, I allow myself to be influenced by the miracle of suggestion; but the afternoons are boring.'

According to Swales, who managed to learn the contents of one letter, Freud told Minna Bernays that if she wanted to know what treatment he was giving Lieben, she should read an American novel, Edward Bellamy's *Dr Heidenhoff's Process*. This futuristic tale, published in 1880, concerns a young woman, 'besmirched' by a seducer, who is tormented by her past. Dr Heidenhoff of Boston has an electrical machine that can extirpate unpleasant memories. (He and his machine turn out to be a dream – induced by morphine – but this doesn't detract from the inventiveness.) The aim of Freud's 'cathartic process' was much the same. The far-seeing Bellamy even introduced the post-Freudian argument that Heidenhoff had invented a means of 'destroying conscience' and thus 'sapping the foundations of society'.

After Nancy, Freud was in Paris for summer conferences on hypnotism and psychology, perhaps travelling there in the company of Bernheim and Liébeault; he didn't see Charcot. Freud was beginning to travel, though his journeys were limited by his means. The two-month summer holidays up mountains and by lakes were in the future.

In 1890 he met Fliess in Salzburg and they went walking in the Berchtesgaden area; going to catch a train, he had an attack of the travel phobia that led him to arrive at railway stations long before he needed to. The following year he made excursions to the Semmering district, where there were mountains he could walk on for days, especially the Rax and Schneeberg. Paths lead up through woods to barren plateaux, where every flower in a crevice looks fluorescent against the grey. For a while in 1891 the Freuds were also there as a family, staying at the village of Reichenau in the valley below.

Vienna was where he spent his time and made his living. Apart from the few famous names or pseudonyms, the patients he saw when he was at Maria-Theresienstrasse have been forgotten. Occasionally they can be glimpsed, like the 'Mathilde S.' who was found in the register of a private clinic, Svetlin's, second only to Obersteiner's in prestige. Freud had her admitted there in October

1889. Mathilde was Jewish, unmarried, twenty-seven years old. An unhappy engagement to a man of 'weak character' had left her sexually unsatisfied, and she had given up men in favour of a 'brilliant career', a move regarded by her family (and perhaps by Freud) as evidence of 'mania', which is why the doors of the clinic clanged behind her. Svetlin's noted that she had 'made a whole cult out of worshipping her doctor, who had treated her with hypnosis during her depressed phase': another patient in love with Freud.

Mathilde S. was not *Studies on Hysteria* material. Nor was Pauline Theiler, wife of his schoolboy friend and confidant, Eduard Silberstein, who went (or was sent) to consult him in the spring of 1891 for 'melancholia'. She was aged twenty-one, not long married. When she arrived at the apartment block, Mrs Silberstein told her maid to wait downstairs, went up to the third floor and jumped; another unhappy woman with a secret history.

Later that year the Freuds outgrew the House of Atonement and moved on. By now they had three children, Mathilde, Martin (born December 1889) and Oliver (February 1891), and from the summer of 1891 Martha was pregnant with a fourth, Ernst, born April 1892. The new apartment, at No. 19 Berggasse, was Freud's choice. Larger and older than their first home, it was a quarter of a mile farther out from the city centre. Martha was not pleased to have to leave the Ringstrasse, and felt they had come down in the world. The junk shops of the Tandelmarkt were at the canal end of Berggasse, which then became a broad, undistinguished thorough-fare where the eighteenth-century building with the Freuds' apartment (and a butcher's shop; he was called Siegmund with an 'e') could be found, after which the road ran uphill and lost itself in a medico-commercial district that contained the general hospital and medical institutes.

Freud, it is said, saw the 'To Let' sign when he walked past one day, went straight in and signed the lease. A stone staircase led to the apartment, which was no better or worse than thousands of other dusty city apartments. Chestnut trees grew in a small courtyard. There was a single bathroom. Perhaps Freud had a sentimental affection for Berggasse. When he had lived with his parents in Leopoldstadt across the canal he must often have gone that way to work in Brücke's laboratory, preparing himself for a career in biological research that never happened. They moved in

at the end of the summer, and Dr Freud's nameplate went up in the
street, alongside the butcher's.

Ultimately Freud would be known for the certainty of his beliefs, a
conviction about the way the mind worked to which he brought the
strength of a moral assurance that made disagreement with him
seem a lapse from virtue. It is tempting to see the later self-
assurance as the counterpart of earlier self-doubt. Neurological
medicine went its stately way. Who was this Freud?

He was not alone among his generation in looking for a psychic
El Dorado. The pure anatomists and physicalists who believed that
biology would solve everything were losing their power, if only
because they were getting old. Theodor Meynert, who had turned
against Freud after his involvement with Charcot and hypnotism,
died in May 1892. Freud went to the house to express his
condolences and was told to take a book or books from the library –
'a rare human pleasure,' he told Fliess, 'somehow like a savage
drinking mead from his enemy's skull'.

Freud had to believe that his own solutions were better than his
rivals', but he had no priority in emergent ideas. The French
psychologist Pierre Janet in particular was on the track of a buried
consciousness that lived a life of its own. Janet was three years
younger than Freud. By 1891 he had revised the vague, romantic
concept of an 'unconscious' that had circulated for most of the
nineteenth century, and was presenting it as a normal part of
personality. His subjects were hysterics in Le Havre, where he was
a professor. He used hypnotism and claimed scientific proof of
'unconsciousness' at work, writing a persuasive account of it in
L'Automatisme psychologique in 1889. Freud had nothing of
psychological significance in print, even an article. At the beginning
of the 1890s Janet was the one in front.

Slowly, the cases of female hysteria that might further Freud's
cause accumulated. He would write up another three, besides
Moser/Emmy and von Lieben/Cäcilie M., in *Studies on Hysteria*.
Miss Lucy R. was a young British governess, probably his first
Anglo-Saxon patient, who was afflicted with a hallucinatory smell of burnt pudding. She was referred by a doctor, very
likely Fliess, who had diagnosed rhinitis, or inflammation of the
nose, a common condition that had a special meaning for Fliess
(more will be heard of it later). Freud treated the governess for nine

weeks. Instead of using hypnotism, he asked her to tell him the origin of the olfactory illusion, then put his hand on her forehead or sometimes held her head between his hands, informing her that she would 'see something in front of you', and that that would be the answer. He had learned from Bernheim that if the therapist insisted, the patient would oblige.

Sure enough, Lucy R. traced the smell to an incident from which Freud was able to deduce that she was in love with her employer. Her ego had found her feelings unacceptable, repressed them and converted them into a physical symptom, a smell associated with the incident, at which time a pudding happened to be over-cooking in the kitchen. Cured of this, she began to hallucinate another smell, this time of cigars, which Freud dealt with in similar fashion to reach the same conclusion.

Lucy R., like others among Freud's early hysterics, has been reassessed by sceptics and her symptoms rediagnosed as a case of olfactory seizure, associated with temporal lobe epilepsy, which can't be ruled out. But a young woman fruitlessly in love with her rich employer makes a better story than an olfactory seizure. Freud had the knack of making an anecdote out of a diagnosis.

The scientist as descriptive writer was a novelty. Freud made conscious use of his literary talent when he wrote these essays about hysterics. The long account of another young woman, Miss Elisabeth von R., aged twenty-four, who suffered from leg troubles and fatigue, showed him uncovering an unhappy life with her family where she nursed her sick father (as Anna O. had done), saw her sisters marry, and was in love with one of her brothers-in-law, though unwilling to admit it to herself.

The sister who was married to the object of Elisabeth's affections died in childbirth. Elisabeth arrived just after her death. Eventually Freud traced the source of her illness to her thoughts at the bedside:

> At that moment of dreadful certainty that her beloved sister was dead without bidding them farewell and without her having eased her last days with her care – at that very moment another thought had shot through Elisabeth's mind, and now forced itself irresistibly upon her once more, like a flash of lightning in the dark: 'Now he is free again and I can be his wife.'

She hadn't told him that the thought shot through her mind. That was his reconstruction of the event. When Elisabeth resisted his explanation, he told her that 'we are not responsible for our feelings', adding that by repressing them, and making herself ill as a result, she demonstrated her moral character. This was a twentieth-century approach to wicked thoughts. Elisabeth accepted the truth and the cathartic cure was complete.

Freud was canny enough to recognise that sceptics, especially sceptical colleagues, might find his accounts too literary, so he made one of his frank confessions, commenting that, having been trained as a neuropathologist, 'it still strikes me myself as strange that the case-histories I write should read like short stories and that, as one might say, they lack the serious stamp of science'. He insisted that his presentation was scientific as well, so getting the best of both worlds.

Last in this parade of hysterics was Katharina, the innkeeper's daughter he met on the top of a mountain and diagnosed as they stood – or sat – there on a summer's afternoon. Katharina, too, was presented in short-story form. Aged eighteen, she worked at an alpine lodge on the mountain where Freud had lunched, saw from the visitors' book that he was a doctor, and went after him to talk about her bad nerves. She suffered from bouts of breathlessness that Freud guessed were anxiety attacks.

Her story was told in a dialogue between the two. She described an 'awful face' she kept seeing, which turned out to be her uncle's. Almost at once she was telling Freud how she had caught him lying on top of her girl cousin ('Perhaps you saw something naked?' 'It was too dark to see anything'), and how the same uncle had jumped into her own bed and made sexual advances when she was only fourteen.

Freud diagnosed hysterical anxiety; she kept reproducing the anxiety aroused by the wicked uncle – or, as Freud admitted in a 1924 footnote to *Studies on Hysteria*, the wicked father, 'uncle' being a disguise in the original version.

It was the first time that Freud wrote about the effects of an explicit sexual episode in childhood. Perhaps a working-class teenager was persuaded to be forthcoming more easily than a baroness or the richest woman in Europe.

A letter to Fliess (unknown till Jeffrey Masson's unexpurgated edition of the correspondence of 1985) identifies the time and place of the episode – 'a nice case for me,' wrote Freud. It was 1893, in August, and he was in the Semmering, staying with his family at

Reichenau. The story was less straightforward than *Studies on Hysteria* made it sound. For one thing, Freud was not alone on the mountain. His paediatrician friend Dr Oscar Rie, who would appear in the 'Irma' dream (and whose future wife, Melanie, was a sister of Fliess's new wife Ida), was with him on a 'complicated tour' of the Rax that lasted two days. Was Rie there when he saw Katharina?

The inn they stayed at, the Otto Haus, named after the Archduke Otto, was just below the summit of the Jakobskogel, a spur off the main mountain. Reichenau was far below in the valley. By 19 August he had met Katharina and diagnosed her problem. Then something strange happened, as he told Fliess in the letter dated 20 August. Martha appeared out of nowhere at the inn, 5,600 feet up: 'Suddenly someone entered the room, completely flushed from the heat of the day, whom initially I stared at as at an apparition and then had to recognise as my wife.' She suggested she spend a few days with him, 'and I felt obliged to afford her this pleasure'.

This was unusual behaviour for Martha, a north German who didn't care for mountains. Although the path from the valley had been improved to encourage tourists, it took several hours to ascend in a pony and trap, a gruelling journey in heavy clothes on a hot day. Evidently she was keen to see her husband.

For six years, he told Fliess, as 'child followed child', there had been 'little room for change and relaxation in her life'. He welcomed the 'coming back to life again of the woman who for the time being does not have to expect a child for a year because we are now living in abstinence; and you know the reasons for this as well'. Avoiding fertility was still a priority with the Freuds. The fifth child, Sophie, had been born four months earlier; the last child, Anna, was not conceived until March 1895, nineteen months away.

Perhaps his celibate state sharpened Freud's curiosity in the girl of eighteen and her sexual history. Perhaps Martha caught a hint of this. There is too little biographical information about her to indicate what exactly her character ran to, apart from her talent for household management and her deference to Sigmund. But her uncomfortable ascent from Reichenau, followed by a request to be allowed to stay, was evidently unusual.

It is just possible that Rie, a strait-laced man, saw Freud and Katharina together, and wondered. The single encounter described in the *Studies* may have conflated several meetings to make a better story. Rie could have used the telephone installed at the inn to send a message via the Reichenau post office, with a poker-faced suggestion that she come at once and give Sigmund a nice surprise.

Thanks to Swales we know the real Katharina's biography. Her name was Aurelia Kronich, and formerly she had lived with her parents on the adjoining mountain, Schneeberg, where her father, Julius, had the tenancy of an inn. Julius, who came from Vienna, went off with Aurelia's cousin, and eventually had four children by her; his wife went to run the newly-built Otto Haus on the Rax, where she and her children were living when Freud was there in August 1893.

Perhaps Aurelia was not as innocent of sexual matters as Freud implied. Perhaps, too, their meeting was not spontaneous. He must have seen Aurelia at the inn, which she helped her mother to run. It may even have been Mrs Kronich who approached him because she was worried about her daughter. Since he was a summer resident in Reichenau, and knew both mountains, he may have heard a rumour about the Kronich husband and wife who metaphorically glared at one another from their twin peaks, and have known something of the background in advance.

A full family history would have given too much away had it appeared in print, so Freud retained the essential detail, added a hint of mystery – the lonely mountain, the girl appearing like a spirit – and made it into another of his stories. Martha and sexual abstinence belonged to a story he didn't write.

11: Erotica

Freud believed that the sexual drive and its effects shaped both individuals and civilisations. His clear-sighted view of sexual needs and consequences was part of a widening resistance to public prudery and ignorance in Western countries. An awakening lay ahead.

Sexual awareness was not the same as sexual licence, though many people, some of Freud's disciples among them, failed to make the distinction. He himself remained outwardly chaste and puritanical, writing with approval (in 1908) of the heroic few who could transcend their animal instincts, an elite to which he knew he belonged.

Freud was anxious to show that sexual phenomena were forced on his professional attention. His own appetites were not mentioned. Since it was not the degree of the appetite that mattered but the strength of character needed to cope with it, it would follow that the more sensual the person, the greater the achievement in behaving otherwise. However, Freud rarely chose to express it like that.

The idea that the neuroses could be explained by 'a sexual aetiology', he explained in 1914, was not his at all. Three of his mentors had influenced him: Breuer, who once told him that the 'secrets of the marriage bed' could be crucial; Rudolf Chrobak, a leading Vienna gynaecologist, who said that the only useful prescription for a wife with nervous troubles and an impotent husband was 'Take a normal penis and repeat the dose'; and Charcot, with his cry of 'always the genitals!'

No doubt it was prudent to keep quiet about his own inclinations. His followers have been minded to keep quiet about them ever since, but even on the most casual view of Freud's life, it is hard to see him as anything but a man with a passionate private interest in sex. Jung, the friend who became an enemy, said that Freud had lost God and replaced him with another compelling image, sexuality, but this is just another analytic stab in the dark.

His thoughts about Actual Neuroses – the neurasthenia and anxiety neuroses that arose from 'abnormal' sexual activity – were worked out in the years after his marriage. He didn't take the moralistic view, common then and for decades to come, that 'birth control' and 'self-abuse' were wicked, but gave technical reasons for condemning them. Neurasthenia and anxiety neurosis, he thought, resulted when the sexual function was inhibited. Freud was on this track in 1887 when he told Fliess about his patient, Mrs A., and by 1892–93 he was discussing it at length with Fliess, and privately nominating him for the job of finding a contraceptive that wouldn't harm the user. Condoms, the two kinds of coitus aimed at preventing pregnancy – interruptus and reservatus – and masturbation were the culprits, as evidenced by numerous examples from his practice. The cases were never described in much detail or quantified in any way.

The symptoms – indigestion, backache, fatigue, anxiety or whatever – were caused, Freud believed, by toxins that the body produced when there was inhibition. To don a condom or to masturbate was to poison the system. The outlook for the educated classes was gloomy, and Freud thought that the lower orders would soon be in the same condition. His published papers on the subject came later in the decade, but already in February 1893 he was writing to Fliess about it, working himself up with apocalyptic logic. The Actual Neuroses were 'entirely preventable as well as entirely incurable'. One of the solutions, that men should stop masturbating, meant exposing them to the risk of syphilis because they would then be driven to use prostitutes. The alternative of 'free sexual intercourse between young men and unattached young women' was feasible only if 'innocuous methods of preventing conception' were available. He raved against the condom, which was neither safe nor acceptable to anyone who was already neurasthenic.

> In the absence of such a solution, society appears doomed to fall victim to incurable neuroses, which reduce the enjoyment of life to a minimum, destroy marital relations, and bring hereditary ruin on the whole coming generation. The lower strata of society, knowing nothing of Malthusianism [contraception] are in full pursuit, and in

the natural course of events, having arrived, will fall victim to the same fate.

Freud's feverish concern with condoms and masturbation (and with abstinence, equally harmful) was of a different order to the more serious work he was doing with hysterics and his attempts to throw light on mental processes and the nature of consciousness. Letter after letter to Fliess examines the consequences. Generalisations abound. 'Every' neurasthenia is sexual, he writes; 'any number' of cases can be traced to coitus interruptus.

The evidence, Freud implied, drove him to these conclusions, which he then fed back to the astonished patients – 'The sexual business attracts people who are all stunned and then go away won over after having exclaimed, "No one has ever asked me about that before!"' We have to take Freud's word for it. He diagnosed a neurosis, questioned the patient about sexual habits, uncovered a history of masturbation or attempts to control fertility, and produced a rabbit from his diagnostic hat.

Freud was a man of broader vision than the pontificating doctors who saw contraception and masturbation as perversions that impaired mankind and brought disease. Yet for years his conclusions about private sexual behaviour were as wrong-headed as theirs, and perhaps more dangerous, since they came as part of a sophisticated theoretical package. His denouncements (first to Fliess, later in published papers) of condoms, interruptus and the rest suggest a personal interest. The anguished prophecy about 'destroying marital relations', made to Fliess on a winter's day early in 1893, was heartfelt.

Freud thought himself neurasthenic, and said so in letters. He used the word to Breuer while on army manoeuvres; he used it to his fiancée, writing from Paris in February 1886 that 'my tiredness is a sort of minor illness; neurasthenia it is called'. Ernest Jones, who saw letters that are still unpublished, said that in those days Freud's symptoms included moodiness and 'an extraordinary feeling of tiredness'. It must have occurred to Freud that enforced abstinence during a long engagement was part of the problem; perhaps all of it. He told Martha that when he was with her, the tiredness vanished 'as though touched by a magic wand'.

Marriage would make things better, except that then he met the fertility problem. His father had made his mother pregnant eight times in ten years. By the time Freud married contraception was gaining acceptance among the professional classes, but the trend passed Sigmund and Martha by. She had six children in just over eight years; her fertility was almost the same as Amalie's. Martha's pregnancies may have been a problem for Freud as well as for her. During their engagement he referred in a letter to 'the three children of whom you have been prematurely dreaming'. Three children meant contraception or less sex.

The birth rate in Germany was falling by 1880. The wives of civil servants and professional men had significantly fewer babies than those in humbler circumstances. Doctors' families were especially quick to shrink. In Austria, or any country where the national religion was Roman Catholicism, fertility rates were slower to change; but Freud was neither a Catholic nor a believer of any sort.

His innate Jewishness has been seen by Ernst Simon as a factor, 'a potent legacy from the orthodox Judaism of his forefathers', with its prescriptive view of sex as duty to the race. It is difficult to see Freud the atheist submitting to this regime. The same author notes that by the 1890s, to have six children in a few years was already rare in 'liberal Jewish bourgeois circles'.

More than once Freud said he hoped that Fliess would discover an acceptable form of birth control. The way he put it, mankind would benefit. But he kept making his wife pregnant; help was needed nearer home. In July 1893, three months after their fifth child was born, Freud said he looked to Fliess as 'the messiah' who would find the answer. In May 1895, when Martha was two months pregnant with their sixth child, Freud was delighted to hear that his friend might have solved 'the problem of conception', adding, 'For me you are a few months too late, but perhaps it can be used next year.'

The question is why existing methods of birth control were not satisfactory to the Freuds. All the barrier contraceptives were in existence. In London they were advertised in illustrated leaflets, sold in shabby lanes off the Strand or available by post in plain packages. Cervical caps, sponges and pessaries came in many varieties, and if rubber condoms were unhelpfully substantial, the membranous kind made of animal gut had been in service for centuries. They were similarly available in German-speaking countries, which is where many of them were manufactured.

Before his marriage Freud was reading about contraception. His personal library at the Freud Museum in London has three pamphlets, all concerned with female methods. The first (by Carl Hasse, 1882) advocated birth control as a 'humanitarian duty' and a kindness to wives; a supplement gave practical advice about how to insert a pessary, together with a pricelist and the name of a supplier in Flensburg. Carl Capellmann (1883), replying to Hasse, said that the pessary, unaesthetic and immoral, made a woman an 'instrument of pollution', turning a wife into a prostitute. Finally a pamphlet by a Dr Otto (1884) restated the liberal argument.

When Freud attacked contraception, he didn't mention female appliances, except obliquely. In 1898 he wrote of the need for something that wouldn't 'wound the woman's sensibilities'. Perhaps Martha, too, found pessaries and caps unaesthetic. The condom, meanwhile, was regularly berated in letters to Fliess. It took its toll; it enfeebled a Mr K.; it left a Mr von F. weak and wretched. As for the non-appliance methods, reservatus and interruptus, Freud was, if anything, more censorious than he was about condoms. It suggests that one or the other, probably interruptus, was his preferred method.

It may be that Martha was persuaded to use a pessary at the beginning of their marriage, disliked it, and felt that the responsibility should be his. Sigmund may have tried the alternatives and come to associate their use with the persistence of his neurasthenia and travel phobia; even with a tendency for them to increase. So the two issues – the avoidance of pregnancy, and his troublesome neuroses for which contraception got the blame – were made to seem complementary.

A pattern can be seen in Martha's fertility. Mathilde, the first child, was conceived in January 1887, four months after the marriage, and born on 16 October. She was breast-fed for only two or three days before Martha engaged a wet-nurse, who arrived on 19 October. The nurse was found wanting and was replaced by another on 24 October.

Since Martha was not suckling the child, her fertility would have been restored sooner rather than later, since lactation acts as a contraceptive. Without breast-feeding, a woman is able to conceive again in about two months; in Martha's case, by January or February 1888. In fact it was March 1889 before her second child (a son, Martin) was conceived, seventeen months after the birth of Mathilde.

The comparable periods between birth and next conception for the following three children were respectively five months, five months and three months; this indicates wet-nurses, regular sexual activity and no contraception. Only in the case of the sixth and last child, Anna, was there another long gap between the birth of her predecessor and her own conception, this one of twenty-three months. At that time, as he told Fliess after the adventure on the Rax in August 1893, he and Martha were not sleeping together.

Early 1888, when Martha was fertile again after the birth of their first child, Mathilde, is thus the likely time when Freud began a determined effort to use contraception. If his neurasthenia happened to worsen during 1888, that might explain the force of his conviction. Perhaps he felt more out of sorts than usual, with oppressive symptoms that he put down to neurosis. Something had to be blamed for it, so Freud blamed contraception. He used it in 1888 to delay a second child, but stopped using it in time for children numbers three, four and five to be born in quick succession.

If this scenario is true, that Freud mistakenly blamed contraception for his loss of well-being in 1888, we are still left needing an explanation for the actual change in his health. Could the answer lie in the dance that his hysterics, von Lieben prominent among them, were leading him? Freud's sensitivity to events is well-established; in the 1890s his anxieties about both his theories and his career would drive him into a cardiac neurosis and daily fears of death.

Sexually hesitant, unmarried until he was thirty, he may have brought with him an intense fantasy life to be incorporated into his married state. Sex was a new delight but with it came new uncertainties. Visiting his hysterics he found himself with neurotic, spirited, not unattractive women, who, if they didn't explicitly tell him about the sex in their own lives (and no one can be sure), made its presence felt. It would be natural if that made him think about the sex in his.

Over the next decade a theoretical structure would be taking shape in the head of the apparently ascetic and hard-working Freud that relied on a concept of erotic needs and frustrations. This process had barely begun when Breuer handed von Lieben on to him because neither he nor anyone else knew what to do with her. Freud's long attendance on so demanding and colourful a patient, which lasted years, must have had emotional consequences. His life

– apartment, children, fastidious Martha who kept her sheets spotless, manuscript pages by the oil lamp at night – was rippled by the presence of the wayward woman he called (to Fliess, on different occasions) 'my prima donna' and 'my teacher'.

Sándor Ferenczi, a colleague and intimate of Freud in the next century, made some private notes about his master at work in the early years, presumably based on conversations with Freud. In May 1932 Ferenczi noted that Freud worked 'passionately' and 'devotedly' at curing his early neurotics, 'if necessary spending hours lying on the floor next to a person in a hysterical crisis'. Was there a particular patient who had to be humoured, and was it Anna Lieben? Helping her pay off her emotional debts was not a task that Freud could leave to others, as he pointed out. Only with Freud did she produce 'all the tears, all the expressions of despair', which were needed for the catharsis. As with Josef Breuer and Bertha Pappenheim, his presence was needed to make the 'talking cure' work. Did he discover, as Josef did with Bertha, that there was a price to pay for their intimacy?

Psychoanalysis would come to recognise an erotic element in the emotional exchanges between patient and analyst, and regard it as unexceptional. The psychoanalyst, Freud wrote in 1914, knows that he is working with explosive forces and needs to 'proceed with as much caution and conscientiousness as a chemist'. In 1888 explosive forces were not anticipated. It would be unsurprising if his visits to Anna Lieben drew him into a verbal intimacy with her, coloured by an eroticism that he found difficult to cope with; this might even be the reason he wrote comparatively little about her in *Studies on Hysteria*. People used to smile knowingly in the nineteenth century about the doctor – any doctor – and his attendant hysterics. Axel Munthe, observing Charcot at the Salpêtrière, said he shared 'the fate of all nerve specialists . . . surrounded by a bodyguard of neurotic ladies'.

Sexual themes appeared in Freud's early cases of hysteria, uncertainly expressed because, on his own admission, he had not yet grasped their importance. Here and there the histories became explicit. Katharina was one such case. The Umbrella Girl, whose case was relegated to a footnote in the *Studies*, was another, a doctor's daughter with leg trouble (she used an umbrella as a walking stick) who, under hypnosis, with her father present, used a 'single significant phrase' that hinted at a traumatic sexual experience involving him. He didn't bring her back for more treatment. Later Freud would build a theory on child molestation, and later still he would knock it down again. He was unsure about his patients' sexuality, and about his own.

Somewhere in that early period was a woman who woke from a hypnotic sleep and 'threw her arms round my neck', at which point a servant came in. Freud described the episode more than once. Was it Anna von Lieben, or perhaps Fanny Moser, who saw many doctors in her lifetime and had a reputation for sleeping with them?

After Freud's death the Wolf Man explained to a journalist why Freud, whom he knew as a friend as well as an analyst, chose to sit at the head of the psychoanalytic couch behind the patient. 'There was a female patient who wanted to seduce him,' said the mischievous Pankejeff, 'and she kept raising her skirt.'

Perhaps it was true, and temptresses were after him. If so, they were disappointed. But one or two of them, we can guess, made him suffer.

12: The Friend

In the 1890s Freud was often unsure and anxious, sustained only by the need to prove himself capable of unpicking the mind, like a man in a legend who faces tasks that are meant to be beyond the powers of mortals. There are hints that he saw his actual survival at stake, that solving the riddles was a matter of life and death. Superstitious fears that he would die at a particular age (the year varied) crept in; his health was mysteriously bound up with his ideas. Little of this would be known if Freud had succeeded in suppressing his letters to Fliess.

Not much happened in the outward life. He presided over a growing family. Patients who came to the consulting room would have heard an occasional cry from a child elsewhere in the flat. Otherwise they encountered only the uniformed maid who showed them into a narrow waiting room (hard chairs, old magazines), and Freud in the room beyond, smart-suited, dark-eyed, his clothes smelling of the cigars he was addicted to. He could get through twenty a day, 'sword and buckler in the battle of life', in his words.

His social outings were unambitious. Card parties where they played taroc, a popular Viennese game, became an institution. Freud spoke ironically of 'an orgy of taroc' on Saturdays. A rich dinner with Leopold Königstein, an eye specialist, and his wife would be followed by cards and, next morning, indigestion. Oscar Rie was another taroc-playing friend, but Freud was less at ease with the Ries. Oscar was not always sympathetic to his work and his wife Melanie gave them chicken and cauliflower, foods that Freud detested.

His parents lived not far away in the 9th District and were regularly visited. From about 1892 they were in a street called Grünenthorgasse, one end of which came out at the canal, a block from Berggasse. Rents were higher than in Leopoldstadt; Freud had been looking after them for years, and wanted them nearby as they got older. Jacob was seventy-nine in 1894, his health beginning to fail. Amalie, twenty years younger, remained vigorous and matriarchal, demanding the deference of her children, especially of her first-born. Freud's Sunday-morning indigestion may have owed less to his meal the previous evening than to the prospect of the regular weekly visit to his mother.

There was no one in the family with whom Freud could discuss his psychological ideas. He told Fliess once or twice that 'the women' didn't approve of what he was doing. Martha was never privy to his work, although later he could talk about it with his sister-in-law, Minna, unmarried and now unmarriageable. Nor were his colleagues much better as confidants. Oscar Rie had his reservations, and so did Breuer, who was collaborating on the book about hysteria but would not commit himself to Freud's sexual generalisations. Freud made him sound difficult, grumbling to Fliess about a 'jewel' that was not going to appear in the book 'because . . . the sexual factor is not supposed to be included'.

Fliess was the man he trusted. Like Freud, he had ambitions beyond his station. His busy private practice as a nose and throat specialist was only a beginning. His first venture did concern the nose, an organ he convinced himself had sexual significance because of physiological connections between noses and genitals, but his second was on a grander scale. As a good Darwinian he knew that mankind was a creature of its tidal, lunar origins. A mathematical theory of 'biorhythmics' arose in his imagination, built around the female menstrual cycle of twenty-eight days and (his own invention) a male cycle of twenty-three days. The theory bestowed the gift of scientific prophecy, since periods of illness and dates of death were predetermined by the mathematics of the system, which Fliess understood even if no one else did. Both the sexually-oriented nose and the prophetic biorhythms appealed to Freud, who never forgot that he had been trained as a physiologist, and hankered for a theory of the mind that had its roots in the body.

In a way Freud and Fliess were two of a kind, men with extravagant ideas seeking a sympathetic ear. Freud seems to have needed Fliess more than Fliess needed him. His admiration was unstinted for a dozen years. There may have been a physical attraction (Freud admitted there was on his side). Fliess had an aggressive self-confidence, helped by affluence; his wife, the former Ida Bondy of Vienna, had money of her own. Freud's letters display touches of envy for his friend's brilliance and certainty. He even lived in the right place for success. Berlin was a modern city, outward-looking in a way that Vienna was not.

In later years Freud came to feel so professionally handicapped by having to use Vienna as a base, more specifically Jewish Vienna, that he determined to broaden his horizon – which was why he turned to Jung and the Swiss. Fliess was an early step in that direction. The Austrian Empire was crumbling at the edges; the Germans, now predominant on the European mainland, developing the best chemical and electrical industries in the world, were planning their world empire of the future. To Jews who came from the east, like the Freuds, Germany had always been the country whose language and culture it was wise to emulate.

If Freud was more tormented about his work than Fliess, he was no less prolific. One of his endeavours was to envisage mind and body as a machine, like a piece of apparatus from some Wellsian science-fiction. Within this system a constant amount of 'excitation' moved hither and thither like a flow of electricity. There were diagrams with squiggles and arrows showing the way the energy, which was essentially sexual energy, flowed like fluid in a pipe. If this hypothetical flow was not disposed of along the appropriate pathways it produced toxic substances that caused the symptoms of neurasthenia: wayward men and women went around poisoning themselves. Freud's attempts to give his speculations a biological foundation are usually put down to his grounding in the anatomical school of Meynert and Brücke. Conceivably his preoccupation with sex also played a part. His important-sounding machine, boiling with lust, leaking somatic sexual excitation at its joints like steam, sounds like a way of keeping sex at a safe distance by making it scientific.

His feeling of isolation was strong. 'They look upon me as pretty much of a monomaniac,' he told Fliess in May 1894, 'while I have the distinct feeling that I have touched upon one of the great secrets of nature', that is, the causes of neurosis. But all he could look forward to was 'respectable failure' in the eyes of the world, which left him 'somewhat bitter'.

This is hardly the cool response of a researcher whose research was still untested. He was right to think that when his theories began to appear they would be attacked from all quarters, but by that time it was a self-fulfilling prophecy. It is as though Freud was preparing himself for a theatrical debut in which the truth of his propositions would be demonstrated by the venom of the criticism.

What his comrade in Berlin had to offer was not only moral support but practical thinking on how the neuroses that Freud was explaining might be treated. All Freud could say about stemming Actual Neurosis was that people had to change their sexual habits. Fliess would have been able to make a sensational contribution (by finding a biological contraceptive) had his biorhythmic system been able to identify days when conception was impossible: a discovery that someone else later made in a different connection, to provide the imperfect 'rhythm' method of birth control. He failed to do this, but he did claim to have a therapy for Actual Neurosis. As an authority on the nose, he believed that some of the sexual habits of his patients were of nasal origin, or at least had nasal implications. By operating on the nose the supposed side-effects of masturbation, such as painful menstruation, could be cured, with beneficial results all round.

Into this minefield Freud was happy to be led. 'Imagine what would happen if one were a physician like you,' he wrote in October 1893, 'able to investigate the genitals and the nose simultaneously; the riddle [of neurosis] should be solved in no time.'

Fliess claimed to have discovered a condition that he called the 'nasal reflex neurosis'. In a work of 1893 he announced that the nose was affected by 'abnormal sexual satisfaction', which caused specific parts of the turbinate bone to become sensitive and inflamed. These lesions then affected other parts of the body, producing, for example, pains in the stomach and menstrual discomfort in women, as well as uterine bleeding. The spots could be treated with cocaine or burnt out by a surgeon; later on, Fliess tried full-scale surgery. Not for the first time a doctor conjured up a condition and supplied his own cure to go with it. Fliess even spoke sternly about 'quacks' who made a mockery of medicine by giving neurasthenics the wrong sort of treatment. Freud was entranced.

The 'nasal neurosis' theory as Fliess developed it had many applications. Women in labour might be relieved of pain; miscarriage could be provoked by interfering with the nose; a simple case of rhinitis was enough to suggest that 'abnormal sexual satisfaction' was being obtained. When Freud saw 'Mr F. from Budweis' he noted the 'suspicious shape' of his nose, and referred him promptly to Berlin for the swellings to be looked at by the expert.

Behind these works of the imagination were some grains of truth. Nose and genitalia have an ancient biological connection. This was known about long before Fliess used it to draw his wild conclusions. Hippocrates spoke of 'vicarious menstruation', nose-bleeding that may occur early in a pregnancy when the menstrual period has been suppressed; in 1898 Mackenzie of Baltimore speculated about the nose and sexual arousal; a condition called 'Honeymoon Rhinitis' was written up in 1919; violent sneezing episodes, of the kind that get into the *Guinness Book of Records*, are common among pubescent girls. The British authority on the subject, the consultant otolaryngologist John Riddington Young, believes that nasal tissue is sensitive to hormonal influence and responds to sexual stimulus. A nose-to-genitals connection may have been established in primitive times, surviving as a physiological oddity. All this, however, falls short of Fliess's imaginary reflex and his faith in hot wires.

Freud let his ideas live comfortably alongside those of Fliess. His interest turned especially to 'anxiety neurosis' which could appear as a chronic state of brooding, depression and health worries, or as an acute episode – what today would be called a 'panic attack'. If the attack included palpitations and shortness of breath, these were merely the side-effects of sexual intercourse that had been converted into anxiety because the energy (Freud's machine model again) was unable to discharge itself satisfactorily. Freud's observations, he claimed, told him that a man who used coitus interruptus to avoid impregnating a woman frequently fell victim to the neurosis. By 1894 he was also putting sexual abstinence high on his list of causes; this occurred during the prolonged period when he himself was abstinent. Whatever its cause, Freud suffered from anxiety.

For about a year – between 1893 and 1894, the same period of abstinence – Freud thought he had something worse, a bad heart. Fliess and others tried to make him give up his cigars, but this was more than he could manage for long. While wanting reassurance that he was not seriously ill, he was reluctant to believe that his symptoms were in the mind. The nerve doctor preferred not to think he suffered from his nerves. 'Something neurotic would be much harder to take,' he informed Fliess. In April 1894, when he had succeeded in lasting three weeks without 'anything warm between my lips', he reported a bout of 'severe cardiac misery', with irregular heartbeat, tension, burning around the heart, shooting pains down the left arm and breathlessness. This was followed by 'visions of death and departure'. He told Breuer he feared chronic myocarditis, a condition that would reduce his life expectancy – Breuer didn't dismiss the possibility – and he was tormented by the thought that Fliess was keeping the truth from him.

One view is that Freud had angina, brought on by the narrowing of a lesser coronary artery that eventually caused a mild heart attack. The other view is that Freud was being neurotic. Fliess, looking for fresh applications of the nasal reflex neurosis, thought it might be his nose, and in 1895 got him to agree to treatment. In any event, after April 1894 the heart trouble grew less severe.

Freud can be seen as a man in turmoil, pursuing a difficult path. This was the context he hinted at, lingering over phrases like 'the secret' and 'the riddle' to Fliess. He once told a Vienna journalist about mankind's longing to 'open all secrets with a single key'. Breuer, looking back on their relationship, told a colleague that his former friend was 'a man given to absolute and exclusive formulations', and had a 'psychical need' of them. Knowledge was not something to be accumulated slowly. A spark would fall, a revelation would be made. The dream at Bellevue, not far away now, would be one of these illuminations of the dark; or it would be presented as such when the time came. Freud was absorbed in his story of a man confronting the unknown.

The 'cardiac' episode uncovered a streak of pessimism. He began to anticipate old age. 'The problem is,' he wrote to Fliess in June 1894, two months after the visions of death, 'that [Martha and I] are about to become old, somewhat prematurely for the little ones.' He was thirty-eight. In his mid-fifties, writing to Ernest Jones on a train, he was careful to explain that it was the motion that made his hand shake, not old age.

Freud's interest in the Actual Neuroses, sharpened by knowing that he was a sufferer, continued to occupy much of his time, but his mind was increasingly on the other varieties of neurosis, of which hysteria was the paradigm. These were the 'psychoneuroses', which could be treated only by altering the patient's perceptions, not by getting him to change his sexual habits.

As early as the middle of 1892, Freud was telling Fliess that

'Breuer has declared his willingness to publish jointly our detailed theory of abreaction, and our other joint witticisms on hysteria.' By 'abreaction' he meant the process of relieving oneself of a painful or difficult emotion, the result being the 'catharsis' or therapeutic purging, the phenomenon that Freud began to use, date unknown, with Emmy von N. and Cäcilie M. Like confessing sins to a priest, the act was therapeutic. Breuer was quick to draw the analogy, but it was not one that Freud the atheist cared to use.

If he could have dispensed with Breuer as co-author of *Studies on Hysteria*, doubtless Freud would have done so. Disenchantment had set in. Breuer was too cautious, too amiably relaxed, too satisfied with life. He was not sufficiently enthusiastic about his friend's ideas. Fliess, the man of the future, was now Freud's confidant, and received regular grumbles on the subject of Breuer. Hysteria – 'my' hysteria, Freud called it – had 'partially evaporated' in Breuer's hands. There were personal matters. His former mentor was now 'an obstacle to my professional progress', while Freud's cardiac troubles found Breuer wanting: he showed 'no concern for me at all'. The debts that Freud had incurred when he was penniless continued to irritate him; now that he was in a position to make repayments, Breuer waved them aside. Derisive references crept into the letter. 'Breuer became a grandmother on February 3.' 'Breuer is like King David; when someone is dead, he becomes cheerful.'

But Bertha Pappenheim's history was Breuer's property, and in any case a book by the little-known Sigmund Freud would have lacked the authority that the other's name gave it. So Freud had no option but to go on working with him. The first product of their collaboration was a 'Preliminary Communication' under both their names (Breuer's coming first), 'On the Psychical Mechanism of Hysterical Phenomena', which appeared in medical journals in Berlin and Vienna in January 1893. No one took much notice, but in London Frederic Myers, a classical scholar who had helped set up the Society for Psychical Research to investigate phantoms and clairvoyance, was sufficiently taken with it to publish an account in the SPR's *Proceedings*. In America the psychologist William James reviewed it in the first number of the *Psychological Review*, and mentioned the similar work that Janet was doing in France; there were many fingers in the pie.

The Breuer–Freud account used the term 'abreacted' for the first time, and spoke of traumatic memories that were 'repressed' by the patient. At the centre of the essay was the claim that bringing memories to light could have a therapeutic effect, summed up in the phrase that hysterics suffered mainly from reminiscences, the first of Freud's epigrams to reach the outside world.

The essay's final paragraph contained a caution. Their step forward had brought them 'nearer to an understanding only of the *mechanism* of hysterical symptoms and not of the internal causes of hysteria'. It is possible that Freud, left to himself, would have written about the sexual origins of hysteria (there is one fleeting reference), but whatever he had learnt from his hysterics, either he was being careful about what he said in print, or Breuer was restraining him.

In 1894, while they were still assembling material for *Studies on Hysteria*, Freud published a less restrained paper, 'The Neuro-psychoses of Defence'. With the concept of defence and its companion, repression, he was laying a foundation stone for psycho-analysis. What he meant by 'defence' was resistance to unacceptable ideas and memories, so that they became repressed and sank from view into the 'unconscious'. Already the mind was acquiring regions.

The matters that alerted the defences were likely to be sexual, since 'it is precisely sexual life which brings with it the most copious occasions for the emergence of incompatible ideas'. By 'incompatible' he meant incompatible with the patient's self-esteem. Hysteria, obsessions and phobias could all be traced back to unacknowledged sexual origins. Freud gave brief accounts of women with sexual secrets that made them ill, and spoke of having 'analysed' their cases.

He knew perfectly well that medicine had always been aware of a relationship between sexual behaviour and nervous illness but had often preferred not to think about it. Instead of behaving like most of his colleagues and discouraging patients who wanted to discuss sexual events, Freud encouraged them to tell him more. A young woman, described in the defence paper, explained that when she was in public places she had a 'dread of being overcome by the need to urinate'. Freud uncovered an erotic day-dream that she had in a concert hall, which so alarmed her that she turned it into a need to relieve herself, setting up a pattern of behaviour that led to the phobia.

These were hardly matters for serious medical men, or if they were, women's conventional shame about the need to use lavatories sufficed as an explanation. Freud, slowly developing his sexual ideas, may have chosen to emphasise them now as a means of outflanking Breuer, who was reluctant to give them such weight in their forthcoming *Studies*. Perhaps, too, his fears for his heart made him anxious to see something in print in case he died prematurely.

The ambitious paper about defence was followed in January 1895 by an equally ambitious paper about anxiety neurosis, his first full-length statement in public to deal with Actual Neurosis, although Fliess had heard it all before. It was detailed, informative and in places autobiographical. When listing the forms that anxiety attacks could take, he spoke about heart disturbances and 'pseudo-angina', very likely with himself in mind.

At about the same time, Fliess treated Freud's nose (presumably cauterising it) in order to help his heart. Whatever Fliess did, it left him 'unbelievably well, as though everything had been erased'. Medically such a procedure makes no sense; to Fliess and the compliant Freud it was progress. One of Freud's patients was less fortunate. She was a woman of thirty, Emma Eckstein, whose family was friendly with the Freuds. References to her were suppressed in pre-Masson versions of the Freud–Fliess letters. Eckstein, being treated as an hysteric, may also have needed treatment for menstrual difficulties, which in turn could be laid at the door of the old enemy, masturbation – a subject she dwelt on in a book about bringing up children, published in 1904. Freud sent her to Fliess, who rolled up his sleeves and operated on her nose in February, using surgery to treat the 'trouble spots' on one of the turbinate bones, not the milder cauterisation. As a result she nearly died. The episode was a test of Freud's friendship; it emerged unharmed, which is more than can be said for Eckstein.

The operation in Berlin was on 21 February 1895. On 2 March she haemorrhaged. Four days later there was further bleeding, and a Vienna surgeon, examining the wound, found that half a metre of gauze had been left behind by Fliess. When this was removed she haemorrhaged so badly that she nearly died. Freud, one of those in attendance, felt faint and had to be given brandy. She nearly died again on 17 March, and again in April, before her recovery was properly under way. Her face was said to have been permanently disfigured where the bone was cut away. She made no complaint.

The nearest Freud came to criticising his friend was when he told him that all the trouble had been caused by 'an operation that was purported to be harmless'. Fliess, the layman's idea of a mad doctor, cast a spell over Freud. Not content with his work on Eckstein's nose, he tried to explain her bleeding with his biorhythmic theories, what he and Freud called 'periodicity'. Once again Freud acquiesced. When they were discussing the case a year later, in 1896, he wrote:

> I shall be able to prove to you that you were right, that her episodes of bleeding were hysterical, were occasioned by *longing*, and probably occurred at the sexually relevant times (the woman, out of resistance, has not yet supplied me with the dates).

The 'longing' was a longing to be loved. Emma's history showed that 'she has always been a bleeder'. She had told Freud of an episode at the age of fifteen when she bled from the nose because she wanted 'a certain young doctor' to treat her (he may have meant himself). The 'sexually relevant times' were the special dates that Fliess spent hours calculating for friends and family like some biological astrologer, using the real twenty-eight-day female cycle and the imaginary twenty-three-day male counterpart to do his preposterous sums.

Her infantile desire to be loved during her illness had somehow caused the bleeding on 20 March and again in April. She nearly died, then, for love of Freud; he doesn't say it in so many words, but spoke of her 'unconscious wish' to entice him to visit her, using her bleeding as 'an unfailing means of rearousing my affection'. He said that she 'bled spontaneously three times and each bleeding lasted for four days, which must have some significance'.

No wonder such passages were suppressed, with their air of private fantasies promoted to scientific status. Breuer was not the kind of friend to share them with, but although in private he later disclaimed many of Freud's ideas, Breuer was nevertheless awed by him. 'Freud's intellect is soaring,' he wrote to Fliess in July 1895. 'I gaze after him like a hen at a hawk.' He had no answer to Freud's moral ferocity and his ability to tell convincing stories – for even the theories were stories, held together by power of imagination rather than weight of evidence. How exactly did Miss Eckstein's emotions make her bleed till she nearly died? The evidence was lacking but the story didn't falter.

He wouldn't waste tears on Eckstein. *Studies on Hysteria* was published in the spring of 1895, with an authors' preface dated April. Chapter 1 was a reprint of the 'Preliminary Communication'. The case-histories followed, beginning with Breuer's account of 'Fräulein Anna O.', which spoke of 'the final cure of the hysteria' and described an illness that ran from July 1880 to June 1882. The cure, as we know, was not what it seemed, but *Studies on Hysteria* was determined to present her as a self-sufficient illustration of a theory. Breuer conveniently forgot what had happened ten years earlier, presumably persuaded by Freud that the principle of catharsis which it was supposed to prove must be demonstrated. If that meant inventing a happy ending for Bertha Pappenheim, so be it.

Her life did, in the end, settle down to normality. In her thirties she found a vocation, becoming a writer and a distinguished social worker, interesting herself in orphanages and women's rights, and even opposing the 'white slave trade' that supposedly lured girls, in this case Jewish girls from Galicia, into European brothels. She never married, and when she died in 1936, aged seventy-seven, she was remembered as a stern idealist. After the war the (West) German authorities put her picture on a postage stamp.

Freud's suspicion that her case had sexual undertones may have been correct. A poem she wrote when she was fifty-two has survived:

> Love did not come to me –
> So I live like the plants,
> In the cellar, without light . . .
>
> Love did not come to me –
> So I bury myself in work
> And, chastened, live for duty.

The hesitant attitude towards sex of *Studies on Hysteria* is usually attributed to Breuer, who was following the conventions of the time. As Freud always said, doctors knew more than they were willing to say. Even so, in the 'Theoretical' section that Breuer contributed to *Studies*, he did write about sexuality, including the assertion that *'the great majority of severe neuroses in women have their origin in the marriage bed'*. Freud himself had uncertainties. He was at his most explicit in the concluding essay, but there he kept away from individual cases. Speculating about the sexual behaviour of bourgeois women with identities, especially Emmy and Cäcilie, might have sounded too informal. The subject was hazardous. It was one thing to condemn self-abuse and condoms – conservative readers of his papers on the Actual Neuroses welcomed his apparent orthodoxy – but the new message, that sexual ghosts lingered in the memories of upright citizens and had the power to upset their lives, was unlikely to be so popular.

Studies on Hysteria was not widely reviewed at first, and some of the notices were unhelpful. The Germans had serious doubts, with one leading neurologist demanding to know if any honourable physician would examine his patients' intimate lives. More encouraging was a humanities professor in Vienna, von Berger, who found the book 'permeated with unconscious and unintended beauty', offering ideas that were 'nothing more and nothing less than ancient poetical psychology'. Prefiguring literary psychoanalysis, he wrote of Lady Macbeth as a woman gripped by 'a true defensive neurosis' who goes sleep-walking because the terrors she has banished from her conscious mind are still at work elsewhere. To von Berger, Freud's apology in the *Studies* for the fiction-like structure of the case-histories lacking 'serious scientific character' was unnecessary. 'A scientist who sails the sea of the human soul,' he declared, 'cannot pretend to cool and sober objectivity no matter how hard he try.'

What von Berger and a few others had noticed was a perceptiveness about people and their curious ways that runs through Freud's work. His contribution to the book rises above its subject, not only in the main argument but in his asides. There is a footnote about von Lieben/Cäcilie M. where he discusses how a person will make an over-optimistic remark – which is soon proved wrong – because their unconscious already has a premonition of the pessimistic truth which they are reluctant to accept. Anna Lieben had suggested to him, and he had agreed, that this might explain the superstitious fear that boasting invites disaster, that pride comes before a fall. Freud wrote:

> We must not vaunt our happiness on the one hand, nor, on the other, must we talk of the worst or it will happen. The fact is that we do not boast of our happiness until unhappiness is in the offing, and we become aware of our anticipation in the form of a boast, because in such cases the subject-matter of what we are recollecting emerges before the feeling that belongs to it.

Freud's private life proceeded quietly in the background. Martha was pregnant in March 1895; abstinence had ended, and he told Fliess he was 'again a human being with human feelings'. He ordered a dozen prints of a photograph of himself and Fliess. He had more riotous evenings playing cards.

At Easter, which fell in mid-April in 1895, he visited Rax and Schneeberg country again with Oscar Rie. A letter to Fliess on 20 April mentions the Easter excursion and says that he also spent 'one day in Abbazia'.

This is a long way for a day trip. Abbazia was a fashionable Adriatic resort on the eastern side of the Istrian peninsula, thirty miles from Trieste, which is across the peninsula to the west. Abbazia was then in the Austrian Empire. The journey by express train from Vienna took thirteen hours, so to go there for the day would be like going from California to London for lunch. Only important patients sent Freud tearing off to foreign parts. One of the women in *Studies on Hysteria*, Emmy von N., really Fanny Moser, is known to have frequented the place. She and a sister spent the winter of 1889–90 at Abbazia (they were there when they heard about the deaths at Mayerling). In April 1895 Freud was still working on the proofs of the *Studies*; he may have wanted to consult Mrs Moser, even to make sure that she wouldn't object to seeing her story in print.

In late spring Martha and the children moved out of Hill Street to spend a few months in Heaven Street, at the Schloss Bellevue. Her sixth pregnancy can't have pleased her; the stay at Bellevue may have been meant as recompense. Freud, coming and going as work allowed, had his dream of Irma's injection there on the night of 23–24 July, a date that Fliess questioned later, but Freud insisted was correct. His own analysis of the dream was given place of honour in *The Interpretation of Dreams*, published five years afterwards. It has been studied ever since in an attempt to discover, among other things, what was revolving in Sigmund's head that night at the Bellevue.

In the dream, which he wrote down when he woke, Freud was anxious not to be blamed for Irma's illness. With him he had 'Dr M.' (who was Breuer), 'my friend Otto' (Oscar Rie) and 'my friend Leopold' (a paediatrician). An injection given by Otto was blamed for causing Irma's infection, probably because the needle was dirty. Detailed but unassuming, the dream consisted of no more than doctors standing around and discussing a case; the medical examination was the sole event. Irma was supposedly Freud's patient Anna Lichtheim, a young widow. But she may well have been the accusing figure of Eckstein, too.

Freud said it was the first dream he interpreted in detail, beginning work at once on 24 July. After taking it apart and brooding over the pieces to see what thoughts about himself and his life they inspired, he concluded that within the dream's absurdities a simple statement was concealed. It told him he was not to blame for Irma's condition, and so *'its content was the fulfilment of a wish and its motive was a wish'*.

As he came to develop the theory after 1895, dreams were not irrational, once the rules were grasped, but serious statements by the unconscious. They could be understood by letting patients find their way from one remark to another, on the 'free association' principle of 'the first thing that comes into your head'. The knowledge that a night-dream (no less than a day-dream) was designed to fulfil a wish, often a wish that no decent person could admit to, forewarned an analyst that his patients' dreams were works of evasion, and that only by dealing with their resistances to the truth could the truth about them be uncovered.

Some came to see the Irma dream as the revelatory moment of psychoanalysis, the instant of its birth. Freud never claimed this in public, but years later he told Fliess that it was the first time he 'grasped the general principle' of wish-fulfilment. It was in his nature to give the episode a dramatic twist, to savour having 'the secret of the dream' revealed to him – the phrase he used, also to Fliess, in 1900.

The revelation was not quite so instant. Dreams were already preoccupying him. Early in 1895 he slept for some weeks on a harder bed than usual, perhaps for health reasons. The change of mattress (he said) gave him unexpectedly vivid dreams, which he wrote down and tried to solve. He made this cryptic statement in one of his long footnotes to *Studies on Hysteria*, months before the Irma dream. On 4 March 1895 he told Fliess about a nephew of Breuer, a young doctor called Rudi, who was so reluctant to wake up when the maid called him that he dreamt he saw a hospital chart with his name on it, decided that he must already be in the hospital, and went back to sleep. Wish-fulfilment was thus on his mind before the Irma dream; and in a letter to Fliess dated 24 July, immediately after the Bellevue dream, he didn't mention wish-fulfilment at all.

The 'particular state of affairs' that he desired – the need to be seen as a model doctor – is a modest wish to emerge from the great dream. Freud says nothing about the Eckstein affair or his wife's sixth pregnancy. Both might have been on his conscience and both can be read into his account. Freud himself said that there were omissions. This has been an incitement to Freudians to discover what was omitted, although for a while after his death the veneration-factor, on which he may have been relying, kept loyal eyes averted. The new Fliess letters show why Eckstein might have troubled his dreams, but it is only one more speculation to add to the rest.

Here are some conjectures by Freudians. Freud was exculpating his friend Fliess for what happened to Eckstein. The patient he was worrying about was not Eckstein but his wife. He was exploring an unsatisfactory sexual relationship with Martha, which included distate on her part for oral sex and desire on his part to indulge in it. He was brooding guiltily on Martha's latest pregnancy. He was taking refuge from the threat (which went back to his childhood) of all-powerful Woman, as evidenced by the pregnant Martha and the bleeding Eckstein, and seeking the companionship of men. He was reliving an act of erotic aggression, aged five, against his sister Anna, aged three. It was a dream of revenge. It sought absolution for his reckless use of remedies, among them cocaine (which he was still using in 1895). It included oblique references to condoms and coitus interruptus.

The dream has been praised as a creative achievement that tells us more about the writer than any lyric poem could ever do; as an exercise in sexuality, birth and death, encompassing his own sexual appetites, his pregnant wife and the approaching death of his father, whose terminal illness (Freud once told a patient) first showed itself that July. In a famous interpretation (by Erik Erikson in 1954) Freud is the middle-aged dreamer, facing the unknown, despairing of his loneliness, constructing for himself a dream that helps to 'appease his conscience, and preserve his identity'. Jung said the dream was an admission of Freud's own neurosis.

Many of the Irma interpretations are persuasive, especially Jung's; some (like Erikson's) make Freud credible enough, a man struggling to survive; most are feasible, since dreams, as Freud pointed out, are in the end too deep to fathom. The flexibility, though, is self-defeating; an interpreter can let his imagination loose on a dream and read into it what he chooses.

The significant thing about Irma's injection may be simply that Freud had a dream that left a profound impression. The wish may have been that he should have a dream that was significant. Why should a dreamer, especially a psychologist, not intervene to his advantage in the business of dreaming?

In the middle of a difficult year, with no sign that recognition was any closer, his unconscious kindly arranged an inspirational experience. It clarified his ideas about wishes and gave his career a powerful thrust in the right direction.

13: Seduction

As time went by, Freud did less visiting and treated more of his patients at Berggasse 19, a crowded apartment by now, with a family of six children, a nursemaid and a governess. Minna Bernays went there to help out in December 1895, shortly before Anna was born, and stayed for ever. The first-floor apartment, gloomy and cramped, was not very healthy, and when children's infections or stomach upsets did the rounds, they lingered for weeks. 'Our home,' Freud said on one occasion, 'is haunted by some kind of illness which refuses to show itself completely.' It may have been the drains; there was only the one bathroom.

Freud's domain was the waiting room that led off the hallway, immediately inside the front door, with his consulting room and its couch beyond, and his study. In 1896 relief came in the shape of a gas explosion in the ground-floor apartment, where a watchmaker lived. The tenant left, and when the place was repaired Freud took it over as his working quarters, seeing patients there by day, and after supper retiring to write into the small hours. Approaching his fortieth birthday in May that year, he was still an obscure figure.

Nothing much is known about the techniques he was using at the time. He may still have been pressing patients' foreheads to clear their minds, rather as gazing into a crystal ball was supposed to do. Hypnotism may still have been a small part of his armoury, but he thought he had a better plan. His new technique, which he had been developing since Anna Lieben and the early hysterics, was 'free association', in which patients were encouraged to speak spontaneously about their dreams or their lives, the assumption being that (with a little help from the analyst) their thoughts would invariably lead to what was significant. This would become the approved way of reading the unconscious, where, in Freud's words, the character of the long-forgotten child lay concealed. 'I dig it out by my work,' he told Fliess in 1897; 'it struggles; and the person who initially was such a good, noble human being becomes mean, untruthful, or obstinate, a malingerer – until I tell him so and thus make it possible for him to overcome this character.'

'Free association' is an early mistranslation that has stuck. What Freud meant was not an 'association' but a 'sudden idea', although in practice there seems little difference. Freud's approach, looking for patterns in apparently disconnected remarks, letting patients ramble on, was a sort of revolution, and its influence survives in modern psychotherapy.

In 1895, still feeling his way, Freud used the phrase 'psychical analysis' in the *Studies*. The following year, in March, it became 'psychoanalysis' for the first time, in a paper he published in France.

At that point, the spring of 1896, the new system shot off in a new direction. Having already put sex at its heart, Freud proposed a simple, brutal explanation of why people became hysterics and obsessional neurotics: they had all been sexually abused in childhood. Fliess had his universal theory of biorhythms; now Freud had a universal theory of seduction.

That life went in predictable cycles (or that sexual behaviour was influenced by the nose) might or might not be true, but such a theory aroused no emotional response. To suggest that every psychoneurotic had been sexually interfered with, however, was likely to upset people in large numbers. Convincing evidence would be needed.

The sexual maltreatment of children was not a concern of the times. In England, incest was not a crime until 1908; as with rape, blame attached more easily to the accuser than the accused. Middle-class parents, or rather middle-class fathers, provided the moral fibre that held society together. If sexual acts took place between adult and child, they were disgusting aberrations, the less publicised the better; the argument was widely used to justify leaving incest, and child abuse in general, outside the law.

Studies on Hysteria had touched on the seduction of minors. Breuer mentioned a boy of twelve who had a sore throat and difficulty in swallowing, and blamed an hysterical response to an incident in a public urinal when a man asked him to perform oral sex. The Katharina case concerned a father-seducer, and the

Umbrella Girl hinted at it, but it was not until October 1895 that Freud told Fliess he was on the scent of a 'strict precondition' for hysteria, that 'a primary sexual experience (before puberty), accompanied by revulsion and fright, must have taken place'. If the victim enjoyed the experience instead of being frightened, the result was obsessional neurosis. Unlike hysteria, this remains a common condition, ruining sufferers' lives with private rituals – compulsive hand-washing is the one always quoted, but there are hundreds – that must be obeyed in order to avoid fearful consequences. Freud, confident that psychoanalysis could cure both the neuroses, told Fliess that 'This gives me a kind of faint joy – for having lived some forty years not quite in vain.'

The idea of bad deeds perpetrated on innocent children was easy to grasp. Like the physiological model of the mind, it was rooted in the physical reality that Freud preferred. So far he had given Fliess no clinical details. Cases must have generated substantial histories and lasted long enough for him to reach conclusions. Early psychoanalyses were comparatively short, but Freud could hardly see an hysteric on Monday and pronounce her cured on Friday. This failure to examine case-histories is puzzling. An account of 'The Neuroses of Defence' that he sent to Fliess on New Year's Day 1896 contained further detail about the principle of the seduction theory but no particulars of the seduced.

Between Christmas and spring 1896 he wrote three papers for publication. In the first, which appeared in a French journal in March (addressed to 'the disciples of J. M. Charcot'), he provided some factual detail 'in order to combat the scepticism with which I expect to meet'. He had made 'a complete psychoanalysis' of thirteen cases of hysteria and six of obsessional neurosis. Some involved assaults by an older child, the others by unspecified adults. As evidence this is not very convincing; it has to be taken on trust.

The second paper, published in Germany in May (with the first use in German of the term 'psychoanalysis'), cited the same thirteen cases, seven of them involving other children, mostly brothers doing things to sisters; the adults to blame in such cases, said Freud, were usually nursemaids, governesses, domestic servants and teachers.

To cause hysteria the assaults had to involve '*an actual irritation of the genitals (of processes resembling copulation)*'. Freud made the remarkable claim that in two of the thirteen cases the time of the earliest seduction lay 'as far back as memory itself', at the age of one-and-a-half or two. Despite glimpses of individual stories, there was again no sustained account of a case and its treatment.

The third paper, 'The Aetiology of Hysteria', was a more substantial affair: longer, more explicit and addressed directly to his medical colleagues in Vienna. Freud gave it as a lecture to the Association for Psychiatry and Neurology in April, and published it soon after.* This was his formal claim to the discovery. In the chair that night was Richard von Krafft-Ebing, Professor of Psychiatry in the university, whose account of sexual perversion, *Psychopathia Sexualis* (1886), had become a standard work, though banned in England where it was seen as another dirty book from across the Channel. Freud owned several copies. Krafft-Ebing was very grand. Kings consulted him, and Crown Prince Rudolf had been one of his patients, as had Anna O. when she was first ill.

Freud's lecture, from its salutation, 'Gentlemen!' to its closing words, 'this new pathway to knowledge', staked his claim in crisp, down-to-earth language. The cases of 'pure hysteria' and 'hysteria combined with obsessions' now totalled eighteen, one fewer than the figure in the first, 'French', paper.

In every one of the eighteen cases, comprising all his analyses (presumably he meant all his analyses of these particular conditions), the sexual connection was apparent. The claim about early memories was repeated: by pursuing the analysis 'as far back as a human memory is capable of reaching', he could 'invariably' bring the patient to reproduce the experiences that caused the neurosis. This involved the assumption that 'even the age of childhood is not wanting in slight sexual excitations'.

Freud's voice was dry and restrained; the rhetoric was in the content, not the delivery. After half an hour he reached the core of his thesis:

> At the bottom of every case of hysteria there are *one or more occurrences of premature sexual experience*, occurrences which belong to the earliest years of childhood but which can be reproduced through the work of psychoanalysis in spite of the intervening decades.

Freud called this 'the discovery of a *caput Nili* [a 'source of the

* The lecture was probably extemporised, or relied on minimal notes. Freud told Fliess that he 'wrote [it] down in full' in May. So any reference to the lecture is strictly speaking a reference to the paper.

Nile'] in neuropathology'. Anthony Stadlen (a psychotherapist and sceptical historian of psychoanalysis), noting the grandiose tone of the paper, thinks that Freud was making a claim for medical immortality before his forthcoming fortieth birthday. As Stadlen points out, Freud compared his announcement of a 'specific aetiology' for hysteria with Robert Koch's discovery of the tuberculosis bacillus, announced four years earlier and applauded all over the world. The *New York Times* called it 'one of the great scientific discoveries of the age'. That was the kind of recognition Freud wanted.

What did the nerve doctors of Vienna make of it? When Freud asked, 'Shall I put before you the actual material I have obtained from my analyses?', the obvious answer would have been, 'Yes, please.' Freud, however, veered off on another course, to meet 'the mass of objections' that he anticipated. The material failed to appear. Freud flashed it in the air again towards the end like a conjuror, citing 'evidence which, if you were given the complete history of a case, would be as clear as daylight to you'. This sounds devious and insulting at the same time. The proof existed but he had no intention of producing it; there would be nothing comparable to the rich narratives in *Studies on Hysteria* that lent conviction to his gallery of women.

The meeting was not impressed. Freud had got on the wrong side of his audience, as he had with the Viennese physicians ten years earlier. 'The donkeys' gave it an 'icy reception', he told Fliess, who was having troubles of his own with donkeys who were not happy with the nasal reflex neurosis. 'They can go to hell,' he added.

Krafft-Ebing, whose career taught him that ideas in psychiatry were often extensions of the psychiatrist's personality, offended Freud by saying that 'it sounds like a scientific fairy tale'. These were almost the words that Freud himself had used on New Year's Day 1896, when he included the seduction theory in the ideas he sent to Fliess. He called the paper 'The Neuroses of Defence (A Christmas Fairy Tale)'. To talk privately of fantasies was permitted because these were code-words between friends. But there was always an element of fairy tale about the seduction theory.

In the closing minutes of the lecture, Freud made another boast, that his findings were 'based on a laborious individual examination of patients which has in most cases taken up a hundred or more hours of work'. The mathematical implications are startling. If the eighteen cases he cited were reduced to fifteen (to allow for the 'in most cases' provision), it meant more than 1,500 hours of psycho-analysis. In later times, working non-stop as an analyst, Freud would expect to have eight one-hour sessions each day in a six-day week. Assuming that all his working days were taken up with these cases, arranged in a gap-free timetable with no holidays, they would have occupied him for seven or eight months before January 1896 when he wrote the first paper that spoke of nineteen patients. Even if spread over a longer period, the cases still represent an improbable commitment. Nor can they have been the only cases he saw, since non-hysterical patients would have presented them-selves as well; and among the hysterics, some would have dropped out or been otherwise unsuitable for his series.

Nothing in the Fliess correspondence makes the claim credible. He was intermittently busy and not busy through 1895. His nose and heart problems distracted him in the early part of the year; so did the operation on Emma Eckstein (who may have been one of the hysterics in the series; Freud claimed a shopkeeper groped an 'Emma' through her clothes when she was twelve). In April he told Fliess that cases of neurosis were 'now very rare' as far as he was concerned, although he was busy with them again a month later. His practice ceased in the summer when he stayed at Bellevue and in the mountains. Nor is there any indication of the seduction theory before 8 October, when he told Fliess that he was on the scent of pre-pubertal sex as 'a strict precondition' for hysteria.

Were his eighteen or nineteen analyses proceeding concurrently, with nothing said about them to his confidant over the months they took to mature, and did he penetrate to the earliest memory in each of them at the same time? On 16 October, eight days after the first intimation, he announced he had 'solved the riddles', and the two neuroses, hysteria and obsessional neurosis, were 'essentially conquered'.

Perhaps he was an opportunist, following a thread – lost times, buried loves, guilty memories – who had heard enough to whet his appetite for the most private evidence of all, the faint memories of childhood shames and pleasures that most of us carry, not wholly remembered or entirely forgotten. Freud himself carried them, as he showed before long. Perhaps his thoughts turned to his earlier cases, from the time before he gave psychoanalysis a name; perhaps he began to make retrospective diagnoses, day-dreaming over the ideas until he could fit them together and present the result as 'science'. For all we know, Freud's hundred-hour cases included old patients like Fanny Moser and Anna von Lieben; he lavished enough time on both of them, and they may have shared sexual memories with him that he never wrote about. We can never be sure what was happening behind Freud's smokescreen.

The methods he used to convince himself went unchallenged for years after his death. Revealing passages in the Fliess letters were not available, and in any case Freud was unchallengeable. Now it seems likely that he arrived at the seduction theory by creative guesswork. This may be how science often works, but it isn't the way that Freud described. He claimed the benefit of hard evidence, meticulously gathered. If the claim was dubious, it was damaging to psychoanalysis, regardless of whether the seduction theory itself was right or wrong.

The evidence lay in the memories. This left scope for every kind of uncertainty, since memories of childhood are fragmentary and hard to verify. Freud agreed in his April lecture that it was difficult. 'Before the application of the analysis,' he wrote, 'the patients know nothing about these [sexual] scenes.' The analyst had to convince them: 'Only the strongest compulsion of the treatment can induce them to embark on a reproduction of them.'

As the memories took shape, patients experienced 'violent sensations' that made them ashamed, and afterwards said that they had 'no feeling of remembering the scenes'. Freud saw this as validating the memories, since why would patients want to discredit what they had themselves invented? In other words, the stronger their resistance, the more powerful the memories locked away in their unconscious must have been.*

Employed more widely, this position became a psychoanalytic stock-in-trade, an argument of exclusivity that was used to demolish disbelievers by telling them that attacks on the doctrine were evidence of their own emotional resistance: what they needed was a dose of psychoanalysis, after which they would see the error of their ways.

---

* Later Freud modified his position. By 1900 he was telling patients that 'the earliest experiences of childhood' were '*not obtainable any longer* as such.' In 1918 he was even more explicit: 'These scenes from infancy are not reproduced during the treatment as recollections, they are the products of construction.'

As for the possibility that he had put thoughts into his patients' heads, Freud dismissed it in the lecture as 'untenable'. His defence (there and elsewhere) was a variant of the exclusivity argument, that only those who used psychoanalysis, which in 1896 meant Sigmund Freud alone, were competent to judge in this 'obscure field'. If you were Freud, you understood. If you were not Freud you were not able to understand, unless possibly you were Fliess.

An authoritarian approach to patients was to be expected, and was implicit in Freud's concept of the job. Robust statements are strewn throughout his early work once he had laid the groundwork in *Studies on Hysteria* with the flat assertion that one should not be afraid of telling patients what their next thought was going to be, since 'it will do no harm'. Memories of a precocious sexual event 'must be extracted from [patients] piece by piece'. The patients' resistance must be conquered 'by emphasising the unshakable nature of our convictions'.

Fliess, privy to first-hand details in the correspondence that were not appearing in the published papers, saw this masterful Freud in action. He had a cousin, Miss G. de B., an hysteric, whose father Freud suspected of seducing her. She suffered from eczema around her mouth; for this and other reasons, Freud thought that as a child she had been forced to commit fellatio.

> When I thrust the explanation at her, she was at first won over; then she committed the folly of questioning the old man himself, who at the very first intimation exclaimed indignantly, 'Are you implying that I was the one?' and swore a holy oath to his innocence.
>
> She is now in the throes of the most vehement resistance, claims to believe him, but attests to her identification with him by having become dishonest and swearing false oaths. I have threatened to send her away and in the process convinced myself that she has already gained a good deal of certainty which she is reluctant to acknowledge.

The story was introduced with the words '*Habemus papam!*', 'We have a Pope!' Freud's glee was evident: another seducer was in the bag.

So here was the process at work. Had Freud been more forthcoming with the Viennese nerve doctors, this was a case that he might have unravelled for them. G. de B.'s memory of something nasty was not so much her memory as Freud's interpretation of events. He 'thrust' his explanation at her and she was 'won over'. She hadn't told him, 'I remember my father came into the bedroom . . .' Freud was working on clues: the eczema by the mouth was one;

a nervous tic that gave her lips an appearance of sucking, and a speech inhibition as a schoolgirl that was associated with 'a *full* mouth', were others.

Krafft-Ebing might have said 'Fairy tale!' under his breath. He might even have inquired what good had been achieved by setting a woman against her father on the basis of, at best, dim circumstantial evidence. But there was nothing apologetic about Freud's reconstruction of childhood memory in the interests of therapy. There was no such thing as the perfect childhood memory, so reconstruction was the only way to reach the evidence of seduction that he had decided was crucial.

In 'Screen Memories' (1899) he suggested that our meagre collection of infantile recollections was not what it seemed. A trivial memory was there to act as a screen for a significant but unacceptable memory concealed behind it. Even that was too plain a statement for the hall of mirrors that Freud was seeking to convey. 'It may indeed be questioned,' he wrote, 'whether we have any memories at all *from* our childhood: memories *relating* to our childhood may be all that we possess.'*

It is a long way from speculation about memories that people possess, to the invention of memories that they ought to possess because an 'interpretation' points that way. Freud's confidence in his powers was alarming.

The seduction theory may have been difficult to swallow. It was, however, a feasible proposition open to proof or disproof. When Freud put his name to it, he must have known that sooner or later others would find – or fail to find – the evidence he claimed to possess. Any dishonesty on his part would be detected. Therefore (one assumes) he must have believed in the theory. But he also fabricated evidence when he talked about the hundreds of hours he spent with the patients. What else did he fabricate? Presumably he was so convinced that he had found the key to neurosis that he felt

---

* I recall about thirty individual events before the age of five, few of apparent consequence, that could be fitted into half an hour. In one, I am being shown the cell at a suburban police station, as a treat, by the policeman to whom my father was reporting an incident that involved me, a delivery boy with a bicycle and a piece of waste land. What the incident consisted of I have no recollection. All I remember is the stone floor, the wooden bunk, the bars, the thrill of crime and punishment. Is that a screen memory for something disagreeable? Reading Freud, with whatever degree of scepticism, you come across these arrows apparently pointing in your direction.

free to embellish the record and help convince the faint-hearted. This intuitive sense that he was right, that he *knew*, ran through his life. Force of imagination, not weight of evidence, was Freud's strength.

In private he was soon less confident than he had seemed when he addressed the psychiatrists. He wrote unhappily to Fliess in 1896 and 1897 about cases of hysteria where treatment had yet to reach a satisfactory conclusion. On 9 October 1896 he wrote, 'I am now very satisfied with my cases'; on 17 December, 'so far not a single case is finished'; on 3 January 1897, 'perhaps by [Easter] I shall have carried one case to completion'; on 7 March, 'I have not yet finished a single case; am still struggling with the difficulties of treatment and of understanding.'

The neurotics came to Berggasse, lay on the couch, stared into space, spilled out their thoughts, added their uncertainties to Freud's. His difficulties with seduction were part of a wider darkening of his life. His father died, probably of cancer, in October 1896, an event that affected him deeply.

His commentary on patients' memories became harsher for a while, around the end of 1896. The details he gave Fliess were lurid, almost pornographic. On 6 December 1896 he wrote, 'she recovered from her unconscious the memory of a scene in which (at the age of four) she watched her papa, in the throes of sexual excitement, licking the feet of a wet nurse'. On 17 December, 'Will you believe that [the patient's] reluctance to drink beer and to shave was elucidated by a scene in which a nurse sits down *podice nudo* [with bare buttocks] in a shallow shaving bowl filled with beer in order to let herself be licked, and so on?' On 3 January 1897 came Fliess's cousin and the tale of fellatio. On 12 January he asked, 'Would you please try to search for a case of childhood convulsions that you can trace back (in the future or in your memory) to sexual abuse, specifically to *lictus* [licking] (or finger) in the anus . . . For my newest finding is that I am able to trace back with certainty a patient's attack that merely resembled epilepsy to such treatment by the tongue on the part of his nurse.'

A new emphasis made fathers the prime seducers of their children. At the same time (24 January 1897) he reported that 'The early period before the age of 1½ years is becoming ever more significant.' On 11 February he wrote explicitly about his own father, whose departure from the scene the previous October had perhaps opened the way for this change. In an anguished passage, like a free association of thoughts, which it probably was, Freud wrote:

> Hysterical cold shivers = being taken out of a warm bed. Hysterical headache with sensations of pressure on the top of the head, temples, and so forth, is characteristic of the scenes where the head is held still for the purpose of actions in the mouth. (Later reluctance at photographer's, who holds head in a clamp.)

Was this the neck clamp that held his own head when he was in the portrait studio, aged eight, for the family to be gentrified in a photograph? In the next sentence he distanced himself by implicating his siblings:

> Unfortunately, my own father was one of these perverts and is responsible for the hysteria of my brother (all of whose symptoms are identifications) and those of several younger sisters.*

Such extreme propositions were separating him from the comfortable limits of bourgeois family life. Nor would his colleagues be likely to understand. His professional isolation was something he drew attention to later on. At the same time, a wish for loneliness was in his nature; he saw himself as the man compelled by destiny to make his own way. In March 1896 he had made the connection in so many words when he told Fliess, 'I ... am contending with hostility and live in such isolation that one might imagine I had discovered the greatest truths.' In April he wrote, 'Of all the advice you gave me, I followed the one concerning my isolation most completely.' Fliess, himself a lonely figure, must have seen them as two innovators in the same boat. In May Freud was still dwelling on his loneliness, this time blaming colleagues: 'I am as isolated as you would wish me to be. Word was given out to abandon me, for a void is forming all around me.'

With his father's death, the feeling of isolation grew worse. 'By one of those dark pathways behind the official consciousness,' he wrote to Fliess, 'the old man's death has affected me deeply ... I now feel quite uprooted.'

His sexual inquiries produced a degree of isolation within the family. In February 1897 he was telling Fliess about his interest in

---

* Both these passages, after the words 'warm bed', were deleted when the Freud–Fliess letters first appeared in the 1950s. Jones made a fleeting reference in the biography.

the appearance, among small children, of feelings of disgust in relation to excrement. The sixth and last child, Anna, was now fourteen months old. 'Why do I not go into the nursery and experiment with Annerl? Because working for 12½ hours, I have no time for it, and the women folk do not support my researches.'

In April he was pursuing the idea that hysterical fantasies could arise from things that children overhear from as young as six months. Oscar Rie, his children's doctor, had implored him to abandon this line of inquiry. 'Probably,' said Freud, 'he has been charged with this mission.' It was the women again, being shocked.

The women would not have liked the letter he sent to Fliess in May 1897, mentioning that 'Recently I dreamed of over-affectionate feelings for Mathilde', his eldest daughter, now aged nine. The wish that the dream fulfilled, said Freud, was 'of course' that he should 'catch *Pater* as the originator of neurosis', and so the dream 'puts an end to my ever-recurring doubts'. But it didn't. The question of who to blame for child seduction, as well as all the other questions, remained unsolved.

Fliess demonstrated how not to have doubts. From time to time they met, in a German city or in the countryside, two men with beards, Freud a stocky figure in a well-cut overcoat, his friend a slighter figure in a cape, full of new findings about noses, about sexuality, and increasingly about the golden numbers twenty-eight and twenty-three which controlled the rhythms of life, soon to be explained. Fliess, too, was meeting professional hostility. At the end of 1896 he told a Berlin audience about his biorhythms and 'the twenty-three-day period, which you are hearing about here for the first time'. Freud, when he read the published text, exclaimed that 'in twenty minutes [it] leads one through the universe'. The Berlin audience was less enthusiastic. Remarks about the importance of birth dates caused laughter, and Fliess lost his temper:

> I see, gentlemen, that this proposal stimulates your laughing muscles in a dubious manner. But I can reveal to you that we are dealing here with a great law of nature, and I promise you, the time will come when you will be struck dumb by the greatness of this law.

The essence of the Fliess system was that important changes in bodily function, including birth and death, followed recurring patterns that could be foreseen, using abstruse calculations based on the twenty-three- and twenty-eight-day cycles. In 1979 the scientific historian Frank J. Sulloway dismissed the idea that

Fliess invented a simplistic mathematics that Freud should have seen through instantly. Fliess's theories were sophisticated and, given the period, had a certain logic; but he let optimism and arrogance distort clinical judgment, so that he was inclined to find what he was looking for. Periodicity in Fliess's all-embracing sense was a chimera. But, while there were many contemporaries who sneered at him, some were impressed.

Freud, for his part, swallowed the theory whole, and in doing so accepted what seems an implicit contradiction of his own theories, since periodicity provided a set of biological rules that made psychological explanations unnecessary. He wanted his own theories to operate in both spheres and thought it possible to reconcile the two, mind and body. At times he even sounded willing to abandon his beliefs for his friend's. A body chemistry that obeyed periodic laws tempted him. 'Perhaps with your help,' he wrote in June 1896, 'I shall find the solid ground on which I can cease to give psychological explanations and begin to find a physiological foundation!'

As interpreted by Freud, periodicity had an amateurish look. Family events were examined to see if they fitted one or other of Fliess's patterns. This could usually be arranged, even if the event was only a new tooth for Anna. There were 'critical' or 'special' dates for everything. The date when Freud's father died had significant numbers attached to it. When Freud's eldest son Martin wrote a poem the day before he developed a throat infection, Freud saw it as 'euphoria before the special date', that is, the special date when he was going to be ill. A month later the boy wrote another poem and lost two teeth; Freud noted it all, hoping to learn something. Oscar Rie's wife had a baby. 'Rumour has it,' Freud wrote to Fliess, 'that you knew date and sex in advance.' Thus Fliess, an unromantic materialist, became endowed with mystical gifts. Behind the professional admiration were Freud's personal feelings. He liked comradeship among men and Fliess was a comrade. Fliess was doubtless flattered to have his theories admired, but was he also uneasy, even privately contemptuous, at his friend's naïve interest in the great system?

The date of his own death still worried Freud, and stemmed from something more than fears for his heart. Certain years in the future were ill-omened. He had told Fliess in 1894 that he expected to die of a heart attack between the ages of forty and fifty, that is, between 1896 and 1906. When the cardiac fears subsided, fifty-one emerged as the death age, which he would reach in 1907. He wrote to Fliess about 'that famous age-limit', which is more likely to have been invented by Freud than worked out by Fliess.

Hebrew number superstitions predisposed him towards such thoughts; a fifty-second birthday was said to be critical for Jewish men. Freud was aware (he later told Jung) of 'the specifically Jewish nature of my mysticism', but someone who prided himself on his rationality must have had neurotic tendencies at work in order to let the superstitions in.

In late middle-age he was still thinking of fatal dates, keeping an eye on 1917–18 when he would be in his sixty-second year, a dangerous age that first occurred to him in 1899 when it replaced the dreaded fifty-first to fifty-second. The reason, which Freud once explained to Jung, was simple. In 1899 he was allocated a new telephone number at Berggasse 19, Vienna 14362. It seemed plausible to Freud that after '43', his age at the time, the '62' signified the end of his life. The underlying thought was that 1899 was a year of special significance because he had completed *The Interpretation of Dreams*, which he regarded, for the moment, as crowning his life's work.

As further evidence, it was 'really uncanny' how the numbers 61 and 62 kept cropping up when he took a holiday in Greece in 1904 with his brother, Alexander. At the hotel in Athens he feared the worst until he found himself given a room on the first floor, which was unlikely to have a high number such as 62; but they gave him room 31 which was half of 62 and almost as bad. This nonsense will be familiar to anyone with obsessive-neurotic tendencies who, like Freud, manages to elevate them into omens of death.

Once, when an appendix operation on his daughter Mathilde went wrong – in 1905 – she became dangerously ill, and the anxious Freud, pacing his study, had a sudden urge to destroy a small marble figure of Venus. He hurled a slipper, knocking Venus from her perch on the wall and breaking her: a sacrificial act to ward off evil and preserve his daughter's life, as he described it, carried out with perfect precision by his unconscious, which managed not to break anything else.

In 1897, uncertain about his work and about himself, Freud was

approaching a climacteric. The seduction theory was still unre-
solved. Any evidence that confirmed the reality of sexual assault in
childhood was clutched at. A patient with 'obsessional ideas'
became convinced as a result of psychoanalysis that his nursemaid
had seduced him in his infancy. He hurried back to his home town
to confront her, now an old woman, and 'received full confirmation'.
Freud hadn't seen the patient for some time and heard about it
from a Mrs F., who got it from a Professor S. That didn't stop the
anecdote being pressed into service and sent to Fliess. Had Freud
possessed better evidence, no doubt he would have used it.

The seduction theory was hedged with qualifications. To cause
neurosis, according to Freud, the assault had to occur in the
earliest years, in infants who had not yet developed the capacity for
continuous memory, so that the trauma remained buried in their
unconscious. Seduction of older children who possessed adult-type
memory didn't count, although earlier events might be concealed
behind later memories.

A young woman came to Berggasse in April 1897, one of the
many unknowns who flicker briefly into life in the letters. She
aroused his suspicions by saying that she felt she had to 'spare
other people'. He wanted to know what people; brought sex into the
conversation; got her to talk about the guilt of certain high-minded
persons, and pounced: 'Well then, let us speak plainly. In my
analyses the guilty people are close relatives, father or brother.'

She confessed at once, and said that her father had regularly
taken her to bed and fondled her when she was between the ages of
eight and twelve. Freud had to tell her that 'similar and worse
things' must have happened when she was still younger –
seductions, that is, that qualified for the theory. As he told Fliess,
convincing the woman of this wasn't difficult.

The classification of seducers was another minefield. The candidates in Freud's 1896 publications included siblings, nursemaids
and teachers, but not fathers. The case for blaming fathers emerged
only in letters to Fliess. They were singled out on 6 December 1896,
in the letter that mentioned the 'highly perverse father' who licked
the nurse's feet. By January 1897 fathers were appearing regularly.
Miss G. de B.'s was suspected of fellatio, there was a 'loathsome
fellow' who had caressed his child and, in February, the skeleton in
the Freuds' own cupboard.

Incestuous fathers became Freud's stereotype for child violators.

In his references to the seduction theory in later years, they were the bogeymen. But when they first appeared in letters to Fliess, the seduction theory was already a year old and he had been finding evidence in his patients for longer than that. How did he come to overlook perverse fathers for so long? No one ever asked him; no one would have dared.

Was there a connection with his father's death? Jacob Freud died in late October 1896, six weeks before the first of the 'fathers-as-seducers' letters. In a 'nice dream' on the night after the funeral (later he said it was the night before), reported to Fliess, Freud was in a barber's shop, the one he visited every day to have his beard trimmed, where he saw a sign that read, 'You are requested to close the eyes.' Freud said it meant that one should do one's duty to the dead. Perhaps, as writers have speculated, it had something to do with closing his eyes to his father's incestuous deeds. By accusing him, Freud ignored the injunction. So was it his father's death that freed him to confide in Fliess? If so, this would explain his shift to the new position of blaming fathers in general: he had suspected them earlier, but said nothing because incestuous fathers were too close to home.

Whatever drove him to make the accusation, we are left to wonder about the nature of his evidence. Could one of his siblings have dropped a hint at Jacob's funeral or in the emotional aftermath? There were five sisters. Anna, the eldest, thirty-eight years old when her father died, lived in New York where her husband, Martha's brother Eli Bernays, was a prospering business-man. Presumably she was not at the funeral. Paula, thirty-two and the youngest, was also in New York, having got married there the previous year to another Austrian emigrant, Valentin Winternitz, whom Freud had never met. The other three sisters are likely to have been in Vienna, or at least central Europe, when their father died. Rosa (thirty-six), who was close to Sigmund, had married a Vienna lawyer, Heinrich Graf, five months earlier. Mitzi (thirty-five) had been married for ten years to a distant relative, Moritz Freud, a Romanian carpet-importer. Sigmund told Fliess that 'none of us has a relationship with her; she has always been isolated and rather peculiar', adding that her three daughters were hysterics and her husband, who was probably responsible, was 'half-Asian'; evidently another pervert.

Finally there was Dolfi (thirty-four), who was single. She was

Freud's favourite, 'the sweetest and best', he once told Martha. Almost certainly she still lived with her parents. Dolfi nursed Jacob through his last illness, the unmarried daughter who suffers in silence.

The identity of the 'several younger sisters' who were molested by their father – according to Freud – can only be guessed at. Dolfi was presumably among them, together with Paula, two years younger, and Mitzi, one year older. No evidence was produced for Fliess; probably there was none of substance. Freud was eager to sniff out any hint of an infant seduction anywhere, and so he inflicted on himself the agony of contemplating unproven and probably non-existent rape or molestation within his own family.

Freud seems never to have suggested that he might have suffered the same fate. Yet not-remembering didn't count as evidence; he had already established that memories must be reconstructed. Eventually he did try reconstructing his own. In the spring or summer of 1897 he began the task of unravelling himself by self-analysis, the next step in the psychological drama that he was making of his life. One of his motives may have been to clear up doubts about what Jacob had or hadn't done. In the event, the only hint of seduction in his own infancy that he ever passed on to Fliess concerned the maid, not Jacob.

Yet his own symptoms, had he seen them in a patient in say 1896, would have made him suspect a victim. To Fliess he used phrases like 'the deepest depths of my own neuroses'. Ernest Jones, Freud's henchman for thirty years, said that during the 1890s 'he suffered from a very considerable psychoneurosis', adding that Freud would 'later doubtless have classified it as an anxiety-hysteria'.

Jones put it more bluntly in a private letter of 1951 to James Strachey, who was translating Freud's works at the same time as Jones was writing the biography. It was odd, wrote Jones, that Freud 'believes his own father seduced only his brother and some younger sisters, thus accounting for their hysteria, at a time when he was suffering from it badly himself. It is all very interesting.'

In the end Freud abandoned the seduction theory altogether. The lurid tales of childhood abuse became figments of his patients' unconscious (or of his), the imaginings of little girls in love with their fathers and little boys in love with their mothers. The ravages of perverts in respectable homes were forgotten. G. de B.'s papa had suffered for nothing. Freud had been misled, or had misled himself.

The tales (or most of them – he left a loophole) that he had diligently reconstructed or invented concerning horrid nursemaids and even more horrid fathers were reclassified as infant fantasy.

Over the next decade Freud would come to see childhood in this new light. The secret of the children was that they masturbated. Their infancy contained the pleasures, as well as the fears and jealousies, that they would carry with them all their lives. This, not sexual abuse, was the world that Freud would reveal for psychoanalysis to conquer.

From the spring of 1897, the letters to Fliess show his views beginning to shift. On 2 May he talked of 'sublimations of the facts, embellishments of them'; on 7 July, 'What we are faced with are falsifications of memory and fantasies'; on 14 August he was staying in the mountains with his family, 'tormented by grave doubts about my theory of the neuroses'. By 21 September, the day after he returned to work in Vienna from more holidays in northern Italy, the struggle was over: 'I no longer believe in my *neurotica*.'

His disappointment was intense. He had been counting on 'complete success', he told Fliess:

> The expectation of eternal fame was so beautiful, as was that of certain wealth, complete independence, travels, and lifting the children above the severe worries that robbed me of my youth . . . Now I can once again remain quiet and modest, go on worrying and saving. A little story from my collection [of Jewish stories] occurs to me: 'Rebecca, take off your gown, you are no longer a bride.' In spite of all this, I am in very good spirits and content that you feel a need to see me again similar to mine to see you.

There is a rough honesty about these admissions. Three years later he told Fliess that he was not a man of science but an adventurer. The seduction theory, then, was an adventure that failed.

His conversion has been debated time and again in recent years. The reasons he gave Fliess included his failure to bring a single analysis to a real conclusion, and the fact that child abuse would have to exist on an enormous scale since (in Freud's theory) abuse led to hysteria, itself a common condition, only where there were other predisposing factors; thus the number of abused children would far exceed the number of adult hysterics. On top of this, 'in all cases, the *father*, not excluding my own, had to be accused of being perverse'. It is as if Freud talked himself into blaming fathers and then wished he hadn't.

Disenchanted with a theory that wouldn't work, appalled by its consequences for his own family, not knowing where to turn, he began a period of intense introspection – the 'self-analysis' – and suffered in the process. More than one writer has suggested that Freud underwent a 'creative illness' which left him shaken but wiser.

The replacement theory that Freud proposed was either a profound insight or a clever strategy, depending on one's sympathies. His need was obvious: to find an alternative explanation for the sexuality that he saw fermenting in his patients' memories, and doubtless in his own. By detaching memories from real events, or rather by proposing that real events in a child's life – in particular, relationships with parents – became the subject of fantasy, a new theory, eventually the 'Oedipus Complex', could arise from the gloomy ashes of seduction.

Freud hammered it out as best he could. He was as serious about understanding human nature as he was about being famous. His insights into child fantasy and his disillusionment with child seduction each catalysed the other. The conversion was uncertain at first and for another year he would come back to the theory for a while, as if moved by nostalgia. He continued to believe, like most people, that some children were molested.

This position, that child abuse existed on a modest scale, remained unexceptional for the best part of a century until, in the 1980s, the issue returned in the shape of the 'Recovered Memory' movement. In the United States, and to a lesser extent in Europe, the ghost of Freud's seduction theory was abroad as a new class of victim emerged: the person (usually a woman) who is sexually abused as a child (usually by her father) and suppresses the memory. Incest was alleged on a large scale, and was sometimes proved retrospectively in the courts.

Freud's seduction theory was the template, although Freud himself was dismissed by many radicals as a cowardly renegade who walked away from the truth: someone who could have made the prevention of child sexual abuse within the family a cause in the 1890s instead of leaving it for the late twentieth century to discover.

Freud certainly began by claiming to have found mass child abuse, but he used dubious means, inventing stories on behalf of patients, eager to find the proofs that would make him famous, until at last he was driven to conclude that they didn't exist. Had he found 'scientific' evidence one suspects he would have pursued it, even at the cost of indicting his own father, but after a year and a half of trying, he was unable to believe any longer. Reading his letters to Fliess you can see the theory slipping between his fingers. Finally he let it go, and put Oedipus in its place.

Reconstructing memories of childhood, as Freud came to understand (and then suspect) the process, presents no obstacle to contemporary therapists who regularly obtain detailed stories of childhood violation and rape from their clients. Since violation and rape undoubtedly occur, it is impossible to stop therapists looking for more of it, just as Freud did a century ago for different reasons and with different results. The accusers uphold 'Recovered Memory' as real and significant. In America, it even shows signs of taking over large areas of psychoanalytic practice. Frederick Crews, an articulate enemy there of the recovered-memory lobby, finds alarming implications in 'the fact that some Freudians can so readily accommodate themselves to a diagnostic outlook that Freud himself came to consider an absurdity'. Meanwhile the other side (which includes the families riven by accusations, spiritual descendants of G. de B. and her father) dismiss it all as a work of the devil and call it 'False Memory Syndrome'.

At a London conference in 1994 which addressed the question of recovered memories of childhood abuse and whether they could be relied upon, protesting women set off the fire alarm at intervals to show their hostility, and handed out leaflets deriding FMS, 'a term invented by men to refute allegations that they have sexually abused children (usually their daughters)'. Freud, 'the first real proponent of FMS', was disposed of with a lie and a half-truth: 'He accepted that girls were sexually abused by men in the family, but, following pressure from colleagues and benefactors [the lie], he recanted his "seduction theory" and then claimed that girls *fantasised* about being raped by their fathers, but that it didn't really happen [the half-truth]'.

For Freud in September 1897, only the world of the unconscious mattered; the seducers had been an aberration. An epigraph had occurred to him nine years earlier for a book he hadn't yet written, *Flectere si nequeo superos Acheronta movebo*, 'If I cannot bend the higher powers, I will move the infernal regions.' Freud later denied that this was a personal statement, but it sounds like one. If he could have no influence on the world at large, he would turn to the dark interior of the mind, the soul, the psyche. He now turned to his.

14: Himself

The process that Freud called his 'self-analysis' began in 1897, and was described in long letters to Fliess that gave a week-by-week account of his memories and dreams, which later became the core material of his book *The Interpretation of Dreams*. The self-analysis made no simple revelations of the flesh-and-blood Freud. What it illustrated was the complexity of psychoanalysis and the arbitrary nature of its conclusions.

The first hints of the analysis came in the spring and summer of 1897 and, as we have seen, it was entwined with his growing doubts about the seduction theory. Before Freud and the rest of bourgeois Vienna went off for their holidays, he told Fliess about a 'neurotic experience' with 'twilight thoughts' and 'veiled doubts' that had brought him to a halt. 'I have never before even imagined anything like this period of intellectual paralysis. Every line is torture,' he wrote, adding that 'I believe I am in a cocoon, and God knows what sort of beast will crawl out'. Another letter soon afterwards (7 July) spoke of 'something from the deepest depths of my own neurosis' that 'set itself against any advance in the understanding of the neuroses'.

The need to understand his sexual nature was involved. In May he had told Fliess the dream of 'over-affectionate feelings' for his nine-year-old daughter. He also reported an erotic dream about walking up a staircase and seeing a woman. The dream had its roots in childhood and the housemaid/nursemaid figure in Freiberg called Resi. In Freudian dream-symbolism (yet to be developed), staircases meant copulation.

Freud had different versions of the staircase dream. In the version he gave to Fliess he was partly dressed, a woman was following him, and he was paralysed, unable to move, but felt only sexual excitement, not anxiety. The dream was prompted by his thoughts earlier that night when he was returning to the first-floor apartment from his working quarters below. He was not wearing a collar and tie and hoped that a neighbour wouldn't see him like that on the stairs. He decided that an 'exhibitionistic wish' was behind it.

In *The Interpretation of Dreams* version he was bounding up the stairs and a maidservant was coming towards him. The published analysis shifted away from his sexual excitement. The servant was older than Freud and unattractive, and the dream staircase was not at Berggasse at all but in an apartment block that he visited daily to give an elderly woman an injection. Freud was in the habit of clearing his throat and spitting on the real-life stairs, since no spittoon was provided for the purpose. The female concierge used to grumble audibly as she cleaned up after him; so did the elderly patient's maid, who objected to his muddy boots on the carpets (he seems to be going out of his way to sound boorish). The staircase dream, Freud concluded, must belong with others he was having about his childhood nursemaid, and it was this woman, a 'prehistoric old nurse', who was the presence behind it, reminding him of the need for personal cleanliness.

What he didn't say in this version was that his self-analysis made the nurse sexually significant to his infant self. He told Fliess about this but otherwise kept it to himself, so that what he said in public about the staircase dream was only half the story.*

Now that he could afford longer holidays, Freud was able to escape from Vienna in the summer. His practice still fluctuated and it was limited by the small number of patients that could be treated in a week; but they seem to have paid him fifteen florins an hour, there were windfalls from consultations in other cities, and the sum he mentioned to Fliess as his annual earnings would be worth £45,000 or £50,000 today.

In mid-July 1897, while he was still debating seduction with himself, he went on a brief walking tour in the Salzburg area with

---

* Additional information was given to a patient, Princess Marie Bonaparte, many years later. What lay behind the spitting on the stairs, said Freud, was contempt for the poor people who lived in the building; that was why he didn't spit in his handkerchief 'like a well-brought-up man'. He was dissatisfied with his career and ambitious for better things, and here he was visiting a house where they didn't even have a public spittoon.

his sister-in-law, Minna, whose company he came increasingly to enjoy. Then he was back in Vienna making arrangements for his father's gravestone, before joining wife and children at Aussee, a fashionable resort and market town at 2,000 feet, amid the mountains and lakes of the Salzkammergut region, 150 miles from Vienna. Baedeker enthused over Aussee's views and drives, Freud over a 'wonderful wood' of ferns and mushrooms where he could wander with the children.

Summer storms flooded the railway lines and cut off the area for days. The 'grave doubts' about seduction were never out of his head. Italy, his next destination, was supposed to take his mind off the subject. Before the end of August he was in Venice with Martha.

One 'magically beautiful day' they were at the windows of their room looking across the blue lagoon, where some English vessels were expected. Martha exclaimed excitedly, like a child, 'Here comes the English warship!' The memory came back to him in a dream of foreboding a year later.

At the start of September – when Martha dropped out of the holiday because of her menstrual period, a date built into the holiday plans by Freud – he began a tour of northern Italy with Alexander and an unsatisfactory pupil who was probably sent to him by Fliess, Dr Felix Gattel. Freud told Fliess he was 'seeking a punch made of Lethe'. Italy's classical past captivated him. He loved antiquities in general, and over the years his study and consulting room in Vienna filled up with pagan statuettes of stone and metal from the Mediterranean, like an archaeological hoard. His random collection has been compared to his unconscious; psychology meant digging up the past.

Freud's feelings about Italy were complicated by his Rome neurosis which stemmed, he believed, from his boyhood hero-worship of the Semitic Hannibal, who marched towards Rome but never got there. To Freud the Jew, the seat of Roman Catholicism meant an obstacle to be overcome. His aim was to go one better than Hannibal and reach it, but this was easier said than done.

His inhibition was real. The essence of Freud was his sensitivity to psychological nuance – the atmosphere of places, the passing of time, the content of dreams, the whisperings in his head. Under his orderly exterior was a buried life of fantasy. Going to Rome (which was full of the antiquities he admired) became a metaphor for fulfilling other 'passionate wishes'.

In September 1897 his tour took him south from Venice to Siena; past Lake Trasimeno, where Hannibal unwisely halted his army, and farther south again to Lake Bolsena. That was forty miles nearer than Hannibal managed, and as far as Freud dared to go. 'Finally,' he wrote in *The Interpretation of Dreams*, 'after having seen the Tiber [I] sadly turned back when I was only fifty miles from Rome.' He went north instead and stayed in Perugia and Florence, less symbolic places. Visiting the Eternal City would have to wait until he knew himself better.

From Italy Freud returned direct to Vienna, and within twenty-four hours he was writing to Fliess to dismiss the seduction theory. His Rome neurosis had not stopped him making a decisive move; abandoning seduction heralded a more colourful round of self-analysis. By the beginning of October he was dreaming furiously, although Fliess was the only one to be told. His nursemaid figure was described to Fliess as an 'ugly, elderly, but clever woman' who was his 'teacher' in sexual matters. As well as telling him about God and damnation, she gave him a high opinion of his capabilities, and was the 'prime originator' – of what, he didn't say. All this came from four nights of dreams and associations. Freud said that if he succeeded in resolving 'my own hysteria', it was the nurse he had to thank because she 'provided me at such an early age with the means for living and going on living'.

None of this was ever explained by Freud. Did 'elderly' mean elderly as perceived by the child? Was she his wet-nurse and so kept him alive with her milk? Whatever happened with her above the blacksmith's forge was not revealed, and may have remained hidden from Freud as well. Perhaps it was no more than soothing a bawling boy by playing with his penis. Memories could only be reconstructed.

The dream-nurse 'washed me in reddish water in which she had previously washed herself', Freud told Fliess, implying that the woman was menstruating. If so, it was hardly a sexual experience at the time, and in any case did it happen? The date of the dream was close to Martha's punctual menstruation; perhaps it was this that put the thought in his head and the dream made something else of it. Fantasies were breeding fantasies. At best, the self-analysis was giving him unclear messages about the sexuality of little Sigmund and by extension of every infant.

He told Fliess that before he was two-and-a-half years old, sexual feelings towards his mother were awakened when he saw her naked as they travelled in a train from Leipzig to Vienna; or that is what he almost says, describing 'a journey . . . during which we must have spent the night together and there must have been an opportunity of seeing her *nudam* (you inferred the consequences of this for your son long ago, as a remark revealed to me)'. Once again it was not a memory but an inference, a may-have-been.

Freud dreamed and made sense of the dreams in the way appropriate to his nature; what other way was there of doing it? He discovered jealousy and ill-wishes in himself towards Julius, the brother born when Sigmund was seventeen months old who had died the following year. Julius and John (the nephew in the primrose field) 'determined . . . what is neurotic, but also what is intense, in all my friendships', Fliess was told. Freud wrote of John more circumspectly in *The Interpretation of Dreams*, of

> how my warm friendships as well as my enmities with contemporaries went back to my relations in childhood with a nephew who was a year my senior; how he was my superior, how I early learned to defend myself against him, how we were inseparable friends, and how, according to the testimony of our elders, we sometimes fought with each other . . . All my friends have in a certain sense been reincarnations of this first figure . . . they have been *revenants* . . . My emotional life has always insisted that I should have an intimate friend and a hated enemy. I have always been able to provide myself afresh with both, and it has not infrequently happened that the ideal situation of childhood has been so completely reproduced that friend and enemy have come together in a single individual.

Josef Breuer was a 'friend and enemy'. So, before long, was Fliess, and later there would be others.

What moved Freud was not the abstract discovery of a truth so much as its rediscovery in terms of his own experience. 'I live only for the "inner work",' he explained to Fliess, who listened with half an ear, having his own theories, which sounded more scientific, to think about. 'Many a sad secret of life is here followed back to its first roots; many a pride and privilege are made aware of their humble origins.' There were days when Freud understood 'nothing of the dream, of the fantasy', others when 'a flash of lightning . . . lets me understand the past as a preparation for the present'.

A thread of nonsense about 'periodicity' ran through his account of the inner marvels. When self-analysis came to a halt for three days, Freud was puzzled until he realised that the same thing had happened twenty-eight days earlier, from which 'one should draw the conclusion that the female period is not conducive to work'. He envied Fliess his numbers, 'harmoniously fitting themselves together.

His own work was out of his hands. We are never told of occasions when ideas came to him – in bed, or walking on the Ringstrasse, or sitting late at his desk downstairs with the cigar smoke irradiated by the gas-lamp. 'I must wait until something stirs in me and I become aware of it. And so I often dream whole days away.' He liked epigrams:

> Happiness is the belated fulfilment of a prehistoric wish. For this reason wealth brings so little happiness. Money was not a childhood wish;

or:

> Immortality, retribution, the entire beyond are all reflections of our psychic internal [world]. *Meeschugge*? [*Crazy?*]. Psycho-mythology.

The theory had to move on. The loss of seduction ripped its heart out, but its successor was ready, and may have been a precondition of the sacrifice. Fliess was given the first hint in May 1897, four months before seduction was formally dropped, when Freud observed that death wishes against parents were involved in neurosis and that it seemed as if sons directed them at their fathers, daughters at their mothers. Post-seduction, in October, Freud admitted that so far the self-analysis had produced nothing that was completely new, with one exception:

> I have found, in my own case too, [the fact of] being in love with my mother and jealous of my father, and I now consider it a universal event in early childhood ... If this is so, we can understand the gripping power of *Oedipus Rex* ... the Greek legend seizes upon a compulsion which everyone recognises because he senses its existence within himself. Everyone in the audience was once a budding Oedipus in fantasy and each recoils in horror from the dream fulfilment here transplanted into reality.

Freud went on to speculate about Hamlet, an hysteric whose reluctance to avenge his father by murdering his uncle ('Thus conscience does make cowards of us all') could be traced to 'the obscure memory that he himself had contemplated the same deed against his father out of passion for his mother'. Shakespeare's unconscious, suggested Freud, understood the unconscious of his hero. Hamlet's 'conscience' was really his hidden sense of guilt.

Freud said all this to Fliess in a letter of 15 October 1897. Three weeks later he wrote plaintively to say he was still waiting for a response. 'Since I have not told it to anyone else, because I can well imagine in advance the bewildered rejection, I should like to have a short comment on it from you. Last year you rejected many an idea of mine, with good reason.' Fliess was the authority, Freud the supplicant.

With or without approval from the sage of Berlin, the idea of Oedipus took hold of Freud. The implications for child sexuality were apparent from the start. He was soon fantasising to Fliess about the infant fantasies that led to masturbation, mankind's 'primary addiction', for which all other addictions – alcohol, morphine, tobacco – were substitutes. When fantasies that accompanied the masturbation were repressed, their hidden presence in the unconscious sowed the seeds of neurosis.

His full theory of how sexual behaviour develops was not yet worked out; infants' catholic curiosity about smells and excrement, as well as about their genitals, made them (Freud was already speculating) like little animals, noses close to the ground, inhabiting a primitive world that needed to be outgrown – but sometimes was not – if they were to become proper humans, walking on two legs.

There was little the child could do about its biological inheritance, but when it came to the relationship with parents, fantasy intervened. Freud's first public statement about the Oedipus theory was a tentative passage in *The Interpretation of Dreams*, which outlined the main provision – that every child was in love with one parent and hated the other – and drew a parallel with the legend of Oedipus, the 'tragedy of destiny'. Although the phrase 'Oedipus Complex' wasn't heard until 1910, from the beginning Freud saw that the principle of erotic and murderous fantasies in childhood helped fill the vacuum left by the seduction theory. As his critics have pointed out, what could be harder to disprove than a theory based on fantasy?

Freud was learning things about human nature, his own included, that he found disturbing. Two or three letters to Fliess in the winter of 1897–98 sound offended by his own observations. Ruminating about a man who rapes his child and has anal intercourse with his wife, he ends, 'Enough of my smut.' The next letter refers to his 'resolutely tramping along in the Dreckology', a term he coins from 'Dreck', the German for 'filth'. He writes ' "dreckological" reports', one of them containing 'wild dreams' which form part of his self-analysis; their content isn't disclosed. These references to 'dreckology' were removed from the Fliess letters before Masson's edition.

The following summer, 1898, while he was anticipating the holidays, Freud had a dream, ostensibly about urine and faeces, immediately after lecturing in Vienna on the connection between neurosis and the sexual perversions. Analysing it in *The Interpretation of Dreams* he wrote, 'I longed to be away from all this grubbing about in human dirt and to be able to join my children and afterwards visit the beauties of Italy.'

Freud was aware of the risks in being seen to embrace 'filth'. He offered an oblique defence in the course of a belligerent paper that he wrote early in 1898 about sex and the neuroses. This began with a sharp criticism of doctors for their prudery. He added to this insult by saying that it was, of course, reasonable for a physician to avoid sexual matters if he felt that he lacked the necessary 'seriousness and discretion' to question neurotic patients, and 'if he is aware that revelations of a sexual character would provoke lascivious thrills in him rather than scientific interest'. As usual the implication was that Freud rose above such matters.

They were unsettling times for him, as they had been for much of the decade. Middle age was just around the corner, and the Ministry of Education was proving reluctant to make him a professor. An *ordinarius*, the most imposing kind, meant a salary and a department; a Jew was unlikely to be appointed unless he converted to Christianity. The rank Freud sought was *extraordinarius*, unsalaried and less imposing, but good for one's reputation and one's practice. A man with his strange ideas needed all the endorsement he could get.

Freud's tastes were conventional enough. In appearance he was as conservative as a banker, wearing suits of dark cloth (although later he had a taste for Scottish tweeds in pepper-and-salt). His apartment was furnished in the popular bourgeois style, fussy as well as heavy, and remained like that as long as he lived in Vienna: lace cloths on tables, glass-fronted cabinets of knick-knacks, dark patterned wallpaper. Photographs and classical scenes were displayed. The modern art of the Secessionists in fin de siècle Vienna, another cultural innovation of the time, would have been out of place in such an apartment, and Freud showed no interest in it.

But his theories were as revolutionary as the paintings, and equally risible to his professional colleagues, the only people apart from patients likely to have heard of him. Nor was he a movement or a school, but simply himself. He knew (he wrote in *The Interpretation of Dreams*) that his ideas were 'bound to excite scepticism and laughter when they were first met with'. When he told patients that impressions from the first year of infancy could leave lasting traces on their emotional lives, they used to make fun of him by suggesting they try and remember what it was like before they were born. Did he smile weakly and wish he had a wealthy wife like Fliess? His skin was still thin enough to pierce. He needed the dignity of a title.

Moves to procure one began in 1897. In January he told Fliess about a rumour that a neuropathologist who was younger by six years had been proposed for *extraordinarius*, and said it left him 'entirely cold', though it might hasten his 'final break' with the university. The body that did the proposing in these matters was a committee of the medical faculty, which, in this musical-comedy land, sent its recommendations via the Imperial-Royal Government of Lower Austria to the High Imperial-Royal Ministry of Religion and Education, where they lay on civil servants' desks for as long as it suited the minister.

In February Freud told Fliess about a visit to one of his former professors, Nothnagel, with a copy of a new work about cerebral palsy in children that he had written – part of his afterlife as a conventional neurologist and his last major publication of this kind. Nothnagel told him, 'spontaneously', that he and Krafft-Ebing wanted to see him nominated for a professorship.

Nothnagel warned him that there was little chance of the minister agreeing. Whether this was because Freud was a Jew (though Jews were often appointed *extraordinarius*), or because he lacked social patronage, or because his reputation was uncertain, apparently was not mentioned. Everyone had stories of anti-Semitism at the ministry, but there was a wider conflict about academic freedom always rumbling in the background between the university faculties, inclined to be liberal, and the dead hand of the

Habsburg civil service. Uncertainty was built into politics and patronage in Vienna because ultimately the system rested on the mysterious workings of an emperor, a court and an imperial-minded bureaucracy.

A new Mayor of Vienna, the jovial Karl Lueger, who knew how to play on anti-Semitism among the city's clerks and shopkeepers, had his election ratified by the emperor that spring after two previous refusals. Liberal Jews were dismayed, Freud among them. Lueger was a populist who made jokes about sending all the Jews to sea in a ship and sinking it. Hitler (still at school in 1897) learned from him.

In May the committee decided to nominate Freud for his preferment. The document recommending him was drawn up by Krafft-Ebing, and spoke enthusiastically of the candidate and his theories of neurosis less than a year after Ebing had dismissed the hysteria-and-seduction lecture as a fairy tale. Masson says the key paragraph was so complimentary that it must have been supplied by Freud. Krafft-Ebing added a rider that the candidate, despite his unusual talent, might have overestimated the importance of his findings.

The nomination went to the Lower Austrian authorities, who had the usual inquiries made about the candidate and, after a few more months, submitted the file 'most humbly' to the ministry. The officials, who got the number of his children wrong, summed up his social standing in a sentence: 'Apparently he lives in very easy circumstances, keeps three servants and owns a practice which is not very extensive but nonetheless lucrative.' They added that Dr Freud was honest.

The ministry received the report and the nomination, and Freud began a long wait. Sometimes he sounded defiant. He told Fliess in January 1898 that in one of his daytime fantasies ('of which I am by no means free as yet') he was putting the Minister of Education in his place – 'You can't frighten me. I know that I shall still be a university lecturer when you have long ceased to be called Minister.' Sometimes he was hopeful. In February he heard a rumour that he was to be made professor at Emperor Franz-Josef's jubilee in December; the old man had been on the throne since 1848. Insisting that he didn't believe it, Freud contented himself with a 'delightful dream' about his elevation. A dream was as far as it got. The ministry did nothing, that year or next or even the year after that.

By 1898 Freud was moving towards the book about dreams. Three years had passed since the dream at Bellevue but he felt his secret was still safe. 'No one even suspects that the dream is not nonsense but wish-fulfilment,' he told Fliess. This was not strictly true. Some of Freud's contemporaries did believe that dreams had meaning – Krafft-Ebing thought that a hidden sexual wish could manifest itself in sleep – but no one thought of putting dreams at the heart of a theory. Obligingly, Freud's unconscious began to produce dreams for all occasions, ready to work into the text. By February 1898 he was 'deep in the dream book'. After the 'hysteria torture' (presumably the seduction fiasco), it was a relief. There was 'nothing but the dream, the dream'.

At Easter he was in Italy again with his brother Alexander, in the north-east of the country, not far from Trieste and the Adriatic. They visited the Roman remains at Aquileia, a 'dump' with a museum, according to Freud, where they saw statues of Priapus. Fliess was reminded rather ponderously that this was the god who 'stood for permanent erection, a wish-fulfilment representing the opposite of psychological impotence'.

The brothers visited a limestone cave with stalactite formations, but Freud was more interested in the guide, whose drunken boasting about the cavern he saw as a neurotic substitute for erotic deeds. When Alexander asked how far one could penetrate inside, the guide said it was 'like with a virgin; the farther you get the more beautiful it is'. In another cave they found themselves in the same party as Karl Lueger, 'the master of Vienna'.

A few weeks later Freud dreamt of a castle by the sea. He was standing at a window with its governor discussing a war. Suddenly the man dropped dead. Ships were rushing across the dark blue water, which was now a canal, brown smoke pouring from their funnels. His brother was with him. They cried out together, 'Here comes the warship!'

The dream left a sinister impression. Its ingredients included the holiday in Venice with Martha the previous year, the visit to Aquileia (where there was a canal) with his brother, and the Spanish–American war; the *Neue Freie Presse* of 10 May had reported the destruction of the Spanish fleet. At one level the dream's associations were of carefree holidays, but behind them lurked a fear of his premature death and how his family would manage; he was the governor who died, and 'it was precisely behind [a] memory of the most cheerful *joie de vivre* that the dream concealed the gloomiest thoughts of an unknown and uncanny future'.

It seemed impossible for Freud to take any experience, waking or sleeping, at its face value. Part of his summer holidays he spent travelling with Martha; part with Minna, walking on glaciers and lying in deckchairs. With Martha he went to the Adriatic again and stayed at Ragusa (now Dubrovnik), a town on the coast of Dalmatia, last outpost in the south of the Austrian Empire. The town was small and picturesque, with a cathedral and avenues of mulberry trees.

Martha, who lacked Minna's stamina when it came to travelling, had one of her gastric disturbances. While she was indisposed, Freud made a day trip into Bosnia-Herzegovina, then under Austrian rule, accompanied by a German lawyer he had met on the holiday. They talked about paintings and Freud mentioned some frescoes of the end of the world and the Last Judgment that had impressed him the year before when he saw them at Orvieto in Italy. The painter was ... a man whose name he couldn't remember. He got as far as 'Botticelli', but had to wait several days until he found someone who could give him the correct answer, which was 'Signorelli'.

Why, Freud asked himself, had he remembered half the word but repressed the remainder? Few people would have bothered, but Freud worked on an explanation and gave Fliess a preliminary version. Paintings, he said, were not the only things that he and the lawyer talked about. 'In the conversation, which aroused memories that evidently caused the repression, we talked about death and sexuality.' A phrase from their conversation which included the word 'Signor' had caused the 'Signor' in 'Signorelli' to slip his mind. 'How can I make this credible to anyone?' he asked, a rhetorical question, since he soon wrote a paper about it, 'The Psychical Mechanism of Forgetfulness', which appeared before the end of 1898.

In the paper, the story was fleshed out. Freud explained that he and his companion had been discussing the Bosnian character, with its 'Turkish' (that is, Muslim) elements. A colleague had told Freud years earlier about the Bosnians' resigned attitude to death, quoting a patient's remark that began *'Herr*, what is there to be said?' Freud quoted the remark to his travelling companion but (he wrote) he suppressed another anecdote that the colleague had also told him about the importance that Bosnian men attached to sexual pleasure, and a patient who once said, *'Herr*, you must know, that if *that* comes to an end then life is of no value.' It was soon after this that the name of the Italian painter eluded him.

His explanation was ingenious, as always. Both the 'sex' story and the 'death' story were linked by the word 'Herr', which introduced the two quotations, and 'Herr' was the German for 'Signor'. The act of suppressing the sex story also suppressed part of the name he was looking for, depriving it of 'Signor' and leaving him with 'elli', so that 'Botticelli' was the best he could manage.

The topic that Freud's mind had censored, he added, was bound up with trains of thought that interested him intensely but were being resisted. 'That this was really true at that time of the topic of "death and sexuality" I have plenty of evidence, which I need not bring up here, derived from my own self-investigation.'

Freud rarely admitted as much as that about his sexual nature, and in future he would admit less, except by accident. We are left to speculate about 'death and sexuality'. Was he concerned that his marital pleasures were ending? Was he replacing Martha in his mind with Minna, with whom he shared intellectual interests, and having carnal thoughts about his sister-in-law? Did the Adriatic coast have sexual undertones that went back to his young-man's summer in Trieste?

Anything is possible in Freudian waters. A Turkish overcoat that Freud wore in a dream he had soon after they returned to Vienna from Dalmatia suggested a condom, among other things, which seems to be stretching credibility. But the opportunities for creative analysis, applied ad lib to dreams and everyday conversations, were infinite.

The mind, said Freud, is a bizarre environment. He worked away at the dream book, determined to prove it.

15: Book of Dreams

*T*he *Interpretation of Dreams* was about the fulfilment of wishes, the book that Freud wrote, in part, to fulfil his own wish for recognition. Dreams, he said, were not simply nonsense-versions of what happened yesterday, they were also disguised versions of one's life long ago in early childhood. What they concealed were primitive wishes driven by lust and hate, a kind of Original Sin (but this was not Freud's terminology) that haunted the world, hidden away in the individual's unconscious.

Most adult dreams were about sex, and the wishes they gave rise to were erotic. Understanding them was not easy; this was the task of psychoanalysis. Freud's ideas about dreams, however, were not only for those who were neurotic and needed analysis. Dream-theory applied to normal people. *The Interpretation of Dreams* was meant for an educated public as well as a medical one.

Most of the book was written or rewritten in 1899, refocusing earlier drafts. It grew to 250,000 words, the longest book he ever wrote. Freud's practice suffered and at one point, worried that he might have to live on his savings, he thought to spend the following summer as physician to a new clinic for neurasthenics at Cobenzl, above Bellevue. He would have felt the humiliation of working there but, in 1899, all that mattered was the book.

For once Freud took an interest in drink, saying he needed it while he was writing. His more usual view was the one he expressed in 1896: 'any drop of alcohol makes me completely stupid'. In December 1898, tired, bored with the literature about dreams that he had to read, he was telling Fliess that he occasionally longed for some wine, 'even if it cannot be a "punch made of Lethe"', but was 'ashamed of acquiring a new vice'. Next year the vice, if it counted as one, had progressed, reaching a climax in July when Freud described his difficulties with *Dreams* and said that

> I cannot manage more than two hours a day without calling on Friend Marsala for help. 'He' deludes me into thinking that things are not really so bleak as they appear to me when sober.

What 'bleak things' gave him a taste for alcohol? The book was intellectually demanding if only because he was now writing very fast, but he was a fluent writer, decisive once he put pen to paper. His mood and sometimes his health could be influenced by work in hand, so had something about his subject left him dispirited and needing consolation? When he was younger he used cocaine to help himself along (and was still an occasional user in the mid-1890s). Why did he need help now?

Most of his writing in summer 1899 was done at a farmhouse in Bavaria, just across the Austrian frontier. The scenic village nearby was called Berchtesgaden. There were no jaunts to Italy, only an extended family holiday in the farmhouse with Freud keeping to himself for much of the time, working in a ground-floor room with a view of mountains, or outside in an 'arbour'. Some of his antiques went with him as paperweights: 'My old and grubby gods,' he told the unromantic Fliess, 'of whom you think so little.'

As he wrote the later chapters and despatched the handwritten sheets to the typesetters from the village post office, proofs of the earlier chapters were arriving and being sent off to Fliess for his comments, which were eagerly awaited. 'Every attempt to make it better than it turns out by itself gives it a forced quality,' wrote Freud. 'So it will contain 2,467 mistakes – which I shall leave in it.' (Later he worked out his unconscious reasons for choosing 2,467: '24' because when he was aged 24 he met an army general whose retirement he had read about in 1899, immediately before he wrote to Fliess; '67' because Freud's present age was 43, and 43 plus 24 = 67, which meant that he wouldn't reach his own retirement until he was 67, and so had many years, 24 of them, ahead of him – altogether a fine piece of numerical mumbo jumbo).

In the second week of September he was still there, exhausted, the last chapter – a theoretical overview – finished at last. The Breuers were in the neighbourhood, 'so that we are bound to meet daily, on which occasions the ladies on both sides make a great show of tenderness to each other. Another reason to wish one were somewhere else.' Autumn had come and the foothills had snow on them. It was time to go back to Vienna for 'another year of this strange life'.

The day he arrived home, another parcel of proofs had just come from the typesetters. He wrote to Fliess about 'tortuous sentences' with their 'parading of indirect phrases and squinting at ideas', that suggested 'insufficient mastery of the material'. There was no more talk of Friend Marsala now that the work was finished, but uneasiness remained between Freud and his project.

Freud had put himself at the centre of the book because it was necessary that his own experience be offered as evidence and justification; he never ceased to dwell on the story of his life and, by doing it here, he could demonstrate the psychoanalytic virtue of knowing oneself. *Dreams* is often praised for its bold passages of autobiography, and it was certainly more honest than most people could manage. But there were limits to what Freud felt he could share with his readers.

One problem, as he explained in the book, was how to write about the dreams of 'normal' people. If he used patients' dreams he must confine himself to neurotics, and go on to examine their case-histories. His friends told him their dreams, but without accompanying analysis they were no more than anecdotes. The only dreams left were his own, offering 'copious and convenient material, derived from an approximately normal person' (Freud was being careful. How neurotic could one be and still be normal?). Having decided to use his dreams, he had to overcome his reluctance to reveal 'so many intimate facts about one's mental life'. The limits he set were announced in a footnote:

> I am obliged to add . . .that in scarcely any instance have I brought forward the *complete* interpretation of one of my own dreams, as it is known to me. I have probably been wise in not putting too much faith in my readers' discretion.

Elsewhere in the book he wrote about the inevitable 'distortions' of his dream interpretation. As we know, there were gaps in his analyses, including 'Irma's injection' and the half-dressed foray on the staircase, where the narrative ignores the sexual implications. If anyone felt inclined to condemn his reticence, he wrote tartly, 'I would advise him to make the experiment of being franker than I am.' When Jung frowned at the reticence, years later, he defended himself by saying that 'I simply cannot expose any more of my nakedness to the reader.'

It has been left to modern researchers to wonder exactly what Freud left out. His unwillingness to give a complete analysis of the dreams created an anomaly at the heart of the book. This may have been the problem that drove him to drink while he was writing it. His dilemma over disclosure is apparent in letters to Fliess. In June 1898 he had agonised about a dream (perhaps involving Martha) that Fliess said was unpublishable. He abandoned it with regret, saying that 'As you know, a beautiful dream and no indiscretion do not coincide.' The following May, when he was driving ahead with the book, he told Fliess that he had decided against using 'disguises'; at the same time, he said, he couldn't afford to give up any material. He offered no solution.

By now the book had become a passion. 'No other work of mine has been so completely my own,' he wrote, 'my own dung heap, my seedling.' But in the act of asserting his freedom from convention he was being forced to compromise. Fliess was used as a censor. Sending him revised proofs from Berchtesgaden in August 1899, Freud wrote, 'I have inserted a large number of new dreams, which I hope you will not delete.' They were 'only *humana* and *humaniora* [of men and their concerns]; nothing really intimate, that is, personally sexual'. Freud's real censor was himself.

His need to prune the book probably provoked the disguised autobiography of the 'Screen Memories' paper, which he wrote in the week preceding Whitsun 1899; this was shortly before he told Fliess about his dilemma over 'disguises' in *The Interpretation of Dreams*. The paper appeared in a medical journal in September, two months before the book came out. When Freud became better known he tried, without success, to restrict the paper's circulation. His indiscretion in writing it in the first place suggests how badly he wanted to unburden himself.

'Screen Memories' is the piece about children in a field of flowers that in 1947 was recognised as describing events from Freud's own childhood. There is no letter to Fliess letting him into the secret. The heart of the paper is its dialogue between Freud and the anonymous patient, under treatment for a 'mild phobia', who is really himself. We are not told if the memories of infancy were taken from the 'patient's' dreams, but it seems likely. The personal fantasies involved made the material too dangerous to use in the book. *The Interpretation of Dreams* made no secret of his imperfections but sexual experiences had to stay hidden, so they found their way into 'Screen Memories'.

Advance copies of *Dreams* were available before the end of October, no more than a month after Freud was still correcting proofs. The date of publication was 4 November 1899, although the title page says 1900. The publisher, Deuticke, printed 600 copies and sold just over 100 in the first month. Freud's second son, Oliver, then eight years old, was walking with his father past the Deuticke bookshop that November. There were copies in the window. 'That's the book I was finishing in the summer,' said Freud, and the occasion impressed itself on Oliver's memory, as his father meant it to.

Dreams sprawls across its subject, changing speed and focus with an eye to the power of contrast, shifting from anecdote to philosophic brooding to confession to set-piece description. No one writes such books any more; few read them, except as curiosities. It is like some magnificent object from a museum, behind burglar-proof glass, opened to a page that the educated visitor (the only kind Freud acknowledged) can recognise; the 'Specimen Dream' about Irma, perhaps, or the passage where he introduces King Oedipus and the force of destiny, 'It is the fate of all of us, perhaps, to direct our first sexual impulse towards our mother and our first hatred and our first murderous wish against our father.' (He meant 'all of us men'; in the theory girls clove to their fathers and wanted to murder their mothers, but in 1900 it was boys who mattered.)

The book begins with a survey of the scientific literature and moves on to methods of dream interpretation, where Freud at once mounts a pre-emptive strike against the received ideas of 'the philosophers and the psychiatrists', who dismiss dreams as aberrations. Lay opinion, 'led by some obscure feeling', has assumed that, on the contrary, every dream has a meaning, though it may be hidden. Freud agrees:

> Here once more we have one of those not infrequent cases in which an ancient and jealously held popular belief seems to be nearer the truth than the judgment of the prevalent science of today. I must affirm that dreams really have a meaning and that a scientific procedure for interpreting them is possible.

This statement set the tone of the book. Determined to show that psychoanalysis was intellectually respectable, Freud gave his dream-system a scientific veneer. Over the years the technicalities of his method, ingenious and complicated, have become largely irrelevant. What has survived is less definable: Freud's perception that dreams show us in touch with ourselves, that they are grounded in the reality of how we live and what we remember. That was the real point of *The Interpretation of Dreams*.

'Free association' was described, with its aim of encouraging 'critical self-observation', made easier if the patient lay in 'a restful attitude': the reason for the couch. The principle of wish-fulfilment was shown not to be a simple matter of dreaming that a bodily need was about to be satisfied, as in clutching a dream glass of water and waking up with a thirst. Freud conceded that the 'secret meaning' which explained the wish had to be 'proved afresh in each particular case by analysis'. In other words, there could never be a general proof of the proposition.

The interpreter had many tasks. The 'manifest' content of the dream – what it appeared to be about, often the experiences of the preceding day – had to be distinguished from the 'latent' content, its true meaning which originated in a wish of which the dreamer could be made aware only by psychoanalysis. The act of dreaming involved 'dream work' by the dreamers, who transformed what was 'latent' and dangerous into the 'manifest' and relatively harmless, which is what they remembered on waking. This unconscious censorship excluded unacceptable wishes that would disturb the sleeper and wake him up if they went unmodified. Dreams were the guardians of sleep and their purpose was to prolong it. 'We dream,' he wrote to Fliess, 'in order not to have to wake up.'

What Freud perceived, in himself and in everyone else, was the intransigent other self below the surface, the infant with untamed desires trying to break loose as we sleep. The lustful desires for one parent and death-wishes against the other lurked there; so did violent jealousy of siblings. Even dreams of nakedness looked back to infancy, to a time before the child felt shame: in other words to paradise, which could be revisited nightly in sleep. 'Paradise,' wrote Freud, always seeking to widen his range, 'is no more than a group fantasy of the childhood of the individual.'

Freud oiled the wheels with anecdotes. A butcher's wife, in love with her husband, told Freud that she had dreamt of being unable to give a supper party. What wish could that possibly fulfil? She liked to give parties; she also liked her food. Analysing her, Freud uncovered a sub-plot involving a friend, a thin woman who got on with the butcher and made the wife jealous. The wife consoled herself that he was a man who liked a plumper figure, and that explained things: the wife's wish was to not give supper parties because they might encourage skinny friend to put on weight.

Another of his women patients ('the cleverest of all my dreamers'), having been told that dreams fulfil wishes, dreamt of a holiday in the country with her mother-in-law. She couldn't stand her mother-in-law, as Freud already knew. He was unflustered when she pointed out mischievously that the dream was doing the opposite of fulfilling a wish. His patient, he knew, had had other reasons for questioning his judgment; all the dream did was confirm her suspicions, fulfilling a wish to see him proved wrong.

In later editions Freud developed the idea of the 'counter-wish' to include masochists who felt a need to inflict mental suffering on themselves. However unpleasant a dream turned out to be, it could be certified as wish-fulfilment if it satisfied the dreamer's masochistic tendencies. This sounds like cheating. Dreams could always be made to fit the theory by a clever interpreter, picking and choosing among the free associations. Such technical ingenuity, perhaps part of Freud's mission to appear scientific, is no longer in fashion. Analysts these days would be more inclined to say that the point of free associating from dreams is to help patients reflect on themselves.

Dream symbolism, popularly seen as crucial to psychoanalysis, was barely mentioned in the 1900 edition. It was not until a colleague, Wilhelm Stekel, developed the idea ten years later that Freud added it to the book. Finding penises in dreams wasn't difficult. Sticks, knives and umbrellas were promptly identified; so, less obviously, were hammers, women's hats, nail-files ('possibly on account of the rubbing up and down'), neckties, airships and snakes. For some reason cigars were not on the list.

Rooms were women and a cupboard was the womb. Landscapes, especially if they contained woods or bridges, could be the genitals. Going up or down stairs meant the sexual act ('A series of rhythmical movements,' explained Freud, 'with increasing breathlessness'). Baldness and teeth falling out, on the other hand, were all too likely to mean castration. It may be that Freud kept clear of symbols at first because his unconscious warned him that this solve-anything code smacked of popular dream-books with lists of answers, and was open to mockery.

Autobiography was never far from the surface of the book. Most of the personal dreams Freud used can be traced to the years when he was either planning or actively writing it. With the exception of what they might say about sex, he was not embarrassed by them, or if he was he hid his feelings. The dreams were raw material, his life an experimental laboratory; he didn't say it in so many words, but there was an air of triumph at being able to read people, and at reading himself in defiance of convention.

He dreamt he was dissecting his legs and pelvis; the dream was about self-analysis. He dreamt about dead colleagues and his own survival, emerging, as he said sarcastically, 'the only villain among the crowd of noble characters who share one's life'. He dreamt about Rome because it had come to mean his unfulfilled wishes. John Freud and their friend-and-enemy relationship appeared in dreams. So did Uncle Josef the forger and his parents.

On a summer's night in 1898, travelling on a train from Vienna to join the family at Aussee, he dreamt of his father. The coach had no corridor so he couldn't use a lavatory. The dream ended with Freud at a railway station with a blind man, to whom he gave a glass urinal. At that point he woke up, wanting to urinate. The blind man was his father. Freud was revenging himself for an episode when he was seven years old:

> One evening before going to sleep I disregarded the rules which modesty lays down and obeyed the calls of nature in my parents' bedroom while they were present. In the course of his reprimand, my father let fall the words: 'The boy will come to nothing.' This must have been a frightful blow to my ambition, for references to this scene are still constantly recurring in my dreams and are always linked with an enumeration of my achievements and successes, as though I wanted to say: 'You see, I *have* come to something.'

That scene, in Freud's analysis, was behind the dream's final episode:

> in which – revenge, of course – the roles were interchanged. The older man ... was now micturating in front of me, just as I had in front of him in my childhood ... Moreover, I was making fun of him; I had to hand him the urinal because he was blind, and I revelled in allusions to my discoveries in connection with the theory of hysteria, of which I felt so proud.

Freud asked himself what secret the dream was trying to withhold. It was simply 'an absurd megalomania which had long been suppressed in my waking life'. So it was a dream about boasting. Other matters were involved, but Freud was unable to deal with them 'out of consideration for the censorship'.

When he dreamt of three women in a kitchen, his analysis led him into a maze of associations, including the childhood memory of his mother showing him flakes of skin from her hand as evidence of mortality. Freud's free associations led him to food, madness, hunger and cocaine, but 'I must desist at this point because the personal sacrifice demanded would be too great.'

In the final chapter, Freud offered a 'psychology of the dream-processes' which was, in effect, his definitive statement about how the mind works. A dream resembled a neurotic symptom. Both arose from an unconscious wish, derived from infancy, that had been repressed. The ideas he had discussed with Fliess five years earlier – about the mind as an apparatus that dealt with energy flashing through the brain – were still recognisable, but wishes were now seen as the fuel for the process; in effect, for living. 'Pleasure' wrestled with 'unpleasure'. The force that drove the mind machine was a wish and nothing but a wish, exciting tensions that clamoured to be got rid of, so that the surplus energy could be discharged, letting the mind settle back to the balanced calm that it always sought to achieve.

All this was as figurative as a poem, although it was presented as a matter of science. Freud had created a framework that he would modify but never abandon. The business of the unconscious mind was the 'primary process', lurking in the background. 'Secondary process' was our conscious thinking, which recognised reality and the need to curb one's behaviour, unlike the greedy unconscious which curbed nothing. The irreconcilable nature of the wish and the reality makes our mental life what it is. Freud would still be trying to explain the intricacies of the relationship when he died.

Reviews of the book disappointed him. Some were favourable, but he may have felt, as authors do, that he had written his heart out and deserved better. To his contemporaries he was just a nerve doctor who had written another tome.

A month after publication he was still waiting for a review, pleased that Fliess had told him of a dozen readers in Berlin, confident he would have some in Vienna as well. 'The time is not yet ripe for followers,' added Freud; 'There is too much that is new and unbelievable, and too little strict proof.' So he was already expecting adherents. Shortly afterwards he found a review in a journal called *The Present*. The article was too low-powered for his liking but gave him a phrase to hold on to, 'his path-breaking work'.

The weather that December was bitter. In the evenings Freud sat in his study downstairs, 'my cellar hole', almost too cold to write. As a New Year (and new century) letter he sent Wilhelm an impenetrable poem to celebrate the birth of a second Fliess son, which seems to praise the father for using his biorhythmic theories to control fertility and restrain 'the power of the female sex'. One wonders if Freud was sitting in his cellar hole with a bottle of Christmas Marsala, contemplating the embers of his sex life and how things might have turned out differently but for the curse of all those pregnancies.

On 8 January 1900, Freud wrote again to Berlin:

> The new century, the most interesting thing about which for us may be that it contains the dates of our deaths, has brought me nothing but a stupid review in the *Zeit* [a popular daily paper in Vienna] by Burckhard, the former director of the Burgtheater ... It is hardly flattering, uncommonly devoid of understanding, and – worst of all – to be continued in the next issue.

Freud added that he didn't count on recognition, 'at least not in my lifetime', pointing out that he had to 'deal in obscure matters with people I am ten to fifteen years ahead of and who will not catch up with me'.

More to Freud's taste was a review later that month for the *Nation*, a Berlin weekly, by a layman, J. J. David. David was acquainted with Freud, who once called him 'an unhappy man and a not inconsiderable poet'. The review made no attempt at a 'scientific' evaluation; what David responded to were the mysterious undertones he read into the book, the 'secret voices in the breast', the way in which the story of Oedipus, 'one of the great poetical creations of all times', stems from 'the dark shadows of early sexuality between parents and children, in Freud's opinion'. Freud found all this 'kind and perceptive' if 'somewhat diffuse'. David was the first of many poets who saw more in Freud than scientists did.

Arthur Schnitzler was another early convert. He seems to have read the book for pleasure, not to review it, and wrote about it in his diary in March. As a result, he said, he dreamt 'more precisely', and his dreams often had Freud in them.

Medical men were not indifferent, although they sometimes cited the book only to dismiss it. A Vienna professor, Dr Raimann, told his students that 'a colleague' was taking advantage of sick people's habit of unburdening their minds so that he could fill his pockets. But medical writers, in Germany if not in Austria, took him seriously, using the reviewer's code-words of guarded commendation: 'ingenious', 'plausible', 'stimulating'. As a rule they failed to come to grips with what Freud was saying about children's oedipal relationships with their parents and the implications of sexual behaviour in childhood. Freud had not entirely come to grips with it himself. There is a well-known passage in *Dreams* where he remarks that 'we think highly of the happiness of childhood because it is still innocent of sexual desires', a statement he contradicts a hundred pages later.

The book is the testament of a man at the pivotal point of his life, defining where he stood. 'Whether or not people like the dream book is beginning to leave me cold,' he wrote to Fliess in July 1900. 'I myself have so far not found anything in need of correction. It is true and no doubt remains true.'

A century later the book attracts curious visitors who admire its reputation while finding it hard to recreate the spirit of its author. The dream as an invariable fulfiller of wishes has itself become a dream, not much believed in. In the 1950s neuroscience was able to define two categories of sleep: one largely dreamless, the other punctuated by bursts of dream-filled brain activity. This pattern doesn't fit the theory that dreams are the guardians of sleep. Far from dreaming in order to be able to sleep in peace, it is more likely that we sleep in order to let dreams reprocess information.

Even so, the tides of memory that flow through dreams, unbidden and unsettling, suggest something more than scavenging designed to leave the brain in good shape for the day ahead. The analyst and writer Charles Rycroft has discussed it persuasively, arguing that dreaming is an imaginative activity which implies 'the existence of some mental entity which is more preoccupied with the individual's total life span and destiny than is the conscious ego with its day-to-day involvement with immediate contingencies'. Dreams, in this view, are 'momentary glimpses of the dreamer's total imaginative fabric, into which are woven all his memories, expectations, wishes and fears'.

These sound like the dreams that many of us would recognise. I dreamt once that a house where I had lived and been happy was burning. I saw the roof fall in. The dream told me what I knew but couldn't admit to myself: that a phase of my life was over. Perhaps Freud's dreams can be fitted into some such scheme.

There was more to *The Interpretation of Dreams* than the intricacies of a theory that tried to offer an impossible completeness. Freud, operating in a more constricted society than ours, was bold enough to take the crazed improprieties of dreams and dreamers seriously and use them to throw light on our nature: forever wishing for the inadmissible. It isn't necessary to take Oedipus and the rest of it as a literal statement in order to get the picture.

Not long after *Dreams* was published, as he waited for the chorus of praise that didn't come, he wrote to Fliess:

> I am actually not at all a man of science, not an observer, not an experimenter, not a thinker. I am by temperament nothing but a conquistador – an adventurer, if you want it translated – with all the curiosity, daring and tenacity characteristic of a man of this sort.

Apologists have said he was being ironic. But it reads like a true confession.

16: Freudian Slips

Nothing seemed right for Freud in 1900. Dissatisfaction nibbled at him. He envied Fliess his certainty and income – the fortunate friend, flourishing in a progressive city – and the letters he sent to Berlin were sprinkled with self-pity. Knowing himself didn't help what he called his 'neurotic swings of mood' any more than they helped his anxieties about money: 'Inwardly I am deeply impoverished', 'My back has become noticeably bent.' What a fool he had been to dream of freedom and well-being, he groaned, just because he had written a dream-book!

In a good week he earned substantial sums, 500 florins, £1,400 today. If this raised his spirits ('money is laughing gas for me,' he once told Fliess), the effect was transitory. Hard work with patients left him weary and longing for 'sunshine, flowers, a bit of blue water, just like a young man'. Like many doctors he was not over-fond of patients, and saw them as 'tormentors'. His spare time was described with heavy irony. He was 'a pleasure-seeking philistine' who indulged his fantasies, played chess and read English novels. Strong cigars were forbidden, alcohol (he had concluded) did nothing for him, and as for carnal things, 'I am done begetting children.'

If only he had more money, or someone to go to Italy with in the summer; if only he could rid himself of Breuer's lingering friendship! He means to buy an iron strong-box that he once saw in a shop window in central Vienna, but he can no longer find the shop when he is out walking, and keeps forgetting to look up the address in the telephone directory. Eventually he forces himself, and discovers that the shop is close to the building where the Breuers live. It is thus in forbidden territory, and his unconscious has been avoiding it.

If Freud's letters told the truth, he was not doing much but vegetate, worry and grow old. His birthday in May 1900 was celebrated with the remark: 'Yes, I really am forty-four now, an old, somewhat shabby Jew.' His family insisted on marking the occasion, but Freud was busy with sackcloth and ashes, telling Fliess that it would be 'a fitting punishment' if 'none of the unexplored regions of psychic life in which I have been the first mortal to set foot will ever bear my name or obey my laws'.

Now and then the melancholy lifts. When it seems that the scientific community may be coming round to Fliess and his periodicity, Freud says dreamily that it will be satisfying to see his friend's critics eat their words.

> Such spiteful glee, such satisfied thirst for revenge plays an important role in my case; so far I have savoured too little of this delicious fare. So I am joining you in nibbling a spoonful of your meal.

Bellevue, where the family stayed in early summer, and which Freud visited daily from Berggasse, aroused pleasing memories of the Irma dream. He day-dreamed about the marble tablet that might be there one day, commemorating the event. Not much else cheered him up except family events, in particular a visit from the Manchester Freuds in the shape of his half-brother Emmanuel and Emmanuel's son Sam. They represented the other life that Sigmund might have had in urban England, where Jews were left alone to get on with their own business and there was no Mayor Lueger in City Hall, blowing on the hot coals of racism.

Emmanuel 'brought with him a real air of refreshment because he is a marvellous man, vigorous and mentally indefatigable despite his sixty-eight or sixty-nine years, who has always meant a great deal to me'. Sam was thirty-five, another engaging Freud-as-Englishman. The visitors went on to Berlin, 'now the family headquarters', where Freud's oldest sister, Anna Bernays, and her daughters were over from New York. Freud saw three of them in Vienna, finding them 'real beauties, precocious like American girls, and very engaging. So occasionally one gets a good impression of one's family.'

Some of Freud's unhappiness was a pose, a protective habit, a superstitious reluctance to be seen to be enjoying himself. Fliess was exposed to more of it than most people because he was Freud's chosen confidant for so many years. Freud seems to have had an almost physical need of the friendship. It is difficult to believe that he was afraid of Fliess, but it may be true that he was afraid of losing him. After receiving a flattering letter from Fliess, which must have pointed out the merits of living in 'splendid isolation', Freud replied (May 1900) that he would have no objection 'if it were not carried too far and did not come between you and me as well'. He added:

> I know, in view of the statistics of human misery, how little one is entitled to. But no one can replace for me the relationship with the friend which a special – possibly feminine – side demands.

Freud admired Fliess as a daring scientist, a new Kepler who would change the way people saw the world; or that was what he *wanted* to admire. The feeling may not have been reciprocated. He may have been too romantic a figure for the cold chemistry of a Fliess.

The theory of biological rhythms and periods was high science as far as Fliess was concerned, and Freud kept acknowledging it as such, even though what interested him was its application to his family: the dates when children would fall ill or men would be at their most creative or when women were least likely to conceive. His interest was in the 'beautiful novelties'.

Some of Fliess's thinking was crucially important to Freud, including ideas about child sexuality and about an underlying bisexuality in human nature. But behind Freud's rapt attention to the ideas was always a warm involvement with Fliess as a person. Freud was the one who made allowances. There is a letter of 1899 in which he recalls a walk near Berchtesgaden, where 'you were, as usual, blind to the beauties of nature and instead raved about the Mannesmanns' tubes [a German engineering invention of the 1890s]. At the time I felt somewhat overwhelmed by your superiority.'

Their relationship was about to change. It may have occurred to them both that the psychology of the one and the biology of the other were hard to reconcile, though it was not something they mentioned in letters. In summer 1900 they met for a brief holiday in the mountains and quarrelled about their ideas, and the friendship began to decline.

According to Fliess, his friend was the one who caused the trouble. Freud never gave a direct account of the meeting. His letters before they quarrelled contain few clues. He says in one that they are becoming estranged, and blames the distance that separates them. In another he sounds irritated at being told he should learn more about nasal therapy.

Perhaps his dissatisfactions got the better of him when they met, and came to a head because Fliess said the wrong things; there must have been a limit to the amount of lecturing that the author of *The Interpretation of Dreams* would put up with from the author of *Relationships between the Nose and the Female Sex Organs.* Perhaps it was something more sinister.

The meeting was arranged, several weeks in advance, for the Austrian Tyrol, where they were to spend four days together, near Innsbruck, from Tuesday, 31 July to Saturday, 4 August, before 'the women' (presumably Martha and Minna) arrived, and Freud crossed into Italy with them. The place they agreed on was beside a lake called Achensee, 3,000 feet up in the Alps. They must have taken rooms in one of the hotels on the shore, the Seespitz or the Scholastika, from which visitors with good legs could set off after breakfast and walk up another three or four thousand feet of mountain, reaching the summit by midday. It was wild, rocky country, with cliffs to fall down and a lake at the bottom to drown in. Fliess later told people in private that Freud had planned to murder him there.

In public, not surprisingly, he said nothing of the sort. His account of the quarrel, published in 1906, said simply that at Achensee, Freud 'showed a violence towards me which was at first unintelligible to me'. Fliess recalled that what led to this outburst were his remarks that 'periodic processes' were at work in the psyche, that these affected a patient's state of mind, and that consequently 'neither sudden deteriorations nor sudden improvements were to be attributed to the analysis and its influence alone'. It is hardly surprising that Freud was upset. He was being told that whatever he did as a psychoanalyst was subordinate to the overriding pattern of biorhythms.

Fliess could see only an envious colleague driven by 'personal animosity'. He quoted an earlier, undated remark by Freud in Vienna, 'It's just as well we're friends. Otherwise I should burst with envy if I heard that anyone was making such discoveries in Berlin!' Fliess, 'astonished', passed this on to his wife Ida, who was no fonder of Freud than Freud was of her.

What Fliess told his family and at least one friend about Achensee was that when they were walking there, Freud meant to give him a quick push when no one was about, so that he would die by falling or drowning and it could be made to look like an accident. The story was unearthed by Peter Swales, who heard it from Fliess's daughter, then in her eighties, in 1981–82; two other accounts confirm it, but it is not clear from them whether the murder-plan was merely a supposition by Fliess or whether anything happened at Achensee. If it was a supposition, did Fliess think of it at the time, or did it occur to him only afterwards?

Fliess, touchy and aggressive in the way that diminutive men sometimes are, might have been susceptible to fears of persecution. Some years later Freud said that Fliess had 'developed a dreadful case of paranoia after throwing off his affection for me'.* But was it paranoia or prudence? A dream of Freud's, published in *Dreams*, hinted at Fliess's death. Freud even drew his attention to it in a letter: 'I am delighted to have outlived you; isn't it terrible to suggest something like this?'

Swales, who believes that Fliess had something to be paranoiac about, finds stronger evidence in a book that Freud published the following year, *The Psychopathology of Everyday Life*. The book is laden with anecdotes illustrating idiosyncracies of behaviour. One of them, trivial in itself, concerns a summer holiday he took with a 'travelling companion'. Swales concludes that the companion was Fliess, the place was Achensee, and that the anecdote was another of those pieces of concealed autobiography to which Freud was addicted, with cryptic allusions to their relationship.

At one point Freud writes how he was

> struck that morning by my companion's rejecting my proposal for a longish expedition and objecting during our short walk to taking a certain path which he said was too steep and dangerous.

Swales goes further and suggests that Freud inserted the reference to the 'dangerous path' with the intention of intimidating Fliess when the book appeared (in a psychiatric journal to begin with) the following year, 1901. 'Here, unmasked,' says Swales, 'is quite a different Freud [to] the man portrayed by his biographers.' The argument is extreme (and Swales takes it further), but the

---

* Fliess was not the only one of Freud's ex-friends to have a convenient diagnosis of paranoia pinned to him over the years. There was no shortage of personal nastiness once psychoanalytic politics got going. But Freud had kinder memories of Fliess as well. 'I once loved him very much,' he wrote in 1911.

Achensee story is disquieting. Freud was a dreamer to be reckoned with.

After these supposed fantasies concerning his friend and colleague Wilhelm come supposed fantasies concerning his friend and sister-in-law Minna. This is a more speculative episode, and Peter Swales is again at work in it, rummaging through the Freudian cellars.

The story that Freud and Minna had a sexual affair has been in circulation for years. Ernest Jones, who wrote about their close relationship, guessed what people might think and declared, 'There was no sexual attraction on either side.' Jones, who presumably knew there were rumours to the contrary, claimed rather too strenuously that Freud was devoted to his wife. Jung claimed to know for a fact that there was a liaison, having been told about it by Minna herself. It would have been incest, technically speaking. There is evidence of a sort that it happened – or that Freud had fantasies about it happening – towards the end of the same summer, 1900.

Minna's chance of marriage had disappeared fourteen years earlier when her fiancé died of tuberculosis. She found work as a governess and a 'lady's companion', lived at times with her mother in Hamburg, and accepted spinsterhood, as women did, but let it sharpen her tongue. From 1896 she lived permanently with the Freuds in Berggasse, the childless aunt that families found invaluable, with a room of her own and a gramophone that played loud music.

Jung, who met her in 1906, is supposed to have said she was 'very good-looking', but this is not evident in photographs. Writing to his sister Rosa in 1886, before he married Martha, Freud is said to have dismissed her as 'very ugly, fat as a hippopotamus'. This didn't reflect his true feelings, or if it did, it was coloured by his eager anticipation of marriage to the other sister.

From the start Freud felt an affinity with Minna, who was not under her mother's thumb in the way he feared that Martha was. 'Minna loves her but doesn't spare her,' he told his fiancée. Nor did Minna set out to be the perfect housewife. Her style when she had to do housework was a duster in one hand and a book in the other. The perfect housewife was what Freud looked for in Martha, and during the engagement to his 'little woman' he dwelt on the domestic virtues he expected to find in her, a devotion to furniture and pretty ribbons and cosy lamps and larder.

Minna had different assets. His letters to her seem to have none of the intellectual condescension that crept in when he wrote to Martha. When Minna's sweetheart died, he advised her not to try and be friendly with his family, since they were sure to blame her for what had happened. 'Burn your letters while it is still winter,' he wrote. After eight years of marriage to one sister he described the other to Fliess as 'my closest confidante'; this was well before she was permanently installed at Berggasse 19.

None of this does more than suggest the possibility of a sexual interest, and Freud's biographers have not been keen to pursue the matter. Better to leave Freud and Minna in peace – admiring one another, sharing intellectual interests, going off for holidays – without wondering too much about the particularity of being alone together: talking over breakfast, grumbling at badly-sprung carriages, climbing ridges, taking steamers on lakes, standing in ruined palaces at midday, sharing sardonic jokes about Englishmen abroad, sleeping side by side on deckchairs, strolling on a terrace after dinner.

Minna was thirty-five years old in summer 1900, an age that sounded older then than now, but was still no obstacle to a spirited woman, the kind that Freud had encountered often enough among his highly sexed hysterics. Freud himself was forty-four, and the word that had gone out to Fliess, 'I am done begetting children,' is supposed to have ended the matter. Oddly, this confession was left untouched by the censors who filleted out almost all the personal references to sex when the Fliess correspondence was first published. The fact that Freud had done 'begetting children' must have been thought of as seemly from the beginning. Presumably the Biblical-sounding phrase was a polite way of saying 'sexual intercourse', although he may have meant no more than he said, that procreation was at an end; pleasure was not addressed.

Whatever he meant, it would be encouraging to think that someone who made so much of sex in his work was able to go on leading a normal sex life of his own for a bit beyond forty-four. In fact he seems to have had sex with Martha as late as 1915, when he was fifty-nine (he noted it in an unpublished dream-analysis). Presumably he did something about contraception between 1896, following the birth of the last child, Anna, and Martha's meno-pause, some time after the turn of the century. (A letter to Fliess in 1900 mentions the holiday trip with Martha, planned for August, when they must 'avoid the period during which she is not capable of enjoyment', presumably a reference to the discomfort of menstru-ation. His wife's thirty-ninth birthday was in July.)

Eduard Hitschmann made an unusual observation. Hitschmann was among the first of the Viennese analysts, and a member of Freud's circle from 1905. In March 1954 he wrote to Ernest Jones, apparently responding to a request for information about Freud's sexual life. He was then in his eighties and living in America, where he had been a training analyst since 1940. 'Never interested in his genitals,' wrote Hitschmann ambiguously, 'I observed once his erection in the trousers after a [psychoanalytic] hour with a pretty woman.' This didn't appear in Jones's biography. Nor did his remark that 'I knew a Colleague who told me, lady patients had to cover their legs and feet, not to be sexually excited during [Freud's] analysis.' These old-man's memories are difficult to evaluate. Most striking of all, in a letter dealing with Freud's sexuality, is a Hitschmann anecdote about Minna:

> Once he gave me an open letter to bring to Minna. There was written: 'When it shall be the evening, we will walk together through the darkness.' June 15 1923.

The year 1923 was a climacteric, when Freud's health and his life changed. The note to Minna (was it left unsealed so that Hitsch-mann could read it and make notes?) may have been written in its shadow.

The events of summer 1900 involving Freud and Minna are loosely documented. After his four days with Fliess at Achensee, Freud crossed into Italy with Martha and perhaps Minna as well. They stayed among more mountains, being driven about through passes and walking on a glacier or two, but Martha, as usual, didn't want much of this, and after a week she returned to Vienna and the children, no doubt because of the days when she was 'not capable of enjoyment'.

By the time Martha left, Freud had met friends from Vienna. He went with them to Venice, where they bumped into his sister Rosa and her husband, after which the party moved back into southern Austria, to see sister Anna and her 'American children' who were holidaying by a lake. It was now the last week in August.

What happened next was described in a long account of the holiday that Freud sent to Fliess; there were no dark echoes of Achensee, just a chatty travelogue that he wrote as soon as he was back in Vienna.

> Finally – we have now reached August 26 – came the relief. I mean
> Minna, with whom I drove through the Puster Valley . . .

They spent nearly two weeks travelling alone in northern Italy, again with lakes and mountains never far away. At the little town of Riva, on Lake Garda, they stayed five days, 'divinely accommodated and fed, luxuriating without regrets, and untroubled'. On 8 September he took Minna to the mountain resort of Merano, in the Austrian Tyrol, where she was to stay for weeks or even months because of an intermittent chest weakness or infection. According to Jones, who may have mixed up the years, he then returned to Vienna via Milan and (inexplicably) Genoa. Freud was in Vienna by 10 September.

The suggestion that they were lovers during the thirteen days comes from Swales, who repeats his stratagem of taking a Freudian text, finding in it a piece of autobiography that has gone unsuspected, and breaking its code with fantasies of his own, rather like Freud cracking a dream. The text is the same *Psychopathology of Everyday Life* in which Swales found an echo of Achensee. Freud, in a chapter called 'The Forgetting of Foreign Words', reports a conversation he had with a 'certain young man of academic background' whom he met while on holiday in summer 1900. As in 'Screen Memories', a dialogue with an anonymous figure is used to make a point about psychoanalysis.

When the acquaintance omits the word 'aliquis' ('someone') from a Latin quotation, Freud uses the man's impromptu free association to trace his thoughts to a church in Naples where a bottle of saint's blood is supposed to liquefy on the same holy day each year. Following other clues, Freud finds the root of the unease that is behind the forgetfulness: the blood that is due to flow at a particular time reminds the acquaintance of his fear that he may have made a woman pregnant, and that he will hear any day that she has missed a menstrual period.

Swales's argument – that the acquaintance was a fiction, that Freud is expressing his own fears that he has made Minna pregnant, that their lovemaking had a significance beyond the act itself – is too complex to reproduce. In a typical invention, Swales decides that the town of Trent, which the couple visited, is where Minna lost her virginity because it was here that the sixteenth-century Council of Trent reaffirmed the sanctity of marriage, and 'it was precisely Freud's nature to want to flout Christian dogma right where it would hurt the most'.* The essay succeeds in making all the 'aliquis' associations apply to Freud's life.

Swales needs to be read in the original to appreciate his intemperate style, part scholar and part bounty-hunter. His writing has been called 'brilliant science fiction' (and less complimentary things) by the psychoanalytic community. Here, his case for detecting Freud's fears behind the other's is eerily convincing. There is something about Freud's dialogue with the well-informed 'young man of academic background' that irresistibly suggests the style of 'Screen Memories'.

A further tranche of Swalesian speculation is devoted to his suspicion that Minna went to Merano in case she needed an abortion, and that very likely an abortion was performed in one of the town's clinics. This is shakier ground. A normal fertility pattern would barely accommodate the two prerequisites – a conception on or after 26 August and a missed menstrual period by 6 or 7 September – and allow time for her and Freud to panic and get her to Merano, a resort where discreet facilities were likely to be available, by 8 September. Fear of a pregnancy sounds more feasible. Fertility cycles were not fully understood at the time. Had Minna's period been due in the first few days of September there was no risk of her conceiving as late as 26 August, but she and Freud were not to know that. However, if Minna was afraid she had conceived, the fear could have delayed menstruation, a well-known paradox. In that case going to Merano was a prudent move. The consequences of Minna bearing a child would have been too awful to contemplate.

She stayed there six weeks. While she was still away, Freud wrote to Fliess, 'I *must*, after all, take an interest in *reality* in sexuality, which one learns about only with great difficulty,' a remark it is tempting to see as significant.

Minna returned to Vienna about 20 October, still unwell and

* When the freethinking H. G. Wells was having an affair with the young socialist Amber Reeves before the First World War, they made love one afternoon in a country church in Kent. Wells said how much they enjoyed the 'flavour of sinfulness'.

causing concern. 'Not everything about her condition is entirely clear,' Freud wrote to Fliess. Early in 1901 she had internal bleeding and an intestinal ulcer was diagnosed. The original reason for her going to Merano, the chest infection, wasn't mentioned.

Swales's arguments make an impressive case for believing that pregnancy was on Freud's mind. Freud was at work on *Everyday Life* immediately after his return to Vienna in September 1900. The 'aliquis' episode occurs in the first few pages. Fresh evidence found in 1997 by a colleague of Swales, and as yet unpublished, shows convincingly where Freud could have obtained, just at the right time, the tale about the liquefying blood in the Naples church on which he then hung his dialogue with the 'certain young man'. But the fact that Freud was worried about pregnancy might have nothing to do with Minna. Martha, aged thirty-nine, could have been the one who missed her period. If that news greeted Freud when he was back in Vienna, it might have been sufficient to set off the 'aliquis' chain of thought.

As far as Minna herself is concerned, the rest is hearsay. Jung's evidence is far from conclusive and comes in more than one version. The most extreme was reported by an American professor of psychology, John Billinsky, who claimed to have heard it from an eighty-two-year-old Jung in 1957. On Jung's first visit to Freud in Vienna in 1907, Minna is supposed to have confided in the visitor that her brother-in-law was in love with her, that they had slept together and that she was tormented by guilt. Billinsky diminished his story by presenting Jung's words verbatim and then admitting that nothing was written down until the interview was over. His account didn't appear until 1969, well after Jung's death, and has been largely ignored ever since.

Billinsky isn't quite alone. Others have claimed they heard the Minna story from Jung, among them his associate Carl Meier and an Italian journalist. Oscar Rie is supposed to have said that for children Freud went with Martha. The possibility remains.

Access to letters between Freud and his sister-in-law is restricted. The historian and Freudian Peter Gay, who was the first to see some of them in the Freud Archives in 1988, found a break in the informal numbering of items between nos. 94 and 161, covering seventeen years, from April 1893 to July 1910. The available letters contained no revelations. But any sexual goings-on would fall within the years for which letters are missing.

*

The summer dreams were over. Freud lost his air of dissatisfaction, accepted that the world was not ready for *The Interpretation of Dreams*, and went back to more productive ways. If he still saw himself as a shabby old Jew – if the shabby old Jew was ever more than a disguise – he was keeping quiet about it. He and Fliess had less to say to each other now; or they had more, but chose not to say it.

The intervals between letters to and from Berlin grew longer, although Fliess was told about work in progress on the new book, *The Psychopathology of Everyday Life*, and about a new patient, 'an eighteen-year-old girl, a case that has smoothly opened to the existing collection of picklocks'. She was 'Dora', the first of the handful of Freud's subjects who would have full-length essays of their own. The analysis ended abruptly on the last day of 1900, Dora having had enough of this nerve doctor who told her what she ought to be thinking about sex, and within days Freud was writing up the case. Dora fascinated him. He was ready with his picklock. The piece was rattled off in weeks, a novella about dreams, oral sex, masturbation and adultery. But it went unpublished for four years.

Everyday Life, which he continued to write alongside Dora's story, was finished by May 1901. It was to be his most popular work, the one that taught people who barely knew his name that if they accidentally used a word or phrase that suggested the opposite of what they intended, they could laugh it off by saying 'Freudian slip!'

The idea that tricks of speech and memory might expose inner conflicts, and make amateur analysts of us all, took time to reach middle-class conversations. The work was not available as a book until 1904, when it appeared as a slim volume of fewer than a hundred pages, swelling year by year in fresh editions until eventually it was three times as long, with a surfeit of anecdotal evidence that Freud couldn't resist. It contained little theory.

In 1914, when an English translation appeared, it was seen in London as 'a most curious and fascinating new system of self-examination which everyone may set about without worrying himself as to the state of his own nerves'. Two years later an American medical journal said that neurotics should not be allowed to read it, since it would only 'make them more morbidly introspective'.

Much of Freud's evidence in the book came from his own experience (often from his period of self-analysis), with sexual matters excluded as they had been in *The Interpretation of Dreams*. Slips of tongue and pen, selective failure of memory, misreadings, mislayings and apparently senseless or bungled acts were all part of the process that Freud called 'faulty function', rendered by his English-language translators as 'parapraxis'.

The principle wasn't new. Freud's phrase, 'there are purposes in people which can become operative without their knowing about them', resembles Thomas Hardy's aside, about men being drawn from their intentions in the course of carrying them out. Writers used slips of the tongue as a convenient literary device. Criminologists were familiar with the idea that witness-statements could be studied for inadvertent disclosure.

To Freud it was part of the psychological scheme of things. 'I fail to see why the wisdom which is the precipitate of men's common experience of life should be refused inclusion among the acquisitions of science,' he wrote, appealing to the world at large as he did in *Dreams*. Parapraxes were not random events but precise evidence of the continuous antagonism between conscious and unconscious, or, in the terms he used in *Dreams*, 'secondary' and 'primary' process. He spoke of 'a continuous current of "personal reference", of which I generally have no inkling', that ran through his thoughts and betrayed itself by parapraxes.

His failure to remember the name of the painter Signorelli, the number '2467' that he thought he had plucked from the air but hadn't, the shop with the strong-box in the window that he couldn't find, were all determined by disturbances in his unconscious. A thousand little instances were collated. A politician opens a session of the Austrian Parliament with the words 'I declare the sitting closed.' A woman says that a man doesn't need to be handsome 'as long as he has five straight limbs'. A woman with a jealous husband who accuses her of 'carrying on like a tart again!' because she dances the can-can at a family party, steps out of a carriage the next day and breaks her leg: a self-punishment, unconsciously willed, that fitted the crime, suggested Freud, since it would be a long time before she would do any can-can dancing again.

None of the slips, lapses and accidents that Freud described was allowed to be purposeless. Each had its rationale. The husband who whispers his mistress's name in his wife's ear betrays the infidelity in his heart. The letter posted without a stamp or sent to the wrong address is never intended to arrive. But *Everyday Life* can be read in two ways. For most of the book Freud seems to be enlarging the scope for understanding oneself, for recognising that slips of speech and memory are the expression of mental conflict. Then, at the end, he tells his readers that what he has demonstrated is that everything is predetermined, that they are merely victims of the inevitable. Perhaps this was Freud the scientist harking back nostalgically to the stern laboratories of his youth where wise men taught him that the body was a chemical engine. Whatever it was, he never reconciled the confused messages.

As well as the autobiographical material he cites in the book, Freud's life offers abundant evidence of parapraxis, not always acknowledged by him as such. In September 1897, when he wrote to Fliess to say he had abandoned the seduction theory, he used the phrase, 'Of course I shall not tell it in Dan.' Anthony Stadlen has mischievously pointed out (for the benefit of Freudians, who haven't noticed) that the Biblical phrase which this echoes, contained in David's lamentation in defeat, is 'Tell it not in Gath' – a city of the Philistines, the enemy. Dan was a dominant tribe of Israel. Thus Freud's unconscious, in Freudian theory, was instructing him to say, 'Don't tell my friends and colleagues about my error. Keep it dark' (which is what he did). Over the years, letters to colleagues often betrayed covert thoughts. With slips of the pen as with dreams, Freud was a tireless producer of the raw materials of his trade.

His account in *Everyday Life* never quite made clear why the unconscious should interfere as he said it did. Freud held that dark thoughts ('egoistic, jealous and hostile feelings and impulsions') offensive to morality used parapraxis as a means of expression. He found it astonishing that 'the urge to tell the truth [that is, to give oneself away by a parapraxis] is so much stronger than is usually supposed'. Elsewhere in the book he said that 'Acquiescence in these parapraxes and chance actions is to a large extent equivalent to a compliant tolerance of the immoral. Among these suppressed impulses no small part is played by the various sexual currents.'

Thus Freud's scenario has the immoral unconscious trying to force its way into everyday behaviour as a salutary reminder of the evil side of one's nature. In dreams, the dark thoughts are censored so that they won't disturb the dreamer and stop him dreaming. Yet in the hours of daylight, such thoughts are allowed to make a nuisance of themselves.

Some critics have savaged the whole concept. Most of us are willing to believe in parapraxis on a modest scale, if only because it agrees with our own experience. For Freud, however, parapraxis was a profound insight into our nature or it was nothing. His more complicated examples (such as 'Signorelli' and 'aliquis') offered interpretations as elaborate as his dream-analyses; and were as open to attack on the grounds that he was including private fantasies.

Everyday Life was first published in consecutive issues of a psychiatric journal in summer 1901. While Freud waited for off-prints to send to Fliess, their friendship was unravelling. A letter from Freud, dated 7 August, replied to one in which Fliess had evidently rubbed salt into the wound that had opened at Achensee almost exactly a year earlier.

'There is no concealing the fact,' wrote Freud, 'that the two of us have drawn apart to some extent.' After referring to Ida Fliess's belief (for which Freud blamed Breuer) that he had somehow interfered with her marriage by his friendship with Wilhelm, he went on:

> You take sides against me and tell me that 'the reader of thoughts merely reads his own thoughts into other people', which renders all my efforts valueless.
>
> If that is what you think of me, just throw my 'Everyday Life' unread into the wastepaper basket. It is full of references to you – manifest ones, for which you supplied the material, and concealed ones, for which the motivation goes back to you.

Take it as 'a testimonial to the role you have played for me up to now', Freud added, with a touch of bitterness. After that the letter became more cordial, but he had cranked the quarrel up.

Freud's confidence in himself was growing. Rome, which he associated with youth and defiance, was still on his mind. He had thought of tackling it at Easter 1901, but again hesitated.

In August the family was on holiday at an inn on the shores of Thumsee, a lake in the mountains not far from Berchtesgaden. They were there when Freud wrote crossly to Fliess. The weather was hot, the lake tempting, and Freud and his sons were less inclined than usual to walk up mountains; they swam and fished instead. Day tourists shouted their orders for lunch to the inn from the far side of the lake. 'Goulash with dumplings!' echoed over the stillness. Freud, in a rowing boat, trailed his fingers in the green water and disapproved.

One morning two of the boys, Martin, aged eleven, and Oliver, aged ten, were fishing near the road when villagers began shouting at them, calling them Jews and thieves. Later in the day a gang of them, this time including women, tried to block the road when father and sons approached. The men were 'armed with sticks and umbrellas', according to Martin, who is the source of the story. Freud swung his walking stick and marched straight at them, at which they dispersed without a murmur, as ruffians are supposed to.

This was not how his own father had behaved in Freiberg when the Christian knocked Jacob's hat into the dirt and Sigmund, the well-read schoolboy, turned for consolation to the myth of Hannibal. Perhaps he thought about Hannibal at Thumsee.

Like other middle-class Jews in Vienna, Freud relied on a network of Jewish colleagues and friends; like others, too, he continued to have mixed feelings about his race. Assimilated families like the Freuds and the Bernays went on feeling antagonistic towards those Jews they saw as inferior. A letter of 1910 to Freud from Minna, who was managing the apartment in the holidays, said that the 'Jewish electricians' had been, and were of course 'too refined to remove the filth they had left'.

But Freud, the Westernised scientist and atheist, was also the Jew with fantasies that connected him to the history of his race. As anti-Semitism grew, so did Freud's concern with his own origins. The hopes of Jews in central Europe, widespread when Freud was young, were weakening. The old Christian dislike of an alien 'them' was reasserting itself.

In Vienna, Mayor Lueger and his friends were busy putting up buildings, electrifying the trams and playing on popular myths about the rosy days of old Vienna, when the wine-gardens in the suburbs were full of well-fed, jolly citizens with hearts of gold and in full employment, speaking the local dialect, not the guttural speech of certain immigrants.

The Leopold Hilsner trials had been in the papers not long before, followed avidly. A vagrant Jew arrested in a Bohemian town (a hundred miles west of Freud's birthplace) was accused of cutting a Christian woman's throat and taking her blood in an act of so-called ritual murder. Hilsner was twice sentenced to death, but the emperor commuted the sentences to life imprisonment. Lueger's men worked hard to stir the accompanying agitation in Vienna. The notorious 'Protocols of the Elders of Zion', which purported to give a verbatim account of Jewish masterminds meeting to devise a plan for world conquest, appeared in Vienna newspapers in 1901.*

In September, Freud, son of Hannibal, finally advanced on Rome in a train. A month earlier he had talked of needing 'eight to twelve days of olive oil and wine' before the summer ended. He must have left Thumsee soon after the altercation with the villagers, which came 'towards the end of our holiday', according to Martin. Did he, at the last minute, decide on Rome, rather than somewhere else in Italy, because of these anti-Semites? He travelled with his brother and stayed twelve days, absorbed by pagan, classical Rome, less so by its other history as the city of Christ. A letter home marvelled that he had been afraid of the place for so long.

As soon as he was back in Vienna he overcame another of his inhibitions and set about acquiring the professorship that years of patient waiting for his merit to be recognised hadn't achieved. Freud himself saw the end of his Roman phobia as clearing the way for this career move. 'Others are that clever without first having to go to Rome,' he told Fliess the following year in almost the last of his letters to Berlin.

Each year since 1897, when Krafft-Ebing and his committee put Freud's name forward, he had been passed over. He began his 1901 campaign by enlisting the help of Elise Gomperz, a former patient, a member of the noted family, well-connected and friendly towards Freud. She failed to move the minister. 'Who is he?' he asked slyly. There were vague reports, Freud heard, that 'certain circles' of officialdom laughed at him.

Perhaps the same circles thought him not only laughable but difficult. Earlier in 1901 Breuer had badgered him into giving a public lecture about his work to the Philosophical Society. Freud pointed out that he would be dealing with 'all sorts of intimate and sexual matters', unsuitable for a mixed audience. When the society sent two delegates to Berggasse to hear a trial run, they said the

* The 'Protocols' had a long life. Hitler embraced them as evidence of Jewish conspiracy when he was developing Nazi ideology in 1920, and the London *Times* took them seriously. They were invented at the end of the nineteenth century by the Russian secret police as anti-Semitic propaganda.

lecture was 'wonderful', and it was announced in the *Neue Freie Presse*. But at the last minute, a letter arrived from the philosophers asking him to begin the lecture with inoffensive examples, then explain that risqué matters were to come and there would be an intermission in which ladies could leave the hall. Freud cancelled the lecture.

In the end the successful lobbyist was another patient with connections, Baroness Marie von Ferstel, a diplomat's wife who was being psychoanalysed by Freud. She may have been determined to show she could do better than Mrs Gomperz. After cornering the minister, von Hartel, the baroness was given to understand that he was anxious to obtain a particular painting, a ruined castle by Böcklin, for a gallery. Her aunt had the painting, but seems to have been unwilling to hand it over. Baroness Ferstel offered him a painting by someone else, and was graciously informed at a dinner party that the papers appointing Freud had been sent to the emperor for him to sigh.

It was not the victory Freud would have wished. After his appointment he had an audience with the minister so he could thank him formally. 'As I was on my way home from this audience,' Freud wrote twenty years later, 'I caught myself in the act of trying to falsify the words that had passed between us and I was never able to recapture correctly the actual conversation.'

Whatever the loss of self-esteem, he had the title at last. 'So it was accomplished,' he said on 11 March 1902 in the last letter he wrote to Fliess for two years, when the friendship finally expired amid recriminations. Anxious to announce his success and needing to confess the moral compromise involved in achieving it, Freud wrote ironically that 'Public acclaim was immense', a newspaper phrase that he liked to make fun of. He went on:

> Congratulations and flowers are already pouring in, as though the role of sexuality has suddenly been officially recognised by His Majesty, the significance of the dream certified by the Council of Ministers, and the necessity of a psychoanalytic therapy of hysteria carried by a two-thirds majority in Parliament.
>
> I have obviously become reputable again ... I myself would still gladly exchange every five congratulations for one decent case suitable for extensive treatment. I have learned that the old world is ruled by authority, as the new is by the dollar. I have made my first bow to authority, and so may hope to be rewarded.

Endorsed, energised, relieved, Freud turned to the business of followers. The suggestion of a professional circle is said to have come from Wilhelm Stekel, a clever and intuitive young nerve doctor with an active interest in women and in sex generally (he published a paper about childhood coitus as early as 1895). He consulted Freud with, as Ernest Jones put it, 'a troublesome neurotic complaint, the nature of which I need not mention', in about 1901. Freud analysed him.

Early the following year, Stekel, who had a second career as a journalist (unkind people said it should have been his first career), reviewed *The Interpretation of Dreams* for a daily newspaper. 'Dr Freud,' he wrote, 'the famous expert on diseases of the soul, opens a new era in psychology.' Stekel soon began to consider a career in analysis, with its rich veins of intimate material and its interesting relationships with women.

In autumn 1902 Freud sent postcards to four Jewish doctors, suggesting they meet regularly at his flat to discuss his work. One of them was the companionable Stekel, whose family, like Freud's, came from the east. Another was Alfred Adler, the socialist son of a Viennese grain merchant, who smoked thin cigars and was inclined to be cantankerous; he was an early feminist. The other two were Rudolf Reitler and Max Kahane. They agreed to meet on Wednesday evenings after supper, and became the 'Wednesday Society'. Freud later summed it up in a sentence: 'From the year 1902 onwards, a number of young doctors gathered round me with the express intention of learning, practising and spreading the knowledge of psychoanalysis.'

To begin with they were master and four admirers, sitting around the table in the waiting room, having cakes and black coffee, filling the room with smoke. Freud, especially, 'smoked like a furnace'. Those who joined him had no reputations to lose, or they might have hesitated to be seen as his allies.

Fritz Wittels, who joined a few years later, said that Freud didn't want to be argued with. He wanted 'a kaleidoscope lined with mirrors that would multiply the images he introduced into it'. Wittels fell into line with the rest. Freud was the father; they were his sons.

17: Unhappy Families

L ike every city in Europe at the beginning of the twentieth century, Vienna was kind to middle-class men who wanted sexual convenience. Strict codes of morality were in force, but these applied largely to women and even in their case could be circumvented. Seduction was a game, carried on in closed carriages, small hotels, bachelor apartments and rooms in restaurants where couples could retire after dinner.

Men of means, usually older, had no difficulty finding hard-up shopgirls, seamstresses or actresses, usually younger. This was Arthur Schnitzler country, as in the story that features the humble Katharina ('Kleimann's glove shop, 24 Wilhelmstrasse'), who provides temporary comfort for the middle-aged hero, a physician, but who can't expect anything permanent since, after all, 'He had only one wish in the world, to be happy, and he would take happiness where it was offered him ...'

Middle-class sex-before-marriage between regular partners was less common then. Respectable young women feared pregnancy and scandal, and were often married young to men who were years, sometimes decades, older. Chastity was supposed to be as natural for single women as it was unnatural for single men. Sometimes women were available under a young man's roof, or his father's. Bourgeois homes had female servants who knew in advance that seduction was habitual and half-expected the young master to try it on.

Here is Freud, commenting on an account of 1907 by a patient (Ernst Lanzer, the 'Rat Man', then aged twenty-nine) of such an incident, involving a servant-girl who was 'neither young nor pretty ... He cannot think why, but he suddenly gave her a kiss and then attacked her. Though she no doubt made only a show of resistance, he came to his senses and fled to his room.' Freud was probably correct; the resistance wouldn't have amounted to much. It was said that clean, attractive young women were recruited as servants so that young sons could be safely initiated. Much the same was alleged in London.

When it came to straightforward, cash-on-the-table prostitution, Europe's cities were well provided for. An American researcher, Abraham Flexner, who visited Europe before the First World War to investigate prostitution, was pained to find that 'male continence has not been required by either tradition or opinion', though he considered Britain to be somewhat less depraved. He found Europe's great capitals proud to be known as sensual cities, while smaller places, Geneva for example, were 'smitten with envy' and tried desperately to be as wicked as Berlin or Vienna.

The Viennese found satisfaction in belonging to a city of pleasure which was also a place of culture and the heart of an empire. Sensuality papered over by propriety was characteristic of the times. London's West End teemed with brothels, tolerated by the police but not licensed because that would have been to condone their existence. Vienna, like most cities on the Continent, had a licensing system, though it covered only some of the street-walkers (Flexner thought that Vienna had 30,000 prostitutes, a wild guess). Their houses sometimes occupied the site of a medieval cemetery or a gallows, where for centuries no one had been keen to live. There was a haunting fear of syphilis among men; it was the one thing wrong with promiscuity.

Fornication thrived all the same. Serious scandal was unlikely, although adultery with a married woman might result in a duel (Schnitzler was nervous about duels). In occasional high-profile cases, where the State felt threatened or someone in high places sought revenge, a nasty outcome was possible. A countess, Louise von Coburg, who had an affair with an army lieutenant, was declared insane by Viennese psychiatrists, among them Krafft-Ebing, who had her locked up because that was what the government wanted; her dangerous symptoms included antipathy towards the count.

The journalist Karl Kraus defended her in 1904 as part of the satirical war he waged on the authorities in the magazine he owned and largely wrote, the *Torch*, where long essays fused evidence and fantasy to depict Vienna as the dark capital of a decaying Habsburg Empire, beset by false dreams and brutalised by hypocrisy. 'The

police and the military have a new function,' he wrote in the von
Coburg piece: 'to channel the sexual drives in new directions.'

Psychiatry came in for regular scorn in the *Torch*, but psychoanalysis was spared to begin with, Kraus and Freud each recognising virtues in the other since they both saw themselves as looking
for truths behind what was false and dishonest. Much of this
dishonesty (most of it, according to Freud) concerned sexual
behaviour. The first contact between the two men occurred when
Kraus was pursuing another scandal of 1904, the Hervay affair.
The marriage of a minor Austrian civil servant to an exotic Jewish
foreigner became public property after a whispering campaign in
newspapers ended in his suicide and her imprisonment for bigamy.

Edward Timms, the historian of Kraus and his circle, sees the
theme of Kraus's *Torch* articles about the affair as 'the collision
between two incompatible worlds – the provinciality of the unfortunate Hervay and the cosmopolitanism of his wife'. Freud sent
Kraus a note written on his visiting card, congratulating him for
perceiving 'the larger implications of a small affair'. A year later
Kraus wrote in the *Torch* of Freud's courage in arguing that
homosexuals were neither mad nor criminal. They were two of a
kind, although Kraus was concerned with society, Freud with the
inward view.

Freud's strange case of 'Dora', dating from 1900 but not
published until 1905, concerned certain private events in a wealthy
bourgeois family that might have interested Kraus, had they
formed part of a public scandal. As it was the events were of no
concern to the outside world. We know about them only because a
daughter was being troublesome and was taken to Freud to be
psychoanalysed.

Fragment of an Analysis of a Case of Hysteria was 50,000 words
long and is the only major psychoanalytic case-history of the five he
published to concern a woman. This reverses the emphasis of the
early, pre-analytic writing in *Studies on Hysteria*, where women
were the only subjects; perhaps Freud, whose women patients are
thought to have outnumbered men two to one – certainly in the
years before 1914 – was anxious not to be seen as a doctor
specialising in women, the less important sex.

Dora, real name Ida, was first taken to Berggasse 19 in the early
summer of 1898 by her father, Philip Bauer, a prosperous

industrialist in his late forties.* Bauer had consulted Freud a few years earlier – as a neurologist, not an analyst – and was treated for ominous symptoms that suggested a return of the syphilis he had contracted before marriage. Dora, born 1 November 1882 and so aged fifteen in summer 1898, had a history of headaches and loss of voice. When Freud saw her she was coughing and hoarse. He thought her hysterical and wanted to try psychoanalysis, but she refused, having been dragged from doctor to doctor already and given doses of hydrotherapy (the baths-and-hoses treatment) and electrotherapy.

Two years later she was worse. She became depressed and unfriendly to her father, declined to help her obsessively house-proud mother, Kathe, and began attending 'lectures for women', very likely on female emancipation. When her parents discovered the draft of a suicide note – left on her writing-desk where they would be sure to find it – they insisted she go to Freud for psychological treatment, and her reluctant analysis began in October 1900 shortly before her eighteenth birthday; this was when Freud told Fliess that her case had 'smoothly opened' to his picklocks.

Freud quickly learned things about the Bauers and the skeletons in their cupboard – he heard some of them from Bauer even before the analysis began – that an onlooker might have thought helped explain Dora's problems. The Bauers and their close friends, another Jewish couple, Hans and Peppina Zellenka (Freud disguises them as the 'Ks'), were like characters in a story about unhappy families written by a melancholy Russian, with Dora the white-faced heroine at the point where the plots and sub-plots, exclusively sexual, intersect. When Bauer had the syphilitic attack that took him to Freud, it was Mrs Zellenka who nursed him, not his wife, and they began a sexual affair, somewhat circumscribed by his state of health.

Dora, who was 'almost a mother' to the Zellenka children, knew about the affair. She had been close to Mrs Zellenka, sharing her marriage secrets, sleeping in the same bedroom with her (the husband was 'quartered elsewhere') and admiring, so she told Freud, the woman's 'adorable white body'. Peppina sounds as odd

* As usual, all identities were concealed in Freud's text. The Bauers were not named and their background explored until researchers tracked them down in the 1980s.

as Dora's mother, but that may be no more than Freud's way of describing women.

Most of these events took place in Merano, disguised as 'B——' in Freud's account, the Austrian resort in the south where Minna went in 1900. The Bauers had moved there because of Philip's health in 1888, and it was there that they met the Zellenkas. Hans was in business, too, but on a smaller scale. The affair between Philip Bauer and Peppina Zellenka had begun in 1894.

Two years later, probably in late spring 1896, Zellenka arranged things so that he was alone with Dora in his shop in the main street of Merano on the day of a church festival, ostensibly to see a procession go past. He seized and kissed her. Freud, reconstructing the event after Dora described it, decided that 'during the man's passionate embrace she felt not merely his kiss upon her lips but also the pressure of his erect member against her body'. Whatever she felt, Dora was disgusted and ran off. In Freud's account she was fourteen years old; in fact she was probably thirteen. His narrative consistently adds a year to her age, a deception simplified by her birthday falling late in the year.

Two years later, in summer 1898, when she was fifteen, Zellenka tried again. This time they were by an Alpine lake where the Zellenkas, Dora and her father were having a summer holiday. Zellenka 'made a proposal' to Dora, telling her that he could 'get nothing out of my wife'. She slapped his face and later told her mother, who told her father, who confronted Zellenka, who not only denied it but said that he had heard from his wife that Dora took an unhealthy interest in sex and had been reading a book called *The Physiology of Love*.

Bauer believed him, or he said he did. He thought his daughter was having sexual fantasies about Zellenka. When she became troublesome in 1900, Bauer told Freud that he considered her fantasies to be the reason for her 'depression and irritability and suicidal ideas'. (He, too, said, 'You know already that I can get nothing out of my own wife.') Freud's function was to stop Dora being such a nuisance.

Sub-plots can be discerned. At one time the Bauers employed a governess who tried to turn Dora against Mrs Zellenka, and who was suspected of being in love with Bauer. The Zellenkas also employed a governess and Hans Zellenka had succeeded in getting into bed with her shortly before he propositioned Dora by the lake.

The governess had told Dora about it, adding that part of Zellenka's wheedling was his general-purpose complaint that he 'got nothing from his wife'. Small wonder Dora slapped his face.

These tales of sexual entanglement made little impression on Freud as evidence in the case of his patient. He didn't doubt their reality, and indeed added to them by 'reconstruction'. Bauer's theory that his daughter was having fantasies about Zellenka was dismissed. Real kisses and no doubt real penises were involved, but Dora as a victim of conditions that confined and denatured young women was not entertained by Freud, any more than by most of his contemporaries; although Karl Kraus might have given it a thought.

Nor was unhappy family life on Freud's list. Unhappy families were a commonplace. Dora had the idea that she had been 'handed over to Herr K. as the price of his tolerating the relations between her father and his wife', but Freud gave no weight to such embittered feelings. She was simply a neurotic, an hysterical young woman whose fate was decided long ago, and not by Mr Zellenka's kisses.

The point of Freud's method was to explore that distant reality, using the art or craft of psychoanalysis. Freud once said that the *Case of Hysteria* was 'a scrupulous and "artistic" presentation'. 'Scrupulous' is questionable but no one could deny him 'artistic'. Nothing was real in the essay until it had gone through the artist's imagination and come out transfigured. The paper is a brilliant concoction of fact and surmise that transcends its subject. Freud dreams his way through Dora's life and finds the proofs that he needs, but the conclusions themselves are dreamlike, the statements, almost, of a fiction-writer who believes in the truths that the story embodies but who would argue that the real truth is the story itself.

Because Dora is a character in a story of a particular kind, Freud has no hesitation in being amazed at her conduct when faced with the predatory Zellenka. When he embraced her in the deserted shop – the assistants had gone, the girl was by the door to the staircase – her 'violent feeling of disgust' was unhealthy, according to Freud. A healthy girl would have felt sexual excitement, marked by a 'genital sensation'. The story called for evidence of hysterical behaviour, and here she was providing it. For a girl aged thirteen to feel disgusted by a kiss, not to mention Mr Zellenka's erect member which presumably should have made things even more enjoyable, was 'entirely and completely hysterical'. Perhaps this robust assumption owed something to a memory of Gisela Fluss. She too was thirteen when Freud was in love with her in Freiberg.

In the published account, 'fourteen' sounded better than 'thirteen'. It was the age of sexual consent in Vienna, and Freud wanted to avoid any hint of illegality on the part of respectable Zellenka. Thirteen was also the age of Freud's eldest child, Mathilde, in 1900; her thirteenth birthday was on 16 October, either just before or just after Dora's analysis began. Would Freud have expected Mathilde to enjoy pleasurable genital sensations when groped by a family friend? But Mathilde was his daughter, not a character in a book.

The essay plunges into Freud's first public account of a psychoanalysis in progress. In *Studies on Hysteria* in 1895 the method was still being invented and he had to keep sex under his hat in case it frightened Breuer and the doctors who sent him patients. By 1900 he was older and braver.

He came to Dora's nervous cough. Dora was telling him how Mrs Zellenka loved her father only because he was 'a man of means'. Freud decided that behind this phrase the opposite was concealed. Her father was 'a man without means'. That could mean only one thing, evidently sexual: he was impotent. Dora agreed with Freud that this was so.

How could a man who was impotent carry on a love affair with his mistress? They arrived, as Freud's inquiries often did, at oral sex, on which Dora was well-informed. The tickling throat and cough, he maintained, were unconscious products of Dora's fantasies of oral sex between the lovers; although whether and how the impotence permitted fellatio was not revealed.

Freud explained Dora to herself: the love she felt for Mr Zellenka (it was no use denying it); the oedipal love for her father that she summoned up from her childhood so that he could protect her against the consequences of loving Mr K.; the homosexual love she felt for Mrs Zellenka (the 'adorable white body' remark was a clue).

How very complicated it all was. Dora dreamt about a house on fire, her father at the bedside, a jewel-case that her mother wanted to save from the flames. Freud traced the dream to bed-wetting and Dora's genitals (the jewel-case), and infantile masturbation, which provoked micturition. The wish behind the dream was that her father should save her from the temptations of Mr Zellenka, as in childhood he had saved her from wetting the bed. Childhood masturbation, associated with the bed-wetting, with vaginal discharges and with self-disgust, was at the root of her hysteria. Freud wrote:

> If Dora felt unable to yield to her love for [Zellenka], if in the end she repressed that love instead of surrendering to it, there was no factor upon which her decision depended more directly than upon her premature sexual enjoyment and its consequence.

On 31 December 1900, Dora broke off the analysis. She shook hands with Freud, wished him a Happy New Year and left his consulting room for good.

Whatever truths he may or may not have uncovered, he had listened to what she had to say. Yet from her point of view, Freud was no less part of the oppressive world of men: paid for by her father, hired to stop her being troublesome, capable of telling her – as he did, in their last session, when she had already announced her departure – that she had seriously wished Zellenka to divorce his wife and marry her.

Generations of analysts saw the *Case of Hysteria* as gospel truth; Dora was unconvinced. Now her history is another museum-piece. Even at the time, Freud admitted that analysis didn't, and by its nature couldn't, provide comprehensive answers.

The case contained unsolved mysteries about Freud, in particular his feelings, if any, for its leading character (or its *other* leading character, since Freud himself was as much a participant in the story as Dora). 'Transference' between patient and analyst later came to be recognised as a process that cut both ways, but at first it was only the patient's emotional responses to the analyst that mattered. In the transference process that Freud was still learning to use at the time of Dora's analysis, patient endowed analyst with the qualities (good and bad) of figures from earlier relationships. Dora, he believed, saw him first as her father and later as Zellenka. But (he said) he failed to recognise this shift of feeling before it was too late to deflect her from her purpose of stopping the analysis and so revenging herself on the Zellenka-figure she saw in Freud.

The contrary process of counter-transference – his emotional attitude towards her – was not included in the story. She plainly irritated him, not least by walking out at the point when he believed (of course) that he was about to cure her. One did not expect to emerge unscathed, he wrote smoothly, when one conjured up and wrestled with 'the most evil of those half-tamed demons that inhabit the human breast'. But Freud's feelings for Dora were presumably as complex as hers for him. Erotic rustlings can be heard throughout the story. His sexual interrogation left no flesh unturned, and although the inquiry was pertinent to the subject, it is hard to see how a man could pursue it day after day with a young woman, reportedly attractive and undoubtedly keen on the subject, while remaining indifferent to sexual tensions between them.

Freud took care to meet general objections to his explicitness. He was aware of many physicians 'in this city, at least', who, 'revolting though it may seem', chose to read a case-history such as Dora's as 'a *roman à clef* designed for their private delectation'; perhaps he was thinking of Krafft-Ebing's histories, but these are colder and more mechanical, lacking the fullness of lives enhanced by a novelist's touch that makes Dora and her circle so vivid and so carnal.

In another passage Freud mounts a defence of his approach to such matters, insisting that his manner with Dora was 'dry and direct', that there was no question of titillation, that 'less repellent' sexual perversions were 'widely diffused among the whole population, as everyone knows except medical writers upon the subject'.

This strengthens rather than weakens the suspicion that Freud was more interested in Dora as a woman than he admitted to himself. Psychoanalysis came to take that sort of thing for granted. In Dora's case the ever-present sexuality gave an edge to the narrative, still perceptible, and may have helped her identify Freud as yet another of the men who made her life difficult. Did she have an inkling, when she walked away from him, that for all its ingenuities and flourishes, Freud's gripping yarn was just a yarn?

Freud kept track of her for a while. She revisited him more than a year later, in 1902, to say she felt better. During that time she had seen Mrs Zellenka and enjoyed a morsel of revenge by telling her she knew about the affair. At the end of 1903 she married a man nine years older, had a child, converted to Protestantism, slipped out of Freud's sight.

Her marriage was unhappy and she devoted herself to playing bridge. In the 1920s, aged forty, she consulted another analyst, Felix Deutsch, Freud's personal physician, who heard a tale of woe about men, sex and constipation. He also found her flirtatious. But Deutsch, as part of the inner circle, knew all the bad things about

Dora, the baddest of which was that she was the woman who had walked out on Freud. He quoted, in 1957, a remark by Freud that she was 'one of the most repulsive hysterics' he ever met, a last word that served as her epitaph until, late in the day, she was rehabilitated by feminists and Freudian revisionists.

One of Freud's grandchildren, Dr Sophie Freud (Martin's daughter, born 1924 and an American citizen), wrote in 1992, in language that would have bewildered her grandfather, how Dora's story was that of 'a promising, intelligent, Jewish middle-class woman who spent her developmental years in a dysfunctional family in misogynistic and anti-Semitic Vienna, emotionally defeated by the hostile environments that shaped her life'. At least Dora achieved one distinction: Freud never wrote another case-history like hers.

By the time her story appeared in 1905, Freud was beginning to define the kind of patients who interested him. They had to be intelligent and civilised: 'If the physician has to deal with a worthless character, he soon loses the interest which makes it possible for him to enter profoundly into the patient's mental life.' The unreliable and the poorly educated, 'good for nothing in life', were unsuitable cases for treatment. The implication was that patients should feel flattered to be accepted for analysis, a procedure that was not intended for the coarse and stupid, the same common crowd Freud shrank from decades earlier when he wrote to Martha about the 'thick skins and easy-going ways' of the mob at Wandsbek Fair.

His Wednesday colleagues were told (1906) that two categories of people were largely free of neurosis, proletarians and princes. After the First World War, everyone had to have second thoughts when it became clear that these had been merely the categories that didn't seek treatment. Psychoanalysis, however, continued to be favoured by the educated, the civilised and the better-off. Already, by 1904, a proper course of treatment was expected to last 'six months to three years'. It was not for the faint-hearted or the hard-up; brain surgery was cheaper. Unlike the democratic Alfred Adler, who sat on one side of him at the Wednesday meetings (Stekel sat on the other), Freud had no vocabulary for talking to tram-drivers and street-sweepers, and would have thought it impracticable to try.

He set himself apart, and created a psychotherapy to match, although trying to pin him down to his own prescriptions is never rewarding. Among the demanding bourgeois clients whose shadows, at least, can be seen flitting across the pavement outside his apartment, there are gentler cases. A psychology student from Switzerland, Bruno Goetz, suffering from headaches and eye trouble, was sent to him around 1905 by his professor, who made sure that Freud read some of the student's poems first. Goetz, later a writer, found himself talking freely and being told, 'Now, my student Goetz, I won't analyse you. You can live happily with your complexes.' Freud gave him a prescription for his eyes, asked when he last ate a steak, and sent him off with an envelope containing 'a small fee for the joy you have brought me with your poems and the story of your youth'. When he got to his room, Goetz found 200 crowns and burst into tears. The money would have taken Freud several hours of analytic time to earn. Reminders of his youth were a fair exchange.

More often he could be seen emphasising how serious his cases were. Psychoanalysis, he wrote, was created 'for the treatment of patients permanently unfit for existence'. He even insisted (1905) that so far he had used psychoanalysis only on 'the severest cases', and that all his earlier patients had 'spent long years in sanatoria'. This can't have been true (had Emma Eckstein been hospitalised for years?), but it was necessary that he dwell on the unhappiness waiting to be conquered, and on his ability to succeed where all others, and especially orthodox psychiatrists, kept failing. With his colleagues he was more subtle now, telling a Vienna medical meeting in December 1904 that 'we physicians' all practised psychotherapy of one sort or another, and could do nothing else, since it was what patients demanded.

His place on the Vienna scene had edged towards prominence, even notoriety. Austrian and German psychiatrists queued up to condemn him. W. Spielmeyer was sarcastic about Dora. A. A. Friedlander, reviewing the *Case of Hysteria*, spoke of 'a growth of jungle weeds of peculiar fantasy choking his intellectual work'. Sex, at the root of Freud's theories, was at the root of the objections. His critics could recognise a bizarre flight of fancy when they saw one, as his critics still can, but their underlying distaste was cultural: they were the voice of the old century, which thought sexual behaviour irrelevant to serious medicine, and they found it offensive that Freud's vision darkened what they saw as the traditional image of man, making him irrational and liable to be dictated to by the private urges that gentlemen didn't talk about and ladies shouldn't even consider.

This attitude was doomed with or without a Freud. Sexuality of one sort or another was prominent in the work of Krafft-Ebing and Moritz Benedikt in Vienna, Fliess in Berlin, Havelock Ellis in England, and many more. Ellis, a non-practising doctor who drew his material from books and personal experience, not from patients, was the first English author to be readable and sane on the subject. He published the opening volume of his heroic *Studies in the Psychology of Sex* in Germany in 1895; it was at the printers in Leipzig when Freud and Breuer's *Studies on Hysteria* appeared. Volume 1 was about homosexuality, an untouchable subject in London, the capital of European prudery, then as now, which is why it first appeared in German. After it was published in English in 1897 (by a German pornographer, who set up a fake university press in England to disguise his intentions), it was prosecuted, and remained a forbidden book for years.

Some of Freud's writing, 'Dora' for example, might have gone the same way had it been translated at that early stage. The *British Medical Journal*'s reviewer had no hesitation in calling Krafft-Ebing's work 'nauseous' in 1902 and advising doctors not to read it. But in the end even the British realised that Ellis, Krafft-Ebing, Freud and Co. were marching with events, not initiating them.

Increasingly certain of his cause, Freud was not thick-skinned. He never forgot a bad review, an unkind word, a professorial snigger. Now a professor in his own right, he continued to lecture to students and postgraduates, spreading the word to Saturday-evening audiences that were measured in dozens and were sometimes not into double figures, but helped send shock-waves through the system. The thought that students might be hoping for scatology distressed him. 'If you have come to hear the sensational or the lewd,' he is supposed to have said, 'rest assured I shall see your efforts aren't worth the trouble.'

His shoulders had the teacher's stoop, his voice was firm though not resonant, his manner conversational, his notes few or non-existent. Asked how he planned his lectures, he was heard to say, 'I leave it to my unconscious.' He always had stories and asides to break up the narrative. Pointing out that some psychologists refused to accept his concept of the unconscious, the 'primary process' that underlaid the 'secondary process' of consciousness, he said it reminded him of the giant in Ariosto's poem who had his head cut off in a battle but was too busy to notice it and went on fighting. 'We cannot help thinking,' said Freud, 'that the old psychology has been killed by my dream doctrine. But it is unaware of the fact, and goes on teaching as usual.'

A winter evening, the frosty air smelling of coal-smoke and wood-smoke; curtains drawn in the apartments of Alsergrund, the 9th District, where Freud has taken a carriage for the short journey from Berggasse to the Allgemeine Krankenhaus, the General Hospital, to lecture in the old psychiatric clinic. Nearby is the Narrenturm, the 'Fools' Tower', where the mad were chained to the walls before Freud's time, whips and straitjackets always to hand. Fanny Moser, the 'Emmy' of *Studies on Hysteria*, had fantasies of madhouses where inmates were drenched in cold water and locked into apparatus that whirled them round till they were quiet. Ten years later the mentally ill were still as much of a mystery as ever, which is why they generated so much fury among psychiatrists. The Fools' Tower was deserted; Vienna's proletarian mad had moved on to new quarters outside the city limits, where they continued to be locked up and forgotten.

A few people turn in from the streets alongside the hospital and find the clinic's lecture hall. It is lit by bulbs dangling above the lecturer's table, leaving the tiered benches in the shadows, most of them empty. Freud is not insulted by the small turn-out, or if he is, he keeps it to himself. He suggests his handful of listeners concentrates itself in front of him, in the light, and his two-hour lecture gets under way.

Hanns Sachs, a young lawyer, later a confidant and an analyst himself, first saw Freud there at the Saturday lectures, drawn to him, as others were, by reading *The Interpretation of Dreams*. He heard affectionate tales of Liébeault and Charcot. Dreams and neuroses were expounded; Sachs found him prophetic, but without the pretentiousness of a prophet. When Freud wanted to make a point about the oblique methods of psychoanalysis, he waved a comic postcard of a yokel in a hotel bedroom, trying to blow out the electric light as if it were a candle. 'If you attack the symptom directly,' said Freud, 'you act in the same way as he does. You must look for the switch.'

Freud, for most people, meant controversy. However hard he

sought to appear as the plain scientist and purveyor of truth, heads shook and tongues wagged. In 1904 he was involved in the Weininger affair, a small scandal involving plagiarism, memory and the friend who had failed, Wilhelm Fliess. For a moment Freud is caught off-balance, not quite master of himself.

Otto Weininger was a deranged young philosopher (born 1880), mild-eyed behind rimless glasses, a pessimist with a blighted view of women and Jews, who published a clever, dangerous book called *Sex and Character* in 1903. Vienna was scandalised and delighted by it, especially when Weininger shot himself soon after in the house where Beethoven died.

Clearly a genius with problems, Weininger condemned sexual intercourse as loathsome and wanted humanity to give it up. Women and Jews were both tainted with the 'feminine principle', which undermined the 'male principle' in men and Aryans. Bisexuality was examined at length, Weininger using algebraic formulas to demonstrate the potency of the 'male' and 'female' substances that were present in everyone, in varying proportions. A 'law of bisexual complementarity' was supposed to explain sexual attraction by drawing a man with twenty-five per cent femininity to a woman with seventy-five per cent of it, and so on. This was Fliessian territory. The jewel in his theoretical crown, the 'periodic law' of twenty-eight days for women and twenty-three days for men, rested on bisexuality.

In summer 1904 the book and its alarming contents came to Fliess's notice. He knew, or found out, that Weininger had been a close friend of a young Vienna psychologist, Hermann Swoboda. Swoboda knew Freud; Fliess smelt conspiracy.

Fliess was visiting Vienna at the time. Freud had already left for summer in the mountains, but even had he been at Berggasse, it is unlikely that either man would have wanted to meet the other face to face. They wrote distressed letters instead.

Fliess began (20 July) by describing his 'consternation' at finding in *Sex and Character* his ideas about bisexuality and the consequent nature of sexual attraction, that 'feminine men attract masculine women and vice-versa'. He had 'no doubt that Weininger obtained knowledge of my ideas via you', and sought a 'frank reply'.

Frankness was more than Freud could manage at first. Bisexuality had been contentious once before. When they had met for what turned out to be the last time, at Achensee in 1900, he had remarked that in order to solve the problems of the neuroses, one had to assume that to begin with we are all bisexual. Wilhelm at once pointed out that it was he who had told Sigmund this, a couple of years earlier when they were at Breslau. At the time Sigmund had brushed it aside, saying he wasn't inclined to consider it. In 1900, however, he was proposing the idea as his own.

Freud admitted this convenient forgetting. He even wrote about it, without identifying Fliess by name, in *The Psychopathology of Everyday Life*, describing his lapse as part of the 'universal' tendency to 'forget what is disagreeable'.

Now, three days after Fliess wrote from his hotel in Vienna, Freud replied from the mountains to say that all Swoboda could have learned from him about bisexuality was what anyone having psychoanalysis learned, that 'a strong homosexual current is found in every neurotic'. He added, 'I did not read [Weininger's] book before its publication': an odd disclaimer, since Fliess had not suggested otherwise.

As soon as he read Sigmund's denial, Wilhelm was able to strike:

> So what Oscar Rie [his brother-in-law in Vienna] told me in all innocence when I mentioned Weininger was incorrect: he said that Weininger went to you with his manuscript and you, after looking at it, advised him against publication because the content was nonsense. I believe that in this case you should have called his attention and mine to the 'burglary'.

Freud responded (27 July) with a mixture of apology and belligerence. It was true, he said, he had seen Weininger's manuscript.

> I must have regretted at the time that via Swoboda, as I already knew, I had handed over your idea to him. In conjunction with my own attempt to rob you of your originality, I better understand my behaviour toward Weininger and my subsequent forgetting.

His unconscious had let him down again, interfering with his memory. It was almost as if Sigmund wanted to put himself at Wilhelm's mercy, his unconscious creating for him a situation where he would have to re-confess to this further and grosser parapraxis: a pitiful gesture that might – who can tell what he was thinking? – touch the sympathy of the former friend whose affection a part of him may still have craved.

The letter of 27 July was inclined to ramble. Having admitted his error, Freud suggested that the harm done by Weininger was slight. Then he snapped at Fliess.

It is not my fault ... if you find the time and the inclination to exchange letters with me again only on the occasion of such petty incidents. The fact is that in the past few years – 'Everyday Life' is the dividing line – you have no longer shown an interest in me or my family or my work. By now I have got over it and have little desire for it any longer; I am not reproaching you and ask you not to reply to this point.

Apparently Fliess did not reply, to that or any point. After seventeen years the correspondence was over.

In 1906 a librarian friend of Fliess published an attack on Swoboda and Weininger, indicting Freud as the go-between. Swoboda threatened to sue; newspapers took an interest. Freud tried to solicit Karl Kraus's support in the *Torch* but otherwise kept his head down and waited for the row to go away, which in the end it did. No doubt both men felt betrayed, and the severance didn't leave Freud unmarked. Over the years he told everyone who would listen that Fliess suffered from paranoia. But Fliess returned to him in dreams as well.

Controversy about something that mattered more accompanied the *Three Essays on Sexuality*, completed in 1904 and published the following year. Freud's views on the sexual origins of neurosis, developed since the 1890s, were at last brought together under one roof. He ranked the book with *The Interpretation of Dreams* and revised it constantly. Its disturbing essays, much reviled to begin with, helped change Western ideas about sexual behaviour. Childhood innocence, in the sense that most people understood it, was summarily dismissed.

Little evidence was presented. Freud drew on information from contemporary observers, among them Krafft-Ebing, Havelock Ellis and Magnus Hirschfeld.* His own self-analysis and his work with patients, few if any of whom were children, played an unquantifiable part. But it is not a clinical study. It is Freud imagining a scenario: that from the cradle, sexual drives are pointing us towards our destinies. Some of his broad statements, outrageous when he made them, are now commonplace; others have become

---

* Magnus Hirschfeld (1868–1935), German sexologist, an acquaintance of Freud, who tolerated him but found him 'unappetising'. Hirschfeld founded and ran an 'Institute for Sexual Science' in Berlin until it was closed down by clean-living Nazis when they came to power in 1933.

historical curiosities. Women, the half of humanity that Freud had trouble coping with, were treated grudgingly. Their nature was secretive and insincere, their erotic life 'veiled in an impenetrable obscurity'; one might ask how he managed to treat so many of them.

The broad subversive sweep of the essays left their mark. The first, a survey of adult 'sexual aberrations', suggested that what the world sees as perversion is no more than the inclinations of a normal infant that have persisted into adult life. This was unwelcome news to sexual moralists and a step towards the utopian goal of freeing people from guilt about their behaviour. The distinction between 'normal' and 'perverted' became blurred under Freud's scrutiny. Homosexuals were not 'degenerate'. Their sexual instinct had taken a particular path, perhaps a variant of the bisexual disposition common to all; he didn't pretend to be certain. Again, contact between the lips of one person and the genitals of another was regarded as a perversion. Yet two people bringing together the mucous membrane of the lips (not part of the sexual apparatus at all, remarked Freud, but 'the entrance to the digestive tract') was highly thought of. So here was 'a point of contact between the perversions and normal sexual life'.

Freud saw a common structure in all erotic behaviour, treating it as part of the human condition, and this dispassionate surveying of the territory gave him the right to be seen as a herald of new attitudes. The small print of *Three Essays* doesn't need to have survived unchallenged, or even to be studied any longer, for the work's authority to be understood. Havelock Ellis acknowledged Freud's priority in the business of calling a spade a spade. Freud, he said, described sexual behaviour without apology and as a matter of course, a thing never done before in medical literature.

The second and third essays dealt with infantile sexuality and the changes of puberty. 'Sex', to a small child, was at first the sensory pleasure to be had from any part of its skin; the genitals came later. This private world of auto-erotic, eventually masturbatory pleasure was then forgotten in the débâcle of infantile amnesia, 'which turns everyone's childhood into something like a prehistoric epoch and conceals from him the beginnings of his own sexual life'.

The speculations were piled high. Adolescence revived the forgotten fantasies of infancy, as the individual came to sexual maturity. At that point the child's oedipal fantasies of love for one parent and jealous hatred for the other might stir in the unconscious. If the individual failed to outgrow these fantasies, the result could be serious neurosis. In garbled form, some of this has long since been diluted into popular psychology: men marry women who remind them of their mothers.

In passing, Freud reluctantly began to change his mind in public about the significance and extent of child seduction. He had taken his time over it. Despite having abandoned the theory in private less than two years after he announced it, he did nothing between September 1897, when the scales fell from his eyes, and the *Three Essays* in 1905. Even then, all he did was concede that he had 'overrated the importance of seduction in comparison with the factors of sexual constitution and development'. He flatly denied that he had 'exaggerated the frequency or importance' of seduction.

This was obfuscation. A year later, in a paper on 'Sexuality in the Neuroses', he admitted what he had denied in 1905, saying that he had 'over-estimated the frequency of such events'. He also made an explicit connection, at last, with the fantasising that lay behind the patients' stories of seduction, explaining that they had misled him by making unconscious use of fantasies to cover up memories of their own infantile masturbation, and that he had taken fantasy to refer to real events. It had taken him nine years to make himself say in print what he had written to Fliess on 21 September 1897, that the seduction theory was untenable.

At first *Three Essays* was widely ignored by medical reviewers, which didn't stop psychiatrists being unkind about it among themselves. Kraus, whose disenchantment with psychoanalysis had not begun, sent his review copy to a novelist, Otto Soyka, who praised it in the *Torch* but gave signs of bafflement, describing it as 'the first comprehensive explanation of the pure physics of love'. Its original edition of 1,000 copies took four years to sell. Freud was paid the modern equivalent of about £300.

A remark at the end of *Three Essays* spoke of the relationship between civilisation and 'the free development of sexuality', and suggested that the one could prosper only at the expense of the other. This was a theme to which Freud returned obsessively over the years, pondering the ill-effects for the individual if he led a sex life that was restricted, and for society if he led a sex life that was not.

Freud himself wavered in his conclusions. Some of the bold spirits who were soon being tempted by psychoanalysis had fewer scruples or coarser appetites. In a broad sense, the sexual basis of psychoanalysis is what commended it to many people more or less sight-unseen because it reflected their own priorities. This didn't make them sexual predators any more than it made Freud one, but it had a special appeal for those with predatory tendencies.

A hint of sexual licence can be assumed to have attracted analysts who were that way inclined, who hoped that the process of erotic transference, or merely the physical proximity and the nature of the subjects being discussed, made female patients susceptible. Such things were rarely mentioned, but they helped give psychoanalysis its flavour in those early days, spicy and dangerous.

18: Dr Joy and Dr Young

The day that Freud met Jung is not a date in the psychoanalytic calendar; it has too many cruel associations, though at the time it was a happy occasion and a sign of progress. The union of Drs 'Joy' and 'Young' seemed full of promise when they met in Vienna on the morning of Sunday, 3 March 1907.

Dr C. G. (Carl Gustav) Jung, a Swiss psychiatrist of thirty-one, had admired Freud (now aged fifty) from a distance for the past year. He and his wife Emma, who was twenty-five, an industrialist's daughter with money, had arrived in Vienna the previous evening after travelling all day by train from Zürich. With them was one of Jung's pupils, an agreeable young doctor called Ludwig Binswanger, son of the Robert Binswanger who ran the Bellevue Clinic.

The visit was originally scheduled for Easter, at the end of March, when Freud would have had more time to spare from his patients. To his annoyance, Jung changed the arrangements at short notice to fit in with his plans for a visit to Budapest followed by a holiday on the Adriatic. Their first meeting was thus arranged to suit the acolyte, not the master.

The relationship was shaped by Freud's need of someone like Jung, as he indicated in an early letter. The confidence he expressed one minute ('the future belongs to us and our views, and the younger men') was tempered the next by his feelings about cut-throat Vienna, 'where, as you know, I am systematically ignored by my colleagues and periodically annihilated by some hack'. Freud had made up his mind before they met, on the basis of their correspondence (which was initiated by Jung) over the preceding eleven months: 'I know . . . of none who is able and willing to do so much for the cause as you.'

Jung left his hotel after breakfast and went to Berggasse and the shabby building at No. 19, where Siegmund the butcher was still in business in the shop by the front door, and replastering work was in progress on the stairs. He was there by ten o'clock and stayed all day, Freud letting him do most of the talking to begin with.

Jung was a physically dominating man, wide-shouldered with a fleshy face, standing six feet two inches tall, so that Freud, at five feet seven, would have been looking at his visitor's chin. A Protestant from a family of pastors, Jung was religious in a broad sense, a Christian mystic as it turned out, although this side of him was in recession during the Freud years. His style was blunt and intimidatory. If Freud used the art of nuance, Jung preferred a pick and shovel; he was the kind of man who spoke his mind, and used directness as a strategy. 'My wife is rich,' he wrote to Freud a few months earlier, to help explain a dream. Once, describing his annual spell of service as a medical officer with the Swiss Army (which he revelled in), he told Freud how instructive it had been to inspect the penises of 500 soldiers. Freud did nothing like that in the Austrian Army, or if he did he kept quiet about it. In their personal lives, Freud was circumspect where Jung had a streak of recklessness. When Freud wanted to be bold and explicit he wrote a book; Jung's cloudier writing didn't express the man in the same way.

The centre of Swiss psychiatry was a State-run mental hospital on the edge of Zürich, the Burghölzli, which came under the wing of the university and was run for investigation and therapy, not as a lock-up for forgotten patients. It has been called a 'monastery' (for its doctors) and a 'factory' (for its inmates). Jung had been on the staff since 1900 and learned to develop relationships with his patients, working-class psychotics, many of them severely disturbed, as opposed to Freud's bourgeois neurotics. Jung believed in trying to communicate with his patients whatever their mental state, and Freud's ideas on psychotherapy found more fertile ground in Zürich than in Vienna.

The Burghölzli's director, Eugen Bleuler (who invented the term 'schizophrenia'), was advising his staff to read *The Interpretation of Dreams* in 1900, and Jung was one of those who did. What he read about repression and the other concepts of psychoanalysis became more relevant when he began to make the long series of word-association experiments at the Burghölzli, published from 1904 onwards, on which his early reputation was based.* The experiments complemented and helped explain the workings of the free association method that Freud had developed by trial and error. They also gave Freud the best of reasons for looking favourably on this newcomer who had approached psychoanalysis from a different direction and ended up endorsing it.

Before they talked that Sunday in Freud's study they had exchanged eighteen letters, beginning with a note from Freud the previous April acknowledging some papers that Jung had sent him about the word-association work. In the first of Jung's letters, 5 October 1906, he managed to express a reservation about Freud's sexual theory, and thus about the basis of Freudian belief. From the start he was an odd sort of acolyte. Having remarked that the effect of psychoanalytic therapy lay partly in 'certain personal rapports', an unexceptional statement, Jung went on to suggest that 'though the genesis of hysteria is predominantly, it is not exclusively, sexual'. The same heresy appeared in a further letter, where Jung suggested that 'the other basic drive, *hunger*', might also play a part in neurosis. 'One feels alarmed by the positivism of your presentation,' he added.

The two then seem to have reached an implied agreement to attribute Jung's doubts to his inexperience. 'I am delighted with your promise to trust me for the present in matters where your experience does not yet enable you to make up your own mind,' wrote Freud, and this conspiracy must have been the basis of their conversations in Vienna. Now and then Freud slipped in a gentle reminder. 'The ancients knew how inexorable a god Eros is,' he wrote on 1 January 1907, a time of year that was apt to make him magisterial.

Jung retained his doubts. 'I could not decide,' he wrote in his memoirs, 'to what extent this strong emphasis upon sexuality was connected with subjective prejudices of his, and to what extent it rested upon verifiable experiences.' But that was written long afterwards, in his eighties, and whether he thought much about Freud's 'subjective prejudices' at the time, if he thought about them at all, is doubtful. They got on, which suggests a degree of authority on Freud's part matched by a degree of deference on his visitor's.

---

* Words are read out to the subject, who responds with the first word that occurs to him. A stop-watch times any delay, which usually indicates an unconscious conflict, the 'repression' that Jung observed. Refinements included measuring skin changes, the principle that led to lie-detector machines.

Freud asserted that authority later in the week when, having by now met Binswanger, he asked the two men to tell him their dreams. Binswanger obliged with a dream about the entrance to Berggasse 19, complete with building works and a decrepit chandelier that the workmen had covered with a piece of cloth. Ah, said Freud, the dream indicated a wish to marry his eldest daughter, Mathilde. But, he added, the dream also repudiated the wish, since 'You won't marry into a house with such a shabby chandelier.'

Binswanger was sceptical but too polite to say so. Getting Mathilde married sounds more like Freud's wish than the visitor's. She was nineteen years old, an obedient young woman with a history of illness, and her father was anxious she should find a husband, at one point eyeing a Hungarian psychiatrist with favour, and reassuring her about her prospects in a friendly letter that said beauty wasn't everything.

After Binswanger's dream it was Jung's turn. Jung dreamt that Freud was walking beside him as 'a very, very frail old man'. Freud said it meant that Jung saw him as a rival. Evidently he didn't feel threatened, viewing Jung not as a heretic but rather as a young man of talents who would come to use them in a way that his mentor approved of.

Old age had been on Freud's mind for a decade, and now that he had reached his fifties, he heard it shuffling nearer. The previous August, 1906, walking up an inhospitable mountain in the Tyrol near the Austrian–Italian border with his sixteen-year-old son Martin, he collapsed with heatstroke and had to abandon the climb; after that he gave up mountain excursions.*

On his next birthday in May 1907, two months away, he would be fifty-one, a prospect that had made him uneasy for years. A man would do well to make plans, and here came this capable Dr Jung, already contemplating psychological revolution on Freudian lines in a distant city. More than one biographer, including Jones, has remarked that Freud was no judge of other people's character. A cannier man-of-the-world (like Dr Jones himself, now hovering in

---

* Father and son were in the Trent–Lake Garda area, where Freud and Minna had drifted in 1900, 'luxuriating without regrets'. The nearby Castel Toblino, on a lake, one of the places they lingered at, is mentioned in Martin's account of the 1906 incident, which quotes his father on its 'dreamlike beauty'. Perhaps it was heatstroke compounded by emotional stress.

the wings, waiting to make his cocksure entrance) would have wanted to know more about Jung's credentials.

Whatever else they talked about that week, it isn't likely that Jung touched on the dreams and visions that accompanied his upbringing as the son of a rural clergyman who preached to peasant congregations. Jung's maternal family claimed to have second sight; his grandfather on that side, a theologian, was said to have kept a chair for the ghost of his first wife who visited him weekly for conversations, to the dismay of the second.

A lonely child, with no siblings until a sister arrived when he was nine, Carl incorporated a world of fables and fairy stories into his existence, or incorporated himself into them. The evidence comes from his memoirs and remains equivocal, like many things about his life.

Aged three he dreamt of a giant penis on a throne in a room below the earth, his initiation (he decided, long afterwards) into the dark side of human experience. As an older child he had difficulties with reality. If he thought about a stone, was the stone also thinking about him? He saw a luminous figure emerge from his mother's bedroom and produce floating heads. Unwell and afraid of choking, he was comforted by a glowing blue circle in the air filled with golden angels.

At the age of nine he carved a small figure of a man from a wooden ruler and concealed it in the attic along with a magic stone painted in two halves. He took it tiny scrolls of paper containing messages written in a secret language: 'a little cloaked god of the ancient world', he thought when he grew up, belonging among the layers of mythological reference that filled his imagination. Like Freud, he saw archaeology as a metaphor for the buried past of the individual, but in Jung's case the past was not a narrow experience of the self but amounted to a visionary pageant, a universal experience of culture and religion that was inherited and shared by humanity.

These were later insights, not developed when Jung met Freud. But to Jung the events that foreshadowed them were important from the start. At high school he developed the idea, which persisted all his life, that he had two personalities, the 'ordinary' Jung and a more romantic figure, perpetually old and wise.

Phenomena were not dismissed because they seemed unusual. As a medical student at Basel, he formed a group of table-rapping spiritualists, where a girl cousin of his (who fell in love with him) functioned as a medium, claiming that the dead spoke through her; one of her guiding spirits was the grandfather who had talked with his departed wife. Jung didn't believe in disembodied spirits, and saw what happened at the seances as projections of the unconscious. A similar process (presumably involving his own unconscious) caused a walnut table at his home to split with 'a report like a pistol shot', and a bread knife to break in pieces in a cupboard. His medical dissertation, 'On the Psychology and Pathology of So-called Occult Phenomena' (1902), was based on the Basel seances and the 'psychological realities' that the events represented.

For the moment Jung subsumed all this in a seemingly orthodox career as a university doctor, and this was still the situation when he met Freud. In Vienna Freud's reputation was tainted, and a rising young psychiatrist would think twice before embracing psychoanalysis; his followers were clever eccentrics, outsiders by nature, not part of the university mainstream. In Zürich, however, he had the authority of being a professor from somewhere else. Jung fell into step with him; but he kept part of himself uncommitted.

On the first Wednesday in April, the visitors were introduced to the weekly meeting in Freud's apartment. The circle was still small. Adler presented a case. Freud read a paper. The guests said little, but one of the group, Dr Max Graf – not a physician but a music critic, whose wife had been analysed by Freud – later recalled their host's enthusiasm for Jung. The men from Zürich were the first non-Jews to attend a Wednesday meeting.

They were not the first visitors from Zürich, a wealthy young Russian Jew, Max Eitingon, an assistant at the Burghölzli, having appeared earlier in the year. He come from Professor Bleuler with a list of questions including some about the sexual implications of psychoanalysis. Upright Swiss Protestants wanted to be reassured.

Jung himself was not impressed with the Viennese analysts, apart from Freud. In Zürich he was heard to say they were degenerates, mediocrities and bohemians, which may have meant they tended towards cloaks and broad-brimmed hats. Was it the stuffy smoke-laden room where they met, the alcohol on someone's breath (Jung was teetotal like his boss Bleuler), the Viennese ribaldry from Fritz Wittels? There is a hint of something athletic and outgoing about Jung, a countryman, needing space to move about in.

Jung was not the only critic. After the meeting, Binswanger was disconcerted when Freud took him aside and said, 'Well, now you've seen the gang.' The visitor thought Freud was disparaging them, and probably he was. The gang were too familiar, too Viennese. Freud saw them as his fractious children, and to begin with they obliged by playing their part: a close-knit group with a weakness for quarrels, but respecting his authority.

By 1908 there were twenty-two members. More than half the group lived near Berggasse, either in the 9th District itself or in the adjoining 1st District, the inner city, the parts of Vienna favoured by middle-class Jews. Most had begun to practise psychoanalysis, and to begin with they were uncomfortably dependent on Freud for their patients. They learnt as they went along; the 'training analysis' for novices, later thought to be indispensable, was yet to be invented by Jung. Max Eitingon went for evening walks with Freud on visits to Vienna, and received bursts of instant analysis as they strode along the Ring or out towards Grinzing. In the Vienna circle itself, only Stekel seems to have had a formal analysis, when Freud treated his 'troublesome complaint' in 1901.

The more they deferred to Freud, the more inclined they were to squabble among themselves. They were men attracted by new ideas, new sources of income and in some cases by sexual opportunity. Isidor Sadger, a Galician Jew whose father was a banker, presented wearying papers, what Freud called 'the interminable flow of Sadger's rubbish', and was rumoured to behave improperly with women patients. Stekel, who had a typewriter on his desk and wrote up cases in his lunch-hour, was so quick to find examples from his files to fit whatever was being discussed at meetings that they were derided as 'Stekel's Wednesday patients' and assumed to be fictitious. Smartly dressed and fond of women, he was quoted by Freud in the 1907 edition of *Everyday Life*, with an example of an act performed accidentally-on-purpose: in greeting a woman whose house he visited, Stekel said that without any conscious intent he extended his hand in such a way that 'I contrived in doing so to undo the bow that held her loose morning-gown together ... with the dexterity of a conjurer.' Stekel – intuitive, amusing and never quite trusted – became a trial to Freud after a few years.

The same was true of Fritz Wittels, a nephew of Sadger, a young doctor-in-training who was invited to join the circle just before Jung's visit, after writing an article about birth control for the *Torch* that appealed to Freud. Wittels put much of his energy into partnering women and writing about them, in particular a promiscuous dumb brunette (Wittels' words, more or less) aged seventeen with whom he fell in love, Irma Karczewska. He made her the basis of a paper about uninhibited female sexuality, 'The Great Courtesan', which he read to the Wednesday meeting in May 1907. Another version was published as 'The Child Woman' in the *Torch* by Karl Kraus. Kraus, too, was Irma's lover.

Promiscuity on his doorstep wasn't welcomed by Freud. He advised Wittels, who was only twenty-six, to be more prudent. Psychoanalysis was not supposed to free people from their inhibitions. On the contrary, Freud said, he wanted to teach them to get the better of their baser instincts, not give in to them. Wittels wrote:

> He was not happy about the influence of the editor of the *Torch* on me. We had developed, he said, strange blind spots for the cultural forces to which civilised men have to yield.

Freud's views were more equivocal than that. He hankered after a society free from harmful inhibitions, and once told a Wednesday meeting of the need for 'an academy of love where the erotic arts would be taught', as in ancient times; the minutes don't say if he was joking. A paper he published early in 1908 spelt out the price of sexual morality. Unsatisfied sexual needs led to neurosis, either by producing toxic substances (the 'Actual Neurosis' syndrome) or by troubling the unconscious with repressed desires. Civilisation was built on the suppression of instincts, as each individual surrendered 'some part of the sense of omnipotence or of the aggressive or vindictive inclinations in his personality'. The sexual instinct was central to this suppression – unfortunately so, since most people 'would have been more healthy if it could have been possible for them to be less good'. Only rare individuals were able to 'sublimate' their feelings, deflecting them to 'higher cultural aims'. Freud evidently convinced himself that he was one of them.* The essay is

---

* The essay, ' "Civilised" Sexual Morality and Modern Nervous Illness', refers bitterly to the constraints that marriage imposes on sexual freedom. 'Satisfying sexual intercourse' occurs only for a few years, after which the marriage 'becomes a

a period piece, a bleak account of mankind struggling with sexual desire before the enlightenments (patchy as they were) of the twentieth century made us slightly more tolerant.

In the eyes of his contemporaries, who ignored the cautions and caveats, Freud was proposing sexual revolution, and Wittels, keen on women and pleased to think he was being progressive as well as libidinous, was easily convinced. One of his early encounters with Freud was at a lecture to medical students where sexual abstinence before marriage was discussed as a means of preventing syphilis. According to Wittels, Freud said he couldn't believe that nature had endowed man with sex organs for the purpose of not using them. If it was necessary to abstain in order to avoid disease, then they should do so, but 'abstain under protest'. This, said Wittels, was taken by his critics as an injunction to students to 'proceed straightaway to the whorehouse'.

If Stekel and Wittels were colourful disciples, some were grey and well-behaved. Paul Federn, who joined in 1903, was sober, serious and loyal, though never a favourite of Freud's. It was Federn who decided, when Mathilde Freud married in 1909, to commission a painting of her father as a wedding present. Either Freud was without a beard at the time (he had a brief beardless phase in 1908 or 1909, but afterwards the family could never agree when and how this came about) or he was painted beardless as a joke by the artist, Maximilian Oppenheimer, best known as the cartoonist 'Mopp'. The clean-shaven Freud was presented to Mathilde at Berggasse 19 shortly before she married Robert Hollitscher. She hated it at sight; a beard was part of Freud's authority. A dressing-table set was hastily substituted, and the painting sent back to Federn; who is said to have fired a pistol-shot at it more than forty years later, a few seconds before he turned the gun on himself and committed suicide.

Among the other unflashy members whom Jung and Binswanger met in 1907 was the secretary who kept the minutes, Otto Rank, a clever artisan in his mid-twenties who had taught himself some

---

failure in so far as it has promised the satisfaction of sexual needs. For all the devices hitherto invented for preventing conception impair sexual enjoyment, hurt the fine susceptibilities of both partners and even actually cause illness.' Thus disillusionment and deprivation puts the partners back where they started, 'except for being the poorer by the loss of an illusion'. Freud is mourning the loss of his own illusions.

psychology and was rescued by Freud from life as a mechanic and brought into the psychoanalytic fold. Born Rosenfeld, he decided to be Rank after the doctor in Ibsen's play *A Doll's House*. He was unprepossessing to look at and lacked personal charm, but he wrote brilliantly about art and artists, and caught Freud's attention by sending him a manuscript. Freud helped him through university to a doctorate, and was rewarded with submissiveness and devotion. 'Little Rank' was how Freud referred to him, an endearment he bore in silence for years. In the end he turned on his patron.

Alfred Adler, one of the speakers when the Swiss were at Berggasse, was the most independent member of the group. An untidy-looking physician with strong socialist views and an unfashionable practice, he lived across the canal in Leopoldstadt. His Russian wife shared his political ideas and later entertained Trotsky and his revolutionary friends when they lived in Vienna.

Already engrossed in plans of his own, Adler was no autocrat like Freud, and didn't believe in the supine patient on the couch with the analyst aloof and out of sight; he and the patient sat looking at one another. His obsession was the individual's drive for power, and he came to see this, not the sexual instinct, as the key to personality. Freud's shadow-world of dreams and memories repelled him. Adler's theory of 'organ inferiority' suggested that what mattered in childhood were bodily weaknesses for which the adult had to compensate; his own sickly childhood may have led him to this conclusion. The body became more important to Adler than the unconscious, the Oedipus theory began to dissolve into fantasy, and it was only a matter of time before his heresies did for him.

Meanwhile, Jung formed his less than enthusiastic impressions of Adler, Stekel, Wittels and the rest, and went back to his own world in Zürich. He took one other impression with him. Somewhere in Vienna that week, according to his account, Minna Bernays told him things about her and Freud. Or (more likely, one might think) she said or implied something that enabled Jung to work out afterwards what it was that Miss Bernays 'really' meant.

To make it a matter of evidence, acceptable to a jury or even a biographer, would very likely have been impossible the next day, let alone the best part of a century later. Jung's evidence may never have been more than a couple of half-finished sentences, improved by the famous intuition. He was a man with hidden forces in his life, as in the case of the knife that shattered and the table that split. He told a story of a wedding at which, over the meal, he made up an individual's life-history for his fellow guests in order to illustrate a criminal's psychology. To everyone's astonishment he described in detail episodes in the life of the man sitting opposite him at the table, whom he had never met.

It often happened, Jung said, that he knew things he couldn't have known by normal means. So did he use his clairvoyance on the formidable Minna? Whether magic or sharp eyes and ears, it comes to the same thing. It is impossible to prove him right or wrong; although his belief that his presence could shatter metal and make doorbells ring, which was another of his stories, doesn't improve his credibility.

Minna's conversation with Jung, assuming there was one, is more likely to have hinted at secrets than to have disclosed them. Imagine it. Jung is writing up his journal:

Later in the week, when we – Emma and I, with Binswanger in tow – were invited to the apartment for supper, the sister-in-law, Miss Bernays, acted as if she was the hostess, doing all the talking, rather than Freud's wife, who concentrated on smiling at everyone and making sure there was hot water in a basin that was ready to sponge the tablecloth if anyone spilt gravy.

Young Binswanger managed to leave a crescent of red wine with the base of his glass (which he wasn't actually drinking, since we were all doctrinaire teetotalers at the Burghölzli in those days), the maid was summoned to erase the impurity, poor B. blushed and wriggled, and Emma, trying to put him at his ease, said something about the madhouse – or the Bellevue Clinic, as one describes it in polite company – on Lake Constance that the Binswangers run as a family concern, which young B. will doubtless take over one of these days.

I was amazed to hear Freud's sister-in-law say, 'Isn't that where Breuer sent that strange Pappenheim girl?' Someone called Bertha Pappenheim was apparently the original of Anna O. in the hysteria book. It was before B.'s time so he didn't have much to say, but I found it intriguing that here was Miss Bernays with an ancient case-history at her fingertips.

She and Freud kept up a jocular intimacy ('Oh do shut up about not liking chicken!' she said once) that concealed a shared affection. I am not often wrong about these things.

I saw her again, the day before we left Vienna, when I called in after luncheon and Freud was still having his post-prandial walk that takes him around half Vienna. She led me into the gloomy consulting room, put me to sit in his chair, and draped herself on the couch. 'Does the professor tell you about all his patients?' I asked her. 'But of course,' she said, in a mysterious voice that may have been meant as a joke. 'We have no secrets, Sigmund and I. I am the sister-in-law and taken to be a sexual neuter, a fitting confidant.'

She was certainly full of surprises. 'You do yourself an injustice,' I said, meaning (I suppose, but can one ever be sure?) to be merely polite. 'Very likely,' she said. 'There are many bitter disadvantages to spinsterhood. But you know, there are compensations.'

Before I could say any more, we heard the front door open and smelt cigar smoke. 'So you are analysing my sister,' he said, as he came in. She smiled and slipped (or rather marched) away; she is heavy on her feet. God knows what they're playing at. When I told Emma she said, 'He wouldn't dare.'

19: Windows on the World

The tone of the letters that arrived from Jung in the spring and summer of 1907 raised Freud's hopes that Zürich was the city that would carry the message of psychoanalysis to Europe and the world. Their technical discussions were cordial, underpinned by Jung's enthusiasm for his new friend.

An emotional transference was at work in Jung. 'I am no longer plagued by doubts as to the rightness of your [sexual] theory . . .' he wrote a month after leaving Vienna; 'I hope and even dream that we may welcome you in Zürich next summer or autumn. A visit from you would be seventh heaven for me personally.' In a letter that described his plan (never realised) to establish a scientific 'laboratory for psychology' and give up working with patients, he said that anyone who knew Freud's science had 'veritably eaten of the tree of paradise' and become clairvoyant: a serious compliment from someone of Jung's persuasion.

Freud, on the receiving end of this agreeableness, needed to do nothing but smile encouragingly and remain single-minded about his aims: 'I could hope for no one better than yourself, as I have come to know you, to continue and complete my work.'

The two knew little about each other. Jung was the better informed, having been to Vienna and seen Freud in action. Also he had read the autobiographical passages in *The Interpretation of Dreams*. The early analysts were interested in their colleagues as case-histories, and liked to use psychoanalysis on them, if only to explain Freudian slips. For the moment, however, Jung and Freud were not interested in rivalry.

Jung himself had various skeletons in the cupboard, such as his weakness for mysticism and parapsychology. He was having, too, a risky relationship with a recently deranged and still abnormal young woman patient, which he kept to himself, although he mentioned her in letters. He sought Freud's opinion in his first letter of substance, months before the visit to Vienna, describing her as a '20-year-old Russian girl student, ill for six years', who had unfortunate obsessions connected with paternal spankings when young, defecation and masturbation. Her name was Sabina Spielrein, but the letter didn't identify her. Nor did it give any hint that Jung was emotionally involved with her, or that she was clever, manipulative and in love with him.

By the time of Jung's letter her condition was improving, and she had enrolled at medical school in Zürich. Jung referred again to her case in July 1907, but wrote only of 'an hysterical patient', so that Freud would not have realised it was the same woman. 'In her dreams,' wrote Jung, 'she is condensed with me. She admits that actually her greatest wish is to have a child by me who would fulfil all her unfulfillable wishes.' More would be heard about the unhappy Spielrein before she emerged as, among other things, the first woman to devote her life to psychoanalysis.

Jung was still finding his feet in 1907. Freud, after years of uneven progress, was emerging as the figure he had dreamt of being. At last he was the leader of a school, his ideas on record in a series of sure-footed books and essays, his practice bringing him patients who paid well for their treatment and supplied the clinical material to feed the writing.

The basic theory was not open to argument. Adjustments could be made, but cases were expected to demonstrate its correctness. A strong case-history that would drive it home was especially prized, and Freud was always on the look-out. In 1907 he looked in the direction of Dr Graf, the musicologist, and his wife, both amateur students of psychoanalysis. The Grafs had a promising child. Herbert was four, a precocious little boy, and his father was analysing him, supervised from a distance by Freud. 'Little Herbert' was encouraged to talk about sexual matters. What he called his 'widdler' fascinated him, as did widdlers in general. By summer 1907, Freud was hoping that the case would provide proofs of child sexuality from a child itself.

In the middle of July, patients were put aside for eleven weeks while Freud went on holiday with the family. Breezy letters from lake-side addresses in the south arrived for Jung, who was preparing for an important conference in early September, billed as 'the First International Congress of Psychiatry and Neurology'. The crowned heads of European psychiatry would be there, looking for the blood of psychoanalysts.

'I hope to be in Sicily when you are reading your paper,' wrote Freud, letting Jung be the front-man while he hiked, swam and picked edelweiss. In telling him what a good time he was having, he remarked that it seemed 'almost cowardly' to be leaving his friend to fight alone, except that Jung was the one 'better fitted for propaganda', to whom all hearts opened. Freud sounded content, a man with a load off his mind. Robust, virile Jung could do the dirty work from now on.

September came, and Freud, having cancelled Sicily because of the weather, turned up in Rome. His family had departed; so had Minna, with whom he had just spent four days in Florence, and he was, he told Jung, 'leading a solitary existence, deep in daydreams'. He thought he might do some writing there: 'Though my main work probably lies behind me, I should like to keep up with you and the younger men as long as I can.' Perhaps he felt as old as he sounded, adding disapprovingly that Eitingon was in Rome, having 'taken up with some woman again. Such practice is a deterrent from theory. When I have totally overcome my libido (in the common sense) I shall undertake to write a "Love-life of Mankind".'

A fatherly letter to the family described watching his first film. In the square near his hotel lantern-slide stills were projected nightly onto a screen fixed to the roof of a house, interspersed with 'short cinematographic performances for the sake of which the old children (your father included) suffer quietly the advertisements and monotonous photographs'. He remained 'spellbound' until 'I begin to feel too lonely in the crowd', and returned to his room to order a bottle of fresh water and write home.

At the Amsterdam conference, where Jung represented him, the anti-Freudians made trouble. Two days out of six were spent discussing hysteria, which meant debating the pros and cons of psychoanalysis. Freud and his theories were now sufficiently important to be taken seriously. The time for laughing at him was over; he had to be denounced.

The principal speaker, Pierre Janet, was sober enough. He disagreed with Freud in a gentlemanly way, damning him with faint praise, incredulous of his sexual theories. Jung, who reported by letter, called him 'a vain old buffer', a phrase that may have struck Freud, since Janet was an old buffer three years younger than he was.

Janet was followed by Gustav Aschaffenburg, Professor of Psychiatry at Heidelberg, barely into his forties but an old enemy of analysis, who, in the course of dismissing Freud, said proudly that a woman he was treating for an obsessional neurosis would have talked to him about sex had he not forbidden it. Jung and the handful of other pro-Freudians present were delighted to note that when Aschaffenburg was talking in private about *Studies on Hysteria* he said 'Breuer and I' instead of 'Breuer and Freud', a slip that Freud made sure got into print, with its implication that the speaker had more sympathy for psychoanalysis than he was willing to show in public.

Jung, occupying the slot that the organisers had intended for Freud, made a robust response and said that his own experience confirmed his colleague's. Unfortunately he overran his allotted thirty minutes, ignored the chairman's signals and, when forced to stop, left the lecture room in a temper. This confirmed the hostile mood of the conference, which throughout applauded attacks on psychoanalysis.

When a Dr Alt, who ran a sanatorium in Saxony, declared that he would never refer a patient to the Freudians, who were filthy and unscrupulous, Theodor Ziehen of Berlin, another leading professor of psychiatry, made a point of congratulating him. Ziehen, like Aschaffenburg, was in his forties; it was not only the old men who hated Freud.

One of the few cheerful pieces of information in Jung's letters about the conference concerned 'a young man from London, Dr Jones (a Celt from Wales!), who knows your writings very well and does psychoanalytic work himself'. The exclamation mark suggests that the Celtic fringe was not where Jung expected analysis to find a friend.

Ernest Jones was a neurologist of twenty-eight, and so twenty-three years younger than Freud. Although well-qualified, he was finding it difficult to get advancement on the London teaching-hospital circuit. There was something odd about Jones, perhaps a deviousness, a wearing of masks; perhaps a coldness that showed through the affability; perhaps a hint of the unreliable. All Jung noticed was a young man who was 'very intelligent and could do a lot of good', and who intended to visit Freud.

It was some time before Jones reached Vienna. Before that he was again with Jung, in November 1907, this time spending five days in Zürich. Again Jung gave him a testimonial, telling Freud that 'Because of his "splendid isolation" in London he has not yet penetrated very deeply into your problems but is convinced of the theoretical necessity of your views.' Jones was no doubt one of those who took easily to a theory based on sex.

The Welsh delight in conclaves, and Jones, a shrewd publicist, decided that psychoanalysis needed its annual reunion. Jung agreed, and Freud was told that they should hold a congress the following spring. Thus Jones, whom no one else had heard of, and whom Freud had yet to meet, initiated the move to internationalise psychoanalysis.

Although he became a public figure in the movement, in some ways the most visible of them all apart from Freud, Jones always carried an air of mysteriousness. Because he was young to start with, never deviated in his respect for Freud or quarrelled seriously with him, and was privy to most of the secrets, he made himself part of the history of psychoanalysis and survived long enough to write his master's biography in three volumes.

At one time he might even have married Freud's youngest daughter Anna, which would have changed many lives. Freud, who didn't want her to marry anybody, would never have trusted her to someone whose private life was as clouded as Jones's. On the other hand, Freud came to place a high degree of professional trust in him. Jones, who had a good opinion of his own abilities mixed with a rueful awareness of his faults, was proud to see himself as Freud's spokesman.

After his first meeting with Jung, Jones had returned to London, then spent a month in Munich doing a postgraduate course under the leading psychiatrist (and opponent of psychoanalysis) Emil Kraepelin. His mistress, who had money, may have paid for the trip, Jones not having much of his own.

He was not at ease in medical London, despite his early promise. Born 1 January 1879, the son of an official at a steelworks, he was brought up in an industrial village in South Wales near Swansea, went to the local grammar school (the one that Dylan Thomas attended thirty years later), qualified in London as a doctor in 1900 amid a shower of gold medals, and by 1905, still in his mid-twenties, was equipped with more than enough postgraduate degrees for a brilliant career. His neurological papers were spectacular displays of learning.

Yet his career was less than meteoric. He was passed over for a junior appointment at a hospital for nervous diseases because a consultant thought he was 'difficult', then for a succession of other posts. Whether the interest he began to develop in psychology and forbidden matters tainted his manner in the eyes of conservative appointment boards, or whether a vaguer presentiment about his character on the part of his seniors affected their judgment and this persuaded Jones to look for unorthodox alternatives, the short-term result was the same, the need to accept jobs for which he was over-qualified.

In 1906, as a part-time medical officer to London County Council, he was arrested and accused of improper behaviour with two girls aged thirteen who attended a school in Deptford for 'mentally deficient' children where he was conducting interviews as part of an inquiry into speech mechanisms. Headlines announcing 'Grave Charges Against West End Physician' were splashed across newspapers, and the affair hung over Jones for six weeks. He was alone with each girl; he said and did things – what things, the newspapers didn't say – and the girls told teachers and parents.

A wily barrister, Archibald Bodkin, was hired for the defence, and Jones, who had an inkling of Freudian ideas by now, is said to have explained to him that the girls must have been playing out a sexual fantasy and projecting their guilt on to him.

Bodkin had no time for such fancies. He concentrated on destroying the girls' credibility, and got Jones freed without a trial.* The medical press gave its support to a wounded colleague, but the damage was done. A London neurologist who was not even born at the time was able to give me, in 1996, a private version of exactly what Jones is supposed to have done, which had been preserved like a folk tale and handed down from one generation to the next.

Two years later, early in 1908 – after Jones had met Jung, but

---

* Contemptuous jokes were exchanged in court about 'romancing' by witnesses. Bodkin: 'Romancing, with illustrated detail, is not unknown, even in courts of justice' (Laughter). Magistrate: 'Particularly by women' (More laughter). Bodkin, later Sir Archibald Bodkin, became famous on the other side of the fence as a moralising and high-minded advocate, and, when he became Director of Public Prosecutions, as the man who banned James Joyce's *Ulysses*.

before he met Freud – a further episode, this time at the West End Hospital for Nervous Diseases where he had a junior appointment, removed any lingering hope of a conventional career. Jones, already dabbling in psychoanalysis, interviewed a ten-year-old girl whose arm was paralysed, and made a diagnosis, on Freudian lines, of hysteria caused by the sexual trauma of an attempted seduction by an older boy. The girl talked, the parents were incensed, and Jones had to resign.

Recklessness on that scale doesn't sound like an accident. Some dissidence or bloody-mindedness seems to have been at work. Perhaps Jones's unconscious had decided that his future lay with the new psychology, so he behaved in an apparently irrational way while arranging matters to achieve the ends he sought. Sex preoccupied him. He wrote that 'the practice of coitus was familiar to me at the ages of six and seven, after which I suspended it and did not resume it till I was twenty-four'. He told Freud that he went into medicine because it offered sexual opportunities. His was another of the Freudian private lives, unexceptional later on, that enraged moralists of the old world when they caught glimpses of them – which is all that anyone ever managed to catch of Jones's.

By the end of 1907 Freud was accustomed to leave things to Jung, so that the conference proposed by the as-yet-unseen Jones was organised from Zürich. Still playing his game of the old man viewing events from afar, Freud wrote that 'I suppose I should be in the way and that you will not invite me', a piece of mock modesty that Jung waved aside. An international journal was another exciting project, and Jung busied himself with plans for it. A movement that would transcend Vienna was taking shape.

Convincing case-histories that would make propaganda for the cause were more necessary than ever; none had appeared since 'Dora' in 1905, the analysis itself dating back to 1900. Freud chose to publish few full histories. The canon of true analytic cases comes to five, and one of those was based on a book, the memoirs of a psychotic. Conclusive success in a complex and novel analysis, the only kind worth reporting, was rare, and Freud may have seen no point in drawing attention to the fact. 'Dora's' case was incomplete and inconclusive, but the fact that she walked out of the analysis meant that she could be blamed for the failure. In 1907–08 Herbert Graf was still a candidate, even if Freud was supervising rather than analysing. But from October 1907 there was a new contender among the full house of ten or so patients whom he was analysing daily.

When he returned to Vienna from Rome, a lawyer and civil servant of twenty-nine, Ernst Lanzer, was waiting for him with a tale of woe. Lanzer was an obsessional neurotic whose life was being ruined by the bizarre rituals of behaviour that make peremptory demands on the victim to do ridiculous things, in order to avoid an unpleasant outcome for himself or those he cares for. Obsessional neurosis – of particular interest to Freud, who saw traces of it in himself – still flourishes as OCD, 'obsessive-compulsive disorder'.

Earlier in 1907, before Lanzer turned up, Freud had published 'Obsessive Actions and Religious Practices', a paper that saw the former as a pathological counterpart of the latter, 'a travesty, half comic and half tragic, of a private religion'. Applying his usual method of finding psychological order in chaos, he insisted that all compulsive acts made sense and that the rituals could be explained, sexual experience being at the root of most of them.

One of his examples was a married woman who had a compulsion that involved straightening the tablecloth so that an imaginary stain on it was visible, then ringing for the maid and sending her away again. According to Freud this was an echo of her wedding night which was spent at an hotel. Her husband, impotent through nervousness, had kept revisiting her room to try again; in the morning he said he would be ashamed if the chambermaid saw the bed unmarked so he poured red ink over the sheet, though in the wrong place. Freud's approach to compulsive neuroses often seems to be explaining one absurdity with another, but his claims for psychoanalysis were so universal that every piece of behaviour had to be solvable, no matter how much tortured ingenuity was needed to make sense of it.

Lanzer's labyrinthine analysis, which began on 1 October 1907, was Freud in action on a grand scale, employing the full machinery of the sexual theory which it was meant to demonstrate, and calling for a corresponding act of faith from the disciples and from those he hoped to convert.

The patient had been 'ill' for years, his obsessions having taken over when he was still a law student, causing him to fail examinations, and he had consulted various doctors without success, among them Vienna's best-known psychiatrist, Julius Wagner von Jauregg. Inner commands told him to cut his throat or kill his girlfriend Gisela's grandmother; he was so horrified by this that he fainted. He had an episodic mania for slimming, and ran up mountains to lose weight, on one occasion being commanded to jump off a precipice, another order he managed to disobey. A command came to move a stone from the road where Gisela's carriage would pass in case it caused an accident; as soon as he moved it, he was ordered to put it back again.

Gisela was one focus of his anxieties. The other was his late father, who had died when Ernst was twenty-one. While studying late at night he waited for his ghost to appear, incorporating this into a ritual of opening the front door ready for his father to come in, meanwhile taking out his penis and looking at it in the mirror. He was able to end this particular ritual by turning it into the threat that if he kept on doing it, some evil would befall his father in the next world.

Like the red-ink story, Lanzer's self-inflicted sufferings were both serious and risible. On the surface he continued to live a normal life. Why not pull himself together? But it was more difficult than that. The full account of the compulsions has a mad intensity. Freud's notes on the case were found after his death and eventually were published, not in their entirety, in the *Standard Edition*, where they occupy sixty pages, the most detailed account of an analysis that he is known to have written.

Lanzer's condition had worsened in the summer of 1907 when, as a lieutenant in the reserve, he spent a month on army manoeuvres in Galicia, and became entangled in an obsession with rats and what they might do to Gisela and to his dead father. It was the rat fantasies that brought him to Freud, after he had come across a copy of the *Psychopathology of Everyday Life*. This sad Jewish patient, trembling, oppressed, with his pince-nez glasses and pale plump cheeks, would find his way into the literature as the 'Rat Man'. When Freud wrote up Lanzer, as *Notes upon a Case of Obsessional Neurosis*, he was nameless except once when he was 'Paul'.

The subject of rats had been introduced to Lanzer by a fellow officer, a 'cruel captain' with sadistic leanings who told him about a supposed Oriental punishment where the victim had a pot clamped to his buttocks with a starving rat (or rats, in Lanzer's version) inside, that then tried to eat its way out. Shortly after telling this story, the cruel captain unknowingly set Lanzer going on another of his compulsions. Just as the manoeuvres were ending, the captain handed over a pair of replacement pince-nez spectacles that Lanzer had sent for from Vienna, adding that a trifling sum of money was owing to an official at a village post office, several hours' journey away.

Lanzer's self-punishment machine took over, inventing a ritual to repay the money that would prevent the rat-torture being inflicted on lady-friend and dead father. A series of crazed railway journeys was involved, although in the end he merely returned to Vienna and sent the money by post.

Freud said that the Rat Man's analysis lasted a year, which was probably untrue, most of the work being done in the first three or four months. His aim was to reduce an incoherent account of behaviour to a series of events for which there were logical explanations. The rat-torture story led back to Lanzer's early fantasies about rats and thence to buried associations with his father and his childhood. Lanzer (decided Freud) had had contradictory feelings of love and hate about his father since he was a small child and had been punished for masturbating; his woman friend was drawn into the same web of ambivalent feelings.

The Rat Man's case thus enabled Freud to demonstrate how child sexuality prepared the ground for a neurosis. But there were many layers to be explored. Rats symbolised all manner of things in Lanzer's life. The rat-theme led Freud to uncover his patient's sadistic appetites, which explained why the cruel captain's tale of torture was able to stir up his unconscious. Once he had been helped to make sense of his disconnected memories, Lanzer understood himself, and in Freud's words, 'The patient's mental health was restored.' Lanzer's family believed this to be true; he married and apparently shook off his obsessions. The freedom to discuss his love life with Freud, which he was able to do in an intimate manner, may have helped him in a comradely sense, rather than the purely psychoanalytic way that Freud was interested in. A few years later, in 1914, Lanzer was back in the Austrian army to fight a real war, only to be taken prisoner by the Russians and die soon after.

The case showed Freud the storyteller in action again, finding solutions to fit theories. No one denies the story was boldly imagined, but did it tell the truth? Some critics say he tampered with the evidence. Freud himself had doubts, not about the rightness of his analysis but about his ability to pin down Lanzer's life in language that could be understood; he wrote to Jung saying, 'how wretchedly we dissect the great art works of psychic nature!' Parallels between Freud's life and Lanzer's may have given the analyst a fellow-feeling for the patient, or suggested a mysterious correspondence between them. Both had obsessional characters, Lanzer's birthplace was not far from Freud's, both families came to Vienna and lived in Leopoldstadt. Freud doesn't comment on any of this. Lanzer even had an emotional attachment to Trieste (where Freud went aged twenty and fantasised about prostitutes), going there aged twenty-six and sleeping with a woman for the first time.

Parts of the account try the patience of a lay reader. Yet Freud's rummaging around in Lanzer's addled head has a haunting quality. It is a fable of a man possessed and the magician who can break the spell; in retrospect a romance of sorts, now that the time for romantic stories has passed and what psychiatry has to offer is the cold charity of Prozac and aversion therapy.

Obsessional neurosis was associated with Jews by Jews themselves. Freud told his colleagues at a Wednesday meeting in 1907, 'The religion of Israel is a compulsive neurosis, which has been continued for hundreds of years.' In 1906 the morose Sadger spoke at the same forum about 'the widespread occurrence of nervousness (especially obsessional neurosis and hysteria) among the Polish Jews' – the unpopular Jews of Galicia, where Sadger came from – a connection which he explained by suggesting that Galician Jews were addicted to 'ruminating'. If Jews were introspective by nature, perhaps that was the reason they took so readily to psychoanalysis. Like everything else to do with Jewishness, there was no shortage of conjecture.

Anti-Semitism in Vienna was more evident than ever. Mad notions circulated of curbing these dangerous aliens. The Austrian Parliament heard a suggestion in 1900 that bestiality laws be used to stop Jews having sexual intercourse with Christians. A whole literature existed about their supposed physical and mental degeneracy, some of it malicious, much of it stamped with what passed for medical authority. Westernised Jews often conspired with their critics; it took Freud himself a long time to start sounding proud of his race.

A man who would be interested in such things arrived in Vienna around the time that Freud acquired the Rat Man as a patient. Adolf Hitler, aged eighteen, a gauche, thin-faced Austrian with a moustache, found lodgings in a dingy house owned by a Polish woman near the Westbahnhof, and presently sat the annual entrance examination to the Imperial Academy of Art. Here, in a building filled with statues and paintings put up near the Ringstrasse in the 1870s, he and more than a hundred others executed two paintings to order, choosing from a list of titles that included 'Expulsion from Paradise' and 'An Excursion'. He passed this part of the test. But the portfolio of drawings he had brought from his home in Linz, a hundred miles away, was inadequate, and he was not one of the twenty-five per cent who were accepted. The examiner's note said, 'Sample drawings inadequate, few heads'; Hitler could do buildings but not people.

For the next year or two he pretended he was an artist, a man of taste who went to the opera, while living on small legacies that finally gave out, forcing him to became a menial worker and for a while, in 1909, a vagrant. The Ring, at first 'like an enchantment out of "The Thousand and One Nights" ', now reminded him of his defeat by the city of culture, loose women and mixed races. A lump sum from an aunt and a precarious career painting Vienna scenes gave him hope again, but he spent his remaining years there in poverty, living in a men's hostel, a respectable one, in the northern district of Brigittenau. He slipped away to Munich in 1913, having managed to evade conscription into the imperial army where he would have had to serve alongside Jews and Slavs.

His wanderings in Vienna, a man in shabby clothes with a greasy black hat, must have taken him many times past the lower end of Berggasse, which was two miles south of his hostel. Brigittenau, the grimy 20th District, was no place for an artist with visions. The inner city, a little further on than Berggasse, remained a paradox. Fine Germanic culture was concentrated there, but so were what he regarded as racial anomalies: a fifth of those who lived in the central district were Jews. In his early days Hitler had seen 'an apparition in a black caftan and black sidelocks' and asked himself, 'Is this a Jew? Is this a German?' Later he marked them off in his mind from the rest of humanity, 'sick to the stomach from the smell of these caftan-wearers' (not that the more successful ones wore anything but suits).

Hitler has been informally assessed as a 'prime example of Freudian psychopathology', ambivalent about his father, who was dead, unhealthily devoted to his mother, who died of cancer soon after Vienna rejected him as an art student. Freud just thought he was mad.

In 1908, Freud's only anxiety for his band of analysts was that they would make a poor showing at the first congress, to be held in April. Jung had chosen the Austrian city of Salzburg, which was a couple of hundred miles west of Vienna in the direction of Zürich but still a much shorter journey for the Viennese. Freud believed that the 'eastern contingent' would be inferior, that the 'talkative Viennese' needed to be made to shut up, that they would show more consideration for Jung than they did for him.

The group got on his nerves. The minutes of the Wednesday circle (which was renamed the Vienna Psycho-Analytical Society on 15 April, ready for the congress) show him opposing a motion in February that wanted him to suppress personal attacks by one member on another. If they couldn't stand each other, he said, they would have to close down. He added that he was still hoping 'deeper psychological understanding' would overcome their personal difficulties: a wish that he expressed more than once without ever finding any evidence that psychological insights turned practitioners into nicer people.

Freud's quarrelsome family of analysts made the relationship with Jung all the sweeter. At first his salutation in letters was 'Dear Colleague'. It took more than a year for this to become 'Dear Friend and Colleague', in November 1907, but only a further three months to reach the plain 'Dear Friend'. In the age of letters such things carried weight, and Jung thanked him for 'the undeserved gift of your friendship'.

A sentence in a letter to Jung referred to Fliess as 'my one-time friend' who had developed 'dreadful' paranoia when their relationship ended. Jung saw this reference as 'surely not accidental' and tactfully asked to be allowed to enjoy Freud's friendship 'not as one between equals but as that of father and son'. Freud made no further comment. He continued with 'Dear Friend' while Jung maintained the respectful 'Dear Professor Freud' he had started with. For the moment, paternal authority and filial piety were evenly balanced.

The day came: forty-two psychoanalysts and hangers-on, more or less the world total, converged on the Hotel Bristol at Salzburg on the last Sunday in April 1908 for their congress the next day, the 27th. It was an agreeable town, not large, astride a river between hills, perhaps overlaid for Freud with memories of meetings there with Fliess. The disgraced Ernest Jones, who had given up hopes of preferment in London and was at present wandering about Europe, met Freud at the hotel soon after he arrived.

Jones noted the Austrian's formal bow and his words 'Freud, Wien', which made him smile, 'for where else did I think he came from?'

Freud's early impressions of Jones were cautious: worthy but fanatical, he told Jung, a lean and hungry man who didn't eat enough and denied that heredity was ever a factor in neurosis. 'To his mind even I am a reactionary. How, with your moderation [Freud was joking], were you able to get on with him?' Jones was never 'Dear Friend' in thirty years, always 'Dear Jones', probably for no other reason than Freud's recognition that 'Friend' as a salutation sounded false to the British.

The Austrians predominated at Salzburg, with the Viennese alone making up over half the total. Of the rest, six delegates were from Switzerland, five from Germany, two each from Hungary and England (Jones had persuaded his best friend to come, a London surgeon called Wilfred Trotter), and one young man from New York, A. A. Brill, who had emigrated there from Hungary aged fourteen, by himself, later returning to Europe to work at the Burghölzli. He looked forward to carrying the flame of the new doctrine back to America.

None of the delegates had been sent by an organisation, since no organisation existed, and their presence was a matter of personal choice. Curiosity or loneliness or exotic tastes or even the lure of a new science had brought them into psychoanalysis in the first place. They can be assumed, if only from Freud's own case, to have had their fair share of neuroses. By definition they were all imaginative enough to embrace a theory of the mind that most people thought outrageous. This sense of apartness must have been evident at the Hotel Bristol.

A few of the delegates would help to shape psychoanalysis, some of them by leaving it, notably Jung and Adler who were both among the nine speakers listed for the Monday. Brill would return as he planned, found the New York Psychoanalytic Society, and make dogged translations of his master's work, best forgotten. Karl Abraham, a young Jewish psychiatrist from Berlin who had been at the Burghölzli, spent his life giving analysis a good name by being calm, authoritative and independent. It took three years of correspondence with Freud before he became 'Dear Friend'. Jones said he was the most normal member of them all.

The ultimately more famous Sándor Ferenczi, a Hungarian, was more erratic, more possessed of passionate ideas that came and went, more dependent on Freud (until Ferenczi, too, packed his bags and left), more muddled and vulnerable in his private life. He was born in 1873 and so was seventeen years younger than Freud. His family were Polish Jews – *Ostjuden* again – who had moved on to Hungary. His correspondence with Freud had barely begun at the time of the Salzburg meeting; the confessions and hand-wringings lay in the future.

Among the inner circle, Ferenczi had the warmest nature. Freud invited him to visit Berchtesgaden in summer 1908 and find himself a boarding-house when the family was in residence, promising that 'now and then you will take a meal with us or climb a mountain with my boys'. Ferenczi was unmarried at thirty-five, and the reason for the invitation, which he accepted, may have been to assess his suitability as a husband for Mathilde, the eldest daughter. But by the summer she was in a nursing home in Merano for her health, and had met the businessman she was to marry. Ferenczi was a 'Dear Friend' within eighteen months of Salzburg.

The most flamboyant delegate was Otto Gross, an Austrian-born psychoanalyst, a self-proclaimed anarchist who sought an end to patriarchal authority by the release of 'subversive sexual energies', or 'free love', which more or less respectable Englishmen like H. G. Wells and Havelock Ellis subscribed to. Gross's views and reckless style placed him at the far extreme of those psychoanalysts (like Fritz Wittels*) who thought that inhibitions stood in the way of social progress. Wittels seems a child compared with Gross, a tousled figure with staring blue eyes who spent half his time in a café in Munich analysing all-comers across a table and spending the fees on morphine, meanwhile taking an assortment of women to

---

* Jones's surgeon friend Trotter, a reticent Englishman abroad, sat between Jones and Wittels at the final dinner. Tired of the garrulous Viennese, he turned to Jones and murmured, 'I console myself with the thought that I can cut a leg off, and no one else here can.'

bed in the name of freedom (two of them committed suicide), or, according to Stekel, persuading other men to make love to his current mistress while he listened in the next room. His moderately promiscuous wife Frieda (not to be confused with the extremely promiscuous Frieda von Richthofen, later D. H. Lawrence's wife, who had enjoyed a brief fling with Gross the previous year) was at Salzburg with him as a co-delegate in 1908.

Freud had already gone out of his way to make constructive remarks about Gross, perhaps because of his own ambivalence about sexual freedom, which was the ambivalence of the movement. Jones, who had his first lessons on psychoanalysis in the Munich café, called him a 'romantic genius'. 'Such a fine man, with such a good mind,' thought Freud, despite having had fragments of Gross's credo passed on to him by Jung. These included a belief that 'The truly healthy state for the neurotic is sexual immorality.'

Jung tried analysing Gross. 'Whenever I got stuck,' he told Freud, 'he analysed me.' Soon after Salzburg, Gross became afraid to stay in his hotel room in Zürich because he thought men were reading his thoughts, and knocking noises came from the wall. Jung detained him at the Burghölzli until he escaped and ran off to more drugs and women.

Whether he was psychotic or under the influence of drugs, his behaviour was a threat to psychoanalysis which needed to seem as respectable as orthopaedics if it were to survive the enmities it created. Fortunately Gross was too obviously disturbed to be a serious contaminant.

Proceedings at Salzburg, which began at eight o'clock on Monday morning, were remembered for Freud's opening address which consisted of an account, without notes, of the Ernst Lanzer case. He spoke for three hours, proposed to sit down at eleven, and was persuaded to continue until noon. According to Freud's published version, which didn't appear until 1909, the analysis must still have been in progress in April 1908, but it is unlikely that the case was presented to the congress as anything less than a triumph. Jones was 'oblivious of the passage of time'. Jung wrote two days later to say he was

> still under the reverberating impact of your lecture, which seemed to me perfection itself. All the rest [including papers by Adler, Abraham, Jones, Stekel, Ferenczi and Jung] was simply padding, sterile twaddle in the darkness of inanity.

An incidental merit of the paper was that it gave Freud's audience insights into the clinical procedures of psychoanalysis. In his writings Freud had avoided formulating rules on how to conduct an analysis. It was not easy to pin down such a fluid process, and in any case he liked to think it was a trade secret. In the Dora case (1905) he said he had omitted details of the technique, which needed 'an entirely separate exposition'. In the same year his paper 'On Psychotherapy' spoke sternly of the 'erroneous impression' that anyone could practise his method, which, however, he could only hint at.

It was probably inevitable that the early analysts should learn by word of mouth and that Freud should find this a congenial state of affairs. The Rat Man lecture, following in detail the progress of a case that was fresh in his mind, must have given the audience an encouraging sense of the founder in action.

Salzburg left Freud feeling 'refreshed ... with a pleasant aftertaste', a rare commendation from a pessimist of his calibre. There was a feeling of work going ahead. Jones and Brill were to visit him shortly in Vienna, and both would soon be in the New World spreading the gospel: Brill in New York, as intended, Jones in Canada, where he went out of desperation because London was hostile and he needed an English-speaking country in which to make a living. Jung had a new journal planned, the biannual *Yearbook*. Abraham was established as Freud's man in Berlin, Ferenczi in Budapest.

As though to give the congress a familial blessing, Emmanuel Freud of Manchester, now aged seventy-five, appeared unexpectedly during the dinner that followed, and he and Sigmund spent the next day together in Salzburg after everyone else had gone, talking about the family. Rosa, Freud's sister, had lost her husband Heinrich the previous month. She was left with two children, grieving and inconsolable.

Emmanuel and Sigmund did the tourist things: cable railway up to the Fortress, steam-tram out to the imperial chateau at Hellbrunn. Emmanuel was still a vigorous companion. But ageing was a process that never escaped Freud's notice. His own birthday was the following week, the unlucky fifty-second, and perhaps he confided his superstitious fears to his half-brother: in order to have them reassuringly dismissed by this common-sensical, almost-English man of affairs.

20: Sons and Heirs

The gentrifying of sex in the twentieth century was brought about by the slow spread of forbidden thoughts and language in print: books first, then the more cautious magazines and newspapers. Freud was a major contributor to the process. By the end of 1908, his psychological (as distinct from neurological) output amounted to twenty-six papers and seven books or book-length studies, overwhelmingly concerned with the sexual interpretation of personality. None of this material was yet available, except by hearsay, in English.

Freud was only one of many writers, although he was the most subversive, who had concluded that sex was too important to be left to the pornographers. The tendency was very noticeable in German-speaking countries, where texts of one sort or another about sexual behaviour found respectable publishers and curious readers.

Why Germany took the lead is not apparent, but scientific study in general was idealised there to an extent unknown in Britain and America. Like German chemists, admired throughout the world, German sexologists (a word lately coined in America) may have been driven by an earnest desire to understand. There were few jokes in sexology. All the sexologists were men, and they were permitted to discuss forbidden subjects because they were also doctors.

Krafft-Ebing, who was dead by 1908, was still in print with non-stop editions of *Psychopathia Sexualis*, the account of sexual aberrations that he had written for a small specialist readership in the 1880s. August Forel, who preceded Bleuler as director of the Burghölzli (and, like him, was a crusader against strong drink), published *The Sexual Question* in 1908, a report by an optimistic moralist who was not afraid to use plain language about sex.

Magnus Hirschfeld began the *Journal of Sexual Science*, also in 1908. His book *Berlin's Third Sex* had already described the city's homosexual delights, of which he was a connoisseur. Iwan Bloch, an authority on venereal diseases, wrote *The Sexual Life of Our Time* in 1906, an all-embracing title (later copied by others) that helped the book to its ninth edition by 1909.

In Britain, Havelock Ellis was writing his *Studies in the Psychology of Sex* – not available in his own country for many years – describing what people did but saying little about why they did it; which was roughly true of all the sexologists. Freud constructed his work around the explanations, not the activities, while not avoiding the sexual deeds themselves.

Freud was widely denounced, but not merely because he wrote about sex. Some of the sexologies (Bloch's and Ellis's, for example) were more explicit; whatever 'scientific' claims were made for them, part of their appeal to publishers was that non-scientific readers enjoyed them as erotica. In general Freud's writing was more restrained. What put him on blacklists was the subversive nature of the theories.

His crime was to say that children were sexual creatures, not little innocents. The *Three Essays on Sexuality* spelt it out in 1905, claiming that infants took pleasure, which could be described as sexual, not only in their genital organs but in their bodily functions, and that their embryonic sexuality had profound implications for their adult lives. This was not how thousands of doctors saw it. 'Sensuality as a sexual feeling,' wrote Professor A. Eulenburg of Berlin at about the same time, 'is in normally constituted children quite dormant.' It was nice to think so. The association between tiny tots and sex was felt to be either disgusting or absurd.

To Freud's dismay, Karl Kraus turned against psychoanalysis. Tales of infant sex were too much for him. In June 1908 the *Torch* said:

> The old science denied the sexuality of adults. The new one claims that the infant feels lust during defecation. The old view was better: it could at least be contradicted by the parties concerned.

Evidence from the front line was needed to refute the critics. The time had come for Herbert Graf, precocious son of the musical Dr Graf, to become a case-history. At last a child had been psychoanalysed. Freud was ready to write it down by summer 1908.

Preliminary findings were used in an essay, 'On the Sexual

Theories of Children'. Did babies come out of grown-ups' bottoms? What was all this about a stork? Freud was anxious to make sense of childhood. The essay mentioned the interest that small girls took in small boys' penises, adding that the girls soon became envious: an aside that later became the theory of 'penis envy'. Freud's idea that penis envy may shape their destiny has exasperated many women. No doubt Freud thought he was being helpful by explaining how the absence of a penis affected women's character through no fault of their own, giving them lifelong feelings of inferiority and jealousy. Belief in penis envy as such has rusted away. But if Freud's phrase is reinterpreted to mean women's envy and anger at male power then the insight was true, since this is what twentieth-century women have come to feel.

Little Herbert, who was disguised by Freud as 'Little Hans', served a simpler purpose. He was living evidence that alongside innocence there was always sensuality. A model child in a model tale, he emerged as a sharp-witted and humorous lad of four (five, by the time the analysis ended) with a lively interest in his penis, in the provenance of babies and in his mother's and sister's widdlers – or their lack of them – as well as in lavatories, bottoms and excrement. The setting was ordinary enough, a bourgeois home with loving Viennese parents. No one sounded degenerate or evil. The knowingness of Hans was itself a kind of innocence, since he had no idea where any of it was leading; widdlers were just fun. But he undeniably had a private life with sex in it, and if one family in the city had a Hans, no doubt others did as well.

This simple fact, that infant sexuality existed, was the common-sense content of the *Analysis of a Phobia in a Five-year-old Boy* – a truism now, but not then. Freud, however, had deeper purposes in studying Hans. The boy was meant to embody a theory, and according to Freud he did. He found his mother erotic, saw his father as a rival, suppressed his feelings and suffered as a result. 'Hans,' Freud wrote happily, 'really was a little Oedipus.'

Dr Graf and his wife were early disciples, perhaps the first to take Freud into their lives without having a professional interest in psychoanalysis. The rise in the West of the intellectual parent who believed in Freud had not begun. A few families in the eastern states of America would be toying with the new fashion before the First World War: it was the 1920s before London and the Bloomsbury set caught up.

The Grafs must have had their own reasons for being so struck with Freud. The husband was only twenty-eight when Hans was born, nearly twenty years younger than Freud, proud to be a friend of the man he admired. His wife had been treated by Freud and after the birth of Hans, their first child, in April 1903, they began to send Freud, at his request, written notes about their son's sexual development and his dreams.

The boy's widdler-interests were noted, as was the fact that when he was three and a half his mother 'found him with his hand on his penis' and said (enlightenment having its limits) that if he didn't stop, a doctor would come and cut it off.

The birth of a sister had left Hans suspicious of storks and interested in her genitals. Graf, reporting events to Freud, added Freudian interpretations. A remark by Hans that he didn't want girls to watch him urinate was put down to the fact that the child had repressed his real wish, which was to exhibit himself.

It must have pleased these avant-garde parents to bring the gift of a talented son to Freud. When Graf sent round the latest packet of notes early in January 1908, he reported that his son was suddenly afraid of horses, specifically of being bitten by one; this in turn was connected with the fear of a large penis, perhaps the horse's. 'My dear Professor,' said Graf's letter, 'I am sending you a little more about Hans – but this time, I am sorry to say, material for a case-history.' Graf, however, knew that case-histories were what Freud wanted. He was always urging friends and pupils to observe their children on his behalf. Now that Hans had turned into a case, the Grafs had more to offer.

Months of analysis began, with Freud advising Dr Graf but letting him do the work. Real horses were involved – a white horse that Hans saw on holiday, the big dray horses pulling carts at a warehouse in the street where they lived – but the child made something different of them in his imagination.

Graf took his son to Berggasse at the end of March 1908; this was the month before the psychoanalysts met at Salzburg, when Freud was preparing his paper about the Rat Man. Freud learned that the child was worried by the appearance of the dray horses, particularly by the harness around the eyes and mouth. This was easily interpreted: the blinkers were a pair of spectacles and the bits were a moustache. Hans was identifying a horse with his father. 'I then disclosed to him,' wrote Freud, 'that he was afraid of his father,

Jung, 1902 or 1903, Sigmund's one-time 'crown prince'. Later he was 'the brutal sanctimonious Jung'.

Emma Jung. She wrote to Sigmund that her husband, like Freud, 'has his own law to fulfil'.

Karl Kraus, Viennese editor, aesthete and thorn in Freud's flesh

Fritz Wittels, bright young analyst and Freud's first biographer

The jaunty Wilhelm Stekel, one of the 'naughty boys' of psychoanalysis who opposed his master.

The 'Celt from Wales', Ernest Jones, the loyal servant. He once had designs on Freud's daughter Anna.

When war broke out in August 1914, Anna Freud was visiting England. She was allowed to return to Austria.

(*Above*) The Hungarian Sándor Ferenczi, one of the inner circle. He grew tired of living in Freud's shadow.

(*Above right*) Serge Pankejeff, the 'Wolf Man', a rich young Russian, was probably Freud's most famous patient. A childhood dream about wolves was supposed to contain the key to his personal problems. He didn't agree.

(*Right*) Lou Andréas-Salomé. She liked to have affairs with intellectuals. Freud gave her flowers but kept his distance.

With his daughter Sophie, whose death at the age of twenty-six may have led him to propose a 'death instinct'.

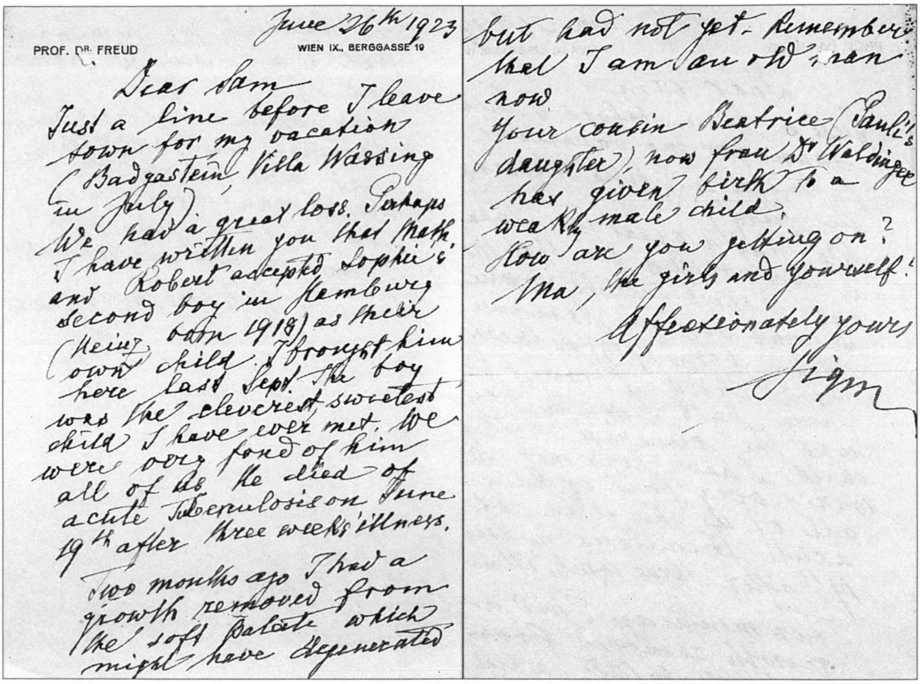

PROF. DR FREUD   WIEN IX, BERGGASSE 19

June 26th 1923

[handwritten letter]
Dear Sam
Just a line before I leave town for my vacation (Badgastein, Villa Wassing in July). We had a great loss. Perhaps I have written you that Math and Robert adopted Sophie's second boy in Hamburg (Heinz, born 1918) as their own child. I brought him here last Sept. The boy was the cleverest, sweetest child I have ever met. We were very fond of him all of us. He died of acute tuberulosis on June 19th after three weeks' illness.

Two months ago I had a growth removed from the soft palate which might have degenerated but had not yet. Remember that I am an old man now.

Your cousin Beatrice (Pauli's daughter), now frau Dr Waldinger has given birth to a weakly male child.

How are you getting on? Ma, the girls and yourself!

Affectionately yours
Sigm

Freud writes to his nephew Sam in Manchester to tell him of the death of his grandson Heinz – three years after Heinz's mother, Sophie, died.

'June 26th 1923. Dear Sam
Just a line before I leave town for my vacation (Badgastein, Villa Wassing in July).

We had a great loss. Perhaps I have written you that Math[ilde] and Robert accepted Sophie's second son in Hamburg (Heinz, born 1918) as their own child. I brought him here last Sept. The boy was the cleverest, sweetest child I have ever met. We were very fond of him all of us. He died of acute tuberculosis on June 19th after three weeks' illness.

Two months ago I had a growth removed from the soft palate which might have degenerated but had not yet. Remember that I am an old man now.

Your cousin Beatrice (Pauli's [Pauline's] daughter), now frau Dr Waldinger, has given birth to a weakly male child.

How are you getting on? Ma, the girls and yourself!

Affectionately yours, Sigm.'

(*Right*) With his daughter Anna, who sacrificed a life of her own for his sake.

The secretive 'committee', high priests of psychoanalytic doctrine, 1922. From left: Rank, Freud, Abraham, Eitingon, Ferenczi, Jones and Sachs.

Horace Frink of New York was Freud's unfortunate choice to lead psychoanalysis in America after the First World War.

Marie Bonaparte, a princess with ideas, admired Freud but declined to hand over the revelatory letters to Fliess that he wanted destroyed.

(*Left*) Amalie Freud (*centre front*) with her five daughters at her ninetieth birthday party, August 1925. Clockwise from extreme left: Rosa, Paula, Dolfi, Mitzi, Anna. All the sisters but Anna were murdered in Nazi death-camps.
(*Above right*) 'I am angry with humanity.'

Extracts from Freud's diary, May–June 1938.
The Nazi terror had begun in Vienna.

May

Sun 1/5	Beer-Hofmann with Princess
Th 5/5	Minna emigrated–Negotiations with Gestapo
Fr 6/5	82 yrs.
Tu 10/5	Emigration within a fortnight
Th 12/5	Received passports
Sa 14/5	Martin left
Sa 21/5	Valuation of the collection
Tu 24/5	Mathilde & Robert departed
Mo 30/5	+ Emilie Kassowitz

June

Th 2/6	Declaration of no impediment
Sa 3/6	Departure 3h 25. Orient Express – 3.¾am Kehl Bridge
London	
Su 4/6	Paris 10h, met by Marie Ernst, Bullitt in the evening to London
Mo 5/6	9 am Dover – London. New house. Minna seriously ill. Columns in newspapers.

Summer 1939. Marie Bonaparte has brought her husband, Prince George of Greece, to visit the dying Freud in London. With them is Hanns Sachs, another exile from Vienna. Freud lies on a hanging couch in the garden at Hampstead: an onlooker now.

(*Left*) The adolescent Freud with his mother, Amalie

(*Below*) Going up in the world: an ill-proportioned oil painting from the 1860s of Sigmund Freud, aged about twelve, and his siblings (*from left, allegedly*) Rosa, Alexander, Anna, Adolphine, Mitzi and Paula

(*Left*) No. 117 Schlossergasse, Freiberg, Moravia, where Freud was born in the room above Zajic the blacksmith's. The house is still there; the town is now Příbor, Czech Republic.

(*Below*) The Freuds and others, *c.* 1878. Sigmund, facing camera at rear, has Anna on his right and (probably) Rosa's fiancé, turned towards Rosa, on his left. Beyond Rosa is Mitzi. Alexander sits at Jacob's feet, looking more like a grandson than a son. The figure seated far left of the picture is Adolfine. Behind the chair is supposedly Pauline, but the historian Peter Swales has evidence that she is a Silberstein daughter, and that Pauline is the girl in white. In any case, would adolescent sisters wear identical dresses?

Freud's teachers: the professors of the Medical Faculty in Vienna, 1882. Brücke is seated, sixth from left. Behind are Billroth, fifth from left, and Meynert, extreme right.

(*Left*) Bertha Pappenheim, 'Anna O.', whose case, now suspect, influenced Freud's development of psychoanalysis. A stamp (*below*), issued by West Germany in 1946, remembers her as something else, the social worker who was a 'helper of humanity'.

Eduard Silberstein, Freud's friend when they were schoolboys, with his wife, Pauline. She committed suicide on her way to an appointment with Freud, May 1891.

Josef Breuer, influential Vienna physician and Freud's mentor as a young doctor. But he outlived his usefulness.

(*Below*) Freud with Wilhelm Fliess, the friend from Berlin. Freud's letters to him from 1887 to 1900 give a matchless picture of psychoanalysis in the making.

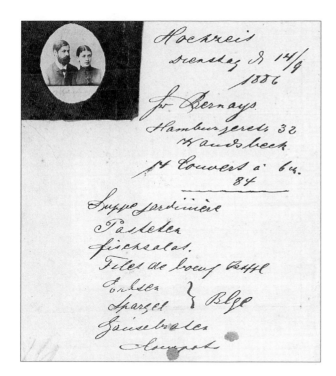

(*Left*) Engagement photograph of Sigmund and his fiancée, Martha Bernays of Hamburg, affixed to the menu of the wedding dinner, Tuesday, 14 September 1886

(*Below left*) No. 19 Berggasse, Vienna, where Sigmund and Martha went to live a few years after their marriage.
(*Below right*) Minna Bernays, Sigmund's sister-in-law. She never married.

The young nerve doctor. 'One manages; and life is generally known to be very difficult and very complicated and, as we say in Vienna, there are many roads to the Central Cemetery.'

Aurelia Kronich. Freud analysed her on a mountain and disguised her as 'Katharina ———'.

Emma Eckstein, the unlucky patient who (in Freud's imagination) bled for love of him.

(*Above*) Schloss Bellevue, where the 'dream of Irma's injection' occurred

(*Right*) The wealthy Anna von Lieben, whose psychological disturbances helped to educate her analyst

(*Above*) Party time, *c.*1898. Rear: Martin and his father. Middle, from left: Oliver, his mother, Aunt Minna, Ernst. Front: Sophie and Anna. Mathilde is absent.

Philipp Freud, Sigmund's half-brother, writes to his half-sister Mitzi (on a postcard bearing his photograph) about the news that they now have a professor in the family. Note the spelling 'Sigismund'.

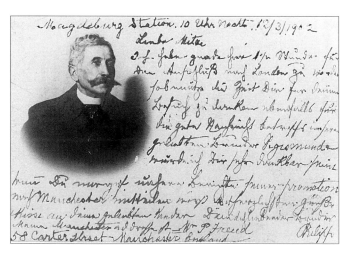

'Magdeburg Station, 10 at night 12/3/1902.
Dear Mitzi
I've got an hour and a half to wait for the connection to London, time to thank you for your visit and the good news regarding our dear brother Sigismund, and I would be very grateful to you if you would send more news about his promotion to Manchester. With regards and kisses to your dearest children and their Mama, your affectionate brother, Philipp
My Manchester address is Hr. P. Freud, 58 Carter Street, Manchester, England.'

precisely because he was so fond of his mother.'

Freud knew he would be criticised for stuffing the child with the very evidence he was seeking. He took the usual pre-emptive course. First he denied that Hans was likely to have been influenced by his father, and complained that the power of 'suggestion', derided by psychologists in his younger days, was now too readily accepted. Next he denied that children made unreliable witnesses, a proposition that had little to do with 'undue influence' but was so elegantly put that who would notice?

> The untrustworthiness of the assertions of children is due to the predominance of their imagination, just as the untrustworthiness of the assertions of grown-up people is due to the predominance of their prejudices. For the rest, even children do not lie without a reason.

Finally Freud threw in the 'sacred-mystery' argument, that only those who conducted an analysis obtained the 'final sense of conviction'. Anyone else was under a disability, a 'regrettable fact', but there it was; if you were not an analyst you could not understand.

There was certainly evidence that Hans was fond of his mother, and that the fondness contained an erotic element. On one occasion he asked her to touch his penis. But the observers kept interfering. Freud had instructed Graf in February to tell his son that the business about the horses was nonsense, and that he was looking for an excuse to be taken into his mother's bed. At a late stage, in April, Graf suggested to Hans that 'perhaps' he wanted Mummy to let go of his baby sister when she was being bathed, so that she would fall in the water. Three days later Graf suggested to him that he didn't want his sister to be alive. Hans agreed, enabling his father to say triumphantly, 'And then you'd be alone with Mummy.'

The analysis sifted through evidence that could be made to fit Freud's interpretations but in itself proved nothing except that Hans's thoughts turned often to penises, babies and lavatories. His pleasure in playing with his penis was seen as part of the problem, and he was threatened more than once with dire consequences, including a 'bag' that he would have to sleep in, and perhaps did. He was a small boy at the mercy of adults, however well intentioned.

The story as it was told,* with its suspiciously perfect proof, has

* The Grafs' relationship with Freud was never satisfactorily explained. Nor was there any mention of a gift from Freud to the child of a rocking horse, which he

troubled many Freudians. Hans is seen arriving at the truth about himself, that he wanted his father out of the way so that he could marry his mother. The admission was made – or it was obtained – in conversations between father and son near the end of April. In one exchange Graf mentioned a funeral that his son had seen on holiday, and went on to say, 'You thought then that if only Daddy were to die you'd be Daddy,' to which Hans said, 'Yes.' Later in the conversation this passage occurred:

> *Graf*: You'd like to be Daddy and married to Mummy; you'd like to be as big as me and have a moustache; and you'd like Mummy to have a baby.
>
> *Hans*: And, Daddy, when I'm married I'll only have one if I want to, when I'm married to Mummy . . .
>
> *Graf*: Would you like to be married to Mummy?
>
> *Hans*: Oh yes.

This conversation was on 25 April 1908, a Saturday, the day before the forty-two delegates, Graf among them, travelled to Salzburg for the psychoanalytic congress. Was Graf anxious to extract the crucial admissions from his son before he left Vienna on Sunday? He may even have hoped to persuade Freud to feature the case in his lecture. As late as 14 April, Freud told Jung that he had been 'toying with the idea of working up my analysis of a hysterical phobia in a five-year-old boy'. For all Graf knew, a dramatic resolution of Herbert's case would change the Professor's mind. So did he approach Freud on the train from Vienna, or tap on his door at the Hotel Bristol, with a pocketful of notes and the wonderful news that his son wanted him gone so he could marry Mummy? If he had hopes, they were disappointed; the Rat Man held the stage.

When he published his account the following year, Freud described how Hans lost his fear of horses and became a wiser child, better able to exercise a conscious control over the forces of his unconscious. Was that a fact or was it wishful thinking? Was the change, whatever the change consisted of, due to Freudian mechanics or to sympathy, affection and the natural decay of a childhood fancy?

---

carried up four flights of stairs to the apartment on Hans's third birthday. Graf referred to the gift in an article he wrote in 1942. Was there a connection between the wooden horse and the horse phobia that came later?

Herbert Graf lived another sixty-five years, until 1973, making his career in the theatre. For more than a decade he was stage director of the New York Metropolitan Opera. He remembered nothing of his analysis.

After a family holiday in Berchtesgaden in summer 1908, writing up Little Hans when he was not walking in the hills or gathering wild strawberries, Freud was in England for the first time in thirty-three years, revisiting the family. He may have noticed that the mood of the British towards Germany was changing. Since his first visit in 1875, when he was still a student, patriotic feelings had taken a new direction. Popular fiction helped to set the mood, notably Erskine Childers' adventure novel *The Riddle of the Sands* (1903) where an invasion of England by cunning Germans is foiled. 'Hun' was creeping into use as a hate-word.

If Freud, who admired the new Germany, read the English newspapers in 1908, he would have found a regrettable unfriendliness. German rearmament, German ambitions, were not popular. The *Daily Mail* was demanding more battleships. Count Zeppelin's airship gave the British a nasty turn when it flew over Europe in the summer, the shape of things to come.

Freud travelled via the Hook of Holland and Harwich, and was in Britain for two weeks. His half-brothers and their families had been absorbed into English life. E. Freud & Son, traders in dry-goods, telegraphic address 'Freud, Manchester', was now run by Emmanuel's son, named Soloman but always known as Sam, who was himself nearly fifty. He and a sister, Bertha, were among five children born to Emmanuel and Marie in Britain; the other three died in infancy.

The two children born before they left Freiberg, the John and Pauline who played with Sigmund as infants, grew up in Manchester. Pauline was still there, but not John. After the 1875 visit to England, Freud had been full of admiration for him, the 'Englishman in every respect'. There is a mystery about this paragon. He vanishes from the family record after the 1870s, and no record exists in Britain of his marriage or death.

Freud's other half-brother, Philipp, was still there with his Birmingham wife and two children, and Freud saw him as well. Like Emmanuel, he was in his seventies. For a family that was so fecund to begin with, the Manchester connection proved curiously sterile. Emmanuel's children – Sam, Pauline, Bertha and (as far as one knows) John – never married; there are hints that their father was a tyrannical figure at home, which might explain why John needed to disappear in order to escape, perhaps doing no more than assume another name and move out of reach. Philipp's daughter married in middle age and had no children. Her death in 1951 marked the end of the Manchester Freuds.

Emmanuel wanted to show Sigmund the English seaside, and they were in Blackpool, pleasure resort of industrial workers, as well as four days in the daintier Lytham St Anne's. Freud's second week was spent on his own in London, walking in the parks, noting the 'fairy-like beauty' of the children, looking at Egyptian antiquities at the British Museum and English paintings at the National Gallery.

Returning to the Continent he had more holiday, of a sort, staying with his ally in Zürich for four days and being taken to see the house that Jung was having built at Kusnacht, on the eastern shore of Lake Zürich, in the style of a gentleman's eighteenth-century residence. A boat house was incorporated for the sailing craft he liked to use on the often stormy waters. Above the entrance to the house a Latin inscription declared that God was present, whether or not one asked him to be.

If the Kusnacht enterprise was pointing Jung towards a future that was more contemplative and less social than his master's, there is no sign that Freud noticed. He needed bursts of rural living and southern sunshine, but the urban apartment and the proximate friendships of the 9th District were the centre of his life. He avoided the loneliness that attracted Jung. In London Freud had complained of being alone and, after the Zürich interlude, when he arranged a few days in the south to round off the holiday season, he made sure he had company: he collected Minna, his best friend, and they went to drowse by an Italian lake.

Yet almost everything that Freud and Jung did drew them closer together. Freud's first letter after his visit addressed him as 'My dear friend and heir'. Issue no. 1 of the *Yearbook* took shape, with the Little Hans paper leading its five contributions. In Freud's mind his fate and Jung's were inseparable. He wrote in January 1909:

> If I am Moses, then you are Joshua and will take possession of the promised land of psychiatry, which I shall only be able to glimpse from afar.

Towards the end of March, Jung and his wife were due to visit Vienna. A date was proving difficult to arrange and, in the course of explaining the problems in a letter of 7 March, Jung came out with the story of a patient who was making trouble for him in Zürich. This was his Russian student Sabina Spielrein, but Freud still wasn't given her name, nor told the truth. Jung said he had cured the woman of 'a very sticky neurosis', and that she had repaid him by causing 'a vile scandal solely because I denied myself the pleasure of giving her a child'. The indignant Jung said he had always behaved like a gentleman, but 'you know how it is – the devil can use even the best of things for the fabrication of filth'.

Freud replied promptly to reassure his son and heir. He had, indeed, heard some story of a woman who introduced herself to a colleague as Jung's mistress, and had presumed she was neurotic. 'To be slandered and scorched by the love with which we operate – such are the perils of our trade,' he observed.

Spielrein was probably Jung's mistress. He was deeply involved with her in any case, an awkward liaison for someone who (it was later apparent) could never convince himself that Freud was right about sex as the key to personality and neurosis: who wanted to find something better in his soul than sexual instincts.

Both men pretended there was nothing at issue. But it could be glimpsed between the lines when Freud sent him a letter about the American view of sex (as he supposed it to be), and referred to 'your' prudery instead of 'their' prudery, a Freudian slip that Jung noted with 'diabolical glee', adding that

> We have noticed this prudishness, which used to be worse than it is now; now I can stomach it. I don't water down the sexuality any more.

The Spielrein business reminded Jung of how powerful his own sexual drives were; perhaps, too, of how he might have benefited if he could have brought himself to confide it all to the master.

Instead (one might speculate) he used the Minna story – that Freud was her lover – as an antidote to his own sexual weaknesses, turning a supposition into a fact so that the man who might have been his confessor was in no position to hear a confession. The question of authority runs through the relationship between the two; from the beginning, Jung had an interest in seeing Freud lose his.

Jung had a bad time with Spielrein, as did Spielrein with him. He was a prominent psychiatrist in a God-fearing city, a prosperous citizen with a growing family; Emma Jung gave birth to a second child at the end of 1908. Spielrein, aged twenty when Jung began to treat her around 1905, was Jewish, slightly built, very bright, with severe personality problems. She had been sent more than a thousand miles from Rostov-on-Don for a cure and a medical education. She was at his mercy; she was also at the mercy of her own imagination, producing fantasies of power and magic which in turn may have become entangled in Jung's mind with his own fantasies of the supernatural.

By 1908 Jung was writing her affectionate letters, one of which made clear the kind of lover he was looking for, someone who could love 'without punishing, imprisoning and draining the other person'. This was not what Spielrein had in mind. She dreamt of having a child by Jung who would be called Siegfried, apparently choosing the name because of its significance in German mythology (and Wagner's operas), where the heroic Siegfried is the son of Siegmund and Sieglinde. Spielrein appears to have thought that this actual/mythical child would draw together the Jewish element – her and Freud, about whom she was well-informed – and the Aryan, in the shape of Jung.

The love affair had disagreeable consequences. In Russia Mrs Spielrein received an anonymous letter warning her to rescue her daughter before Jung ruined her. It was probably written by Mrs Jung, but the story is blurred, the dates uncertain, much of Jung's correspondence still locked up, and the best evidence comes from the victim herself, Sabina. Mrs Spielrein wrote to Jung begging him to desist, which produced the brutal response that doctors didn't overstep the mark with their patients, because they were paid to be considerate.

> I would suggest that if you wish me to adhere strictly to my role as doctor, you should pay me a fee as suitable recompense for my trouble. In that way you may be *absolutely certain* that I will respect my duty as a doctor *under all circumstances*.

Sabina had scenes with him, culminating – date unknown – in a physical struggle, with her holding a knife in a bloodstained hand. This may have happened in Jung's office at the Burghölzli. She rushed out to a group of women colleagues crying 'That's not my blood, that's his. I murdered him!' Following this episode she began to think of Freud as 'an angel of deliverance'.

When Jung sent his 'vile scandal' letter to Freud on 7 March, he knew that trouble was coming. If Freud had heard about a mistress, there must have been rumours in Zürich. Bleuler, director of the Burghölzli, was no fonder of sexual misdemeanour than he was of alcohol. His views on psychoanalysis were equivocal, and Jung was already drawing away from him. At the end of March Jung resigned from the hospital. No doubt this was part of a wider intention to live on his own terms; the house at Kusnacht, which belonged to the same strategy, was ready for occupation that spring. But fears about Spielrein may have precipitated the break.

The Jungs' visit to Vienna lasted from 25 to 30 March 1909, a Thursday to a Tuesday. The Jungs stayed at the Regina, the hotel favoured by psychoanalysts, in the shadow of the Votive Church just outside the north-west corner of the Ring and within a few blocks of Berggasse. What Freud and Jung discussed and did is unknown, except on the last evening.

As the climax of the visit, Freud made a formal declaration that Jung was to be his 'successor and crown prince', an event he had anticipated in letters. They might have drunk a toast in Marsala, except that Jung had signed the pledge. An Egyptian god may have changed hands. Perhaps the ceremony was confined to eye contact, a handshake and a tear. As Freud recalled when he wrote to Jung the following month, 'I formally adopted you as eldest son and anointed you *in partibus infidelium*' ('in the regions of the unbelievers').

This took place in the apartment, in the second of two rooms that he reserved for himself.* Later the same evening, as they sat talking, Jung brought up the subject of the occult; the first time, perhaps, that this happened in the presence of Freud, who said predictably that it was all nonsense. Irritated, Jung became aware of a 'curious sensation' in his chest, 'as if my diaphragm were made of iron and were becoming red-hot – a glowing vault'. This was followed by a loud noise in the bookcase.

Both men were alarmed. Jung then made a remark to the effect that it had been a 'catalytic exteriorisation phenomenon' (what parapsychologists would later call psychokinesis), and Freud made a remark to the effect that it was rubbish. 'Herr Professor,' said Jung, 'in a moment there will be another loud report,' and indeed

---

* Until 1907 Freud's sister Rosa and her husband, Heinrich Graf, together with their two children, lived in an apartment adjoining the Freuds. When they moved out, a year before Graf died, the two sets were knocked into one, enabling Freud to vacate the rooms below and thereafter work from the enlarged apartment.

there was. The other Jung had shown his face, the clairvoyant who read thoughts and shattered knives. 'My spookery', he called it afterwards.

It was a peculiar evening, pointing to future troubles. Jung's mood when he next wrote to Freud was aggressively independent:

> That last evening with you has, most happily, freed me inwardly from the oppressive sense of your paternal authority. My unconscious celebrated this impression with a great dream which has preoccupied me for some days and which I have just finished analysing. I hope I am now rid of all unnecessary encumbrances. Your cause must and will prosper.

This can't have been the response Freud wanted from the new crown prince, and he may have wondered at Jung's cryptic reference to the 'great dream'.

Jung, like Freud, would turn dreams to his own ends. In his case he interpreted them as personal adventures in space and time, not a raking out of cellars that were filled, as he saw it, with grubby junk from childhood. He later described a number of 'great dreams'. The post-Vienna dream could have been one he described in which, walking though mountain country on the Swiss–Austrian border, he encountered a peevish old customs official. The official was dead but he was 'one of those who still couldn't die properly'. Jung identified the 'border' as the boundary between the conscious and the unconscious mind, between Freud's views and his. The ghost was Freud and the dream, whenever it occurred, was a death-wish. Yet, as Jung wrote when describing it long after, at the time he dreamt it he wanted to go on working with Freud 'and, in a frankly egotistic manner, to partake of his wealth of experience'.

Freud, replying to the letter, remained calm. His reproof, if it was a reproof, said merely that he found it strange that on the evening Jung was elevated to crown-prince status,

> you should have divested me of my paternal dignity, which divesting seems to have given you as much pleasure as I, on the contrary, derived from the investiture of your person.

Most of the letter was taken up with the occult. Freud admitted that at the time, he was impressed by the 'poltergeist'. Since then he had paid attention to the shelves, and all he heard were creaks, unrelated to his thoughts, and never when he was thinking about Jung. His willingness to believe had 'vanished with the magic of your personal presence', and

I confront the despiritualised furniture as the poet confronted undeified Nature after the gods of Greece had passed away [a reference to a poem by Schiller]. Accordingly, I put my fatherly horn-rimmed spectacles on again and warn my dear son to keep a cool head.

So Freud had not dismissed the incident. He had sat thinking about Jung, trying to make it happen again. And having disposed of the episode in the first half of the letter, he went on in the second half to talk about his obsession with numbers and death, as if he wanted Jung to know that he sympathised with irrational beliefs, while realising that there were rational explanations for them.

Freud's affection for Jung was unwavering in 1909. He took the Sabina Spielrein affair in his stride. When she approached him at the end of May, writing from a Zürich boarding-house that she wanted to see him about 'something of [the] greatest importance to me', he passed her letter to Jung, asking innocently who she could be: busybody, chatterbox, paranoiac? He probably guessed she was Jung's anonymous scandal-maker, and Jung had to tell him she was, explaining that he had broken with her because she was 'systematically planning my seduction ... Now she is seeking revenge.' She was also spreading a rumour that he meant to divorce his wife and marry her.

A consoling response came from the old hand at hysteria. Although he had never been taken in quite so badly, Freud had 'come very close to it a number of times and had [he used the English phrase] *a narrow escape*'. Only the fact that he was ten years older when he came to psychoanalysis, he said, had saved him from experiences like Jung's. But they helped the analyst develop a thick skin. They were (English again) 'a *blessing in disguise*'.

Anxious letters went to and fro between Vienna and Zürich. Freud assured Spielrein that his friend Jung was incapable of ignoble behaviour. Spielrein assured Freud that her dearest wish was to part from her friend with love, and quoted from the insulting letter Jung had written to her mother. Freud advised Jung not to be contrite, since 'little laboratory explosions' (patients evidently being experiments) were unavoidable. Spielrein told Freud, 'you are a sly one', because he was listening to both sides of the story. She said she had spoken to 'the miscreant', who promised to tell Freud the truth. Jung confessed that Spielrein was not to blame, that his letter to her mother was 'a piece of knavery which I very reluctantly confess to you as my father'; all the same, he went on lying about the relationship. Freud apologised to Spielrein and told Jung not to worry. Peace reigned; Jung was safe; another woman had been put in her place.

Both men had more exciting things to think about in summer 1909: they were going to America, and so was Sándor Ferenczi of Budapest.

Freud's invitation had arrived the previous December, and was not well received. He had already shown signs of European ambivalence towards the New World, which in his youth he had contemplated (as he had England) as a place to escape to, while remaining set in the mould of a world he understood better. Beyond the Atlantic he saw a caricature-land, peopled by prudes who worshipped dollars. Now, when Clark University at Worcester, Massachusetts invited him to give a series of lectures in July 1909, he was annoyed that the dollars he was offered by way of honorarium were too few. 'Naturally,' he told Jung, 'the Americans pay only $400 for travel expenses.'

July was now a busy month in his practice, packing in the patients before he went on holiday. He declined, letting it be known among his circle that it was presumptuous of Clark to think he was going to make sacrifices in order to give lectures. 'America should bring money, not cost money,' he wrote to Ferenczi, adding a word about the other half of the caricature, prudery: 'By the way, we could soon be "up shit creek" the minute they come upon the sexual underpinnings of our psychology.' He said the same thing to Jung; when the sexual implications were understood, 'they will drop us'.

His view of America was insolently European. Both he and Jung groaned about a leading Boston psychiatrist, Morton Prince, who was attracted by psychoanalysis but alarmed by its sexual implications. Two years older than Freud, he had the genial self-confidence that novices were not encouraged to show unless they showed exceptional talent. Jung noted 'the gentle zephyrs of prudery blowing across from America, for which Morton Prince seems to have a quite special organ'.

Beyond Prince was a less-defined impression of puritan values. Freud might have pointed to the same tendencies in Englishmen, but he was fond of England and overlooked them.

If he had any serious doubts about visiting America, and it's unlikely that he did, they disappeared in February 1909 when Clark University renewed its invitation. The honorarium went up to $750, the lectures were to be given in the second week of September and he would receive an honorary degree. An invitation to Jung followed early in June, as the Spielrein affair was ebbing.

Seven weeks before they sailed, Freud was planning his wardrobe: suits, a dress coat, a 'salon jacket', a thick coat for the ocean voyage. One should buy a top hat on arrival, he told Ferenczi jovially, 'on account of the difficulty of transporting it', then 'throw it into the ocean before the return trip'. But he knew that America was serious business. Psychoanalysis was a commodity, and Freud was the sole exporter.

21: America

The small and unorthodox Clark University, forty miles from Boston, was founded in 1887 by a farmer's son, Jonas Clark, whose own education had been neglected. Its elderly president, who also ran the postgraduate school, was a tenacious psychologist, G. Stanley Hall, devoted to making Clark famous and to sending out alumni with doctorates in psychology. The week of lectures to which Freud and Jung were contributing formed part of celebrations to commemorate Clark's twentieth anniversary. When Freud told Jung about it, he wrote 'twentieth (!) anniversary' to show what he thought of American time-scales compared with European.

Freud would have known that Clark was worthy but not in the first rank, and that his rival Pierre Janet had preceded him to America three years earlier as the guest of Harvard, Columbia and Johns Hopkins. The Americans knew more about Janet, whose views on the unconscious lacked Freud's insistence on the sexual origins of neurosis and were less disturbing. Still, Clark was a foothold.

Hall's own career had included long stints in Europe, six years in all, some of it spent on word-association experiments long before Jung began them. The idea of sexual theories in psychology didn't worry him, although he knew that anyone concerned with education had to tread carefully. In America, as in Britain, there were powerful public inducements to go along with the moralists' fiction that sexual activity had only one aim for decent people: to produce children and to do so within marriage. By American standards, continental Europe was noticeably immoral, Britain only slightly less so.

Hall was a refugee from a puritanical childhood on a New England farm. He devoted 'half a dozen shelves' in his personal library to books on sexual matters, and Clark University offered a course on the psychology of sex, the topics including morality, disease, divorce, modesty, prostitution, fecundity and eugenics. This wasn't bad going for a man of sixty-five in the conservative climate of New England. As a remark by Freud after he had been to America suggests, Hall did not fit the caricature:

> Who could have known that over there in America, only an hour away from Boston, there was a respectable old gentleman waiting impatiently for the next number of the *Yearbook*, reading and understanding it all, and who would then, as he expressed it himself, 'ring the bells for us'?

In the months before Freud sailed, Ernest Jones kept him informed about the New World from his exile in Canada where he had wangled some modest university posts in Toronto. There he saw patients and wrote papers, and confidently expected to be a professor of psychology before long.

Accompanying him was a woman he described as his wife, a wealthy and vivacious Dutch Jewess, Loe Kann. (It was Kann who had helped finance his travels in Europe.) For decency's sake he said they were married. In a letter to Freud he mentioned that he was house-hunting in Toronto on behalf of 'my harem', a light-hearted phrase to describe the domestic set-up of 'wife', his two sisters from Wales who had joined him there, and two servants. Three months later – it was shortly after the first of Jung's confessions about Spielrein – Freud passed on the harem remark to Jung, perhaps thinking that a joke at this point would be helpful. Jung, however, took it literally. 'What you say about Jones is astonishing,' he replied, 'but it fits in with certain expressions of his that have struck me.' Jones was stuck with his reputation.

To Freud he was already a shrewd disciple, a role he filled for the rest of Freud's life, never crowned with glory like Fliess and Jung and thus on safer ground when it came to friendship; when Jones disillusioned him, as he did sometimes, it caused no heartache. From the beginning Jones bombarded his master with letters, advising him like an old friend, flattering him when necessary, warning of pitfalls, making sly comments on colleagues: an unofficial chief of staff. In 1909, already an expert on America after one visit to Boston, he said that psychiatrists there were only out to make money, warned of local reservations about sex, and reported that Brill, now established in New York, had written a silly article.

More constructively, he advised Freud against his intention to speak in German and confine the lectures to the subject of dreams. Freud refused to use English, but let himself be persuaded to give a broad introduction to psychoanalysis.

The three travellers, Freud, Jung and Ferenczi, met in Bremen on 20 August, the day before they sailed in style aboard the new liner of the North German Lloyd company, the *George Washington*. Thousands of emigrant east-European Jews were continually passing through Hamburg and Bremerhaven, the port of Bremen at the mouth of the Weser, travelling in rather less style to new lives in America; 750,000 from these two ports alone in the ten years before 1914, some of them shipped economically across Europe in sealed wagons. If Freud and party saw anything of them, they made no comment.

At the shipping office Freud was annoyed to learn that William Stern, Professor of Philosophy at Breslau, was a fellow-passenger and another Clark lecturer. Stern, whose later career took him to Duke University, was not undistinguished; soon after, he introduced the concept that led to IQ testing. But he had once given *The Interpretation of Dreams* a cool review, as a result of which he was damned, 'a repulsive person'. Freud was further irritated that the passenger list, which managed to spell Stern's name correctly, had him down as 'Freund'.

They spent the day sightseeing, Ferenczi waving 'a large bundle of dirty notes . . . black on one side and green on the other', the first dollar bills that Freud had seen. At the cathedral they inspected a lead-lined cellar where the environment preserved corpses by mummifying them, a visit that had repercussions.

Over lunch in a restaurant, Jung announced that he had decided to abandon abstinence. They all drank to this. Shortly after, as he was eating salmon, Freud 'broke into a bad sweat with a feeling of faintness', and had to leave the food. Having slept badly and drunk beer on the night train that brought him to Bremen, he saw nothing significant about his momentary attack. The story is told in the diary that Freud kept for the first part of the trip.*

Jung, describing the incident more than fifty years later, said that Freud fainted, and that what had upset him was a conversation they were having about the corpses in the cellars. Freud had

* The diary is sealed up in the Library of Congress. It was allowed out briefly when Anna Freud was alive, used in a book that didn't appear until 1992, and then locked up again.

complained that this talk about the dead meant that Jung had a death-wish towards him. Jung, recalling it, said he had been 'alarmed by the intensity of [Freud's] fantasies'.

Whatever happened, it had no effect on the sightseeing, which continued in a car that Jung insisted on hiring. They met a military unit returning to the city from summer manoeuvres, Freud observing sarcastically (in his diary) that 'of course, [it] has to be carefully inspected by the Captain of the Swiss army'.

The following afternoon they sailed from Bremerhaven, calling at Southampton and Cherbourg, where more passengers came on board, before leaving Europe behind for the seven-day crossing. The weather was wet and misty, with calm seas. The three psychoanalysts were together most of the time. When Freud saw the scoundrel Stern buttonhole Jung on deck, he called out, 'Now, Doctor, when are you going to bring that conversation to an end?' At which, Freud told his diary, 'the shabby Jew in embarrassment departed'. No doubt Stern was another of the wrong sort of Jews, like the clamouring masses from the east on the run from pogroms and poverty who crammed the emigrant ships.

As they crossed the Atlantic, the three psychoanalysed one another, but it is not clear at what length or under what conditions. In a letter to Freud when they were back in Europe, Ferenczi wrote about the 'meditation in which I immersed myself on the ship after the somewhat painful acknowledgement of my *infantility* about you'. In another letter he spoke of 'the "ménage à trois" on the George Washington'. Jones's account in his biography said it was 'group analysis', implying that each was analysed simultaneously by the other two.

Jung said nothing about Ferenczi but described, in a famous passage in *Memories, Dreams, Reflections* denigrating Freud, how the latter withheld details of his private life that would have helped explain a dream, saying 'I cannot risk my authority', with the result that he lost all his authority as far as Jung was concerned. Jung doesn't say if this was on board the *George Washington*, and he wrote elsewhere that he analysed Freud in America itself, but his account in *Memories* naturally favours himself. He wrote it more than twenty years after the death of his rival and five years after the death of Ernest Jones, so there was no one to contradict him.

Dreams kept them all busy. Somewhere on the tour Jung had the best-known of all his dreams, about a house whose rooms become older as he descends until, in the cellar, he finds Roman walls and below the cellar a cave containing fragments of primeval pottery and two skulls. Perhaps suggested by the lake-side house that he had built for himself, the dream told him that within personality were memories that belonged to human history, not merely to one's own life, a concept that he developed as the 'collective unconscious'. It was an appropriate dream for a man who wanted to escape the shadow of someone else's theories in order to advance his own.

In *Memories* he took pleasure in describing how Freud made feeble attempts to interpret the dream, wondering whose skulls they were and what death-wish was involved. Eventually Jung made a patronising concession. He said the skulls must belong to 'my wife and my sister-in-law', knowing (he wrote) that this wasn't true, since he was newly married at the time and had no reason to entertain death-wishes. On the contrary: Jung had been married six years, had recently escaped from the troublesome Spielrein and had an uneasy relationship with his wife. But the dream came in handy for belittling Freud. To bring in wives and sisters-in-law could even be taken as a cruel hint about Freud's supposed adultery with Minna.

Reading about these private visions creates an illusion of insight into the minds of the analysts. The information is incomplete and prejudiced, even by the standards of biography, which relies on incomplete and prejudiced information. The events under scrutiny are often states of mind, leading nowhere as far as the reader can tell. Inward lives are glimpsed to no purpose. Freud was echoing some private intimacy when he wrote to Jung, after the American adventure, to say that 'My Indian summer that we spoke of on our trip has withered lamentably under the pressure of work', adding that 'I am resigned to being old.' What iceberg was that the tip of? By 'Indian summer' did Freud mean the freedom he felt now that Martha, forty-eight in August 1909, had passed the menopause? We hear a few words and have to guess the rest.

They came to New York, and as they entered the Upper Bay, Freud is supposed to have turned to Jung and said, 'Don't they know we're bringing them the plague?' Newspapers duly reported the arrival of Professor Freund.

The celebrations at Clark were not due to begin for more than a week, and the party spent most of that time in New York City, with Brill as their guide. He had an apartment at Central Park West, which Freud thought 'the nicest part of the city', and where psychoanalysts have lived and worked ever since.

They saw the Jewish quarter on the Lower East Side and Chinatown next to it, the Metropolitan Museum of Art, a cinema show (in more comfort than Freud had enjoyed at the open-air films in Rome), the American Museum of Natural History, a lunatic asylum and, one evening, Coney Island, where the rides and blazing lights of the new Luna Park must have made the pleasure gardens of the Prater seem far away. All three had chronic indigestion and diarrhoea.

Freud took a hired car to call on his sister Anna and her husband Eli Bernays at Morningside Heights, near Columbia University. Eli was now wealthy, which made him no more attractive to his brother-in-law, who still thought of him as a bankrupt, a philanderer and a draft-evader. There was no one at home. Freud presumed that Anna and the children were away. 'For Eli alone, who perhaps is in the city,' he wrote to his family, 'I will not take even one step.'

It was in the vicinity of Columbia, after Brill had taken them to visit the university's psychiatric clinic where he worked, that the episode of the weak bladder took place. They – Freud and Jung, probably Ferenczi and Brill as well – were on or near Riverside Drive, which runs beside the Hudson River, admiring the view across the water of the Palisades, the great cliffs of New Jersey. Freud was taken short and wet his trousers. The source of the story is Jung, not in his 1961 memoirs but in a 1951 conversation with Professor Saul Rosenzweig of Toronto, who used it in a book published forty-one years later. Rosenzweig added that Jung 'appeared to be deriving some special satisfaction from the disclosures he was making about Freud'.

Jung's account gave no further details of the mishap itself but said that Freud was afraid the same thing might happen at Clark University, at which Jung offered to analyse him and seek to uncover whatever psychic problem was involved. Jung believed that ambition was to blame: the impulse to urinate represented an infantile attempt to draw attention to one's importance.

Freud himself, in 1908, had made a connection between urinary incontinence (as in bed-wetting) and ambition. But he denied to Jung, as he did in general, that he had such a trait. As the analysis proceeded (where, how often, for how long?) Freud reported a dream that required some personal details to help Jung's interpretation. He refused to give them, because that would mean losing his authority. This is evidently the dream that may have occurred aboard the *George Washington*, and that Jung described in the 1961 *Memories* without mentioning the bladder incident. In the Rosenzweig interview it was being used in a context that damaged Freud twice over by making him look both evasive and a frail old man of overriding ambition who couldn't control a bodily function.*

None of the qualifications disproves the story. Freud himself admitted to bladder problems, caused, he said, by prostatic hypertrophy, the enlargement of the prostate that afflicts many middle-aged and elderly men, making them need to micturate frequently; he suffered from it later. In conversation with Jones, date unknown, he blamed America for causing him the discomfort: 'They escort you along miles of corridors and ultimately you are taken to the very basement where a marble palace awaits you, only just in time.'

Older men, knowing that frequent visits to the lavatory are a sign of age, are reluctant to reveal their weakness in the company of their juniors. None of the others in the group on Riverside Drive had reached the age of prostate problems. Freud's pride may have led him to miss the chance to visit a marble palace at Columbia, with unfortunate consequences half an hour later. It is hardly the stuff of human drama. Very likely, too, it had nothing to do with Freud's ambition. But these are the games that Freud taught analysts to play.

Ernest Jones, who had been back to Europe for a conference, joined them in Manhattan two days after the Columbia visit, and that night, 4 September, they went by multi-decked steamer down Long Island Sound to Fall River, and thence by train to Boston and on to Worcester, where assorted scientists were gathering for the celebrations.

Americans were interested in psychology. A 'Boston School' of psychotherapy already existed, an eclectic group, more sophisticated than anything in London. There was, too, a popular appetite

---

* The suspect 1957 interview with John Billinsky, in which Jung allegedly said that Freud's dreams on the trip were about himself, Martha and Minna, includes the remark that '[Freud] had psychosomatic troubles and had for instance to urinate about every half an hour.' Few great men can have had their bathroom habits so ruthlessly annotated.

for new ideas in psychology (and in 'science' generally), respected by many intellectuals who, unlike their British counterparts, saw no harm in encouraging newspapers and magazines to spread the word. The view in Britain was that simplistic accounts for lay readers did more harm than good; a superior silence was preferable. In America, journalism was not despised. Freud attracted interest at both levels.

For the first time he met distinguished Americans who took his ideas seriously. William James, the country's leading psychologist, who turned up later in the week, was sceptical but curious. A formidable man, inclined to mysticism, impressed by spiritualism and tortured by sexual anxieties, he said he went to Clark 'to see what Freud was like'. Freud's host, G. Stanley Hall, was already half converted to the cause.

Another promising recruit was also at Worcester that week, the Harvard Professor of Neurology, James Jackson Putnam, who was drifting towards psychoanalysis at the age of sixty-three. (Old Americans had more open minds than old Europeans; William James was sixty-seven.) Putnam, who said he was disgusted when he first read Freud, had been led to think again by Jones who, less than half his age, had softened him up on a foray to Boston earlier in the year. Jones found him 'a delightful old man, meek, humble, learned, well-read, idealistic, but easily swayed in all directions'.

Meeting Freud at Worcester completed his conversion, although the version of psychoanalysis that he came to favour was not one that Freud cared for. It tempered the unconscious and gave it moral undertones, viewing psychoanalysis almost as an exercise in character-building and taking a generally more optimistic view of human nature, as many analysts were later to do in America. But Putnam's painful honesty was endearing; Jones said he was the only man he ever knew who would admit in public that he was wrong.

Freud and Jung stayed with Hall and, for a week, as the programme of lectures and social events unfolded, they had little time to reflect on America. Psychology was one conference subject among many. In all there were twenty-nine lecturers, among them two Nobel prize-winners, in disciplines that included astronomy, chemistry, physics, biology and history. To be surrounded daily by scientists endorsed Freud's own standing in science, which Americans had no trouble in accepting.

His five lectures, delivered at eleven a.m. each day from Tuesday to Saturday, 7 to 11 September, were given without notes, and the published version in *Five Lectures* is a reconstruction. Oedipus and sexual aspects were dealt with in the fourth lecture, without too much worrying detail but plainly enough. In Rosenzweig's own reconstruction of the lectures as delivered, using contemporary reports, Freud moved into his theme by pointing to the lack of candour in sexual matters. He went on:

> Is there a sexuality of infancy? you will ask. On the contrary, is not the time of childhood just the period of life which is characterised by a lack of sexual drive? No, Gentlemen, it is not true that the sexual drive entered into children at puberty as, in the Gospel, the Devil enters into the swine. The child has sexual drives and sexual behaviour from the outset.

No violent attacks seem to have followed this and other disclosures; perhaps the forum was too distinguished for the critics, although Jones's Professor of Psychiatry in Toronto complained that the average person would think the Viennese were advocating free love and a return to savagery. To Freud, the week at Clark had the sweetness of revenge:

> In Europe I felt as though I were despised; but over there I found myself received by the foremost men as an equal. As I stepped on to the platform at Worcester . . . it seemed like the realisation of some incredible day-dream.

Whatever had been troubling him on Riverside Drive, Freud was at ease. When he arrived at the university building to give his first lecture, he was smoking a cigar. As he started up the three flights of stairs, a woman usher indicated a 'No Smoking' sign. Freud nodded politely but kept the cigar. The same thing happened for three days, after which the usher gave up. Europeans spat on staircases and smoked cigars on them; Americans would have to put up with it.

Freud's view of America remained irrational. It upset his bowels (he was still blaming the food years later, although his digestive troubles predated America) and his prostate; it was full of garrulous people who mumbled their words and were liable to slap him on the back and say 'Hi, Doc!' In a way he was too proud and insular for a foreign country he couldn't understand; at the same time he craved its respect.

Jung, who took the practical view that America was a place

where he could earn large fees (and later did), wrote to his wife to say that after they received their doctorates, Freud was 'in seventh heaven'. Ferenczi, recalling the visit twenty years later when he was no longer the humble acolyte, said that Freud appeared 'somewhat ridiculous, when almost with tears in his eyes he thanked [Stanley Hall] for the honorary doctorate'.

The Americans were good listeners, as European lecturers always found them to be. A month before Freud was there, Bertha Pappenheim, 'Anna O.' of the *Studies on Hysteria*, had been lecturing in America, having left her unhappy youth far behind. When Freud spoke about her at the start of his lectures as the first patient of the new psychology, the fifty-year-old woman had just been warning audiences in Chicago and New York about the evils of the white slave trade.

The rest of the tour was anti-climax. Putnam took Freud, Jung and Ferenczi another 200 miles to an American wilderness of peaks and lakes, the Adirondack Mountains of upstate New York, where he had his 'camp': the log-cabin version of the English 'country cottage'. There was too much tramping up and down steep trails, an unsettling informality of steaks grilled on charcoal and first names used in conversation. 'Ferenczi and I were taught a board game by two young girls,' he wrote to his wife. 'Amazing!' When he had a mild attack of what he called appendicitis, all his hosts could say was 'Gee, that's too bad.' No doubt they were in a frontier frame of mind; he was nostalgic for Berggasse perhaps, or the familiar backwoods of Berchtesgaden and the Tyrol. His abdominal pains made him think of death.

Two weeks and another Atlantic crossing later, they were back in Europe. Freud left behind a core of converts who would take no more than two years to establish themselves as the most active and successful of the new nerve doctors in America. By 1910 they were identifying themselves in public as 'psychoanalysts', and the following year, encouraged by Freud and the Europeans, the New York Psychoanalytic Society was set up by Brill and others; it is still the heart of the movement in America. Magazines and popular fiction dwelt on dreams and Freudian slips (but rather less on sex), the case-histories of *Studies on Hysteria* were recycled for magazines, and the psychoanalyst began to emerge as a figure that middle-class readers felt at home with, expensive but responsible, brilliantly clever, high-minded, explaining Americans to themselves. When the latest wave of dance mania arrived with the tango and the turkey trot before the First World War, Brill explained in the *New York Times* that it was merely a matter of repressed emotions breaking through. An audience existed to hear such things. In London there was an undercurrent of derision, a reluctance to believe, as Americans so often did, that this new priest-and-doctor figure of the times had the power to alter lives.

Freud's spirits were raised by his visit. America made him uneasy. But he had spread the word.

The day after the three travellers returned and went their own way, Freud kept imagining he saw Jung. Freud had remained in Hamburg, perhaps to see Mrs Bernays and Minna. He told Jung that wherever he went in the city, 'your light hat with the dark band kept turning up. And the same in Berlin.' Jung returned a thinner compliment. 'Occasionally a spasm of homesickness for you comes over me,' he wrote, 'but only occasionally.' Freud must have noticed the offhand tone. Unless, circumspectly, he made it his business not to.

22: Naughty Boys

In the beginning there was Freud, then Freud and a few colleagues in Vienna, and by 1910 the first glimmerings of an international community. No one had much idea how psychoanalysis should organise itself, and there was an undercurrent of distaste for doing it at all.

'Internal politics' had consisted of quarrels among the Viennese, usually about who thought of something first, arbitrated by Freud. Maturity meant having larger issues to quarrel over. The second annual conference was planned for early in the year, to make up for not having one in 1909 when the high command was in America. Before it was held, in March, while Freud continued to 'scuffle with my ill-mannered boys in Vienna', he was dreaming of a new era in which the centre of gravity would move to the west, specifically to Zürich, and of the regimes to go with it.

He kept his administrative plans to himself, except for Jung, who had little interest in them, and Ferenczi, who received hints in letters and probably oral instructions when he visited Vienna. Ferenczi advocated a Freudian way of life that went 'beyond the infantile', making it unnecessary to tell lies in private or in public. The bickering Viennese analysts were a poor advertisement for this utopia, Freud noting sadly that psychoanalysis had no 'ennobling influence' on them, but Ferenczi was undeterred. 'Just think what it would mean,' he enthused to Freud in February, 'if one *could tell everyone the truth*, one's father, teacher, neighbour and even the king. All fabricated, imposed authority would go to the devil.' Alongside the hare-brained idealist was an old-fashioned authoritarian. 'I do not think,' he wrote in the next sentence but two, 'that the psychoanalytic worldview leads to democratic egalitarianism; the *intellectual elite of humanity* should maintain its hegemony.'

This was more the kind of thing that Freud had in mind. He,

Ferenczi and Jung made plans for the 1910 conference, to be held at Nuremberg immediately after Easter. Jung had been away for three weeks, two of them just getting to Chicago and back, because a manic-depressive millionaire, Harold Fowler McCormick, needed him. He returned just in time.

Delegates assembled at the Grand Hotel heard Ferenczi on the first afternoon propose an international association to be run from Zürich by a newly created president, Jung, who would be appointed for life. His powers would be dictatorial, giving him the right to censor any article or lecture by a psychoanalyst. In passing, Ferenczi made disparaging remarks about the Viennese, the kind that Freud made in private, then put on his idealistic hat and lectured delegates on the need to behave like sensible children in Father Freud's family, able to face the truth, however sobering, 'without childish sensitivity and vindictiveness'.

Uproar followed. The conference had to be suspended. A private meeting of Viennese convened by Stekel was discussing what to do when Freud arrived uninvited. Wittels was there and wrote an account of the impassioned leader at bay, telling them that Jews couldn't win friends for the new ideas, that he was too old to be attacked continually, that they were all in danger, that 'the Swiss will save us – will save me, and all of you as well'.

Compromises were made next day. The president's life-term became two years, and the powers of censorship were removed. No one tried to stop Adler and Stekel starting a magazine in Vienna, the *Zentralblatt für Psychoanalyse* ('Central Journal for Psychoanalysis'). Adler, too potent to be disregarded, was made chairman of the Vienna society to keep him quiet, leaving Freud with the real power as chairman of the scientific sessions. But some of the Viennese never forgave him; the naughty boys became naughtier.

Freud believed that with Nuremberg, 'the infancy of our movement has ended', and he read an optimistic paper that hinted at psychoanalysis as the new religion; behind the nerve doctor was the prophet. Few civilised people, he said, could exist without reliance on others, or were even capable of reaching an independent opinion. The intensity of their 'inner lack of resolution and craving for authority' couldn't be exaggerated, and 'The extraordinary increase in neuroses since the power of religions has waned may give you a measure of it.'

Freud added correctly that society would be in no hurry to

concede this authority to psychoanalysis. Describing his early struggles to be heard, he noted that 'People simply did not believe me, just as even today people do not much believe any of us.' But a more rational future lay ahead. Freud offered a practical example; he knew how to keep an audience awake. Suppose, he told them, that

> a number of ladies and gentlemen in good society have planned to have a picnic one day at an inn in the country. The ladies have arranged among themselves that if one of them wants to relieve a natural need she will announce that she is going to pick flowers. Some malicious person, however, has got wind of this secret and has had printed on the programme which is sent round to the whole party: 'Ladies who wish to retire are requested to announce that they are going to pick flowers.' After this, of course, no lady will think of availing herself of this flowery pretext, and, in the same way, other similar formulas, which may be freshly agreed upon, will be seriously compromised. What will be the result? The ladies will admit their natural needs without shame and none of the men will object.

Thus Freud defined one small corner of utopia.

Psychoanalysis irritated people by invading other specialities. Writers, painters and famous figures in general offered tempting subjects, and some of the Viennese analysts indulged themselves with the new 'psychobiography'. A Wagner or a Stendhal could be examined posthumously to see where his creativity came from, though the answer was usually disappointing. Karl Kraus, who was outraged to be told that Goethe's writing contained 'indisputable evidence of the masturbatory drives of its creator', wrote in the *Torch* that 'nerve doctors who pathologise genius should have their heads bashed in with the collected works of the genius'. Stekel and Sadger were both keen to show poets as neurotics.

Freud was above such banalities and he tried to dissuade his pupils from perpetrating them, but he believed in psychobiography and when he wrote it the critics were out in force. His study *Leonardo da Vinci and a Memory of His Childhood*, published May 1910, attracted praise as well as derision. Even a hostile review in a Vienna journal conceded that 'Freud's greatness puts him beyond the reach of ordinary means'; the label of 'great man' was creeping in.

Whether *Leonardo* was 'true', and whether Freud intended it to be read as a documentary account, was another matter. A short book or a long essay, it was a flight of fancy in a manner he

developed over the years, the daring (or dotty) historical speculation. If attacked for having 'merely written a psychoanalytic novel',
he said, his reply would be that he claimed no certainty for the
results, but that he had, like others before him, 'succumbed to the
attraction of this great and mysterious man'. As for the charge that
psychobiography set out to 'drag the sublime into the dust', he
replied innocently that great men deserved to be seen as they were.
His Plutarchian view of biography was long forgotten.

The book used what little is known about the artist's youth to
suggest that as an illegitimate child he was brought up by women,
and that his mother's 'excessive tenderness' and his intense erotic
attachment to her made him homosexual. Freud was less interested in Leonardo's sex life, which he thought was probably non-
existent, than in his idea that the infant's sexual curiosity can
become the adult's intellectual stimulant: that Leonardo 'converted
his passion into a thirst for knowledge'. Even Leonardo's interest in
flight was given Freudian origins, childish dreams of flying being
interpreted as a longing to be capable of sexual performance.

Freud undoubtedly liked to think of himself as a (heterosexual)
artist in the same mould as Leonardo: 'a man whose sexual need
and activity were exceptionally reduced, as if a higher aspiration
had raised him above the common animal need of mankind'.
Leonardo had other hints of Freud the ascetic. Carried away, he
wrote that among the 'higher and more refined' classes, 'it is only
with reluctance that the majority of those alive today obey the
command to propagate their kind; they feel that their dignity as
human beings suffers and is degraded in the process'. This would
be news to most people, including the higher and refined.

Freud the novelist, unconfined by biographical rules, seized on
Leonardo's childhood memory of a vulture that flew into his cradle,
opened his mouth with its tail, and 'struck me many times with its
tail against my lips'. This unlikely event is interpreted as a fantasy
with sexual implications that illuminates Leonardo's relationship
with his mother and thus his character.

The particular significance of the vulture was that the ancient
Egyptians believed there was no male of the species – the female
being impregnated by the wind – so the bird was a symbol of
motherhood. Leonardo was assumed to have known this fable as an
adult, and to have used it unknowingly to construct the fantasy of

the visitation in the cradle, which in turn enabled Freud to see him as the child brought up without a father, and so on.

The vulture perception appealed to other analysts, who carried it a stage further by claiming to have found the outline of the bird concealed in Leonardo's *Madonna and Child with St Anne*. Oskar Pfister, a Zürich clergyman and analyst, saw the painting at the Louvre in 1910 soon after the essay appeared and detected an unmistakable vulture in a blue cloth draped over Mary's hips. 'I saw one too,' cried Jung, 'but in a different place: the beak precisely in the pubic region.' Ferenczi saw it as instructed, 'astonished not to have found the bird oneself'.

A dozen years later the vulture became an embarrassment, when someone discovered that Leonardo's reference had been mistranslated. The bird he wrote about was a kite. Despite this, the essay remained a provoking piece of imaginative reconstruction, and if Freud had brought himself to acknowledge the vulture error when it was detected in 1923 he could have taken it in his stride. But 1923 was a bad year for facing up to facts, and he left the essay as it was. He was too attached to his fiction.*

Freud was caught up in someone else's attempts to write psychobiography when Fritz Wittels began a vendetta with Karl Kraus of the *Torch*. Apart from occasional sighs of regret that his pupils couldn't control themselves, Freud took little interest in their private lives. But this time he feared that scandal would damage the cause.

Wittels had already struck Freud as imprudent by his affair with Irma Karczewska, the young actress he and Kraus had shared in 1907. Three years later, on 12 January 1910, when Kraus had already decided that psychoanalysis was a fraud, and the two men had fallen out – over the voluptuous Irma, among other things – Wittels read a psychobiographical paper about Kraus to Freud and his colleagues called 'The *Torch* Neurosis'. This played on the supposed connections between art and psychopathology, and poked fun at Kraus as the proprietor with a small organ, the *Torch*, ranged against the big organ of the *Neue Freie Presse*, the

---

* James Strachey, while preparing the *Standard Edition*, contemplated altering Freud's text to take account of the error. Jones, then working on the biography, wrote to him in 1952, 'Re the vulture, which is awkward. I don't see how we can tamper with the Holy Scripture.' It was thirty years since the error had been pointed out, but the vulture was still a nuisance.

newspaper Kraus hated. The Vienna Psycho-Analytic Society swallowed all this, though Freud was not enthusiastic. He added that Wittels should guard against saying these things to a wider circle, 'who would not have scientific esteem for them'.

Details soon reached Kraus, and on 13 February Freud wrote to Ferenczi to say that 'psychoanalysis is being threatened by a vicious attack from the *Torch* because of Wittels' lecture', and complained about 'the boundless vanity and insubordination of this talented beast, Karl Kraus', as if jokes about small organs were no excuse. The beast bit back. Little Hans was dragged in.

> Psychoanalysts' children do not fare well. In infancy, the son must admit to experiencing erotic feelings while defecating. Later, he must tell his father what goes through his mind when, on the way to school, he sees a horse defecating. He is lucky indeed if he reaches the age when he can confess to dreaming that he raped his mother.

The Vienna society was told to ignore these 'stupid rockets', as Freud called them, but Wittels decided privately that he would demolish his enemy by putting him in a satirical novel. Kraus tried to stop publication, having seen the manuscript that a mutual woman-friend had shown him without Wittels' knowledge, and his lawyer visited Freud to point out how much damage Kraus might do to the cause. Eventually Freud insisted on seeing the proofs, and informed Wittels that 'Psychoanalysis is more important than your silly controversies. Why should I allow it to be damaged by your inconsiderate book?'

Wittels ignored his warnings, published the satire in the autumn of 1910, was involved in a libel action, and sold many copies; he left Freud's circle, later wrote his unauthorised biography, later still lived and worked in America. The cause was unaffected, but Freud never entirely forgave him. When they met in 1933 he was still grumbling about the episode. Wittels pointed out how long ago it all was. 'I know,' said Freud, 'but you were close to me.'

Those who showed loyalty were rewarded with friendship and a professional leg-up. Jones, still seen as not quite reliable at the time of the Clark lectures, took care soon after to secure his position, writing to say that Freud had been right to suspect him of wanting to lead the movement in England and America, but that now his 'resistances' were at an end.

Jones had no difficulty in recognising Father Freud. He was not a mute uncomplaining follower, but in the early years he watched his step. Genuine feelings and a measure of sycophancy coloured the Jones approach. Words like 'genius' and 'rare treat' were slipped in. A reprint that Freud sent him was, like all his writings, too short. 'We crave, like Oliver Twist, for more.' When a letter from Berggasse failed to arrive in Toronto in April 1912, Jones surmised that it had gone down with the *Titanic*, which had sunk in the icefields on 14 April. 'If so,' he added, 'the sorrow of that disaster will be even more far-reaching than was at first thought.'

The Welshman was never as toadying as the oily words suggest. He knew that he and others like him were perceived as docile, submitting to authority, but in his biography of Freud he suggested they were 'better described as men who had come to terms with their childhood complexes and so could work in harmony with both an older and a younger generation'. His self-description in a letter of June 1910 puts a finger on his masochistic streak:

> The originality-complex is not strong with me; my ambition is rather to know, to be 'behind the scenes', and 'in the know', rather than *to find out* . . . To me work is like a woman bearing a child; to men like you, I suppose it is more like the male fertilisation. That is crudely expressed, but I think you will understand what I mean.

If it suited both men to agree that mind-fucking was the Father's speciality, what was there to complain about? Freud accepted what Jones had to offer without irony. He told Jung early in 1910 that the Welshman, his resistances broken for good, was being more contrite than necessary. To Jones he wrote, as though in a school report, 'you seem to have changed in a most thorough and satisfactory manner'.

The continuing saga of Jones in Toronto showed him isolated and in need of moral support from Vienna. Friends begged him to be careful, and he gave the impression that he was, but things continued to happen to him. Sexual references were removed from his articles, a journal he edited was banned, obscure forces worked against him behind his back, lies were circulated: that he recommended masturbation, sent young men to prostitutes and advised young women to go in for debauchery.

A New York neurologist, Joseph Collins, followed Jones from meeting to meeting in America, making public attacks on him because, Jones said, he had psychoanalysed Mrs Collins in England, after which she divorced her husband. As usual he breathed injured innocence.

James Putnam wanted him considered for a post at Harvard's psychological laboratory, a move that would have changed his life and perhaps the history of psychoanalysis in the United States. But the head of the laboratory, Hugo Münsterberg, while agreeing he was an attractive candidate, was worried that the emphasis on sex in a course available to non-medical students might attract 'the loafers'.

Harvard had a point. In February 1911 a woman whom Jones was treating in Toronto, a 'severe hysteric', went to a woman doctor who was also secretary to the local Purity League, alleging that Jones had slept with her 'to do her good'. The respectable explanation was that she had undergone an erotic transference to her analyst, an occupational hazard as Freud told Jung, but as usual there was a Jones dimension. The woman, a divorcee, had a revolver and made threats, and Jones hired a detective for Loe Kann's peace of mind; when he visited Chicago, the detective went along too. Jones said that altogether it cost him (no doubt, cost Loe) more than $1,000.

Why not sue for slander? Freud asked mildly. The answer was in a letter from Jones to Putnam in Boston, giving a different version of the story. The woman was blackmailing him, and he paid her $500 'to prevent a scandal'.* There were those in London who would have said they always knew.

Nothing like this ever happened to the Professor. His life was always different but always the same: the self-discipline, the patients, the family, the disciples, the foolscap sheets of writing, the necessary holidays. In his fifties, he needed more than ever to escape each summer. In April 1910 he told Ferenczi, 'I count eighty-one days until the beginning of vacation,' and proposed they go to Sicily later in the season. Psychoanalysis was hard work, a struggle with demons. It had become a more complicated business. The patient's transference to the analyst was now seen as crucial, enclosing the two of them in a highly charged relationship that invoked the ghosts of childhood for him or her to confront and understand.

Among his new patients in 1910 was a troubled young man, Serge Pankejeff, the Wolf-Man-to-be. It would take four years to

---

* Jones admitted to a general interest in women without giving much away. His memoirs, *Free Associations*, explained that the record it gave of his erotic life was 'entirely truthful' but incomplete. Perhaps the woman with the revolver was the former wife of the angry Mr Collins.

analyse him. A letter to Ferenczi, telling him about Pankejeff, hints at what a painful business it was:

> On the whole I am only a machine for making money and have been working up a sweat in the last few weeks. A rich young Russian, whom I took on because of compulsive tendencies, admitted the following transferences to me after the first session: Jewish swindler, he would like to use me from behind and shit on my head. At the age of six years he experienced as his first symptom cursing against God: pig, dog, etc. When he saw three piles of faeces on the street he became uncomfortable because of the Holy Trinity and anxiously sought a fourth in order to destroy the association.

Summer came. Adolf Hitler, now resident at the Brigittenau hostel, was busy trying to sell watercolours in the sunshine. Jung went off to potter about Lake Constance in his sailing boat. Freud said goodbye to Pankejeff and the rest of them till the autumn and went to the seaside in Holland, within reach of Hamburg, where Martha could visit old Mrs Bernays who was on her death-bed, though she lingered until the autumn.

Flat beaches at a place called Noordwijk were not Freud's idea of fun. From the balcony of the Pension Noordzee he contemplated a sunset, thinking about his mother-in-law and death. Cold winds blew in from the North Sea; a day's hard sailing up the coast to the north-east, where the chain of islands changed from Dutch to German, would reach the waters where brave Britons foiled the Huns in *The Riddle of the Sands*.

Jones arrived, after a conference in Brussels, to stay briefly at a villa that Kann's sister owned in Noordwijk. ('My patience with Canadian civilisation suddenly reached a breaking point, and I fled to Europe.') They took long walks on the beach, Freud prodding at seaweed with his stick. Jones asked him what he expected to find. 'Something interesting,' said Freud. 'You never know.'

He found time to write a gloomy letter to Jung, 'my dear son and successor', to say that he, Freud, had been in too much of a hurry to form the International Association. The first months of Jung's reign had 'not turned out brilliantly', due to a lack of seriousness on Jung's part: 'One who wishes to rule must carefully cultivate the art of winning people.' Freud missed the hints that Jung was not interested in being a ruler in his elder's mould. A friendly reply cheered him up.

He let work intrude again when the composer Gustav Mahler – who lived a few tram-stops away in Vienna, although they had never met – sent a telegram asking to see him urgently. He was too important to refuse but, when Freud assented, Mahler kept cancelling the appointment. Eventually they met at a restaurant in Leiden, just inland, and an analysis of a kind was conducted as they walked around the town. Mahler, a tormented man with a difficult young wife, is said to have been troubled by impotence. Freud claimed that he uncovered a 'mother-fixation' and 'achieved much' in an afternoon; strangely, when time was short, psycho-analysis could dispense with years of therapy.

Freud's real holiday was in September, with Ferenczi in Sicily. But it was not as relaxing as he hoped. The problem was Ferenczi, who, like most in Freud's circle in those days, was troubled by having such an intimidating father-figure to relate to. They all knew too much about the theory of parental complexes and behaved accordingly, actors in a Freudian drama.

In Ferenczi's case there was no apparent rebellion, only an appetite for demonstrating his dependence, a subject he never tired of analysing. He and Jones had something in common, but the Welshman saw Freud's authority as a practical matter, deferred to it and didn't let it worry him. Ferenczi, more original than Jones, lacked his everyday skills.

In Sicily, visiting ruins from their base at Palermo, he was disappointed that Freud, the object of his admiration, was behaving like a tourist trying to enjoy himself. What Ferenczi wanted was profound discourse between him and the Professor, in which they would tell each other the truth about everything. What Freud wanted was a travelling companion.

One of the books he had with him was the memoirs of a German appelate judge, Paul Schreber, who had been intermittently mad but recovered sufficiently to write an autobiography before his condition became irreversible; in 1910 he was in a mental hospital, nearing the end of his life, and Freud planned to analyse him on the basis of the memoirs. Ferenczi hoped that he and Freud would collaborate in the project, but the first evening at the hotel, when Freud wanted him to act as secretary and take some dictation about Schreber, he sulked and said he expected something better to do. Thereafter Freud worked alone in the evenings. On the return journey he wrote to Jung from Rome, calling Ferenczi 'a dear fellow, but dreamy in a disturbing kind of way, [whose] attitude towards me is infantile'.

The mood was wrong in Sicily. In general Freud enjoyed Ferenczi's warmth (and perhaps his adulation, when no one was looking), and was happy to be confided in. He listened to Ferenczi's complaints about his health. He heard his sexual confessions. Ferenczi, deep in a dispiriting affair with a mother and daughter, Gizella and Elma Pálos, agonised for months and years about which he should marry. Freud was always ready – too ready, given the deadly egocentricity that his friend inflicted on the unlucky women – with advice and a cheering word. Despite Ferenczi's gaucheness he was taken seriously for his technical skills as an analyst and his intuitive way with patients. His greatest asset to Freud was that, like Jones, his loyalty was not in doubt.

In order to be seen as loyal, the comrades needed not only to sympathise in a broad way with psychoanalysis. They had to accept certain articles of faith, especially sex as the root of neurosis, and the central role of the Oedipus Complex.

Alfred Adler was the first to challenge Freud. He came to think that Freud's genius lay in creating a technique that was available for his pupils to develop as they chose. As early as 1907 he was telling the Vienna society that 'there is more than one way in psychoanalysis', drawing a sharp response from Freud about 'the arbitrariness of individual psychoanalysts'.

After the 1910 conference, when revolt was in the air, Adler, the 'common man' who treated poor patients and looked at times like a poor patient himself, dishevelled and unstylish, found the courage to fight. Stekel lined up behind him. So did a handful of other, lesser, Viennese.

In Adler's version of analysis the instinct that mattered was aggression, the drive for power. A child was motivated by the will to survive, and the weaker the child the greater the need to compensate for its deficiencies (Adler himself had been a sickly child, suffering from rickets and other ailments). Neurosis was not repression but compensation. Sex was a demonstration of the will to power. Social conflicts helped to shape personality.

At first Freud leaned towards tolerance. It was Jung, complaining to Freud in October 1910 about having to 'dirty my hands' with the machinations of internal politics, who grumbled about Adler's 'total absence of psychology', and Freud who replied soothingly that 'the insides of other great movements would have been no more appetising if one could have looked into them'. A month later Adler was still 'a very decent and highly intelligent man', but he was now 'paranoid' and his theories were unintelligible. By the end of the year, Freud sounded anxious:

> The crux of the matter – and that is what really alarms me – is that he minimises the sexual drive and our opponents will soon be able to speak of an experienced psychoanalyst whose conclusions are radically different from ours. Naturally in my attitude towards him I am torn between my conviction that all this is lopsided and harmful and my fear of being regarded as an intolerant old man who holds the young men down.

Jung's own reservations about the sexual drive had never gone away. For the moment he had no need to press them. In any case, he was the favoured son to whom anything – almost anything – was permitted. Adler enjoyed no special protection.

Where Freud was all flights of fancy and distinguished prose, Adler's psychology sounded more like common sense, and when he wrote about it he made it sound more banal than ever. Adler was bloody-minded, a bit of a philistine. He lacked the patrician manner that distinguished both leaders of the movement. Freud, his beard barbered daily as it had been for decades, emerged from his large apartment – which had several servants – in a fur-lined overcoat, carrying an ivory-handled stick, smoking a fat cigar. Adler's caricature is a man with an insipid moustache and fleshy features, arguing with socialists in a café in Leopoldstadt, which the Freuds had escaped from thirty years earlier, brandishing a cheap cheroot.

'Paranoia' was now well-established as a label for enemies. Freud believed that repressed homosexual feelings were its cause (his paper about the mad judge, Schreber, explored the matter), and he again applied the diagnosis retrospectively to his lost friend, Wilhelm Fliess, describing Adler as 'a little Fliess *redivivus*'. He even told Jung that the reason he found the quarrel with Adler so upsetting was that it 'opened up the wounds of the Fliess affair'. Underneath, he was less confident than he seemed.

A process of cleansing got under way. Nothing was too small to be used against the rebels. Minor errors in editing an issue of the *Zentralblatt* in January 1911, the journal for which Adler and Stekel were responsible, were noted by Freud as psychological weaknesses.

The Vienna society held meetings in January and February 1911 for Adler's case to be stated and discussed. Most of the speakers denounced him. After the final meeting he resigned as the society's president, and Stekel, the vice-president, went with him. His views, Freud wrote to Jones, were clever but dangerous; his behaviour throughout neurotic. Freud was the visionary whose trick was never to fall to earth. Adler, stubborn and persevering, never left it.

Max Graf was at the meetings and saw Freud's relentless exercise of authority. Graf had decided already that the atmosphere at Freudian conclaves was that of 'the foundation of a religion'. Outsiders often attacked the movement for its intolerance, as when a professor at Würzburg, Wilhelm Weygandt, said that Freud's followers compared him to Galileo and refused to hear any criticism. Graf, however, was not an outsider but a follower and amateur analyst, the father of Little Hans. What he found unsettling was the excommunication of Adler, whom he respected, by the founder of the church. The time came when Graf was 'unable and unwilling to submit to Freud's "do" or "don't" – with which he once confronted me'. Then he left, too.

For a few months, Adler remained in the Vienna society, an enemy within. Stekel made his peace with Freud and returned to favour for a while. 'The other boy', the wicked Adler, was beyond redemption. '[He] fixes himself in mute resistance and ill-suppressed anger,' Freud wrote to Jones in May. 'He is a paranoiac I am sorry to say.' Soon he was 'an abnormal individual driven mad by ambition'. This monster left the society in June.

In October 1911 the remaining Adlerians were told to choose between the two camps. In all, including Adler, ten members resigned, and went off to form their own society. No contact with them was allowed. This had absurd consequences. A year later (November 1912), when Lou Andréas-Salomé* was staying in Vienna and beginning an intellectual love affair with Freud, she told him that Adler had invited her to one of his Thursday-evening discussions. Freud pointed out that there was no contact between the groups, and guests of the Vienna society had to choose one or the other. Grandly, he waived the rule in her case. 'I would never

---

* Louise Andréas-Salomé (1861–1937), a Russian general's daughter, was a formidably clever (and when young, extremely beautiful) woman with a reputation. Among her intellectual, in some cases physical, conquests were Tolstoy, Strindberg, Schnitzler, Rilke and Nietzsche. It was said of her that nine months after she began an affair with a man he gave birth to an idea. With Freud she was meek and adulatory.

dream, dear lady,' he said, 'of imposing such a restriction.' All the same, he asked her to 'make no reference to your contact with us when with them, and vice versa'.

The Adlerians became a lost tribe, surviving as the school of 'individual psychology', written off by Freudians as simplistic, socialistic and unpsychological. Adler's ideas did rather better. Freud borrowed some of them himself, like the 'destructive instinct', proposed in 1920, which derived from Adler's 'aggressive drive' of 1908.

Only historians of psychology know or care about these shifts; the fury of quarrels long ago often seems disproportionate. By the second half of the twentieth century, Adlerian heresies were becoming part of psychoanalytic thinking. Social conflicts in the patient's adult life were emphasised; uncovering the memories of infancy became less significant; the sex drive ceased to be the key to all understanding. But in 1911, all Freud cared about was that Adler had been driven into the wilderness, and had ceased to be a threat.

23: The Break with Jung

In 1911 the psychoanalyst entered fiction via a German novel called *The Intellectuals*, by Grete Meisel-Hess, in which a doctor with piercing eyes and a beard he likes to stroke is seen treating a neurotic woman who is suffering from repressed memories about sex. After she has told him her dreams, he cures her by hypnosis and suggestion. The American pre-analytic novel of 1880, Edward Bellamy's *Dr Heidenhoff's Process*, groped in the same direction. As Dr Heidenhoff put it, 'Macbeth's question, "Canst thou not minister to a mind diseas'd, Pluck from the memory a rooted sorrow, Raze out the written troubles of the brain?" was a puzzler to the sixteenth century doctor, but he of the twentieth, yes, perhaps of the nineteenth, will be able to answer it affirmatively.'

By 1911, having shown psychoanalysis to the world, Freud was as contemptuous as ever of popular attempts at explanation. It was a doctrine for the educated. Neither he nor Jung was interested in the public's vulgar curiosity. When, the following year, Zürich newspapers stirred up a campaign against analysis, Jung's first instinct was to consult a lawyer and see if he could sue the vermin for libel (he couldn't, or didn't). If 'the public' mattered at all, it was something for subordinates to worry about. Ferenczi wrote to Freud (August 1911) that in the Hungarian part of the Austrian Empire, at least, 'the youth and the intelligent public' were already won over, even if they were easily led astray by 'the vituperation of the professors'. Freud showed no interest.

He and Jung were practising analysts – Freud more so than Jung because he lacked a rich wife and had no income without his patients – but more importantly they were the leading theoreticians in their field. Jung's specialty was the treatment and understanding of madness, in Anthony Storr's phrase a 'search for meaning in the apparently incomprehensible'. His work complemented Freud's with neurosis, and both were formidable exponents. Together they dominated psychoanalysis. Adler's departure in 1911 produced no differences between them; if anything, Jung, intolerant of all the Viennese except Freud, was the more anxious to see the back of him. The duopoly worked satisfactorily as long as both men were agreed about the order of rank.

However this was dressed up, Freud had to be the senior partner. They could disagree, but ultimately there would be a limit to the disagreement. Their comparative status is caricatured in the official group photograph at the Weimar congress, September 1911, where Freud, much shorter than Jung, towers over him; either Freud was standing on a box or Jung's feet were below ground level.

From the beginning, each had something the other wanted. Freud made no secret of his friend's value as chief organiser and propagandist. Jung confessed in his memoirs that he wanted to benefit from Freud's experience. Behind the self-interest they must have liked one another as well. But the fiction of father and son, proposed by one and accepted by the other, was mentioned too often to sound natural.

Taking the bleakest view, they were close colleagues who wanted or needed to give an appearance of friendship. By now their letters steered carefully around topics, like ships avoiding sandbanks. They corresponded regularly about the politics of the movement, gossip, their enemies; less than before about theoretical matters. The letters were complicated mechanisms, often implying more than they said.

The topic that flickered in the background in 1911 was an essay (eventually a book) about mythology being written by Jung, which had acquired an air of mystery. Jung brought in a family legend that he was Goethe's great-grandson, via an ancient illegitimacy, in order to make a joke about work in progress and to say that Goethe would have approved of it, the implication being that Freud would not. Jung to Freud, 18 January:

> it is a risky business for an egg to try to be cleverer than the hen. Still, what is in the egg must eventually summon the courage to creep out. So you see what fantasies I must resort to in order to protect myself against your criticism.
>
> They say here that your son Martin has broken his foot skiing. Is that true?

Martin had broken his leg on the Schneeberg. Freud to Jung, 22 January:

> He lay motionless in the snow for five hours before help came and some of his appendages would certainly have frozen if a friend had not watched over him ... I don't know why you are so afraid of my criticism in matters of mythology.

Their lives were very different. Jung, whose doubts about sex as the explanation of everything were as strong as ever, was unfaithful to his wife, something she had to put up with. Freud, who placed sexuality at the core of human affairs, led the dimmest of sex lives with Martha. Jung, in his lake-side house, had ancient texts on the wall of his study, and a photograph of the Shroud of Turin that he kept covered with a cloth to hide the image of Christ's face. Freud, cooped up in his apartment, had his statuettes of 'old and grubby gods', not to be taken too seriously. By Jung's robust standards his life seems cramped, turned in on itself.

Working in his study late at night in January 1911, Freud began to have headaches, followed in the daytime by forgetfulness. He thought it was old age (he was now fifty-four) and hardening arteries, and told Jung that his health was troubling him. Then someone noticed that the rubber tube that fed the gas lamp on his desk had a faulty connection. Every night he was slowly poisoning himself.

Informed of this, Jung wrote laconically, 'Couldn't anyone smell the gas?' This drove Freud to a more detailed account ('I smelled nothing because I sat swathed in cigar smoke') and the touching boast that, faced with memory-lapses about people and events, 'I am still very proud of the fact that I did not attribute all this to neurosis'. One imagines Jung laughing with his wife about how the old boy had come close to gassing himself while worrying about his unconscious.

The prospect of Jung's essay about mythology intrigued Freud because of his own close interest in the subject. He believed that myths revealed their neurotic origin. Thus Eve was really Adam's mother, and the story in Genesis distorted an original myth where Adam was being punished for committing incest with her. This approach, typical of Freud, was rather less typical of Jung, who thought that myths had a reality and a value of their own and were not merely a reflection of the unconscious. He told Freud of 'wandering alone through a strange country, seeing wonderful things that no one has seen before'. Freud saw no harm in this. But he badly wanted to see what was going to creep out of Jung's egg.

All was revealed during the Weimar congress, where Jung spoke, and then at greater length in Part 1 of the essay itself, published in the *Yearbook*, a spectacular work that impressed readers with its range, its bravura and most of all its obscurity. Under the title *Transformations and Symbols of the Libido*, and drawing on many sources in literature and anthropology, Jung sought to interpret the myths of primitive cultures and ancient civilisations as a common property, drawing on the same symbolic figures and images: part of what he later called the 'collective unconscious'.

Much of Jung's evidence, in *Transformations* and elsewhere, came from people in states of altered consciousness, including visionaries and schizophrenics, who supposedly had superior access to these universal myths. In particular he was influenced by the published fantasies of someone he never met, a young American woman who wrote poetry and went into trances, Miss Frank Miller. Her outpourings about God, the sun and an Aztec hero bitten by a green snake seem to have encouraged Jung to use *Transformations* as an outlet for his own visions.

Besides Miss Miller, who was distinctly odd, there were the psychotic patients he encountered whose fantasies, he believed, contained the same mythological ingredients. He made the point with an epigram at the Weimar meeting – 'In [schizophrenia] the patient suffers from the reminiscences of mankind' – which neatly rephrased Freud's remark of the 1890s in which it was the hysteric who suffered from reminiscences, not mankind's but her own.

Freud, bemused by these new directions, could find nothing heretical in them. One of his own projects in 1911 concerned primitive man and his practices (which became a book, *Totem and Taboo*), and he told Jones that he and Jung were 'on the same track', which they were not. Jones, back in Europe for Weimar in September, claimed to Freud, but not till fifteen years later, that Jung took him aside at the conference and spoke of the day when he would be superior to Freud. Jones told him he should analyse the 'father complex' that made him say such things, to which Jung replied, 'It is my fate.'*

* Neither Jung nor Freud was backward about making such claims. In 1912, winding up a seminar at the Vienna Psycho-Analytical Society, Freud defended his views by saying, 'I know that I have a destiny to fulfil. I cannot escape it and I need

No rift between the two was apparent at Weimar. But their lines of communication were out of order. During the previous week Freud had stayed with the Jungs at Kusnacht, when he failed to say anything about *Transformations*, Part 1, published almost a month earlier. Jung couldn't bring himself to ask, and it was left to Mrs Jung, writing covertly to Freud in October and November, to say things that so far had been left unspoken. She was 'tormented' to think that his relation with Jung was 'not altogether as it should be'. She spoke of her husband's 'misgivings' and 'trepidation' about *Transformations*, thus alerting Freud to nuances in Part 1 that he might have missed, and to the likelihood that Part 2 would give him something to complain about.

Mrs Jung's marriage was troubled, partly because of Jung's sexual activities. Two of his supposed mistresses – Toni Wolff, who began as a patient, and a nurse, Mary Moltzer, both of them middle-class women who later became analysts – attended Weimar. Freud may have seemed a comforting figure. In one letter Emma sighed that of course the women were all in love with Carl, adding that she felt unable to compete with him in any way, so that 'I usually have to talk extra stupidly when in company.' A woman's place in Zürich was the same as it was in Vienna. But Mrs Jung was not too downtrodden to give Freud advice. She ended her letter of 6 November with a warning:

> You may imagine how overjoyed and honoured I am by the confidence you have in Carl, but it almost seems to me as though you were sometimes giving too much – do you not see in him the follower and fulfiller more than you need? Doesn't one often give much because one wants to keep much? ... And do not think of Carl with a father's feeling: 'He will grow but I must dwindle,' but rather as one human being thinks of another, who like you has his own law to fulfil.

This motherly advice from young Mrs Jung must have made Freud grit his teeth. But she knew what she was talking about. Part 2 of the masterpiece, still being written, began to cast its shadow, as Part 1 had done.

'In my second part,' said a letter from Jung on 14 November, 'I have got down to a fundamental discussion of the libido theory.' In Freud's vocabulary, 'libido' meant the all-powerful sexual drive. There were signs that Jung meant to tamper with this sacred word

---

not move towards it. I shall await it.'

in the psychoanalytic vocabulary, extending its definition to energy that was not merely sexual. Edgy letters went to and fro, disagreeing politely without having anything explicit to disagree about.

In 1911 Freud had published an historical fragment about Ephesus, for no apparent reason, describing how the Apostle Paul formed a dissident community there, which 'did not long remain faithful to him', and came under the influence of another apostle, John, who introduced mystical tendencies. Some authorities assume it was aimed at Jung, the latter-day apostate, although it is so feebly done that it is hard to see it having much effect on someone so hardboiled.

The spiral into animosity had begun. 'I would never have sided with you in the first place had not heresy run in my blood,' wrote Jung in March 1912, perhaps with an eye on St John at Ephesus. He began to express doubts about the Freudian concept of incest-wishes in small children, which implied a re-examination of the Oedipus Complex. To the uninitiated, much of their disagreement about the origins of the taboo against incest is impenetrable. Freud himself didn't always grasp instantly what Jung was saying.

In May 1912 they found a trivial occasion to quarrel over and deflect attention from the real issue, the nature of their partnership. Freud went to visit Ludwig Binswanger, the young Swiss psychiatrist he had first met in Vienna with Jung. Binswanger, who was fonder of Freud than he was of Jung, thought he was dying of cancer (but lived for another fifty-four years) and planned to write a valedictory essay; this was the reason for Freud's visit.

Binswanger had taken over the family's Bellevue Sanatorium at Kreuzlingen, on Lake Constance, where Bertha Pappenheim was treated, and it was at the family estate there that Freud visited him over the Whitsun weekend; he noted that Count von Zeppelin, the airship man, lived on the estate next door.

Jung, on Lake Zürich to the south, was not more than forty miles away, but Freud either failed to give him sufficient notice of the visit or Jung pretended that he didn't learn of it in time. Freud sent a letter at the last minute giving his movements; Jung had gone sailing on Lake Zürich; there was malice by Freud (as some Jungians still assert) or merely confusion compounded by a reluctance in either party to meet the other.

Jung, whether genuinely hurt or seeking a tactical advantage, called it Freud's 'Kreuzlingen gesture'. 'I understand the Kreuzlingen gesture,' he said darkly. 'Whether your policy is the right one will become apparent from the success or failure of my future work.'

In July Freud wrote to Ferenczi, asking rhetorically what it all meant, and supplied his own answer:

> Jung must now be in a florid neurosis. However this turns out, my intention of amalgamating Jews and goyim in the service of psychoanalysis seems now to have gone awry. They are separating like oil and water.

Ferenczi obliged on 6 August with instant hostility to Jung and his fantasies; once Freud gave the word, the central Europeans were quick to voice their pent-up feelings against the alien. Ferenczi added that the Swiss in general were a 'bunch of anti-Semites', and advised his master to keep an eye on Jones as well.

But Jones was safe enough; safer than any of them. Having returned to Europe for the rest of the year, though still hoping that Canada might change its mind and embrace him, he was busy making plans that didn't include Jung. In early summer he and Loe Kann had visited Vienna so that she could have her morphine habit, no doubt aggravated by life in Toronto, treated by Freud, who was instantly taken with the 'deeply neurotic Jewess'.

While he was there, Jones heard the latest about Jung, and seized on a remark by Ferenczi that a small group of men could represent (in Jones's words) 'the pure theory unadulterated by personal complexes, and thus build an unofficial inner circle'. Freud was delighted, calling it a 'secret council', and he and Jones between them talked it up into a romantic vision of a band of brothers against the world, 'designed,' sang Jones, 'like the Paladins of Charlemagne, to guard the kingdom and policy of their master'. Its purposes were strategic, not scientific. 'I dare say,' wrote Freud, 'it would make living and dying easier for me if I knew of such an association existing to watch over my creation.'

Freud insisted that everything be kept private. He gave his orders for the membership: Jones, Ferenczi and Abraham, who were physicians; and two laymen: Rank and the lawyer Hanns Sachs, a newcomer to the group. All were Jews except Jones, who, being a Celt from Wales, tried to claim solidarity with them as a member of another 'oppressed race', perhaps a joke. These were to be the high priests charged with doctrinal vigilance; or, depending on the mood of the less austere members – Jones, possibly Sachs,

Freud in his happier moments – the brave lads of adventure stories who were to swear eternal oaths in blood and stick together whatever happened.

In 1912 there was no annual congress to prepare for. Plans to hold it in Munich were abandoned when Jung announced that in September he would be in America, giving nine lectures at the Jesuits' Fordham University, New York City. Whether by accident or design, this got him out of Europe just as news of *Transformations* Part 2 began to leak out.

A few days before Jung left, Jones was in Bavaria with a friendly analyst who had proofs of Part 2 as it would appear in the *Yearbook*. There were nearly 300 pages. Jones made of them what he could. Libido, he informed Freud, was evidently 'no longer sexual in the individual child'. Jung wasn't denying infantile sexuality altogether, but, Jones advised, the work was obscure and rambling, a 'disconnected shovelling in of mythology with occasional remarks of his own'.

Freud was soon able to read it for himself, as Mrs Jung sent him an off-print a week later when her husband was in mid-Atlantic. He said he took his time reading it. The 300 pages went with him to Rome, where he spent the second half of September, and he finished them on the way back to Vienna.

Their theoretical content he brushed aside, saying that Jung's errors didn't matter; it was the man's character that worried him, for who could respect 'greatness proclaiming itself'? Still, the errors, as they sank in, had to be faced. The Part 2 that everyone had been waiting for turned out to be a bewildering lyric about the Hero whose progress through self-sacrifice and rebirth is driven by mysterious psychic forces ('that driving strength of our own soul'), not the sexual energy of the libido as laid down by Freud.

The lectures that Jung gave in New York, which were soon filtering back to Europe in second-hand reports, were more direct. He redefined libido as a vital force, he denied infant sexuality in Freud's sense, he marginalised the Oedipus Complex. Human nature danced to a different tune, spiritual rather than biological.

In November 1912 Jung wrote from Zürich, for the first time in three months, to boast what a 'very great deal' he had been able to do for the movement in America. 'Naturally,' he said, 'I also made room for those of my views which deviate in places from the hitherto existing conceptions.' He was out for revenge:

I found that my version of psychoanalysis won over many people who until now had been put off by the problem of sexuality in neurosis. As soon as I have an offprint, I shall take pleasure in sending you a copy of my lectures in the hope that you will gradually come to accept certain innovations already hinted at in my libido paper.

Jung knew what the response would be, and there was a certain contempt about pretending otherwise. But invective was taking over from argument. 'Your Kreuzlingen gesture has dealt me a lasting wound,' he added, to which Freud replied that 'I find your harping on [it] both incomprehensible and insulting.' The salutation was 'Dear Doctor', not 'Dear Friend'.

Later in the month they met on the neutral ground of a row about one of the international journals, the *Zentralblatt*, whose editor, Stekel, was clinging to his contract despite attempts by Freud to remove him for general misbehaviour. At Freud's instigation, Jung, as President of the International Association, called a meeting of branch presidents to dispose of the editor and approve a new journal in its place. Perhaps both realised that sooner or later they must meet before they parted, like lovers having the goodbye lunch.

Seven men, including Freud and Jung, gathered at the Park Hotel in Munich on 24 November. Jones, who was in Florence, received a card from Jung to say the meeting was on 26 November, but was given the correct date by his mistress, Kann, who was in Vienna being analysed. In Munich he told Freud that no doubt Jung had made an unconscious slip. 'A gentleman wouldn't have that sort of unconscious,' said Freud.

Stekel was dealt with as Freud suggested, by removing the *Zentralblatt*'s official status, and at eleven a.m., two hours before they were to reconvene for lunch, Sigmund and Carl left the hotel together and (Freud told Ferenczi) 'took our appointed walk for the purpose of having a talk'; so the move had been planned.

The letter that described the meeting was written two days later. They began by arguing about the Kreuzlingen gesture. Then the 'unbelievable and unexpected' happened. Jung appeared to capitulate:

He was absolutely crushed, ashamed, and then admitted everything: that he had already feared for a long time that intimacy with me or with others would damage his independence, and for that reason he had decided to withdraw; that he had certainly construed me according to his father complex and had been afraid about what I would say about his modifications . . .

> I spared him nothing at all, told him calmly that a friendship with him couldn't be maintained, that he himself gave rise to the intimacy which he then so cruelly broke off; that things were not at all in order in his relations with men, not just with me but with others as well ... He totally ceased contradicting me and admitted everything. I think it did him good.

This change of heart, Freud added, would not be permanent because of Jung's 'kernel of dishonesty'.

Ferenczi heard a less forthcoming version of events that followed in Munich. At the hotel, 'I got a similar anxiety attack at the table as I did that time ... in Bremen; I wanted to get up, and for a moment I felt faint.' A sleepless night on the train was blamed.

The truth was more interesting. A mild dispute arose over lunch. In one version, it concerned an Egyptian pharaoh who was supposed to have erased his father's name from monuments; death again, as in Bremen. In another, Freud was upset that his own name had been omitted from some Swiss work on psychoanalysis. Very likely both things happened. All at once Freud collapsed and slid off his chair. Jones saw Jung pick him up and carry him out to a sofa. As he came round he murmured, 'How sweet dying must be.' In Jung's memoirs, 'he looked at me as if I were his father'.

Freud's emotions or his digestion had got the better of him. He was afraid that by collapsing he had lost, as he told Jones, a 'portion of my authority', but for a day or two the signs were promising. A contrite letter from Jung followed him to Vienna, admitting that his mistakes had been inexcusable, reassuring Freud that their 'personal relationship' would continue, and hoping that the journey home hadn't overstrained him.

Replying, Freud thanked him and dismissed the Park Hotel incident as 'a bit of neurosis that I ought really to look into'. He added that Jung's *Transformations* had 'brought us a great revelation, though not the one you intended', and made a remark about mysticism that sounded like disparagement.

On 3 December, Jung asked how Freud could possibly understand his work while underestimating it; as for the 'bit of neurosis', Freud should take it seriously. On 5 December, Freud suggested that each of them should pay attention to his own neurosis, not his neighbour's. On or about 11 December, in a brief letter dissociating himself from Adler, Jung meant to write that 'Even Adler's cronies do not regard me as one of theirs', but instead wrote 'one of yours'.

On 16 December Freud wrote to point out this Freudian slip and asked if Jung could consider it 'without anger'.

Jung could not. On 18 December he finally lost control. It was a mistake, he thundered, for Freud to treat his pupils as if they were patients, thus producing either slavish sons or 'impudent puppies' like 'Adler-Stekel and the whole insolent gang now throwing their weight about in Vienna'. Out poured the insults; Jung, as uncertain about his new concepts as Freud had once been about his, may have found the brutality therapeutic.

> I am objective enough to see through your little trick. You go around sniffing out all the symptomatic actions in your vicinity, thus reducing everyone to the level of sons and daughters who blushingly admit the existence of their faults. Meanwhile you remain on top as the father, sitting pretty . . .
>
> You see, my dear Professor, so long as you hand out this stuff I don't give a damn for my symptomatic actions; they shrink to nothing in comparison with the formidable beam in my brother Freud's eye. I am not in the least neurotic – touch wood! I have submitted . . . to analysis and am much the better for it. You know, of course, how far a patient gets with self-analysis: *not* out of his neurosis – just like you . . . I shall continue to stand by you publicly while maintaining my own views, but privately shall start telling you in my letters what I really think of you.

Freud to Jung, 3 January 1913: 'I propose that we abandon our personal relations entirely.'

Jung to Freud, 6 January: 'I accede to your wish that we abandon our personal relations, for I never thrust my friendship on anyone. You yourself are the best judge of what this moment means to you. "The rest is silence." '

The central Europeans and Jones stood firm. Freud discussed Jung with them in a tone of contempt. 'He can go jump in the lake,' he wrote to Ferenczi. Jones was told about Jung's boast that, unlike Freud, *he* had been psychoanalysed. 'With the Moltzer? [Mary Moltzer, the nurse and presumed mistress] I suppose; you may imagine what the treatment was.'

Psychoanalysis, split the previous year by Adler's defection, had fragmented again, this time on racial as well as ideological lines. But Jung, who faced a long personal crisis after the break, crawling with dreams and visions, was in no fit state to found a school and recruit members, even if that had been his intention. *Transformations*, incoherent text of Jung's new psychology, was a poor substitute for Freud's clarity. Nor did he have a circle of analytic friends as Freud did, many of them bound to him because they needed the patients he referred to them or depended on him emotionally.

Ferenczi relied on Freud as father and mentor, bombarding him with dreams and confessions, chattering about the unsolvable problem of the mother and daughter, Gizella and Elma, describing visits to prostitutes, worrying he had syphilis, worrying that he *wanted* to have syphilis so that he could appear to Gizella as a despised syphilitic, comforted by her love.

Jones needed the patronage of someone more forgiving than the medical cabals of London and Toronto. Whatever information he had kept from Freud, Loe Kann was no doubt passing it on as part of her analysis. While it was still in progress, Jones returned to Canada for the last time. Freud wrote to Ferenczi to say how charmingly Loe had behaved (Jones had been in trouble again, this time for sleeping with her companion, Lina). 'I am now altogether satisfied with my adopted children,' beamed Freud.

Like Ferenczi, they were part of the network. So was the secret committee. Even Sabina Spielrein, now planning a career for herself in psychoanalysis, had chosen Freud's ideas, not Jung's. His sons and daughters may have lacked the stature of Jung, but they were all that Freud needed. Unlike Jung, who agonised for years over the break, Freud shrugged and moved on.

24: Fables

When they were still friends and colleagues in 1910, Freud is supposed to have sought a promise from Jung never to abandon the sexual theory, because it was an 'unshakable bulwark' against 'the black tide of mud of occultism'. Jung's supernatural hankerings were no secret. When it came to Part 2 of the *Transformations* essay, with its visions and mysterious psychic energy, his intentions became clearer. Ferenczi saw it (May 1913) as 'none other than his hidden confession of *occultism* in the guise of science'.

Yet Freud was not as fiercely doctrinaire about the occult as the 'black tide of mud' anecdote, which comes from Jung's memoirs, suggests. Had Jung continued to uphold sexual libido as the great force of life, Freud might have been happy for him to dabble in the supernatural and the unexplained, since in his own way he dabbled in it himself.

Freud had been unconcerned in June 1911 by the news that his friend's evenings were taken up with astrology. 'I dare say,' wrote Jung, 'that we shall one day discover in astrology a good deal of knowledge that has been intuitively projected into the heavens.' No paternal reproof about black tides followed. Freud said merely that 'I promise to believe anything that can be made to look reasonable', having 'grown humble' in matters of occultism since 'the great lesson Ferenczi's experiences gave me'.

These experiences (which Jung knew about) took place in 1910 and 1911 when Ferenczi lured Freud into the occult, at least into its milder regions, 'thought transference' or telepathy. A strange correspondence resulted. Something in Freud's nature wanted to believe the unbelievable.

His long-standing weakness for magic numbers and fateful dates, however he chose to explain it by 'scientific' means, has often distressed his followers. Jones, a rationalist from a religious-minded nation, was shocked at any activity that was tainted with supernatural beliefs. Telepathy was included in this category, if only because those who toyed with it often toyed with phantoms and seances as well.

The phenomena were imperfectly defined. In 1910 the paranormal – the 'beyond' or the 'unseen' were the fashionable terms – still had a degree of scientific credibility. Such marvels of the age as wireless telegraphy and X-rays had confused people's ideas of what lay in the realm of the normal. Sir William Crookes, the eminent English physicist who invented the cathode-ray tube, was the same William Crookes who believed he had danced with a materialised spirit called Katie. Victorian spiritualists with their ectoplasm and levitations had come and largely gone, most but not all of them discredited.

The respectable face of the paranormal in England was the Society for Psychical Research, set up in 1882 by representatives of science, church and learning to offer a working compromise for the thoughtful. It published erudite papers, some of them sceptical, and hoped to find proofs of immortality while remaining 'scientific'. Thought-transference was an important sideline.

In a way that would have been unthinkable a few decades later, bishops, scientists, philosophers and writers hurried to join the society. Frederic Myers, its visionary, saw the unconscious as a 'subliminal self' with mystical overtones, but his views were eclectic and he was lecturing in London about the Breuer–Freud work on hysteria three months after it was published in Vienna.

Affiliates of the society included Charcot, Janet and Jung. In 1911, when it was already in decline, Freud was invited to become a 'contributing member'. The psychologist William James, a friend of Myers and a tentative believer in life beyond the grave, died at about the same time, just when Freud was asking Jones what he knew about the society. Jones replied contemptuously that it went in for 'spook-hunting', adding, 'It does not seem that your researches lend much support to spiritism, in spite of William James' ardent hope. Poor James. One hasn't even the consolation of thinking that he knows better by now.'

Freud was unmoved, and the following year he contributed a paper to the society on 'The Unconscious in Psychoanalysis'. This, however, was a strict exposition of how he viewed the unconscious mind, with nothing in it to alarm a rational Welshman.

The same couldn't be said about the correspondence between Freud and Ferenczi. Their letters mentioned telepathy as soon as they returned from America in autumn 1909, which suggests that their interest, which was mainly Ferenczi's interest to begin with, arose during the visit. Both of them could have discussed telepathy at Worcester with William James or with Stanley Hall, who didn't believe in the paranormal but was an active sceptic, familiar with the Boston medium Leonora Piper, and knowledgeable about conjuring tricks. *Appleton's Magazine* published a popular article by him in 1908, 'Spooks and Telepathy'.

After the party returned from America, Freud and Ferenczi were briefly in Berlin before they went home. Freud may have gone there to meet Emmanuel, in Germany on one of his visits, as well as his colleague Karl Abraham.

Ferenczi, who had a brother living in the city, went by himself to visit a clairvoyant, Mrs Seidler, for what he called a 'seance', and showed her one of Freud's letters. Seidler thought it had something to do with Vienna, and spoke about the writer's dissatisfaction with his colleagues (which could have described Freud) and other trifles. It was a thin harvest, typical of clairvoyants, but sufficient to draw the response from Freud that 'there seems to be something to the thing', despite the fact, as he pointed out to Ferenczi – who seems not to have noticed – that 'Vienna' was printed on the stationery. 'Absolute silence' was to be maintained.

Ferenczi, convinced that Seidler had read his thoughts, sent his brother to see her, taking more letters for inspiration. The resulting evidence failed to impress Freud, and soon Ferenczi was patronising a Budapest clairvoyant, Mrs Jelinek, who sat with him in a smelly parlour and told him things of little consequence. Again Freud was unimpressed. But he didn't withdraw his support, which might have put a stop to the dabbling.

Ferenczi now interested himself in telepathic exchanges between analyst and patient. In 1910, shortly before their trip to Sicily, he sent Freud material that, for the first time, had some merit. The patient was a homosexual man. Ferenczi thought he could explain the patient's free associations as he lay on the couch: his unconscious was picking up information from Ferenczi's unconscious.

On 25 July: 'The patient lies down as usual. But he immediately jumps up excitedly ... "What kind of worms do you have on the couch?" ' Ferenczi interpreted for Freud:

> I had sexual intercourse on the same day. The thought occurred to me that it is not right to use the same couch for one's occupation and for making love. The woman with whom I had intercourse calls spermatozoa 'little worms'.

On 26 July the patient described a fantasy. 'I am lying [down]. My clothes are empty, as if there were no body in them at all.' Ferenczi had been reading a newspaper piece by Anatole France, where a lunatic is described putting clothes on an armchair with a pole as a backbone.

On 16 August the patient said, 'The sun lay on the moon, the moon on the stars. They carry out the movements of coitus.' An earlier patient, a printer, had told Ferenczi about a philosophical work he was handling in which gravitation and magnetism were identified with sexual attraction. The printer had used the phrase, 'Sun and Earth are having coitus with each other.'

Freud was convinced. The observations 'seem to me finally to shatter the doubts about the existence of thought transference'. It was simply a matter of getting used to the idea. Ferenczi was alarmed to think that he now bore the responsibility for converting the Professor. But Freud's interest was unfocused. It was the fact that telepathy existed, an anomaly in the fabric, that intrigued him, rather than any specific application. He believed one minute and doubted the next.

When Ferenczi wrote (November 1910) to say that he had become '*a great soothsayer, that is to say, a reader of thoughts!*' able to read patients' minds via his own free associations, Freud referred sarcastically to 'your earth-shaking communication to the effect that you were yourself a medium'. Ferenczi had declared that 'the future methodology of psychoanalysis' must take note of the discoveries. Gently, Freud dissuaded him. 'I see destiny approaching, inexorably,' he wrote, 'and I note that it has designated you to bring to light mysticism and the like ... Still, I think we ought to venture to slow it down.'

That was sensible, given the fragile nature of the evidence for telepathy. In Britain a scandal about thought-reading had shaken the Society for Psychical Research. Ferenczi carried on in a quiet way, scraping together evidence. In 1912 he came across horses that could do advanced mathematics by means of telepathy –

'deriving square and cube roots, division, subtraction of large numbers' – in what he believed were 'flawlessly correct' experiments.

Freud had no views on mathematical horses. No doubt he knew that Ferenczi's enthusiasm ran away with him. Nevertheless, it was Ferenczi who taught him about telepathy. It was his evidence alone that impressed Freud, who had no telepathic experiences of his own, and once said that his life had been 'particularly poor in an occult sense'. He was willing to contemplate strange beliefs from a man he trusted: as he had twenty years earlier with Fliess, who appeared in Freud's dreams when he and Ferenczi visited Sicily.

In 1913 Freud was feeling so positive about telepathy that he could tell the annual conference, in words that must have made Jones wince:

> I have had good reason for asserting that everyone possesses in his own unconscious an instrument with which he can interpret the utterances of the unconscious in other people.

He said much the same thing in *Totem and Taboo*, his history of civilisation that had just appeared – the second of his eccentric historical dramas – in which the origin of religion and civilisation itself was supposed to have been the primeval murder of an autocratic tribal father by his downtrodden sons. The horror of the event impressed itself on those who were there, and the acquired guilt and remorse somehow altered the way their minds worked. The change was then passed on to future generations, and from this built-in guilt came social order and morality. Freud was undeterred that by 1913 orthodox biology was beginning to reject the idea that 'acquired characteristics' of any kind could be inherited.

How, exactly, it all worked was left vague, but some mental 'apparatus' (or 'instrument', in the conference version) was involved. Freud suggested that an 'unconscious understanding' of the historical events (the primal murder and its sequel) 'may have made it possible for later generations to take over their heritage of emotion'. Mixed up in this was the idea of thought-transference.

Freud didn't persevere with telepathy; he left it as raw material he might devote himself to one day, but never did. In yet another reference (in a paper of 1915) he said it was 'a very remarkable thing that the unconscious of one human being can react upon that of another, without passing through the consciousness. This deserves closer investigation.'

The wild fable of *Totem and Taboo* was the only serious use he found for the phenomenon. The 'heritage of emotion' was evidently circulated in the manner of Jung's 'collective unconscious', which was also communicated in some unspecified fashion. But *Totem and Taboo* is odd enough as it is, so its hints about telepathy are politely overlooked.

The enormous conjectures in *Totem and Taboo*, which is subtitled 'Some points of agreement between the mental lives of savages and neurotics', form another of Freud's personal statements, brilliantly executed. Less autobiographical and less readable than *The Interpretation of Dreams*, its attempt to describe the origins of civilised society made it, he told Jones, 'the most daring enterprise I ever ventured . . . God help me!'

Using the anthropological literature of his day and the principles of psychoanalysis, he produced a series of essays, and in particular the culminating Chapter 4, where he claimed to be describing real events while protecting himself with an equivocal sentence here and there: 'It would be as foolish to aim at exactitude in such questions as it would be unfair to insist upon certainty.' The book was visionary or dangerously speculative, depending on the reader's sympathies.

The 'taboos' were the primitive prohibitions that existed within a tribe, in particular the prohibition against incest. The 'totem' was the sacred animal from which the tribe claimed to be descended and which, according to Freud, was originally a man.

Freud had read about the taboos that applied to the totem: that it mustn't be killed, and that, within the clan, the males may not have sexual relations with the females. It was obvious to him what he was looking at: prohibitions against the two wishes of the Oedipus Complex, to get rid of one's father and sleep with one's mother. Whatever was responsible for these taboos had shaped the central neurosis of human beings and laid the foundations (which were of course neurotic) of religion, self-control and all the other apparatus that makes up civilised society. All stemmed from the primitive need to curb personal excesses.

Freud had made the connection as though in a dream, but instead of presenting the work as a fantasy with implications for the human race – which might have made it sound unacceptably Jungian – he set out to anchor it in real events that took place in the primitive 'hordes' that Darwin envisaged, or perhaps in one particular horde, a quibble that Freud brushed aside with the remark about not aiming at exactitude.

The argument is inseparable from the style. In this passage from his autobiography (1925) he is summarising *Totem and Taboo* and talking about two elements that were crucial to his understanding: the ritualised killing of the totem, which was then eaten and mourned over, and the nature of life in Darwin's hordes, in each of which the men lived under the domination of one powerful, violent and jealous male:

> There rose before me out of all these components the following hypothesis, or, I would rather say, vision. The father of the primal horde, since he was an unlimited despot, had seized all the women for himself; his sons, being dangerous to him as rivals, had been killed or driven away. One day, however, the sons came together and united to overwhelm, kill, and devour their father, who had been their enemy but also their ideal. After the deed they were unable to take over their heritage since they stood in one another's way. Under the influence of failure and remorse they learned to come to an agreement among themselves; they banded themselves into a clan of brothers by the help of the ordinances of totemism, which aimed at preventing a repetition of such a deed, and they jointly undertook to forgo the possession of the women on whose account they had killed their father. They were then driven to finding strange women.

The totem meal was the festival that commemorated the 'fearful deed', and it was from this deed that sprang

> man's sense of guilt (or 'original sin') . . . which was the beginning at once of social organisation, of religion and of ethical restrictions.

Having described the murder and its consequences, Freud conceded that the event might be a fiction. But he badly wanted to see it as the literal truth, to believe that 'primitive men actually *did* what all the evidence shows that they intended to do'. Despite its scholarly flourishes, *Totem and Taboo* had the childlike air of a longed-for wish, and maintained it till the last sentence, where, 'without laying claim to any finality of judgment', Freud thought – hoped – that 'in the case before us it may safely be assumed that "in the beginning was the Deed" '.

Anthropologists have had little patience with it as history, but Freud remained good-humoured and adamant. He was amused when an English anthropologist called it a 'Just So Story', after Kipling's fables for children, and he was even said to have told an American pupil that he invented the theory on a wet Sunday afternoon. Making jokes may have helped to hide personal motives, his interest in murderous offspring reflecting a fantasy-view of himself as a primal father whose fantasy-sons meant to kill him: especially his son Jung.

Murder, incest and the origins of man made a good story in 1913. Today biologists speak more soberly of the incest taboo having arisen from a need to harmonise social behaviour. Freud would have thought this pitiful, but, unfortunately for his interpretation, it is probably correct.

The long last chapter, written in the late winter and early spring of 1913, was fitted in around the patients, who nowadays queued to see him. Shortly after he finished the book in May he told Ferenczi that he was working an eleven-hour day, which meant eleven patients under analysis.

For a man who thought himself doomed at forty, he had reached fifty-seven in good shape, apart from grumblings in his bowels that all the hot salt-water of Karlsbad couldn't wash away.* His winter relaxations still included taroc on Saturdays and excursions to familiar places, including Sunday visits with friends to eat at Cobenzl, under the Kahlenberg.

Women pleased him, perhaps more visibly than before, now that their temptations were a diminishing threat. He enjoyed the attentions of Lou Andréas-Salomé, the predatory Russian, who spent six months in Vienna from autumn 1912 to spring 1913, and often on Sundays they would talk in his study for hours. In February he told her about the fantasy of parricide that he was getting ready to write about in *Totem*.

Salomé, who has been called 'a near-mad near-genius', was fifty-one, a big handsome woman who married a German professor (engaged in a lifelong work on Persian philology) because he threatened to kill himself; she then refused to sleep with him, ever. The bright young men who still attracted her were another matter. In Vienna she had an affair with Victor Tausk, one of Freud's rising disciples, 'a blond fellow with a big head' eighteen years her junior, but with Freud she liked to think she was operating on a higher plane.

Her interests, he assured Ferenczi, were purely intellectual. She was a woman of significance, 'even though all the tracks around her

---

* In May 1914, shortly after his fifty-eighth birthday, Freud decided he had rectal cancer. An internal examination showed otherwise. 'So I have been restored to life,' he wrote to Ferenczi.

go into the lion's den but none come out'. It was her presence, rather than her convoluted speculations about psychoanalytic theory, that appealed to him, as it had appealed to Nietzsche, Rilke and the rest.

Within a few weeks of her arrival in Vienna, when she missed one of his university lectures, he wrote to say that 'I stared as if spellbound at the vacant chair reserved for you.' When she visited him on Sundays, to discuss analysis and gossip about childhood, he gave her flowers to take away, 'pink tulips and pale lilac' once, roses after her farewell visit in April.

Ernest Jones's common-law wife, Loe Kann, was also a favourite. Her treatment for morphine addiction and other problems, one of which was Jones, was coming to an end in spring 1913. Freud knew things that Jones didn't, including the fact that, following her analysis, Kann was now involved in Vienna with a near namesake, Herbert Jones, a wealthy American who wrote poetry. Psychoanalysis threw spanners in the works, as it was meant to. Freud had analysed Elma Pálos, as a result of which she didn't want to marry Ferenczi, who found himself landed with Gizella, her mother, whether he liked it or not. To be the analyst of his disciples' mistresses made Freud even more of a power in their lives.

His feelings for Loe, 'a jewel', were enthusiastic. By the summer, when she had decided to break with Ernest, she was 'blooming', now that she was free, and had become 'extraordinarily dear' to him. He told Ferenczi, 'I have produced with her a very warm feeling with complete sexual inhibition, as has rarely been the case before (probably owing to my age),' a rare admission about warm feelings in the past. In a paper about 'Transference-love' written in 1914, where Freud said that a woman patient must recognise falling in love with her male analyst to be part of the treatment, he discussed the temptations facing the poor analyst, who must convince her by his self-control that it was safe to tell him her fantasies. Did he have Loe in mind? If not her, certainly other attractive women among the hundreds who had stretched out on his couch.

The essay had a touch of sadness, noting the 'incomparable fascination' of 'a woman of high principles who confesses her passion', and suggesting that what tempted the analyst was not a patient's 'crudely sensual desires'. Rather it was her subtler behaviour, not overtly sexual, that might make a man forget himself 'for the sake of a fine experience'. Like the street of brothels in Trieste, they offered the rewards of self-denial.

In 1913, Ernest Jones had to come to terms with the post-analytic Loe. He was stoical, admitting to Freud that he had an inclination to blame him ('a passing phenomenon'), going to Budapest to be analysed by Ferenczi, abandoning Canada for good and leasing a London apartment in Great Portland Street, which was a damaging few hundred yards outside the medical district; picking up where he left off nearly five years earlier. Kann, who took her time about abandoning him altogether, helped him furnish the apartment. Freud was sent details of the dying affair, as if his imprimatur was required, receiving a detailed account of how Kann brought home a stray kitten, overfed it, then gave it laxatives followed by an enema. Because Jones didn't take all this seriously enough, she became enraged and 'kept me for three hours running "urgent messages" as a punishment'. She needed a special syringe to give the cat bromide. Then she needed prussic acid in case it was so ill that they had to kill it. 'She certainly has the power of gratifying and developing the masochistic side of a man,' said Jones bravely, but if he hoped for a soothing response from Freud, none came. Jones let him know that she was still taking morphine.

Each of the five members of the committee was presented by Freud in May 1913 with a small antique seal suitable for mounting in a gold ring; he already had such a ring of his own with a head of Jupiter. When Freud finished writing *Totem and Taboo*, some of them gave him a dinner at a restaurant in the Prater where he was presented with an Egyptian figurine, which he put in front of his plate and called his totem. The cause was advancing, but they still needed to feel themselves a band of brothers in a hostile world.

Vienna went about its business, a city seething with ideas that left the imperial authorities unmoved. Emancipation was not an issue for Emperor Franz-Josef and his squadrons of bureaucrats. Intellectuals and artists who wanted to change the old repressive world were left to chatter among themselves, whether they were Freud and his followers; or Karl Kraus, who grew apocalyptic and announced in the *Torch* that Austria was an 'experimental station for the end of the world'; or painters with disturbed visions that upset traditionalists, like the Expressionist Oskar Kokoschka, who claimed to have smelt crisis in the air in 1910, and to have realised 'suddenly, intuitively', that 'the whole of humanity was smitten with an incurable disease'.

Repression was the basis of civilised society. Freud acknowledged authority and at the same time subverted it. The rulers of the Austro-Hungarian Empire, along with the rulers of other empires, could hardly be expected to do anything but go on endorsing it.

What worried them most were specific outrages, like the case of Colonel Alfred Redl, the empire's gallant head of espionage, who turned out to be a spy and to have sold Russia the plans of fortresses in Galicia and the army's order of battle for invading Serbia should Austrian interests in the Balkans ever need defending. The colonel, a homosexual, was encouraged to shoot himself so that a trial could be avoided, and obliged in May 1913. The following year, when war came, the battle plans turned out to be more important than anyone would have supposed.

Later in 1913 and into 1914, Jung was troubled by vivid dreams or visions of international catastrophe that may have been evidence of his own drift into temporary insanity, but which he came to see as prophetic. He went into a trance on a train journey and saw Europe overwhelmed by blood-ridden seas filled with corpses. Switzerland, of course, was saved. He had the same dream twice on the same journey. Another dream, repeated three times, showed him Europe frozen over in summer. Amid the ice he found a tree of grapes and fed the starving.

Jung was not himself. He decided to 'let himself drop' (his own words) during Advent, December 1913. An exploration of his unconscious got under way, and he began to frequent an underworld of spirit-heroes and spirit-friends; detractors say he was a schizophrenic for several years to come.

Before he began these psychic journeys, he had time to attend one more annual psychoanalytic congress, at Munich in September, where he and Freud were in the same room for the last time. The meeting renewed Jung's presidency of the International Association, with many of the Freudian delegates abstaining, but by now his tenure was a formality. In October he gave up the editorship of the *Yearbook* for reasons 'of a personal nature, on which account I disdain to discuss them in public', and six months later, April 1914, he resigned the presidency.

'So my prediction has come true,' Jones wrote to Freud, 'that "if you give a dog enough rope, he will hang himself".' Freud had already written a pithy, tendentious history of the movement, dated February 1914 and published in the *Yearbook*, which dismissed Jung's heresy as being of less importance than Adler's, and derided the pretensions of 'the Swiss':

> The truth is that these people have picked out a few cultural overtones from the symphony of life and have once more failed to hear the mighty and primordial melody of the instincts.

The history may have speeded Jung's departure, with its cool and autocratic manner.

> No one need be surprised at the subjective character of the contribution I propose to make here to the history of the psychoanalytic movement, nor need anyone wonder at the part I play in it. For psychoanalysis is my creation.

Only once did Freud equivocate, when he felt the need to say he was 'without any strong personal motive' for writing the essay. The text contradicted him, and he told at least one of his friends the truth, writing to Salomé in June that 'I intentionally gave everyone a good clobbering.'

The movement had survived; expansion could continue. In London, Jones was planning to evangelise the educated English, encouraged by the way 'better-class magazines and literary journals' had begun referring to psychoanalysis. This was a less informed process than in America, where a professor could write a popular article without being derided for it. London journalists took to the idea of a mysterious 'unconscious' that everyone possessed, though they kept away from sex. The *Strand* magazine gave analysis a favourable mention in a 1912 piece, modishly titled 'Is love a disease?' When *The Psychopathology of Everyday Life* appeared in Brill's translation in 1914, Freud became 'the Sherlock Holmes of the mind'.

Such vulgarity didn't impress the medical establishment, which had no time for Jones (who was told privately that he would be ostracised if he remained in London) or for Freudian indecencies. The first time psychoanalysis was aired at a British Medical Association meeting, in 1911, Dr David Eder, a recent convert, described a case of hysteria to a specialist audience of nine neurologists; when he came to sex, they all walked out.

Undeterred, Jones and Eder formed the London Psycho-Analytical Society in October 1913, and made each other president and secretary respectively. By the following January Jones's private practice was thriving, with eight patients daily, giving him an income of £60 or £70 a week, which meant affluence in 1914. He told Freud that he would soon be in a position to marry, 'which I hope will be the next step in my life'. Loe married the other Jones in Budapest in June, when Freud was among the guests.

That summer, 1914, Freud's daughter Anna was being allowed to go by herself to England for a holiday. She was eighteen years old, a shy, serious-minded woman given to day-dreams and self-sacrifice. It was as though she and her father conspired from an early age to implicate her in his affairs at the expense of her own.

At thirteen she would sit in a corner at meetings of the Vienna society. If allowed, she would have accompanied him to America in 1909. Freud thought her 'a little odd', saw how her nearest sister, Sophie, overshadowed her, and gave her kindly advice but not the overt affection of hugs and kisses; these were always in short supply in the Freud household.

Gentler parents might have relaxed their rule for the last child, the darling of the brood, as they sometimes do. Instead, Freud offered serious advice about how to be sensible and look life in the face. Anna had a stormy relationship with Sophie, who was two and a half years older and prettier, and who became engaged in 1912 to a photographer from Hamburg, Max Halberstadt. (Mathilde had been married since 1909.) Freud referred to Anna playfully as his 'only daughter'. The three sons were young men, no longer living at home. Perhaps she pondered the fate of daughters left as the sole comfort of ageing families.

At the time of Sophie's engagement, Anna was sixteen and just finishing high school. Freud had promised her a taste of the south in the autumn and winter, travelling for months with Aunt Minna to broaden her mind and improve her uncertain health. The grand tour now had to be cancelled because preparations for the wedding made it inconvenient for Minna to be absent; bourgeois families had inflexible ways. Anna was dumped in Merano for the winter, in the care of a distant relative, and told she would not be going to Sophie's wedding in January 1913.

A surviving letter to her father from Merano is full of anxiety about her failure to be a 'reasonable' person, and begs him to help her achieve this state. Her reward came at Easter 1913, when Freud took her from Merano to spend a few days in Venice and

Trieste, making her, at last, the travelling companion she wanted to be.

The journey by herself to England in 1914 came after she had passed a preliminary examination to become a schoolteacher, and before she began as an apprentice in the autumn. At eighteen, she was seven months younger than her father when he crossed the English Channel for the first time in 1875 and discovered the sombre glories of Manchester. The plan for Anna was that she would remain in the south of England, staying in Sussex at a 'ladies institution' and also with a family. Twenty pounds was sent to Sam Freud in Manchester, Freud's nephew, so he could act as banker.

It seems not to have occurred to Freud that Ernest Jones, the wayward bachelor who had announced his intention of looking for a wife, might decide he need look no further than the daughter of psychoanalysis. Not until after she had arrived in mid-July did Freud warn her in a letter that 'I know from the most reliable sources that Dr Jones has serious intentions of wooing you.' No doubt the reliable source was Loe, the new Mrs Herbert Jones.

He told Anna that there was no question of her being given the same freedom of choice as her sisters. She had 'lived more intimately with us than they', and he believed that she would 'find it more difficult to make such a decision for life without our – in this case my – consent'. A letter to Jones, who had already met her with flowers on arrival and shepherded her to her destination, followed: 'She does not claim to be treated as a woman, being still far away from sexual longings and rather refusing man.' It was a father speaking, not a psychoanalyst.

Jones replied with the air of a man misunderstood, remarking on Anna's 'beautiful character', adding slyly that she would 'surely be a remarkable woman later on, provided that her sexual repression does not injure her'. He was insolent because he was disappointed. A whole history of psychoanalysis, with Ernest Jones as the founder's son-in-law, never happened.

At the end of June 1914 the heir to the Austrian throne, Archduke Franz Ferdinand, a stout man in a tight uniform, was on a visit to Bosnia, part of the empire, to support the Bosnians against the neighbouring Serbs who were making trouble. A tuberculous youth with a revolver shot him and his wife dead at Sarajevo, hoping to advance the Serbian cause. Ferdinand was the second heir-apparent to be killed, his cousin Rudolf having committed suicide at Mayerling a quarter of a century earlier.

In the park at Baden, outside Vienna, the band stopped playing in the middle of a tune. Serge Pankejeff, who had finished his analysis with Freud the previous week, remembered returning from a stroll in the Prater and being handed a special edition of the *Neue Freie Presse* with the news. Freud, writing to Ferenczi that Sunday, spoke of consequences that could not be foreseen, although it appeared that 'personal involvement here is slight'. But the faded Austrian Empire, a 'worm-eaten galleon' as someone called it, decided to be bold and punish Serbia.

It took a month of threats and ultimatums to invoke alliances and draw the rest of Europe into the quarrel. There was time for Jung to leave the International Association, severing his last connection, and for the Zürich analysts to resign with him. 'So we are rid of them,' Freud wrote to Abraham on 26 July, 'the brutal sanctimonious Jung and his pious parrots.'

Countries were mobilising by now; the generals were nearly ready to begin. Freud was caught up in the same fever as the rest of Vienna. He admitted that for the first time in thirty years he felt himself an Austrian, willing to give 'this not very hopeful Empire' another chance.

In England, Jones took Anna and a party for a leisurely Saturday on the River Thames. He heard rumours of 'a general Armageddon', and volunteered to escort her back to Germany. Mrs Herbert Jones meanwhile was buying up quantities of morphine, claiming it was for foreign armies to treat their wounded.

By early August everyone had declared war on everyone else. Anna was able to return home with the departing Austrian Ambassador and his party, travelling via Gibraltar and Genoa. Soon there was encouraging news for Germany and her allies, the 'Central Powers', of battles against Russians and French. As for England, Abraham wrote encouragingly from Berlin that 'we may rely on Krupp and Zeppelin'.

Freud was as absorbed by events as by the Franco-Prussian war when he was a schoolboy. Staying in Hamburg with Sophie and her husband, whose son Ernst, born earlier that year, was his first grandchild, Freud wrote to Abraham that when he and his family talked about 'our' battles and 'our' war loans, he retained only a faint memory of 'discussions about an earlier battle which after some partial successes ended in nothing'. It was, he said, 'like remembering an earlier life'. He meant the great war with Jung.

25: War

As a child in Russia, Lou Andréas-Salomé had affectionate brothers who made her feel safe among men, confident of their goodwill. 'Do you still believe that all the big brothers are so good?' Freud wrote to her in November 1914. She replied from her home in Germany that the world's big brothers had 'all gone stark staring mad', adding loyally that the reason for this was that countries couldn't be psychoanalysed.

It was too easy an answer for Freud, with his pessimistic view of human nature and his belief that many lacked the character to be helped by psychoanalysis.

> I do not doubt that mankind will survive even this war, but I know for certain that for me and my contemporaries the world will never again be a happy place. It is too hideous. And the saddest thing about it is that it is exactly the way we should have expected people to behave from our knowledge of psychoanalysis. Because of this attitude to mankind I have never been able to agree with your blithe optimism. My secret conclusion has always been: since we can only regard the highest present civilisation as burdened with an enormous hypocrisy, it follows that we are organically unfitted for it. We have to abdicate, and the Great Unknown, He or It, lurking behind Fate will someday repeat this experiment with another race.

Freud added that the Germans, 'perhaps because [they are] certain of victory', were behaving better than other nations; a view he didn't maintain.

His sons were caught up in the war. Oliver, training to be a civil engineer, worked on construction projects before he was conscripted. Once described by Freud as 'my pride and my secret hope', he disappointed him by showing signs of Freud's own obsessional neurosis.* The other two sons, Martin and Ernst, were fighting

* Oliver was psychoanalysed, not by his father, in the 1920s. His character was

men from the start. By January 1915 Corporal M. Freud was already in the trenches in Galicia, facing the Russians. Freud dreamt of their death more than once and concluded (since dreams were wish-fulfilments) that this meant a hidden desire to see them done away with because he envied them their youth.

Anna went on living at home, became a student teacher, began to translate articles between German and English, described her dreams to her father, and delighted him by turning into 'a charmer': she had selected herself as the disciple in the family. The sons' lack of scholastic distinction disappointed Freud. Anna would make up for them.

The war inhibited travel and reduced the number of patients. Few could come from other countries. The 'outside world' that the International Association had been set up to penetrate was further off than ever. Occasional letters passed between Jones and Freud, sent via neutral countries. In autumn 1914 it took three weeks for news of Emmanuel Freud's death in Manchester to reach Sigmund.*

There was more time for writing. Freud began with the Wolf Man, whose analysis lasted from February 1910 to June 1914, the last of his cases to be written up in detail. Serge Pankejeff had returned to Russia before war broke out and was living on his estates. His name was not used in the paper, and has become widely known only in recent years. Nor was he officially the 'Wolf Man', any more than his predecessor was the 'Rat Man', although towards the end of his life, Pankejeff would answer the phone with 'Wolf Man speaking'.

The paper, 116 pages in the *Standard Edition*, was called *From the History of an Infantile Neurosis*. Written towards the end of 1914, it was, as the title implied, not a full recital of Pankejeff's condition, but dealt only with childhood events and their implication. The Jung and Adler heresies were fresh in Freud's mind. A colourful account of a child's sensual life was a reassertion of orthodoxy.

By turning a handful of dreams and memories into an erotic fairy

---

faultless, Freud said, until 'the neurosis came over him and stripped off all the blooms'.

* Emmanuel Freud, who was eighty-one, was killed in a railway accident on 17 October, when he fell from a moving train near his home. War hysteria in Britain in 1914 led to violent ill-will against those with German names and connections, and property was attacked. Conceivably Emmanuel the anglophile committed suicide.

tale, Freud plunged as deeply into a fiction that served his purpose as he had done with the crime story of murderous sons in *Totem and Taboo*. Freud's skill as writer and advocate enabled an unlikely tale to be taken at his valuation for many years. Nothing was too much for Freud; no plot too startling.

Pankejeff, a wealthy young man suffering from depression and various obsessional symptoms who went from psychiatrist to psychiatrist before he found Freud, spent his earliest years in a palatial house on his father's estates in southern Russia, where the route to the world outside was by river-boats down the Dnieper to the Black Sea. They were a melancholy family. Pankejeff Senior went off to a sanatorium in Germany from time to time, and was diagnosed by the eminent Professor Kraepelin as a manic-depressive. Serge's sister Anna killed herself with poison in 1906; she was twenty-one, he was nineteen. Two years later his father was found dead in an hotel bedroom, probably from an overdose of veronal.

Following these traumas, Pankejeff, now twenty-three, arrived in Vienna in January 1910 accompanied by a revolver-carrying doctor, and devoted himself to cafés, the Prater and prostitutes, while Freud analysed him for an hour a day, Sundays and the summer months excepted, over the next four years. Pankejeff's problems, as far as the analysis was concerned, lay in his childhood. According to Freud he was 'entirely incapacitated' by his neurosis, unable to do anything for himself, but there is contrary evidence, some of it from Pankejeff in his old age.

At the start of the treatment, Freud told Ferenczi that he had taken him on because of his 'compulsive tendencies', by which apparently he meant that his patient was compulsively amorous. He was certainly active with women, leading what Freud described, with a hint of distaste, as a 'completely unbridled instinctual life'. He also had chronic constipation.

A dream, remembered from childhood, came to dominate the analysis. Pankejeff was four years old. As he lay in bed, the window opened of its own accord and he saw six or seven white wolves sitting motionless in a walnut tree, staring at him. He woke in terror. Convinced that behind this nightmare lay an important memory, Freud reconstructed an event from his patient's earliest childhood that, if it were true and if psychoanalysis were valid, explained where Pankejeff's troubles arose. The Russian didn't remember the episode: Freud remembered it for him, using detail from the dream and associations from the analysis, but relying chiefly on his own vision of what might have been, which in Freud's creative fever became what was.

The revelation was precise and circumstantial. When he was eighteen months old, in 1888, Pankejeff (said Freud) saw his parents making love on a summer's afternoon when he was lying in a cot in their bedroom; in Freud's language, he witnessed the 'primal scene' of parental intercourse. The act was 'three times repeated', a remarkable feat. It was probably five o'clock. Their underclothes and the bedclothes were white, and they were doing it '*a tergo*', in Freud's discreet phrase, the woman on her hands and knees, the man kneeling behind her. The child saw their genitals. Eventually he soiled himself and called their attention to him by screaming.

The white wolves of the dream were his white-clad mother and father. The discrepant number (two parents, several wolves) was merely an attempt by the unconscious to conceal the meaning of the dream. Other anomalies were explained by Freud's elastic principles of dream distortion. His skilful marshalling of detail in a way that makes sense – a psychoanalytic sense – has convinced true believers and even half-believers. But it is the reality of a fairy tale.

The coital position was deduced from Pankejeff's fear, as a child, of a picture in a book of a wolf standing upright. So the father, kneeling behind the bowed-down mother, was the wolf on its hind legs.

To follow Freud's account, itself the distillation of so many hours of analysis, is to sense the preposterous grandeur of his concept. A butterfly with yellow stripes that frightened Pankejeff as a child becomes both a woman parting her legs – the opening and shutting of the wings – and the Roman 'V', representing '5', which was the hour he saw his wolf-parents copulating. Later on, the yellow stripes remind him of a pear, 'Grusha' in Russian, which turns out to be the name of a nursery-maid whom he saw kneeling to scrub the floor, 'with her buttocks projecting', when he was aged two and a half, a sight that aroused him because of its connection with the primal scene.

One consequence of this was a lifelong taste for lower-class women. Thus, aged seventeen, he saw a peasant girl kneeling by a pond to wash clothes, and, said Freud, 'fell in love with the girl instantly and with irresistible violence', even before he saw her face (another strand in the fairy story – 'Once upon a time a handsome young prince was walking through a village' – sadly, she gave him gonorrhoea).

To his analyst he was a child with disturbed relationships, who saw his mother as a castrated wolf (no visible sexual organs) and his father as the castrating wolf. His anxiety was directed towards his bowels, which, beginning with the episode in the cot, plagued him for the rest of his life, as did his attitude towards men (which was too deferential) and women (who had to be of humble birth).

What Pankejeff thought of all this when he came to recollect it in the future is a story in itself. He didn't believe in the bedroom scene ('terribly far-fetched'), he knew that Freud hadn't cured him – he remained obsessive and anxious all his life – but at the same time Freud was 'a genius' with 'very serious eyes that looked to the very bottom of the soul'. Because of Freud, he said, he felt able to marry Theresa, a nurse in Munich he was in love with. Freud became the father he didn't have, 'a new father with whom I had an excellent relationship'. In psychoanalytic terms there was a 'positive trans-ference', a banal but probably sufficient explanation of how Freud helped Pankejeff and many other patients. He was a friend and counsellor.

Even among psychoanalysts there are sceptics who find the case-history too fanciful, but for most it remains a fine old specimen that it is wiser to leave undisturbed. A few commentators mutter about anomalies and general unbelievability. Among the not unreason-able questions (unasked until recent years) is how, exactly, an observer can see details of both persons' genitals during dorsal copulation. Echoes of Freud's own infancy above the blacksmith's can be heard or imagined. 'Are we confronting biography or autobiography?' asks a critic, but in psychoanalysis there is no such thing as a straight answer. Whatever the truth, to an outsider the improbable triple copulation and highly visible genitalia have a familiar air. It is the way things happen in pornography.

After the Wolf Man study, Freud wrote few papers based on material from specific cases. Theoretical statement and speculation became his staple offering. Earlier in 1914, *On Narcissism* had considered what happens when the self-love of infancy matures. When the Wolf Man book had been written (though it was not published until 1918), Freud settled down in 1915 to produce a series of papers on what he called 'metapsychology', while the war turned into stalemate and he felt sometimes (he told Salomé)

> as alone as during the first ten years, when I was surrounded by a desert; but I was younger then and still endowed with infinite energy and perseverance.

This metapsychology, to which he devoted a dozen papers, was an attempt to examine the mind as an abstraction and produce a general theory of how it worked. It thus marked a return to the ground he covered when he was devising his schemes of mental energy flows for Fliess in 1895, and the daunting last chapter of *The Interpretation of Dreams*. Hints about his new 'synthesis' were given in letters, and the papers were written at a rate of more than two a month between spring and summer 1915.

Perhaps he saw them as a final offering, his theoretical testament to the future. Who knew what would come after the war? A group of powerful essays, describing the operating processes of the mind and their manifestations in neuroses and dreams, would help him along the road to immortality.

Freud wrote the prescribed twelve, destroyed seven and published five. The most substantial are the three he wrote first, 'Instincts and Their Vicissitudes', 'Repression' and 'The Unconscious'. Embedded in Their abstractions is the old scheme of the mind developed from nineteenth-century models, a machine for managing the stimuli or 'excitation' received from the external world. Finely drawn, as difficult to follow as an engineer's blueprints, the essays invoke an imaginary machine in which consciousness is protective, desiring to rid itself of harmful stimulation from the world outside.

> The nervous system is an apparatus which has the function of getting rid of the stimuli that reach it, or of reducing them to the lowest possible level; or which, if it were feasible, would maintain itself in an altogether unstimulated condition.

But the neurological premises behind this striving for nirvana are not true, and Freud's metapsychology has little to do with the real nervous system and even less with the practice of psychoanalysis.

Why he destroyed the seven papers is not known. Ernest Jones regretted not asking him. Lou Salomé did ask, after the war, and was told that the metapsychology had not yet been written, that 'the sporadic character of my insights' was an obstacle. This contradicted what he was telling her and others in summer 1915. Presumably Freud became dissatisfied with the concept and felt unable to rework whatever had gone wrong with it. If he regarded the essays as his last word on theory, he may also have been afraid to see them in print lest they mark the completion of his life's work. In the 1899 calendrical fantasy, based on a new telephone number, his sixty-second year, from May 1917, was going to be his last.

Freud had become an isolated figure. The war was helping to uncover the lonely contemplative who had been there all the time, waiting to exercise the prerogatives of old age. J. J. Putnam, the American psychologist who had embraced psychoanalysis but insisted on its moral virtues, sent him a copy of his book, *Human Motives*, in summer 1915. In his reply of Thursday 8 July, which made appropriate gestures towards religion and ethics, Freud had the air of a man evaluating his life. Were he to meet the Almighty, 'it is rather I who should reproach Him, than he me. I would ask him why he had not provided me with a better intellectual equipment.'

His views on his personal ethics were as predictable as most people's on theirs, and fitted into a sentence, 'I consider myself a very moral human being [who has] never done anything shameful or malicious.' He added that he used morality in the social, not sexual, sense, sounding as if he might have a confession to make. None came.

> Sexual morality as society – and at its most extreme, American society – defines it, seems very despicable to me. I stand for a much freer sexual life. However, I have made little use of such freedom, except in so far as I was convinced of what was permissible for me in this area.

If a confession hovers in the cryptic *in so far as I was convinced*, it is too vague to mean anything. He approached the subject and drew back. Oddly some unpublished notes, apparently by Freud, about a series of dreams he had that week, mention 'successful coitus Wednesday morning', 7 July, in connection with a dream about Martha. The letter to Putnam was written the following day. They are the two most direct recorded references by Freud to his sexual affairs, and they both concern the same forty-eight hours.

His sexual life, then, wasn't over; there was no reason why it should be, despite his attempts to suggest otherwise. His working life was vigorous enough. Free of patients, more or less, he made work for himself by writing and lecturing. He gave two series of expository lectures at the university's psychiatric clinic in successive winter terms, 1915–16 and 1916–17, to a mixed medical and lay audience that contained, as Freud thought it worth noting, both men and women. Among those who heard his first lecture in October 1915 were two of his daughters, Mathilde and Anna, and a medical student, Ella Haim, who was about to marry Oliver and become Freud's first daughter-in-law.*

The lectures were a reworking of earlier versions – 'The old material, which is abhorrent to me,' he told Ferenczi – but he attracted audiences of up to a hundred people, large by his standards, and this made him and his publishers see the possibilities. The material was later incorporated in two volumes of the *Standard Edition*, one-twelfth of the whole, where, as the *Introductory Lectures*, it remains the most accessible account of Freud's work.

Perhaps the state of the world was inviting a new curiosity about human nature. The growing horrors of the war mocked the casual optimism about 'civilisation' and 'progress' that prevailed before 1914. Freud's sanguine views on the unconscious, where demons lived, were making him sound prophetic. It didn't take much imagination to extend his meaning from private affairs to public when he spoke in a lecture about dreams of revenge and death against one's intimates, 'censored wishes [which] appear to rise up out of a positive Hell'.

Isolated in Vienna, travelling infrequently and seeing little or nothing of his key colleagues – Ferenczi, Jones, Abraham, Rank – Freud relied on letters to tell him about the movement. A flourishing correspondence with Ferenczi, who was in Budapest, kept him informed about his friend's tormented love-life. The affair with Gizella Pálos continued through the war. Her daughter, Elma, still appealed to him. She had married an American, but was still potentially available as a soul-mate.

The owlish Ferenczi tried to look unflinchingly at his feelings, but succeeded only in tying himself and everyone else in knots. Freud had to hear how a fortune-teller told him he would marry

* Oliver, at the time an engineer working on a tunnel in the Carpathians, got married in December 1915. His wife came from an affluent family and had no intention of giving up her career. The marriage soon foundered and Freud persuaded his son to seek a divorce.

twice; how his stuffed-up nostrils made him breathless when making love to Mrs Pálos; how she had broken the umbrella he gave her, a 'symptomatic action' which could only mean she didn't want to marry him; how his worries about marrying a woman who was now middle-aged (they had been lovers since the start of the century) was giving him diarrhoea. Liaisons with prostitutes and Gizella's sister were gone into. Nothing was too trivial to bring to the master's attention. When he altered a word in a sentence about Gizella, he hinted that the crossing-out might be a significant parapraxis.

It would be hard to find anything less likely to inspire confidence in the therapeutic value of psychoanalysis than this sad self-dissection by one of the movement's leaders, who spent a decade or more trying to make up his mind while privately blaming Freud for having guided him away from the younger woman towards the older. Freud's comments were inclined to be terse and pragmatic, declining to 'go into your autoanalytic communications', a wise course. 'One must be able,' he suggested, 'to decide whether one loves a woman or not even with stuffed-up nostrils.'

Freud had worries of his own. He told Abraham, now pressed into service as a military surgeon, that he grew 'old and rather frail and tired' and had 'more or less given up work . . . I believe I have had my time.' His sixtieth birthday in May 1916 was mentioned in newspapers and brought a surfeit of flowers. Anxiety about his sons nagged at him. At Karlsbad, taking the waters with Martha, there were 'officers with Iron Crosses instead of ladies in fantastic dresses'. Food shortages and general privation made him pessimistic about the outcome. One of Jones's letters got through in 1916 with the news that he had bought a country cottage ('built in 1627') together with a motorcycle and sidecar.* Freud mistook 'motorbike' for 'car' and passed the news on to Ferenczi with a sigh, saying 'Still happy England. That doesn't look like an end to the war.'

In summer 1917 the Freuds went to the Tatra Mountains in Slovakia, where Ferenczi had relatives, and Freud could 'wallow in

* In 1917 there was further domestic news of Jones. First he discarded Lina, Loe Kann's former maid, with whom he had been living. Then he married a talented Welsh musician, Morfydd Owen, aged twenty-five, who had an emerging reputation as a composer. She was also very religious. 'He regards himself as a reformed character,' Freud informed Abraham. The truth was more disturbing. Jones thought that his wife's talents and her religious beliefs could both be subordinated to his needs. Their marriage was stormy and came to a tragic end.

a superfluity of bread, butter, sausages, eggs and cigars, rather like the chief of a primitive tribe'. There were even mushrooms to be hunted; sometimes, he said, he could forget the war for as long as half a day. Just before they left Vienna, his sister Rosa Graf, widowed before the war, heard that her only son Hermann, twenty years old, had been killed on the Italian front. 'Her grief,' said Freud, 'surpassed description.'

The Austrian harvest that summer was disastrous. Meanwhile German submarines were at last being subdued, and the threat of starvation receded for the British. The United States had entered the war in April 1917. 'Our future is pretty dim,' wrote Freud.

Worries about money, never far from the surface even when he was prosperous, sharpened now that his practice had dwindled and prices were rising. There was some talk about a Nobel Prize. Freud claimed to want it only for the money. 'My mental constitution,' he wrote ironically to Abraham,

> urgently requires me to earn and spend money on my family as the fulfilment of my well-known father complex. In these circumstances, entirely against my will, my hopes turn to the Nobel Prize.

He was hardly indifferent to honours, and the tone of his letters is ambivalent. 'It would be ridiculous to expect a sign of recognition when you have seven-eighths of the world against you,' he told Ferenczi. The prize didn't come his way. When he spoke in letters of 'raging and grousing' against the times, of his 'powerless embitterment', it may have reflected a fear, along with apprehensions of approaching death, that his fame was dissolving back into the obscurity he had spent so many years struggling to escape.

In a short paper of 1917 written for a Hungarian periodical, 'A Difficulty in the Path of Psycho-Analysis', Freud examined 'three severe blows' that science had dealt to human vanity: the cosmological, which removed us from the centre of the universe; the biological, which showed our animal origins; and now the psychological, 'probably the most wounding', which rearranged the mind to make it subject to a dilatory unconscious and so demonstrated that *the ego is not master in its own house*'. In this brief essay, written for a lay audience, Freud casually asserted one of his principal claims for the world's attention.

In doing so he named Copernicus as the author of the first blow and Darwin the second, leaving Freud himself (despite a prudent credit in the last paragraph for Schopenhauer, 'whose unconscious

"Will" is equivalent to the mental instincts of psychoanalysis') as the implicit provider of the third. Abraham made a sly comment about 'your colleague Copernicus'. Freud admitted nothing but denied nothing either:

> You are right to point out that the list [in the essay] is bound to create the impression that I claim a place side by side with Copernicus and Darwin. However, I did not wish to relinquish an interesting idea just because of that semblance, and therefore at any rate put Schopenhauer in the foreground.

The world remained wary of psychoanalysis. It was easily perceived as the eccentric cult that its enemies described. Freud was always wary of adherents who might contaminate it, not because they were heretics like Adler and Jung but because they were unstable or inferior. Otto Gross, long gone from the analytic scene, was one of the failures. The roguish Stekel, ejected before the war, was found wanting, and so was Wittels, on the grounds that he was personally unreliable.

Georg Groddeck, who appeared on Freud's scene in 1917, scraped in as a comrade who was eccentric but tolerable. A German physician, a physiotherapist and masseur converted to psychoanalysis who ran a clinic at Baden-Baden, he called himself a 'wild analyst' and contrived to sit at Freud's feet while holding mystical views. Being good-natured and unambitious, he was unlikely to do any harm. He was fifty-one when he introduced himself with a long letter in summer 1917, launching at once into his fixed idea: that body and mind were indistinguishable, driven by a force that 'lives us while we believe we are living', which he called the 'It', in German the 'Id'.

His system had clinical consequences, since it meant that bodily ailments had mental origins not in the limited sense believed in by Freud, where, say, an hysterical response could produce a cough or a limp, but in a more profound way. It was an exaggerated version of 'psychosomatics', that unproven branch of medicine.

> When a person has bad breath, his unconscious does not want to be kissed ... and when he vomits, it wants to get rid of something harmful ... and when somebody loses his sight then he has merely taken a little too far a habit of the It, which is not to notice most things.

Freud chided him for trying to 'spiritualise nature' with mystical ideas, noting that 'your position on the question of the distribution between the somatic and the mental is not quite ours', but welcomed him to the fold.

At the same time, Freud himself was dabbling in the mind-and-matter question with Ferenczi – an extension of their shared interest in telepathy – and hoping to prove that unconscious ideas could affect biological development. Ferenczi was supposed to be seeking evidence for the kind of process that Freud had envisaged in *Totem and Taboo*. He mentioned the work to Groddeck in the summer, spelling out his belief that 'the unconscious act exerts an intensive, decisive influence on somatic processes such as conscious acts never do'. It is impossible to know what he meant, assuming he knew himself.

To Abraham in November 1917 he said that he hoped for a psychoanalytic account of adaptation, Darwin's theory of how organisms modify themselves and adapt to their environment. Freud thought it would 'put the coping stone on psychoanalysis'. This grand design was not pursued; the ultimate conjunction of mind and matter remained as mysterious for Freud as it did for Groddeck.

Winter shortages of food and fuel in Vienna grew worse every year.* As 1917 came to an end, Freud was tired and dejected. A photograph sent to Abraham showed how he had aged. The latest variant in his death-neurosis said his life would end in February 1918, three months before his sixty-second birthday. The superstition, he told Ferenczi in November 1917, seemed 'downright friendly'.

The same month another letter to Ferenczi noted the effect of one of his brief abstentions from smoking:

> I have been grumpy and tired, got heart palpitations and an increase in the painful swellings of my gums (carcinoma? etc) ... Then a patient brought me fifty cigars, I lit one, became cheerful, and the gum irritation rapidly abated! I wouldn't have believed it if it weren't so striking. Totally Groddeck.

For the moment, no more was heard of the swelling.

In January 1918 the daily flour ration was reduced from seven ounces to just over five. Potatoes were like gold, jam was made with

---

* The Allied blockade of the Central Powers had serious consequences after 1915. Malnutrition encouraged epidemics and even affected the birth-weight of babies. In Germany alone, three-quarters of a million civilians died of starvation during the war.

turnips, cats and dogs were eaten by the poorest. At Berggasse 19 they did comparatively well, thanks to patients and friends. 'We live on gifts, like a doctor's family in the old days,' Freud wrote to Abraham, putting cigars at the top of the list, followed by flour, lard and bacon. But he missed meat – 'I have always been a carnivorous animal' – and blamed his listlessness on the diet. Vienna was short of everything, including fuel. Poor-quality brown coal and chopped-up fences had to suffice, electricity was intermittent, few trams were to be seen, and at night apartments were lit feebly or not at all. Unswept snow topped with soot was piled in the streets. Freud wrote 'Shivering with cold' at the head of a January letter to Abraham. February came and went, and so did May; he had survived his sixty-second year.

The Bolshevik revolution of October 1917 had effectively removed Russia from the war, but the Central Powers derived little benefit. German and Austrian armies invaded the new Communist State (Vienna dreamt of trainloads of grain from the Ukraine, which never came), and landowners in the overrun territories of Russia were able to survive a little longer.

The Wolf Man's estates were outside Odessa, on the Black Sea. When the Austrians arrived there in spring 1918, Pankejeff, his lands and fortune still intact, sought permission to bring his wife to Vienna because she was ill. His friend Professor Freud was asked to supply a medical certificate. Eventually the Wolf Man reached the West, and even had some more analysis at Berggasse after the war. He never saw Russia again.

In summer 1918 Freud escaped again to the Tatra Mountains, cheered up by a rich Hungarian benefactor who planned donations to the cause, Anton von Freund. Freud had previously analysed his wife. He was 'the sort of person whom one would have to invent if he did not already exist', Freud wrote from the mountains. Von Freund ('a doctor of philosophy and a brewer'), who was in his late thirties, had been operated on for testicular cancer, then treated by Freud for a subsequent neurosis, after which he decided to shower money on psychoanalysis. An institute was to be set up in Budapest, and a publishing house in Vienna would be financed.

Freud, accompanied by his 'little daughter' (Anna was twenty-two), stayed at Freund's villa before going up to the hills, and worked on a new edition of *The Interpretation of Dreams*, the fifth, commenting in the preface that he couldn't bring himself to make any fundamental revision for fear of destroying its 'historic character'. It was part of his autobiography. Its unFreudian statement that 'we think highly of the happiness of childhood because it is still innocent of sexual desires' – which occurs immediately after a memory of the infant Anna dreaming of 'wild stwawbewwies' – was later accompanied by a dissenting footnote, but the statement itself was untouched.

As another winter approached the war was in its final stages, although few expected the end to come so rapidly. In September Freud and his skeletal organisation staged the first wartime congress, in Budapest, with unheard-of support from the authorities. The scale of battle-neurosis and shell-shock had made armies think again about the nature of 'malingering'. Some military doctors applied Freud's concept of the 'flight into illness', the escape into neurosis from an intolerable situation, to behaviour on a battlefield. The Budapest meeting was accordingly blessed with one Austrian general, two officials from the War Ministry in Berlin, a civic reception and a banquet.

A month later the Central Powers were collapsing, destroyed from within by civil unrest. On the Western Front the German Army was in retreat from the Allies. Vienna looked on, helpless. The Hungarians, Bohemians, Serbs, Croats and other subjects of the Austrian Empire left abruptly to pursue their own destinies. Italy, the old, despised enemy in the south, routed the Austrian army with Allied help and scooped up hundreds of thousands of prisoners (Lieutenant Martin Freud was among them). Trieste was Italian again by 3 November.

What remained of the Austrian army began to break up. Trainloads of dissident troops came home to Vienna, disillusioned, still carrying their rifles. The Habsburg Empire ceased to exist, and so did the Habsburg dynasty after more than 600 years. Franz-Josef had died in 1916, causing Karl Kraus to remark that he could believe the emperor was dead, but couldn't convince himself that he had ever lived. His successor, Emperor Karl, faded away. Freud claimed to feel only relief at the end of the old Austria, adding to Ferenczi that 'The Habsburgs have left behind nothing but a pile of crap.' There were armed gangs and red flags in the streets. When Freud and his daughter Mathilde were out walking, two blocks from Berggasse, they came briefly under fire.

A day or so before a general armistice came into force on 11

November, the terms dictated by the Allies, a letter arrived from Jones, written five weeks earlier, with the news that Morfydd Owen, his 'darling wife' of nineteen months, was dead. There seemed no end to Jones's misfortunes with women. The events, not described to Freud, had the familiar Jonesian whiff of melodrama. Morfydd, taken ill when they were on holiday in South Wales at the end of August, was operated on by a local surgeon for appendicitis, probably with Jones as the anaesthetist, and died a few days later. She was twenty-seven. There are hints that initially Jones viewed her symptoms as psychological. He spoke of her death being due to 'delayed chloroform poisoning'. A death certificate was not issued for more than two weeks, and, despite the innocent nature of the medical findings, and Jones's evident grief, traces of gossip have persisted ever since. Freud's letter of condolence, dated 10 November, said that 'the years of separation have done little to change my feelings for you'.

There were many contacts to renew, but for a long time Austria was cast aside from the stream of events, isolated and penurious. It was nearly a year before Jones was allowed to travel to Vienna; almost as long before Freud saw his eldest son again. Friends urged him to settle in a less disagreeable place, and he engaged a teacher 'so as to get my English polished up', with a vague intention of going to Britain when they would let him in.

Improved English came in useful in Vienna, which he didn't leave, because the Austrian currency was already ruined by inflation and the only worthwhile patients were those, mainly Anglo-Saxons, who could pay in pounds, dollars and Swiss francs. Middle-class savings had evaporated. Freud said he lost a sum worth about £200,000 today.

Failure to be seen as solvent and prosperous was wounding to his self-esteem, whatever the circumstances. Dependants relied on their famous relative to provide for them in hard times. They included his sons, until they found work, his daughter Anna, his mother, his sister-in-law Minna, his widowed sisters Rosa and Paula, his unmarried sister Dolfi. Assistance on this scale was beyond his means.

Eli Bernays, his unloved brother-in-law in New York, found ways of transferring substantial sums. Freud's letters after the war to his nephew Sam in Manchester refer several times to Eli's gifts, always with the reminder that it is the 'female' or the 'passive' members of the family who are benefiting. Freud didn't want to be seen as living on his brother-in-law's charity. His dislike of Eli, to whom he had been beholden when he was young and poor and in love with Martha, lasted down the years, not helped by Eli's unfaithfulness to his wife. When he sent $5,000 to a children's home in Vienna, it was 'a nice way of paying back his debts to friends when he left Vienna as a bankrupt'. When conditions improved, 'I am glad to say none of the family is still dependent on the scarce and irregular subsidies from Eli.' Freud knew how to harbour a grievance; the two were unreconciled when Eli died in 1923.

Eli's son, Edward,* found favour with 'Uncle Sigi', arranging for the *Introductory Lectures* and other works to be published in America. Eventually Freud received substantial royalties. He told his nephew that 'You are the only one of my relatives who has ever, or at least since many years, done me any service.'

That, in turn, was unfair to his nephew Sam, busy sending food parcels from Manchester to Berggasse in the two years of intense hardship that followed the end of the war. Some were stolen in transit or eaten by mice. Although Freud insisted on paying for the food as soon as he was able to, Sam kept saying he didn't want the money. Shopping lists arrived in Manchester:

> The articles most desirable to Martha are: milk, extract of meat, *coffee*, oats & some spices as: white pepper, cinnamon. I am very fond of cheese . . . all things in tin boxes are welcome, marmalade is very good, but corned beef is quite common here.

Vienna was a thousand miles from London, a far-off place regarded by the victors as having brought its sufferings on itself. Civilisation had receded. Nothing worked properly. Foreign entrepreneurs haunted hotel corridors looking for people anxious to sell their jewels.

Freud was spared the worst indignities, thanks to the hard-currency patients. He might have to sit in his study wearing overcoat and hat to keep warm – and a woman he analysed in 1920

---

* Edward L. Bernays, public relations consultant, was a marketing pioneer whose campaigns used psychology as cleverly as a psychoanalyst. For his first campaign, to make a New York play about venereal disease acceptable, he created a fund to support sex education, presenting its influential donors with tickets for the first night. The waspish Jones described him to Freud as 'an American "sharper" and quite unscrupulous'. Bernays didn't die until 1995, aged 103, a legendary figure.

remembered an unheated apartment with only cold water in the taps – but the pounds and dollars began to add up in bank accounts abroad. While the poor made do with trousers cut from sacking, Freud was writing to Sam (22 February 1920) asking him to choose a cloth in soft Shetland wool, of a shade recommended by Martha – 'pepper and salt or mouse-grey or tete de negre' – so that he could have a suit made for the spring. 'I am,' he added, 'accumulating foreign money in Amsterdam to pay for this.'

Jones sent encouraging platitudes as well as patients. Science was the rock. Storms could be withstood. The poet Clough was quoted: 'But westward, look, the land is bright!' Taking his own advice, Jones got married again, in 1919 – to an attractive young Viennese intellectual, Katharine Jokl, less than two months after they were introduced in Switzerland – and lived with her happily ever after; reformed at last. Soon he was busy helping to reorganise the cause in Europe and America.

The committee took shape again. Gizella Pálos obtained a divorce and Ferenczi married her; her ex-husband dropped dead of a heart attack on the wedding day. 'Something demonic, in Groddeck's sense,' suggested Freud.

The old routines reasserted themselves. Patients came to Berggasse on the hour. There was a new routine: unknown to almost everyone, in the evenings Freud was psychoanalysing his daughter Anna, drawing her deeper into his life.

As old age – real, now, not imagined – began to overtake him, he maintained the cold dedication of a leader whose duty it is to survive. Rumours in America in 1919 that he had been driven to suicide irritated him. His life wasn't over after all.

26: Hard Times

No psychoanalyst, in Vienna or anywhere else, could begin to match Freud for reputation and authority. His prudent intentions before the war to broaden the base of the movement would be fulfilled by the steady development of his theories in other hands and other places, not always as he envisaged. For the moment his word remained law. Unable to tolerate dissent, he reigned alone.

Colleagues in Vienna were more than ever beholden to him where money was concerned, since from time to time he had hard-currency patients to offer them. Among the needy was 'Little Rank', the intimate who knew his place. Freud had more than once praised and patronised him in the same breath when writing to other colleagues – 'indispensable helpmate' and 'ever-faithful', the acolyte who 'keeps his honest character unharmed'. Rank had spent much of the war editing an army newspaper, where he specialised in abusing the British Prime Minister, Lloyd George; the years had hardened him, and his gaze behind the thick spectacles was not quite as meek. Still, he remained a poor man, and now that he was back in Vienna, Freud had him on the list of favoured analysts who could be sent an American or two.

There was no shortage of Viennese patients, but even when Freud charged hundreds of crowns an hour the devalued currency was worth very little. Americans paid in proper money: $10, cash. The movement as a whole needed funds, especially to subsidise the publication of books and journals, and Freud was the only figure who could attract them. The notional fortune from Anton von Freund, the Hungarian benefactor, dwindled to a more modest sum, partly because of inflation, partly because Freund's cancer returned and carried him off early in 1920. But it was better than nothing.

A new generation of analysts was emerging in Vienna, eyes fixed as firmly as their predecessors' on father Freud. Among them was Wilhelm Reich, one of the strangest practitioners of the century, then young and poor, studying medicine; a tormented man who found in Freud's writing confirmation of his belief that we continually deceive ourselves. 'Man flees from himself!' he wrote in his diary in July 1920.

> All lies – even the best, most sincerely desired truth. 10.30 pm. The wind is howling again – no, it's the tram! What is going on in Vienna at this moment: people getting drunk, bodies wildly intertwined, everywhere, from the ground floor to the top – do I want it, too? Yes or no?

Born in 1897 to well-off Jewish parents in Galicia, Reich was as obsessed by sex as Freud had ever been, but perhaps enjoyed too much of it, whereas Freud's problem was that he enjoyed too little. His personal life had been unhappy. As a child he participated in an oedipal drama with real sex and real death, spying on Mother when she made love to his tutor and lusting after her himself, then being forced to betray her by Father, a violently jealous man, after which she killed herself by drinking bleach. While he was still at medical school after the war, he visited Freud and was entranced by him, finding everything he did and said 'shot through with tints of irony', and he became a practising analyst even before he qualified as a doctor.

Patronage soon came his way. 'I am alive,' he told his diary in January 1921, 'have two *paying* patients sent to me by Freud himself!' Before his wilder ideas about the power of the orgasm surfaced, he was seen as a brilliant if unorthodox recruit to the movement, 'a shark in a pond of carp', as he once put it, but devoted to his mentor.*

Helene Deutsch, the first 'modern woman' to be an analyst and interest herself in female sexuality, was another recruit who enjoyed the founder's patronage. Born Helene Rosenbach in 1884,

---

* The movement expelled Reich in 1934. Eventually, disappointed with Freud, he progressed to the United States in 1939, and became infamous as the inventor of the 'orgone energy accumulator', a cubicle that allegedly concentrated energy from the atmosphere and could cure conditions from the common cold and sexual impotence to cancer. His activities landed him in prison, where he died in 1957. The 'permissive society' of the 1960s promptly resurrected him as a standard-bearer of sexuality. So Reich came to embody the sensual appetites that Freud was attacked for having promoted, though Freud never sought or indulged them himself.

she, too, came from the Jewish east, from Galicia, and in 1913 qualified as a doctor at the Vienna medical school, where one of her examiners refused to let any woman attend his lectures, and addressed her, whenever he had to, as 'Mr Rosenbach'. She and the Viennese doctor she married, Felix Deutsch, both became part of the inner group. Freud analysed her in 1918 as a prelude to her becoming an analyst, and she fell in love with him as analytic patients were supposed to.

The essential quality of the Viennese community was cosiness. Freud found Helene's husband a post at the English legation in Vienna, which meant access to coffee and butter. Presently Felix became Freud's personal doctor. When Freud had problems with a quarrelsome disciple, Victor Tausk, who had come back disturbed by the war and was begging to be analysed, Freud refused and passed him on to Helene Deutsch.

Tausk, a troubled but significant figure who vanished from the history of psychoanalysis because he was seen as an embarrassment, committed suicide soon after, in July 1919, at the age of forty, simultaneously shooting and hanging himself, for reasons that probably included his rejection by Freud. Unhealthy dependencies were habitual. Freud's response to his death, in a letter to Lou Salomé, once Tausk's lover, contained an unnerving home-truth, 'I confess I do not really miss him; I had long taken him to be useless, indeed a threat to the future.' It was Freud's proclaimed intention always to face reality, whether it was his or anyone else's. That makes the frankness no less chilling.

Another analyst, Herbert Silberer, fell out with Freud – probably because Silberer took sides with the disgraced Stekel before the war – and was refused an audience when he wrote asking for one in 1922. 'I no longer desire personal contact with you,' said the letter of rejection. No doubt Silberer, too, was a disturbed individual, and had unconnected reasons for hanging himself in spectacular fashion soon afterwards, his features lit by torchlight so that his wife would see him when she came in. But Freud's presence hovers in the background.

The crowd of faces around Freud, often in dispute for his favours, never had quite the same importance after the war. He had less energy to spare for them, and the matter of who would succeed him came to be settled in favour of his youngest daughter, Anna. She was not to be the organiser and editor of psychoanalysis, roles that

Rank, Eitingon and Jones would fill. Freud's need by the time he reached his mid-sixties, which he did in 1921, was to have someone at his side he could rely on in the present and trust to keep faith with his ideas in the future: ultimately a guardian of the flame, a fundamentalist, a censor, although these roles were still half a lifetime away for the shy young woman of the early 1920s.

A wife might have remained at his side until she herself grew old, but Martha had never been part of his work. Of his children, Anna was the only one who cared tuppence about psychoanalysis, a happy accident, or probably not an accident at all, since her father did all he could to encourage her interest, edging her towards decisions that would deprive her of a private life and give her a professional one instead. Whether the second choice was better or worse than the first, it was clearly the one that Freud wanted.

A letter to Salomé in March 1922, written when Anna had been away from Vienna for eleven days on family visits to Hamburg and Berlin, says how much he misses her; adds that for a long time he has pitied her 'for still being at home with us old folks'; then confesses his overriding need:

> if she really were to go away, I should feel myself as deprived as I do now, and as I should do if I had to give up smoking! As long as we are all together, one doesn't realise it clearly, or at least we do not.

These are 'insoluble conflicts', says Freud, and so 'it is good that life comes to an end some time or other'. It was a hint that nothing would change until he was dead, that Anna's contract would last as long as he lived.

He made sure that people knew he was concerned for her well-being. Sam Freud was told in the week of Anna's twenty-sixth birthday, in December 1921, that she was a 'faultless blessing', except for the fact that she was 'still at home', that is, unmarried. It may be that he felt compassion. But he did nothing about it.

Anna's psychoanalysis by her father was part of the process. It began in October 1918, just before the war ended, and lasted three and a half years, an incestuous exercise that went against Freud's own version of the ideal therapy, if only because it confused their real-life relationship with the relationship inside the analysis. How could there be a transference to a father-figure when the real father was the man sitting at the head of the couch? Being the founder he was of course free to do as he pleased, but there was an air of secrecy, and few people heard that he had analysed his daughter.

Neither of them spoke of it outside a small circle, and for decades it went unmentioned in published material, including the Jones biography.

The analysis, and a second one that began in 1924, told Freud about Anna's 'suppressed genitality' and the difficulties she had in freeing herself from him; he wrote about them to Salomé, who had become Anna's friend as well as his. His daughter had fantasies about being beaten. This has been inferred from a paper that Freud wrote in 1919, 'A Child is being Beaten', and a second by Anna (with which she began her career), 'Beating Fantasies and Day-dreams', written in 1922. Both deal with unnamed patients, but there is evidence that she was one of the subjects in Freud's paper, and the sole subject in her own, which was written six months before she had treated anyone.

A young woman describing masturbation fantasies to her father sounds incongruous. Was it supposed to help her overcome personal difficulties? Whatever the analysis taught father and daughter, it either did nothing to stop her becoming an ascetic, or it confirmed her in an asceticism that already existed.

The small muster of Anna's would-be suitors begins with Ernest Jones, who probably didn't expect to succeed, and continues with Hans Lampl, a bearded doctor without much money who had been a schoolfriend of Martin. He appears in an anecdote about taking Anna to a ball one New Year's Eve in the early 1920s. They looked in at her father's study and he gave them a coin for luck before returning to his papers. The ball is not described; the anecdote is about Freud.

It was not Anna who concluded that Lampl was unsuitable but Anna in collusion with her father. Instead of parents keeping an eye on their daughter's potential seducer, the daughter was keeping her own eye on him and reporting back. She wrote to Freud in July 1921 that she and Hans were 'often together' in a 'friendly relationship', which gave her 'daily opportunities to confirm our judgment of him from last year and to rejoice that we judged correctly'. Hans wisely went off and married a Dutch psychiatrist.

Siegfried Bernfeld, another of the new generation of analysts (he would later deconstruct 'Screen Memories'), was spoken of as a candidate; he was a rising star but no more successful with Freud's daughter. Max Eitingon, member of the committee since 1919, rumoured to have been a Russian spy, and fourteen years older than Anna, is said on small evidence to have inspired her with deep affection. But her potential for loving a man had been extinguished.

Her cousin Edward Bernays, the young American who was in the process of inventing public relations, makes a guest appearance to keep up the numbers. He was on a walking tour of Europe in 1920. Edward and Anna are said to have walked a short distance in western Austria. Perhaps the entire list of suitors – with the exception of Jones, who had his own strategic agenda – exists to sustain the fiction that after 1918 there was ever the slightest chance of Anna marrying.

Her siblings were all in marriages of one sort or another. Ex-Lieutenant Martin Freud married a barrister's daughter in December 1919, and his father-in-law found him a job in a bank. Oliver, married and divorced during the war, tried again in 1923, marrying a teacher from Berlin. The equable Ernst, the architect, also married a Berliner, in 1920, and seems to have lived in more harmony than either of his brothers.*

Their father found the idea of divorce in the family distasteful, and Oliver's first marriage doesn't appear in Freud genealogies. Martin's marriage lasted until 1938, when his philandering proved too much for his wife Esti and she left him. Their daughter, Sophie, who became a sociologist, suggests that her 'chaste and ascetic grandfather had delegated the fulfilment of sexual pleasure to his oldest son'.†

Anna's two sisters were married before the war. Mathilde was childless, having had a pregnancy terminated for health reasons early in the marriage. Sophie's two sons, Ernst, born 1914, and Heinz, born 1918, were the first of the grandchildren. At the birth of Ernst, Freud sent Ferenczi a postcard saying, 'Very strange! An oldish feeling, respect for the wonders of sexuality!'

Although he took an austere view of small children and the dangers of over-indulgence, he seems to have made an exception for Heinz, describing him variously as 'a little devil' and 'the cleverest, sweetest child I have ever met'. Heinz's mother, Sophie, was dead

---

* Two of Ernst Freud's sons became prominent, Lucian as a painter, Clemens (his name anglicised to Clement) as a writer and British Member of Parliament.

† Among Martin's possessions was a handsomely bound volume of works by his father, titled *Vier Krankengeschichten*, 'Four Case-Histories', which began with Freud's analysis of the mad Judge Schreber, but suddenly became a blank-page album. This was where Martin secreted photographs of his lovers. Sophie Freud has it now.

by 1920. Post-war epidemics of influenza killed millions of people in many countries, and she may have succumbed to one of the virulent strains, 'blown away,' wrote Freud, 'as if she had never been'.

Her death, in January 1920, was seen by some of Freud's circle as having influenced the book he completed in May and published later the same year, *Beyond the Pleasure Principle*. The title was ironic: what lay beyond pleasure was death. One of its ideas, pursued with logical diligence, was that a primitive psychological 'compulsion to repeat' could be observed in normal people, a desire for the same things to happen again and again. Freud convinced himself that this suggested an unconscious drive to restore former circumstances. Since life was preceded by non-life, the aim of the organism was thus to achieve an inorganic state.

'So,' wrote Ernest Jones, explaining it in the biography, 'the ultimate aim of life must be death,' and the life instinct, or 'Eros', was in perpetual and hopeless conflict with the death instinct. This news was not well received by the faithful. In private James Strachey called it 'a lamentable muddle'.

The origins of the death instinct may have been in Freud's frame of mind: his natural pessimism, his age and his response to the war. At the best of times he was ready to pronounce on reality as he saw it. 'Better . . . that the truth should be told by psychologists,' he wrote, 'than that the task should be left to cynics.' Sophie's death, making 1920 the worst of times, was the last straw, although Freud denied any connection between the theory and the tragedy – such an unscientific motive could hardly be admitted – and insisted that the death instinct was already included in the draft text by the time Sophie died. Recent evidence suggests that additions were made to the manuscript after her death. Times were hard; Freud was melancholy; a book about death was a natural consequence.

The patients with pounds and dollars were light relief of a sort, breaths of the outside world that set the tone of Freud's practice for the rest of his life. Many of his patients were 'pupils', learning to become analysts by being analysed themselves. Whether they came from home or abroad, they were no longer cases to be quarried for fresh insights, but rather a succession of worthy, sometimes less worthy, men and women to whom Freud applied the methods that by now had been, in his eyes, perfected.

In the immediate post-war years, he sometimes took candidates who would have failed to meet his rigorous standards in the past. A dentist from New York, passed on by Jones and accepted at half-price – on the grounds that he was 'only half of an American. The other half a Hungarian Jew' – was not, observed Freud, very clever, in fact was 'rather a young ass'. But '5 Doll. are 750 K[ronen]!!' Before the war the Wolf Man paid forty crowns an hour and thought it expensive. Now forty crowns wouldn't buy a cheap cigar. Pankejeff was a patient again after the war, but his money was worthless and the Bolsheviks had his land. Freud treated him for nothing.

The Anglo-Saxons came with strong views of their own. To the English, the novelty of a bearded professor in Vienna with scatty ideas about sex was so excitingly wicked that at first only the strong-minded and the eccentric were likely to be attracted.

James Strachey (whose family, in recent years much documented, was distinctly odd and strikingly clever – an older brother was the biographer Lytton Strachey) encountered Freud's work through Frederic Myers and the Society for Psychical Research in 1912. Psychoanalysis appealed to him, in as much as he understood it, and after consulting Ernest Jones he set out to become a doctor, enrolling at a London teaching hospital. After three weeks he had had enough, and in 1920 he decided to go straight to Vienna and train with the founder.

Freud had no objection to non-medical analysts and accepted him at a reduced rate, one pound an hour instead of two, on the understanding that he would remain in analysis for a year. Strachey was not intimidated by the Professor and his unheated apartment. He wrote to his brother Lytton in November 1920, after something over a month's analysis:

> Each day except Sunday I spend an hour on the Prof's sofa (I've now spent 34 altogether) – and the 'analysis' seems to provide a complete undercurrent for life. As for what it's all about, I'm vaguer than ever; but at all events it's sometimes extremely exciting and sometimes extremely unpleasant – so I daresay there's *something* in it . . . During the early part of the hour all is vague – a dark hint here, a mystery there – then it gradually seems to get thicker; you feel dreadful things going on inside you, and can't make out what they can possibly be; then he begins to give you a slight lead; you suddenly get a clear glimpse of one thing; then you see another; at last a whole series of lights break in on you; he asks you one more question; you give a last reply – and as the whole truth dawns upon you the Professor rises, crosses the room to the electric bell, and shows you out at the door.

Other times were not so good, when 'you lie for the whole hour with a ton weight on your stomach simply unable to get out a single word'.

Freud, who had difficulty understanding Strachey's soft-spoken English, was favourably inclined towards him because Jones had pointed out that as a member of a literary family he might make a useful translator. If Freud were to be made accessible to the English-speaking world, something better than Brill's renderings was needed.

Jones was more sensitive to this than Freud, whose manner sometimes implied that one translation was very much like another, as if to say that his works spoke for themselves whatever the language. When Freud decided to entrust papers for translation to whichever Americans happened to be having analysis, Jones shuddered and lectured him on how rare it was to be able to write correct English, 'of course even rarer in America than in England'. James Strachey was Jones's choice, and in time he became Freud's as well.

Strachey's Anglo-American wife, Alix Sargant-Florence, whom he married shortly before the analysis began, travelled with him to Vienna, and, after an attack of 'palpitations', joined her husband on the couch, although not at the same time. His hours were in the mornings, hers in the afternoons. Mrs Strachey (who became a co-translator with her husband) decided that Freud was a simple man, liberal-minded but orthodox, inclined to be gullible. These confident judgments, at times patronising, came naturally to the Stracheys, who were soon familiar with Freudians in Vienna and Berlin. Anna Freud was a 'sentimentalist', Bernfeld a 'hopeless pedagogue', Lampl a 'hard-hearted and selfish beast'. Ernest Jones, who had negotiated their entry into the charmed circle, was 'the little brute'.

The Stracheys were not afraid to stereotype whole populations in half-jokes with sharp edges. The typical Viennese was 'extremely provincial'. Germans as a race were 'very, very simple minded' and in matters of culture 'trebly damaged idiots'. Virginia Woolf, another star of the Bloomsbury group, was dismissive both of psycho-analysis and its practitioners, although her husband's forward-looking Hogarth Press was soon publishing Freud's works.* The

* Mrs Woolf, having read the publisher's proof of Freud's paper 'Obsessive Actions and Religious Practices' – it appeared in English in 1924 – wrote scathingly to a friend about the incident of the wedding night and the red ink, which the

Bloomsburys kept abreast of developments but reserved the right to sneer. The English intelligentsia in the 1920s had an undisturbed sense of their own importance.

Freud's two-fold interest in the English-speaking countries, to earn their currencies and to see psychoanalysis implanted in them, centred on the United States. Britain was an admirable place and his old liking for it remained, but he knew that the real territories to conquer were across the Atlantic. The scorn and distaste he often expressed for American culture was probably enhanced by the knowledge that psychoanalysis had found an easy foothold there, and must be encouraged despite his reservations about brashness and commercialism. It was also disturbing to need American money so badly.

In October 1920 he contacted his nephew Ed Bernays, offering to write popular articles for a New York magazine as long as it was reputable, and suggesting a less than enthralling title for the first, 'Don't Use Psychoanalysis in Polemics'. Bernays approached *Cosmopolitan*, which said it would pay $1,000 per article, an enormous sum, as long as the subjects were on the lines of 'The Wife's Mental Place in the Home'. Freud backed away. His definition of 'popular' was something that would instruct the well-educated layman.

At about the same time, Sam Freud in Manchester, reading an old copy of *Punch* while he waited to see the dentist, saw with 'astonishment and delight' that it contained a poem about Freud and Jung. He sent it off to his uncle, but it was not well received. The poem was silly; popularity, sighed Freud, was a threat to more serious achievements.

Yet the rise of psychoanalysis had to take place amid the shifting sands of public taste. He accepted promptly when, a few years later, Bernays proposed he head an 'international psychoanalytic foundation', with a 'scientific fund' to be subscribed by the public that would promote the cause. Unfortunately the public was not interested in scientific funds; psychoanalysis raised other expectations.

The *Chicago Tribune* offered him $25,000 in June 1924 to psychoanalyse the murderers in the sensational case of two

---

husband threw on the bed-sheets 'to excuse his impotence to the housemaid but threw it in the wrong place which unhinged his wife's mind – and to this day she pours claret on the dinner table. We could all go on like that for hours; and yet these Germans think it proves something – beside their own gull-like imbecility.'

university students, Leopold and Loeb, who killed a boy of fourteen because, it was said, they saw themselves as 'Nietzschean supermen'. But by then he had health reasons for declining, and so didn't have to resist the temptation of a sum that would have meant security for life.

In the same year the Hollywood producer Sam Goldwyn offered him a fortune, the figure reported being $100,000, to help make a movie about 'the great love stories of history', beginning with Antony and Cleopatra. No doubt the real value to the studios would have been Freud's name on the screen and in the publicity material. To a growing public, and despite his best efforts to the contrary, Sigmund Freud now stood for sexual revelation of a superior kind, vaguely scientific but daringly post-war. He declined Goldwyn's offer.

The following year, 1925, a German film producer, Hans Neumann, tried to draw him into a project to make an educational film about psychoanalysis. Freud, not at all keen, left the negotiations to Abraham, now President of the International Association, and a popular-science film, *The Secret of a Soul*, was duly made and shown in cinemas. The publicity said it was 'supervised' by Freud, which was untrue and annoyed him intensely. Jones tried to have the film banned in London, without success.*

Because Freud's name was so widely known by the 1920s, he was both more sought-after and more vulnerable for precisely the reason he feared, that his reputation made him 'news', subjecting him to vulgar scrutiny. In the lurid case of an American patient and his lover, Dr Horace Frink and Mrs Angelika Bijur, he narrowly avoided public exposure in an episode that newspapers would have loved at the time.

Frink, who graduated at Cornell in 1905, set up as a psychiatrist, dabbled in hypnosis and was an early convert to psychoanalysis, becoming the first secretary of the New York Psychoanalytic Society in 1911. He and his wife, Doris Best, were both analysed the following year by a colleague, Dr Thaddeus H. Ames, and he planned to visit Vienna in 1915 for further analysis by Freud. The war made this impossible.

* Psychoanalysis attracted film-makers for sound commercial reasons. The script of an unmade German movie of the period, *Sensational Revelations from the Night Life of the Human Soul*, called for a choreographed version of Freud's *Three Essays on Sexuality*, the boy star Jackie Coogan as Young Oedipus and the Tiller Girls as erotic dancers.

Ernest Jones initially thought him 'an honest fellow, but very limited', but he published a useful book about compulsive behaviour in 1918, and when someone was needed to lead psychoanalysis in the United States after the war, and in particular to be American editor of the international journal, Frink's popularity with the New York society – and Brill's irritating habit of not replying to Freud's letters – made him a serious candidate.

In February 1921 he went to Europe for his long-delayed training analysis, a tall, amusing fellow who confirmed Freud's expectations during the several months he was in Vienna. Thereafter he was the chosen candidate. No one seems to have been unduly worried by this imperialism on the part of Vienna. Freud knew best. One of his private reasons for favouring Frink, who was not a Jew, may have been his old bias in favour of Gentiles when it came to finding missionaries for the Anglo-Saxons.

Frink had what appeared to be mild psychological problems. A year or two earlier he had suffered 'toxic headaches' and some memory loss, and in Vienna he was sleeping badly. No details of the analysis were ever published. But he told Freud about a continuing liaison with a married woman, Angelika Bijur, that had begun before the war when she came to him as a patient. Freud encouraged him to admit to his feelings about her, telling him (as he explained later to Dr Ames) that

> I thought it the good right of every human being to strive for sexual gratification and tender love if he saw a way to attain them, both of which he had not found with his wife. When he grew uncertain of his mind I had to take the side of his repressed desires and in this way become the advocate of his wish for divorce and marriage with Mrs B.

Angelika's husband, Abraham, was a wealthy businessman from a New York family of Orthodox Jews. Angelika Bijur had money of her own. They had quarrelled more than once, both about his sexual performance and her friendship with Frink, which she insisted was innocent. When Frink's analysis with Freud (which she had paid for) was ending in summer 1921, she came to Europe to see him. On the way she stopped off in Paris where her husband was staying. She slept with him the same afternoon and on several subsequent occasions. Thaddeus Ames, who was now Abraham's analyst – and also President of the New York Psychoanalytic Society – knew the details. Angelika, it was reported, enjoyed satisfactory orgasms on each occasion. She also gave her husband a present of some pearl studs worth $5,000.

Mrs Bijur then continued to Vienna, joined Frink, saw Freud, and heard from him that Frink's love for her was genuine. She said later that her lover was suffering from depression when she arrived. Freud, according to her, 'advised my getting a divorce, both because of my own incomplete existence, and because "If I threw Dr F[rink] over now he would never again try to come back to normality and probably develop into a homosexual though in a highly disguised way." ' She claimed to have regarded some of Freud's ideas as 'insane delusions'.

Angelika Bijur doesn't sound too reliable a witness, but evidently both she and Frink believed they were being told by an expert that divorce followed by remarriage was the preferred course of action. By this time Freud had chosen Frink as his American standard-bearer and so had a vested interest in his recovery. Frink's future in the movement, he reminded Ernest Jones, 'depends on a complete change in his private affairs he is now planning, the success of which is not yet assured'.

Frink and Mrs Bijur set about making the change. They took a train to Paris, where Abraham was waiting for his wife at the station, walked up to him smiling and said they meant to get married. The three then returned to New York in separate ships, and Abraham consulted his lawyers – egged on, it appeared, by his family. He wrote an unposted letter to Freud asking, 'Great Doctor, are you savant or charlatan?'

The first Freud heard of these rumblings was when Thaddeus Ames wrote to him in September, one doctor to another, explaining the background and warning that Bijur's lawyers were ready, 'on sufficient provocation', to give the story to the newspapers and 'attack Dr Frink and Psychoanalysis'. Bijur was prepared to grant his wife a divorce but he wanted Frink expelled from the New York society. If he wasn't expelled, said Ames, and the story became public, 'the newspapers would damn every analyst in America'.

This was not the way newspapers or cuckolded husbands behaved in central Europe. Freud's reply, courteous but indignant, laid into American 'hypocrisy and sham morality' and suggested, unrealistically, that New York's analysts should stand by Frink whatever happened. He distinguished between advising the couple, which he had not done, and making them face reality, which he had: 'for me it was a case of honourable serious love versus convention, there my interest ended'. The public, he admitted, might not grasp the difference.

Freud was splitting hairs. His view of sexual behaviour was always equivocal. Conventional morality and the single man concerned him when he was a young doctor, the frustrations of his own bachelor life still fresh in his memory. He disliked the conventions but fell short of condemning them. Later he developed the view that civilisation involved the renouncing of instincts. No doubt this reflected the fact that he had renounced them himself. But in private he sympathised with those who seized their sexual opportunities.

A wish to see Horace and his Angelika marry for love hovers behind the story. 'Mrs B. is a treasure of the heart,' he wrote to Frink (12 September 1921). 'The prize is well worth the struggle . . . Mrs B. will become beautiful when she is happy.' Abraham was dismissed contemptuously as 'the famous husband of Mrs B.' (Freud to Jones, 6 November 1921).

The bleak tale gets bleaker. Frink was a more unstable character than Freud realised. His wife wrote him pathetic letters, unhappy but not angry, which he showed anxiously to Freud, who thought they were 'cool and reasonable', and that after the divorce 'she will become what she has been before'. Frink remained unsure of what to do, begging Freud for more analysis. Meanwhile the divorces went ahead unpublicised in states distant from New York. Doris Frink, in New Mexico with her two children, did as she was told by Mrs Bijur's solicitors. Luckily perhaps for Freud, the following year Abraham conveniently died of cancer, an event that 'has simplified the state of [Frink's] affairs and abolished all possibilities of scandal in virtuous America' (Freud to Jones, 11 May 1922).

In summer 1922 Freud relented and let Frink return to analysis. He and Angelika went to Berchtesgaden, where the Freuds spent the summer, and 'at times' was given an hour of treatment. It was not Freud's custom to compromise his holidays, but Frink, leader-elect in America and a man who deserved to be happy, was evidently a special case. There are hints in the correspondence, too, that Freud hoped some of Angelika's money might come the way of the movement.

When the Freuds returned to Vienna, Frink and Mrs Bijur seem to have gone with them. The couple then went to Paris to make arrangements for the wedding. Frink returned alone to Vienna and had a psychotic breakdown, behaving violently at his hotel, with powerful mood-shifts and hallucinations; he thought his bathtub was a grave. Freud had to engage someone to guard him. When Angelika arrived he struck her. Despite all this they were married in December and went to Egypt for their honeymoon.

But Frink was never the same again. Elected president of the New York society (whose members knew little of what was going on) in January 1923 while he was still on his honeymoon, he caused trouble as soon as he returned with a book review denigrating Brill. The former Mrs Frink died of pneumonia in May – he was not allowed to visit her – and he began quarrelling with Angelika. By the end of 1923 he was too ill to work, and could no longer serve as president.

The following year he was twice admitted to the Phipps psychiatric clinic at Johns Hopkins in Baltimore; Angelika decided to divorce him; he cut an artery and nearly bled to death. Eventually he made a recovery of sorts, and lived another twelve years, dying of a cardiac condition in 1936 when he was fifty-three.

At the Phipps clinic, Frink was treated by Adolf Meyer, a distinguished psychiatrist who had emigrated to the United States from Switzerland in the 1890s. A moralist in the Zürich mould who had no sympathy with psychoanalysis, he found the Frink affair distasteful, and wrote privately of 'the supposed American leader of psychoanalytic work and his revolting wife', meaning Angelika. Meyer concluded that both she and Frink 'acted more or less under forcible suggestion by Freud'.

No doubt Freud did what he thought best, but it seems that he used his technical skills and personal authority, as so often before, to convince his clients that he knew their minds better than they did. He misread Frink and Mrs Bijur. His judgments ring hollow, as if he failed to grasp that these were real lives, not the elements of another essay. And when the drama was over, leaving Frink suicidal, his second divorce pending, and the other husband and wife dead, Freud wrote to Jones (25 September 1924):

> What is the use of Americans, if they bring no money? They are not good for anything else. My attempt at giving them a chief in the person of Frink, which has so sadly miscarried, is the last thing I will ever do for them.

This was written after Freud himself became seriously ill, and allowances need to be made. He, too, would never be the same again.

27: Cancer

In the busy and often difficult years immediately after the war, Freud's health was not a particular issue. He complained about old age, as usual. Two days after his sixty-fifth birthday, in May 1921, he told Ferenczi that on 13 March

> I quite suddenly took a step into real old age. Since then the thought of death has not left me, and sometimes I have the impression that seven of my internal organs are fighting to have the honour of bringing my life to an end.

No explanation occurred to him, except the implausible one that Oliver happened to be leaving for Romania. Ten years earlier he would have been more likely to analyse the feeling and see where it came from. Now he just accepted it. Also in May, Georg Groddeck, still pursuing the psychology of disease, wanted Freud and Anna to stay with him at Baden-Baden. The rational reason for saying no, replied Freud, was that his summer holidays were already planned:

> The real reason is different. Because I have lost my youth ... In reality one has only a single need in old age, a need for rest. It is a quite transparent calculation. Since I shall not be able to pick the fruit of this tree I shall not bother to plant it. Mean but honest.

These intimations of mortality occurred while he was analysing Frink for the first time. Perhaps what now seems like callousness towards Frink and his affairs was simply weariness; but if Freud was jaded, he was not as decrepit as sometimes he implied. He continued to find the energy to see a full list of patients six days a week – in June 1922 he told Jones that '9 hours [a day] may soon be too much for my powers' – and the committee and his rivalrous lieutenants demanded attention, though he was often reluctant to give it.

The last ten days of the long summer break in 1921 were spent on a working holiday with the committee in the Harz Mountains of northern Germany, the only occasion they went away together. Abraham, who knew the area, acted as their guide. Eitingon, the new member, Rank, Sachs, Ferenczi and Jones were all there. Sightseeing and walking (when Freud, according to Jones, was 'swift and tireless') alternated with discussions.

Freud, having another of his enthusiasms for the occult, chose the occasion to read his colleagues a paper, eventually called 'Psychoanalysis and Telepathy', that he had written earlier in the summer. Freud's original text was untitled. It wasn't published until after his death, and his editors supplied an innocuous title which does it an injustice. For the first and only time, Freud looked, briefly, beyond telepathy.

The paper began robustly by claiming that the impetus to investigate 'psychical forces other than the human and animal minds with which we are familiar' was now 'irresistibly strong'. This was explained by the post-war sense that life on earth had somehow lost its value, and by the prevailing doubts about scientific certainty raised, for example, by Einstein's theory of relativity. The analyst had to beware of surrendering his impartiality. Yet there was little doubt, said Freud, that if occult phenomena were examined, 'the outcome will very soon be that the occurrence of a number of them will be confirmed'. Which ones, he didn't say.

Spiritualism was referred to, and the threat to psychoanalytic methods that would arise if 'ultimate explanations' available to alleged 'spiritual beings' became available.

> So, too, the methods of analytic technique will be abandoned if there is hope of getting into direct touch with the operative spirits by means of occult procedures, just as habits of patient humdrum work are abandoned if there is a hope of growing rich at a single blow by means of a successful speculation.

Having advanced into this alien territory, Freud at once retreated, declaring that 'My personal attitude to the material remains unenthusiastic and ambivalent', and spent the rest of the lecture examining instances of fortune-telling and thought-transference. He had forgotten to bring details of a particular episode that had impressed him,* and included the fact of the

---

* The episode concerned an English doctor called Forsyth, an Austrian patient who was interested in Galsworthy's stories in *The Forsyte Saga*, and various coincidences of name and idea.

forgetfulness in the lecture to his tiny audience as proof that 'I discuss the subject of occultism under the pressure of the greatest resistance.'

Freud lived comfortably with his uncertainties about the occult. Three subsequent papers dealt with the subject and left no one any wiser. A remark of 1933, 'It may be that I too have a secret inclination towards the miraculous,' has to suffice.

After the Harz excursion, the committee went back to rebuilding the movement. The inner circle was still dominant, and psycho-analysis in general was becoming institutionalised. Matters that had always been decided by personal preference and the need to conform to Freud's wishes had begun to formulate themselves as issues that needed guidance or even rules. Should homosexuals be allowed to join constituent societies of the International Associ-ation? Not really, since homosexuality was a neurosis that inter-fered with the treatment of patients' neuroses, although homosex-uals couldn't be banned outright. Should non-medical analysts be encouraged? The answer had always been yes, but the Americans insisted on medical qualifications, and there was nothing that Europe could do about it.

The publishing arm of psychoanalysis, the Internationaler Psycho-analytischer Verlag, set up in January 1919, was the movement's most visible activity, and the one that caused most trouble. Referred to always as 'the *Verlag*' (the publishing house), it was Freud's guarantee of independence from the caprice or cupidity of commercial publishers. Its finances were uncertain because of the impoverishment and demise of the man who was meant to finance it, von Freund.

Running the *Verlag* in a way that reconciled national interests was not easy, and Freud, who didn't want to be bothered with operating details, left them to others, mainly Jones and Rank, who quarrelled. Jones, editing the *International Journal* from London, found Rank in Vienna overruling his instructions, or complaining about 'transatlantic rubbish': an objection that seemed preposter-ous to Jones, who once remarked to Freud in another context that, while he had some sympathy with anti-Americanism, one could hardly indict a nation, especially one that in fifty years would be 'the arbiters of the world'. Freud found himself drawn into disputes, complaining to Jones about his interference, then having to digest the long justifications that came back by return of post. He was neither happy nor competent as a business manager, but he could never entirely detach himself from *Verlag* affairs.

His life no longer had the imperatives that formerly drove him from one task to the next. He had become aware of the hesitations of age. Writing to Ferenczi before the 1922 conference, to be held in Berlin, he sounds sad and reminiscent:

> Something in me rebels against the compulsion to go on earning money which is never enough, and to continue with the same psychological devices that for thirty years have kept me upright in the face of my contempt for people and the detestable world. Strange secret yearnings rise in me – perhaps from my ancestral heritage – for the East and the Mediterranean and for a life of quite another kind: wishes from late childhood never to be fulfilled, which do not conform to reality as if to hint at a loosening of one's relationship to it. Instead of which – we shall meet on the soil of sober Berlin.

During his summer holidays at the Pension Moritz in Berchtesgaden, when he was preparing his lecture for the conference in September – and intermittently analysing Frink – he heard that his sister Rosa's daughter Caecilie, known as 'Mausi', had killed herself with an overdose of veronal.* She was twenty-three, unmarried and pregnant. Freud's letter to Sam telling him of the tragedy mentioned a love affair that went wrong, but made it seem that a poor relationship with 'Auntie Rosa' was to blame. Perhaps no one told Freud the truth because of his views about scandal in the family.

At Berlin about 250 analysts and interested parties gathered for the usual lectures, gossip and meals. Fewer than a dozen Americans made the journey, among them Frink and Mrs Bijur, who were in Europe in any case. American psychoanalysis was becoming self-contained, prosperous, needing no guidance from Europe; or, as Freud put it, obsessed with success and money.

His lecture dealt with another refinement of his general theory, his 'metapsychology' – as it turned out, the last – which was to add further abstractions to the crowded guesswork of the Freudian maps. The full account appeared in April 1923 as *The Ego and the Id*.

In German the title was *Das Ich und das Es*, which translates

---

* Rosa was the unluckiest of Freud's siblings, losing her husband before the war, her son during it, and now her daughter. She lived for another twenty years, only to die in the gas chambers.

literally as 'The I and the It'. The 'It' was the term used by Groddeck to suggest the unknowable part of the self, the force that 'lives us while we believe we are living'. Many people have this perception of a something-else beyond the 'I' that we think we know. Freud, however, took it over as a technical term to help him redefine the 'unconscious', a word that no longer meant what he wanted it to mean. His translators decided against 'I' and 'It', either because the terms were too confusing, or because they sounded insufficiently learned. 'I' was Latinised into 'Ego' and 'It' into 'Id'. As a result, in English 'the Id' became convenient shorthand for the dark side of human nature.

Freud's essay was another of his attempts to know the unknowable. Unlike the books he wrote at the start of the century, which drew on the evidence of dreams and parapraxis, he was describing hypothetical structures for which no scientific evidence existed. A super-ego (first hinted at by Freud in 1914) was given the task of conscience, born out of responses in childhood to parental authority. The ego had to live between the conflicting demands of the super-ego and the id, and cope with the outside world as well. In Freud's analogy, the id was the horse and the ego was the rider. Both ego and super-ego did much of their work unconsciously, which is why the specific unconscious that contained what Freud called 'the dark inaccessible part of our personality', where the unruly sexual instincts were to be found, was henceforth defined as the id.

Many psychoanalysts would come to use *The Ego and the Id* as the basis of an 'ego-psychology' that ultimately paid less attention to the threatening contents of the id and more to the rational ego, the moral self that patients recognised, and that analysts of later generations increasingly felt at home with.

Two or three months before the book was published in the spring, Freud became aware of an ulcer in his mouth, on the right-hand side of the palate. At the time he was smoking up to twenty cigars a day. Apart from the war, when supplies were short, he had been a serious smoker for most of his working life. His addiction was deep-seated, and his attempts to overcome it in the 1890s because of fears that it was affecting his heart were fruitless.

In 1897 he had confided his view to Fliess that all addictions, to alcohol, morphine, tobacco or anything else, were only substitutes for the 'primary addiction', masturbation. Even if that were true, knowing it made no difference. Like humbler smokers, he acknowledged that the habit helped with 'the battle of life'.

The ulcer persisted but he did nothing about it, although he must have been aware of the possibilities from the start. A connection between pipe and cigar smoking (then the most common habits) and oral cancer was widely suspected in the nineteenth century, and commented on in the literature. Freud would have known that doctors called carcinoma of the mouth 'the rich man's cancer' because of the cost of cigars.

When it suited him he was as careful of his health as most doctors are. In 1914, when he had the rectal examination to exclude cancer, he greeted the negative result by saying, 'So this time I am let off.' There was a similar episode in 1916. A year later came his swollen gums, which he described to Ferenczi, adding '(?carcinoma)' and saying that cigars had cured them. Perhaps in 1923 he let himself think that some other kind of magic would dispose of the ulcer.

Freud had no doctor he consulted regularly. Early in April he spoke to a dermatologist he knew, hardly the first choice for an ulcer in the mouth, who examined the lesion and said it was benign, but advised having it excised. Shortly afterwards Felix Deutsch was asked informally to have a look when he was at Berggasse on other business. Freud said his visitor would 'see something you won't like'. Deutsch looked, thought the lesion was cancerous, but didn't say so. He said it should be seen to immediately.

A dangerous charade ensued. As though reluctant to be seen to take the matter seriously, Freud, who must have suspected the truth, arranged to have the surgery performed by an acquaintance, Professor Marcus Hajek, who had made his reputation with research but, as Freud knew, was an indifferent surgeon. Hajek admitted him to the outpatients' department of the public hospital where he worked, and Freud went there in a cab one morning, without telling his family, to have the suspect growth excised. He expected to be allowed home soon after, but there was too much bleeding for him to leave until the next day, and Martha received a telephone message asking her to bring a nightshirt. She arrived with Anna to find him sitting on a chair, his clothes spattered with blood.

Visitors were not allowed during lunch-time, so the two were sent away. Freud was put in a bed in an isolated room where there was already a patient, described by Felix Deutsch as an 'imbecile dwarf'. With his wife and daughter still absent, he began to haemorrhage. The emergency electric bell was broken and the other patient ran for help, perhaps saving Freud's life, since the staff, even when they came, found it difficult to stop the bleeding. Returning after lunch, Anna refused to leave, and spent the night at her father's bedside. In the morning Hajek added insult to injury by treating Freud like a charity patient, demonstrating the case to a crowd of students around the bed before sending him home.

Max Schur, who later took over as Freud's physician, hinted that Hajek may have disliked or feared psychoanalysis, and was unconsciously taking it out on the founder now he had him at his mercy. This explanation would have appealed to Freud, who may even have thought of it himself: although for the sake of his sanity, he presumably had to ration the number of times he looked for Freudian explanations of what people were up to in his vicinity.

The operation was on 20 April 1923, shortly before his sixty-seventh birthday, and the pathological report confirmed the cancer. Incomprehensibly, nobody told Freud the truth. Treatment with X-rays and radium was prescribed; perhaps it was assumed that this was enough to let him work things out for himself.

Letters he wrote to Salomé and Jones implied that he knew more than he was saying, yet he conspired with the silent doctors. Afterwards there was talk of fears that he might have killed himself had he learned about the cancer, which sounds like an excuse for not having had the courage to tell him. As far as his friends could judge, the event that distressed him most that summer was the death in Vienna on 19 June of his grandson Heinz, whose mother Sophie had died three years earlier. The child had tuberculosis; another victim of the war.

The holidays were spent convalescing with his family, who were presumably ignorant of the truth. In August they were at the Hotel du Lac in Lavarone, high up in the mountains shared between Austria and Italy. The committee had decided to meet in the vicinity, and its members gathered at San Cristoforo, 2,000 feet below, around the other side of Freud's mountain.

No one ever explained why they chose to follow their leader on his holiday. Quarrelling within the committee was worse than usual, but Freud had made it clear that they must settle their differences without reference to him. Had his operation in April given them a sense of his mortality, frightening them into his presence?

The silent Dr Deutsch had arrived at the Hotel du Lac, and seems to have told his patient that more surgery was going to be needed, still without mentioning the dreaded word. But we have little idea of what was said, thought, implied or guessed at, either at the top of the mountain or the bottom. We know that Jones wrote to his wife in London on 26 August to say that 'Freud has a real cancer slowly growing and may last many years. He doesn't know it and it is a most deadly secret.' We know that Deutsch told the committee, who endorsed the need for silence, then took their minds off the news by attending to internecine quarrels, condemning Jones for allegedly calling Rank (though not to his face) 'a swindling Jew'. We know that Anna Freud wrote to Salomé on 29 August, 'You are right, I would not leave him now under any circumstances.'

Shortly afterwards, she and her father travelled to Rome, and stayed there for several weeks. Freud had planned the trip in April, at the time of his operation, and he enjoyed her pleasure at seeing the city for the first time. It was only an interlude. Even before they arrived, when they were having breakfast on the Rome-bound express, Freud bit on a crust of bread, and blood spurted from his mouth.

It may have been easier for Freud to keep up the same pretence as everyone else. Perhaps he felt the need, for once, of the comfort that comes from going along with the mood of others. He must have known his fate from the start. The timing of the decision to take his daughter to Rome, his city of dreams, is hardly a coincidence.

After a lifetime of thinking about dangerous periods and fatal ages, perhaps he thought, too, that the prophetic year had arrived, and resigned himself to it. Max Schur made a suggestion that is no wilder than some of his master's. He took the random figure that Freud used to Fliess in 1899, '2467 mistakes', which Freud later analysed on the grounds that 'nothing in the mind is arbitrary and undetermined', and wondered if the figure still had a potency. Was it not possible, wrote Schur, that a memory of the '2467', which had entered his head 24 years earlier and contained the age he reached in May 1923, 67, came back to haunt him with a warning of his death? This, of course, is ridiculous; but any compulsive neurotic will recognise the logic.

The holidays over, Freud learned the truth officially. Another professor, Hans Pichler, examined him and confirmed a fresh neoplasm, or an extension of the old one. Pichler was an oral surgeon inclined to radical methods who had made his reputation restoring the mouths of wounded soldiers. Invited to operate, he prepared himself by experimenting on a corpse. On 4 October he did preliminary surgery, followed a week later by the principal operation, in the course of which the entire upper jaw and palate on the right side were removed. This meant that the nasal cavity and the mouth were open to one another, and had to be separated by a device like an enormous denture. A month later more surgery was needed. Freud described himself to Sam in Manchester as 'very much broken and enfeebled'.

The operations were fearful but successful. The cancer was eradicated for many years, and Freud lived on, as an invalid with restricted horizons that effectively removed him from public view. He withdrew into his family and a small circle of friends. His prosthesis, in its many versions, could never be made to fit properly, caused constant pain and impaired his ability to talk and eat. He no longer spoke in public, and when he ate, it was never in the company of strangers. His mouth and jaw were regularly monitored with minor operations.

None of this stopped him seeing patients, and he began work again on 2 January 1924. Nor did it stop him smoking. When he found he was unable to open his mouth sufficiently to wedge a cigar between his teeth, he used a clothes-peg to force them apart. The prosthesis had to fit tightly (thus causing painful pressure) so there would be enough suction to make the cigar burn properly.

In his new existence he would find consolation in seeing himself transcended, a figure in a story that unfolded around him. 'You know there is a character in epochs which you cannot change,' he wrote to Sam while he was still at the Auersperg sanatorium on 20 October recovering from his two-part surgery. He liked to think of himself as part of history: as he had done for most of his life.

28: Defections

Freud was no sooner stricken by his cancer than a defection in the camp, the first on any scale since Jung's, was threatened by Otto Rank, who for some time had been developing unorthodox ideas. Defection wasn't easy for Freud's sons. Rank was trusted, envied by some for his closeness to Freud, and owed his career to his master. When the committee was having supper at San Cristoforo, the day they heard about the cancer, he burst into hysterical laughter at the mention of Freud's name. The news destabilised everyone, but especially a friend with rebellion on his mind.

A Hungarian analyst, Sándor Radó, remembered his first glimpse of Freud before the war, a man with an aristocratic air, dressed in a fur-lined overcoat and carrying an ivory-handled walking stick. With him was his faithful Rank, 'a young, poorly dressed boy who was agitated, fidgety and talked to him all the time'. Now he was in his fortieth year, and he had decided it was time to stop being 'Little Rank'.

He and Ferenczi (who was himself toying with change) collaborated in 1923 on a book about psychoanalytic techniques that questioned the value of long-drawn-out reconstructions of childhood. Shortly after, Rank published a book of his own, *The Trauma of Birth*, which calmly announced that what lay behind neurosis was the shock of being born and the consequent fantasy of returning to the womb, the lost paradise. Therapy should be directed accordingly. Without the need to rake through memories, a sharp dose of analysis lasting a few months would do the trick.

Freud was slow to condemn. How could Rank be unfaithful to him? Trying to welcome the theory as 'the most important progress since the discovery of psychoanalysis', he succeeded only in smelling deceit. 'Rank's "birth trauma" and your activity,' he wrote to Ferenczi in 1924, '. . . both derive from attempts to speed up the analytic process.' Their method could become 'a path for travelling salesmen', another swipe at America.

Ferenczi drew back from confrontation, but in the spring Rank went off to New York where he had friends among analysts he had trained in Vienna (courtesy of Freud, who passed them on to him), and talked about, among other things, the undervaluing of women, using his theory to explain that it was men's unconscious memories of the shock of birth that distorted their view of women. The analysts of Central Park West paid $20 an hour, four or five times the going rate, to be trained by the new man.

Soon, the poor relation come into his own, he was boasting to Ferenczi that he had 'saved psychoanalysis here, perhaps the life of the whole international movement'. Having found that New York analysts were 'for the most part uncured and dissatisfied with the Professor's analysis', he claimed to have restored their confidence in themselves.

The Old World waited crossly for the renegade to come to his senses. Freud, declaring that a psycho-neurosis must be at work, at first took a sympathetic view, then concluded that Rank had been fatally 'attracted by the dollar'. No sooner was Rank home than he veered off again to Paris, returning by Christmas 1924 to apologise to everybody, making Freud briefly happy, before another cycle of travels began, ending with a final break in 1926. One of his last misdeeds was to question the interpretation of the Wolf Man's dream of the six wolves in the walnut tree.

Freud received a parting gift, perhaps ironic, of Nietzsche's works in twenty-three volumes, bound in white leather. This, he said, was Rank boasting of his new affluence, and also Rank being self-destructive, determined to get rid of his money. Jones, his warnings vindicated, put it about that Rank had a manic-depressive psychosis. 'We have to bury him,' said Freud, and the movement vilified him for decades.*

With no idea how long he had to live, but fearing the worst, Freud began to write *An Autobiographical Study* in 1924. Non-scientific scrutiny had already begun, to his disgust. A year earlier his former pupil Fritz Wittels had written the first biography,

---

* Rank lived at first in Paris, where, in the early 1930s, he was the analyst and lover of the writer Anaïs Nin. Eventually he settled in America.

which had brought a polite reply, followed by the truth some time later that Freud thought it a 'hateful caricature', produced as 'a sop to the world's gossipy tendencies'.

The autobiography was written in the mountains of the Semmering, where he had spent holidays in his earlier years because he couldn't afford to travel further; now he went there because of the need to remain within easy reach of doctors, who could get to the valley below from Vienna in under three hours. The book was short, sixty-odd pages in the *Standard Edition*, and not always reliable.

An English-language edition of his collected papers was being prepared for publication by Jones, and Freud worked on those, too, in his mountain villa. Perhaps he heard that the family of Katharina, the young woman from the Rax who appeared in *Studies on Hysteria* thirty years earlier, was dead or had left the district, because it was then that he added the footnote to her story to say that the would-be seducer was her father, not her uncle.

The past, at Freud's age, was easily evoked. Emma Eckstcin, who may have led him to his ill-fated seduction theory, died in July 1924, not yet sixty, after years as an invalid. Breuer, his name barely known to a new generation, died the following year at the age of eighty-three. According to the Breuer family, he once saw Freud in Berggasse after their break, and went towards him with open arms, only to see his former friend cross over to the other side of the road. Freud managed a good, sonorous obituary notice.

Another disturbing name was conjured up when Abraham, fatally ill, as it turned out, with a lung infection, consulted Fliess in Berlin in 1925 and reported to Freud that the phases of his illness had 'strikingly confirmed' his new doctor's theory of periodicity. Abraham died before the end of the year, aged forty-eight; another stalwart gone.

When Fliess himself died in 1928, his widow, the Ida whom Freud never liked, wrote to ask if he had kept her husband's letters, which she would very much like to read. Freud said they had probably been destroyed some time after 1904, adding that he would be happy to learn that the other half of the correspondence, his letters to Fliess, had 'found a fate that will assure their protection against any future use'. Mrs Fliess, who was in possession of almost every letter of the hundreds that Freud had written to her husband, said nothing and kept them for a rainy day.

Abundant glimpses of Freud in decline can be found. Those who met him in the 1920s and '30s, whether as friends, patients or journalists, were more willing to describe what they saw than their predecessors. Karl Kraus had been mocking Freud in print from the early 1900s and was still doing it after the war. 'Psychoanalysis, we are warned, has become a menace,' he wrote in 1924. 'Nonsense. It was a menace from the day it was born.' But Kraus would have thought it below his dignity to scrutinise Freud in a personal way. Those who came for analysis and went away to write memoirs, or who made it their business to speculate about what went on at Berggasse 19, were less restrained. They were curious, unlikely to be awed, occasionally hostile, frequently irreverent even when they were sympathetic.

A Canadian scholar, Paul Roazen, made his reputation with *Freud and His Followers* (1975), a biography of the movement for which he interviewed many survivors. His sketches of late-period Freud have not been bettered: the rumpled tweed suit, the thin hands like a grandmother's, the aphoristic speech, the obsessive-compulsive tendencies – always worse in old age – that spilled over into trivial anxieties. 'Once he knocked at Tante Minna's door because she had left a pencil in his study that he wanted to return.'

Fame was a satisfaction as far as it went. Freud's Christmas letter to Sam in 1925 said that he was 'considered a celebrity', that 'writers and philosophers who pass through Vienna, call on me to have a talk', that 'Jews all over the world boast of my name pairing me with Einstein. After all I have no reason to complain.' There were hints of the special quality of his life. 'The other day while we were talking,' Anna wrote to Lou Salomé (1926),

> Papa and I agreed that analysis is not a business for mere humans, but that one needs to be something much better – who knows what! It is not the analytical work that is so difficult, for one can accomplish that with some human reason, it is the everlasting dealing with human fates.

In such a context, what did physical frailty matter? The Freuds, anyway, had encouraging strains of longevity. His mother reached her ninetieth birthday in 1925. Relatives flocked to the mountain resort of Bad Ischl where she spent her summers, deaf but composed, and kept in ignorance of as many family deaths as possible. Freud didn't join the visitors. Sometimes he dreamt of the family dead. Approaching his seventieth birthday, he told Sam that he was 'not what my father and your father were at that age'.

Shortly afterwards he demonstrated the point with two attacks of angina in the street to add to his general shakiness.

When he reached seventy, in May 1926, the Mayor of Vienna gave him a diploma as freeman of the city. The Nobel Prize committee gave him nothing, that year or ever, despite rumours. He went on hoping in private. 'Passed over for Nobel Prize,' he wrote on 31 October 1929, the first entry in a skeletal diary that he began to keep that year. 'Conclusively passed over for Nobel Prize' followed in 1930, although by that time he had received the next best thing, the Goethe Prize for Literature; 'a great honour although not a big sum,' he told Sam, practical as ever.

Interesting women sat at his feet, or lay on his couch; they always had done, but in his declining years they seemed to gather around him as if it was now safe and proper to reach out and touch this monument to sexuality. One of the more unlikely adherents of psychoanalysis, Princess Marie Bonaparte of France, entered his life in 1925, demanding he treat her.* She was hardly through the door when she was engaged in a passionate transference, telling him she loved him.

He had warned her that he was in poor health. Bonaparte wept and clutched at the hand behind the couch; Freud was flattered. Because she was a sort of beauty with a sort of beast, nothing was denied her, except that when she demanded his sexual confidences in exchange for hers they were not forthcoming. 'You must have had a supernormal sexual development,' she wheedled. 'Of this,' he replied, 'you will not learn anything. Perhaps not so super.'

He let her make copious notes (or was unable to stop her), and although many of them are still interred in one of the basements where the history of psychoanalysis languishes, published fragments add their mite to the portrait. When she told him he was a combination of Einstein and Louis Pasteur, he replied with a variation of the 'conquistador' remark he first used on Fliess, disclaiming intellectual status in favour of a role as man of action. 'Who has changed the world more than Christopher Columbus? Now who was he? An adventurer!' So the fantasy of being bold and

* Princess Marie, who was also Princess George of Greece, was forty-three, wealthy, neurotic, frigid, promiscuous (one of her lovers was a French Prime Minister), an admirer of the pioneering French analyst, René Laforgue. Thirty years earlier she would have been a candidate for *Studies on Hysteria*, alongside Anna von Lieben and the other rich, dreamy hysterics.

ruthless, which ran alongside the fantasy of being the pure and dedicated man of science, was undimmed.

One New Year's Eve when Bonaparte was at Berggasse 19, Martha confided 'how much her husband's work had surprised and shocked her, in that it treated sexuality so freely'. As a result she had tried to take no notice of it. Bonaparte told Freud, who made the only possible response, 'My wife is very bourgeois.' But on another occasion he told her that he was a petit bourgeois himself, who wouldn't want one of his daughters to have a 'liaison'.

Women like the princess, who were clever enough to make him feel at ease, were always welcome. He liked the idea of the independent woman. The norm was still the one in force when he was a sweetheart and young husband in the last quarter of the nineteenth century, when a wife was an 'obedient jewel', her future in her husband's keeping. The fact that Freud enjoyed the companionship of clever women and encouraged a few of them to have analytic careers is not particularly significant. Almost always they offered deference and a measure of adoration, sometimes with sexual mysteriousness added on, like a dab of scent on the wrist.

Minna seems to have been a match for him, but she was a special case, the sister-in-law he talked to because his wife wasn't up to it. Sabina Spielrein, who had original ideas and a sense of her own importance, may have been another exception, and notably failed to do any sitting at his feet. Most of them, however, conformed to male expectations: the coquettish Bonaparte; Salomé who hung on his words (he was scathing about her to Bonaparte: 'She is a mirror'); Loe Kann confessing her sexual sins and telling tales about Jones.

Freud had a straightforward liking for glamorous women. In 1929, aged seventy-three, he got himself to the theatre where Yvette Guilbert, the French *diseuse* and singer, whom he first heard in Paris in 1889, was performing. She was now in her sixties; he took Martha and Anna to have tea with her at her hotel, and quoted a phrase from one of her songs to Ferenczi, 'I said all that? It's possible, but I don't remember.'

References to women's 'mysteriousness' have always been useful to men, as if no further comment were needed. As Peter Gay – quoting a question that Freud asked the princess, 'What does woman want?' – remarks in his biography of Freud, 'men for centuries had defended themselves against their obscure fear of woman's hidden power by describing the whole sex as unfathomable'. It was not indifference; on the contrary, Freud was haunted by women when young, when he could still, in theory, have done something about it, even been a conquistador of the bedroom. He didn't share the barmier medical beliefs of the time (especially prevalent in England) about the absence of sensuality in women. Corresponding with Fliess about 'the sexual theory' in 1899, he wrote that 'I do not yet have the slightest idea what to do with the ††† female aspect', printing crosses to ward off danger.

When it came to treating patients, throughout his career Freud saw fewer men than women. His theories reversed the emphasis, reflecting the world he was brought up in, in which men were the principals, women the assistants. A sustainable charge against him is that he was inclined to ignore women, to write them out of the plot. Quotations are available for anyone who wants to go further and nail him as a bigot, as in the *Three Essays* (1905), where he describes women's erotic life as 'veiled in an impenetrable obscurity, which is 'partly owing to the stunting effect of civilised conditions and partly owing to their conventional secretiveness and insincerity'.

But bigotry is relative. A paper of 1908 noted 'the undoubted intellectual inferiority of so many women', attributing it to 'the inhibition of thought necessitated by sexual suppression'. Freud's argument was that women's upbringing forbade them to take an intellectual interest in sexual problems, making them see curiosity as something sinful, thus blunting their ability to think. The sexologist Magnus Hirschfeld, who was fiercely radical and regarded in his day as a supporter of feminism, drew the same conclusion from the evidence, that 'woman's mental inferiority' was undeniable.

Freud didn't respond to feminist propaganda, such as it was in the early part of the century. Local movements operated at too low a temperature to make an impact on men as a whole or on Freud in particular. Neither Germany nor Austria had anything to match the hectic solidarity of the English suffragettes before the First World War with their fire-raising and their little hammers to smash shop windows. It was only after the war, when the first feminist currents were felt in psychoanalysis, that Freud was moved to make any comment, and even then he took his time and said little. But he must have been aware of the changing climate, because he wrote several papers after 1924 that touched on 'female psychology'.

Karen Horney, a young doctor in Berlin before the First World War who became enthralled by Freud's writings, was one of the new women of analysis, like Helene Deutsch, long ahead of her time. She was analysed by Karl Abraham, became an analyst herself, and began to raise questions that no one felt inclined to answer; as in her paper 'The Flight from Womanhood' (1926), where she complained that psychoanalysis measured women by masculine criteria, and asked 'how far therefore does this picture fail to present quite accurately the real nature of women?'

She had harsh words for penis envy, sang the praises of motherhood, and implied that it was men who ought to be envying women for their 'by no means negligible physiological superiority'. Ernest Jones was impressed; Freud was not. Horney's opinion on penis envy, he wrote five years later, 'does not tally with my impressions'. Most analysts agreed with him.

All Freud could do now was cling to his beliefs and ignore the rest. If ever he could have been persuaded to view women differently, the time was long past. In 1925 he announced that they lacked the austere super-ego that gave men their sense of high morality; the movement must not be deflected by feminists 'anxious to force us to regard the two sexes as completely equal in position and worth'. The paper, written for the annual conference, was presented in his absence by a woman, his daughter.

Seven years later, in a paper addressing the 'riddle of femininity' in the *New Introductory Lectures* of 1932 (which were written to be read, not spoken), Freud seemed at first to be shifting an inch or two. It wasn't enough, he said, to see the male as active, the female as passive. His 'excellent women colleagues' had important things to say about female development.

A few pages later he was back on the ravages of penis envy. It was penis envy that made women susceptible to envy and jealousy of all kinds. Furthermore, a point he had been making for decades, women were less able than men to sublimate their sexual instincts; although what else was Bertha Pappenheim doing when she made over her life to teaching and fighting the chimerical white slave trade? What else was his own daughter doing?

Patients heard prejudice mixed up with analysis. Joseph Wortis, a young American doctor who was analysed in the thirties, often heard Freud grumble about American women, who 'lead men around by the nose, make fools of them'. Matriarchy ruled across the Atlantic. In Europe, 'Men take the lead. That is as it should be.' Wortis asked cautiously if equality might not be the answer. 'A practical impossibility,' snapped Freud.

Reports from the consulting room by those on the receiving end accumulated. The musty smell was recorded, the fingertip hand-shake, the cufflinks and watch-chain that reminded one man of his father, Freud's sudden pounding of his chair-arm or the head of the couch for emphasis, Freud getting to his feet the moment time was up and saying softly, 'I have listened.' A biographer, Emil Ludwig, visiting out of curiosity, was told that his life of Napoleon should have said more about the childhood; Freud put him right but in the process muddled up Napoleon's brothers, an error that Ludwig enjoyed and stored up for future use.

Eva Rosenfeld, a Prussian Jewess who worked with difficult children and was drawn into the Freud family circle in the 1920s through a friendship with Anna, was analysed by Freud in 1929. She found analysis rewarding because it changed her perception of what mattered in her life without affecting her personality: 'I did not become someone other than who I had always been.'

Staring up from the couch, she noticed a shade in the six-lamped chandelier that was different from the rest, and drew this to Freud's attention. He said she was wrong, and they argued for a moment before he switched on the light and got up to have a closer look. 'You are right,' he said. 'This fact will not, however, prevent me from saying that you mean to tell me Anna's position among my six children is different from that of all the others.' As Ludwig the biographer noted, 'in that room a simple question seldom got a simple answer'.

Wortis, whose analysis was short and combative, respected Freud but took nothing for granted. He dreamt of a picture that showed a line of servants emerging from the door of a hut. Freud's suggestion, that the building was the womb and the servants were children, struck him as far-fetched, and he said so. His frankness was not well received, although Freud had said at the beginning that honesty was the basis of an analysis. 'You must learn to absorb things and not argue back,' he said, at which Wortis began to argue about not arguing. The American suggested that to understand was to forgive. It wasn't a question of forgiving, said Freud, it was a question of *getting on*.

Wortis was forever picking holes in the method. How could he let his thoughts flow naturally in free association, he asked, when the man listening was Freud, who brought to mind sex and neurosis? Freud ignored the objection and told him to get on with it.

The need to keep going and push an analysis towards some sort of conclusion was a practical matter of which Freud had always been aware. Was there, even, a natural end to an analysis, or in theory could it go on for ever? One of the last papers he wrote, in 1937, was called 'Analysis Terminable and Interminable'. Time was a problem. For an old man in precarious health it was the only problem that mattered.

His essential relationship was the one for which he had so carefully prepared: with the daughter who had been his patient and whose patient he now became, the unattached woman, always at hand, who was his voice in public and his confidant in private. In the end she became his nurse as well.

Her life can't be compared with that of her Aunt Dolfi, who was the family drudge, caring for Jacob and then Amalie. But the pattern was still there under the surface. Although she had her own life – working as a child analyst, contributing to the literature, deferred to by the movement – it remained an extension of Freud's. Many thought she was too self-effacing for her own good, too devoted to the idea of goodness, too willing to sacrifice herself on her father's behalf. After his death this faithfulness became a jealous anxiety to preserve his memory undamaged, an outcome he may have had in mind. Cupboards were locked against the release of possible skeletons. Freud, the anti-biographer, could not have found a better censor.

The day-dreams Anna called 'unseemly', which contained the fantasies of being beaten, led to a further analysis by Freud in 1924, the year after his cancer was diagnosed. Her analysis, or perhaps simply the friendships with women and their families that she built up, made her more at ease with herself in years to come. Whispers of a lesbian relationship with the most important of the women, Dorothy Burlingham,* are unlikely to have been true. But they can still be heard among those who find something sinister in

* Mrs Burlingham, who came from the rich Tiffany family, left her marriage in 1925 and took her four children from New York to Vienna, where she was analysed by Freud. Eventually the family lived hand-in-glove with the Freuds. They rented

the thought of this dark, pretty daughter burying her desires in the interests of a man like Freud.

The idea that she might marry was still being brandished by her father at the end of 1925. He wrote proudly to Sam about her work as a 'pedagogic analyst', treating 'naughty American children' (the Rosenfelds and the Burlinghams) and earning good money:

> Yet she has just passed her 30th birthday, does not seem inclined to get married, and who can say if her momentary interests will render her happy in years to come when she has to face life without her father?

If he thought she might marry after his death, he gave no indication of it. She was bound to him for ever. Since it was what Anna appeared to want as much as her father, there is little point in trying to unravel the conspiracy between them that had begun in her adolescence. Like all profound relationships, what mattered was the thing itself.

In June 1929, when Freud's condition was stable enough to let him go further afield, the family were staying in the mountains at Berchtesgaden, in a house called Schneewinkel, or 'Snow Corner'. It was the summer solstice, celebrated with fires on the peaks gleaming through the clouds and rain. Anna (now aged thirty-three) wrote to Eva Rosenfeld:

> there is one thing I must ask you. What am I going to do when I can no longer remain where I am now, when I am left alone and thus lose all that gives meaning to my life? I have always wished that I would then be allowed to die.

A month later she was in England to read a paper to the annual congress, held that year at Oxford. Freud, in his 'idyllically quiet and beautiful Schneewinkel', had no shortage of company. Visitors who came and went that summer included his three sons, Brill from America, Ferenczi, and Jones with his wife Kitty, but it was Anna he wanted. Her dog, a German shepherd called Wolf, 'spends half the day lying apathetically in his basket', he wrote to Salomé. 'Like Wolf, I can hardly wait for her return.'

---

an apartment at Berggasse 19, and Dorothy had a private telephone line to Anna in her father's quarters. The Burlinghams, together with Eva Rosenfeld and her brood, became part of an extended family, replete with children, that surrounded Anna and replaced some of what was missing from her life.

Yet even with Anna, restraint had to be exercised. A fragment of film exists that shows the two of them in a wintry Berggasse piled with snow, probably during the late 1920s. Dressed in long black overcoat and black hat, Freud flings a cigar butt on the ground and stalks along, giving the camera a nasty look. His daughter, smiling, tries to slip her arm through his, but he rejects the approach and clasps his hands firmly behind his back. As they walk away, Anna has managed to get an arm inside his, but the hands are still locked behind the overcoat, uncooperatively. Evidently her gesture was too affectionate to be encouraged for the world to see. Anna was indispensable, but austerity remained the hallmark of life with Freud.

29: Waiting and Hoping

No further papers of importance about the theory and practice of psychoanalysis were to be expected from Freud. His writings up to 1926 would eventually fill the first twenty volumes of the *Standard Edition* when James Strachey and his team came to prepare it in the 1950s. Three volumes were sufficient for work after 1926, a more than respectable output for an old man with a serious illness. The later work either restated and clarified basic principles, or it discoursed on cultural themes, using psychoanalysis to throw light on human behaviour and belief in a wider historical sense. On the whole it was well received, although late Freud on 'Civilisation' and 'Religion' is less rewarding than early Freud on dreams, lust and memory.

If he sounded pessimistic, that was in the nature of psychoanalysis; his awareness of wickedness and folly had been cultivated over a lifetime. His short book *The Future of an Illusion* (1927) dealt summarily with religion, seeing its beliefs as the wish-fulfilments of children which had failed to make them either more happy or more moral. The evidence was deployed crisply enough, but Freud's conclusion, that 'science is no illusion', brought up the rear rather limply. The Christian T. S. Eliot, giving it a hostile review in the *Criterion*, the quarterly magazine he founded in London five years earlier, waved it aside, saying 'Thus dreams the wizard of the dream world.'

Another short book, *Civilisation and Its Discontents* (1930), dwelt on the curbing of 'instinctual behaviour' that was necessary to attain a civilised society, and on the never-ending conflict between desires and restraints: the stuff of neurosis. Communism was dismissed as a delusion, since human nature couldn't be modified by a political system. If inequality in wealth were ended, it would

merely reappear somewhere else, for example in sexual relationships. The argument was aimed in part at Wilhelm Reich, who by
that time was a communist as well as an analyst.

Freud, wearing his rationalist's hat, began the book with a
defence of his ideas about religion, as set out in *The Future of an
Illusion*, which had led to a correspondence with his friend the
writer Romain Rolland. Rolland had spoken of an inner feeling of
'eternity', of something unbounded, 'oceanic', which Freud took to
mean 'a feeling of an indissoluble bond, of being one with the
external world as a whole'. According to Rolland this 'oceanic
feeling' was the source of religious sentiment. Freud wasn't
impressed. Others might experience it; he never had, and offered a
psychoanalytic explanation: that the 'feeling' was merely a
'shrunken residue' of the infant's earliest sensations when it is
unable to differentiate between itself, its mother and the world
beyond. Freud was superstitious but not religious: there was no
more to be said about it.

The book was written at Snow Corner in the mountains. A letter
to Salomé said it contained 'banal truths' and didn't spring from
'inner necessity', as his earlier work did, but was written because
he had to do something more than smoke and play cards all day,
and he was no longer much good at walking. But he had a long
history of denigrating his own books. This one carried a gloomy
conviction; it also sold an edition of 12,000 copies within a year to
readers who were aware of their own discontents with the way the
world was going.

The basic precepts of Freudian thinking had now been around for
twenty or thirty years. Although psychoanalysis had a foothold
everywhere (Freud was encouraged to learn that neuroses among
Indian Muslims were the same as those in Vienna), orthodox
psychiatry carried on as though nothing had happened. Assertions
like Ferenczi's before the war, that 'youth and the intelligent public'
were already won over in Hungary, were wildly over-optimistic,
and Freud avoided such claims.

Ideas filtered down and became common currency. 'The unconscious', which long predated Freud, came to be seen as Freudian.
'Meaningless' behaviour was perceived to have meaning after all.
The 'Freudian slip' caught on at an early stage; so did observations
about sexual symbols in dreams, putting bananas and staircases in
a new light. It was sex that directed interest towards psychoana-

lysis in the first place; a set of theories based on the instinct of hunger wouldn't have been the same thing.

The range and subtlety of Freud's insights left their mark. If his attempt at a universal theory of human behaviour eluded him, as it has eluded everyone else, his psychological canvas was crowded with figures in whom all could recognise themselves. His theories, suggests Charles Rycroft, are not a unitary structure, 'more a collection of miscellaneous ideas, insights and intuitions ... propounded over a span of fifty years'. Like the Bible, his millions of words can be endlessly interpreted. Schools of variant Freudians arose to prove it.

Many of Freud's ideas were subversive of the nineteenth-century complacency towards human progress that came to an end in his lifetime. He caught the tide of history as well as helping to create it, and for many in the disillusioned aftermath of the First World War he came to represent equivocal modern values.

'I pointed out to [the Rat Man],' wrote Freud, 'that he ought logically to consider himself as in no way responsible for any of these traits in his character; for all of these reprehensible impulses originated from his infancy, and were only derivatives of his infantile character surviving in his unconscious.' Freud's own moral values were strict, his ideal that of development towards moral responsibility, but his belief that behaviour was inexorably determined was seen as contributing to the general retreat from the old morality.

A British murderer, Ronald True, a wartime pilot who had suffered head injuries and become a morphine addict, was sentenced to death in 1923 for killing a prostitute, despite evidence of insanity. Reprieved by the Home Secretary, he became the centre of a debate about the perils of making allowance for the mentally disturbed. Newspapers complained about sinister psychoanalytic doctrines which, if taken to their logical conclusion, meant that no one was to blame for anything. Robert Graves touched the same nerve in his nihilistic memoirs of 1929, *Goodbye to All That*, though he didn't mention psychoanalysis:

> In the Punch-and-Judy show of our century ... there are no more guilty and also, no responsible men. It is always, 'We couldn't help it' and 'We didn't really want that to happen.' And indeed, things happen without anyone in particular being responsible for them. Everything is dragged along and everyone gets caught somewhere in the sweep of events. We are all collectively guilty, collectively bogged down in the

sins of our fathers and of our forefathers ... That is our misfortune,
but not our guilt.

The number of practising analysts was modest. The Vienna
society had forty-one members in 1924. European medicine
remained suspicious. Its conservative hierarchies, controlling
specialties through the universities, marginalised the 'Freudian
science'. Anti-Semitism smouldered below the surface, a hidden
agenda, exactly as Freud had feared it would when he looked to
Jung to change the movement's racial characteristics.

In America things were different. The medical profession dominated psychoanalysis – after 1923 every analyst had to be a doctor
of medicine – but the new psychology was seen as opportunity, not
threat. University departments, free from interference by State or
specialist cliques, took a benign interest in it almost from the start.
Individual physicians, less inhibited about money than Europeans,
saw the financial opportunities. Psychoanalysis in American hands
became a more positive doctrine, with less emphasis on the malign
powers of the unconscious.

Ernest Jones had a story about a Boston conference he addressed
as early as 1909. A woman protested that egocentricity might be a
feature of dreams in Vienna, but it was certainly not so in America,
where dreams were altruistic. Freud found this 'delicious'.

The British experience was less clearly defined, despite the
presence in London of Jones, the lobbyist and fixer. The small
British Psycho-Analytic Society had no standing in the medical
profession and was run as Jones's private domain, on well-
disciplined lines; he once threatened to expel Bertrand Russell's
niece because she gave lectures without his permission. Few people
even knew the society existed. Outside a small circle of intellectuals, attentive to Freudian ideas, the British were less impressed
than Americans by visions of the future. More cynical or more
realistic, they added psychoanalysis to the list of peculiar innovations that would end in tears.

Psychoanalysis was something that featured in newspaper
inquiries, usually hostile, and in the scornful rhetoric of judges and
bishops. To be analysed was to be 'psyched', an unfriendly coinage
of the time, as in the London *Daily Express* of 1928: 'While for some
patients being "psyched" may be a step towards being cured, to
others it may amount to being infected.' A leading article in *The
Times* complained that psychoanalysis could reveal 'the lover of

cruelty or the sensual person' to him or herself, and so 'fill with horror and dismay minds which were accustomed to view their tendencies in an entirely different light'. The writer saw no point. 'To what end is such a revelation made?'

Dislike of Germany and her allies after the war didn't help, given the origins of the founder. Jones fought with Rank over German phrases that appeared in the proofs of *International Journal* articles, typeset by Austrian printers who were liable to put 'Frau' instead of 'Mrs', an insult to British eyes. Impropriety – *foreign* impropriety – was widely assumed to go hand in hand with 'Freudism'. Freud was seen as a medical purveyor of filth, in the manner of Havelock Ellis. As a rule Freud went into less detail than Ellis about sexual behaviour, but the tone of his work was more subversive.

The medical profession, which might have been expected to show a measure of tolerance, was as anxious as the vice squad to keep out filth. The publishers Kegan Paul were nervous about *Leonardo* when they brought out an English translation in 1922, because of its references to homosexuality. Infant sexuality was especially offensive. The *Three Essays*, available in the United States from 1910 because a core of professionals took a serious interest in the subject, didn't appear in a British edition until 1949. Many doctors in the conservative British Medical Association would have been delighted to see Jones deprived of his flourishing private practice, since he was seen as doubly wicked, dealing in unclean topics and profiting handsomely as a result.

The Sussex branch of the BMA heard about 'improper sexual practices' connected with girls and psychoanalysis in 1925. They were uncertain allegations, never published or pursued, perhaps containing an echo of the pre-war tales about Jones whose country cottage was in the same county. The following year the BMA set up a committee, which included Jones, to look into psychoanalysis, and it meandered through the evidence for several years. A girl aged thirteen was supposedly forced to take a bath 'stark naked' at her boarding school in the presence of the headmaster. 'This was a school run on psychoanalytic lines,' said the doctor who had complained. 'There is no school in England run on psychoanalytic lines,' smiled Jones, the only member of the committee who knew anything about the subject.

They heard long exchanges about the supposed absurdities of

psychoanalysis. A 'Freudian' had treated the victim of a wartime bombing raid by airships. The unidentified analyst was supposed to have drawn a sausage-shaped device on a piece of paper and asked the patient what he thought it was. 'A Zeppelin?' said the man. 'Does it not,' pressed the analyst, 'suggest to you the *male organ*?'

Jones, suave and persuasive, let his opponents make fools of themselves and gently converted the committee to open-mindedness. 'It means fighting step by step against an invincible opposition,' he wrote to Freud in January 1929, but the report later in the year did no damage. Jones's hand can be seen behind long sections of it, including a passage about 'the popular belief that [Freudian analysis] encourages the patient to indulge in socially forbidden impulses, although all the alleged instances of this brought before the Committee were found to be devoid of foundation'. He was taking a long-delayed revenge on the profession that had hounded him out of London long ago.

Whatever Freud thought of these activities, far off in the empire, they came to him as echoes of conflicts from which he had withdrawn. The only issue in London that aroused his interest – and anger – concerned Anna, whom Jones dared to criticise. Jones seemed to go out of his way to annoy Freud: another humble acolyte, perhaps, tired of the years of humility, puffing himself up a little while the emperor slept.

Behind the quarrel was the figure of Melanie Klein, a woman analyst with an overpowering personality who thrived on controversy. An Austrian (born 1882), lacking academic credentials, she was analysed by Ferenczi and became a child analyst, with dogmatic ideas about the violence and complexity of infant fantasies. When Karl Abraham, her mentor, died in 1925, Jones invited her to work in London, with the idea that she would bring new ideas and stir up British psychoanalysis, which, for all the activity that Jones generated, was like a stage army, mustering fewer than a dozen practitioners. In the event she stirred it up for the next thirty-five years. An occasional member of the British society can still be heard calling her 'that bitch'.

The remarks that upset Freud were in a letter of May 1927. Jones described the successful analysis of his two small children, and in the same breath spoke of a book by Anna, an introduction to child analysis, recently published. It pained him, he said, that there were parts of the book he couldn't agree with, adding gratuitously,

'I cannot help thinking that they must be due to some imperfectly analysed resistances.' What the letter didn't say, but what Freud would have known, was that the Jones children were in the hands of Klein, whose methods were not Anna's.* Klein had decided that infants were more mature than Freud or anyone else supposed, incubating murderous oedipal fantasies when they were barely six months old. No doubt the women's contrasting natures – one a flamboyant divorcee with children, the other anxious and virginal – enhanced their doctrinal differences.

To suggest that Anna had been 'imperfectly analysed' was impertinence on a grand scale, even if Jones was not aware that the analyst was her father. At first Freud did no more than remind him that such accusations cut both ways. In September 1927 he lost his patience and accused the Welshman of organising a campaign. 'Is anyone actually analysed enough? I can assure you that Anna has been analysed longer and more thoroughly than, for example, you yourself.' Tell me, said Freud, what is going on in England and in your mind. 'I have learned to bear much, and have no illusions about a golden age in which the lamb grazes next to the wolf.'

Jones reassured him: 'The mood here is one of entire devotion to your personality and fidelity to the principles of psychoanalysis.' This was true, and both Jones and the British society remained loyal to the cause. But Freud feared betrayal in his old age. He denounced Jones behind his back, calling him dishonest, an unoriginal thinker whose 'application of my ideas has stayed on a schoolboy level', a disappointed lover who was taking revenge on Anna because she rejected his advances in 1914; encouraged, he might have added, if he himself wanted to be honest, by her father.

One aspect of Freud's life in the 1920s was more agreeable than he might have expected. Now that Austria was a republic and the Habsburgs a memory, the socialists ran Vienna, and chose to see Freud as a representative of the new post-imperial order that would bring peace and prosperity to the workers. It was they who made him a freeman of the city, citing the 'special obligation and gratitude' felt by socialists for 'the new roads which he has opened

---

* One of the children was the writer Mervyn Jones, aged five at the time. He wrote in his autobiography that analysis didn't cure him of neurotic traits. 'Anyway, I have forgotten – or, I should presumably say, repressed – everything about my sessions with Mrs Klein except the journey to her house and the look of her room.' His analyst friends were surprised. But the same thing happened to Little Hans.

for the education of the children and the masses'. The tribute sat uneasily on someone who was as contemptuous as Freud of the common people, of the 'deformed skulls and potato noses' of the mob, but he was pleased to receive it, and wrote to Sam to say so.

Political parties made him sceptical, and the more they offered, the more sceptical he became. It was hard to see what anyone could offer the new Austria, its backbone broken by inflation and unrest, that would make it noticeably happier than the old. Many of all classes regretted the vanished glories, and various dissidents roamed the streets with angry speeches in their fists and knives in their pockets.

'Red Vienna', as people called it, was only half the story. The national government, as well as provincial Austria – as much of it as remained after the war – was Catholic and conservative, controlled by the Christian Socialists. Supporting them was the strong pro-German element that wanted 'Anschluss', union with Germany, forbidden by the peace settlement. Speakers warned of the need to defend Germanic values against the new threat from the east, godless Bolshevism, and against the old threat that proved as reliable as ever at rousing emotions, the 'Jewish peril'. Each side used paramilitaries.

In an incident near the Hungarian border in 1927, a band of war veterans fired on some Social Democrats, killing an invalid and a child. At the trial in Vienna the accused men were acquitted. Workers demonstrated, stormed the Palace of Justice, alarmed the authorities, were fired on by the heavily-armed State police. Three hours later, almost 90 people were dead and more than a thousand injured, the worst violence Vienna had experienced since 1848. Among those who saw the carnage, and had to run for his life, was Wilhelm Reich. It was soon after this that he joined the Communist Party.

The times were breeding extremists. 'A rotten affair,' Freud wrote to Ferenczi from the mountains, where he read about it in the newspapers. The events of the summer were 'as though a large comet stood in the sky'.

There was nothing to be done except wait and hope. 'Vienna is going downhill and may be lost if we don't get the famous "Anschluss",' he wrote to Sam at the end of 1928, presumably because he saw union with Germany as a lesser evil than a badly governed Austria at war with itself. Germany itself had long ceased to be an inspiration. Its psychiatrists had ruined themselves in his eyes by the 'arrogance' and 'coarseness' of their hostility to psychoanalysis. Its politicians and generals had proved untrustworthy in war. When he wrote his autobiography in 1924, Max Eitingon saw the draft and begged him to remove a reference to German 'barbarism'. Freud refused.

Like the rest of Europe, he was aware that the bombastic German politician Hitler had acquired a following for his *National-sozialist* party – the 'Natsies', the 'Nazis'. By 1929 the party was organised in districts throughout Germany and Austria. Street violence was its method of choice. On 7 November that year, Freud made the entry 'Antisemit[ic] disturbances' in his minimalist diary. A lecture by a Jewish professor at the Anatomical Institute, near the top of Berggasse, had been disrupted by Nazi students. People escaped through windows. But Jew-baiting of one sort or another had gone on throughout Freud's lifetime, and the general feeling was that Germany would be able to contain the National Socialists. Staying in Berlin in May 1930 to have work done on his prosthesis, Freud met an American diplomat and journalist, William Bullitt.* 'A nation that produced Goethe,' he told Bullitt, 'couldn't possibly go to the bad.'

The unknown quantity was Hitler himself, who had spent the post-war decade sharpening his claws. His 'spiritual home', where he went to brood on his apocalyptic visions, was the same mountain country around Berchtesgaden that Freud was devoted to. The year after Freud and family were there in 1922, when the unfortunate Fricks were among the visitors, Hitler 'fell in love with the landscape' and chose the same guest-house, the Pension Moritz, where he strutted about waving a rhinoceros-hide whip to impress the owner's wife. His autobiography, *Mein Kampf*, 'My Struggle', which announced on page one that Austria must return to 'the great German mother-country', was completed in 1926 elsewhere in the Berchtesgaden area, which he continued to visit. When Freud spent the summer there in 1929, they were not far apart.

---

* Bullitt's wife had been psychoanalysed by Freud in Vienna. In 1930 Freud and the American agreed to collaborate on a study of the late Woodrow Wilson, US President when the war ended, a man little liked in Europe. Freud contributed to the psychological assessment. Strachey didn't include it in the *Standard Edition*, Jones having suggested to him that it would 'not do Freud much good in the eyes of impartial historians'.

*

One more professional upheaval was to come. Sándor Ferenczi, the exasperating Hungarian who had trouble with his health, his women and his self-esteem, parted company with Freud, whose approval he had craved through much of his life, and whose intimate he had been for more than twenty years.

Had Ferenczi cared less about Freud, he might have gone with Rank in 1924. Jones claimed to have drawn him 'forcibly back from the precipice'. Now, Ferenczi was disillusioned with psychoanalysis. After a few years of agonising he made his views public at the age of fifty-nine, offended Freud and became an outcast. Denigrated at the time, with the implication that he was mad, he was ignored by the movement till recent years, when rehabilitation began.

From the start Ferenczi had extravagant ideas about relationships, as if they could be purified by the truth. 'Yours, thirsty for honesty,' he signed himself in a letter of 1910 to Freud. The authoritarian side of therapy made him uneasy. He wanted people to approach one another without reservations, and dreamt once that he saw Freud standing naked in front of him, symbolising 'the longing for absolute mutual openness'. Telepathy appealed to him because he liked to think of the patient's thoughts melting into the analyst's.

Freud, seventeen years older, was patient and gentle over the years, helping him overcome what he saw as infantile tendencies. A thousand or two letters passed between them, more than in the case of any other colleague; Ferenczi's warmth and extravagances had an enduring appeal. In the 1920s they were exchanging friendly views about refinements of analytic technique. From 1927, however, Ferenczi was developing methods that he kept to himself, although stories began to circulate about what he was up to.

His patients were indulged and treated as equals and the disciplined structure of the analysis was collapsed in favour of a kind of friendship. There was kissing, even cuddling. Analytic sessions could go on for hours at a time, if necessary behind drawn curtains at the homes of patients. Tales of a dancer called Elisabeth Severn, said to be clairvoyant, who was in turbulent analysis with Ferenczi for years, caused amusement. Freud told Jones after Ferenczi's death that the Hungarian 'believed that she influenced him through vibrations across the ocean', a story that didn't help Ferenczi's reputation when it appeared in the Jones biography.

By the end of 1931 Ferenczi was talking openly about his new vision, and Freud was raising objections. Kissing people was all very well, he said, but this wasn't post-revolutionary Russia, where everyone did it. A kiss was an erotic intimacy. The next thing might be petting-parties, 'resulting in an enormous increase of interest in psychoanalysis among both analysts and patients'. Freud's tone remained friendly, but he slipped in a wounding sentence, omitted by Jones from the biography, where he said that

> According to my memory the tendency to sexual playing-about with patients was not foreign to you in pre-analytic times, so that it is possible to bring the new technique into relation with the old misdemeanours.

In other words, Freud knew that Ferenczi as a young doctor had had sexual relations with his patients, and was implying that the new technique was part of the same pattern.

Shortly after this, in January 1932, Ferenczi began to keep a 'clinical diary', unpublished until the 1980s, where, among other things, he denounced his profession for its insincerity and said it was more concerned with making life comfortable for analysts than for patients. Ferenczi spoke of 'the advice' – Freud's advice – 'not to let patients learn anything about the technique', and 'the pessimistic view, shared with only a trusted few, that neurotics are a rabble, good only to support us financially and to allow us to learn from their cases: psychoanalysis as a therapy may be useless'. The worm had turned with a vengeance; although the views of his master that he now found so upsetting, contempt for some clients and impatience with many, had been no secret to his colleagues for decades.

Once, said Ferenczi, Freud truly believed in analysis, working devotedly to cure neurotics at the time of Breuer, lying on the floor for hours when a patient had an hysterical crisis. Was it Freud who told him that, and was it true? Did the young doctor really get down in the dust with Anna von Lieben and Fanny Moser, holding their hands, whispering consolations? In his anxiety to bring compassion into the psychoanalytic relationship, Ferenczi sought a golden past where his hero had once lived and worked, where doctor and patient were absorbed in one another, and no electric bell sounded to bring the rapture to an end.

Another, more ominous, ghost appeared. Ferenczi concluded that what mattered to the small child was not only internal fantasy but external reality. The 'seduction theory' of 1896 came back to haunt Freud, in the shape of a paper that Ferenczi wrote for the 1932 annual conference at Wiesbaden.* 'Confusion of Tongues Between Adults and the Child', a watered-down version of what Ferenczi believed, told analysts they should listen to their patients and to children. With that in mind, it addressed the issue of sexual abuse, contrasting the 'languages' of adult passion and childish innocence. Ferenczi was not far from shedding the concept of child sexuality.

Before he delivered the paper, Ferenczi insisted on reading it to Freud in private. He arrived with his wife, Gizella, at Berggasse 19 on 30 August 1932; 'an icy cold emanated from him,' Freud told Anna.

Ferenczi at once began the reading, which must have lasted half an hour or more. Freud (and Brill, who was in Vienna, and joined them after the reading had begun) listened in silence. Ferenczi's comment that 'Even children of respected, high-minded puritanical families fall victim to real rape much more frequently than one had dared to suspect' echoed the findings that Freud had announced as an unknown practitioner.

Those early papers on seduction had cited questionable evidence. 'Confusion of Tongues' cited no evidence at all. It particularised only once, mentioning 'an educator' who had recently told Ferenczi of 'five families of good society in which the governess lived in a regular conjugal state with nine-to-eleven-year-old boys'.

It is not known whether Freud remonstrated with him. When the Ferenczis had gone, he told Brill one of his Jewish jokes, about an old Jew who promises a Polish baron that he can teach his dog to talk in three years. 'Why not?' he says to a friend. 'In three years either the baron will be dead, or the dog, or me.' Fatalism was Freud's best defence. Describing to Anna how shocked he had been, he said that Ferenczi spoke of childhood traumas in almost the words he himself had used thirty-five years earlier. He told Eitingon that the paper was stupid and inadequate, though harmless.

That didn't stop attempts to prevent Ferenczi delivering it, but

---

* The previous year's meeting had been cancelled at short notice because of political and financial crisis in Europe in the wake of the Wall Street crash. Austria's leading bank, the Kreditanstalt, was the first major institution to collapse, in May 1931.

he was too important to be silenced; it was he who had founded the International Association, whose congress he would be addressing. He was given a cold reception, as cold as the one Freud received when he told the psychiatrists of Vienna about child seduction. Freud himself was not there; he had stopped attending public meetings years earlier. Later, as editor of the *International Journal*, Jones suppressed the paper.

Illness disposed of the Ferenczi problem. He was already unwell at the time of the Wiesbaden meeting, suffering from pernicious anaemia which was then an irreversible condition. He died of it in May 1933.

In a letter to Jones soon after, Freud wrote that 'Ferenczi takes a part of the old era with him', which would be replaced by a new era 'when I step down . . . Fate, resignation, that is all'. Freud went on to describe Ferenczi's condition:

> For years Ferenczi has no longer been with us, indeed, not even with himself. It is now easier to comprehend the slow process of destruction to which he fell victim. During the last two years it expressed itself organically in pernicious anaemia . . . In his last weeks . . . a mental degeneration in the form of paranoia developed with uncanny logical consistency. Central to this was the conviction that I did not love him enough . . . His technical innovations were connected with this, as he wanted to show me how lovingly one has to treat one's patients in order to help them . . . But let us keep his sad end a secret between us.

Mental instability was a recognised by-product of advanced anaemia. But paranoia was the traitor's sickness, and Freud, leaving uncertainties in his letter for the recipient to interpret as he chose, managed to make Ferenczi sound as if he had been unbalanced for years; it was the familiar technique.

Jones ignored the injunction to say nothing; Freud can't have thought he would do anything else. He duly improved the story. When he wrote his life of Freud, the world was told about 'lurking demons' against whom Ferenczi struggled for years before he was overcome, dragged down into psychosis. This travesty became the accepted version. He was certainly idealistic, odd, neurotic and no doubt a suitable case for treatment, but if that constituted madness, he would not have been alone among the analysts.

As far as the movement was concerned, Ferenczi's ideas were best forgotten, since they were not only insulting but impractical. The Freud who had been on call to his more interesting hysterics and who spent countless hours with them, whether on the floor or anywhere else, could hardly have based a therapeutic method on such prodigal use of time. Nor could the authority of the analyst as Freud developed it be set aside, when authority and discipline were what gave the therapy its structure.

Forty years later psychoanalysis was changing. The importance of mothers (paid scant attention by Freud) was being recognised. The emphasis began to shift from child fantasy to child environment. These things were at least distantly related to Ferenczi's methods. The structure of the analysis ceased to be sacrosanct, and people spoke of 'the therapeutic alliance', as Ferenczi had spoken of 'empathy'. Even childhood seduction came roaring back in the shape of the child-abuse fever that raged from the 1980s, with excesses of overstatement to balance those of understatement in the past. This world would have been beyond Freud's comprehension.

30: 'A Fanatical Jew'

Amalie Freud, the matriarch, was at the mountain resort of Bad Ischl as usual in summer 1930, a minor celebrity in the little town of salt-springs and doctors that the Austrian royal family (and the Pappenheims) used to patronise; the old imperial villa was now a tourist attraction. She shared her birthday, 18 August, with the late Emperor Franz-Josef, and in 1930, when she reached ninety-five, there was a photograph of her in the newspaper that she complained 'makes me look a hundred'. Her health was failing. Her blood-relatives included seven children, fourteen grandchildren and nineteen great-grandchildren. Dolfi, always in attendance, is supposed to have remarked in 1930, when she was sixty-eight, that 'Unfortunately I am not married.' Amalie said, 'Is that any way for a young girl to talk?'

Freud was staying at Grundlsee, not far away, and was taken by car to visit her three times in August. The third visit, on her birthday, was the last time he saw her. She was in pain and drugged. His colleague, Paul Federn, brought her back to Vienna to die. Anna represented Freud at the funeral in September. Afterwards he wrote to Jones to say that all he felt was freedom from the fear that he might have died before her, and satisfaction at her 'deliverance' after so long a life. 'Otherwise,' he said, 'no mourning', and raised an eyebrow at the display of grief by his brother Alexander, 'ten years younger than I'. Alexander, who had prospered, now had a rabbinical look about him, with his broad-brimmed hat and white beard, and a strong resemblance to Jacob.

Freud's own health went from one minor crisis to the next. In October 1930 he had a touch of pneumonia. The prosthesis, 'the monster', was forever being readjusted, and suspicious tissue was burnt or cut away once or twice a year. Freud cursed the torments of the device and insisted that otherwise his health wasn't too bad.

More clouds gathered on the European scene. At the German elections in September 1930, Hitler's National Socialists won more than a hundred seats in the Reichstag, making them the second party. People still asked, who was this Hitler? Perhaps he was no more than a reincarnation of Vienna's Mayor Lueger, and would have his day and be forgotten. No sleep seems to have been lost at Berggasse 19. The political outlook had been gloomy for years; one managed to survive. Freud groped his way forward like everyone else. In 1931 he had his mind on the need for a summer residence in the city – a suitable house with a garden was found in a suburb – and the emerging differences with Ferenczi.

Had his health permitted, he would have visited his birthplace, formerly Freiberg, now Příbor, situated in a country invented at the end of the First World War, Czechoslovakia. A street had been renamed Freudova in his honour, and the blacksmith's house was given a plaque.* Anna represented him, looking wistful in a beret and a fur coat, and read a small crowd his words about the happy child of Freiberg.

Spectator now, not participant, he 'almost' caught sight of Charlie Chaplin in the streets of Vienna. But Chaplin was in a hurry. 'He invariably plays only himself as he was in his grim youth,' Freud wrote to Max Schiller, the husband of Yvette Guilbert, and couldn't stop himself adding that Madame Yvette's entire repertoire of characters, from prostitutes to artless girls, was doubtless traceable to the fantasies of *her* early youth – only 'I know that unwarranted analyses call forth antagonism.'

He sat without much patience for a young sculptor, Oscar Nemon, wished on him by Federn, who was 'usually highly inept in discovering unacclaimed geniuses'. Nemon was a 'gaunt, goatee-bearded artist' and a 'slavic eastern Jew', evidently not a fact in his favour, who fashioned 'from the dirt – like the good Lord' a head that Freud was forced to admit was 'astonishingly lifelike'. The Freuds' housekeeper complained that it made him look angry. 'But I am angry,' said Freud. 'I am angry with humanity.'

Nothing was certain any more. Other banks failed after the Kreditanstalt, and the *Verlag* and its book-publishing operations was threatened, though it survived. Hitler, banned from entering

---

* In 1996 the *Jerusalem Post* reported that the building was now in use as a massage parlour. The headline said, 'Freud's Birthplace Offers Another Kind of Therapy.'

Austria, slipped into Vienna when no one was looking in September 1931 because he wanted to visit a cemetery.* While there, he told a local Nazi who called himself *Gauleiter* of the city, Alfred Frauenfeld, that by 1933 at the latest he would be in power in Germany.

On 30 January 1933 Freud was writing 'Hitler Reichs Chancellor' in the diary, misdating it as the 29th. The National Socialists still lacked a mandate to govern, but Germany's president, the elderly von Hindenburg (who said that 'I already have one foot in the grave'), was finally persuaded that only 'this fellow Hitler', whom he detested, could bring order to the political chaos into which the country had fallen, and made him chancellor, the head of government.

National elections, the last that Germany would see under Hitler, were held early in March, and left the National Socialists as the governing party. On 23 March the Reichstag passed an enabling act that gave Hitler dictatorial powers, and the revolution began: against the socialists, the Jews, the memories of defeat in 1918. The historian William Shirer wrote, 'Hitler was liquidating the past, with all its frustrations and disappointments.'

Beatings, murders and arrests became a commonplace in Germany. Shop windows carried photographs of Hitler; every pole flew its red and black swastika. Stormtroopers blew bugles wherever they went, if it was only a mission to collect old clothes. In May the authorities burnt books on ritual bonfires in Berlin and other university cities. Stage-managed by the Propaganda Ministry, professors made patriotic speeches while students fed the fires and chanted indictments. The works of Freud were committed to the flames for their 'soul-disintegrating exaggeration of the instinctual life'. He was in the company of, among others, Thomas Mann, Albert Einstein, Arthur Schnitzler, Upton Sinclair, Zola, Proust and Havelock Ellis.

Material looted from Magnus Hirschfeld's Institute for Sexual Science was added to the fires. Hirschfeld, as a Jew and a

* A twenty-three-year-old niece with whom Hitler had a romantic liaison, Geli Raubal, killed herself with a bullet through the heart at his apartment in Munich on 18 September. Raubal had Viennese connections, and her body was taken there for burial. Hitler, deeply distressed (whether for love or for fear of political damage), risked crossing the border in his Mercedes, a carload of bodyguards close behind, and went to Vienna where he put flowers on her grave at the Central Cemetery. Afterwards he told his driver to go past the Opera House on the Ringstrasse.

homosexual, was an easy target for National Socialists denouncing the 'decadence' of the old Berlin; although some of his homosexual patients, their files stored in the building, were said to have been Nazis, thus explaining why the premises were attended to so promptly. Hirschfeld himself had fled before the terror began.

Many Jews soon followed. It was easier to get away at the beginning. Ernst and Oliver Freud were both in Berlin with their families. Oliver, the unlucky son, was unemployed in 1933. He went first to Vienna, then to France, ultimately to America. Ernst, a stronger character, had a career as an architect to take with him. Hearing that one of his sons was being called 'Jew Freud' at school helped him make up his mind. Clemens, then aged nine, may have been the child involved. He told his grandfather, 'How different things would be for me today if I were an Englishman.' Presently he was.

Few people grasped the scale of events. Freud made optimistic noises about Austria. He thought the country was moving towards a right-wing dictatorship, but put his trust in the League of Nations, which would never allow legalised persecution of the Jews. 'Besides,' he reasoned to Jones, 'Austrians are not inclined to the German brutality.' Freud was correct about the move towards a dictatorship, wrong about the rest.

Probably he was never as optimistic as he let himself sound. 'The world is turning into an enormous prison,' he wrote to Marie Bonaparte. To his fury, a respectable Austrian journalist, Ludwig Bauer, to whom he talked at the end of 1933, wrote an article that presented him as a helpless old man, trembling with fear, saying over and over again, 'Do you think they will turn me out, do you think they will take my books away?' This was trumped-up Freud. The article brought a letter from a Swiss psychiatrist offering him a safe haven at the Burghölzli in Zürich if it would comfort him in his depression. That was Jung's old hospital. It was the sort of comfort Freud could do without.

As expected the Austrian Chancellor, Engelbert Dollfuss, abolished parliamentary government. Democracy gave its last twitch in February 1934 when the Social Democrats and a handful of Communists called a strike that turned into four days of civil war in Vienna. The modern apartment blocks of Karl Marx Hof, built by the socialists to house working-class families, became a fortress. The buildings still line the main road in a northern suburb, not far from Brigittenau where Hitler lived in the men's hostel. Women dropped burning coals on the troops below. The Dollfuss government responded with artillery and killed a thousand people.* Freud wrote to the American poet Hilda Doolittle ('H.D.'), who had been his patient in 1933:

> No doubt, the rebels belonged to the best portion of the population, but their success would have been very short-lived and brought about military invasion of the country. Besides they were Bolshevists and I expect no salvation from Communism. So we could not give our sympathy to either side of the combatants.

Austria was almost invaded. Home-bred Nazis increased their activity. Terrorist bombing began in May. There were explosions on railways, at power stations, in churches. A pump-room at Ischl was blown up. Stink bombs were used in government offices. As the violence increased, it was uncertain how Italy would respond. The Italians had their own dictator, Mussolini, who was suspicious of Hitler and saw Austria as part of his own country's business. They met in Italy on 14 June. Freud wrote to Jones two days later from his summer retreat below the Kahlenberg, where it was beautiful but 'one does not enjoy life. The foundations are rocking.' At that very moment, perhaps, 'the intriguer M. in Venice is selling us to the captain of the thieves H.' But Hitler assured Mussolini that Austria would remain independent.

This didn't save Dollfuss, who was assassinated in his office on 25 July. The conspirators were not quick enough to take control, and what had been planned as a Nazi uprising was put down by the government, which even hanged some of them. Still unsure of himself outside his own country, Hitler drew back, and Austria settled down to a slow process of Nazification, the long-awaited Anschluss postponed. It was still possible for Vienna's Jews to hope and do nothing.

Germany was already an unhealthy place to be. Several dozen psychoanalysts left when they could. Karen Horney, who wasn't a Jew, and Hanns Sachs, who was, had both been invited to work in America before Hitler came to power. Helene and Felix Deutsch went to America in 1934; Max Eitingon to Palestine in 1935, a few

---

* Kim Philby, later the British secret service agent who spent his career spying for the Russians, is said to have been in Vienna that February, and to have joined the Communist Party as a result of what he saw.

months after the 'Nuremberg Laws' which began the outlawing of Jews by depriving them of German citizenship and forbidding marriage or sexual relations between Jew and Aryan. The Freudian diaspora extended to Australia and South America, although the United States was and always would be the chief attraction.

Jones, still dreaming in London about the future of psychoanalysis, looked at these developments without enthusiasm. Writing to Eitingon, before he emigrated, Jones said that the 'quarrelsome Central Europeans seem to have retained their home habits in other countries', and were doing their best to 'infect' them.

Like most of the British, he mistrusted immigrants. Doctors were particularly suspicious. So was the handful of analysts in London, who were afraid of being overwhelmed by rivals for business. 'We cannot create patients,' wrote Jones. At the same time he found hospital jobs for some German analysts who arrived in 1933, and by the end of the year there were six of them in London, the first of many. But England was not America. As Jones once told Anna, without embarrassment, 'Here there is a considerable prejudice against people speaking with a foreign accent.'

The analysts who remained in Germany were able to go on practising as long as they conformed to Nazi requirements. Jews were discouraged and later excluded (as they would eventually be excluded from the practice of all medicine and all law), but psychotherapy, if not the discipline Freud had in mind, carried on, and even flourished under official patronage. This curious situation came about because the doctor who emerged as the leading figure was a psychiatrist and Adlerian psychoanalyst, M. H. Goering, whose cousin was Field Marshal Hermann Goering. Under such auspices the lesser Goering could indulge himself as the mastermind of Nazi psychoanalysis, all set to create a 'German healing art of the soul', a flesh-creeping phrase that he used in speeches.

Classic Freudian analysis itself was unacceptable, the science of sexual perversion. The Oedipus Complex was replaced with the Family Complex. Freud was vilified for being one of the traitors to humanity (Darwin was another) who subverted the higher values of the fair-skinned races. Jung, the Aryan, still busy by his lake in Zürich, was seen as a proper figure to be associated with M. H. Goering's new arrangements, and he lent them his authority in the 1930s. Perhaps he was deliberately improving his position at the expense of Freud. If he was not anti-Jewish he was aggressively pro-Aryan: a distinction too fine for Hitler's Europe. Later he was heard to say, 'Well, I slipped up.'*

Freud's response to the Nazis was to emphasise his own Jewishness, which itself was far from straightforward. He was an atheist who avoided Jewish rituals. When he went through a Jewish wedding ceremony it was against his will. Apparently none of his three sons was circumcised. But Freud couldn't ignore his origins; nor, in the end, did he want to. Ernest Jones in his obituary said that Freud's achievements would have been impossible without his racial characteristics, among them 'a peculiar native shrewdness' and 'a sceptical attitude towards illusion and deception'. More sophisticated critiques, for example by Sander L. Gilman, show Freud, and Jews in general, defining themselves by the things that Gentiles say about their appearance, sexuality and character, described in hostile, often obscene terms.

Exactly what Jewishness meant to Freud was something he claimed not to be able to express. He told a correspondent in 1935, 'I have always held faithfully to our people, and never pretended to be anything but what I am: a Jew from Moravia whose parents come from Austrian Galicia.' Even that simple statement contains a qualification. Galicia had been a province of the Austro-Hungarian Empire, so to qualify it with 'Austrian' was unnecessary. Doing so, however, made the place sound nearer and more civilised. 'Galicia' by itself suggested the eastern wildernesses, sending their unEuropean villagers streaming to the West, arousing antagonisms that harmed those who had already Westernised themselves. The leering Israelites who were hatefully caricatured in Nazi literature had a kinship with the figures from whom Freud once sought to distance himself, when, like thousands of other Jews, the ideal was German.

Times changed and Freud changed with them. On his seventy-fifth birthday, in 1931, he responded to greetings from the chief rabbi of Vienna by saying that to his surprise, he had discovered

---

* Jung's relationship with the Nazis remains controversial. It is undeniable that he wrote about an 'Aryan psychology' that was different to the Jewish variety, and used alarming phrases like 'the most precious secret of the Germanic peoples – their creative and intuitive depth of soul' (1934). Jung said that Freud failed to understand the 'Germanic psyche'. But the Austrian may have understood it better than the Swiss.

that 'in some place in my soul, in a very hidden corner, I am a fanatical Jew'. This may have been a variant of the romantic feeling he had expressed nine years earlier to Ferenczi about the 'secret yearnings' he found in himself, 'perhaps from my ancestral heritage'. But the equivocations remained. Gilman says that 'Freud spent his life defining and redefining his sense of the Jew.'

Freud's response to the new anti-Semitism was to distance himself from the contemporary world and write another of his fictional histories, the last. He produced a book about Moses, using psychology to speculate about the origins of the Jewish people. In other words, he made it up. Its genesis was described in a letter of 1934 to Arnold Zweig, a writer who had escaped from Germany to Palestine. When faced with 'the new persecution', said Freud, he asked himself once again 'how the Jews have come to be what they are and why they have attracted this undying hatred'. The book, begun in 1933 and written over the next four years, was originally called 'The Man Moses, a historical novel', changed before publication to *Moses and Monotheism*.

The book offered few comforts. First there was a new history of the Jews. Moses, in this version, was a high-born Egyptian priest who led the Semitic slaves out of captivity and made them adopt his own monotheistic belief in an abstract, invisible God who demanded high moral standards of behaviour. They were the 'chosen people' because Moses chose them; they were circumcised because he wanted to differentiate them, and circumcision was an Egyptian custom: a crucial element in Freud's argument.

Tired of his severity, and presumably his high moral standards, the followers killed him. Other tribes absorbed them and converted them to a 'barbarous god of volcanoes and wildernesses', Yahweh, resident on Mount Sinai. Together they became the Jews, worshipping the violent volcano-god. The Biblical Moses began as someone else, a minor local priest with whom the 'real' Moses, the Egyptian, was later combined. Repressed memories of the murdered Moses and his religion persisted over the years, handed on, like the memories in *Totem and Taboo*, by the process of inherited guilt that Freud still believed in. These shadows of the past changed the volcano-god into the original deity, the one who believed in truth and justice, and who made circumcision a requirement. Moses triumphed.

Freud wasn't interested in religious belief as such, only how it came about – the *Totem and Taboo* school of history – and in the way that the beliefs of the Jews stamped them as unique. It was Moses, said Freud, who created the Jews by giving them a religion in which they were a chosen people, spiritual and tenacious, superior to others. Among Freud's explanations of anti-Semitism were the Jews' own insistence on their apartness, and the unconscious fear among Gentiles of castration, aroused, he said, by the Jews' mutilating custom of circumcision; a custom that has also been widespread among middle-class Gentiles in Anglo-Saxon countries this century without doing much (as Jones wrote sarcastically when reviewing *Moses*) to diminish their prejudices.

No doubt Freud saw traces in himself of a latter-day Moses. Uncertain about his Jewish identity, he sought consolation by rewriting history and looking in his own unconscious. He said that Moses haunted him for years, plaguing him 'like "a ghost not laid" '.

Austria drifted towards fascism. In 1933, at the beginning of the Nazi regime in Germany, Anna Freud wrote to Jones to say that 'Sometimes I am amazed that in such times as the present, spring and summer come as if nothing had happened.'

The entries in Freud's diary, never more than a few words, marked the progress of a closed-in life: 'Princess', 'Martha 74 yrs', 'Nose bleed'. Michael Molnar of the Freud Museum, who has annotated them all, points out that the entry immediately preceding 'Nose bleed'. on 27 October 1936, is on 24 October, and says 'date of Fliess's birthday', the only time in the ten years of the diary that Freud recalls the anniversary. 'Fliess' and 'Nose bleed' might go together, since it was his operation on Emma Eckstein's nose in 1895 that nearly killed her when she haemorrhaged.

Are we supposed to believe that Freud's nose bled on a Tuesday because he had been thinking about Wilhelm Fliess on the Saturday, or that he made the entry about Fliess because he was unconsciously aware of a nasal problem that became a nose-bleed three days later? It is not impossible, or at least it is not impossible that Freud thought it was possible. Once upon a time, he believed that Eckstein bled through love of him.

The death of Bertha Pappenheim, in March 1936, isn't in the diary. At seventy-seven she was only three years younger than Freud, with a lifetime of social work separating her from the young woman whom Breuer treated, and told Freud about to such powerful effect. There were mysteries about her case, never solved by Breuer or anyone else.

Whatever the truth, she became someone else, a reformer. 'If there is any justice in the next life,' she wrote (1922), 'women will make the laws there and men will bear the children.' Nothing in her later years suggested her existence as Anna O., whom she so successfully subdued into the stern philanthropist and writer.

When he was younger Freud no doubt would dearly have liked to know about her dreams. If she had kept a journal all her life, if in old age she still recorded a dream or two because of a never-extinguished curiosity about herself . . .

I had been travelling since supper with my companion, who bore a faint resemblance to my mother. She carried a horsewhip wrapped up in brown paper 'so that men will know who I am'. The railway station when we got to Rovno was lit with long jets of blue gas that smelt of sulphur.

'They must think we're fools,' said my companion. We could actually see a Russian criminal in a shabby suit putting two young women on a train. Their heads were small, like potatoes. The man gave them a packet of roubles tied up with string and said that when they reached Buenos Aires they could be dancers or companions to rich ladies or anything they chose. We shouted 'Liar!' and 'White Slave scum!' as loud as we could, but nobody heard us.

Rovno being a bad place for abduction, it was imperative to find the chief of police. I walked down a filthy street – I was on my own by this time – and came to a set of iron gates with spikes on top. A boy sweeping the gutters said, 'You can go in now.'

Beyond the gates it was like a park, with a building I recognised at once. I was very frightened. Two wild duck with blue feathers flew off a lake, and I thought: Now I've got to go through all that again.

A nurse took me inside and I could hear men whispering. It was the sanatorium at Kreuzlingen. Dr Breuer had only been gone an hour. He had abandoned me – I had that feeling in my pubic bone, the same feeling as when I saw the bloody sheets after Dadda died, the same feeling I got riding at Coblenz when a man with a straight back at the stables spoke out loud about my 'fine figure', and I turned away in disgust but kept hearing the words in my head, fine figure, fine figure, fine figure.

The superintendent was holding a hypodermic syringe. I wanted

to tell him not to be silly, I was a mature woman who did good
works and wrote books. Every time I opened my mouth I coughed
like I did when I was nursing Dadda. The coughs meant, 'Listen,
my good man, I was in charge of an orphanage. I founded a league
of women. I saved hundreds of girls from being sold into prostitution.'

It was important that he understand I was on my way to address
a meeting in Berlin about the need for Jews to live alongside
National Socialists. I told him to take his morphia away, and they
put a cloth over my face to keep the coughs in. I shouted at them
that I wasn't the Anna of those articles they kept publishing, the
dumb little fräulein they gave the talking cure to, which didn't
work anyway. We all knew what their problem was, they were men.
Breuer thought he knew everything. So did that impertinent friend
of his I never met, that Freud, who wrote about me afterwards as if
he knew me. None of them got anywhere near Anna. She played
women's games with them.

Then the needle went in with a pop, and I saw a blue flash of
feathers over the lake.

I woke at dawn in the sleeping car with a slight headache, but it
was almost gone by the time we reached Berlin.

31: Exodus

Various institutions were on their last legs. The *Torch*, which came to an end in February 1936, gave psychoanalysis a dying kick. Analysts, said Karl Kraus in the final issue, had been ambushing victims outside their hotels on the Ringstrasse. Some, he added, 'among them the most miserable ones', had already left for America 'to set up where the money is', perhaps a dig at Wittels, now prospering in New York.

A French woman journalist went to Vienna in the same year to write a humorous piece about Freud that saw him and his Jewish science as an easy target. Calling herself Madame Dubois and pretending to be frightened of dogs, she used Paul Federn as an intermediary.

Federn, who saw her (she implied) only because she claimed to be 'disgustingly rich', had 'a rabbinical nose such as one sees only in anti-Semitic caricatures'. He took money from her and made an appointment with Freud, whom she saw at 'a beautiful house, freshly painted, with chestnut-coloured shutters gleaming in the sunshine' – a rented house in the shady road at Grinzing that climbs to Heaven and Bellevue. Federn was there as well.

Looking, she said, sixty rather than eighty, Freud wore 'a natty grey suit like a gigolo's, but it did not seem ridiculous because there was still so much youth in his way of walking and moving about'. His hands, too, were youthful, 'a little red and heavy, but without wrinkles, without those spots which usually cover the hands of old men'. She noticed 'a great lump' under his chin that moved as he talked, and supposed that this was because of 'a grave disease of the larynx' from which surgery had miraculously saved him. The extent of his handicap eluded her; what she saw was a mouth 'lined with gold ... like an old cannibal fresh from the hands of an American dentist'.

A real patient might have been awed, or at least attentive, but Mme Dubois sat back and enjoyed herself.

'Why do you insist on my treating you?' he asked her in English. 'A treatment by psychoanalysis is very long. It will take at least a year, probably more, and meanwhile I may die. Then what are you going to do? Eh? Kill yourself? Don't you ever want to kill yourself? You do, don't you?'

From her point of view he was a caricature, a curious old Jew with gold teeth who dabbled in human gullibility. Perhaps by this stage in his life a caricature is all he was. His creative days were over; the world was still digesting him; the Vienna that had been his laboratory was dissolving.

When Mme Dubois mentioned that she used to like dogs *before*, and agreed that she meant before her marriage, 'The two prophets exchanged a look pregnant with the modest triumph of men who are never wrong.'

'What did I tell you?' said Freud.

'Absolutely, Herr Professor.'

'It is a classic case.'

'I thought as much, Herr Professor.'

Now that sex had been introduced, the lightning-sketch was complete. The old boy even agreed he would psychoanalyse her.

'Freud rose. He extended a hand; I extended an envelope. His gesture seemed friendly rather than professional. But he took the envelope.'

It was beside the point that he might actually have needed the money: for Martha and Minna, for family widows and spinsters, for the *Verlag* (whose central bookstore at Leipzig had just been seized by the Gestapo), for Anna and the future.

As for the physical sufferings of Freud, most accounts take the view that the fewer details the better. Near the end of 1936 there is a rare glimpse of him in torment with his mouth, temporarily unable to cope. A small surgery with dental chair adjoined his consulting room, and he was examined there every morning. One Saturday Professor Pichler was burning out a suspect ulcer in his cheek using local anaesthetic when Freud exclaimed, 'I can't go on any longer.' Pichler completed the operation; there was no further complaint. The surgeon's notes state merely, 'Patient feels no pain at first, but says towards end that he cannot stand it any more. No real reason.'

Five days later, when he wrote to Marie Bonaparte, Freud said the subsequent pain had been so severe that when analysing patients – nothing seemed capable of stopping the analyses – he needed a fresh hot-water bottle every half-hour to hold against his face.

In passing he let the princess know that he was following the vicissitudes of the ex-King of England, Edward VIII, who had abdicated a week earlier so that he could marry the American divorcee, Wallis Simpson. 'What is going on with the King?' he asked, and impaled him with a diagnosis:

> I think he is a poor fellow, no intellectual, none too bright, probably a latent homosexual who came to this woman by way of a friend and found his potency with her and therefore cannot get by without her.

Bonaparte was about to acquire the letters to Fliess. She told Freud on New Year's Eve that she had been offered them for 12,000 francs by a Berlin dealer, who had acquired them from Mrs Fliess. They were said to have been intended for the National Library of Prussia, until the Nazis burnt Freud's books and he became a blacklisted author.

His response to the news was to say how private the letters were, how embarrassing it would be should they fall into the hands of strangers: 'Our correspondence was the most intimate you can imagine . . . I do not want any of them to become known to so-called posterity.' In conversation he told her a joke. Question: How do you cook a grouse? Answer: 'First you bury it in the earth. After a week you take it out again.' What then? 'Then you throw it away.'

Perhaps he could persuade her to let him pay half? 'All the hunches and false paths connected with the birth of analysis' were there. The princess stood firm; the more he wanted the letters destroyed, the more valuable they seemed as historical documents. A condition of her purchase, she told him, was that she must never sell the material 'directly or indirectly' to the Freud family in case they destroyed it. She spoke vaguely of depositing the papers in a national library – Geneva, perhaps – embargoed for a century after his death. In the end she read him selected passages, and left all the material in a safe-deposit box with Rothschild's in Vienna.

Germany continued to provide fearful evidence of what life in Austria would be like, if – or when – the Anschluss came. The concentration camps were well established. They were not yet seen as a means of mass extermination, rather as a violent way of dealing with political prisoners. Oblique references in letters to Arnold Zweig suggest that Freud had heard of them; the point of the camps was that people should know there were places called Dachau and Buchenwald, and be terrorised by their existence.

In Austria local Nazis, financed by Berlin, ranted and demonstrated. Bombs went off daily. The chancellor, Kurt von Schuschnigg, who had succeeded the murdered Dollfuss, governed by appeasement, and was anxious to do nothing to upset Germany. 'Our political situation seems to become more and more gloomy,' Freud wrote to Jones in March 1937. 'The invasion of the Nazis can probably not be checked; the consequences are disastrous for analysis as well.' The Turkish siege of 1683 was often in his mind, when another enemy was at the gates. Then, a relieving army came over the Kahlenberg; now there was no salvation on the way, certainly not from Britain, and 'If our city falls, then the Prussian barbarians will swamp Europe.' He said he would like to live in England, like Ernst.

Pierre Janet, visiting Vienna that spring, wanted to call on Freud. He was seventy-seven, no doubt intending to exchange greetings and forget former differences. Freud was having none of it. If he saw the man, he told Bonaparte, he would have to reproach him for having 'behaved unfairly to psychoanalysis and also to me personally and having never corrected it'. Ancient wrongs were aired: when French writers spread the libel that Freud stole his ideas, Janet did nothing to stop them. Freud refused to make a polite excuse for saying no: 'Honesty the only possible thing; rudeness quite in order.'

His memory for dissenters was as sharp as ever. Alfred Adler, in Scotland to lecture during summer 1937, had a heart attack and died in an Aberdeen street. Writing shortly after to Zweig, who had commented sadly on the death, Freud said:

> I don't understand your sympathy for Adler. For a Jew boy out of a Viennese suburb a death in Aberdeen is an unheard-of career in itself and a proof of how far he had got on. The world really rewarded him richly for his service in having contradicted psychoanalysis.

As far as one knows, Freud and Adler had no personal differences. But Adler had dared to present theories of his own. When Ernst Freud edited the Freud–Zweig letters in 1970, he silently removed this passage, doing a kindness to Adler, or, more likely, to his father.

By 1938 the Germans were ready to move against Austria. Hitler invited the Austrian chancellor to visit him for a friendly chat, and Schuschnigg went secretly across the border to Berchtesgaden for the meeting on 12 February, fourth anniversary of the storming of Karl Marx Hof in Vienna. By the end of the day, terrorised by Hitler, he had effectively signed away Austria.

Weeks of propaganda and uncertainty followed. Anna wrote to Jones on 20 February to say that 'We are not in agreement with the sense of panic of the others. It is still too early to judge exactly what is taking place.' As late as 9 March, Schuschnigg announced a national plebiscite in which the Austrian people would vote for or against an independent Austria. It was to be held in four days' time, on Sunday 13 March.

Hitler was infuriated, or pretended to be. The plebiscite gave him the excuse to order an invasion. On Friday morning, Germany closed the frontier at Salzburg and moved up troops. Vans were still driving around Austria, urging citizens to vote 'Yes' on Sunday. Leaflets with the same message were showered on Vienna from the air. Schuschnigg sent a desperate message to London, but as Freud (and most people) knew, Britain had no intention of doing anything. Schuschnigg resigned and the Viennese National Socialists took over government buildings and the streets.

Freud had already been visited by a US diplomat, the chargé d'affaires in Vienna, a sign that the Americans would be protective. Few could expect help of that kind. That evening, Friday 11 March, Wilhelm Stekel, Freud's one-time colleague, abandoned everything – home, clothes, books – and went to the Westbahnhof, where he caught the nine p.m. train to Zürich and freedom.

At eight o'clock on Saturday morning, 12 March, German troops began moving into Austria, without opposition. One armoured division used a Baedeker guidebook and stopped at petrol stations to refuel. When troops began arriving in Vienna, the crowds were said to have been silent at first, but this may be a retrospective fiction. They were soon cheering and helping to round up Jews. The Viennese Nazis had little to learn from the invaders when it came to cruelty.

Some Jews were set to work with buckets and brushes, scrubbing off anti-Nazi slogans and generally cleaning the pavements ready for Hitler's arrival on Monday. Serge Pankejeff, who had been a clerk with an insurance company for years and lived quietly with his wife Therese, noted that on the first day of the new order they began work in the office by singing the German national anthem.

A Saturday-evening edition of the *Neue Freie Presse* contained the official news of the Anschluss. Freud crumpled it in his hand. In his diary he wrote *Finis Austriae*. After that he stopped seeing patients.

The following day the board of the Psycho-Analytical Society met at Berggasse 19 for the last time. In a nice theatrical gesture, Freud told them they should follow the example of the rabbi Johanan ben Zakkai, who fled Jerusalem after the Romans destroyed the temple and began a religious school in his place of refuge. The board agreed that the society should be reconstituted wherever Freud might end up; it remained dormant in his lifetime, though it reappeared in Vienna after the war.

Ernest Jones and Marie Bonaparte both hurried to Vienna. Jones flew there via Prague on 15 March, the day that the American chargé cabled Washington to say, 'Fear Freud, despite age and illness, in danger.' This message seems to have been shown to the President, Franklin Roosevelt, and from then on the Americans made sure that the Nazis knew they were being monitored. Among the guardians was William Bullitt, Freud's co-author, now US Ambassador to France. The British did nothing on this scale, although Jones's efforts as a freelance were supported.*

Before Jones arrived, a ragged band of stormtroopers were at Freud's apartment, where their chief interest was burglary. They made off with a sum equal to £300, say £9,000 today: the kind of money that the prudent central-European kept by him for emergencies. They showed no interest in Freud, although another elderly Herr Freud is said to have been attacked in the street by mistake. A few doors away, at Berggasse 7, where the *Verlag* had its premises, more bandits arrived and briefly arrested Martin Freud. Jones walked in while this was going on, and they arrested him, too, for an hour.

Years later what was taking place in the city blurred into folk-memories, each one a random event with a random witness. Someone saw elderly Jewish men being rounded up in the Prater,

---

* The Foreign Office took a relaxed view of Hitler's Germany. Its files include an extract from a House of Commons debate on 12 April 1938 which reports the remark of an MP, Oliver Locker-Lampson, that 'We are still shuddering from the shock of the recent rape of Austria.' Alongside it an official has written, 'Are we?'

made to strip naked and run about on all fours. A Jewish child, Leah Sachs, and her brother saw three Jews being made to kneel and scrub the pavement near the Südbahnhof, watched by a group of stormtroopers. One of them unbuttoned his trousers and urinated in a Jew's face. Then they kicked and beat all three.

According to Jones, Freud was still reluctant to leave Vienna and had to be persuaded. It is more likely that by now he wanted to go, as long as the Germans would let him – there were expensive formalities before Jews were allowed to leave – and someone would have him.

Any remaining doubts were settled when, a week later, the Nazis returned to Berggasse 19, this time in the more serious shape of the Gestapo, and Anna was taken away for questioning. Bonaparte, who had remained in Vienna after Jones returned to London, was in the flat and tried to get herself arrested as well, but the Gestapo didn't want a princess on their hands. Anna was held until early evening, when she was allowed to leave (perhaps after intervention by the Americans) and returned to the apartment and her distraught parents. Freud's doctor, Schur, had provided Anna and Martin with lethal doses of Veronal, for use if they faced torture. Freud wasn't told.

America was too far to go. Jones busied himself in high places in London, canvassing for the Professor as an acceptable immigrant. Later, his story was that he fixed things for Freud. In practice it is inconceivable that the British would have said no. A month later, at the end of April, the passport-control department of the Foreign Office issued definitive instructions to overseas consulates about the issue of immigrant visas. 'Distinguished persons, ie those of *international* repute in the field of science, medicine, research or art' could be admitted without reference to London, and visas in this category couldn't be refused until London had been consulted. Freud would have qualified automatically.

What Jones did was speed up the process, and ensure that not only Freud but his entourage could come to Britain, as well as certain other analysts.* The Home Secretary, Sir Samuel Hoare, was an ice-skater who belonged to the same skating club as Jones

* Jones was able to decide who came and who did not. Hans Lampl, Anna's one-time suitor, and his wife, who had left Berlin for Vienna in 1933, wanted to go to London. But they were not on his list, he told Anna, because 'opinion', unspecified, was against them. They went to Amsterdam instead.

and they had a nodding acquaintance. Jones approached him via a distinguished physicist who was President of the Royal Society, and Hoare promised work permits for Freud, family and associates. Early in April, as the first train-loads of political prisoners were leaving Vienna for the camps, Anna was studying maps of London.

Among less fortunate middle-class Jews, demand for visas far exceeded supply, in the case of both America and Britain. British passport officers were told to be suspicious of temporary visitors who might be refugees in disguise. Anyone who looked Jewish was to be 'discreetly questioned'. Many occupations were undesirable; the 1930s had seen too many people out of work. Retail traders, small shopkeepers and 'minor musicians' were not wanted; nor were the rank and file of professionals: lawyers, doctors, dentists. The medical establishment whipped up strong feelings about alien doctors who were held not to understand the British way of life.

Domestic workers – the house servants who were still common in middle-class homes in Britain – found it comparatively easy to enter the country because they were doing work that the British found uncongenial. Thousands of Jewish women were allowed in from Austria. Accountants and teachers pretended to be servants so they could obtain visas. The 'Personal' columns of *The Times* carried daily lists:

> Young Viennese Girl (Jewish), can cook well, seeks position as Nurse or Parlourmaid.
>
> Two dressmakers, first-class (Non-Aryan) seek position.
>
> Viennese D. Phil, 24, Jew, seeks position as tutor, companion to gentleman or private secretary.

Many of those who were unable to leave – as well as some of those who were, and who found a new life unbearable – committed suicide. It became an epidemic in Vienna. Max Schur reported Anna's words to her father, 'Wouldn't it be better if we all killed ourselves?' 'Why?' said Freud. 'Because they would like us to?'

Theresa Pankejeff had grown introverted and unhappy over the years. She and her husband had enough money to live on; the once-millionaire earned a modest salary, and Theresa, who was German, received a small legacy. After the Anschluss they had nothing in particular to fear, since neither of them was Jewish. But one day she said to him, 'Do you know what we're going to do? We'll turn on the gas.' He remonstrated with her, but later decided that it was wiser to ignore the remark.

One night there was a storm, and the heavy swastika flag that was displayed on every building (including Berggasse 19) began to flap against the window of their top-floor apartment. Mrs Pankejeff said she was afraid it would break the glass. The following day, 31 March, her husband went to the office as usual. When he returned, the kitchen was filled with gas and his wife sat at the table, dead. She had taken money from the bank and left it for Pankejeff on the table; she had also fastened the flag. In his grief the Wolf Man went to Berggasse, hoping to see Freud. But the maid said, 'He is ill. He cannot receive you.'

Preparations were being made for the Freuds to leave Vienna. He had some gold bullion – coins or bars, another sign of the prudent European – that Bonaparte arranged to have smuggled out of the country via the Greek Embassy's diplomatic bag. Bonaparte helped Freud and Anna go through papers and see what could be destroyed. The Vienna Society archives were examined and the early minutes sent to New York. Part of Freud's library was sold. A young photographer, Edmund Engelman, made a pictorial record of the apartment, not using flash-bulbs in case they attracted attention. He also took the photograph for a new passport. Before Freud could leave, his assets had to be accounted for and an exit tax levied; until a figure was agreed and the money paid, no one, not even President Roosevelt, could extricate him.

Because of this delay, some of the entourage got away before Freud himself. The list had fifteen names beside his: Martha, Minna, Anna, Martin and his wife Esti (with two children), Freud's grandson Ernst Halberstadt, his daughter Mathilde and her husband, Max Schur and his wife (also with two children), and the Freuds' housekeeper. Minna left on 5 May; Martin on 14 May, preceded by his wife and children; Mathilde and her husband on 24 May. Freud wrote to Minna, safe in London, that they were still hindered by the exit tax: 'We are standing in the doorway like someone who wants to leave a room but finds that his coat is jammed.'

On 25 May Freud heard that the tax, at twenty-five per cent of his notional assets, came to 31,329 Reichsmarks, payable on 21 June. Since his bank accounts had already been sequestered, and his funds in Holland were there illegally, he couldn't have found this sum in Vienna. Marie Bonaparte paid it for him, $4,824, and he repaid her later. Among her other services that spring, to the history of psychology if not to Freud, she removed the Fliess letters from the Rothschild vaults, now in the possession of the Gestapo, and took them to France.

He was free to go. He had to sign a document to say that the authorities had treated him 'with all the respect and consideration due to my scientific reputation'. Jones said in his biography that Freud asked if he might be allowed to add something, and wrote an ironic sentence, 'I can heartily recommend the Gestapo to anyone,' but Jones heard the story from Martin and it wasn't true. The document, since discovered, merely has Freud's signature; perhaps he told his son that it was what he would have liked to write.

The party would consist of himself, Martha, Anna, a doctor who had to replace Schur at the last minute because he was ill, the housekeeper and Freud's chow, Lun. Four of Freud's sisters were living in Vienna; they went nowhere. The fifth sister, Anna, Eli's widow, was safe in New York, a wealthy woman. In Vienna were three widows – Rosa, Mitzi and Paula – and the unmarried Dolfi. Jones says that Freud and his brother Alexander left behind money for their upkeep, 160,000 Austrian schillings or £8,000, nearly £250,000 today. It isn't clear how Freud could dispose of such a sum without attracting attention and a crippling level of exit tax.

A letter Freud wrote to Bonaparte from London later in the year said that 'To maintain them in England is beyond our powers', and surmised that the funds he left for them 'may have been confiscated already, and are certain to be lost if they leave'. He added that he had been considering a home for them on the French Riviera, 'But would this be possible?' Four old women, who in any case might have hated being uprooted, were not seen as much of a priority. The death camps had not been invented.

Freud said goodbye to them for the last time. He and the others left the Westbahnhof aboard the Orient Express at 3.25 p.m. on Saturday 4 June. A member of the US legation staff in Vienna accompanied them. In the small hours of Sunday morning, after travelling for twelve hours across Austria and Germany, the train reached the frontier at Kehl. The German Customs took no interest in them, and they crossed the Rhine bridge to Strasbourg, France and safety. The princess and William Bullitt were on the platform in Paris to meet the train, and the Freuds rested at her house. She gave him a receipt for his gold, waiting for him in London.

In the evening they left for Calais and the night ferry to England. During the journey Freud dreamt he was landing at Pevensey Bay, where William the Conqueror went ashore in 1066. The source of the story is Jones again, which arouses one's suspicions. But the powerful invader, still dreaming of conquest, sounds like the man we expect. The frail refugee with the stick and the white beard and the glasses too heavy for his face was just a disguise. There is enough truth to signify in Auden's obituary poem:

> He wasn't clever at all: he merely told
> the unhappy Present to recite the Past
> like a poetry lesson till sooner
> or later it faltered at the line where
>
> long ago the accusations had begun . . .
>
> if often he was wrong and, at times, absurd,
> to us he is no more a person
> now but a whole climate of opinion
>
> under whom we conduct our different lives . . .

He passed through Dover on Whit Monday, a Bank Holiday. Crowds were leaving London for the south coast as Freud's train travelled north. Twenty years earlier, Whit Monday 1918, London had its last air-raid of the First World War, when German Goths and Giants flew up the Thames. In 1938 the Spanish Civil War was in progress, and the following morning's newspapers carried reports of 'unidentified bombers' over the Pyrenees.

Mathilde and Martin were at Victoria Station to welcome him, together with Jones and his wife. Freud's temporary home in the suburb of St John's Wood, which he described to Eitingon, was a rented house to the north of Regent's Park, at 39 Elsworthy Road, chosen and furnished by Ernst. 'The enchantment of the new surroundings . . . make one want to shout "Heil Hitler!" ' Primrose Hill was adjacent; it reminded him of Grinzing. He told Eitingon about the triumph he felt at being freed, mingled 'too strongly' with grief, since he had 'always greatly loved the prison from which I have been released'. Now that he had left it for good, Vienna at last defined itself for him as home.

To his brother Alexander, who had got as far as Switzerland (he and his wife didn't come to Britain until the autumn, and they left soon after for Canada) he wrote on 22 June:

This England – you will soon see for yourself – is in spite of everything that strikes one as foreign, peculiar and difficult, and of this there is quite enough – a blessed, a happy country inhabited by well-meaning hospitable people. At least this is the impression of the first weeks. Our reception was cordial beyond words. We were wafted up on the wings of a mass psychosis. (I feel compelled to express myself poetically.) After the third day the post delivered letters correctly to 'Dr Freud, London' or 'Overlooking Regent's Park'; a taxi driver bringing Anna home exclaimed on seeing the number of the house: 'Oh, it's Dr Freud's place.' The newspapers have made us popular. We have been inundated with flowers and could easily have suffered serious indigestion from fruit and sweets.

The mass-circulation newspapers were probably not on his breakfast table. He would have seen in them traces of the same anti-Semitism that was thriving across the Channel, but a milder anglicised strain, social rather than political. Three days before Freud wrote to his brother, the *Sunday Express*, then a powerful newspaper in tune with middle-class values, had this to say:

There is a big influx of foreign Jews into Britain. They are overrunning the country. They are trying to enter the medical profession in great numbers . . . Worst of all, many of them are holding themselves out to the public as psychoanalysts . . . [the psychoanalyst] often obtains an ascendancy over the patient of which he makes base use if he is a bad man.

A leaflet prepared by British Jews suggests the nervous climate that greeted immigrants. They were told to learn English and its correct pronunciation, not to make themselves conspicuous, not to criticise the government or the way of life. 'Talk halting English rather than fluent German and *do not talk in a loud voice*. Do not read German newspapers in public.'

Freud was insulated from all this. He worked on, acquiring a few patients, writing a little. The last section of *Moses and Monotheism* was completed in July, and Freud arranged early publication. Earlier portions had appeared already, but it was the final synthesis that he expected would cause most offence, as it did. Visitors came, some distinguished: H. G. Wells; Salvador Dali (who brought his wife and a millionaire); emissaries from the Royal Society (which had elected him a foreign member) with its 'Charter Book' to sign. Sam Freud came down from Manchester.

A permanent home was found a mile away, in Maresfield Gardens, Hampstead, just off the Finchley Road: a detached house built after the war that Ernst gutted and rearranged, ready for them to move into in the autumn. Martha was in occupation from 27 September. Freud – who had undergone radical surgery at the London Clinic, a private hospital, earlier in the month – joined her three days later.

It was the week of the Munich crisis, when Germany, having swallowed Austria, seemed about to swallow the next country to the east, Czechoslovakia. The British Prime Minister, Neville Chamberlain, was nudged by his colleagues into a show of strength. Trenches, to be used as air-raid shelters, were dug in London parks, and the nation's stock of anti-aircraft guns, forty-four of them, was wheeled out. The fleet was mobilised.

But Chamberlain remained an appeaser, telling the British people in a radio broadcast, 'How horrible, fantastic, incredible it is that we should be digging trenches and trying on gas-masks here because of a quarrel in a faraway country between people of whom we know nothing.' He flew to do a deal with Hitler in Munich and returned in triumph ('I believe it is peace for our time'), as seen in a hundred television documentaries, a bank-manager figure by the plane, waving his piece of paper. Freud wrote 'Peace' in his diary. Six months later the Germans took Czechoslovakia, and the mood in Britain finally changed.

By this time, March 1939, Freud's cancer was active, spreading and inoperable. He was also suffering from heart failure. At the end of July he gave up his practice. Apart from pain and general debility, decaying bone gave off a foul smell that drove away his dog. A gangrenous cavity appeared in his cheek, and mosquito netting had to be used on his bed to deter flies. This terrible ending of his life he faced with apparent equanimity. Anna nursed him, getting up several times each night to spray his mouth with analgesic. Max Schur, who had reached England safely, was there most of the time. Discussing Hitler and what would happen next, Schur asked Freud if he thought the coming war would be the last. '*My* last war,' said Freud. His name was on the Gestapo's 'Special Search List' to be rounded up when Britain fell.

On 1 September Hitler invaded Poland, and two days later, on a Sunday morning, Chamberlain told Britain that 'we are now at war with Germany'. Freud's bed was moved to a safer part of the house when the first air-raid sirens sounded soon after Chamberlain's broadcast; it was a false alarm.

On 21 September, a Thursday, Freud took Schur's hand and said,

'My dear Schur, you certainly remember our first talk. You promised me then not to forsake me when my time comes. Now it's nothing but torture and makes no sense any more.' Schur said that he understood. 'Thank you,' said Freud. 'Talk to Anna, and if she thinks it's right, make an end of it.'

Forty years earlier, in one of his rhetorical letters to Fliess, he asked, 'What has the individual come to, how negligible must be the influence of the religion of science, which is supposed to have taken the place of the old religion, if one no longer dares to disclose that it is this or that man's turn to die?'

After Schur had spoken to Anna, the doctor injected him with a powerful dose of morphine, which was repeated, perhaps twice, over the next thirty-six hours. In effect, this was euthanasia; Schur consulted a lawyer before he wrote his report of the episode.

Freud lapsed into a coma and died at three a.m. on Saturday, 23 September 1939. He was eighty-three and had outlived all the calendrical omens. It was Yom Kippur, the Jewish Day of Atonement, a time of collective repentance: a coincidence that he might have analysed into something more than coincidence, given the opportunity.

32: Afterwards

Freud's generation showed a proper respect. Anna, left as her father's representative on earth, was deferred to as the keeper of his memory, not to mention his papers in the house at Maresfield Gardens. She was a therapist in her own right but she lived in Freud's shadow, and would not have wanted it otherwise. People took care not to offend 'Miss Freud'.

The house was a repository of the past. All Freud's surviving antiquities and books were there. Aunt Minna died during the war, but Martha, the elder sister, outlived her, a silent old woman of fixed habits who insisted on going out to the Finchley Road to buy the household groceries, as she had always done in Vienna. She was ninety when she died in 1951.

Anna was then in her mid-fifties, busy and vigorous. She stood for the need to conserve and cherish, which was unhelpful to those seeking impartial assessment of her father but admirable in its loyalty to him; he had been her life. For all its psychoanalytic comings and goings, the house at Maresfield Gardens made visitors feel they had crossed a border into another land. Jeffrey Masson, when he first visited it in the 1960s, was

> struck by a certain smell, a palpable mustiness. It was very dark and almost completely silent. As soon as I entered, I felt weighted down. Mementoes were everywhere.

A distinguished British analyst went there during his training:

> It was as if they were all in Vienna still. An old servant offered me a sandwich without meat, as in the hard times. They dressed in the same way, Anna in a long black dress, part of another world. When I was in analysis I dreamt of Anna Freud's legs. My analyst said, 'You're the only man to see them.'

For Anna, as for the majority of psychoanalysts, the life of Sigmund Freud was a property to be safeguarded. When the

Second World War ended in 1945, there were ominous signs that popular interest was reviving. A biography appeared in America in 1946, and a second the following year, a perceptive book by a magazine writer, Helen Walker Puner. Both dismayed Freud's circle. Authorised versions of Freud's life were needed.

The first came in the shape of a collection of letters, the ones Freud wrote to Wilhelm Fliess, prophet of biorhythms and nasal reflexes. The letters, 284 of them, spent the war at the Danish Legation in Paris, where Princess Marie Bonaparte had taken them from Vienna. Bonaparte brought them to London in May 1946 for Anna to read.

Anna was reluctant to see them published, and so was her brother Martin. Bonaparte was equally keen to see them in print, and she was a persuasive woman, in a strong position as the one who had saved the collection, and who might even find another home for it if the Freuds were not interested. Between the legal niceties and the need to present the true Freud, thus rendering other people's books superfluous, Anna decided the letters should appear. But first they had to be censored.

The editing was done between 1946 and 1949 by a former Viennese analyst, Ernest Kris. One of Freud's favoured disciples in the 1930s, he settled in New York during the war, and was happy to work with Anna at his elbow when he visited London every summer. They could hardly have been closer: he was having analysis with her all the time they were engaged on the letters.

Camouflaging Freud began, however the process may have been perceived at the time. The book was to be called *The Origins of Psycho-analysis*, but material that Anna and Martin thought too seamy in the picture it gave of their father's interests disappeared. A paragraph about female circumcision, lurid details of 'seductions', the fact that Freud experienced sexual desire, were among the casualties. So was the business of Emma Eckstein, the woman who was supposed to have nearly bled to death for love; she wasn't allowed to exist. Money, debts, ambition and cocaine were seen as equally sensitive subjects. Altogether more than a hundred letters didn't appear at all, and deep cuts were made in some of the remainder. A German-language version, with a substantial introduction by Kris, was the first to appear, in 1950, followed by the English edition in 1954. Kris told Anna that his conscience was clear; a note in the book said that the editing followed a principle of 'omitting or abbreviating [whatever] would be inconsistent with professional or personal confidence', a phrase vague enough to mean anything. In fact Kris and Anna stripped the correspondence of much that had haunted Freud at the time. Psychoanalysis accepted what it was given – even the emasculated version contained undreamt-of insights – and was grateful.

Long before *Origins* appeared, Anna and her advisers were agonising about a biography. An American publisher asked Jones to write one in 1946, but at first he hesitated, or pretended to, because he was sixty-seven and in uncertain health. Anna would have preferred Kris, and there was even talk of another candidate from old Vienna, Siegfried Bernfeld, one of Anna's ghostly suitors in the 1920s, who now lived in San Francisco. Bernfeld collected much biographical material about Freud's early years. Perhaps his talent for discovery told against him; his idea of creating an accessible Freud archive was later brushed aside in favour of reticence and obfuscation. Bernfeld was before his time, wanting answers to biographical questions that no one else was asking. In 1947 he published the article that identified Freud's 'Screen Memories' paper as autobiographical. It was this pioneering effort that inspired Peter Swales's rampant curiosity thirty years later.

Bernfeld didn't become the official biographer, and nor did Kris. Jones decided that he would do it after all. Whatever Anna thought about his reputation for deviousness, he was too eminent a figure, and had worked alongside Freud for too many years, to be denied.

By 1950 Jones was at work on the first volume of what turned out to be a three-volume biography, the kindly Bernfeld supplying him with information. The most important material was Freud's correspondence, which the family handed over with misgivings. Trunkloads of papers were taken down to Jones's house in Sussex, where he lived in comfortable semi-retirement with his wife and a couple of servants. Sigmund and Martha's letters during their engagement were initially withheld. Some of the Freuds wanted to destroy them. Only Ernst Freud, now established in Britain as an architect, seems to have been on Jones's side. Eventually Anna produced two thousand letters written between Sigmund and Martha, Jones having sworn he wouldn't show them to 'another living soul', except Mrs Jones who had the job of translating them. He almost sank under the weight of this and other material. By the time he finished Volume One it was the end of 1952, and he was seventy-four.

Because it was an official biography, the family, and Anna in particular, had their eye on him. His style was often vivid, his approach direct and rarely sycophantic. But he came to praise Freud, who had shaped Jones's own life, and he omitted many things and modified others. He used the Fliess correspondence with discretion, he gave a bland account of Freud and cocaine (a subject that disturbed Anna), he skipped lightly over Freud's own neuroses, in general he took Freud at his own valuation. Anna, apprehensive at what to expect, was relieved as she saw Jones's drafts.

The biography, his last service to Freud, remains a monumental work. The third volume appeared in 1957; soon afterwards he was found to have cancer. Like others in Freud's early circle, Jones had some bizarre characteristics, but unlike them he remained consistently loyal to Freud. On his death-bed he was disturbed to hear choirs singing hymns in his dreams, as if religion were trying, unsuccessfully, to reclaim the old rationalist. He chose to cut short his suffering, as Freud had done, and put an end to his life with drugs in February 1958.

The wish to protect the papers and deter inquisitive researchers created an archive whose aim was to lock things away. Freud was to be spared the indignity of having his methods used publicly on himself. This was at odds with the implied purpose of psychoanalysis, to seek truth behind façades, but went nicely with the authoritarian side of Freud. Dr Kurt Eissler, a leading New York analyst, took it upon himself to build up this collection and watch over it. Another of the Viennese refugees from Hitler, Eissler corresponded with Anna Freud during the war and cultivated her friendship. By 1950, when he and others at the New York Psychoanalytic Society had decided that a Freudian archive should be established in America, her support was forthcoming.

No one took any notice of Siegfried Bernfeld, whose ideal, tentatively expressed in letters to Eissler, was an archive in the form of a workshop open to researchers. Anna was horrified by this, preferring the plans for a safe place where material would be handled 'with great discretion'. By the time Bernfeld died in 1953, the Sigmund Freud Archives had been legally incorporated, and Eissler was at work, seeking out letters and other papers, and embarking on a programme to tape-record ageing analysts and patients.

In a separate endeavour, selections of letters were published in unreliable editions, several of them edited by Ernst Freud, who left out whatever he and Anna thought might cause offence: a miscellany in 1961, letters to Karl Abraham in 1965, letters to Arnold Zweig in 1970. Ernst had effective control of the rights to his father's material in those days. Freud had left the copyrights to five of his grandchildren – they still receive the income – and Ernst managed Sigmund Freud Copyrights, which had been set up in 1946 to handle them. Anna had no direct control of the material, but she was a trustee of her father's will, and was always consulted; her brother was unlikely to go against her wishes.

The first letters to be treated properly were those to Jung, published, together with Jung's side of the correspondence, in William McGuire's edition of 1974, after years of negotiation with both families. Anna Freud did her best to intervene. Among other things, she didn't want Stekel referred to as a 'swine', Morton Prince as an 'arrogant ass', or anything said about the Jung–Sabina Spielrein liaison. By this time, however, the copyright business – raising income for the grandchildren by licensing the right to reproduce Freud texts – had been put on a professional footing. Ernst died in 1970. McGuire resisted Anna Freud's proposals, and Sigmund Freud Copyrights let the unexpurgated edition go ahead.

Eissler's archive continued to grow. All material was deposited at the Library of Congress and made subject to restrictions on access. These were often extravagantly cautious. Embargoes of twenty, thirty, fifty years were common. Occasional items were withheld into the next century but one, the twenty-second. Freud's patients and their living descendants, it was said, must be protected (although Freud himself was often casual about confidentiality); similarly, interviewees would stay silent if they thought their views would be revealed. There was some substance in these restraints, but they were applied wholesale, without imagination. When Ernest Jones identified Anna O. as Bertha Pappenheim in the biography, the sky didn't fall in; nor when Henri Ellenberger named Emmy von N. as Fanny Moser in 1977.

Absurd situations arose over some of Eissler's interviews. Having embargoed his long conversations with Wilhelm Reich in 1952, he was dismayed to find that a copy of the transcripts returned to Reich was used as the basis of a book a mere fifteen years later. Martin Freud's estranged wife, Esti, gossiped happily to Paul Roazen, and let him read her copy of her interview with Eissler, which, she was surprised to be told by Roazen, was inaccessible at the Library of Congress until 2053.

The Wolf Man, whom Eissler identified in Vienna and interviewed year after year, was another disappointment. Pankejeff fell into enemy hands when an enterprising Viennese journalist, Karin Obholzer, tracked him down for herself in 1973 and persuaded him to talk to her. Eissler failed to head her off, and eventually Pankejeff sold her the rights in his story, which included the forty hours of interviews she had recorded, on the understanding that nothing would be published until his death; at the time he was eighty-six. Her book appeared in 1980, a year after he died, and showed a refreshing scepticism on the part of Freud's most famous patient. Eissler's interviews with him gather dust in the Library of Congress.

Eissler's most significant coup was to persuade Anna Freud to bequeath the Freud papers at Maresfield Gardens. She died in 1982, and eventually an emissary came from New York to enforce the terms of the will. By this time the house had become the Freud Museum, displaying Freud's artefacts – his couch, his statuettes, his library – and there was reluctance to see the papers go. Photocopying machines worked long hours, but much of the material went uncopied. Resentment at the British because they had made too little fuss of her father may explain why she succumbed to Eissler.

The British Psycho-Analytic Society has the Jones papers, which are available to researchers, although they have been tampered with on at least one occasion. In 1972 Anna Freud visited the library accompanied by Dr Masud Khan, a controversial analyst who was then the society's archivist. They removed papers that she said belonged to the family, among them material relating to Emma Eckstein. Presumably they, too, have long since gone to America.

A peculiar series of events undermined Eissler and his archive shortly before Anna died. In the 1970s he befriended Jeffrey Moussaieff Masson, then a young American psychoanalyst in training, who had another existence as a professor of Sanskrit in Toronto. Impressed by Masson's talents, within a few years he decided to make him his successor.

Eissler evidently wanted a protégé who was not over-burdened by the past and its deified image of Freud. Perhaps he had suffered more than he showed from the barbs of Freud scholars, angry at his restrictive policy, and decided to amaze them with an activist who had an appetite for disclosure.

Before Eissler sounded him out about the appointment, at the same time inviting him to become a director of Sigmund Freud Copyrights, Masson got to know Anna Freud and, with Eissler's endorsement, made himself at home in Maresfield Gardens, 'a gigantic treasure chest', where he unearthed many papers. He worried her by proposing an unexpurgated edition of the Fliess letters, a matter that became an obsession with him, but in the end she agreed even to that.

The formal offer of Eissler's succession was made in October 1980, and by 1981 Masson was familiarising himself with the classified material in the Library of Congress, and planning to make everything available. Eissler, while hating the idea, said he must do as he pleased.

But at the last minute, Masson ruined himself in the eyes of Eissler and the psychoanalytic establishment. He became convinced (not least from material in Eissler's archives) that Freud had betrayed himself and humanity by abandoning his own 'seduction theory' of large-scale child abuse and replacing it with a theory of childhood fantasy that became the Oedipus Complex. In summer 1981, at a New England psychoanalytic meeting, he told a questioner that Freud had made a 'gigantic mistake' by treating reality as fantasy. The *New York Times* got wind of his heresy, and the result – since psychoanalysis without Oedipus is rather like Christianity without the Resurrection – was publicity, rancour, dismissal and lawsuits. Masson says innocently that he had made no secret of his views to Eissler, and that he was shocked at the response.

An attempt to stop his splendidly uncensored edition of the Fliess correspondence, which he translated as well as edited, failed because the publishing contracts were in place. Some analysts still pretend it doesn't exist because they dislike Masson so much; some radicals are irritated by what they see as his self-indulgence in not keeping quiet until he had opened up the archives. Masson himself has long since abandoned psychoanalysis as a hopeless case and moved on.

Eissler, a sad figure, retired in the aftermath of the Masson affair, and under a new director the archives appear to be less restrictive than they were; although only a fantasist would expect to see all the seals broken this side of the millennium.

Psychoanalysis has evolved and adapted, becoming a less clearly defined discipline than the one Freud offered to the world. No one could accuse its practitioners of having stagnated. Freud's original concept of the instinctual drives has been watered down; even the Oedipus Complex is less binding, as emphasis has shifted from the events of childhood to include adult life and relationships. The individual's unconscious has become, to some analysts, a creation of society, not a closed inner world. The school of 'object relations', which concentrates on the patient's relationship with other people, has done much to humanise psychoanalysis, although the phrase 'object relations' is itself dehumanising. Freud's perception of people in general, and infants in particular, as creatures struggling like animals to tear simple pleasures from a hostile environment, has been modified by a belief that we start life adapted to our surroundings.

The style of analysis has changed. Patients tend to be invited to collaborate rather than made to feel they are submitting to superiors. Some analysts have abandoned the couch and do it face-to-face; others find the old posture is still best for removing distractions and encouraging free association. Regular sessions, four or five times a week for months or years, remain an ideal in some quarters, but the classical analysis has been in decline for years. Paul Federn, Freud's friend, could write as early as 1972 that in the United States psychoanalysis had become 'a popular, generally misunderstood method of treating emotionally sick people'. Briefer treatments for specific problems have crept in. Psychoanalysis at the edges now dissolves into the less specific 'psychotherapy', which in turn becomes the ubiquitous 'counselling', where psychology and commonsense are often indistinguishable. In general the psychoanalytic community has diluted the pure doctrine in favour of a more user-friendly set of beliefs that is (they hope) less vulnerable to attack because less specific.

For some practitioners, psychoanalysis is still a rigid and unyielding discipline; at times they sound stricter than Freud himself, certainly the early Freud, adjusting the system as he went along. Dr A. is a therapist who believes in Freud if not always in psychoanalysis. He has no time for today's proliferation of ad hoc therapies 'to be used if your father dies or your dog dies'. Freudian therapy is something else.

It would be unhelpful, says A., to let a social relationship develop between him and a patient. He never stands up when the client enters; there is no greeting; should someone fail to keep an appointment, he sits patiently, waiting. Those who ask direct questions don't receive direct answers. Individuals must find their own solutions; it is their unconscious, after all, not his. 'There is no resolution to an oedipal situation, but there is a recognition of it, and if we recognise it, we probably lead a more interesting life than otherwise.'

Freud himself, to A., was an Oedipus, a man confronting riddles about life, a realist who 'always said he would be maligned, because he saw us as we are, not only as we would want to be'. Faced with life's traumas, suggests A., what matters is to find ways of managing the 'noble enterprise' of self-recognition.

He may be right. The outsider's problem with psychoanalysis is that it evidently contains truths, but never the single absolute truth that Freud the magician claimed; or, as A. prefers to put it, 'the absolute truth that some people like to think that Freud claimed to have found'.

The audacious claims made for psychoanalysis, whether by its founder or his successors, have been slowly undermined. When Freud achieved general recognition after the First World War, to believe in 'the unconscious' meant accepting the version that he proposed. In the second half of the century, psychology has come to recognise alternatives that don't depend on the grinding Freudian mechanisms of repression and conflict. Freud's solution to the riddle was no more proof against time than anyone else's. His monument is his search for one.

The site of Bellevue, the guest-house under the Kahlenberg, where a plaque commemorates the dream of 1895, still attracts the occasional pilgrim. On a summer's day it makes a charming place for a picnic. Freud went there once with Ernest Jones, and they ate on the terrace in front of the building, under the north-east corner. It was there, Jones was told, that 'the great event' occurred. One can guess at the precise spot, but it hardly matters any more. Air, branches and a bird or two fill the space where Freud slept and dreamed.

Notes

The source of letters can be identified from the Bibliography under the editors' names as follows:

> Freud to Fliess: Masson (1985), refered to simply as 'Masson' in the Notes
> Freud and Karl Abraham: Abraham and Freud
> Freud and Andréas-Salomé: Pfeiffer
> Freud and Ferenczi: up to and including June 1914, Brabant; from July 1914, Falzeder
> Freud and Jones: Paskauskas
> Freud and Jung: McGuire
> Freud and Silberstein: Boehlich

Rylands = unpublished ms correspondence between Freud and Sam Freud at John Rylands University Library, Manchester

Letters = the selection of Freud letters, edited by Ernst Freud, published in 1961

Jones Papers = material (chiefly correspondence) used by Ernest Jones when writing Freud's biography, now deposited at the British Psycho-Analytical Society

Other abbreviations:

F. = Freud; F.P. = Frink Papers, at Johns Hopkins Medical Institutions; Fer. = Ferenczi; J. = Jung; M.B. = Martha Bernays; SE = Standard Edition of Freud's works

'In conversation' means in conversation with the author.

Papers by Peter Swales are identified as follows:

1982a   'Freud, Minna Bernays, and the Conquest of Rome: New Light on the Origins of Psychoanalysis', *New American Review* (Spring/Summer 1982)

1982c   'Freud, Johann Weier, and the Status of Seduction: The Role of the Witch in the Conception of Fantasy', L. Spurling (ed.), *Sigmund Freud: Critical Assessments*, Vol. 1 (1989). Condensed as 'A Fascination with Witches', *The Sciences*, New York Academy of Sciences, 22 (Nov. 1982)

1982d   'Freud, Fliess, and Fratricide: The Role of Fliess in Freud's Conception of Paranoia', Spurling (ed.), ibid.

1983a   'Freud, Martha Bernays, and the Language of Flowers: Masturbation, Cocaine, and the Inflation of Fantasy', privately printed, New York

1983b   'Freud, Cocaine, and Sexual Chemistry: The Role of Cocaine in Freud's Conception of the Libido', Spurling (ed.), ibid.

1983c   'Freud, Krafft-Ebing, and the Witches: The Role of Krafft-Ebing in Freud's Flight into Fantasy', Spurling (ed.), ibid.

1986   'Freud, His Teacher, and the Birth of Psychoanalysis', P. E. Stepanksy (ed.), *Freud: Appraisals and Reappraisals*, Vol. 1 (1986)

1988   'Freud, Katharina, and the First "Wild Analysis"', Stepansky (ed.), ibid., Vol. 3 (1988)

1: *Tales from the Vienna Woods*

2   Martha's stockings: Ernest Jones, I, 141.
  The case of Katharina: SE2:125ff.
3   Swales on Katharina: Swales (1988). Throughout I have used some of Swales's discoveries (and have said where I do so) without attempting to convey the Freud who obsesses him, a man of sinister complexity 'whose dreams were his life and whose life was a dream'.
4   Nazis at the gates: to Jones, 2 March 1937, Paskauskas.
4ff Bellevue history: Dr Wilhelm Schlag, Vienna, in conversation, 1995.
5   'we move to Heaven': to Fliess, 25 May 1895, Masson.
  'a man like me': to Fliess, ibid.
6   The unconscious in the nineteenth century: Ellenberger; Whyte.
  'Internal perception': to Fliess, 25 May 1895, Masson.
  'Hysterics suffer': SE2:7.
7   'wild and yearning': to Fliess, 2 April (letter begun 28 March), 1895, Masson.
7ff The Irma dream: SE4:107.
9   Vision of a middle-aged man: E. E. Erikson, 'The Dream Specimen of Psychoanalysis', *Journal of the American Psychoanalytic Association*, 2 (1954).

2: *Out of the East*

12   Hofmann and Freit: Krüll, 89ff. Krüll's important information about the family is used throughout the chapter. Ellenberger, 420ff, touches on eastern Jews in general and the Freuds in particular.
15   Freud's caul: Ernest Jones, I, 5.
  Sigismund: Gilman, 'one of the essential Jewish names in the comic literature of the period', 70.
  Martin on Amalie: Martin Freud, 11.
16   'strange riddle': SE6:46.
  'about God Almighty and hell': to Fliess, 3 Oct. 1897, Masson.
  'always carrying you off': to Fliess, 15 Oct. 1897, ibid.
  'my teacher': to Fliess, 4 Oct. (letter begun 3 Oct.) 1897, ibid.
17   The Wolf Man: 'From the History of an Infantile Neurosis', SE17:7.
  Dishonest maid: to Fliess, 4 and 15 Oct. 1897, Masson.
  Freud revealed: Siegfried Bernfeld, a Viennese, by then living in San

Francisco, was the first seriously to begin unravelling Freud's life. His
paper, 'An Unknown Autobiographical Fragment by Freud', appeared in
The American Imago, IV (1947).

18 Leaving Freiberg: Ernest Jones, I, 13–15; Roazen (1992), 27.
Philipp and the new baby: SE6:49–51.

19 The birds'-beaks dream: SE5:583.
Freud's 'associations': Krüll, 125; Ernest Jones, I, 10n.
'Deeply buried': Molnar, 110.
Breslau station: to Fliess, 3 Dec. 1897, Masson, 285.
First addresses in Vienna: Krüll, 148.

20 'potato noses': to Martha Bernays (hereafter 'M. B.'), 16 Dec. 1883,
Letters.

3: *The Field of Flowers*

21 Jacob's income: Krüll, 149.

22 Café poet: SE4:192–3.
Piano lessons: Anna Freud Bernays, 'My Brother Sigmund Freud',
American Mercury (1940), 51.
Rich uncle: A. F. Bernays, quoted by Krüll, 257.
Jacob's cap: SE4:197.

23 Made of dust: SE4:205.
'As for the biographers': to M.B., 28 April, 1885, *Letters*.
Biography as concealment: to Arnold Zweig, 31 May 1936, Ernst Freud.
Josef in Freud's dream: SE4:137.

23–4 Josef as the forger: Krüll, 164ff, citing Gicklhorn; Public Record Office,
Memo No. 217, 19 Jan. 1979, by Joffre de Galles (pseud. for Peter
Swales).

24 'From my youth': to Fliess, 21 Sept. 1899, Masson.

25 Philipp's trade and marriage: Krüll, 173, 269; to Silberstein, 9 Sept. 1875,
Boehlich.
Studying the war: A. F. Bernays (1940) op. cit.
To Silberstein, undated: Boehlich, 1.

26 Fluss family details: Boehlich, Introduction; Krüll, 262.
Amalie at Roznau: Boehlich, Introduction.
'knowing my character': 17 Aug. 1872, Boehlich.
'nonsensical Hamlet': 4 Sept. 1872, ibid.
Gisela's appearance: 4 Sept. 1872, ibid.
'Only in summer': 21 Feb. 1875, ibid.
'miserable life': 17 March 1873, 'Some Early Unpublished Letters of
Freud' *International Journal of Psycho-Analysis*, 50 (1969).
'Natural Scientist': 1 May 1873, ibid.

27 'You never know!': 16 June 1873, ibid.
Sardonic letter: 1 May 1873, ibid.
Contemporary account of Fair: *Illustrated London News*, 10 May 1873.

28 'for the world of the aesthete': 16 June 1873, *International Journal of
Psycho-Analysis* 50, (1969).
Lincoln's letters: A. F. Bernays (1940) op. cit.
Exam results: 10 July 1873, Boehlich; subjects and essay title: to Emil
Fluss, 16 June 1873, *International Journal of Psycho-Analysis* 50, (1969).
'My father': 2 Aug. 1873, Boehlich.
Unable to visit England: 6 Aug. 1873, ibid.
Given up Gisela: 20 Aug. 1873, ibid.

30 References to masturbation: The fictional character in 'Screen Memories' mentions childhood masturbation. S. Bernfeld, in his 1947 paper that identified 'Screen Memories' material as autobiographical, tactfully avoided any suggestion that Freud's own experiences might be involved. But he wrote to Ernest Jones, 13 Feb. 1952: 'I have come to suspect that one of the reasons for the secrecy with which Freud surrounded [the fictional character's story] might be just its close connection with masturbation.' Jones Papers.

4: *Dissection*

31 'a sort of curiosity': SE20:8.
'age-old dossiers': to Emil Fluss, 1 May 1873, *International Journal of Psycho-Analysis*.
Charitable grants: E. Laible, '"Through Privation to Knowledge": Unknown Documents from Freud's University Years', *International Journal of Psycho-Analysis*, 74 (1993).
'troubled medical student': 2 Dec. 1874, Boehlich.
'roaming': 21 Feb. 1875, ibid.
Freud's curriculum: 7 and 13 March 1875, ibid.
32 'academic happiness': 11 April 1875, ibid.
Vacation plans: 13 June 1875, ibid.
'I am not insensitive': 28 June 1875, ibid.
'a splendid specimen': A. F. Bernays, 'My Brother Sigmund Freud', *American Mercury*, 51 (1940).
33 Freud's Manchester letters: 3 Aug. and 9 Sept. 1875, Boehlich.
Immigrant city: Sebald, 191–2.
New Year's Eve: 1 Jan. 1875, Boehlich.
'"touching" Gisela': 24 Jan. 1875, ibid.
'imprudent affection': 27 Feb. 1875, ibid.
34 'Epithalamium': 1 Oct. 1875, ibid.; the draft, p. 188.
34–5 Claus and the eel project: S. Bernfeld, 'Freud's Scientific Beginnings', *American Imago*, 6 (1949).
35–6 Freud on Trieste: between 28 March and 23 April 1876, Boehlich.
36 'deserted streets': SE17:237.
37 Reworking the essay: to Ferenczi, 12 May 1919, Falzeder.
'demand of a determinism': SE15:106.

5: *Vocation*

38 Rokitansky's cadavers: A. Castiglioni, 'The Second Viennese School: From Rokitanksy to Freud', *Ciba Symposia*, 9, 3/4 (June–July 1947).
'no other forces': Hirschmüller, 38.
39 Brücke's appearance: Ellenberger, 431.
Mathilde on Amalie: Mathilde to Ernest Jones, 6 Dec. 1951. Jones Papers.
39–40 'even the God-denier' and following: 18 Sept. 1874, Boehlich.
40 'I began to understand': SE4:196.
'expected to feel myself inferior': SE20:9.
The radical students' society: Rice, 193ff.
Freud on the Polish Jew: 28 June 1875, Boehlich.
40–41 Jews on the train: to Fluss, 18 Sept. 1872, *International Journal of Psycho-Analysis*, 50 (1969).

41 Billroth and the Jews: Rice, 194–6, 239; Gilman, 18.

42 Charitable grants: E. Laible, '"Through Privation to Knowledge": Unknown Documents from Freud's University Years', *International Journal of Psycho-Analysis*, 74 (1993).
Freud in the laboratory: S. Bernfeld, 'Freud's Scientific Beginnings', *American Imago*, 6 (1949).
With the Bettelheims: 14 Aug. 1878, Boehlich.
Salivary glands: ibid.
Flaying or torturing: F. to Wilhelm Knöpfmacher, a friend, 6 Aug. 1878, *Letters*.

43 Fleischl and 'exclusive society': to M.B., 27 June 1882, *Letters*.
Borrowing from Fleischl: e.g. F. to M.B. 10 March 1885, *Letters*; from Paneth: e.g. Masson 60, n1.
Fluss family at graduation: Ernest Jones, I, 63.
Gisela marries Popper: Swales (1983a), 8n.

43–4 Marie Bonaparte and Freud's virginity: Appignanesi and Forrester (1992), quoting Swales, 340.

44 Inaccessible journals: see Note to page 146n.
Gedo's anecdote: 'On the Origins of the Theban Plague', in Stepansky, Vol. 1 (1986); phone conversation with J. E. Gedo, 1997.
Doing it well: E. Hitschmann to Ernest Jones, 26 March 1954, Jones Papers.
F. meets Martha: Ernest Jones, I, 114–15; to M.B., 26 June 1885, *Letters*.

45 First love letter: Ernest Jones, I, 116.
Bernays's bankruptcy: Hanns W. Lange to the author, 6 March 1995.

46 £2,000 grant: E. Laible, *International Journal of Psycho-Analysis*, 74 (1993).
'a very poor Jew': ibid.
Freud–Martha letters: Until they eventually appear in a scholarly edition, everyone has to rely on the passages that Jones used in his biography (1953), and the ninety-odd letters that were included (no doubt after passages were deleted) in the *Letters*. About 2,000 letters written before their marriage are thought to exist; this means that no more than 7 or 8 per cent of the total has been published so far.
'Martha must give up': Ernest Jones, I, 122.
'Unruly dreams': 30 June 1882, Ernest Jones, I, 385.
Quoting Shakespeare: to M.B., 14 July 1882, *Letters*.

46–7 In the park: to M.B., 14 Aug 1882, *Letters*.

47 Poor nursing: Johnston, 228.
Two boiled eggs: to M.B., 29 May 1884, *Letters*.
Sixpence on cigars: to M.B., Sept. 1882, Ernest Jones, I, 170.
'The sponger's existence': to M.B., 17 Nov. 1884, *Letters*.
Breuer's bathroom: to M.B., 13 July 1883, *Letters*.

48 Owing Breuer money: to Breuer, 7 Jan. 1898, when the debt of 2,300 florins was being paid off, *Letters*.
'My stormy longing heart': 30 June 1883, Ernest Jones, I, 140.
Longing for England: to M.B., 16 Aug. 1882, Ernest Jones, I, 195.
Paradise Lost: Book 1, lines 190–1.
Three rooms and a larder: 18 Aug. 1882, *Letters*.
Indescribable longing: Aug. 1882, Ernest Jones, I, 186.

49 'You are quite right': 22 Aug. 1883, *Letters*.
'silent savagery': 16 Jan. 1884, *Letters*.

'violent and passionate': 6 Oct. 1883, Ernest Jones, I, 214.
The mindless poor: 29 Aug. 1883, *Letters*.
50   On Nathan Weiss: to M.B., 16 Sept. 1883, *Letters*.

6: *Nerve Doctor*

52   Tailor's apprentice: to M.B., 18 Jan. 1884, *Letters*; SE3:232 has 'cobbler's' apprentice, no doubt to conceal his identity.
'at least a beginning': to M.B., 18 Jan. 1884, *Letters*.
Weiss's ghost: to M.B., 10 Jan. 1884, *Letters*.
Alcoholic innkeeper: to M.B., 28 Jan. 1884, *Letters*.

52–3   Never a 'proper' doctor etc: SE20:253.

53   In Meynert's laboratory: S. Bernfeld, 'Sigmund Freud, M.D., 1882–1885', *International Journal of Psycho-Analysis*, 32 (1951).
'Brain mythology': Webster, 178.
Meynert as poet, and brain anatomy as hobby: Bernfeld to Jones, 23 July 1951, Jones Papers; as chloroform addict, F. to Fliess, 4 Jan. 1898, Masson.

54   'to make the world sit up': 14 Feb. 1884, *Letters*.
'chasing after money': 7 Jan. 1885, *Letters*.
'a poor little devil': 28 Aug. 1884, *Letters*.

54–5   The Oedipus medallion: Ernest Jones, II, 15.

55   'Master Koch': 9 Oct. 1883, *Letters*.
'I will quench my thirst': 17 Aug. 1884, *Letters*.
'traumatic events': 23 June 1884, *Letters*.

55ff   The cocaine story: S. Bernfeld, 'Freud's Studies on Cocaine, 1884–1887', *Journal of the American Psychoanalytic Association*, 1, 1953; to M.B., 1884–6, *Letters*, passim; Ernest Jones, I, 86–108, passim; Andrews and Solomon; Nahas; Thornton; D. F. Musto, 'A Study in Cocaine', *History of Medicine* (Autumn 1970). Freud's writings on cocaine are mentioned only briefly in SE. They were published in Byck.

59   Martha's fault: SE20:14.
Freud the menace: 27 May, Jones Papers
'clear dividing line': *Letters*.
Destroying papers: 28 April, *Letters*.

60   Treating with personality: 5 Aug. 1883, Ernest Jones, I, 221.
Midwife story: SE16:397.

60–1   Obersteiner's clinic: to M.B., 6, 8 and 19 June, *Letters*; E. Shorter, 'Women and Jews in a Private Nervous Clinic in Late Nineteenth-century Vienna', *Medical History*, 33 (1989).

61   Casino Zögernitz: Schnitzler (1971), 142–3.

7: *French Lessons*

62   A worldly priest: to M.B., 21 Oct. 1885, *Letters*.

63   Children's brains: SE1:8.
Brouardel's mortuary: ibid.; Masson (1992) 36; to M.B., 20 Jan. 1886, *Letters*.
'Dirty knees': SE1:8n.
Feeling lonely: Ernest Jones, I, 200, using letters to M.B.
To Minna Bernays: 3 Dec.: *Letters*.

63–4   Life in Paris: to M.B., 21 Oct., 8 Nov. and 24/26 Nov. 1885, *Letters*; brothel incident, to M.B., 5 Dec. 1885, Ernest Jones, I, 206.

64   Green bed-curtains: Ernest Jones, I, 200.

Hallucinations: SE6:261.

The day-dream: SE6:149.

1916 paper: SE15:98.

65 Freud's change of plan: to M.B., 12 Dec. 1885, *Letters*.

65–7 Charcot's hysterics: Munthe; Ellenberger, 95ff; Sulloway, 33–4; Thornton, 94ff.

67 'I drank beer': to M.B., 20 Jan. 1886, *Letters*.

'Something alien': to M.B., 2 Feb. 1886, *Letters*.

67–8 Charcot mentions sex: SE14:13–14.

68 Back in Vienna: Ernest Jones, I, 156–7.

'paralyses and anaesthesias': SE20:14.

68–9 Janet's paper: see M. Macmillan, 'New Answers to Old Questions: What the Complete Freud–Fliess Correspondence Tells Us', *Psychoanalytic Review*, 77, 4 (1990). The paper, 'L'Anesthésie Hystérique', read at the Salpêtrière on 11 March 1892, spoke of 'the habitual associations of our sensations, the ideas we conceive of our organs'.

Article of 1888: SE1:41ff, esp. 49.

Freud puts up his plate: Ernest Jones, I, 157.

Early cases: to M.B., 13 May 1886, *Letters*; 5 June 1886, Ernest Jones, I, 259.

Quarrel with Bernays: Ernest Jones, I, 149ff.

69–70 Eli gaoled: Hanns W. Lange to the author, 6 March 1995.

70 Army service: to Breuer, 1 Sept. 1886, *Letters*.

The wedding: Ernest Jones, I, 165.

'Who is this Freud?': E. Rice, 'The Jewish Heritage of Sigmund Freud', *Psychoanalytic Review*, 81 (1994).

The ecgnonin dream: to M.B., 11 Nov. 1884, Ernest Jones, I, 386.

Swales: (1983a) 22.

8: *Secret Lives*

72 Pawning watches: Ernest Jones, I, 166.

72n Saved by a miracle: S. Bernfeld to Jones, 19 June 1951, Jones Papers.

73 Male hysteria episode: S. and S.C. Bernfeld, 'Freud's First Year in Practice, 1886–1887', *Bulletin of the Menninger Clinic*, 16 (March 1952); Ernest Jones, I, 252ff; Sulloway, 35ff; F.'s account, SE20:15–16.

Freud's autobiography: *An Autobiographical Study*, SE20:7–74.

74n Conductor's cramp: letter to *The Times* from J.N. Blau, 22 June 1994.

74 'crowds of neurotics': SE20:17.

'thin and lacks blood': Dowse, 128, 129.

Mrs A.: to Fliess, 24 Nov. 1887, Masson.

75 'It may be': 4 Feb. 1888, ibid.

76 Menacing comparisons: W.S. Playfair, contrib. to Albutt.

Review of neurasthenia book: SE1:35.

Freud on making a living: SE20:16.

Schnitzler in Berlin: Schnitzler (1971), 243.

77 'Unluckily': SE20:16.

'brave and sweet': F. to Emmeline and Minna Bernays, 16 Oct. 1887, *Letters*.

77n Original edition: Kris et al.

78 Breuer's method: SE1:56.

79 Crab and chicken: Hirschmüller, 94.

Schnitzler's patient: Schnitzler (1971), 270.

9: *The Talking Cure*

80   To Martha: Ernest Jones, I, 248.
     Siegmund Pappenheim as guardian: Swales (1986).
     Pappenheim family history: H.F. Ellenberger, 'The Story of "Anna O": a
     Critical Review with New Data', *Journal of the History of the Behavioral
     Sciences*, VIII (1972).

80–1 Bertha's upbringing: ibid; Hirschmüller, 98ff.

81   'insipid trivia': ibid., 100.
     'monotonous family life': SE2:41.

81–3 The case history: Breuer's account in SE2, *Studies on Hysteria*, was
     commented on in the same book by Freud, who subsequently made many
     references to it. So did numerous other writers (Ernest Jones, I, has a
     detailed account) but, as often happens with Freudian history, the
     original episode went unquestioned. Then Henri Ellenberger used an 1882
     photograph of Pappenheim in riding habit to discover her stay at the
     Bellevue Sanatorium, where Breuer had deposited her real case-history
     that year (Ellenberger, 1972, above). This and other significant material
     was recovered in 1972 by Albrecht Hirschmüller, and reproduced in
     Hirschmüller, 276.

84   'quite unhinged': 5 Aug. 1883, Ernest Jones, I, 247.

85   Letters to Martha: 31 Oct. and 11 Nov. 1883, Ernest Jones, I, 247.
     'astonishingly undeveloped': Hirschmüller, 277

86   'has never been in love': ibid., 278.
     'It was discovered': SE15:83.

10: *Hysterical Women*

89   Fanny Moser revealed: Henry Ellenberger, 'The Story of "Emmy von N.":
     A Critical Study with New Documents', in Micale. Ellenberger credited
     Ola Andersson with the original investigation.
     Mentona's account: her *Autobiography*, see Micale, op cit.

90   Swales on Anna Lieben: Swales (1986), passim.

91   'hysterical psychosis': SE2:69n.
     Sensual Vienna: cf. Ellenberger, 291: Kerr, 130; Timms.
     (1986) passim.

91–2 Jews and neurosis: Gilman, 120ff; E. Simon, 'Sigmund Freud, the Jew', in
     Leo Baeck Institute, *Year Book II* (1957), which quotes Freud at second-
     hand in 1907, 'The religion of Israel is a compulsive neurosis which has
     been continued for hundreds of years'.

92   Crude legends: analysed by Gilman, passim.

92–3 The Nancy school: Ellenberger, 85ff; Crabtree, 164ff.

93   Freud not impressed: to Fliess, 29 Aug. 1888, Masson.
     Freud visits Moser: Swales (1986) 33–4.
     Freud in Nancy: SE20:17–18, SE23:285; Swales (1986) 34ff.

93–4 Letters to Minna: Swales (1986) 35–6; Masson, quoting from letter of 28
     July 1889, 17n.

94   Walking with Fliess: to Fliess, 11 Aug. 1890 and 3 July 1899, Masson.

94–5 'Mathilde S.', Svetlin's clinic: E. Shorter, 'Women and Jews in a Private
     Nervous Clinic in Late Nineteenth-century Vienna', *Medical History*, 33
     (1989).

95   Mrs Silberstein's suicide: Boehlich, xiv–xv, 192.

95–6 Moving to Berggasse: Ernest Jones, I, 361; M. Grotjahn, 'A Letter by
     Sigmund Freud with Recollections of His Adolescence', *Journal of the*

American Psychoanalytic Association, 4 (1956).

96 'a rare human pleasure': 12 July 1892, Masson.

~ Janet c. 1891: 'J. C. N.', 'Book Forum', *American Journal of Psychiatry*, 148 (Dec. 1991); Ellenberger, 358ff.

97 Olfactory seizure: Thornton, 208; Webster, 158–9.

100 Aurelia Kronich: Swales (1988).

11: *Erotica*

101 Heroic few: Freud in '"Civilised" Sexual Morality and Modern Nervous Illness' says that 'mastering' the sexual instinct can 'steel' the character, but only in the case of 'a few specially favourably organised natures'. SE9:193, 196.

Three mentors: SE14:13–15.

102 Replacing God: Jung, 174.

Discussing with Fliess: e.g. 8 Feb. 1893, 'Draft B', Masson.

Mrs A.: 24 Nov. 1887, ibid.

Seeking a harmless contraceptive: to Fliess, 10 July 1893, ibid.

The culprits: 'Draft B', ibid.

Theory of toxins: Ernest Jones, I, 285; SE7:113, SE7:215–16, SE16:388–9; to Fliess, 2 April 1896, Masson. Swales (1983b) proposes that the toxin theory was 'derived by extrapolation specifically from cocaine, the drug having provided a model for the toxin'.

In February 1893: 'Draft B', Masson, 39.

103 'The sexual business': to Fliess, 6 Oct. 1893, ibid.

'my tiredness' and 'magic wand': to M.B., 2 Feb. 1886, *Letters*.

Jones on neurasthenia: Vol. I, 186.

104 'the three children': 10 Feb. 1886, *Letters*.

'potent legacy': E. Simon, 'Sigmund Freud, the Jew', in Leo Baeck Institute, *Year Book II* (1957).

'the messiah': 10 July 1893, Masson.

'a few months too late': 25 May 1895, ibid.

104–5 Three pamphlets: they were found in 1994 by a Bulgarian researcher, Chris Tögel.

105 'woman's sensibilities': SE3:277.

Messrs K. and F.: 23 Aug. 1894, Masson.

Wet-nurses: to Emmeline and Minna Bernays, 21 Oct. 1887, *Letters*.

105–6 Martha's fertility: John M. McGarry, F.R.C.O.G., has reviewed the evidence.

107 'prima donna': 12 July 1892; 'teacher': 8 Feb. 1897, Masson.

Ferenczi's notes: Dupont, 93.

emotional debts: SE2:69n, 'It might be called a "hysterical psychosis for the payment of old debts".'

'all the tears': ibid., 70n.

In 1914: SE12:170.

Munthe, 230.

Umbrella Girl: SE2:100–101n.

108 'threw her arms': SE20:27.

Fanny Moser's reputation: O. Andersson, 'A Supplement to Freud's Case History of "Frau Emmy v. N." in Studies on Hysteria 1895', *Scandinavian Psychoanalytic Review* 2 (1979). 'She nearly always seems to have had lovers and erotic relationships, sometimes with doctors whom she

consulted at the spas, or who lived in her house as her personal doctors.'
Wolf Man explains: Obholzer, 169.

12: *The Friend*

109 Twenty cigars a day: Ernest Jones, II, 430.
'Sword and buckler': F. to Lou Salomé, 8 May 1930, Pfeiffer. The
translator's phrase echoes Psalm 91, v. 4, 'his truth shall be thy shield
and buckler' (Authorised Version). Freud's German translates literally as
'protection and weapon'. German bibles, like the English, don't give the
phrase an aggressive connotation. But Freud evidently saw cigars as
weapons of attack as well as defence.
'orgy of taroc': to Fliess, 11 March 1900, Masson.
Sunday indigestion: Ernest Jones, II, 436.
Chicken and cauliflower: to Fliess, 25 May 1899, Masson.
Grünenthorgasse: Krüll 262.

110 Disapproving women: 8/11 Feb. 1897, Masson.
The 'jewel': 21 May 1894, ibid.
Physical attraction: c.f. F. to Ernest Jones, 8 Dec. 1912, 'some piece of
unruly homosexual feeling', Paskauskas.

111 The machine analogy: SE1:295, 'Project for a Scientific Psychology' (1895).
It is hard going. There is an extensive literature; Sulloway, 101–31, gives
an authoritative account. Freud's undated letter to Fliess, 'Draft G' (?Jan
1895), includes his 'schematic diagram of sexuality'.
'monomaniac': 21 May, Masson.

112 'Imagine': 6 Oct., ibid.
'abnormal sexual satisfaction': Masson (1992) 76.
Relieving women in labour: hostile review of Fliess, in Masson, 310n.

113 'Mr. F.': to Fliess, 14 May 1893, ibid.
Nose and genitalia: J. Riddington Young, F.R.C.S., personal
communication.
Perils of interruptus: to Fliess, 6 Oct. 1893, Masson; 'Draft E' (?June
1894).
Perils of abstention: SE3:150.
Freud's heart: more than a dozen letters to Fliess between 18 Oct. 1893
and 20 June 1898 refer to it.

114 'Something neurotic': 11 Dec. 1893, Masson.
'visions of death': 19 April 1894, ibid.
The 'angina' view: Schur, 62. Schur was Freud's doctor in the 1930s.
Treatment by Fliess: Ernest Jones, I, 366.
'The secret': 15 Oct. 1895, Masson; 'the riddles': 16 Oct. 1895, ibid.
'a single key': Masson, 25n, citing a 1904 interview with Freud in the
Neue Freie Presse.
'exclusive formulations': P.F. Cranefield, 'Josef Breuer's Evaluation of His
Contribution to Psychoanalysis', *International Journal of Psycho-Analysis*,
39 (1958), quoting from a Breuer letter to August Forel, 21 Nov. 1907.
'The problem is': 22 June, Masson.
Writing on a train: 7 Sept. 1912, Paskauskas.

115 'Breuer has declared': 28 June, Masson.
Breuer draws the analogy: SE2:211, 'We meet the same urge as one of
the basic factors of a major historical institution – the Roman Catholic
confessional.'
'partially evaporated': 12 July 1892, Masson.

'an obstacle': 29 Sept. 1893, ibid.
'no concern': 22 June 1894, ibid.
'a grandmother': 7 Feb. 1894, ibid.
'King David': 13/15 March 1895, ibid.
Myers's account: June 1894.
James's review: Clark, 258.

116 'abreacted': SE2:8.
The Neuro-psychoses': SE3:43; 'it is precisely', 52; 'dread of being overcome', 56.

117 Anxiety neurosis paper: SE3:87.
Eckstein's book: Masson (1992) 245.

117–18 Emma Eckstein: Masson (1992) 55–106 and 241–58. Swales thinks that Eckstein prompted Freud's 'seduction theory' (1982c, 1983c). Eckstein is thought to have been the 'Emma', molested as a child, described in SE1:353. Eckstein's operations: Eight letters to Fliess, between 4 March and 26 April 1895, describe events.

118 'I shall be able': 26 April 1896, Masson.
'unconscious wish': 4 May 1896, ibid.
'Freud's intellect': ibid., 134n.

119 Pappenheim's life: H. F. Ellenberger, 'The Story of "Anna O": A Critical Review with New Data', *Journal of the History of the Behavioral Sciences*, VIII (1972); Hirschmüller, passim.

120 Intimate lives: Kiell, 68; von Berger's review, ibid., 69.

121 'again a human being': 13 March 1895, Masson.

122 A harder bed: SE2:69n.

123 Erik Erikson: 'The Dream Specimen of Psychoanalysis', *Journal of the American Psychoanalytic Association*, 2 (1954).
Jung on the dream: 3 Dec. 1912, 'the mournful admission of your own neurosis', McGuire.

124 Too deep: SE4:111n, 'There is at least one spot in every dream at which it is unplumbable.'

13: *Seduction*

125 Minna comes to stay: to Fliess, 29 Nov. 1895, Masson.
'Our home': 9 Oct. 1899, ibid.
Gas explosion: to Fliess, 22 Nov. 1896, 'my new quarters', Masson; family accounts in Young-Bruehl, 33, 465.

126 'I dig it out': 27 Oct. 1897, Masson.
Published in France: SE3:143, 'Heredity and the Aetiology of the Neuroses'; 151: 'I owe my results to a new method of psycho-analysis'. The *Standard Edition* uses the hyphenated form, which is retained by many psychoanalytic journals, institutions and adherents as being more traditional than the lay person's 'psychoanalysis'.
A boy of twelve: SE2:211–12.

127 'strict precondition': 8 Oct. 1895, Masson.
'faint joy': 16 Oct. 1895, ibid.
Paper in French journal: SE3:143.
Second paper: SE3:162, 'Further Remarks on the Neuro-psychoses of Defence'.

128 Third paper: SE3:191.
Krafft-Ebing and Pappenheim: Hirschmüller, 103.

128n 'in full': 30 May 1896, Masson.

128   Freud's speaking style: Hanns Sachs, 'Freud: Master and Friend' (1945),
      in Ruitenbeek.
129   Stadlen: 'Tell it Not in Dan: The Untold Story of Freud's Seduction
      Theory', transcript of an unscripted talk at the Institute of Contemporary
      Arts, London, 19 March 1994. Many have written about the theory and
      Freud's reasons for setting it aside. Cf F. Cioffi, 'Was Freud a Liar?'
      Listener, 7 Feb. 1974; Masson (1992), a full-length study which concludes
      that the theory was correct and should never have been revoked; Krüll,
      ·24–70 passim; J.G. Schimek, 'Fact and Fantasy in the Seduction Theory:
      A Historical Review', *Journal of the American Psychoanalytic Association*,
      35 (1987); Swales (1988) 130–2, 154–5; H. Israëls and M. Schatzman,
      'The Seduction Theory', *History of Psychiatry*, IV (1993); K.R. Eissler,
      'Comments on Erroneous Interpretations of Freud's Seduction Theory',
      Journal of the American Psychoanalytic Association, 41 (1993); M.B.
      Macmillan, 'Freud's Expectations and the Childhood Seduction Theory',
      Australian Journal of Psychology, 29, 3 (1977); Webster, passim.
130   Groping 'Emma': SE1:353–5, the 'Scientific Project'. The paper was never
      edited for publication; if it had been, no doubt Freud would have changed
      the name to protect Eckstein's identity.
131n 'earliest experiences': SE4:184; 'These scenes': SE17:50–1.
132   'it will do no harm': SE2:295; 'must be extracted': SE3:153; 'by
      emphasising': SE3:269.
      Fliess's cousin: to Fliess, 4 Dec. 1896, Masson.
      'When I thrust': to Fliess, 3 Jan. 1897, ibid.
133   'It may indeed': SE3:322.
135   In March (1896): 16; in April: 26/28; in May: 4. All Masson.
      'By one of those': 2 Nov. 1896, ibid.
      In February (1897): 8/11; in April: 6; in May: 31. All Masson.
136   'in twenty minutes': to Fliess, 29 March 1897, ibid.
      Fliess derided: ibid., 233–4n.
137   In June: 30 June 1896, ibid.
      'euphoria': 12 April 1897, ibid.
      Martin's teeth: 16 May 1897, ibid.
      'Rumour has it': 31 Oct. 1897, ibid.
      Told Fliess in 1894: 22 June, ibid.
138   'That famous age-limit': 29 Sept. 1896, ibid.
      Critical for Jewish men: Schur, 25.
      'specifically Jewish nature': to Jung, 16 April 1909, McGuire.
      The dangerous age: ibid.
      Mathilde's operation: Young-Bruehl, 44–5.
      Attacking Venus: SE6:169.
139   'obsessional ideas': 3 Jan. 1897, Masson.
      Young woman patient: to Fliess, 28 April 1897, ibid.
140   'nice dream': 2 Nov. 1896, ibid.
      'none of us': 27 April 1898, ibid.
141   'the deepest depths': 7 July 1897, ibid.
      Jones on Freud's psychoneurosis: Vol I, 334–5.
      Jones to Strachey: 27 Oct., Jones Papers.
144   Crews; 1994 conference: 'Recovered Memories of Abuse: True or False?'
      17–18 June, organised by the Psychoanalysis Unit of University College,
      London, in association with the Anna Freud Centre.
      The epigraph: to Fliess, 4 Dec. 1896, 17 July 1899, Masson.

Freud on the epigraph: to Werner Achelis, 30 Jan. 1927, *Letters*, but c.f. Bettelheim, 15, who suggests that Freud used the motto to 'deny importance to the world at large by concentrating all interest on the dark aspects of the psyche'.

14: *Himself*

145 'neurotic experience': 22 June 1897, Masson.
Erotic dream: 31 May 1897, ibid.

146 *Dreams* version: SE4:247–8.
Annual earnings: 4 June 1896, '[my] laboriously earned sixteen to seventeen thousand [presumably florins]', Masson. In 1896 1 fl. = 21 English pre-decimal pence, so 16,500 fl. = 346,500 pence = approx. £1,440 × 32 for a century's inflation = £46,000. F. to Fliess, 8 Feb. 1897, says he earned 700 florins the previous week, evidently more than usual; a forty-week year at that rate would produce a present-day £78,000.

146n Bonaparte version: F.R. Hartman, 'A Reappraisal of the Emma Episode and the Specimen Dream', *Journal of the American Psychoanalytic Assocation*, 31, 3 (1983). Hartman was quoting from two Bonaparte documents about her analysis with Freud, a manuscript and a typescript, which few people have seen: another Freud mystery. Borch-Jacobsen has an entertaining Appendix about the secrecy surrounding Bonaparte material.

146 Walking tour: Ernest Jones, I, 367.

147 'wonderful wood': to Fliess, 22 June 1897, Masson.
'grave doubts': to Fliess, 14 Aug. 1897, ibid.
'magically beautiful': SE5:463ff.
Martha's period: to Fliess, 8 Aug. 1897, Masson.
'a punch made of Lethe': 6 Sept. 1897, ibid.

148 'Finally': SE4:196.
Freud's 'teacher': 3–4 Oct 1897, Masson.
Reddish water: ibid.

149 'a journey': ibid.
'determined . . .': ibid.
'how my warm friendships': SE5:483.
'I live only': 27 Oct. 1897, Masson.

150 'one should draw': 15 Oct. 1897, ibid.
'harmoniously': 5 Nov. 1897, ibid.
'I must wait': 3 Dec. 1897, ibid.
'Happiness': to Fliess, 16 Jan. 1898, ibid.
'Immortality': to Fliess, 12 Dec. 1897, ibid.
First hint: 31 May, 'Draft N.', ibid.

151 'Since I have not told it': 5 Nov. 1897, ibid.
'primary addiction': 22 Dec. 1897, ibid.
Like little animals: to Fliess, 14 Nov. 1897, ibid.
Tentative passage: SE4:260ff.

152 'Enough of my smut': 22 Dec. 1897, Masson; 'Dreckology': 29 Dec. 1897, ibid.; 'wild dreams': 4 Jan. 1898, ibid.
'I longed': SE5:468–71.
Belligerent paper: SE3:265.
Scottish tweeds: to Sam Freud, 22 Feb. 1920, Rylands.

153 'bound to excite': SE5:451–2.
'entirely cold': 24 Jan., Masson.

Visiting Nothnagel: 8 Feb., ibid.
Wider conflict: Barea, 301–2.

154 Lueger's jokes: J. Meyers, 'Freud, Hitler and Vienna', *London Magazine*,
Aug.–Sept. 1974.
Freud nominated: Masson, 231n; further details, including the officials'
report, H. Leupold-Löwenthal, 'Years of Isolation', *Sigmund Freud House
Bulletin*, 1, 2 (1977).
Daytime fantasy: 4 Jan., Masson.
Jubilee rumour: to Fliess, 9 Feb. 1898, ibid.

155 'No one even suspects': 16 May 1897, ibid.
Krafft-Ebing and sexual wishes: R. Sand in Gelfand and Kerr, 228.
'deep in the dream book': 9 Feb., Masson; 'torture': 18 May, ibid.; 'the
dream, the dream': 24 May, ibid.
At Aquileia: to Fliess, 14 April 1898, ibid.
The castle dream: SE5:463ff.
Newspaper report: Anzieu, 315.

156 Summer travels: Ernest Jones, I, 368.

156–7 The 'Signorelli' episode: Freud's accounts are in SE3:289–97, 'The
Psychical Mechanism of Forgetfulness', and Chapter 1 of *The
Psychopathology of Everyday Life*, SE6:2–7; also to Fliess, 22 Sept. 1898,
Masson.

157 Turkish overcoat: SE4:204–6.

15: *Books of Dreams*

158 Most adult dreams: SE5:396, 'the majority of the dreams of adults deal
with sexual material and give expression to erotic wishes'.
Cobenzl clinic: to Fliess, 9 Oct. 1899, Masson.
'any drop of alcohol': to Fliess, 16 April 1896, ibid.
'punch made of Lethe': 5 Dec., ibid.

159 'I cannot manage': to Fliess, 8 July 1899, ibid.
At Berchtesgaden: Ernest Jones, I, 369.
'grubby gods': 1 Aug. 1899, Masson.
'Every attempt': 27 Aug. 1899, ibid.
Explaining 2,467: SE6:242–3.
'bound to meet': to Fliess, 16 Sept. 1899, Masson.

160 'another year' and 'tortuous sentences': 21 Sept. 1899, ibid.
'copious and convenient': SE4:105.
'I would advise': ibid., 121.

161 'I simply cannot': 17 Feb. 1911, McGuire.
'As you know': 9 June 1898, Masson.
'disguises' and 'No other work': 28 May 1899, ibid.
Revised proofs: 6 Aug., ibid.

162 Printing history of *Dreams*: Ernest Jones, I, 395.
Oliver at the bookshop: Roazen (1993) 184.
'It is the fate': SE4:262; 'Here once more': SE4:100.

163 'secret meaning': SE4:146.
'We dream': 9 June 1899, Masson.
'Paradise': SE4:245.

163–4 The butcher's wife: SE4:147ff.

164 the clever patient: SE4:151–2.

165 'the only villain': SE5:485.
'One evening': SE4:216.

166 'I must desist': SE4:206.
 Wish versus reality: to Fliess, 19 Feb. 1899, Masson.
 A dozen readers: 9 and 14 Dec., ibid.
167 'path-breaking' work: 21 Dec., 1899, ibid.
 'my cellar hole': ibid.
 New Year letter: 29 Dec., ibid.
 David's review: Kiell, 114–18.
 Freud on David: 'unhappy man', to Fliess, 6 Aug. 1899, Masson;
 'somewhat diffuse', to Fliess, 1 Feb. 1900, ibid.
168 'more precisely': B. Urban, 'Schnitzler and Freud as Doubles',
 Psychoanalytic Review, 65, 1 (1978), 152.
 Dr Raimann: Ernest Jones, I, 395–6.
 'we think highly': SE4:130; contradicted, 256ff.
 'Whether or not': 10 July, Masson.
 Rycroft, 'the existence': *The Innocence of Dreams*, xi.
169 'conquistador': 1 Feb. 1900, Masson.

16: *Freudian Slips*

170 'neurotic swings': 12 Feb., Masson; 'impoverished', 'back bent', 23 March,
 ibid.
 'laughing gas': 21 Sept. 1899, ibid.
 'sunshine, flowers' and 'philistine': 11 March 1900, ibid.
 Iron strong-box: to Fliess 20 May 1900, ibid., c.f. SE6:137–8.
171 'Yes, I really am': to Fliess, 7 May 1900, ibid.
 'Such spiteful glee': 1 July 1900, ibid.
 The tablet: 12 June 1900, ibid.
 Emmanuel and Sam: ibid.
172 'I know': 7 May 1900, ibid.
 The new Kepler: to Fliess, 27 June 1899, ibid.
 'beautiful novelties': to Fliess, 22 Dec. 1897, ibid.
 Walk near Berchtesgaden: to Fliess, 3 July 1899, ibid.
172–3 Before they quarrelled: to Fliess, 1 and 12 Feb. 1900, ibid.
173 Holiday plans: to Fliess, 10 July 1900, ibid.
 Murder plans: Swales (1982d). A strange book by an American clinical
 psychologist, Paul Scagnelli, *Deadly Dr Freud. The Murder of Emmanuel
 Freud and Disappearance of John Freud*, includes the Fliess episode in
 its chronicle of Freud as villain.
 Fliess's account: Sulloway, 220–1.
174 'a dreadful case': to Jung, 17 Feb. 1908, McGuire.
174n 'I once loved him': to Karl Abraham, 3 March, Abraham and Freud.
 'I am delighted': to Fliess, 21 Sept. 1899, Masson.
174 'struck that morning': SE6:210–11.
175 Jones, 'no sexual attraction': Vol I, 168.
175–80 Jung's tales about Minna: J. Billinsky, 'Jung and Freud',
passim *Andover Newton Quarterly*, 10 (1969). Kerr, 135ff, examines the evidence,
 including unpublished notes of Billinsky's interview with Jung.
 Minna as governess: Young-Bruehl, 29.
 Gramophone: Harald Leupold-Löwenthal, in conversation, 1994.
 'very good-looking': Kerr, 136.
 'very ugly': Han Israëls, who saw the letter, in conversation, 1994.
 'Minna loves her': Ernest Jones, I, 129.
175–6 'little woman': 6 Jan. 1885; pretty ribbons: 18 Aug. 1882; both to Martha,
 Letters.

176 'Burn your letters': 7 Feb. 1886, ibid.
'closest confidante': 21 May 1894, Masson.
'done begetting': 11 March 1900, ibid.
Sex in 1915: Gay (1989), 163.

177 'avoid the period': 1 July 1900, Masson.
Hitschmann's letter: 26 March 1954, Jones Papers.
Freud's travels: Ernest Jones, I, 369–70, quoting letters that are still
unpublished. His account may not be accurate.

178 Travelogue: to Fliess, 14 Sept. 1900, Masson.
Swales's account: (1982a).

179 'I *must*, after all': 24 Sept. 1900, Masson.

180 'Not everything': 25 Nov. 1900, ibid.

180 Missing letters: Gay (1990) 178–9. C.f. Gay (1989) 752–3, where he
examines the evidence for an affair between Freud and Minna and is
unconvinced but uneasy.

181 Work in progress: 14 Oct. 1900, Masson.
'fascinating new system': 'What Freudism Is', *Saturday Review*, 11 July.
'morbidly introspective': M. Solomon, *Journal of Abnormal Psychology*
(1916), quoted in Kiell.

182 'purposes in people': the phrase is not from *Everyday Life* but from the
section on parapraxes in *Introductory Lectures*, SE15:74.
'I fail to see': *Everyday Life*, SE6:159.
'continuous current': ibid. 24.

183 Gath, not Dan: Stadlen, 'Tell it Not in Dan: The Untold Story of Freud's
Seduction Theory', transcript of an unscripted talk at the Institute of
Contemporary Arts, London, 19 March 1994.
'egoistic': SE6:276; 'the urge', 221; 'Acquiescence', 276.

184 Some critics: notably Timpanaro.
At Thumsee: Martin Freud, 68–71. But Freud's eldest son was not always
reliable.

185 'Jewish electricians': Gay (1990) 168.
Lueger and the myths: Barea, 318–19.

185–6 Hilsner trials: L. Wolff, 102–104.

186 Freud in Rome: Ernest Jones, II, 21–2; to Fliess, 19 Sept. 1901, Masson.
'eight to twelve days': to Fliess, 7 Aug. 1901, ibid.
Letter home: Ernest Jones, II, 22.
'Others are that clever': 11 March 1902, Masson.
Freud seeks patronage: ibid.; two letters to Elise Gomperz, 25 Nov. and 8
Dec. 1901, *Letters*.
'all sorts': to Fliess, 15 Feb. 1901, Masson.

187 Marie von Ferstel: to Fliess, 11 March 1902, ibid.
'on my way home': SE18:190.

188 Jones on Stekel: Ernest Jones, II, 8.
Stekel on *Dreams: Neue Wiener Tagblatt*, 29 and 30 Jan. 1902.
Four postcards: Ernest Jones, II, 8–9. Phyllis Bottome, an early
biographer of Adler, said, 62–3, that others who 'joined the psychoanalytic
circle' included Arthur Schnitzler and Karl Kraus, but gave no details.
Schnitzler was certainly an admirer, and Kraus was not yet hostile to
psychoanalysis.
'From the year 1902': SE14:25.
'like a furnace' and 'kaleidoscope': Wittels, 133–4. Wittels was Freud's
first biographer.

17: *Unhappy Families*

189 Humble Katharina: 'A Confirmed Bachelor', Schnitzler (1973).
    Lanzer and the maid: SE10:261.

190 Flexner: *Prostitution in Europe*.
    Brothel sites: Zweig, 74.
    von Coburg affair: extracts from *Die Fackel*, 'The Torch', quoted in Szasz, 133ff.

191 Hervay affair: Timms (1986) 64ff.
    Visiting card: ibid., 94.
    Freud's courage: 'Torch', 8 Nov. 1905, in Timms (1986) 94.
    Women patients: B. Brody, 'Freud's Case-load' (1970) in Ruitenbeek found 66 women in 107 cases. My casual survey of 43 patients, omitting the all-female cast of *Studies on Hysteria* but including some cases that Brody wouldn't have known about, contains 26 women; not a very different proportion.

191–8 Dora's story: SE7:7–122. The case has attracted dozens of
passim commentaries. C.f. Decker's exhaustive *Freud, Dora, and Vienna 1900*; P.J. Mahony's meticulous *Freud's Dora*; Ernest Jones, I, 398, who sees the case as 'really a continuation of *The Interpretation of Dreams*'; Malcolm (1988), who thinks the 'prurient interest [in Dora] that Freud attributes to others was his own'; S. Marcus, 'Freud and Dora: Story, History, Case History', *Partisan Review*, 41 (1974), who sees it as 'a new form of literature', its narrative enriched by Freud's dislike of Dora.

193 Bauer's shop: Freud raises the tone by calling it a 'palace of business' and referring to 'clerks'. Anthony Stadlen says it was undoubtedly a shop.
    Physiology of Love: by Paolo Mantegazza (1831–1901), an Italian doctor and early sexologist, widely read.

197 Dora's marriage and after: Decker, 151ff.
    Consulting Deutsch: ibid., 171.

198 'repulsive': F. Deutsch in *Psychoanalytic Quarterly* (1957).
    Malcolm Sophie Freud: reviewing Decker in *Psychoanalytic Books* 3, 3 (Fall 1992).
    'If the physician': SE7:254.
    'good for nothing': ibid., 263.
    Proletarians and princes: *Minutes*, 5 Dec. 1906, Nunberg and Federn.
    'six months to three years': SE7:254.

199 Bruno Goetz: 'Some Memories of Sigmund Freud' (1952), in Ruitenbeek.
    'unfit for existence' and 'severest cases': SE7:263.
    'we physicians': ibid., 258.
    Spielmeyer and Friedlander: quoted in Kiell, 286, 294.

200 Ellis's *Studies*: Ferris, 5–6.
    'nauseous': 8 Feb. 1902.
    'If you have come': Ernest Jones, I, 376.
    The teacher's stoop: Roazen (1992) 174.

200–1 Freud as a lecturer: Ernest Jones, I, 375; Wittels, 130. At the clinic: H. Sachs, 'Freud: Master and Friend' (1945), in Ruitenbeek.

201 New quarters for the mad: P. Haiko et al., '"The White City" – the "Steinhof" in Vienna', *Sigmund Freud House Bulletin*, 5, 2 (Winter 1981).

202 The Weininger affair: Gilman, 77ff; Johnston, 158ff; Sulloway, 223ff; SE10:36n.
    'consternation': Masson, one of three letters from Fliess to Freud included in the book.

202–3 The Achensee and Breslau story: Fliess to F., 26 July 1904, Masson; Ernest Jones, I, 344–5; SE6:143–5, where Freud misdates the 1900 meeting with Fliess to 1901. Students of Freudian slips assume he was wishing their friendship had lasted longer than it did.

203 'strong homosexual current': 23 July, Masson.
'So what Oscar Rie told me': 26 July, ibid.

204 Returned in dreams: to Fer. 6 Oct. 1910, 'My dreams at the time [the previous month, in Sicily] were, as I indicated to you, entirely concerned with the Fliess matter . . .', Brabant.

204–6 *Three Essays*: SE7:130–243; c.f. A. Stone, 'Book Forum', *American Journal of Psychiatry*, 148, 12 (Dec. 1991).

204n 'unappetising': to Jung, 2 Nov. 1911, McGuire. C.f. C. Wolff and, for a warm appraisal, Isherwood, 19ff.

205 Ellis on Freud: 'Freud's Influence on the Changed Attitude Toward Sex', *American Journal of Sociology*, XLV, 3 (Nov. 1939).

206 'overrated the importance': SE7:190.
'over-estimated the frequency': SE7:274; c.f. Esterson, 21–2.
Soyka's review: 21 Dec. 1905.
Printing history: Ernest Jones, II, 321.

18: *Dr Joy and Dr Young*

208 Emma Jung: Ellenberger, 668.
Jung's visit: Jung (hereafter, J.) to Freud, 20 and 26 Feb. 1907; to J., 21 Feb; McGuire, 24n.
'the future' and 'I know of none': 1 Jan. 1907, ibid.

209 replastering: L. Binswanger, 'My First Three Visits with Freud in Vienna' (1957), in Ruitenbeek.
'My wife is rich': J. to F., 29 Dec. 1906, McGuire.
500 penises: J. to F., 4 Oct. 1911, ibid.
Jung and his patients: Storr (1986) 30–1.

210 'hunger': 23 Oct. 1906, McGuire.
'I am delighted': 6 Dec. 1906, ibid.
'I could not decide': Jung, 172.

211 Freud asks for their dreams: Binswanger, in Ruitenbeek.
Hungarian psychiatrist: Sándor Ferenczi.
Two-edged letter: 19 March 1908, *Letters*.
Jung's dream: J. to F., 2 Nov. 1907, McGuire.
Heatstroke: Martin Freud, 125–30.

212 Visions and second sight: Ellenberger, 661.
Lonely child and world of fables: Jung, 21–39 passim.
Two personalities: Jung, 61–2.

212–13 Table-rapping: H.F. Ellenberger, 'C.J. Jung and the Story of Helene Preiswerk: a Critical Study with New Documents', in Micale; Jung, 127–8.

213 Table and bread knife: Jung, 125–7.
At the Wednesday meeting: Kerr, 132ff.
Graf's recollection: 'Reminiscences of Professor Sigmund Freud', *Psychoanalytic Quarterly*, II (1942).
Eitingon and Bleuler: Kerr, 127–8.
degenerates: Ernest Jones (1990) 157.

214 'the gang': Binswanger, in Ruitenbeek.
22 members: Ernest Jones, II, 9; half near Berggasse: Decker, 259. E. Shorter, 'The Two Medical Worlds of Sigmund Freud', in Gelfand and Kerr, is an authoritative account of the society in 1910, when it had 27 medical members, of whom 21 were Jewish, including one woman.
Instant analysis: Ernest Jones, II, 35–6.
'Sadger's rubbish': to J., 2 Jan. 1910, McGuire.
Sadger's improprieties: Wilhelm Reich, quoted in M. Sharaf, 107–8.
'Wednesday patients': Ernest Jones, II, 153.
Fond of women: Edward Timms in conversation, 1994.
Undoing the bow: SE6:176.
Never quite trusted: Ernest Jones, II, 152–3.
215 Wittels, Kraus and promiscuity: Timms (1995) 56–75 passim.
'academy of love': *Minutes*, 12 Feb. 1908, Nunberg and Federn.
1908 paper: '"Civilised" Sexual Morality and Modern Nervous Illness', SE9:181.
216 'abstain under protest': Timms (1995) 49.
Beardless Freud: six letters to Ernest Jones, 1952–5, from Ernst Freud, Oliver Freud and Mathilde Hollitscher, often contradictory. Jones Papers, CFB/FO4, FO5, FO6.
Shooting a picture: Roazen (1993) 131.
217 Rosenfeld into Rank: Fitch, 164.
'Little Rank': to Ferenczi, 12 March 1911, 'little Rank . . . has held on very valiantly alongside me', Brabant.
Entertaining Trotsky: Ernest Jones, II, 151.
218 Wedding story: Jung, 68.
Ringing doorbells: ibid., 215–16.

19: *Windows on the World*

220 'no longer plagued': 31 March 1907, McGuire.
'tree of paradise': 30 May 1907, ibid.
'I could hope': 7 April 1907, ibid.
221 The Russian girl: 23 Oct. 1906, ibid.
'In her dreams': 6 July 1907, ibid.
222 'I hope to be in Sicily': 10 July 1907, ibid.
'almost cowardly': 2 Sept. 1907, ibid.
'solitary existence': 19 Sept. 1907, ibid.
At the movies: 22 Sept. 1907, *Letters*.
Amsterdam conference: Ellenberger, 796–8; Ernest Jones, II, 125–7.
'vain old buffer': 11 Sept. 1907, McGuire.
223 'Breuer and I': J. to F., 11 Sept. 1907, ibid.
Alt and Ziehen: ibid.
'a Celt from Wales!': ibid, 1–33.
224 'splendid isolation': J. to F., 30 Nov. 1907, ibid.
In Munich: Ernest Jones (1990) 153.
Jones's childhood: ibid, 1–33.
225 Deptford scandal: ibid., 135–8; Brome, 39–42; *News of the World*, 25 March–6 May 1906, passim.
225–6 Hospital scandal: Jones (1990) 139–41; Brome, 49–50.
226 'practice of coitus': Jones (1990) 21.
sexual opportunities: Jones to F., 28 June 1910, Paskauskas.
'I suppose': to J., 8 Dec. 1907, McGuire.

227 'Obsessive Actions': SE9:117.
An imaginary stain: SE9:121.

227–30 Lanzer's analysis: SE10:155, 'Notes upon a Case of Obsessional Neurosis'.
Commentaries on the case include Mahony (1986), which first disclosed
the patient's name; Rosenzweig's unsettlingly discursive *Freud, Jung, and
Hall the King-Maker*, 28–32, 268ff; R.M. Gottlieb, 'Technique and
Countertransference in Freud's Analysis of the Rat Man', *Psychoanalytic
Quarterly*, LVIII (1989); F.J. Sulloway, 'Reassessing Freud's Case
Histories: The Social Construction of Psychoanalysis', *Isis*, 82 (June 1991).

229 Pince-nez spectacles: Anthony Stadlen has the only known photograph of
Lanzer.
What Lanzer's family believed: Stadlen, in conversation.

230 'how wretchedly': 30 June 1909, McGuire.
'The religion of Israel': E. Simon, 'Sigmund Freud the Jew', in Leo Baeck
Institute, *Year Book II* (1957).
Bestiality proposal: J.S. Jones, 110.

231–2 Hitler in Vienna: J.S. Jones, passim; Shirer, 25–7.

232 Hitler as psychopath: Rosenzweig, 72–3.
Freud on Hitler: Gilman, 82.
Freud on the Viennese: to J., 31 Jan. and 17 Feb., McGuire.
Change of name: Ernest Jones, II, 10.
'my one-time friend': 17 Feb. 1908, McGuire.
'surely not accidental': 20 Feb., ibid.

233–6 Salzburg meeting: McGuire, 143n; Ernest Jones, II, 45–9; Ernest Jones
(1990) 156ff.

233 'Freud, Wien': Ernest Jones (1990) 156.
'to his mind': 3 May 1908, McGuire.
Brill the emigrant: Brabant, 10n.

234 Ferenczi's biography: A. Haynal in Brabant, xvii–xviii.
'now and then': to Ferenczi, 10 May 1908, Brabant.

234–5 Gross's career: Ernest Jones (1990) 163–4; Maddox, 91–106, passim; M.
Stanton, 'The Case of Otto Gross: Jung, Stekel and the Pathologisation of
Protest', in Timms and Robertson.

234n Trotter's consolation: Ernest Jones (1990) 158.

235 'a fine man': to J., 29 May 1908, McGuire.
'truly healthy': J. to F., 25 Sept. 1907, ibid.
'he analysed me': 25 May 1908, ibid.
Knocking noises: J. to F., 26 June 1908, ibid.
'reverberating impact': 30 April 1908, ibid.

236 omitted details: SE7:112.
'erroneous impression': SE7:261.
'refreshed': to J., 3 May 1908, McGuire.
Emmanuel at Salzburg: to Martha Freud, 29 April 1908, *Letters*.

20: *Sons and Heirs*

237–8 Hirschfeld; Bloch: C. Wolff, 53, 79, 119.

238 Prof. Eulenburg: in Senator and Kaminer, 334.
'On the Sexual Theories of Children': SE9:209.

239 Little Herbert/Little Hans: relevant commentaries include P. Chodoff, 'A
Critique of Freud's Theory of Infant Sexuality', *American Journal of
Psychiatry*, 123, 5 (Nov. 1966); Gay (1989) 255–61; Esterson, 56–62;
Eysenck; J. Wolpe and S. Rachman, 'Psychoanalytic Evidence: A Critique

Based on Freud's Case of Little Hans', *Journal of Nervous and Mental Diseases*, 131 (1960).

'a little Oedipus': SE10:111.

241 'the untrustworthiness': SE10:102–3.

241–2n Graf's article: *Psychoananalytic Quarterly*, II (1942).

242 'You'd like to be Daddy': SE10:92.

243 Graf in later life: McGuire, 587; Rosenzweig, 160.

Family holiday: to Anna Freud, 7 July 1908, *Letters*; Ernest Jones, II, 57.

Freud in England: ibid., 57–8; SE6:227.

243–4 Philipp's daughter: Pauline ('Polly') Hartwig.

244 Jung at Kusnacht: McGuire, 224n; Ellenberger, 682.

'My dear friend': 15 Oct. 1908, McGuire.

'If I am Moses': 17 Jan., ibid.

245–7 The Spielrein story: Kerr has a definitive account.

245 'To be slandered': 9 March 1909; McGuire.

'your' prudery: 17 Jan 1909, ibid.

'We have noticed': 19 Jan., ibid.

246 'without punishing': Carotenuto, 168. This Italian account of the Spielrein affair was written with access to Spielrein's papers, found in Geneva in 1977.

A child called Siegfried: ibid., 86.

246 Love affair, letters, the bloodstains: ibid., 93–7.

247 Jungs in Vienna: McGuire, 215n.

'crown prince': to J., 16 April 1909, ibid.

247n The Graf apartment: Oliver Freud to Ernest Jones, 16 April 1953, Jones Papers.

247 Episode with bookcase: Jung, 178–9.

248 'That last evening': J. to F., 2 April 1909, McGuire.

The 'Customs' dream: Jung, 186–7.

'my paternal dignity': 16 April, McGuire.

249 Spielrein writes from Zurich: Carotenuto, 91.

Freud asks innocently: 3 June 1909, McGuire.

'seeking revenge': 4 June 1909, ibid.

'*a narrow escape*': 7 June 1909, ibid.

249–50 Freud–Spielrein exchanges: Carotenuto, 113–15, 92, 94.

249 'little . . . explosions': 18 June 1909, McGuire.

'a sly one' and 'the miscreant': Carotenuto, 104.

249–50 'a piece of knavery': 21 June 1909, McGuire.

250 Freud apologises: Carotenuto, 114–15.

Invitations to America: Rosenzweig, 23–4.

'Naturally': 30 Dec. 1908, McGuire.

'America should bring': 10 Jan. 1909, Brabant.

'they will drop us': 17 Jan. 1909, McGuire.

'gentle zephyrs': J. to F., 11 Nov. 1908, ibid.

251 Planning his wardrobe: 4 July 1909, Brabant.

21: *America*

252f Clark University, its founder and G.S. Hall: Rosenzweig, passim.

252 'twentieth (!) anniversary': 30 Dec. 1908, McGuire.

Janet in America: Hale (1995) 143.

252–3 Hall and morality: ibid., 100–4; Rosenzweig, 105–6.

253 'Who could have known': to Oskar Pfister, 4 Oct. 1909, Ernest Jones, II, 64.
Jones in Canada: Ernest Jones to F., 26 Sept. 1908, Paskauskas.
'my harem': Ernest Jones to F., 10 Dec. 1908, ibid.
Freud tells Jung: 9 March 1909, McGuire.
'What you say': 11 March, ibid.
Out to make money: Ernest Jones to F., 7 Feb. 1909, Paskauskas.

254 Meeting in Bremen: Ernest Jones, II, 61.
Emigrants; sealed wagons: Aschheim, 36–7.
Stern; the day in Bremen: Freud's travel diary, quoted in Rosenzweig, 51–7.

255 'alarmed by the intensity': Jung, 180.
'meditation': 5 Oct. 1909, Brabant.
'ménage à trois': 9 July 1910, ibid.
'group analysis': Ernest Jones, II, 61–2.
Famous passage: Jung, 181–2.

255–6 Best-known dream: ibid., 182–3.

256 'My Indian summer': 2 Feb. 1910, McGuire.
'Don't they know': quoted as hearsay in Noll, 47.

256–7 In New York: Ernest Jones, II, 62; Rosenzweig, 253.

257 'the nicest part': Roazen (1992) 382.
Hired car: Rosenzweig, 61.
'For Eli alone': ibid.

257–8 Freud's weak bladder: ibid., 64ff, 292.

257 Ambition and incontinence: SE9:175.

258n Freud's dream: Rosenzweig, 65.

258 'miles of corridors': Ernest Jones, II, 67.
'Boston School': Hale (1995) 116ff.

259 Formidable James: Rosenzweig, 14ff; 'what Freud was like', ibid., 3.
Putnam's disgust: Hale (1971), Introduction, 21; second thoughts: Ernest Jones, II, 65.
'delightful old man': Ernest Jones to F., 7 Feb. 1909, Paskauskas.
the only man: Ernest Jones, II, 65.
Lecture programme: Rosenzweig, 119.

260 'Is there a sexuality': ibid., 426.
Jones's professor: Ernest Jones to F., 20 April 1910, Paskauskas.
'In Europe': SE20:52.
Freud's cigar: Rosenzweig, 307.

261 'seventh heaven': 14 Sept. 1909, Jung, 402.
'somewhat ridiculous': Dupont, 184, entry of 4 Aug. 1932.
Pappenheim in America: Rosenzweig, 108–9.
At Putnam's camp: Hale (1971) Introduction, 23–4; Freud's letter to his wife, 16 Sept. 1909, ibid.
Abdominal pains: to Ferenczi (hereafter, Fer.) 10 Jan. 1910, Brabant.
Core of converts: Hale (1995) 177–8; identifying themselves, 223; New York Society, 317.

261–2 Popular psychoanalysis: ibid., 397–415, passim; Brill in the *New York Times*, 416.

262 'your light hat': 4 Oct. 1909, McGuire.
'occasionally': 14 Oct. 1909, ibid.

22: *Naughty Boys*

263 'ill-mannered boys': to Fer., 3 March 1910, Brabant.
Hints to Ferenczi: 1 Jan. 1910, ibid.
'beyond the infantile': Fer. to F., 5 Feb. 1910, ibid.
No 'ennobling influence': to Fer., 3 April 1910, ibid.

264 In Chicago: Emma Jung to F., McGuire, 301.
Jung's millionaire: McLynn, 247; McGuire, 240, 241n. McCormick, a wealthy industrialist, was married to a Rockefeller.
Nuremberg meeting: McGuire, 304n; Grand Hotel, ibid., 573.
Ferenczi speaks: Kerr, 285–6; Ernest Jones, II, 76–7.
At Stekel's meeting: Wittels, 140; Brome, 77.
Compromise: Kerr, 287.
Zentralblatt: SE20:50.
Appointing Adler: to Fer., 3 April 1910, Brabant, where Freud says he means to 'withdraw from all official influence'. This is not what happened.
'the infancy': ibid.
Optimistic paper: 'The Future Prospects of Psycho-analytic Therapy', SE11:141.

265 Kraus outraged: *Torch*, 5 June 1908.
'Freud's greatness': in Kiell, 377.

266 Defending *Leonardo*: SE11:134, 63, 130–1.
'a man whose sexual need': ibid., 101; 'only with reluctance', ibid., 96–7.

266–7 Vulture fantasy: SE11: 61–2, 82–125, passim.

267 Pfister and Jung see it: J. to F., 17 June 1910, McGuire; so does Ferenczi: to F., 12 June 1910, Brabant.

267n 'Re the vulture': 27 May 1952, Jones Papers.

268 Freud cautions Wittels: *Minutes*, 12 Jan. 1910, Nunberg and Federn.
'Psychoanalysts' children': *Torch*, 9 April 1910.
'stupid rockets': to Fer., 12 April 1910, Brabant.
'Psychoanalysis is more important': Timms (1995) 98.
Novel and libel action: ibid., 93–103.
'you were close to me': ibid., 143.
Jones stops resisting: Ernest Jones to F., 18 Dec. 1909, Paskauskas.

269 'like Oliver Twist': 19 March 1909, ibid.
Titanic letter: 7 May 1912, ibid.
'better described': Ernest Jones, II, 144.
Masochistic streak: 19 June, Paskauskas.
Contrite Jones: 2 Jan. 1910, McGuire.
'you seem to have changed': 22 May 1910, Paskauskas.
Jones and sex in Toronto: Ernest Jones to F., 30 March 1910, 8 Feb. 1911, ibid.
Joseph Collins: Ernest Jones to F., 4 May 1910, ibid.; Ernest Jones, II, 31

270 Post at Harvard: Hale (1971) 206
Woman with revolver: Jones to F., 8 Feb. 1911, Paskauskas.
Why not sue?: to Jones, 26 Feb. 1911, ibid.
Jones to Putnam: 13 Jan. 1911, Hale (1971).

270n 'entirely truthful': page xxi.

270 'eighty-one days': 24 April, Brabant.

271 'On the whole': 13 Feb., ibid.
Brigittenau hostel: J.S. Jones, 143–4.
Jung goes sailing: J. to F., 6 Aug. 1910, McGuire.

Old Mrs Bernays: Ernest Jones, II, 87.
Sunset at Noordwijk: to J., 10 Aug. 1910, McGuire.
'My patience': Ernest Jones to F., 25 July 1910, Paskauskas.
'Something interesting': Ernest Jones, II, 88.
'my dear son': 10 Aug. 1910, McGuire.

271-2 Analysing Mahler: Ernest Jones, II, 88-9; Kennedy, 3-4, 72-3.
First evening at hotel: Brabant, 214-15n.
'a dear fellow': 24 Sept. 1910, McGuire.; c.f. F. to Fer., 2 Oct. 1910, Brabant.

273 Ferenczi and the Pálos women: Brabant, passim.
'more than one way': *Minutes*, Nunberg and Federn.
'dirty my hands': 29 Oct., McGuire; F.'s reply, 31 Oct. ibid.

274 A decent man: to J., 25 Nov. ibid.
'The crux': 3 Dec. 1910, ibid.
Fur-lined overcoat: Lieberman, 147, quoting the Hungarian analyst, Sándor Radó.
The mad judge: SE12:9-82, 'Psycho-analytic Notes on an Autobiographical Account of a Case of Paranoia'.
'a little Fliess': to Fer., 16 Dec. 1910, Brabant.
'opened up the wounds': 22 Dec. 1910, McGuire.
Minor errors: to Fer., 19 Feb. 1911, Brabant.

274-5 Series of debates: Ernest Jones, II, 148ff; to Ernest Jones, 26 Feb. 1911, Paskauskas, which also has 'clever, but . . . dangerous'.

275 Graf's views: *Psychoanalytic Quarterly*, II (1942).
Weygandt and Galileo: Ellenberger, 798.
Stekel makes his peace: to Fer., 2 May 1911, Brabant.
'The other boy': to Ernest Jones, 14 May 1911, Paskauskas; 'abnormal individual', to Ernest Jones, 9 Aug. 1911, ibid.

275-6 Salomé, Adler and Freud: Salomé to F., 3 Nov. 1912, Pfeiffer; F. to Salomé, 4 Nov., ibid.

23: *The Break with Jung*

277 Jung sees a lawyer: J. to F., 23 Jan. 1912, McGuire.
Won over: 3 Aug., Brabant.

277-8 Anthony Storr: (1986) 29.

278 Goethe's 'great-grandson': Jung, 52 and n.; J. to F., 18 Jan. 1911, McGuire.

279 Shroud of Turin: Donn, 131-2
The gas episode: to J., 22 Jan., 9 Feb., 17 Feb. 1911, McGuire.; J. to F., 14 Feb., ibid.
Eve as Adam's mother: to J., 17 Dec. 1911, ibid., citing Rank.
'wandering alone': 17 April 1910, ibid.

280-1 *Transformations*: Jung's title is sometimes given as 'Symbols
passim of Transformation' or 'Psychology of the Unconscious'. I have used Kerr, McLynn, Noll; Storr (1986).

280 'reminiscences of mankind': Steele, 234.
'on the same track': 5 Nov. 1911, Paskauskas.
Jung's fate: Ernest Jones to F., 25 March 1926, ibid.

280-1n Freud's destiny: SE12:250.

281 Freud at Küsnacht: McGuire, 443n.
Mrs Jung's letters: 30 Oct., 6 Nov., 14 Nov., 24 Nov. 1911, McGuire.

282 Ephesus paper: SE12:342.

'I would never': 3 March, McGuire.

Doubts about incest: J. to F., 23 May 1912, ibid.

Binswanger at Kreuzlingen: McLynn, 194; to Fer., 30 May 1912, Brabant, which also mentions Zeppelin.

283 The 'Kreuzlingen gesture': to J., 23 May and 13 June, McGuire; J. to F., 8 June and 18 July, ibid. All 1912.

'florid neurosis': 28 July, Brabant.

Kann's addiction: F. to Ernest Jones, 8 Nov. 1912 etc. Paskauskas.

'deeply neurotic': F. to Fer., 23 June 1912, Brabant.

'the pure theory': Ernest Jones to F., 30 July 1912, Paskauskas.

'secret council': to Ernest Jones, 1 Aug. 1912, ibid.

'like the Paladins': 7 Aug. 1912, ibid.

'I dare say' and membership orders: to Ernest Jones, 1 Aug. 1912, ibid.

284 Jung announced: J. to F., 22 March 1912, McGuire.

Jones reads proofs: Ernest Jones to F., 4 Sept. 1912, Paskauskas.

Freud reads them: to Ernest Jones, 22 Sept. 1912, ibid.

Fordham Lectures: McGuire, 513n.

284–5 Jung boasts: to F., 11 Nov. 1912, ibid.

285 'your harping': 14 Nov. 1912, ibid.

The Stekel row: ibid.

Meeting in Munich: ibid., 521–2n.

A gentleman's unconscious: Ernest Jones (1990) 211.

285–6 Freud's account: to Fer., 26 Nov. 1912, Brabant.

286 'Pharaoh' version: Jung, 180–1; 'name omitted' version: Ernest Jones (1990) 212.

'my authority': 8 Dec. 1912, Paskauskas.

Contrite letter: 26 Nov. 1912, McGuire.

'a bit of neurosis': 29 Nov. 1912, ibid.

287 'jump in the lake': 30 Dec. 1912, Brabant.

'With the Moltzer?': 26 Dec. 1912, Paskauskas.

288 Visiting prostitutes: Fer. to F., 26 Dec. 1912, Brabant; fearing syphilis: Fer. to F., n.d., Brabant, 412–13.

Sleeping with Lina: Ernest Jones to F., 30 Jan. 1913, Paskauskas.

'altogether satisfied': to Fer., 2 Feb. 1913, Brabant.

24: *Fables*

289 'unshakable bulwark': Jung, 173.

'none other': 12 May 1913, Brabant.

'I dare say': 12 June 1911, McGuire.

'I promise': 15 June 1911, ibid.

290 Myers on hysteria: SE2:xv.

Freud invited: to Ernest Jones, 26 Feb. 1911, Paskauskas.

'spook-hunting' and 'poor James': 17 March 1911, ibid.

Freud's SPR paper: SE12:260.

291 At Mrs Seidler's: Fer. to F., 5 Oct. 1909, Brabant.

Freud's response: 6 and 11 Oct. 1909, ibid.

At Mrs Jelinek's: Fer. to F., 20 Nov. 1909, ibid.

291–2 The homosexual man: Fer. to F., 17 Aug. 1910, ibid.

292 Freud convinced: 20 Aug. 1910, ibid.

'*a great soothsayer*': 22 Nov. 1910, ibid.

'earth-shaking': 3 Dec. 1910, ibid.

'methodology' and 'destiny approaching': letters of 22 Nov. and 3 Dec., ibid.

SPR scandal: A telepathic hoax had been exposed.

292–3 Horse tales: Fer. to F., 5 June 1912, Brabant.

293 'particularly poor': SE18:193.

In Freud's dreams: see Note to page 204.

'I have had good reason': SE12:320.

Totem and Taboo: SE13:xiii–161.

'unconscious understanding': SE13:159.

'very remarkable thing': SE14:194, 'The Unconscious'.

294 'God help me!': 9 April 1913, Paskauskas.

'It would be': SE13:143n.

295 'There rose before me': SE20:67–8.

'actually *did*' and 'may safely be assumed': SE13:161.

'Just So Story': SE18:122.

295–6 Wet Sunday afternoon: Clark, 355.

296 Eleven-hour day: 24 May 1913, Brabant.

296n 'restored to life': 12 May 1914, ibid.

296 Fantasy of parricide: Andréas-Salomé, 104.

'near-mad': Binion, ix. C.f. Peters.

Salomé and Tausk: Roazen (1970); 'a blond fellow': Andréas-Salomé, 37.

296–7 'lion's den': 20 March 1913, Brabant.

297 'as if spellbound': to Salomé, 10 Nov. 1912, Pfeiffer.

'pink tulips': Pfeiffer, 215, quoting Salomé's journal, 9 Feb.; roses: Andréas-Salomé, 131.

Another Jones: to Fer., 4 May 1913, Brabant; also, 482n.

The Pálos triangle: Fer. to F., 12 May 1913, ibid.

'a jewel': to Fer., 13 May 1913, ibid.

'blooming . . . very warm feeling': 9 July 1913, ibid.

Analyst's temptations: SE12:164–6.

'incomparable fascination': ibid., 170.

298 Stoical Jones: Ernest Jones to F., 11 June 1913, Paskauskas.

London apartment: Ernest Jones to F., 19 Nov. 1913, ibid. Ernest Jones (1990) 227.

Kann's kitten: Ernest Jones to F., 13 Sept. 1913, Paskauskas.

Antique seals: Ernest Jones, II, 175; Grosskurth, 57.

Dinner in the Prater: to Fer., 17 June 1913, Brabant; Ernest Jones, II, 398.

298–9 'incurable disease': R.N. Stromberg, '1910: An Essay in Psychohistory', *Psychoanalytic Review*, 63, 2 (1976).

299 Colonel Redl: Zweig, 160ff; Johnston, 55.

Jung's dreams: Jung, 199–200.

Jung's detractors: McLynn, 240.

At Munich: Ernest Jones, II, 114ff; McGuire, 549n.

'a personal nature': 'Statement by the Editor', in the *Yearbook*, McGuire, 551n.

'my prediction': 22 April 1914, Paskauskas.

300 'the truth is': SE14:62; 'no one need be': ibid., 7; 'without any': ibid., 49.

'a good clobbering': 29 June, Pfeiffer.

'better-class magazines': Ernest Jones to F., 22 Aug. 1913, Paskauskas.

Articles in London: D. Rapp, 'The Early Discovery of Freud by the British General Educated Public, 1912–1919', *Social History of Medicine*, 3, 2 (1990).

Ostracism threatened: Ernest Jones (1990) 227.

Neurologists walk out: E. Glover in Hobman.

London Society: ibid.

301 £60 or £70: calculated from Ernest Jones to F., 9 Jan. 1914, Paskauskas.

Loe's wedding: to Jones, 2 June 1914, ibid.

301–2 Anna's girlhood: Young-Bruehl 53ff; 'a little odd': Gay (1989) 432.

301 'only daughter': to Anna Freud, 21 July 1912, quoted in Gay (1989) 431.

Letter from Merano: Young-Bruehl, 57–8.

302 Anna in England: ibid., 65ff; to Sam Freud, 7 July 1914, Rylands.

'I know': Young-Bruehl, 67.

'She does not claim': 22 July 1914, Paskauskas.

'beautiful character': 27 July 1914, ibid.

303 Pankejeff hears the news: Gardiner, 90.

'personal involvement': 28 June 1914, Brabant.

'So we are rid of them': Abraham and Freud. The editors changed 'pious parrots' to 'disciples'.

'not very hopeful': to Abraham, 26 July 1914, ibid.

On the Thames; rumours; escorting Anna: Ernest Jones to F., 27 July, Paskauskas.

Buying up morphine: 3 Aug., ibid.

'Krupp and Zeppelin': Ernest Jones, II, 193. The letter, undated in Jones, is evidently the one in Abraham and Freud dated 13 Sept., but the words 'Krupp and Zeppelin' have been removed.

Faint memory: 22 Sept. 1914, Abraham and Freud.

25: *War*

305 'Do you still': 14 Nov., Pfeiffer.

'stark staring mad': 19 Nov., ibid.

'I do not doubt': to Salomé, 25 Nov., ibid.

Oliver the engineer: his letter to Jones, 23 Nov. 1953, Jones Papers.

'my pride': Young-Bruehl, 115.

305–6n 'the neurosis came': to Arnold Zweig, 28 Jan. 1934, quoted in Gay (1989) 429fn, which also reports Oliver's analysis. The letter was included in *The Letters of Sigmund Freud and Arnold Zweig* (1970), but the references to Oliver's neurosis were removed by the editor, who was Ernst Freud, Oliver's brother.

306 In the trenches: to Salomé, 31 Jan. 1915, Pfeiffer.

Dreaming of death: Ernest Jones, II, 202–3; to Fer., 10 July 1915, Falzeder.

Anna's dreams: Young-Bruehl, 72–3.

Freud disappointed: Roazen (1993) 129; c.f. F. to Sam Freud, 28 July 1926, 'None of them [Oliver, Ernest, Martin] can boast of a satisfactory position or a good income': Rylands.

'Wolf Man speaking': Mahony (1984), 146. There are numerous commentaries on the case. Among them: Storr (1989) 104ff; F. Crews, 'The Unknown Freud', *New York Review of Books*, 18 Nov. 1993; P.J. Mahony, 'Freud's Cases: Are They Valuable Today?', *International Journal of Psycho-Analysis*, 74 (1993); D. Carroll, 'Freud and the Myth of the Origin', and S. Fish, 'Witholding the Missing Portion: Power, Meaning and Persuasion in Freud's "The Wolf-Man"', in Spurling, Vol. II (1989); Esterson, 67–93.

307 Pankejeff's early life: his 'Memoirs' in Gardiner.

In Vienna: ibid.; Obholzer, 38–9, 94–5.
'incapacitated': SE17:7.
'compulsive tendencies': 8 Feb. and 13 Feb. 1910, Brabant.
'unbridled': SE17:104.
The wolves: ibid., 29ff.
308 Making love: ibid., 37–8.
309 What Pankejeff thought: Obholzer, passim.
'a new father': Gardiner, 89n.
'Are we confronting': Mahony (1984) 78.
309–10 'as alone': 30 July 1915, Pfeiffer.
310 Seven papers destroyed: see B. Silverstein, '"Now Comes a Sad Story":
Freud's Lost Metapsychological Papers', Stepansky, Vol. 1 (1986).
Freud's metapsychology: see Holt, passim.
'The nervous system': SE14:120.
'sporadic character': 2 April 1919, Pfeiffer.
What Freud said earlier: to Salomé, 30 July 1915, ibid.; to Ernest Jones,
30 June 1915, Paskauskas.
311 To Putnam, 8 July: Hale (1971).
Unpublished notes: Gay (1989) 163, 673.
312 At Freud's lecture: to Fer., 31 Oct. 1915, Falzeder.
312 and n Ella Haim: Falzeder, 79n; persuaded by Freud: Oliver to Ernest Jones, 23
Nov. 1953, Jones Papers.
312 'The old material': to Fer., 31 Oct. 1915, Falzeder.
'censored wishes': SE15:143.
312–13 Fortune-teller: 16 Dec. 1915, Falzeder; stuffed-up, 9 March 1916, ibid.;
umbrella, 17–22 Oct. 1916, ibid.; middle-aged woman, 17 Jan. 1916, 20 Nov.
1917, ibid.; liaisons and parapraxis, 18 Nov. 1916, ibid.
313 Freud's comments: 4 Feb. and 12 March 1916, ibid.
'rather frail': 20 May 1917, Abraham and Freud.
Surfeit of flowers: to Abraham, 8 May 1916, ibid.
Iron Crosses: 1 Aug. 1915, ibid.
Jones's letter: 30 May, Paskauskas.
'happy England': 13 July 1916, Falzeder.
Tatra Mountains: Ernest Jones, II, 216.
'a superfluity': to Abraham, 21 Aug. 1917, Abraham and Freud.
313n Discarding Lina: Ernest Jones to F., 15 Jan. 1917, Paskauskas; marrying
Morfydd: Ernest Jones to F., 20 Feb. 1917, ibid.
313 'reformed character': Ernest Jones to F., 31 Oct. 1916, Paskauskas; F. to
Abraham, 20 May 1917, Abraham and Freud.
Subordinating his wife: Ernest Jones (1990), Mervyn Jones's Introduction,
xii, 244.
314 Rosa's grief: to Abraham, 13 July 1917, Abraham and Freud.
'Our future': to Abraham, 11 Nov. 1917, ibid.
'My mental constitution': 18 Dec. 1916, ibid.
'ridiculous': 31 Oct. 1915, Falzeder.
'raging': to Abraham, 22 June 1917, Abraham and Freud; 'embitterment', to
Abraham, 29 May 1918, ibid.
'A Difficulty': SE17:137.
Lay audience: the article was written for a well-known Hungarian literary
magazine, Nyugat ('West').
315 'your colleague Copernicus': 18 March 1917, Abraham and Freud.
'You are right': to Abraham, 25 March 1917, ibid.

Groddeck's long letter: 27 May 1917, Schacht.

'When a person': to Freud, June 1917, ibid., 40.

315–16 'your position': 29 July 1917, ibid.

316 'the unconscious act': to Groddeck, 5 June 1917, ibid.

'the coping stone': 11 Nov. 1917, Abraham and Freud.

Looking older: to Abraham, 5 Oct. 1917, ibid.; Abraham to F., 2 Nov. 1917, ibid.

'downright friendly': 20 Nov., Falzeder.

'grumpy and tired': 6 Nov., ibid.

Food shortages: Pick, 37; Hamilton, 130ff.

316n Effects of blockade: Peter Loewenberg, 'Germany, the Home Front (1)', in Cecil and Liddle, 556.

317 'We live on gifts': 29 May 1918, Abraham and Freud.

'carnivorous': to Abraham, 22 March 1918, ibid.

Vienna, 1918: Pick, 20–42, passim.

'Shivering with cold': 18 Jan. 1918, Abraham and Freud.

Pankejeff leaves Russia: to Salomé, 29 May 1918, Pfeiffer.

Tatra Mountains: Ernest Jones, II, 222.

Von Freund's biography: Falzeder, 96n; Ernest Jones, II, 221.

'the sort of person': to Abraham, 27 Aug. 1918, Abraham and Freud.

'little daughter': to Salomé, 1 July 1918, Pfeiffer.

318 'we think highly': SE4:130.

First wartime congress: SE17:206; SE20:54.

Civic reception: to Salomé, 4 Oct. 1918, Pfeiffer.

'pile of crap': 17 Nov. 1918, Falzeder.

Under fire: Ernest Jones, II, 227.

319 Morfydd Owen's death: Rhian Davies, her biographer-to-be, suggests (personal communication) that Jones's delay may have contributed to her death. She has also discovered that Morfydd left her husband more than once during their short marriage. His own account of the death, Ernest Jones (1990) 245, said that a wartime low-sugar diet contributed to the chloroform poisoning, not a viable explanation. His pocket diaries, with the Jones Papers, are unhelpful.

Polishing his English: Ernest Jones, III, 5.

What Freud lost: ibid., 3.

320 Eli's unfaithfulness: Young-Bruehl, 31.

'a nice way': to Sam Freud, 27 May 1920, Rylands.

'I am glad to say': 4 Dec. 1921, ibid.

320 and n Edward Bernays: 'Uncle Sigi' by Bernays, *Journal of the History of Medicine and Allied Sciences*, 35, 2 (1980), which includes Freud's letter (Aug. 1923); Rosenzweig 236–7; *The Times* obituary, 14 March 1995; 'an American "sharper"', 28 June 1920, Paskauskas.

320 'most desirable': 15 Oct. 1920, Rylands.

321 Unheated apartment: V. Brome, 'The View from the Couch', *Sunday Times Magazine*, 21 March 1971, quoting Alix Strachey.

Quoting Clough: 10 June 1919, Paskauskas.

Katharine Jokl: Mervyn Jones in Ernest Jones (1990) 249; Brome, 124ff.

Marriage and death: Fer. to F., 1 March 1919, Falzeder.

'Something demonic': to Fer., 4 March 1919, ibid.

Rumours: Ernest Jones, III, 26.

26: *Hard Times*

322 Abusing Lloyd George: Lieberman, 152.
   Favoured analysts: e.g. F. to Dr Thaddeus H. Ames, 11 June 1922. Frink
   Papers, Johns Hopkins Medical Institutions. See Note to 332–6
323 'Man flees': Higgins, 112ff.
   Reich's childhood: Sharaf, 36–47, passim.
   Visited Freud: ibid., 57.
   'I am alive': Higgins, 147.
   'a shark': Sharaf, 73.
323–4 Helene Deutsch: see Appignanesi and Forrester, 307–28, passim.
324 Tausk's suicide: Roazen (1970) 131. Roazen saw Tausk as rejected by Freud.
   He was attacked by Freudians for saying so.
   'I confess': 1 Aug. 1919, Roazen (1970), 139–40.
   Silberer and Stekel: Roazen (1992) 339.
325 'if she really were': 13 March, Pfeiffer.
   'faultless blessing': 4 Dec., Rylands.
   Anna's analysis: Young-Bruehl, 80–90, passim.
326 Second analysis: ibid., 122.
   'suppressed genitality': to Salomé, 10 May 1925, Gay (1989) 441. The version
   in Pfeiffer was censored.
   Beating fantasies: Young-Bruehl, 103ff.
   Lampl anecdote: ibid., 95–6.
   'often together': ibid., 96.
326–7 Lampl, Bernfeld and Eitingon as suitors: Roazen (1992) 438, citing
   interviews with contemporaries. Roazen (1993) 80, cites Eva Rosenfeld, who
   was in Freud's circle: she 'told me that Anna had confided to her a hopeless
   love for Max Eitingon'.
326 Eitingon as spy: Roazen (1993) 80, 209.
327 Bernays as suitor: Young-Bruehl, 95.
   Martin's marriage: to Sam Freud, 27 Oct. 1919, Rylands.
327 and n Martin's philandering: Sophie Freud (his daughter), 291–7.
327 Mathilde's abortion: to Ernest Jones, 3 Sept. 1912, Paskauskas.
   'Very strange!': 11 March 1914, Brabant.
   'the cleverest': to Sam Freud, 26 June 1923, Rylands.
328 'blown away': Ernest Jones, III, 20.
   'the ultimate aim': ibid., 293.
   'lamentable muddle': Strachey to Jones, 11 Sept. 1955, Jones Papers.
   'Better . . . that the truth': SE15:206, *Introductory Lectures*, XIII.
   Recent evidence: M. Solms, *International Journal of Psycho-Analysis*, 75
   (1994), reviewing Ilse Grubrich-Simitis, who is the queen of Freudian textual
   revisionists.
329 New York dentist: Ernest Jones to F., 25 Nov. 1919, Paskauskas; F. to Ernest
   Jones, 11 Dec. 1919, ibid.
   Forty crowns: Obholzer, 34.
   Strachey discovers Freud: Meisel and Kendrick, 26–7.
   'Each day': ibid., 29–30.
330 Difficulty understanding: to Ernest Jones, 12 Oct. 1920, Paskauskas.
   Useful translator: Ernest Jones to F., 7 May 1920, ibid.
   Freud on translation: to Ernest Jones, 12 April 1921, ibid.
   'even rarer': Ernest Jones to F., 6 May 1921, ibid.
   Alix Strachey on Freud: V. Brome, *Sunday Times Magazine*, 21 March 1971.
   She also quoted Freud as saying, 'The greatest invention some benefactor can

give mankind is a form of contraception which doesn't induce neurosis.' So his obsession of the 1890s was still flourishing.

Stracheys on others: Meisel and Kendrick, passim.

330–1n Red ink incident: SE9:121; Woolf's letter: Nicolson, 134.

331 Popular articles: Ernest Jones, III, 30–1.

Poem in *Punch*: Sam Freud to F., 20 Oct. 1920; F. to Sam, 16 and 28 Nov. 1920, Rylands.

Scientific fund: Bernays, *Journal of the History of Medicine and Allied Sciences*, 35, 2 (1980).

$25,000: Ernest Jones, III, 108–9.

332 $100,000: ibid., 121. Paul Ries, who has studied Freud's associations with the cinema, says that Goldwyn, visiting Europe in 1924, sent a telegram asking, 'Let me know when I can see you.' Freud replied, 'Never.' Personal communication.

The Secret of a Soul: Ries's 'Popularise and/or Be Damned: Psychoanalysis and Film at the Crossroads in 1925', *International Journal of Psycho-Analysis*, 76 (1995), is a definitive account.

332n *Sensational Revelations*: ibid.

332–6 Frink and Bijur: the story, ignored or played down in most accounts, is based here on the Frink Papers, hereafter FP, at Johns Hopkins Medical Institutions (See Acknowledgements). The letters from Freud are typescript and handwritten copies.

332 Ames's biography: Paskauskas, 428n.

Plans for 1915 visit: Ernest Jones to F., 1 July 1914, ibid.

333 'honest fellow': ibid.

Frink's book: Ernest Jones to F., 31 Dec. 1918, ibid.

Irritating habit: Ernest Jones, III, 39.

'I thought it': to T. H. Ames, 9 Oct. 1921, FP.

Angelika and Abraham: Ames to F., 10 Sept. 1921, FP.

Mrs Bijur paid: a typescript 'statement' by her, undated, headed 'Re Dr Horace W. Frink over period of years 1920–24', FP.

334 Mrs Bijur in Vienna: letter of 10 Sept., FP.

Frink's love for her: letter of 9 Oct., ibid.

Freud advised divorce: the 'statement', ibid.

'depends on': 27 July 1921, ibid.

'savant or charlatan?': letter of 10 Sept., ibid.

'sham morality': letter of 9 Oct., ibid.

335 'cool and reasonable': to Frink, 12 Sept. 1921, ibid.

The divorces: undated 27-page typescript by Helen Frink Kraft (Frink's daughter), headed 'Events in the life of Horace W. Frink, M.D.', 12–13, FP.

At Berchtesgaden: to Ernest Jones, 24 Aug. 1922, Paskauskas.

Hints about money: to Frink, 17 Nov. 1921, 'you are not yet aware of your phantasy of making me a rich man. If matters turn out all right let us change this imaginary gift into a real contribution to the Psycho-analytic Funds'. FP. C.f. to Ernest Jones, 24 Aug. 1922, 'I think it would do [Frink] good to . . . impress his future wife who is rich and not mean', Paskauskas.

336 Striking Angelika: the 'statement', FP

Frink's hallucinations: L. Edmunds, 'His Master's Choice', *Johns Hopkins Magazine* (April 1988), 44; to Ernest Jones, 25 Sept. 1924, Paskauskas.

Denigrating Brill and subsequently: 'Events' typescript, FP.

Frink's decline and death: ibid.

'the supposed leader': typescript headed 'Hedonistic Periods of Human

History', filed as 'Meyer n.d. c. 1924', Meyer Papers at Johns Hopkins.
'forcible suggestion': typescript headed 'Dr Frink – May 27th 1924', ibid.

27: *Cancer*

338 'The real reason': 29 May 1921, Schacht.
'9 hours': 4 June, Paskauskas.
338–9 Harz trip: SE18:175; Ernest Jones, III, 85.
339 'Psychoanalysis and Telepathy': SE18:177.
340 Three subsequent papers: 'Dreams and Telepathy' (1922), SE18:197; 'Some
Additional Notes on Dream-Interpretation' (1925), Part C, 'The Occult
Significance of Dreams', SE19:135; *New Introductory Lectures* (1932), XXX,
'Dreams and Occultism', SE22:31.
'secret inclination': SE22:53.
Allowing homosexuals: Grosskurth, 110.
Lay analysts: ibid., 109–10.
The *Verlag*: Ernest Jones, III, 31–2.
Rank v. Jones: ibid., 48ff.
'arbiters of the world': 29 Sept. 1924, Paskauskas.
Freud drawn in: to Ernest Jones, 6 April 1922, ibid.; Ernest Jones to F., 10
April 1922, ibid.
341 'Something in me': 30 March 1922, in Ernest Jones, III, 88.
Pension Moritz: to Sam Freud, 20 Aug. 1922, Rylands.
Rosa's daughter: ibid.; her pregnancy, Ernest Jones, III, 91.
Berlin meeting: ibid. 91–2.
As Freud put it: to Ernest Jones, 12 April 1921, 'And success means money',
Paskauskas.
342 Groddeck's 'It': Groddeck to F., 27 May 1917, Schacht.
Redefining the unconscious: SE19:4ff.
Horse and rider: SE19:25.
'dark inaccessible': SE22:73.
342–6 Freud's cancer: Ernest Jones, III, 94–104; Schur, 347–66; J. C. Davenport,
'Sigmund Freud: The Inside Story', *Medical Historian* (Liverpool Medical
History Society) July 1993; to Ernest Jones, 25 April 1923, Paskauskas; to
Joan Rivière, 8 May and 2 July 1923, *International Review of Psycho-
Analysis* 19 (1992); to Salomé, 10 May 1923, Pfeiffer.
344 At San Cristoforo: Ernest Jones, III, 97–8; Gay (1989) 423–5; Grosskurth,
131–4; Ernest Jones to F., 12 Sept. 1923, Paskauskas.
345 Ernest Jones to his wife: Brome, 139.
Anna to Salomé: Young-Bruehl, 118.
To Rome: Ernest Jones, III, 98–9.
Schur's suggestion: Schur, 356–7.
346 Pichler operates: Schur, 361–3.
'enfeebled': to Sam Freud, 25 Oct. 1923, Rylands.
Back to work: to Abraham, 4 Jan. 1924, Abraham and Freud.
Clothes-peg: Ernest Jones, III, 107.

28: *Defections*

347 Rank laughs: Ernest Jones, III, 98.
'young, poorly-dressed': Lieberman, 147.
Rank and Ferenczi collaborate: Ernest Jones, III, 58–9.
The Trauma of Birth: Lieberman, 230; Gay (1989) 472ff; SE23:216.
'most important progress': to Fer., 24 March 1924, in Ernest Jones, III, 61

'Rank's "birth trauma"': 4 Feb. 1924, 'Six Letters of Sigmund Freud and Sándor Ferenczi [etc]', introduced by Ilse Grubrich-Simitis, *International Review of Psycho-Analysis*, 13 (1986).

348 Rank in New York: Lieberman, 225, 227ff.
Boasting to Ferenczi: ibid., 245.
Rank's neurosis: Ernest Jones, III, 72.
'attracted by the dollar': to Salomé, 17 Nov. 1924, Pfeiffer.
Rank comes and goes: Ernest Jones, III, 74ff; Lieberman, 246–60.
Rank boasting: to Ernest Jones, 27 Sept., 1926, Paskauskas.
'bury him': Lieberman, 260.

349 Polite reply: to Wittels, 24 Dec. 1923, Timms (1995) 104.
'hateful caricature': to Wittels, 8 Jan. 1929, ibid., 132.
Within easy reach: to Sam Freud, 11 July 1924, 'Here we are on the top of a mountain, 2700 ft. high, two and a half hours by rapid train from Vienna', Rylands.
Footnote to Katharina: SE2:134.
Eckstein's death: F. R. Hartman, 'A Reappraisal of the Emma Episode and the Specimen Dream', *Journal of the American Psychoanalytic Association* 31, 3 (1983); Masson (1992) 255–6.
Breuer snubbed: Hirschmüller, 191.
'strikingly confirmed': Abraham to F., 8 Sept. 1925, Abraham and Freud.
Ida Fliess/Freud correspondence: Masson, Introduction, 5–6.

350 'a menace': *Torch*, Dec. 1924, in Szasz, 123.
Anna to Salomé: Young-Bruehl, 207.
Kept in ignorance: to Sam Freud, 21 Aug. 1925, Rylands.
Dreaming of the dead: to Sam Freud, 6 May 1928, ibid.
'not what my father': 19 Dec. 1925, ibid.

351 Angina: Ernest Jones, III, 127.
Skeletal diary: Molnar, with copious annotations.
'Conclusively': 6 Nov. 1930, ibid.
'a great honour': to Sam Freud, 18 Aug. 1930, Rylands.
Passionate transference: Bertin, who had access to a range of Bonaparte material. Much remains undisclosed.
'You must have had': ibid., 156.

351n Bonaparte biography: Appignanesi, 329–51, passim.

351–2 'Who has changed': Bertin, 155; 'her husband's work', ibid., 174; 'liaison', ibid., 155.

352 'a mirror'; ibid., 155.
Tea with Guilbert and Ferenczi letter: Molnar, 47.

352–3 'men for centuries': Gay (1989) 501.

353 'I do not yet have': 5 Nov., Masson.
'veiled': SE7:151.
Paper of 1908: '"Civilised" Sexual Morality and Modern Nervous Illness', passage quoted, SE9:199.
Hirschfeld on women: C. Wolff, 87.

354 Karen Horney: see Quinn, 'Flight from Womanhood', 220–1; penis envy, 223ff.
'does not tally': SE21:243.
Lacked superego: SE19:257–8. The paper is 'Some Psychical Consequences of the Anatomical Distinction Between the Sexes'.
'excellent women': SE22:116.

354–5 What Wortis heard: 'Fragments of a Freudian Analysis', *American Journal of*

Orthopsychiatry, X (1940).
355 'I have listened': ibid.
Emil Ludwig: Ruitenbeek, 213; the interview was in 1927.
'I did not become' and chandelier story: 'personal memoir' by Victor Ross, in Heller, 35–6.
Wortis and the dream: Ruitenbeek, citing Wortis.
356–7n Burlingham's biography: Heller, 74ff; Roazen (1993) 47.
357 Summer solstice: Heller, 114–15.
'there is one thing': ibid., 116.
Oxford and Schneewinkel: to Salomé, 28 July 1929, Pfeiffer.
'Like Wolf': ibid.

29: *Waiting and Hoping*
360 'oceanic': to Rolland, 14 and 20 July 1929, *Letters*.
'indissoluble bond': SE21:65.
'banal truths': 28 July 1929, Pfeiffer.
12,000 copies: Ernest Jones, III, 158.
361 'more a collection': *New York Review of Books* (April 1975).
'I pointed out': SE10:185.
True's reprieve: E.T. Dean, Jr, 'War and Psychiatry: Examining the Diffusion Theory in Light of the Insanity Defence in Post-World War I Britain', *History of Psychiatry*, iv (1993).
361–2 Robert Graves: cited in Fussell, 203–4.
362 Forty-one members: E. Federn in Freud Supplement to *Journal of the History of the Behavioral Sciences*, VIII, 1, (Jan. 1972), 29.
In America: ibid., 25; N. G. Hale., Jr, 'From Berggasse XIX to Central Park West: the Americanization of Psychoanalysis, 1919–1940', *Journal of the History of the Behavioural Sciences*, 14 (1978).
Altruistic dreams: Ernest Jones to F., 2 Jan; F. to Jones, 27 Jan. 1910, Paskauskas.
Russell's niece: T.G. Davies, '"Truth Is a Point of View": An Account of the Life of Dr Ernest Jones', in Murray and Turner.
Daily Express: 31 Dec. 1928.
362–3 *Times* leader: 31 Dec. 1925.
363 'Frau' and 'Mrs': Ernest Jones, III, 49–50.
Nervous publishers: ibid., 87.
Improper practices: minutes of the Psycho-Analysis Committee, 20 Dec. 1928, BMA Archives.
'There is no school': ibid.
364 'A Zeppelin?': 6 Dec. 1928, ibid.
'step by step': 21 Jan. 1929, Paskauskas.
The report: *Report of the Psycho-Analysis Committee*, British Medical Association, July 1929.
365 'I cannot help': 16 May, Paskauskas.
365n 'Anyway': Mervyn Jones, 14.
365 Cut both ways: to Ernest Jones, 31 May 1927, Paskauskas.
'Is anyone': 23 Sept., ibid.
'The mood here': 30 Sept. 1927, ibid.
'schoolboy level': to Eitingon, 14 Jan. 1929, in Young-Bruehl, 172.
365–6 'special obligation': H. F. Ellenberger, 'The Story of "Anna O": A Critical Review with New Data', *Journal of the History of the Behavioral Sciences*, VIII (1972), 26.

366 Border incident: Johnston, 75; Sharaf, 124.
'rotten affair': 16 July 1927, in Gay (1989) 589.
'going downhill': 6 Dec. 1927, Rylands.
367 German psychiatrists and barbarians: SE20:49.
Eitingon begs him: Ernest Jones, III, 123.
Meeting Bullitt: ibid., 160–1.
367n The collaboration: Jones to Strachey, 16 and 18 July 1956, Jones Papers.
367 Hitler at the Moritz: Toland, 142.
368 'from the precipice': Ernest Jones to F., 9 Sept. 1932, Paskauskas.
'thirsty for honesty': 3 Oct. 1910, Brabant.
Freud naked: ibid.
Ferenczi's methods: Dupont, passim.
'vibrations': 29 May 1933, Paskauskas.
369 Kissing people: to Fer., 13 Dec. 1931, Ernest Jones, III, 174–6.
Wounding sentence: quoted in Masson (1992) 159–60.
Freud's advice: Dupont, 185–6.
Lying on the floor: ibid., 93.
370 'Confusion of Tongues': Masson (1992) quotes from it extensively, 149ff.
Ferenczi at Berggassse: Masson (1992), 171.
Talking dog: ibid.
Telling Anna and Eitingon: Gay (1989) 583–4.
371 Suppressed by Jones: Masson (1992) 152–3.
'the old era': 29 May 1933, Paskauskas.
'lurking demons': Ernest Jones, III, 190.

30: *'A Fanatical Jew'*

373 'makes me look': Ernest Jones, I, 3.
'unfortunately': Roazen (1993) 192.
Amalie's death: Ernest Jones, III, 162; Molnar, 79, 80, 82.
'no mourning': 15 Sept. 1930, Paskauskas.
Torments: to Ernest Jones, 4 Jan. 1931, ibid.
374 summer residence: Molnar, 96. The house was on the main road in
Pötzleinsdorf, not far from Grinzing and the Kahlenberg.
Freiberg ceremony: Molnar, 110–11.
To Max Schiller: 26 March 1931, *Letters*.
374n Massage parlour: *The Times* (London) 9 Dec. 1996, quoting from the
Jerusalem Post. The Sigmund Freud Professor of Psychoanalysis at the
Hebrew University in Jerusalem suggested that 'Freud would have regarded
the house's current usage with some amusement.'
374 Nemon and Federn: to Eitingon, 3 Aug. 1931, quoted in Molnar, 100.
'I am angry': Molnar, 100.
375 and n Hitler in Vienna: Toland, 254–6; Shirer, 132.
375 Burning books: Molnar, 149; Gay (1989) 592.
376 'Jew Freud': Molnar, 149.
'How different': to Ernest Jones, 23 July 1933, Paskauskas.
'Besides': 7 April 1933, ibid.
'The world': Ernest Jones, III, 194.
Bauer's article: to A. Zweig, 28 Jan. 1934, Ernst Freud (1970).
377 Letter to H.D.: 'H.D.', 192.
378 Quarrelsome Europeans: Ernest Jones to Anna Freud, 2 July 1934; Ernest
Jones to Eitingon, 3 July 1934, both quoted in R. Steiner, 'It Is a New Kind of
Diaspora . . .', *International Review of Psycho-Analysis*, 16 (1989), 65.

'We can't create': Ernest Jones to Eitingon, 12 July 1933, ibid., 47.
'considerable prejudice': Ernest Jones to Anna Freud, 29 April 1938, ibid., 66.
Goering's psychotherapy: Cocks; G. Cocks, 'Psychotherapy in the Third
Reich: A Research Note', *Journal of the History of the Behavioral Sciences*,
14 (1978); M. G. Ash, 'Whose History? Whose Therapy? Psychoanalysis and
Psychotherapy in the Third Reich', *Bulletin of the History of Medicine*, 61
(1987).

379 'I slipped up': Jaffé; c.f. McLynn, 344–67, passim.
379n 'precious secret' and 'Germanic psyche': Jung ('The State of Psychotherapy
Today', 1934) quoted by Rosenzweig, 75.
379 Uncircumcised sons: Swales is usually credited with this arresting
information. E. Rice, 'The Jewish Heritage of Sigmund Freud',
Psychoanalytic Review, 81, 2 (1994) has supporting testimony: (1) from
Elliott Philipp, a cousin of Martha Freud (2) from Albrecht Hirschmüller,
Breuer's biographer, who consulted the birth records of Viennese Jews.
These leave space to include the fact of circumcision and the name of the
Mohel, the official circumcisor. In the case of Martin, Ernest and Oliver, the
space is blank.
Freud's obituary: *International Journal of Psycho-Analysis*, XXI (1940).
'held faithfully': to Siegfried Fehl, 12 Nov. 1935, quoted in Gay (1989) 597.
380 'in some place': Gilman, 35.
'secret yearnings': 30 March 1922, Ernest Jones, III, 88.
'defining and redefining': Gilman, 10.
'the new persecution': 30 Sept. 1934, Ernst Freud (1970).
'The Man Moses': ibid.
Moses and Monotheism: SE23:7–137. I have used these commentaries: Rice;
E. Rice, 'The Jewish Heritage of Sigmund Freud', *Psychoanalytic Review*, 81,
2 (1994); C.E. Schorske, 'Freud's Egyptian Dig', *New York Review of Books*,
27 May 1993; Gilman, 183–6, 190, 193; Ernest Jones, review of *Moses and
Monotheism*, in *International Journal of Psycho-Analysis*, XXI (1940).
'barbarous god': to A. Zweig, 13 Feb. 1935, Ernst Freud (1970).
381 'like "a ghost"': to Ernest Jones, 28 April 1938, Paskauskas.
'I am amazed': 27 April 1933, Molnar, 139.
382 'If there is any justice': Ernest Jones, I, 247n.

31: *Exodus*

384 The French journalist: Odette Panettier, Ruitenbeek, 103–111. Freud had
been renting the house, in Strassergasse, each summer since 1934.
385 Freud's oral treatment: Ernest Jones, III, 224, 518; Molnar, 210.
386 The letters to Fliess: Masson (1985), Introduction 4–10, quotes extensively
from the correspondence between Freud and Bonaparte.
The grouse joke: Molnar, 214.
'a poor fellow': 17 Dec. 1936, ibid., 210.
387 'more gloomy' and 'if our city falls': 2 March, Paskauskas.
Janet's visit: Ernest Jones, III, 228.
'I don't understand': 22 June 1937, Ernst Freud (1970). Ernest Jones, III, 223
gives the censored passage. Both misdate the letter to 1936.
'behaved unfairly ... rudeness': 9 April 1937, Ernest Jones, III, 228.
388 Anna to Jones: Jones Papers.
Visited by diplomat: Molnar, 229.
Stekel flees: M. Stanton, 'Wilhelm Stekel: A Refugee Analyst and His English
Reception' in Timms and Segal. Stekel killed himself with poison in an hotel
room in London, 25 June 1940.

388–9 First day of the new order: Pankejeff's 'Memoirs' in Gardiner, 117.
  389 Theatrical gesture: Molnar, xxiv, 230.
    Jones and Bonaparte in Vienna: Ernest Jones, III, 233ff, Molnar, 231.
    Stormtroopers at Berggasse: Ernest Jones, III, 234; Molnar, 231.
    Another Herr Freud: Young-Bruehl, 225.
389n 'Are we?': Public Record Office, FO371/21871.
389–90 Jews in the Prater, on the pavement: Stevens, 76ff.
  390 Still reluctant: Ernest Jones, III, 234.
    Anna questioned: ibid., 239; Molnar, 232.
    Veronal: Schur, 498.
    Visa instructions: B. Wasserstein, 'The British Government and the German Immigration 1933–1945' in Hirschfeld, 71–2.
    Hoare and Jones: Ernest Jones, III, 237; Molnar, 232.
390n Lampls excluded: Jones to Anna Freud, 29 April 1938. Quoted in R. Steiner, 'It is a New Kind of Diaspora . . .', *International Review of Psycho-Analysis*, 16 (1989) 67.
  391 Studying maps: ibid., 56.
    Domestic workers welcome: Tony Kushner, 'An Alien Occupation: Jewish Refugees and Domestic Service in Britain, 1933–1948', typescript at the Wiener Library, London, 8ff.
    Suicides: Stanton in 'Stekel', Timms and Segal, says that 'it has been estimated that up to one-fifth of European refugees committed suicide (around 160,000), either in the process of fleeing, or afterwards, through the inability to assimilate to their new country'.
    'Wouldn't it be better': Schur, 499.
391–2 Theresa Pankejeff's death: Pankejeff's 'Memoirs', in Gardiner, 118–23.
  392 'He is ill': Obholzer, 61.
    Smuggling gold: Ernest Jones, III, 238; Molnar, 239.
    Going through papers: Molnar, 232.
    Engelman's photographs: Molnar, 236; Bettelheim, 18.
    Fifteen names: Schur, 501.
    Departure dates: Molnar, 235–6.
    'standing in the doorway': 20 May 1938, Molnar, 236.
    Paying the tax: Molnar, 236; Bertin, 200.
  393 Fliess letters: Bertin 197.
    The 'Gestapo' story: Ernest Jones, III, 241 and Martin Freud, 217; debunked, *Journal of the International Association for the History of Psychoanalysis*, 8 (1989).
    Money for the sisters: Ernest Jones, III, 246.
    'To maintain them': 12 Nov. 1938, *Letters*.
    Leaving Vienna: Molnar, 237.
  394 Pevensey Bay; Ernest Jones, III, 244.
    Auden's poem: 'In Memory of Sigmund Freud (d. Sept. 1939)'.
    At Victoria Station: Molnar, 239.
    'The enchantment': 6 June 1938, *Letters*.
394–5 To Alexander: *Letters*.
  395 Leaflet for British Jews: *While you are in England: Helpful Information and Guidance for Every Refugee*, issued by the German Jewish Aid Committee in conjunction with the Jewish Board of Refugees, Wiener Library.
395–6 Last days in London: Ernest Jones, III, 247–63; Molnar, 239–64; Schur, 504–29.
  397 'Talk to Anna': Gay (1989) 739–40 (but not Schur or Jones) has the words,

'make an end of it'. Gay's version, drawing on an unpublished memorandum by Schur and other sources, makes it clear that the doctor gave Freud a lethal dose of morphine.

'What has the individual': 6 Feb. 1899, Masson.

32: *Afterwards*

398 Martha goes shopping: Young-Bruehl, 308; Ernest Jones, III, 248.
'a certain smell': Masson, *Final Analysis* (1992b), 163.
'It was as if': in conversation, 1994.

399 Puner's book: *Sigmund Freud: His Life and Mind*; as catalyst to authorised publications, Paul Roazen's Introduction to Puner (1992 reissue), ix.
Fliess letters in London: Ernest Jones, I, 317.
Anna and Martin oppose publication: Young-Bruehl, 296–7, which quotes from Anna's letters.
Kris as editor: Young-Bruehl, 303.
Expurgating the letters: C.f. M. Macmillan, 'New Answers to Old Questions: What the Complete Freud–Fliess Correspondence Tells Us', *Psychoanalytic Review*, 77, 4 (1990).

400 Jones asked to write: Young-Bruehl, 305. The publisher was Simon & Schuster.
Bernfeld inspired Swales: Swales in a lecture, 'Freud and the Unconscionable: the Obstruction of Freud Studies, 1946–2113', given in London and New York in 1991–2 but not published. Tape recordings are in circulation.
The Freuds and Jones's biography: H. Trosman and E.S. Wolf, 'The Bernfeld Collaboration in the Jones Biography of Freud', *International Journal of Psycho-Analysis*, 54 (1973).

401 Anna relieved: Young-Bruehl, 307.
Death-bed dreams: mentioned in BBC recordings made by the author for an obituary radio programme about Jones in 1959. A member of the family said, 'I could tell he was awfully disturbed by that, because he told me that he hadn't heard people singing hymns, or been to anything religious, since his Sunday-school days.' This passage wasn't broadcast.
Jones's death: Brome, 218.
Eissler, Bernfeld and the Archive: Swales's 'Unconscionable' lecture, New York, 1992, see note to p. 400.

402 Anna Freud and McGuire: S. Shamdasani, '"Should this Remain?" Anna Freud's Misgivings Concerning the Freud–Jung Letters', *International Forum of Psychoanalysis*, 5 (1996).
Censoring Freud: among the widespread criticisms, often savage, in recent years of the policy are Masson (1992b), passim; M. Macmillan, 'New Answers to Old Questions: What the Complete Freud–Fliess Correspondence Tells Us', *Psychoanalytic Review*, 77, 4 (1990); Roazen (1993) 200–1; F. J. Sulloway, 'Reassessing Freud's Case Histories: The Social Construction of Psychoanalysis', *Isis*, 82, 312 (June 1991) 246–51; P. J. Swales, passim.

402–3 Eissler and Reich: Roazen (1993) 136; Eissler and Esti Freud, ibid.

403 Freud Museum and the papers: information from the Museum.
Removing Jones papers: information from the British Psycho-Analytic Society.

403–4 Masson and Eissler: Masson (1992b); Malcolm (1985); Masson to the author, 12 March 1997.

407 Dr A: in conversation, 1996; letter to the author, 24 March 1997.
The great event: Ernest Jones, I, 388.

Bibliography

Abraham, Hilda C., and Ernst L. Freud (eds), *A Psycho-Analytic Dialogue: The Letters of Sigmund Freud and Karl Abraham 1907–1926* (Hogarth Press and the Institute of Psycho-Analysis, 1965)

Albutt, Playfair and Eden, *A System of Gynaecology* (Macmillan, 1895)

Andréas-Salomé, Lou, *The Freud Journal* (Quartet, 1987) [1964]

Andrews, George, and David Solomon (eds), *The Coca Leaf and Cocaine Papers* (Harcourt Brace Jovanovich, 1975)

Anon, *Recollections of a Royal Governess* (Hutchinson, 1915)

Anzieu, Didier, *Freud's Self-Analysis* (Hogarth Press and the Institute of Psycho-Analysis, 1986) [1975]

Appignanesi, Lisa, and John Forrester, *Freud's Women* (Weidenfeld & Nicolson, 1992)

Ascheim, Steven E., *Brothers and Strangers: The East European Jew in German and German Jewish Consciousness, 1800–1932* (University of Wisconsin Press, 1982)

Barea, Ilsa, *Vienna: Legend and Reality* (Secker & Warburg, 1966)

Bateman, Anthony, and Jeremy Holmes, *Introduction to Psychoanalysis: Contemporary theory and practice* (Routledge, 1995)

Bellamy, Edward, *Dr Heidenhoff's Process* (Frederick Warne, 1891) [1880]

Bertin, Celia, *Marie Bonaparte: A Life* (Quartet, 1987) [1982]

Bettelheim, Bruno, *Recollections and Reflections* (Thames and Hudson, 1990)

Binion, Rudolph, *Frau Lou: Nietzsche's Wayward Disciple* (Princeton University Press, 1968)

Bloch, Iwan, *The Sexual Life of Our Time in its Relations to Modern Civilization* (Rebman, 1908)

Boehlich, Walter (ed.), *The Letters of Sigmund Freud to Eduard Silberstein 1871–1881* (Harvard University Press, 1990)

Borch-Jacobsen, Mikkel, *Remembering Anna O: A Century of Mystification* (Routledge, 1996)

Bottome, Phyllis, *Alfred Adler: A Biography* (G. P. Putnam's Sons, New York, 1939)

Brabant, Eva, Ernst Falzeder and Patrizia Giampieri-Deutsch (eds), *The Correspondence of Sigmund Freud and Sándor Ferenczi*, Vol. 1, 1908–1914 (Harvard University Press, 1993)

Brome, Vincent, *Ernest Jones: Freud's Alter Ego* (Caliban Books, 1982)

Bullock, Malcolm, *Austria 1918–1938: A Study in Failure* (Macmillan, 1939)

Byck, Robert (ed.), *Cocaine Papers by Sigmund Freud* (Stonehill, New York, c.1974)

Carotenuto, Aldo, *A Secret Symmetry. Sabina Spielrein: Between Jung and Freud* (Routledge & Kegan Paul, 1984)

Cecil, Hugh, and Peter H. Liddle (eds), *Facing Armageddon: The First World War*

Experienced (Leo Cooper, 1996)

Clark, Ronald, W., *Freud: The Man and the Cause* (Jonathan Cape and Weidenfeld & Nicolson, 1980)

Cocks, Geoffrey, *Psychotherapy in the Third Reich: The Goring Institute* (Oxford University Press, 1985)

Crabtree, Adam, *From Mesmer to Freud: Magnetic Sleep and the Roots of Psychological Healing* (Yale University Press, 1993)

Crews, Frederick, *The Memory Wars: Freud's Legacy in Dispute* (Granta Books, 1997)

Davies, Thomas Gruffydd, *Ernest Jones, 1879–1958* (University of Wales Press, 1979)

Decker, Hannah, S., *Freud, Dora, and Vienna 1900* (The Free Press, New York, 1991)

Donn, Linda, *Freud and Jung: Years of Friendship, Years of Loss* (Scribner, New York, 1988)

Dowse, Thomas Stretch, *Lectures on Massage & Electricity in the Treatment of Disease* (Hamilton, Adams & Co., c.1890)

Dupont, Judith (ed.), *The Clinical Diary of Sándor Ferenczi* (Harvard University Press, 1988)

Ellenberger, Henri F., *The Discovery of the Unconscious: The History and Evolution of Dynamic Psychiatry* (Basic Books, 1970)

Erb, Wilhelm, *Handbook of Electro-Therapeutics* (William Wood, New York, 1883)

Esterson, Allen, *Seductive Mirage: An Exploration of the Work of Sigmund Freud* (Open Court, Chicago, 1993)

Eysenck, H. J., *Fact and Fiction in Psychology* (Penguin Books, 1965)

Falzeder, Ernst, and Eva Brabant (eds), *The Correspondence of Sigmund Freud and Sándor Ferenczi*, Vol. 2, 1914–1919 (Harvard University Press, 1996)

Ferris, Paul, *Sex and the British* (Michael Joseph, 1993)

Fisher, Seymour, and Roger P. Greenberg, *The Scientific Credibility of Freud's Theories and Therapy* (Columbia University Press, 1985) [1977]

Fitch, Noël Riley, *Anaïs: The Erotic Life of Anaïs Nin* (Little, Brown, 1993)

Flexner, Abraham, *Prostitution in Europe* (Century, New York, 1914)

Fordham, Frieda, *An Introduction to Jung's Psychology* (Penguin, 1973) [1953]

Fordham, Michael, *Freud, Jung, Klein – The Fenceless Field: Essays on psychoanalysis and analytical psychology* (Routledge, 1975)

Freud, Ernst L. (ed.), *Letters of Sigmund Freud 1873–1939* (Hogarth Press, 1961)
   The Letters of Sigmund Freud and Arnold Zweig (Hogarth Press and The Institute of Psycho-Analysis, 1970)

Freud, Martin, *Glory Reflected: Sigmund Freud – Man and Father* (Angus and Robertson, 1957)

Freud, Sigmund, *Standard Edition of the Complete Psychological Works of Sigmund Freud*, trans. James Strachey et al., Vols 1–24 (Hogarth Press, 1955–1975)

Freud, Sophie, *My Three Mothers and Other Passions* (New York University Press, 1991) [1988]

Fussell, Paul, *The Great War and Modern Memory* (Oxford University Press, 1977) [1975]

Gardiner, Muriel (ed.), *The Wolf-Man and Sigmund Freud* (Karnac Books and the Institute of Psycho-Analysis, 1989) [1972]

Gay, Peter, *A Godless Jew: Freud, Atheism, & the Making of Psychoanalysis* (Yale University Press, 1987)
   Freud: A Life for Our Time (Papermac, 1989) [1988]
   Reading Freud: Explorations & Entertainments (Yale University Press, 1990)

Gelfand, Toby, and John Kerr (eds), *Freud and the History of Psychoanalysis* (The Analytic Press, 1992)

Gicklhorn, Renée, *Sigmund Freud und der Onkeltraum: Dichtung und Wahrheit*

(Vienna, 1976)

Gilman, Sander L., *Freud, Race, and Gender* (Princeton University Press, 1993)

Groddeck, Georg, *The Book of The It* (Vision, 1940) [1923]

Grosskurth, Phyllis, *The Secret Ring: Freud's Inner Circle and the Politics of Psychoanalysis* (Jonathan Cape, 1991)

Grubrich-Simitis, Ilse, *Zurück zu Freuds Texten: Stumme Dokumente sprechen machen* ('Retrieving Freud's Texts: Making Silent Documents Speak') (S. Fischer Verlag, Frankfurt, 1993). Not yet available in English

Gunn, Daniel, and Patrick Guyomard (eds), *A Young Girl's Diary* (Unwin Hyman, 1990) [1919]

Hale, Nathan G. Jr (ed.), *James Jackson Putnam and Psychoanalysis: Letters between Putnam and Sigmund Freud, Ernest Jones, William James, Sándor Ferenczi, and Morton Prince, 1877–1917* (Harvard University Press, 1971)

    Freud and the Americans: The Beginnings of Psychoanalysis in the United States, 1876–1917 (Oxford University Press, 1995) [1971]

Hamilton, Cicely, *Modern Austria as Seen by an Englishwoman* (Dent, 1935)

Hannah, Barbara, *Jung: His Life and Work* (Michael Joseph, 1977)

'H.D.' (Hilda Doolittle), *Tribute to Freud* (Carcanet, 1985) [1970]

Heller, Peter (ed.), *Anna Freud's Letters to Eva Rosenfeld* (International Universities Press, Madison, Conn., 1992)

Higgins, Mary Boyd (ed.), *Passion of Youth: An Autobiography* [of Wilhelm Reich], *1897–1922* (Picador, 1989) [1988]

Hirschfeld, Gerhard (ed.), *Exile in Great Britain* (German Historical Institute, 1984)

Hirschmüller, Albrecht, *The Life and Work of Josef Breuer: Physiology and Psychoanalysis* (New York University Press, 1989) [1978]

Hobman, J. B. (ed.), *David Eder: Memoirs of a Modern Pioneer* (Gollancz, 1945)

Holmes, Colin, *A Tolerant Country* (Faber & Faber, 1991)

Holroyd, Michael, *Lytton Strachey, Vol. 2: The Years of Achievement (1910–1932)* (Heinemann, 1968)

Holt, Robert R., *Freud Reappraised: A Fresh Look at Psychoanalytic Theory* (Guilford Press, 1989)

Hunter, Ian M. L., *Memory*, (Penguin, 1964)

Hynes, Samuel, *The Edwardian Turn of Mind* (Princeton University Press and Oxford University Press, 1968)

Isherwood, Christopher, *Christopher and His Kind 1929–1939* (Eyre Methuen, 1976)

Jaffé, Aniela, *From the Life and Work of C. G. Jung* (Harper & Row, New York, 1971)

Johnston, William M., *The Austrian Mind: An Intellectual and Social History 1848–1938* (University of California Press, 1972)

Jones, Ernest, *Sigmund Freud: Life and Work, Vol. I, The Young Freud 1856–1900* (Hogarth Press, 1980) [1953]

    Vol. II, Years of Maturity 1901–1919 (ibid., 1967) [1955]

    Vol. III, The Last Phase 1919–1939 (ibid, 1980) [1957]

    (American editions of Jones's biography have a different title for Volume I and, unfortunately, different pagination throughout all three volumes.)

    Free Associations: Memories of a Psychoanalyst (Transaction Publishers, 1990) [1959]

Jones, J. Sydney, *Hitler in Vienna 1907–13: Clues to the Future* (Blond & Briggs, 1983)

Jones, Mervyn, *Chances: An Autobiography* (Verso, 1987)

Jung, Carl Gustav, *Memories, Dreams, Reflections* (Fontana Press, 1995) [1961]

Kennedy, Michael, *Mahler* (Dent; Master Musicians series)

Kerr, John, *A Most Dangerous Method: The Story of Jung, Freud, and Sabina Spielrein* (Sinclair-Stevenson, 1994)

Kiell, Norman (ed.), *Freud Without Hindsight: Reviews of His Work (1893–1939)* (International Universities Press, Madison, Conn., 1987)

Kris, Ernst, Marie Bonaparte and Anna Freud (eds), *The Origins of Psycho-analysis: Letters to Wilhelm Fliess, Drafts and Notes, 1887–1902* (Imago, 1954)

Krüll, Marianne, *Freud and His Father* (W. W. Norton, 1986) [1979]

Leo Baeck Institute, *Year Book II* (East and West Library, 1957)

Lesky, Erna, *The Vienna Medical School of the Nineteenth Century* (Johns Hopkins University Press, 1965)

Lieberman, E. James, *Acts of Will: The Life and Work of Otto Rank* (The Free Press, New York, 1985)

McGrath, William J., *Freud's Discovery of Psychoanalysis: The Politics of Hysteria* (Cornell University Press, 1986)

McGuire, William (ed.), *The Freud–Jung Letters: The Correspondence between Sigmund Freud and C. G. Jung* (Hogarth Press and Routledge & Kegan Paul, 1974)

McLynn, Frank, *Carl Gustav Jung* (Bantam Press, 1996)

Maddox, Brenda, *The Married Man: A Life of D. H. Lawrence* (Sinclair-Stevenson, 1994)

Mahony, Patrick J., *Cries of the Wolf Man* (International Universities Press, New York, 1984)

    Freud and the Rat Man (Yale University Press, 1986)

    Freud's Dora: A Psychoanalytic, Historical, and Textual Study (Yale University Press, 1996)

Malcolm, Janet, *In the Freud Archives* (Vintage, New York, 1985) [1984]

    Psychoanalysis: The Impossible Profession (Maresfield Library, 1988) [1982]

Masson, Jeffrey Moussaieff, *Against Therapy* (Harper Collins, 1993) [1989]

    The Assault on Truth: Freud and Child Sexual Abuse (Fontana, 1992) [1984]

    Final Analysis: The Making and Unmaking of a Psychoanalyst (Fontana, 1992b) [1990]

    (ed.) *The Complete Letters of Sigmund Freud to Wilhelm Fliess 1887–1904* (Harvard University Press, 1985)

Meisel, Perry, and Walter Kendrick (eds), *Bloomsbury Freud: The Letters of James and Alix Strachey 1924–1925* (Chatto & Windus, 1986)

Meisel-Hess, Grete, *The Intellectuals* (Oesterheld, Berlin, 1911)

Micale, Mark S. (ed.), *Beyond the Unconscious: Essays of Henri F. Ellenberger in the History of Psychiatry* (Princeton University Press, 1993)

Mitchell, Stephen A., and Margaret J. Black, *Freud and Beyond: A History of Modern Psychoanalytic Thought* (Basic Books, 1995)

Molnar, Michael (ed.), *The Diary of Sigmund Freud 1929–1939: A Record of the Final Decade* (Hogarth Press, 1992)

Morton, Frederic, *A Nervous Splendor: Vienna 1888–1889* (Weidenfeld & Nicolson, 1980)

Mosse, Werner E. (ed.), *Second Chance* (J. C. B. Mohr, Tubingen, 1991)

Munthe, Axel, *The Story of San Michele* (John Murray, 1946) [1929]

Murray and Turner (eds), *Lectures on the History of Psychiatry* (Royal College of Psychiatrists, 1990)

Nahas, Gabriel G., with Helene Peters, *Cocaine: The Great White Plague* (Paul S. Eriksson, c.1989)

Nicolson, Nigel (ed.), *A Change of Perspective: The Letters of Virginia Woolf 1923–28*, Vol. III (Hogarth Press, 1994)

Niederland, William G., *The Schreber Case: Psychoanalytic Profile of a Paranoid Personality* (Quadrangle / The New York Times Book Co., 1974)

Noll, Richard, *The Jung Cult: Origins of a Charismatic Movement* (Princeton University Press, 1994)

Nunberg, Hermann, and Ernst Federn (eds), *Minutes of the Vienna Psychoanalytic Society* (4 vols., 1962–1975)

Obholzer, Karin, *The Wolf-Man Sixty Years Later: Conversations with Freud's controversial patient* (Routledge & Kegan Paul, 1982) [1980]

Paskauskas, R. Andrew (ed.), *The Complete Correspondence of Sigmund Freud and Ernest Jones 1908–1939* (Harvard University Press, 1993)

Peters, H. F., *My Sister, My Spouse: A Biography of Lou Andréas-Salomé* (Gollancz, 1963)

Pfeiffer, Ernst (ed.) *Sigmund Freud and Lou Andréas-Salomé: Letters* (Hogarth Press and Institute of Psycho-Analysis, 1972)

Pick, Robert, *The Last Days of Imperial Vienna* (Weidenfeld & Nicolson, 1975)

Puner, Helen Walker, *Sigmund Freud: His Life and Mind* (Transaction, New Jersey, 1992) [1947]

Putnam, James Jackson, *Human Motives* (Little, Brown, 1915)

Quinn, Susan, *A Mind of Her Own: The Life of Karen Horney* (Macmillan, 1988) [1987]

Rice, Emanuel, *Freud and Moses: The Long Journey Home* (State University of New York, 1990)

Roazen, Paul, *Brother Animal: The Story of Freud and Tausk* (Allen Lane, The Penguin Press, 1970) [1969]

    Freud and his Followers (Da Capo Press, New York, 1992) [1975]

    Meeting Freud's Family (University of Massachusetts Press, 1993)

    How Freud Worked: First-Hand Accounts of Patients (Jason Aronson, New Jersey, 1995)

Rosenzweig, Saul, *Freud, Jung, and Hall the King-Maker: The Historic Expedition to America (1909)* (Hogrefe & Huber Publishers, Seattle, 1992)

Rubin, David C. (ed.), *Autobiographical Memory* (Cambridge University Press, 1987)

Ruitenbeek, Hendrik M. (ed.), *Freud as We Knew Him* (Wayne State University Press, Detroit, 1973)

Rycroft, Charles, *The Innocence of Dreams* (Hogarth Press, 1991) [1979]

    Viewpoints (Hogarth Press, 1991b) [1964]

Sandler, Joseph, and Anna Ursula Dreher, *What Do Psychoanalysts Want? The Problems of Aims in Psychoanalytic Therapy* (Routledge, 1996)

Scagnelli, Paul, *Deadly Dr Freud: The Murder of Emmanuel Freud and Disappearance of John Freud* (Pinewood Publishing Co., Durham, North Carolina)

Schacht, Lore (ed.), *The Meaning of Illness: Selected Psychoanalytic Writings by Georg Groddeck* (Maresfield Library, 1988) [1977]

Schnitzler, Arthur, *My Youth in Vienna* (Weidenfeld & Nicolson, 1971)

    Vienna 1900: Games with Love and Death (Penguin Books, 1973)

Schorske, Carl E., *Fin-de-Siècle Vienna: Politics and Culture* (Cambridge University Press, 1981) [1961]

Schur, Max, *Freud: Living and Dying* (International Universities Press, New York, 1972)

Sebald, W. G., *The Emigrants* (Harvill Press, 1996) [1993]

Senator, H., and S. Kaminer, (eds), *Marriage and Disease* (Rebman, 1907)

Sharaf, Myron, *Fury on Earth: A Biography of Wilhelm Reich* (André Deutsch, 1983)

Shirer, William L., *The Rise and Fall of the Third Reich: A History of Nazi Germany*

(Secker & Warburg, 1960)

Spiel, Hilde, *Vienna's Golden Autumn 1866–1938* (Weidenfeld & Nicolson, 1987)

Spurling, Laurence (ed.), *Sigmund Freud: Critical Assessments*, Vols 1, 2, 3 and 4 (Routledge, 1989)

Squire, Larry R., *Memory and Brain* (Oxford University Press, 1987)

Steele, Robert S., *Freud and Jung: Conflicts of Interpretation* (Routledge & Kegan Paul, 1982)

Stepansky, Paul E. (ed.), *Freud: Appraisals and Reappraisals* (Analytic Press, New York, Vol. 1 1986; Vol. 2, 1987; Vol. 3, 1988)

Stevens, Austin, *The Dispossessed: German refugees in Britain* (Barrie & Jenkins, 1975)

Storr, Anthony, *Jung* (Fontana, 1986) [1973]
    Freud (Oxford University Press, 1989)
    Feet of Clay: A Study of Gurus (Harper Collins, 1996)

Sulloway, Frank J., *Freud, Biologist of the Mind: Beyond the Psychoanalytic Legend* (Harvard University Press, 1992) [1979]

Sutton, Nina, *Bettelheim: A Life and a Legacy* (Basic Books, 1996) [1995]

Szasz, Thomas, *Anti-Freud: Karl Kraus's Criticism of Psychoanalysis and Psychiatry* (Syracuse University Press, 1990) [1977]

Thomas, D. M., *Pictures at an Exhibition* (Bloomsbury, 1993)

Thornton, E. M., *Freud and Cocaine: The Freudian Fallacy* (Blond & Briggs, 1983)

Timms, Edward, *Karl Kraus, Apocalyptic Satirist: Culture and Catastrophe in Habsburg Vienna* (Yale University Press, 1986)
    (ed.), *Freud and the Child Woman: The Memoirs of Fritz Wittels* (Yale University Press, 1995)

Timms, Edward, and R. Robertson (eds), *Austrian Studies*, No. 3 (Edinburgh University Press, 1991)

Timms, Edward, and Naomi Segal (eds), *Freud in Exile: Psychoanalysis and its Vicissitudes* (Yale University Press, 1988)

Timpanaro, Sebastiano, *The Freudian Slip: Psychoanalysis and Textual Criticism* (New Left Books, 1976) [1974]

Toland, John, *Adolf Hitler* (Doubleday, New York, 1976)

Turner, E. S., *Taking the Cure* (Michael Joseph, 1967)

Webster, Richard, *Why Freud Was Wrong: Sin, Science and Psychoanalysis* (Harper Collins, 1995)

Weiss, Edoardo, *Sigmund Freud as a Consultant: Recollections of a Pioneer in Psychoanalysis* (Intercontinental Medical Book Corporation, New York, 1970)

Whyte, Lancelot Law, *The Unconscious before Freud* (Tavistock Publications, 1962) [1960]

Wittels, Fritz, *Sigmund Freud: His Personality, His Teaching, & His School* (George Allen & Unwin, 1924)

Wolff, Charlotte, *Magnus Hirschfeld: A Portrait of a Pioneer in Sexology* (Quartet, 1986)

Wolff, Larry, *Child Abuse in Freud's Vienna: Postcards from the End of the World* (New York University Press, 1995) [1988]

Wortis, Joseph, *Fragments of an Analysis with Freud* (Simon & Schuster, New York, 1954)

Woycke, James, *Birth Control in Germany 1871–1933* (Routledge, 1988)

Young-Bruehl, Elisabeth, *Anna Freud* (Papermac, 1991) [1988]

Zanuso, Billa, *The Young Freud: The origins of psychoanalysis in late nineteenth-century Viennese culture* (Basil Blackwell, 1986) [1982]

Zweig, Stefan, *The World of Yesterday: An Autobiography* (Cassell, 1943)

Index

I have writte[n]

[a]nd Robert a[s]

second boy

their born

own child

here last

was the ele[...]

hild I have

ere very p[...]

all of us

a cute Rober[t]